STEPS IN THE ACCOUNTING CYCLE

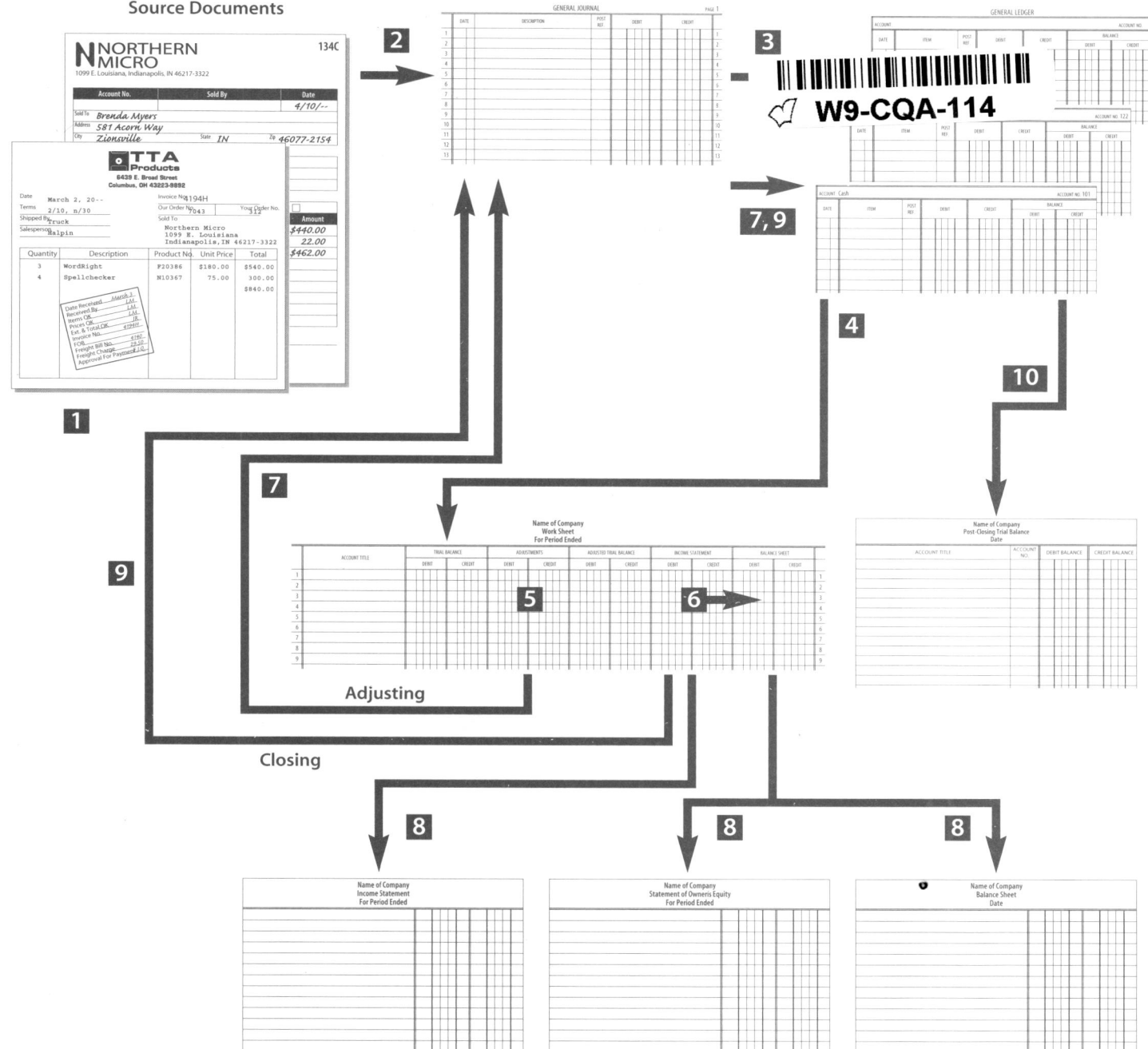

Steps in the Accounting Cycle

During Accounting Period:
1. Analyze source documents.
2. Journalize the transactions.
3. Post to the ledger accounts.

End of Accounting Period:
4. Prepare a trial balance.
5. Determine and prepare the needed adjustments on the work sheet.
6. Complete an end-of-period work sheet.
7. Journalize and post the adjusting entries.
8. Prepare an income statement, statement of owner's equity, and balance sheet.
9. Journalize and post the closing entries.
10. Prepare a post-closing trial balance.

Chapters 1-15

College Accounting

19th Edition

James A. Heintz
DBA, CPA
Professor of Accounting
School of Business
University of Kansas
Lawrence, Kansas

Robert W. Parry, Jr.
Ph.D.
Professor of Accounting
Kelley School of Business
Indiana University
Bloomington, Indiana

THOMSON

SOUTH-WESTERN

Australia · Brazil · Canada · Mexico · Singapore · Spain · United Kingdom · United States

THOMSON
SOUTH-WESTERN

College Accounting, 19th edition, Chapters 1–15
James A. Heintz and Robert W. Parry, Jr.

VP/Editorial Director
Jack W. Calhoun

Publisher
Rob Dewey

Executive Editor
Sharon Oblinger

Developmental Editor
Aaron Arnsparger

Marketing Manager
Kristen Hurd

Senior Content Project Manager
Tim Bailey

Manager, Editorial Media
John Barans

Technology Project Manager
Robin Browning

Website Project Manager
Brian Courter

Manufacturing Frontlist Buyer
Doug Wilke

Production House
LEAP Publishing Services, Inc.

Compositor
GGS Book Services, Inc.

Printer
Quebecor World
Versailles, KY

Art Director
Bethany Casey

Internal Design
Pop Design Works LLC

Cover Design
Pop Design Works LLC

Cover Images
JUPITERIMAGES and
Getty Images, Inc.

Rights Acquisition Account Manager-Image
Deanna Ettinger

Photo Researcher
Charlotte Goldman

Student Edition ISBN 13:
978-0-324-38249-5

Student Edition ISBN 10:
0-324-38249-9

Instructor's Edition ISBN 13:
978-0-324-38251-8

Instructor's Edition ISBN 10:
0-324-38251-0

Library of Congress Control Number:
2006910206

For more information about
our products, contact us at:

Thomson Learning Academic
Resource Center

1-800-423-0563

Thomson Higher Education
5191 Natorp Boulevard
Mason, OH 45040
USA

Dedication

We are grateful to our wives

Celia Heintz and Jane Parry

and our children

Andrea Heintz, John Heintz, Jessica Jane Parry, and Mitch Parry

for their love, support, and assistance during the creation
of this 19th edition. We especially appreciate
Jessie Parry's willingness to let us use her name
throughout the first six chapters.

LEADING THE PACK—
OUR PROMISE OF EXCELLENCE

Edition after edition, Heintz & Parry's *College Accounting* has been the leader in providing solid, tested content to hundreds of thousands of students. The 19th edition continues that tradition of excellence. We've kept intact everything that has made *College Accounting* so successful, then added new features, supplements, and technology to ensure that it remains **the best text** on the market. Our main objective has and always will be to make accounting understandable to every student and to do so without sacrificing crucial substance and technical correctness. Our step-by-step, straightforward approach helps build practical accounting skills that are needed when entering the world of work. The text presents basic topics first and builds to more advanced coverage so that students are never overwhelmed. Likewise, the narrative approach covers a simpler example of a service business before moving on to a merchandising business and then to a manufacturing environment. In the end, *College Accounting, 19e*, combines an easily readable style throughout the text with helpful reinforcement through its unparalleled learning package. By building practical accounting skills and developing an understanding of concepts, students will be prepared for success in the business world. We're confident that this new edition represents a text that achieves our goals and continues its tradition of fundamental excellence.

PROVEN TO BE THE BEST!

A Proven Approach

Heintz & Parry has proven that students excel when they're not rushed into financial statements or overloaded with theory. This text presents concepts simply and ensures the best, most accurate coverage, which allows students to build on their foundation of knowledge one topic at a time.

Forward-Thinking Enhancements

The 19th edition refines the many improvements of earlier editions that were made in response to both instructors' feedback and our own commitment to meet the evolving needs of the learning environment. In response to increased importance of this topic today, a newly added appendix to Chapter 7 provides students with a brief discussion of internal controls. A complete discussion of periodic and perpetual methods of accounting for inventory has been enhanced in Chapter 13 and moved up to immediately follow coverage of sales and cash receipts and purchases and cash payments. A new "Revisiting the Opener" end-of-chapter assignment has been added that serves as a direct follow-up from the chapter opening scenario. These are just a few of the many enhancements made to this edition.

Pedagogy with Purpose

College Accounting, 19e, employs time-tested, classroom-proven educational techniques. Repetition of key topics, a continuing topic example, and relevant demonstration problems are some of the methods used to ensure—and enhance—student progress.

Superior Supporting Products

A helpful instructor's resource manual, colorful teaching transparencies tied to the text as well as transparencies of assignment solutions, and excellent PowerPoint® slides are just a few of the features that constitute the extensive supplement package. See descriptions of these and other ancillary products on pages xvii–xix of this preface.

Powerful Technology Solutions

Our ThomsonNOW technology solution offers exceptional online homework, multimedia, and classroom management tools for high-impact assistance to students and instructors.

Unmatched Service

You have our commitment to always provide you with the best of everything accompanying our products. From your Thomson South-Western sales representative, to the Academic Resource Center staff, to the authors themselves, our professional resources and support team are committed to helping you.

**Take a closer look at *College Accounting, 19e,*
and see for yourself why it's THE choice for college accounting!**

PROVEN TO BE THE BEST!

A PROVEN APPROACH: DEVELOPING NECESSARY SKILLS FOR ENTERING THE WORLD OF WORK

Quality and creative suggestions and other feedback from instructors and students provide excellent opportunities for our ongoing refinement and enhancement of each edition. As always, we listened and responded in this new edition. Skill development and mastery are encouraged and assisted by a number of features.

College Accounting, 19e, presents simple concepts first and builds to more advanced content. In each chapter, students focus on only one major topic or procedure, ensuring that they master each new concept before moving on.

- **Real-world skills** are developed to help students get jobs after graduation.
- **Careful development of topics** prevents "information overload."
- **Repetition of key topics** throughout helps students master important concepts and procedures.
- **Narrative approach** covers the simpler example of a service business before moving on to a merchandising business and later a manufacturing business. Along the way, the company structure moves from sole proprietorship to partnership to corporation.
- **Demonstration problems** can be used as study aids or in-class examples.
- **Comprehensive problems** provide important opportunities to review skills.
- **Three versions** of the text (9, 15, or 27 chapters) create a custom fit for your course.

WHAT'S NEW WITH THIS EDITION?

Self Study and Applying Your Knowledge Sections

New to this edition, the end-of-chapter material has been divided into these two new categories to better reflect the purpose of the material and to enhance student performance in the course. The *Self Study* section includes activities that can be used as a study aid prior to working the chapter exercises and problems or as a quick review before an exam or a quiz. This section includes Key Points

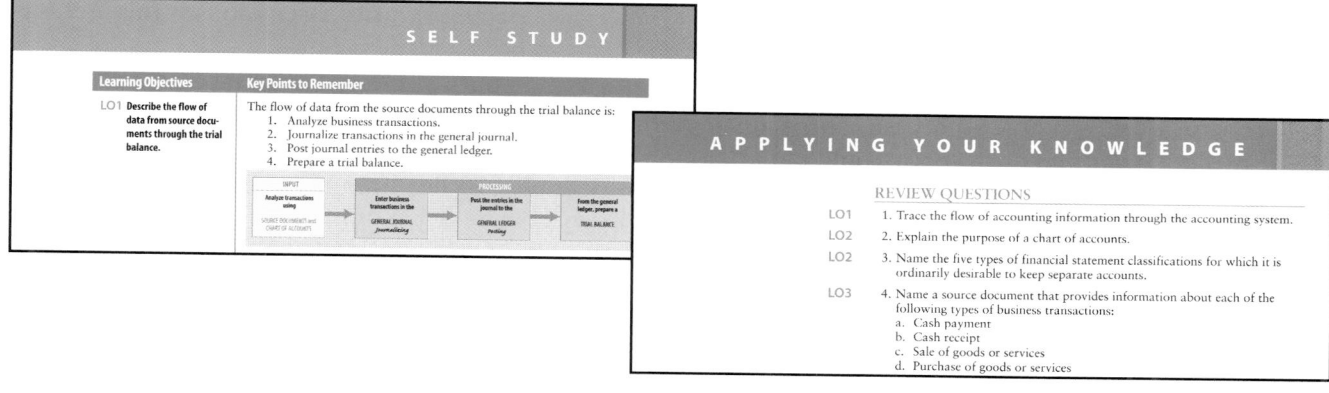

PROVEN TO BE THE BEST!

to Remember, a Demonstration Problem (with solution), Key Terms, and Self-Study True/False and Multiple-Choice questions. Answers are provided at the back of the text for the Self-Study questions. *Applying Your Knowledge* offers an expansive selection of exercises and problems (both A and B sets), review questions, a new "Revisiting the Opener" assignment, Mastery and Challenge problems, and writing and ethics related activities. The exercises and problems include learning objective references and check figures for students to check their work as they progress.

Computers and Accounting

Accounting Software—Gary P. Schneider, University of San Diego, and Toni Hartley, Laurel Business Institute

People use computers to help them do many common tasks in business, at school, and in everyday life. For example, instead of writing a homework assignment using pen and paper or a typewriter, many students use software on a personal computer to create the homework assignment. If the homework requires calculations, students might use spreadsheet software to perform those calculations and paste the results into the document. If the homework requires

Figure A

Clicking this button instructs the software to create the same entry each accounting period.

The software automatically enters the account number when an account name is selected from a drop-down list.

The software automatically calculates running totals and warns the accountant if the total debits do not equal the total credits.

Completely Revised and Expanded! Written by Gary Schneider of the University of San Diego, and updated for this edition by Toni Hartley of Laurel Business Institute, *Computers and Accounting* puts computers in the context of their importance to accounting in the real world. This coverage, which has been increased, now appears in Chapters 2, 6, 9, and 12. The coverage:

- Describes the computer skills that are used in accounting.
- Explains how computer software aids bookkeeping.
- Examines the use of the computer in payroll accounting.
- Tells how the computer helps process cash receipt, cash payment, sales, and purchase transactions through a special journal environment.

CHAPTER UPDATES AND ENHANCEMENTS

- **Chapter 1:** In 2002, the Sarbanes-Oxley Act (SOX) was passed by Congress to help improve reporting practices of public companies. A brief discussion of this Act has been added.

- **Chapter 5:** In this edition, we include a discussion of the cash, modified cash, and accrual methods of accounting. In prior editions, we addressed cash and modified cash in Chapter 10 when discussing accounting for a professional service business. Chapter 10 has been moved to a module at the end of the text.

- **Chapter 7:** A new appendix on internal controls has been added in response to user and reviewer requests. The appendix emphasizes control of cash receipts and cash disbursements because of its location in the text, but general coverage of internal control concepts is also included.

PROVEN TO BE THE BEST!

Chapter 7 Appendix
Internal Controls

Objectives

Careful study of this appendix should enable you to:

LO1 Explain the importance of internal control.

LO2 Define internal control and describe its key components.

LO3 Describe selected internal controls over cash receipts.

LO4 Describe selected internal controls over cash payments and the use of a voucher system.

In Chapter 7, we introduced the concept of internal control and provided some examples of good internal control over cash transactions. Here, we examine internal control in greater depth. We (1) explain why it has achieved greater

LO2 Define internal control and describe its key components.

KEY COMPONENTS OF INTERNAL CONTROL

Internal control is really important. So what exactly do we mean by internal control? Both the concept and attempts to define it have existed for many years. For our purposes, the following is a good definition:

> Internal control is a system developed by a company to provide reasonable assurance of achieving (1) effective and efficient operations, (2) reliable financial reporting, and (3) compliance with laws and regulations.

Several internal control frameworks have been developed that are consistent with this definition. The most widely accepted framework in the United States contains the following five components:

* Control environment
* Risk assessment
* Control activities
* Information and communication system
* Monitoring processes

* **Chapter 13:** A complete discussion of the periodic and perpetual methods of accounting for inventory is addressed in Chapter 13. This change was made to address the suggestions of our current users. Thus, Chapters 10 through 13 in *19e* offer the following coverage:

* **Chapter 10—Accounting for Sales and Cash Receipts:** Includes calculation of net sales.

* **Chapter 11—Accounting for Purchases and Cash Payments:** Includes the calculation of gross profit, but costs for merchandise inventory are provided.

* **Chapter 12—Special Journals:** Illustrates use of special journals for entries made in Chapters 10 and 11. Some faculty may choose to skip this chapter.

* **Chapter 13—Accounting for Merchandise Inventory:** Includes how to compute the cost of goods sold and the cost of ending inventory using various inventory methods under the periodic and perpetual systems.

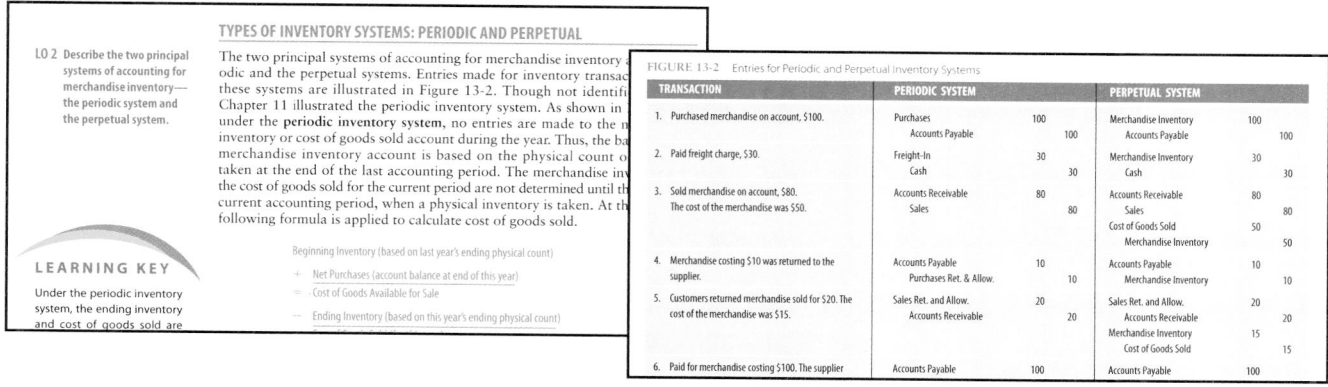

LO 2 Describe the two principal systems of accounting for merchandise inventory—the periodic system and the perpetual system.

TYPES OF INVENTORY SYSTEMS: PERIODIC AND PERPETUAL

The two principal systems of accounting for merchandise inventory are the periodic and the perpetual systems. Entries made for inventory transactions under these systems are illustrated in Figure 13-2. Though not identified Chapter 11 illustrated the periodic inventory system. As shown in under the **periodic inventory system**, no entries are made to the inventory or cost of goods sold account during the year. Thus, the balance merchandise inventory account is based on the physical count taken at the end of the last accounting period. The merchandise inventory the cost of goods sold for the current period are not determined until the current accounting period, when a physical inventory is taken. At the following formula is applied to calculate cost of goods sold.

Beginning Inventory (based on last year's ending physical count)
+ Net Purchases (account balance at end of this year)
= Cost of Goods Available for Sale
− Ending Inventory (based on this year's ending physical count)

LEARNING KEY

Under the periodic inventory system, the ending inventory and cost of goods sold are

FIGURE 13-2   Entries for Periodic and Perpetual Inventory Systems

TRANSACTION	PERIODIC SYSTEM		PERPETUAL SYSTEM	
1. Purchased merchandise on account, $100.	Purchases	100	Merchandise Inventory	100
	Accounts Payable	100	Accounts Payable	100
2. Paid freight charge, $30.	Freight-In	30	Merchandise Inventory	30
	Cash	30	Cash	30
3. Sold merchandise on account, $80. The cost of the merchandise was $50.	Accounts Receivable	80	Accounts Receivable	80
	Sales	80	Sales	80
			Cost of Goods Sold	50
			Merchandise Inventory	50
4. Merchandise costing $10 was returned to the supplier.	Accounts Payable	10	Accounts Payable	10
	Purchases Ret. & Allow.	10	Merchandise Inventory	10
5. Customers returned merchandise sold for $20. The cost of the merchandise was $15.	Sales Ret. and Allow.	20	Sales Ret. and Allow.	20
	Accounts Receivable	20	Accounts Receivable	20
			Merchandise Inventory	15
			Cost of Goods Sold	15
6. Paid for merchandise costing $100. The supplier	Accounts Payable	100	Accounts Payable	100

* **Chapter 14 (*18e*):** This chapter on vouchers has been deleted in response to limited coverage of this topic in the course today. Relevant control-oriented material has been retained in the new appendix to Chapter 7.

PROVEN TO BE THE BEST!

CONSISTENT COLOR-CODING OF ACCOUNTS

College Accounting, 19e utilizes an improved color scheme to highlight specific accounts and help students visualize important relationships.

- Assets in blue
- Liabilities in yellow
- Ownership equity in purple
- Revenues in green
- Expenses in red
- Drawing accounts in light purple
- Net income in orange
- Contra-revenues in light green
- Conta-costs in light red

Consistent with past editions of the text, all journals appear on blue rulings to differentiate them from ledgers and other processing documents, which are shown in yellow. Financial statements are white.

FIGURE 2-1   Summary of Transactions Illustrated

Trans-action	Cash	+	Accounts Receivable	+	Supplies	+	Prepaid Insurance	+	Delivery Equipment	=	Accounts Payable	+	Jessica Jane, Capital	−	Jessica Jane, Drawing	+	Revenues	−	Expenses	Description
										Assets (Items Owned)		**= Liabilities + (Amounts Owed)**		**Owner's Equity (Owner's Investment + Earnings)**						
Balance (a)	2,000												2,000							
Balance (b)	2,000 (1,200)								1,200				2,000							
Balance (c)	800								1,200 900		900		2,000							
Balance (d)	800 (300)								2,100		900 (300)		2,000							
Balance (e)	500 500								2,100		600		2,000				500			Deliv. Fees
Balance (f)	1,000 (200)								2,100		600		2,000				500		200	Rent Exp.
Balance (g)	800 (50)								2,100		600		2,000				500		200 50	Tele. Exp.
Balance (h)	750		600						2,100		600		2,000				500 600		250	Deliv. Fees
Balance (i)	750 (80)		600		80				2,100		600		2,000				1,100		250	
Balance (j)	670 (200)		600		80		200		2,100		600		2,000				1,100		250	
Balance (k)	470 570		600 (570)		80		200		2,100		600		2,000				1,100		250	
Balance (l)	1,040 (300)		30		80		200		2,100 1,500		600 1,200		2,000				1,100		250	
Balance (m)	740 (650)		30		80		200		3,600		1,800		2,000				1,100		250 650	Wages Exp.
Balance (n)	90 430		30 620		80		200		3,600		1,800		2,000				1,100 1,050		900	Deliv. Fees
Balance (o)	520 (150)		650		80		200		3,600		1,800		2,000		150		2,150		900	
Balance	370	+	650	+	80	+	200	+	3,600	=	1,800	+	2,000	−	150	+	2,150	−	900	

Cash	$ 370	Accounts Payable	$ 1,800	
Accounts Receivable	650	Jessica Jane, Capital	2,000	
Supplies	80	Jessica Jane, Drawing	(150)	Amounts in ( ) are subtracted
Prepaid Insurance	200	Delivery Fees	2,150	
Delivery Equipment	3,600	Rent Expense	(200)	
Total assets	$ 4,900	Telephone Expense	(50)	
		Wages Expense	(650)	
		Total liabilities and owner's equity	$ 4,900	

PROVEN TO BE THE BEST!

PEDAGOGY WITH A PURPOSE

This text facilitates student learning by employing a classroom-proven pedagogy.

- **A narrative approach** uses a continuing example to help students understand topics.
- **Repetition of key topics** benefits students by repeated exposure to important concepts and techniques.
- **Learning objectives** preview the skills that will be studied and mastered in that chapter.
- **Chapter openers** present the topic in context and are revisited by an assignment at the end of the chapter.
- **Margin notes** enrich student understanding of concepts and terms beyond what is contained in the text narrative.
- **Learning Keys** emphasize important new points and help students gain a clearer understanding of the key coverage in each chapter.

- **A Broader View** provides students with interesting examples of actual events or situations that tie to accounting.
- **Profiles in Accounting** feature real people successfully working and using their College Accounting skills.
- **Arrow pointers** and **text pointers** emphasize the sources and calculations of numbers.
- **Key steps** demonstrate steps to accomplish specific objectives, such as how to prepare a bank reconciliation or work sheet.
- **Accounting forms** are presented on rulings to emphasize structure and help students quickly learn how to prepare these documents.
- **Depreciation methods** are introduced in Chapter 5 with some detailing in that chapter's appendix.
- The most current **payroll information** is presented in two chapters (Chapters 8 and 9).
- The **combination journal** is featured in a module in the back of the book and provides flexibility

---

> Most firms also prepare a statement of cash flows. Given the complexity of this statement, we will postpone its discussion until later in this text.

LEARNING KEY

Permanent accounts contain the results of all transactions since the business started. Their balances are carried forward to each new accounting period.

LEARNING KEY

The owner can make withdrawals from the business at any time, as long as the assets are available. These withdrawals have nothing to do with measuring the profitability of the firm. Thus, they are closed directly to the owner's capital account.

A BROADER VIEW

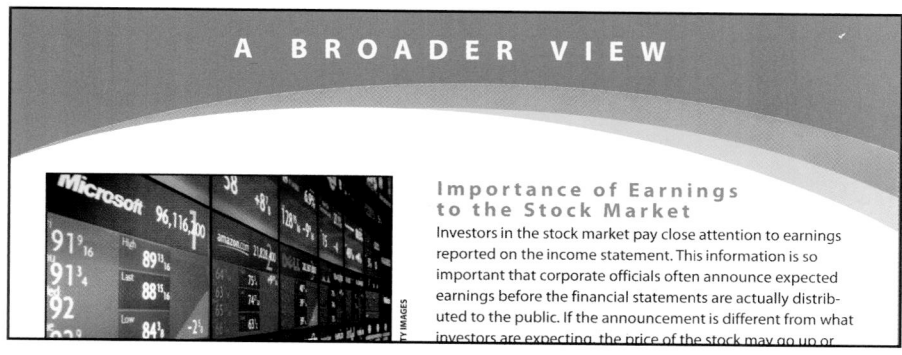

Importance of Earnings to the Stock Market

Investors in the stock market pay close attention to earnings reported on the income statement. This information is so important that corporate officials often announce expected earnings before the financial statements are actually distributed to the public. If the announcement is different from what investors are expecting, the price of the stock may go up or

PROVEN TO BE THE BEST!

for those instructors not wishing to cover this topic.

- The topics of **sales and cash receipts** and **purchases and cash payments** in a general journal system are presented consecutively in Chapters 10 and 11.

- **Special journals system** coverage (Chapter 12) immediately follows the sales and cash receipts and purchases and cash payments chapters.

- **Text and Supplements carefully verified** to guarantee an accurate and error-free text and package.

Some additional specific examples include:

- Transactions reflected in the accounting equation (Page 21)
- The articulation of the key financial statements (Page 32)
- Owner's equity umbrella (Page 56)
- Source documents (Page 94)
- General journal and general ledger relationship (Page 98)
- Work sheet development (Page 142)
- Linkages between the work sheet and the financial statements (Pages 183 and 184)
- Tax forms (Pages 288 and 289)

End-of-chapter activities reinforce learning.

- **Key Points to Remember** provide an effective review of important information covered in each chapter.

- **Key Terms** are defined at the end of each chapter, and the page of their first appearance is listed.

- **Demonstration Problems** bring together key concepts and principles. Students can work through the problems and solutions independently to gain confidence before working the homework assignments. The problems are also effective for in-class examples.

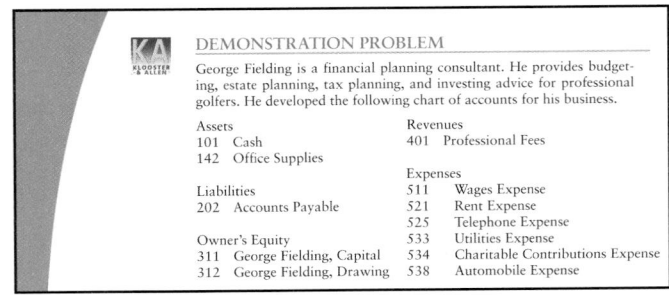

PROVEN TO BE THE BEST!

- **Review Questions** for each chapter help students understand and assimilate the important points covered and determine where additional review is required.

> **MANAGING YOUR WRITING**
>
> You are a public accountant with many small business clients. During a recent visit to a client's business, the bookkeeper approached you with a problem. The columns of the trial balance were not equal. You helped the bookkeeper find and correct the error, but believe you should go one step further. Write a memo to all of your clients that explains the purpose of the double-entry framework, the importance of maintaining the equality of the accounting equation, the errors that might cause an inequality, and suggestions for finding the errors.

- **Managing Your Writing,** introduced in a Chapter 1 module and written by Ken Davis of Indiana University—Purdue University, guides students through an easy-to-follow, 12-step process for honing writing skills. An assignment at the end of each chapter allows students to apply critical thinking and writing skills to issues raised by material in that chapter.

- **Ethics Cases** help students think through what they would do in various situations. Case problems for individual and group use allow students to weigh the merits of various ethical considerations related to accounting.

- **Self-Study Test Questions,** consisting of multiple-choice and true/false items, allow students to assess their understanding of chapter material to determine if further study is required before proceeding to the exercises and problems. Answers to the questions are provided at the end of the text.

- **A & B Exercises and Problems,** keyed to chapter learning objectives, provide a range of instructional choices. One set can be used in class and the other for assignments. Alternatively, both sets can be used for practice for students needing extra assistance.

> **MASTERY PROBLEM**
>
> ✓ Cash bal., June 30: $45,495;
> Trial Bal. total debits: $96,200
>
>
>
> Barry Bird opened the Barry Bird Basketball Camp for children ages 10 through 18. Campers typically register for one week in June or July, arriving on Sunday and returning home the following Saturday. College players serve as cabin counselors and assist the local college and high school coaches who run the practice sessions. The registration fee includes a room, meals at a nearby restaurant, and basketball instruction. In the off-season, the facilities are used for weekend retreats and coaching clinics. Bird developed the following chart of accounts for his service business.
>
> Chart of Accounts
>
> | Assets | | Revenues | |
> |---|---|---|---|
> | 101 | Cash | 401 | Registration Fees |
> | 142 | Office Supplies | | |
> | 183 | Athletic Equipment | Expenses | |
> | 184 | Basketball Facilities | 511 | Wages Expense |

- **Mastery Problems** challenge students to apply the essential elements introduced in the chapter. Selected assignments may be solved using Klooster and Allen General Ledger software. These are designated by icons shown here.

> **CHALLENGE PROBLEM**
>
> *This problem challenges you to apply your cumulative accounting knowledge to move a step beyond the material in the chapter.*
>
> ✓ Total debits: $19,150
>
> Journal entries and a trial balance for Fred Phaler Consulting follow. As you will note, the trial balance does not balance, suggesting that there are errors. Recall that the chapter offers tips on identifying individual posting errors. These techniques are not as effective when there are two or more errors. Thus, you will need to first carefully inspect the trial balance to see if you can identify any obvious errors due to amounts that either look out of proportion or are simply reported in the wrong place. Then, you will need to carefully evaluate the other amounts by using the techniques offered in the text, or tracing the journal entries to the amounts reported on the trial balance. (Hint: Four errors were made in the posting process and preparation of the trial balance.)

- **Challenge Problems**—Perhaps the most important measure of student understanding is the ability to apply newly learned concepts to new and unfamiliar situations. At the end of each chapter, the Challenge Problem tests the ability of more advanced or ambitious students to apply concepts to transactions, events, or economic conditions one step beyond what is laid out in the text.

> **COMPREHENSIVE PROBLEM 1:**
> **THE ACCOUNTING CYCLE**
>
> Bob Night opened "The General's Favorite Fishing Hole." The fishing camp is open from April through September and attracts many famous college basketball coaches during the off-season. Guests typically register for one week, arriving on Sunday afternoon and returning home the following Saturday afternoon. The registration fee includes room and board, the use of fishing boats, and professional instruction in fishing techniques. The chart of accounts for the camp operations is presented below.

- **Comprehensive Problems**—Comprehensive review problems are built directly into the text, providing an opportunity to review topics from multiple chapters.

PROVEN TO BE THE BEST!

OUR SERVICE COMMITMENT

The entire Heintz & Parry team is ready to help instructors. Your Thomson South-Western representative is always available to provide individualized assistance.

- Call the Academic Resource Center for desk copies and product information: 800-423-0563
- Career College Customers: 800-477-3692
- Community College or University Customers: 800-423-0563
- E-mail the authors or the publisher through the hot link at **http://www.thomsonedu.com/accounting/heintz**

The Product Web Site Is a Rich Resource

The Heintz & Parry Web site gives you access to supplement downloads, teaching ideas, hot links, and more. The Heintz & Parry Web site (**http://www.thomsonedu.com/accounting/heintz**) provides easy access assistance to both students and instructors. Links for Web Work assignments provide a helpful way to connect with assignment resources. Online quizzes with solutions help students test themselves as they study. Instructors have online access to many other resources, such as the solutions and instructor's manuals in Microsoft® Word, which are all password protected.

PROVEN TO BE THE BEST!

ACKNOWLEDGMENTS

We thank the following individuals for their helpful contributions in assisting us in this revision of *College Accounting*.

Lelia Austin, *Lake City Community College*

Cathie Bishop, *Parkland College*

Becky Hancock, *El Paso Community College*

Patti Fedje, *Minot State University*

Judy Toland, *Bucks County Community College*

William Hood, *Central Michigan University*

Aaron Reeves, *Saint Louis Community College—Forest Park*

James Farris, *Golden West College*

Jane Bloom, *Palm Beach Community College*

William Parrish, *Delgado Community College—City Park*

Marc Newman, *Hocking Technical College*

Cathy Collins, *Waubonsee Community College*

Anna Boulware, *St. Charles Community College*

Richard Dugger, *Kilgore Community College*

Del Spencer, *Trinity Valley Community College*

Sonja Lolland, *Sierra College*

Norma Lawless, *Panola College*

Scott Steinkamp, *College of Lake County*

Al Aspelund, *Century College*

Jerry Lafferty, *National College of Business and Technology*

William Schlemmer, *Normandale CC*

Claudia Gilbertson, *North Hennepin Community College*

Norma Hunting, *Heald College*

Patricia Lopez, *Valencia Community College*

Claire Moore, *Heald College*

Marlane Sanderston, *Minnesota State University—Moorhead*

Barbara Schulz, *Mott Community College*

Kenneth Utley, *Western Kentucky University*

David Zagorodney, *Heald College*

We'd like to thank the following faculty for their helpful responses to our most recent Web survey:

David White, *Missouri State*

Paul Muller, *Western Nevada Community College*

Scott Wange, *Davenport University*

PROVEN TO BE THE BEST!

Nancy Fallon, *Albertus Magnus College*

Lisa Nash, *Vincennes University*

Gary Reynolds, *Ohio Technical College*

Karen Marbot, *Hudson Valley Community College*

James Stanton, *MiraCosta College*

Donald Curfman, *McHenry County College*

Melissa Meeboer, *Eastern Wyoming College*

John Varelli, *Rogers State University*

Anne Wessely, *St. Louis Community College*

Michelle Stobnicke, *Santa Fe Community College*

Susan Winchester, *Highland Community College*

Tatyana Pashnyack, *Bainbridge College*

John Hartwick, *Glendale Community College*

Joann Dawe, *Front Range Community College*

Mary Bridges, *South Plains College*

Bunny Brosman, *Lake Land College*

Daniel Small, *J. Sargeant Reynolds Community College*

Roger McMillian, *Mineral Area College*

Elizabeth Crooks, *Fresno City College*

Donald Uecke, *Milwaukee Area Technical College*

Tamela Jarvais, *Blackhawk Technical College*

Laura Merfeld, *North Iowa Area Community College*

Michelle Meyer, *Joliet Junior College*

In addition, we would like to thank all who have assisted in providing the supporting materials. These individuals are listed in the supplements section on pages xvii–xix. We would like to thank Richard Dugger of Kilgore College and Donna Larner of Davenport College for their diligent verification of the solutions and working papers.

Special thanks to Jane Parry and Andrea Heintz for assistance in the development of this text. Finally, we thank Tina McCarty, owner of Pass It On Pet Supplies in Cincinnati, Ohio, for providing the location site for the Parkway Pet Supplies store photos used in the last two editions.

Through 19 editions, *College Accounting* has helped millions of students understand and employ basic accounting skills. But we know we can't rest on past success. The business world continues to change, and so do we. To prepare today's generation for a lifetime of accounting skills, the solution is simple. Depend on the text that's simply better than ever. *College Accounting, 19e.* From the leader in college accounting, you expect the best.

Jim Heintz
Rob Parry

Student Supplements and Resources	ISBN	Authors, Affiliations, Description
ThomsonNOW		ThomsonNOW provides all the tools you need to save you time studying and completing homework, and to help you succeed in class and on exams.
		• Complete chapter problems on-line and obtain instant feedback, hints, and grades.
		• See your grades, which homework and class assignments you've completed, and what work you need to complete in the future.
		• Reference the class syllabus on-line at any time.
		• Review personalized study plans to take advantage of the shortest path to learning.
		• Read the entire text as an eBook! Link to integrated eBook pages from specific assignments.
Study Guide and Working Papers		James Heintz and Robert Parry
Chapters 1–9 + Combination Journal Module	0-324-64021-8	Written by the authors, the Study Guide and the working papers for the end-of-chapter assignments in the text are provided
Package: Chapters 1–9 and Chapters 10–15	0-324-64012-9	together in one convenient resource. The Study Guide offers students the opportunity to reinforce their learning experience with brief discussions of the key points and learning objectives for each chapter. In addition, the Study Guide provides a third set of "C" assignments consisting of review questions, exercises, and problems similar to those at the end of each chapter. The solutions to the Study Guide assignments are available separately.
		The working papers are tailored to the text's end-of-chapter assignments. Journals, ledgers, work sheets, and other documents are provided to make preparation of the solutions less time consuming for the student. The text solutions manual contains the solutions to the end-of-chapter assignments on forms similar to those provided in the working papers.
Klooster and Allen General Ledger Software and Data Files CD		James Heintz and Robert Parry
Chapters 2–27	0-324-64738-7	Available for use with selected problems found in the main text (identified by icons). As students use the opening balances, chart of accounts, and set-up functions to complete problems, they gain valuable, hands-on experience with full-functioning general ledger software.
Jet Stream Cleaning Service Practice Set with Student CD		Janet Caruso, Nassau Community College
Appropriate for use after Chapter 7	0-324-64751-4	This practice set is a sole proprietorship service business simulation. It reviews the accounting cycle and accounting for cash. The practice set can be solved manually, with Klooster and Allen General Ledger software, or with Peachtree 2007 Educational Version by Sage. The student CD includes the installation files for both software packages as well as the relevant data files.

Keystone Furniture Practice Set with Student CD Appropriate for use after Chapter 15	0-324-64764-6	**Toni Hartley, Laurel Business Institute** This practice set contains information about a sole proprietorship merchandising business, covering payroll. It can be completed by using either the general journal alone or special journals. The practice set can be solved manually, with Klooster and Allen General Ledger software, or with Peachtree 2007 Educational Version by Sage. The student CD includes the installation files for both software packages as well as the relevant data files.

Instructor Supplements and Resources	**ISBN**	**Authors, Affiliations, Description**
Solutions Manual Chapters 1–15	0-324-63991-0	**James Heintz and Robert Parry** The complete, carefully verified solutions for all text assignments. Accounting rulings are used where appropriate. (*Note:* These are also the solutions to the working papers.)
Study Guide Solutions Chapters 1–9 + Combination Journal Module Chapters 10–15	0-324-54775-1 0-324-64735-2	**James Heintz and Robert Parry** Solutions to all set "C" assignments found in the Study Guide. **This may be packaged with the Study Guide at the instructor's discretion.**
Solutions Transparencies Chapters 1–15	0-324-64743-3	**James Heintz and Robert Parry** Contains solutions for the Series A & B Exercises and Problems, Mastery Problems, Challenge Problems, and Comprehensive Problems in the text. Where appropriate, solutions appear on accounting rulings.
Teaching Transparencies Chapters 1–15	0-324-64745-X	**James Heintz and Robert Parry** Colorful teaching transparencies of many of the text illustrations for use in classroom presentations.
Test Bank Chapters 1–15	0-324-63996-1	**Janet Caruso, Nassau Community College** These tests have been revised and carefully verified. AACSB tags have been added to aid in assessing competency reporting. The electronic test bank (ExamView) is available on the Instructor's Resource CD-ROM, as described on the next page.
Instructor's Resource Guide Chapters 1–15	0-324-64747-6	**William CK Alberts and Linda Alberts, National Business College** This guide contains a wealth of resources to help instructors create an exciting and productive classroom experience. Included are enhanced chapter outlines and teaching tips; references to exhibits, PowerPoint® slides, and teaching transparencies; suggested enrichments and activities; check figures for text assignments; pretests tied to learning objectives; and Ten Questions Your Students Will Always Ask to help anticipate student learning needs.
Achievement Tests Version A, Chapters 1–15 Version B, Chapters 1–15	0-324-64024-2 0-324-63997-X	These tests, grouped in "A" and "B" sets, allow for maximum flexibility in assigning in-class and out-of-class work for students.
Achievement Test Keys Version A, Chapters 1–15 Version B, Chapters 1–15	0-324-64008-0 0-324-64010-2	Solutions for the Achievement tests.

Instructor's Resource CD-ROM with **Exam** *View* ® Chapters 1–27	0-324-64742-5	A wealth of instructor resources can be found electronically on one convenient CD-Rom. The CD contains: • ExamView 5.0, an enhanced, easy to use electronic test bank that contains the questions found in the two printed test banks. • A complete set of PowerPoint® presentations, which reinforce text content by using engaging visuals that are paced well for student comprehension. • The solutions manual, instructor's manual, and text check figures are provided as Microsoft® Word files. • Inspector software files with solutions for instructors who use the Klooster and Allen General Ledger Software.
Jet Stream Cleaning Service Practice Set Key w/ Inspector CD	0-324-64752-2	**Janet Caruso, Nassau Community College** Instructor's Key for the Jet Stream Cleaning Service student practice set which includes the Inspector software for checking the solutions in the Klooster and Allen General Ledger software.
Keystone Furniture Practice Set Key w/ Inspector CD	0-324-64764-6	**Toni Hartley, Laurel Business Institute** Instructor's Key for the Keystone Furniture student practice set which includes the Inspector software for checking the solutions in the Klooster and Allen General Ledger software.
JoinIn on TurningPoint Visit http://www.turningpoint.thomsonlearning connections.com to find out more!	0-324-64933-9	JoinIn™ on Turning Point™ is interactive PowerPoint® and is simply the best classroom response system available today! This lecture tool provides interactive questions that provide immediate feedback on the students' understanding the topic at hand. As students are quizzed using clicker technology, instructors can use this instant feedback to lecture more efficiently.

Additional Resources

Using Peachtree Complete 2007 for Accounting (w/ CD-ROM) 1e	0-324-37797-5	**Glen Owen, Allan Hancock College** This text allows faculty to easily incorporate computerized accounting into the first accounting course. The textbook takes a user perspective by illustrating how accounting information is both used and created. In addition, the text uses proven and successful pedagogy to demonstrate the software's features and elicit student interaction. The text's foremost goal is to help students learn fundamental accounting concepts through the use of Peachtree and the analysis of business events. The content complements the first course in accounting and is therefore best used in conjunction with a core text on accounting or after students have had a first accounting course.
Using Quickbooks Pro 2007 for Accounting (w/ CD-ROM) 7e	0-324-37875-0	**Glen Owen, Allan Hancock College** Similar in description to the Peachtree text above, this book introduces students to Quickbooks Pro 2007.

CONTENTS IN BRIEF

PART 1   ACCOUNTING FOR A SERVICE BUSINESS   1

Chapter 1   Introduction to Accounting   3
Chapter 2   Analyzing Transactions: The Accounting Equation   19
Chapter 3   The Double-Entry Framework   53
Chapter 4   Journalizing and Posting Transactions   89
Chapter 5   Adjusting Entries and the Work Sheet   133
Chapter 6   Financial Statements and the Closing Process   181
Comprehensive Problem 1: The Accounting Cycle   225

PART 2   ACCOUNTING FOR CASH AND PAYROLL   231

Chapter 7   Accounting for Cash   233
Chapter 8   Payroll Accounting: Employee Earnings and Deductions   283
Chapter 9   Payroll Accounting: Employer Taxes and Reports   317

PART 3   ACCOUNTING FOR A MERCHANDISING BUSINESS   353

Chapter 10   Accounting for Sales and Cash Receipts   355
Chapter 11   Accounting for Purchases and Cash Payments   397
Chapter 12   Special Journals   439
Chapter 13   Accounting for Merchandise Inventory   491
Chapter 14   Adjustments and the Work Sheet for a Merchandising Business   531
Chapter 15   Financial Statements and Year-End Accounting for a Merchandising Business   575
Comprehensive Problem 2: Accounting Cycle with Subsidiary Ledgers, Part 1   619
Comprehensive Problem 2: Accounting Cycle with Subsidiary Ledgers, Part 2   622

Module 1: Accounting for a Professional Service Business: The Combination Journal   625

Answers to Self-Study Questions   659

Index   661

CONTENTS

PART 1   ACCOUNTING FOR A SERVICE BUSINESS   1

Chapter 1   Introduction to Accounting   3

The Purpose of Accounting   4
The Accounting Process   4
Generally Accepted Accounting Principles (GAAP)   5
Three Types of Ownership Structures   6
    Sole Proprietorship 6; Partnership 6; Corporation 7
Types of Businesses   7
Career Opportunities in Accounting   8
    Accounting Clerks 8; Bookkeepers and Para-Accountants 8; Accountants 8; Job Opportunities 10
To Do List   12
Key Points to Remember   14
Key Terms   14
Review Questions   16
Exercises   17
Managing Your Writing   18

Chapter 2   Analyzing Transactions: The Accounting Equation   19

The Accounting Elements   20
    Assets 20; Liabilities 20; Owner's Equity 20
The Accounting Equation   21
Analyzing Business Transactions   22
Effect of Transactions on the Accounting Equation   22
    Expanding the Accounting Equation: Revenues, Expenses, and Withdrawals 24;
    Effect of Revenue, Expense, and Withdrawal Transactions on the Accounting Equation 25
Financial Statements   31
    The Income Statement 31; The Statement of Owner's Equity 33; The Balance Sheet 33
Overview of the Accounting Process   34
Key Points to Remember   37
Demonstration Problem   38
Key Terms   41
Self-Study Test Questions   42
Review Questions   44
Exercises and Problems   44
Managing Your Writing   49
Mastery Problem   50
Challenge Problem   51

Chapter 3   The Double-Entry Framework   53

The T Account   54
Balancing a T Account   54
Debits and Credits   55
    Assets 55; Liabilities and Owner's Equity 55; The Owner's Equity Umbrella 55; Owner's Capital 56;
    Drawing 56; Revenues 56; Expenses 56; Normal Balances 56
Transaction Analysis   57
    Debits and Credits: Asset, Liability, and Owner's Equity Accounts 58;
    Debits and Credits: Including Revenues, Expenses, and Drawing 60;
    Summary of Transactions 69
The Trial Balance   70
Key Points to Remember   72
Demonstration Problem   73

Key Terms   76
Self-Study Test Questions   76
Review Questions   78
Exercises and Problems   78
Managing Your Writing   85
Mastery Problem   86
Challenge Problem   87

Chapter 4   Journalizing and Posting Transactions   89
Flow of Data   90
The Chart of Accounts   90
Source Documents   91
The General Journal   93
Journalizing 93
The General Ledger   98
General Ledger Account 98; Posting to the General Ledger 99; The Trial Balance 105
Finding and Correcting Errors in the Trial Balance   106
Ruling Method 107; Correcting Entry Method 108
Key Points to Remember   109
Demonstration Problem   110
Key Terms   115
Self-Study Test Questions   115
Review Questions   117
Exercises and Problems   118
Managing Your Writing   129
Mastery Problem   129
Challenge Problem   130

Chapter 5   Adjusting Entries and the Work Sheet   133
End-of-Period Adjustments   134
Supplies 135; Prepaid Insurance 137; Wages Expense 138; Depreciation Expense 139;
Expanded Chart of Accounts 141
The Work Sheet   142
The 10-Column Work Sheet 142; Preparing the Work Sheet 142; Preparing the Work Sheet 144G
Finding Errors on the Work Sheet   145
Journalizing Adjusting Entries   145
Posting Adjusting Entries   145
Methods of Accounting: Cash, Modified Cash, and Accrual   147
Key Points to Remember   151
Demonstration Problem   152
Key Terms   155
Self-Study Test Questions   156
Review Questions   157
Exercises and Problems   157
Managing Your Writing   170
Mastery Problem   172
Challenge Problem   173

Appendix   Depreciation Methods   175
Straight-Line Method   175
Sum-of-the-Years'-Digits   176
Double-Declining-Balance Method   176

Modified Accelerated Cost Recovery System 177
Key Points to Remember 178
Key Terms 178
Review Questions 179
Exercises 179

Chapter 6   Financial Statements and the Closing Process 181
The Financial Statements 182
The Income Statement 182; The Statement of Owner's Equity 182;
The Balance Sheet 185; Additional Investments by the Owner 186
The Closing Process 187
Journalize Closing Entries 190; Post the Closing Entries 190
Post-Closing Trial Balance 193
The Accounting Cycle 194
Key Points to Remember 199
Demonstration Problem 200
Key Terms 203
Self-Study Test Questions 204
Review Questions 205
Exercises and Problems 206
Managing Your Writing 215
Mastery Problem 215
Challenge Problem 217

Appendix   Statement of Cash Flows 219
Types of Business Activities 219
Preparing the Statement of Cash Flows 220
Key Points to Remember 222
Key Terms 223
Review Questions 223
Exercises and Problems 223

COMPREHENSIVE
PROBLEM 1   THE ACCOUNTING CYCLE 225

PART 2   ACCOUNTING FOR CASH AND PAYROLL 231

Chapter 7   Accounting for Cash 233
Checking Account 234
Opening a Checking Account 234; Making Deposits 234; Writing Checks 237; Bank Statement 239
Reconciling the Bank Statement 240
Deposits 240; Cash Payments 240; Reasons for Differences Between Bank and Book Balances 241;
Steps in Preparing the Bank Reconciliation 241; Illustration of a Bank Reconciliation 242; Journal
Entries 243; Electronic Funds Transfer 245
The Petty Cash Fund 245
Establishing a Petty Cash Fund 246; Making Payments from a Petty Cash Fund 246; Petty Cash
Payments Record 246; Replenishing the Petty Cash Fund 248
The Change Fund and Cash Short and Over 249
Establishing and Operating the Change Fund 249; Cash Short and Over 250
Key Points to Remember 251
Demonstration Problem 252
Key Terms 254

Self-Study Test Questions   255
Review Questions   256
Exercises and Problems   257
Managing Your Writing   265
Ethics Case   265
Mastery Problem   266
Challenge Problem   267

Appendix   Internal Controls   269
Importance of Internal Control   269
Key Components of Internal Control   270
   Control Environment 271; Risk Assessment 271; Control Activities 271; Information and
   Communication System 272; Monitoring Processes 272
Internal Controls Over Cash Receipts   272
Internal Controls Over Cash Payments   273
   Voucher System 273
Key Points to Remember   278
Key Terms   278
Review Questions   279
Exercises and Problems   279

Practice Set: Jet Stream Cleaning Service

This set is a service business operating as a sole-proprietorship. It reviews the accounting cycle and accounting for cash, utilizing general journals. It can be solved manually, with K&A general ledger software, or Peachtree 2007 by Sage. Appropriate for use after Chapter 7.

Chapter 8   Payroll Accounting: Employee Earnings and Deductions   283
Employees and Independent Contractors   284
Employee Earnings and Deductions   284
   Salaries and Wages 284; Computing Total Earnings 285; Deductions from Total Earnings 287;
   Computing Net Pay 292
Payroll Records   293
   Payroll Register 293; Payroll Check 294; Employee Earnings Record 296
Accounting for Employee Earnings and Deductions   296
   Journalizing Payroll Transactions 296; Wages and Salaries Expense 298; Employee Income Tax
   Payable 299; Social Security and Medicare Taxes Payable 299; Other Deductions 299
Payroll Record-Keeping Methods   300
Key Points to Remember   301
Demonstration Problem   302
Key Terms   305
Self-Study Test Questions   306
Review Questions   307
Exercises and Problems   307
Managing Your Writing   314
Ethics Case   314
Mastery Problem   315
Challenge Problem   316

Chapter 9   Payroll Accounting: Employer Taxes and Reports   317
  Employer Payroll Taxes   318
    Employer FICA Taxes 318; Self-Employment Tax 319; Employer FUTA Tax 320; Employer SUTA Tax 320
  Accounting for Employer Payroll Taxes   321
    Journalizing Employer Payroll Taxes 321; Payroll Taxes Expense 322; Social Security and Medicare Taxes Payable 322; FUTA Tax Payable 323; SUTA Tax Payable 323; Total Payroll Cost of an Employee 323
  Reporting and Payment Responsibilities   324
    Federal Income Tax Withholding and Social Security and Medicare Taxes 324; FUTA Taxes 326; SUTA Taxes 330; Employee Wage and Tax Statement 330; Summary of Employee Wages and Taxes 331; Summary of Taxes, Reports, and Payments 331
  Workers' Compensation Insurance   333
  Key Points to Remember   337
  Demonstration Problem   338
  Key Terms   340
  Self-Study Test Questions   340
  Review Questions   341
  Exercises and Problems   342
  Managing Your Writing   350
  Ethics Case   350
  Mastery Problem   350
  Challenge Problem   351

PART 3   ACCOUNTING FOR A MERCHANDISING BUSINESS   353

Chapter 10   Accounting for Sales and Cash Receipts   355
  Merchandise Sales Transactions   356
    Retailer 356; Wholesaler 357; Credit Memorandum 358
  Merchandise Sales Accounts   359
    Sales Account 360; Sales Tax Payable Account 361; Sales Returns and Allowances Account 361; Sales Discounts Account 362
  Journalizing and Posting Sales and Cash Receipts Transactions   363
    Sales 363; Posting Sales to the General Ledger 364; Posting Sales to the Accounts Receivable Ledger 365; Sales Returns and Allowances 367; Cash Receipts 367; Posting Cash Receipts to the General Ledger and Accounts Receivable Ledger 370
  Schedule of Accounts Receivable   371
  Key Points to Remember   373
  Demonstration Problem   375
  Key Terms   381
  Self-Study Test Questions   382
  Review Questions   383
  Exercises and Problems   383
  Managing Your Writing   392
  Ethics Case   393
  Mastery Problem   393
  Challenge Problem   396

Chapter 11   Accounting for Purchases and Cash Payments   397
  Merchandise Purchases Transactions   398
    Purchase Requisition 398; Purchase Order 399; Receiving Report and Purchase Invoice 400; Cash and Trade Discounts 400

Merchandise Purchases Accounts   **401**
Purchases Account 402; Purchases Returns and Allowances Account 403; Purchases Discounts
Account 403; Freight-In Account 404; Computation of Gross Profit 405
Journalizing and Posting Purchases and Cash Payments Transactions   **407**
Purchases 407; Posting Purchases to the General Ledger 408; Posting Purchases to the Accounts
Payable Ledger 409; Purchases Returns and Allowances 410; Cash Payments 411; Posting Cash
Payments to the General Ledger and Accounts Payable Ledger 411
Schedule of Accounts Payable   **412**
Key Points to Remember   **415**
Demonstration Problem   **416**
Key Terms   **421**
Self-Study Test Questions   **421**
Review Questions   **422**
Exercises and Problems **423**
Managing Your Writing   **432**
Ethics Case   **432**
Mastery Problem   **433**
Challenge Problem   **434**

Appendix   The Net-Price Method of Recording Purchases   435
Net-Price Method   **435**
Recording with the Net-Price Method   **435**
Key Points to Remember   **436**
Key Terms   **436**
Review Questions   **437**
Exercises   **437**

Chapter 12   Special Journals   439
Special Journals   **440**
Sales Journal   **441**
Posting from the Sales Journal 442
Cash Receipts Journal   **444**
Posting from the Cash Receipts Journal 447
Purchases Journal   **451**
Posting from the Purchases Journal 452
Cash Payments Journal   **455**
Posting from the Cash Payments Journal 456
Key Points to Remember   **462**
Demonstration Problem   **466**
Key Terms   **472**
Self-Study Test Questions   **472**
Review Questions   **473**
Exercises and Problems   **474**
Managing Your Writing   **485**
Ethics Case   **486**
Mastery Problem   **486**
Challenge Problem   **488**

Chapter 13   Accounting for Merchandise Inventory   491
The Impact of Merchandise Inventory on Financial Statements   **492**
Types of Inventory Systems: Periodic and Perpetual   **494**

Assigning Cost to Inventory and Cost of Goods Sold   495
Taking a Physical Inventory 495; The Periodic Inventory System 498; The Perpetual Inventory System 502; Lower-of-Cost-or-Market Method of Inventory Valuation 503
Estimating Ending Inventory and Cost of Goods Sold   504
Gross Profit Method of Estimating Inventory 505; Retail Method of Estimating Inventory 505
Key Points to Remember   507
Demonstration Problem   509
Key Terms   511
Self-Study Test Questions   512
Review Questions   514
Exercises and Problems   515
Managing Your Writing   522
Ethics Case   522
Mastery Problem   523
Challenge Problem   524

Appendix   Perpetual Inventory Method: LIFO and Moving-Average Methods   525
Perpetual LIFO   525
Perpetual Moving-Average   526
Key Points to Remember   527
Key Terms   528
Review Questions   528
Exercises and Problems   528

Chapter 14   Adjustments and the Work Sheet for a Merchandising Business   531
Adjustment for Merchandise Inventory: Periodic Inventory System   532
Adjustment for Unearned Revenue   535
Expanded Chart of Accounts 536
Preparing a Work Sheet for a Merchandising Business   537
Adjustments for Northern Micro 537; Preparing a Work Sheet for Northern Micro 537
Adjusting Entries   544
Preparing and Journalizing Adjusting Entries Under the Perpetual Inventory System   544
Key Points to Remember   546
Demonstration Problem   547
Key Terms   550
Self-Study Test Questions   551
Review Questions   552
Exercises and Problems   552
Managing Your Writing   565
Ethics Case   567
Mastery Problem   567
Challenge Problem   569

Appendix   Expense Method of Accounting for Prepaid Expenses   571
The Expense Method   571
Adjusting Entries Under the Expense Method   571
Key Points to Remember   573
Key Terms   573
Exercises   573

Chapter 15   Financial Statements and Year-End Accounting for a Merchandising
Business   575
The Income Statement   576
The Statement of Owner's Equity   580
Balance Sheet   580
Current Assets 582; Property, Plant, and Equipment 582; Current Liabilities 582; Long-Term
Liabilities 582; Owner's Equity 583
Financial Statement Analysis   583
Balance Sheet Analysis 583; Interstatement Analysis 584
Closing Entries   586
Post-Closing Trial Balance 588
Reversing Entries   588
Key Points to Remember   591
Demonstration Problem   594
Key Terms   600
Self-Study Test Questions   601
Review Questions   602
Exercises and Problems   603
Managing Your Writing   616
Ethics Case   616
Mastery Problem   617
Challenge Problem   617

COMPREHENSIVE
PROBLEM 2   **ACCOUNTING CYCLE WITH SUBSIDIARY LEDGERS, PART 1   619**

COMPREHENSIVE
PROBLEM 2   **ACCOUNTING CYCLE WITH SUBSIDIARY LEDGERS, PART 2   622**

Practice Set: Keystone Furniture

This set is a merchandising business operating as a sole-proprietorship. It
includes accounting for payroll, and can be solved using either general
journals or special journals. It can be solved manually, with K&A general
ledger software, or Peachtree 2007 by Sage. Appropriate for use beginning
with Chapter 12, continuing up through Chapter 15, where students will
be asked to prepare a simple income statement and balance sheet.

Module 1   Accounting for a Professional Service Business:
The Combination Journal   625
The Modified Cash and Accrual Bases of Accounting   625
Accounting for a Professional Service Business   626
The Combination Journal   628
Journalizing in a Combination Journal 629; Proving the Combination Journal 630
Posting from the Combination Journal   632
Determining the Cash Balance 634
Performing End-of-Period Work for a Professional Service Business   634
Preparing the Work Sheet 634; Preparing Financial Statements 634;
Preparing Adjusting and Closing Entries 638
Key Points to Remember   639

Demonstration Problem   640
Key Terms   645
Self-Study Test Questions   645
Review Questions   646
Exercises and Problems   646
Managing Your Writing   655
Ethics Case   655
Mastery Problem   655
Challenge Problem   657

Answer to Self-Study Questions   659

Index   661

Accounting for a Service Business

1 Introduction to Accounting

2 Analyzing Transactions: The Accounting Equation

3 The Double-Entry Framework

4 Journalizing and Posting Transactions

5 Adjusting Entries and the Work Sheet

6 Financial Statements and the Closing Process

Objectives
Careful study of this chapter should enable you to:

LO1
Describe the purpose of accounting.

LO2
Describe the accounting process.

LO3
Define GAAP and describe the process used by FASB to develop these principles.

LO4
Define three types of business ownership structures.

LO5
Classify different types of businesses by activities.

LO6
Identify career opportunities in accounting.

Introduction to Accounting

So, you have decided to study accounting. Good decision. A solid foundation in accounting concepts and techniques will be helpful. This is true whether you take a professional position in accounting or business, or simply want to better understand your personal finances and dealings with businesses.

Throughout Chapters 2 through 6, we will introduce Jessie Jane's Campus Delivery service. By studying Jessie's business transactions and accounting techniques, you will learn about business and accounting. This is a major advantage of studying accounting. While studying accounting, you also learn a lot about business.

Knowledge of how accounting works will help you evaluate the financial health of businesses and other organizations. It will also give you a solid approach to dealing with financial and business transactions in your personal life. How do you plan to use the accounting skills developed in this class?

Accounting is the language of business. You must learn this language to understand the impact of economic events on a specific company. Common, everyday terms have very precise meanings when used in accounting. For example, you have probably heard terms like asset, liability, revenue, expense, and net income. Take a moment to jot down how you would define each of these terms. After reading and studying Chapter 2, compare your definitions with those developed in this text. This comparison will show whether you can trust your current understanding of accounting terms. Whether you intend to pursue a career in accounting or simply wish to understand the impact of business transactions, you need a clear understanding of this language.

THE PURPOSE OF ACCOUNTING

LO1 Describe the purpose of accounting.

The purpose of accounting is to provide financial information about the current operations and financial condition of a business to individuals, agencies, and organizations. As shown in Figure 1-1, owners, managers, creditors, and government agencies all need accounting information. Other users of accounting information include customers, clients, labor unions, stock exchanges, and financial analysts.

FIGURE 1-1   Users of Accounting Information

USER	INFORMATION NEEDED	DECISIONS MADE BY USERS
Owners—Present and future	Company's profitability and current financial condition.	If business is good, owners may consider making additional investments for growth. If business is poor, they may want to talk to management to find out why and may consider closing the business.
Managers—May or may not own business	Detailed measures of business performance.	Managers need to make operating decisions. How much and what kinds of inventory should be carried? Is business strong enough to support higher wages for employees?
Creditors—Present and future	Company's profitability, debt outstanding, and assets that could be used to secure debt.	Should a loan be granted to this business? If so, what amount of debt can the business support, and what interest rate should be charged?
Government Agencies—National, state, and local	Company's profitability, cash flows, and overall financial condition.	The IRS will decide how much income tax the business must pay. Local governments may be willing to adjust property taxes paid by the business to encourage it to stay in town.

THE ACCOUNTING PROCESS

LO2 Describe the accounting process.

Accounting is a system of gathering financial information about a business and reporting this information to users. The six major steps of the accounting process are analyzing, recording, classifying, summarizing, reporting, and interpreting (Figure 1-2). Computers are often used in the recording, classifying, summarizing, and reporting steps. Whether or not computers are used, the accounting concepts and techniques are the same. Information entered into the computer system must reflect a proper application of these concepts. Otherwise, the output will be meaningless.

FIGURE 1-2   The Accounting Process

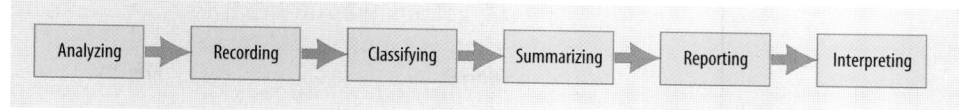

- **Analyzing** is looking at events that have taken place and thinking about how they affect the business.
- **Recording** is entering financial information about events into the accounting system. Although this can be done with paper and pencil, most businesses use computers to perform routine record-keeping operations.
- **Classifying** is sorting and grouping similar items together rather than merely keeping a simple, diary-like record of numerous events.
- **Summarizing** is the aggregation of many similar events to provide information that is easy to understand. For example, a firm may buy and sell baseballs during the year. Summarizing provides information on the total baseballs bought and sold and the change in the number of baseballs held from the beginning to the end of the period.
- **Reporting** is telling the results. In accounting, it is common to use tables of numbers to report results.
- **Interpreting** is deciding the meaning and importance of the information in various reports. This may include ratio analysis to help explain how pieces of information relate to one another.

GENERALLY ACCEPTED ACCOUNTING PRINCIPLES (GAAP)

LO3 Define GAAP and describe the process used by FASB to develop these principles.

Soon after the stock market crash of 1929, the federal government established the Securities and Exchange Commission (SEC). The purpose of this government agency is to help develop standards for reporting financial information to stockholders. The SEC currently has authority over 12,000 companies listed on the major stock exchanges (New York, American, and NASDAQ). It has the power to require these firms to follow certain rules when preparing their financial statements. These rules are referred to as **generally accepted accounting principles** (GAAP).

Rather than developing GAAP on its own, the SEC encouraged the creation of a private standard-setting body. It did so because it believed the private sector had better access to the resources and talent necessary to develop these standards. Since 1973, the Financial Accounting Standards Board (FASB) has filled this role. In developing accounting standards, FASB follows a specific process and relies on the advice of many organizations. When an accounting issue is identified, the following steps are followed.

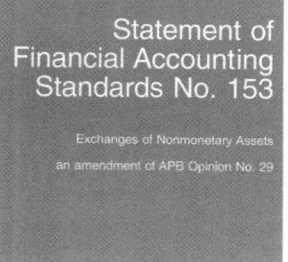

1. The issue is placed on FASB's agenda. This lets everyone know that the Board plans to develop a standard addressing this issue.

2. After researching an issue, FASB issues a **discussion memorandum**. This document identifies the pros and cons of various accounting treatments for an event.

3. To gather additional views on the issue, the Board will often hold **public hearings** around the country. Interested parties are invited to express their opinions at these hearings.

4. Following these hearings, the Board issues an **exposure draft**. This document explains the rules that FASB believes firms should follow in accounting for this event.

5. After considering feedback on the exposure draft, the Board issues a final **statement of financial accounting standards** (SFAS).

Throughout this process, many parties participate by testifying at public hearings, or by sending letters to the Board explaining why they agree or disagree with the proposed standard. These parties include the American Institute of Certified Public Accountants (AICPA), the American Accounting Association (AAA), the Institute of Management Accountants (IMA), the Financial Executives Institute (FEI), corporate executives and accountants, representatives from the investment community, analysts, bankers, industry associations, and the SEC and other government agencies. Clearly, FASB considers the views of a wide range of parties. By doing so, it maximizes the likelihood of developing and gaining acceptance of the most appropriate accounting and disclosure requirements.

THREE TYPES OF OWNERSHIP STRUCTURES

LO4 Define three types of business ownership structures.

One or more persons may own a business. Businesses are classified according to who owns them and the specific way they are organized. Three types of ownership structures are (1) sole proprietorship, (2) partnership, and (3) corporation (Figure 1-3). Accountants provide information to owners of all three types of ownership structures.

Sole Proprietorship

A **sole proprietorship** is owned by one person. The owner is often called a proprietor. The proprietor often manages the business. The owner assumes all risks for the business, and personal assets can be taken to pay creditors. The advantage of a sole proprietorship is that the owner can make all decisions.

Most businesses in the United States operate as sole proprietorships or partnerships. However, corporations earn the highest amount of revenue. The

FIGURE 1-3   Types of Ownership Structures—Advantages and Disadvantages

TYPES OF OWNERSHIP STRUCTURES		
Sole Proprietorship	**Partnership**	**Corporation**
• One owner	• Two or more partners	• Stockholders
• Owner assumes all risk	• Partners share risks	• Stockholders have limited risk
• Owner makes all decisions	• Partners may disagree on how to run business	• Stockholders may have little influence on business decisions

largest corporations in the United States are known as the "Fortune 500."

Partnership

A **partnership** is owned by more than one person. One or more partners may manage the business. Like proprietors, partners assume the risks for the business, and their assets may be taken to pay creditors. An advantage of a partnership is that owners share risks and decision making. A disadvantage is that partners may disagree about the best way to run the business.

Corporation

A **corporation** is owned by stockholders (or shareholders). Corporations may have many owners, and they usually employ professional managers. The owners' risk is usually limited to their initial investment, and they often have very little influence on the business decisions.

TYPES OF BUSINESSES

LO5 Classify different types of businesses by activities.

Businesses are classified according to the type of service or product provided. Some businesses provide a service. Others sell a product. A business that provides a service is called a **service business**. A business that buys a product from another business to sell to customers is called a **merchandising business**. A business that makes a product to sell is called a **manufacturing business**. You will learn about all three types of businesses in this book. Figure 1-4 lists examples of types of businesses organized by activity.

FIGURE 1-4 Types and Examples of Businesses Organized by Activities

SERVICE	MERCHANDISING	MANUFACTURING
Travel Agency	Department Store	Automobile Manufacturer
Computer Consultant	Pharmacy	Furniture Maker
Physician	Jewelry Store	Toy Factory

A BROADER VIEW

© DAVE BARTRUFF/INDEX STOCK IMAGERY/JUPITER IMAGES

All Kinds of Businesses Need Accounting Systems

Even small businesses like those that provide guided horseback tours of the Rocky Mountains need good accounting systems. Proper records must be maintained for the cost of the horses, feed, food served, tour guides' salaries, and office expenses. Without this information, the company would not know how much to charge and whether a profit is made on these trips.

CAREER OPPORTUNITIES IN ACCOUNTING

LO6 Identify career opportunities in accounting.

Accounting offers many career opportunities. The positions described below require varying amounts of education, experience, and technological skill.

Accounting Clerks

Businesses with large quantities of accounting tasks to perform daily often employ **accounting clerks** to record, sort, and file accounting information. Often, accounting clerks will specialize in cash, payroll, accounts receivable, accounts payable, inventory, or purchases. As a result, they are involved with only a small portion of the total accounting responsibilities for the firm. Accounting clerks usually have at least one year of accounting education.

Bookkeepers and Para-Accountants

Bookkeepers generally supervise the work of accounting clerks, help with daily accounting work, and summarize accounting information. In small-to-medium-sized businesses, the bookkeeper may also help managers and owners interpret the accounting information. Bookkeepers usually have one to two years of accounting education and experience as an accounting clerk.

Para-accountants provide many accounting, auditing, or tax services under the direct supervision of an accountant. A typical para-accountant has a two-year degree or significant accounting and bookkeeping experience.

Accountants

The difference between accountants and bookkeepers is not always clear, particularly in smaller companies where bookkeepers also help interpret the accounting information. In large companies, the distinction is clearer. Bookkeepers focus on the processing of accounting data. **Accountants** design the accounting information system and focus on analyzing and interpreting information. They also look for important trends in the data and study the impact of alternative decisions.

Most accountants enter the field with a college degree in accounting. In fact, since many states require 150 credit hours to sit for the CPA exam, many students are also earning a masters degree in accounting before entering the profession. Accountants are employed in public accounting, private (managerial) accounting, and governmental and not-for-profit accounting (Figure 1-5).

FIGURE 1-5 Accounting Careers

ACCOUNTING CAREERS		
Public Accounting • Auditing • Taxation • Management Advisory Services	**Private Accounting** • Accounting Information Systems • Financial Accounting • Cost Accounting • Budgeting • Tax Accounting • Internal Auditing	**Governmental and Not-for-Profit Accounting**

ACCOUNTING CLERK I
Performs accounting activities such as maintenance of the general ledger and preparation of various accounting statements and financial reports. Requires a high school diploma or its equivalent with 0–3 years of experience in the field or in a related area. $25,000–$32,000

BOOKKEEPER
Maintains and records business transactions. Balances ledgers and prepares reports. May require an associate's degree or its equivalent with 2–4 years of experience in the field or in a related area. $29,000–$38,600

BUDGET ANALYST I
Analyzes accounting records to determine financial resources required to implement programs and makes recommendations for budget allocations to ensure conformance to budgetary limits. Also responsible for reviewing operating budgets periodically in order to analyze trends affecting budget needs. Requires a bachelor's degree and 0–2 years of experience in the field or in a related area. $39,800–$50,000

ACCOUNTS PAYABLE
MANAGER
Responsible for all activities in the accounts payable function. Ensures timely payments of vendor invoices and expense vouchers and maintains accurate records and control reports. Reviews applicable accounting reports and accounts payable register to ensure accuracy. May require a bachelor's degree in a related area and at least 7 years of experience in the field. Familiar with a variety of the field's concepts, practices, and procedures. Relies on experience and judgment to plan and accomplish goals. Manages a staff of administrators/clerks and typically reports to the controller. $56,000–$77,000

CHIEF AUDIT OFFICER
Oversees all aspects of an organization's auditing function. Responsible for planning and directing all accounting and financial data. Requires a bachelor's degree with at least 15 years of experience in the field. Familiar with a variety of the field's concepts, practices, and procedures. Relies on extensive experience and judgment to plan and accomplish goals. Performs a variety of tasks. Leads and directs the work of others. A wide degree of creativity and latitude is expected. Typically reports to top management. $119,000–$180,000

Public Accounting

Public accountants offer services in much the same way as doctors and lawyers. The public accountant can achieve professional recognition as a **Certified Public Accountant** (CPA). This is done by meeting certain educational and experience requirements as determined by each state, and passing a uniform examination prepared by the American Institute of Certified Public Accountants.

Many CPAs work alone, while others work for local, regional, or national accounting firms that vary in scope and size. The largest public accounting firms in the United States are known as the "Big Four." They are Deloitte and Touche, Ernst & Young, KPMG, and PricewaterhouseCoopers.

Services offered by public accountants are listed below.

- **Auditing.** Auditing involves the application of standard review and testing procedures to be certain that proper accounting policies and practices have been followed. The purpose of the audit is to provide an independent opinion that the financial information about a business is fairly presented in a manner consistent with generally accepted accounting principles.

- **Taxation.** Tax specialists advise on tax planning, prepare tax returns, and represent clients before governmental agencies such as the Internal Revenue Service.

- **Management Advisory Services.** Given the financial training and business experience of public accountants, many businesses seek their advice on a wide variety of managerial issues. Often, accounting firms are involved in designing computerized accounting systems.

In 2002, the **Sarbanes-Oxley Act** (SOX) was passed by Congress to help improve reporting practices of public companies. The act was in response to accounting scandals at firms like Enron, WorldCom, and others. A contributing factor to these accounting scandals may have been a lack of independence between the auditor and the company. For example, many believe that it is not appropriate for the same accounting firm to provide management advisory and audit services to the same company. First, it may be difficult to find fault with actions taken by the company based on advice from the same accounting firm. Second, management advisory fees often exceed audit fees. Thus, accounting firms may have been reluctant to disagree with some of the client's accounting practices because it may have resulted in losing lucrative fees for management advisory services. As a result, although public accounting firms provide the above services, SOX prohibits providing management advisory and audit services to the same company. Further, audit and tax services may be provided to the same company only if preapproval is granted by the audit committee of the company.

Private (Managerial) Accounting

Many accountants are employees of private business firms. The **controller** oversees the entire accounting process and is the principal accounting officer of the company. Private or managerial accountants perform a wide variety of services for the business. These services are listed below.

- **Accounting Information Systems.** Accountants in this area design and implement manual and computerized accounting systems.

- **Financial Accounting.** Based on the accounting data prepared by the bookkeepers and accounting clerks, accountants prepare various reports and financial statements and help in analyzing operating, investing, and financing decisions.

- **Cost Accounting.** The cost of producing specific products or providing services must be measured. Further analysis is also done to determine whether the products and services are produced in the most cost-effective manner.
- **Budgeting.** In the budgeting process, accountants help managers develop a financial plan.
- **Tax Accounting.** Instead of hiring a public accountant, a company may have its own accountants. They focus on tax planning, preparation of tax returns, and dealing with the Internal Revenue Service and other governmental agencies.
- **Internal Auditing.** Internal auditors review the operating and accounting control procedures adopted by management to make sure the controls are adequate and are being followed. They also monitor the accuracy and timeliness of the reports provided to management and to external parties.

A managerial accountant can achieve professional status as a **Certified Management Accountant** (CMA). This is done by passing a uniform examination offered by the Institute of Management Accountants. An internal auditor can achieve professional recognition as a **Certified Internal Auditor** (CIA) by passing the uniform examination offered by the Institute of Internal Auditors.

Governmental and Not-for-Profit Accounting

Thousands of governmental and not-for-profit organizations (states, cities, schools, churches, and hospitals) gather and report financial information. These organizations employ a large number of accountants. Since these entities are not profit-oriented, the rules are somewhat different for governmental and not-for-profit organizations. However, many accounting procedures are similar to those found in profit-seeking enterprises.

Job Opportunities

Job growth in some areas will be much greater than in others. Newspaper advertisements often indicate that accountants and accounting clerks are expected to have computer skills. Computer skills definitely increase the opportunities available to you in your career. Almost every business needs accountants, accounting clerks, and bookkeepers. Figure 1-6 shows the expected growth for different types of businesses. Notice that growth will be greatest in the service businesses. Chapters 2 through 9 introduce accounting skills that you will need to work in a service business. Chapter 10 begins the discussion of merchandising businesses. Accounting for manufacturing businesses is addressed in the last chapters of the book.

Figure 1-7 shows the expected demand for accounting skills. A small increase in demand is expected for bookkeeping, accounting, and auditing clerks, and these types of positions will offer the highest number of job opportunities over the next several years. The next highest demand is for accountants and auditors, and this demand is expected to increase over the next several years.

Regardless of the type of career you desire, writing skills are important in business and your personal life. Becoming a good writer requires practice and a strategy for the process used to prepare memos, letters, and other documents. On pages 12 and 13, Ken Davis offers an excellent approach to managing your writing. Take a moment to read Ken's tips. Then, practice his approach by completing the writing assignments as you finish each chapter.

FIGURE 1-6   Expected Growth

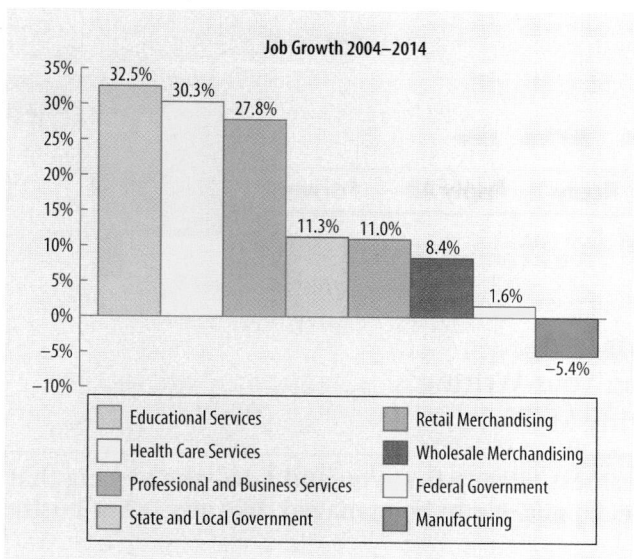

The growth in the number of new jobs from 2004 to 2014 will vary according to industry. The major area of growth will be in service businesses. Businesses providing educational, health care, and professional/business services are expected to have the strongest employment growth. There is expected to be fairly strong growth in merchandising businesses and state and local governments. Job growth in the federal government will be small, and there is expected to be about a 5% reduction in employment in manufacturing businesses. Total employment for all industry sectors will increase 13.0%.

Source: U.S. Department of Labor—Bureau of Labor Statistics (http://www.bls.gov) as of January 18, 2006.

FIGURE 1-7   Expected Demand

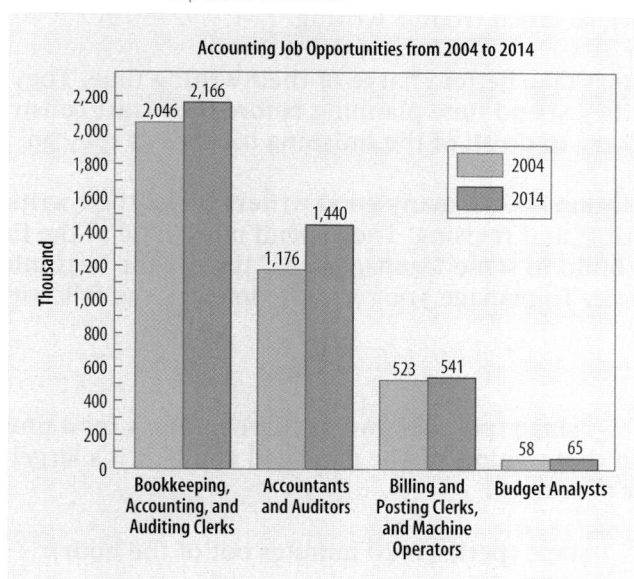

The highest number of jobs available will be for bookkeepers, accounting and auditing clerks, and accountants and auditors. The growth for each area shown from 2004 to 2014 will be:

	Thousands	Percentage
Accountants and auditors	264	22.4%
Budget analysts	8*	13.5%*
Bookkeeping, accounting, and auditing clerks	120	5.9%
Billing and posting clerks, and machine operators	18	3.4%

*Differences due to rounding.

Source: Daniel Hecker, "Occupational Employment Projections to 2014," *Monthly Labor Review,* November 2005.

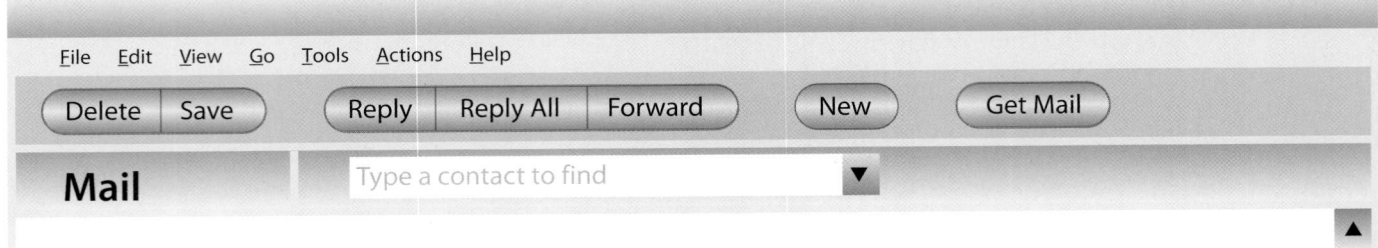

File   Edit   View   Go   Tools   Actions   Help

Delete   Save   Reply   Reply All   Forward   New   Get Mail

Mail

Type a contact to find ▼

From: Ken Davis
Subject: Managing Your Writing
To: Accounting Students

Here's a secret: the business writing that you and I do—the writing that gets the world's work done—requires no special gift. It can be managed, like any other business process.

Managing writing is largely a matter of managing time. Writing is a process, and like any process it can be done efficiently or inefficiently. Unfortunately, most of us are pretty inefficient writers. That's because we try to get each word, each sentence, right the first time. Given a letter to write, we begin with the first sentence. We think about that sentence, write it, revise it, even check its spelling, before going on to the second sentence. In an hour of writing, we might spend 45 or 50 minutes doing this kind of detailed drafting. We spend only a few minutes on overall planning at the beginning and only a few minutes on overall revising at the end.

That approach to writing is like building a house by starting with the front door: planning, building, finishing—even washing the windows—before doing anything with the rest of the house. No wonder most of us have so much trouble writing.

Efficient, effective writers take better charge of their writing time. They *manage* their writing. Like building contractors, they spend time planning before they start construction. Once construction has started, they don't try to do all of the finishing touches as they go.

As the following illustration shows, many good writers break their writing process into three main stages: planning, drafting, and revising. They spend more time at the first and third stages than at the second. They also build in some "management" time at the beginning and the end, and some break time in the middle. To manage *your* writing time, try the following steps.

	To Do List
✓	At the MANAGING stage (perhaps two or three minutes for a one-hour writing job), remind yourself that writing *can* be managed and that it's largely a matter of managing time. Plan your next hour.
	At the PLANNING stage (perhaps 20 minutes out of the hour):
	1. **Find the "we."** Define the community to which you and your reader belong. Then ask, "How are my reader and I alike and different?"—in knowledge, attitudes, and circumstances.
	2. **Define your purpose.** Remember the advice a consultant once gave Stanley Tool executives: "You're not in the business of making drills: you're in the business of making holes." Too many of us lose sight of the difference between making drills and making holes when we write letters and memos. We focus on the piece of writing—the tool itself—not its purpose. The result: our writing often misses the chance to be as effective as it could be. When you're still at the planning stage, focus on the outcome you want, not on the means you will use to achieve it.

3. **Get your stuff together.** Learn from those times when you've turned a one-hour home-improvement project into a three- or four-hour job by having to make repeated trips to the hardware store for tools or parts. Before you start the drafting stage of writing, collect the information you need.

4. **Get your ducks in a row.** Decide on the main points you want to make. Then, make a list or rough outline placing your points in the most logical order.

At the DRAFTING STAGE (perhaps 5 minutes out of the hour):

5. **Do it wrong the first time.** Do a "quick and dirty" draft, without editing. Think of your draft as a "prototype," written not for the end user but for your own testing and improvement. Stopping to edit while you draft breaks your train of thought and keeps you from being a good writer. (*Hint*: If you are writing at a computer, try turning off the monitor during the drafting stage.)

At the BREAK STAGE (perhaps 5 minutes):

6. **Take a break and change hats.** Get away from your draft, even if for only a few minutes. Come back with a fresh perspective—the reader's perspective.

At the REVISING STAGE (perhaps 25 minutes):

7. **Signal your turns.** Just as if you were driving a car, you're leading your reader through new territory. Use "turn signals"—*and, in addition, but, however, or, therefore, because, for example*—to guide your reader from sentence to sentence.

8. **Say what you mean.** Put the point of your sentences in the subjects and verbs. For example, revise "There are drawbacks to using this accounting method" to "This accounting method has some drawbacks." You'll be saying what you mean, and you'll be a more effective communicator.

9. **Pay by the word.** Reading your memo requires work. If your sentences are wordy and you are slow to get to the point, the reader may decide that it is not worth the effort. Pretend you are paying the reader by the word to read your memo. Then, revise your memo to make it as short and to the point as possible.

10. **Translate into English.** Keep your words simple. (Lee Iacocca put both these tips in one "commandment of good management": "Say it in English and keep it short.") Remember that you write to express, not impress.

11. **Finish the job.** Check your spelling, punctuation, and mechanics.

Finally, at the MANAGING STAGE again (2 to 3 minutes):

12. **Evaluate your writing process.** Figure out how to improve it next time.

By following these 12 steps, you can take charge of your writing time. Begin today to *manage your writing.* As a United Technologies Corporation advertisement in *The Wall Street Journal* admonished, "If you want to manage somebody, manage yourself. Do that well and you'll be ready to stop managing and start leading."

Dr. Kenneth W. Davis is Professor of English and Adjunct Professor of Communication Studies at Indiana University-Purdue University, Indianapolis. He is also president of Komei, Inc., a communication consulting and training company.

Learning Objectives	Key Points to Remember
LO1 Describe the purpose of accounting.	The purpose of accounting is to provide financial information about a business to individuals and organizations.
LO2 Describe the accounting process.	The six major steps of the accounting process are analyzing, recording, classifying, summarizing, reporting, and interpreting.
LO3 Define GAAP and describe the process used by FASB to develop these principles.	Generally accepted accounting principles (GAAP) are the rules that businesses must follow when preparing financial statements. FASB takes the following steps to develop an accounting standard: 1. The issue is placed on the Board's agenda. 2. After researching the issue, a discussion memorandum is issued. 3. Public hearings are held. 4. An exposure draft is issued. 5. The statement of financial accounting standards is issued.
LO4 Define three types of business ownership structures.	Three types of business ownership structures are the sole proprietorship, the partnership, and the corporation.
LO5 Classify different types of businesses by activities.	Different types of businesses classified by activities are a service business, a merchandising business, and a manufacturing business.
LO6 Identify career opportunities in accounting.	Career opportunities in accounting include work in public accounting, private accounting, and governmental and not-for-profit accounting.

KEY TERMS

accountant (8) Designs the accounting information system and focuses on analyzing and interpreting information.

accounting (4) A system of gathering financial information about a business and reporting this information to users.

accounting clerk (8) Records, sorts, and files accounting information.

accounting information systems (9) Accountants in this area design and implement manual and computerized accounting systems.

analyzing (5) Looking at events that have taken place and thinking about how they affect the business.

auditing (9) Reviewing and testing to be certain that proper accounting policies and practices have been followed.

bookkeeper (8) Generally supervises the work of accounting clerks, helps with daily accounting work, and summarizes accounting information.

budgeting (10) The process in which accountants help managers develop a financial plan.

Certified Internal Auditor (10) An internal auditor who has achieved professional recognition by passing the uniform examination offered by the Institute of Internal Auditors.

Certified Management Accountant (10)   An accountant who has passed an examination offered by the Institute of Management Accountants.

Certified Public Accountant (9)   A public accountant who has met certain educational and experience requirements and has passed an examination prepared by the American Institute of Certified Public Accountants.

classifying (5)   Sorting and grouping similar items together rather than merely keeping a simple, diary-like record of numerous events.

controller (9)   The accountant who oversees the entire accounting process and is the principal accounting officer of a company.

corporation (7)   A type of ownership structure in which stockholders own the business. The owners' risk is usually limited to their initial investment, and they usually have very little influence on the business decisions.

cost accounting (10)   Determining the cost of producing specific products or providing services and analyzing for cost effectiveness.

discussion memorandum (5)   The first document issued by FASB when developing an accounting standard. This document identifies the pros and cons of various accounting treatments for an event.

exposure draft (6)   This document explains the rules that FASB believes firms should follow in accounting for a particular event. Based on the responses to the exposure draft, the Board will decide if any changes are necessary before issuing a final standard.

financial accounting (9)   Includes preparing various reports and financial statements and analyzing operating, investing, and financing decisions.

generally accepted accounting principles (GAAP) (5)   Procedures and guidelines developed by the Financial Accounting Standards Board to be followed in the accounting and reporting process.

internal auditing (10)   Reviewing the operating and accounting control procedures adopted by management to make sure the controls are adequate and being followed; assuring that accurate and timely information is provided.

interpreting (5)   Deciding the meaning and importance of the information in various reports.

management advisory services (9)   Providing advice to businesses on a wide variety of managerial issues.

manufacturing business (7)   A business that makes a product to sell.

merchandising business (7)   A business that buys products to sell.

para-accountant (8)   A paraprofessional who provides many accounting, auditing, or tax services under the direct supervision of an accountant.

partnership (6)   A type of ownership structure in which more than one person owns the business.

public hearing (5)   Following the issuance of a discussion memorandum, public meetings are often held by FASB to gather opinions on the accounting issue.

recording (5)   Entering financial information about events affecting the company into the accounting system.

reporting (5)   Telling the results of the financial information.

Sarbanes-Oxley Act (9)   An act passed by Congress to help improve reporting practices of public companies.

service business (7)   A business that provides a service.

sole proprietorship (6)   A type of ownership structure in which one person owns the business.

statement of financial accounting standards (6)   A standard issued by the Financial Accounting Standards Board. These standards must be followed when preparing financial statements.

summarizing (5)   Bringing the various items of information together to determine a result.

tax accounting (10)   Services focused on tax planning, preparing tax returns, and dealing with the Internal Revenue Service and other governmental agencies.

taxation (9)   See tax accounting.

REVIEW QUESTIONS

LO1   1. What is the purpose of accounting?

LO1   2. Identify four user groups normally interested in financial information about a business.

LO2   3. Identify the six major steps of the accounting process and explain each step.

LO3   4. What are generally accepted accounting principles (GAAP)?

LO3   5. Describe the steps followed by the Financial Accounting Standards Board when developing an accounting standard.

LO4   6. Identify the three types of ownership structures and discuss the advantages and disadvantages of each.

LO5   7. Identify three types of businesses according to activities.

LO6   8. What are the main functions of an accounting clerk?

LO6   9. Name and describe three areas of specialization for a public accountant.

LO6   10. What is the purpose of the Sarbanes-Oxley Act?

LO6   11. Name and describe six areas of specialization for a managerial accountant.

REVISITING THE OPENER

In the chapter opener on page 3, you are asked to consider how you plan to use the accounting skills that you will learn in this class. Prepare a one-page memo to your instructor that explains what you hope to learn in this course and how this knowledge will be useful to you.

SERIES A EXERCISES

E 1-1A (LO1)

PURPOSE OF ACCOUNTING Match the following users with the information needed.

1. Owners
2. Managers
3. Creditors
4. Government agencies

a. Whether the firm can pay its bills on time
b. Detailed, up-to-date information to measure business performance (and plan for future operations)
c. To determine taxes to be paid and whether other regulations are met
d. The firm's current financial condition

E 1-2A (LO2)

ACCOUNTING PROCESS List the six major steps of the accounting process in order (1–6) and define each.

_____	Recording
_____	Summarizing
_____	Reporting
_____	Analyzing
_____	Interpreting
_____	Classifying

SERIES B EXERCISES

E 1-1B (LO1)

PURPOSE OF ACCOUNTING Describe the kind of information needed by the users listed.

Owners (present and future)
Managers
Creditors (present and future)
Government agencies

E 1-2B (LO2)

ACCOUNTING PROCESS Match the following steps of the accounting process with their definitions.

Analyzing
Recording
Classifying
Summarizing
Reporting
Interpreting

a. Telling the results
b. Looking at events that have taken place and thinking about how they affect the business
c. Deciding the importance of the various reports
d. Aggregating many similar events to provide information that is easy to understand
e. Sorting and grouping like items together
f. Entering financial information into the accounting system

MANAGING YOUR WRITING

Take a moment to think about what it would be like to run your own business. If you started a business, what would it be? Prepare a one-page memo that describes the type of business you would enjoy the most. Would it be a service, merchandising, or manufacturing business? Explain what form of ownership you would prefer and why.

Objectives

Careful study of this chapter should enable you to:

LO1
Define the accounting elements.

LO2
Construct the accounting equation.

LO3
Analyze business transactions.

LO4
Show the effects of business transactions on the accounting equation.

LO5
Prepare and describe the purposes of a simple income statement, statement of owner's equity, and balance sheet.

LO6
Define the three basic phases of the accounting process.

Analyzing Transactions: The Accounting Equation

Have you ever heard the expression "garbage in, garbage out"? Computer users commonly use it to mean that if input to the computer system is not correctly entered, the output from the system will be worthless. The same expression applies in accounting. In this chapter, Jessica Jane enters into many transactions while running her delivery business. For example, she purchases a motor scooter to make deliveries. To understand the impact of this event, Jessie needs to know how to properly measure the cost of the asset, estimate its useful life, and keep records of whether she paid cash or promised to make payments in the future. If Jessie does not understand the economic events affecting her delivery business and their impact on the accounting equation, the events will not be correctly entered into the accounting system. This will make the outputs from the system (the financial statements) worthless. What kinds of questions do you think Jessie should ask herself to improve her understanding of an event and its impact on the business?

The entire accounting process is based on one simple equation, called the accounting equation. In this chapter, you will learn how to use this equation to analyze business transactions. You also will learn how to prepare financial statements that report the effect of these transactions on the financial condition of a business.

THE ACCOUNTING ELEMENTS

LO1 Define the accounting elements.

Before the accounting process can begin, the entity to be accounted for must be defined. A **business entity** is an individual, association, or organization that engages in economic activities and controls specific economic resources. This definition allows the personal and business finances of an owner to be accounted for separately.

Three basic accounting elements exist for every business entity: assets, liabilities, and owner's equity. These elements are defined below.

Assets

LEARNING KEY

Pay close attention to the definitions for the basic accounting elements. A clear understanding of these definitions will help you analyze even the most complex business transactions.

Assets are items that are owned by a business and will provide future benefits. Examples of assets include cash, merchandise, furniture, fixtures, machinery, buildings, and land. Businesses may also have an asset called **accounts receivable**. This asset represents the amount of money owed to the business by its customers as a result of making sales "on account," or "on credit." Making sales on account simply means that the customers have promised to pay sometime in the future.

Liabilities

Liabilities represent something owed to another business entity. The amount owed represents a probable future outflow of assets as a result of a past event or transaction. Liabilities are debts or obligations of the business that can be paid with cash, goods, or services.

The most common liabilities are accounts payable and notes payable. An **account payable** is an unwritten promise to pay a supplier for assets purchased or services received. Acquiring assets or services by promising to make payments in the future is referred to as making a purchase "on account," or "on credit." Formal written promises to pay suppliers or lenders specified sums of money at definite future times are known as **notes payable**.

Owner's Equity

LEARNING KEY

The business entity's assets and liabilities are separate from the owner's nonbusiness assets and liabilities.

Owner's equity is the amount by which the business assets exceed the business liabilities. Other terms used for owner's equity include **net worth** and **capital**. If there are no business liabilities, the owner's equity is equal to the total assets.

The owner of a business may have business assets and liabilities as well as nonbusiness assets and liabilities. For example, the business owner probably owns a home, clothing, and a car, and perhaps owes the dentist for dental service. These are personal, nonbusiness assets and liabilities. According to the **business entity concept**, nonbusiness assets and liabilities are not included in the business entity's accounting records.

If the owner invests money or other assets in the business, the item invested is reclassified from a nonbusiness asset to a business asset. If the owner withdraws money or other assets from the business for personal use, the item withdrawn is

A B R O A D E R V I E W

Assets and the Cost of Products We Buy

Next time you buy something, think of all the assets a company needs to produce that product. If the product comes from a capital-intensive industry, one that requires heavy investments in assets, the company must price the product high enough to cover the cost of using the assets and replacing them when they wear out. For example, General Motors recently reported that the cost of property, plant, and equipment used for operating purposes came to over $65 billion.

AP IMAGES

reclassified from a business asset to a nonbusiness asset. These distinctions are important and allow the owner to make decisions based on the financial condition and results of the business apart from nonbusiness activities.

THE ACCOUNTING EQUATION

LO2 Construct the accounting equation.

> *The left side of the equation represents the assets. The right side of the equation shows where the money came from to buy the assets.*

The relationship between the three basic accounting elements—assets, liabilities, and owner's equity—can be expressed in the form of a simple equation known as the **accounting equation.**

Assets	=	Liabilities	+	Owner's Equity

This equation reflects the fact that both outsiders and insiders have an interest in the assets of a business. *Liabilities represent the outside interests of creditors. Owner's equity represents the inside interests of owners. Or, viewed another way, the left side of the equation shows the assets. The right side of the equation shows where the money came from to buy the assets. When two elements are known, the third can always be calculated.* For example, assume that assets on December 31 total $60,400. On that same day, the business liabilities consist of $5,400 owed for equipment. Owner's equity is calculated by subtracting total liabilities from total assets, $60,400 − $5,400 = $55,000.

LEARNING KEY

If you know two accounting elements, you can calculate the third element.

Total assets	$60,400
Total liabilities	−5,400
Owner's equity	$55,000

Assets	=	Liabilities	+	Owner's Equity
$60,400	=	$5,400	+	$55,000
$60,400	=		**$60,400**	

If during the next accounting period, assets increased by $10,000 and liabilities increased by $3,000, owner's equity must have increased by $7,000 ($10,000 − $3,000) as shown below.

Assets	=	Liabilities	+	Owner's Equity
BB $60,400	=	$5,400	+	$55,000
10,000	=	3,000	+	7,000
EB $70,400	=	$8,400	+	$62,000
$70,400	=		$70,400	

BB: Beginning balance
EB: Ending balance

Note also that after computing the ending balances for assets, liabilities, and owner's equity, the accounting equation remains in balance.

ANALYZING BUSINESS TRANSACTIONS

LO3 Analyze business transactions.

A **business transaction** is an economic event that has a direct impact on the business. A business transaction almost always requires an exchange between the business and another outside entity. We must be able to measure this exchange in dollars. Examples of business transactions include buying goods and services, selling goods and services, buying and selling assets, making loans, and borrowing money.

All business transactions affect the accounting equation through specific accounts. An **account** is a separate record used to summarize changes in each asset, liability, and owner's equity of a business. **Account titles** provide a description of the particular type of asset, liability, or owner's equity affected by a transaction.

Three basic questions must be answered when analyzing the effects of a business transaction on the accounting equation. These questions help address the steps in the accounting process discussed in Chapter 1.

1. **What happened?**
   - Make certain you understand the event that has taken place.

2. **Which accounts are affected?**
   - Identify the accounts that are affected.
   - Classify these accounts as assets, liabilities, or owner's equity.

3. **How is the accounting equation affected?**
   - Determine which accounts have increased or decreased.
   - Make certain that the accounting equation remains in balance after the transaction has been entered.

EFFECT OF TRANSACTIONS ON THE ACCOUNTING EQUATION

LO4 Show the effects of business transactions on the accounting equation.

Each transaction affects at least two accounts and one or more of the three basic accounting elements. A transaction increases or decreases specific asset, liability, or owner's equity accounts. Assume that the following transactions occurred during June 20--, the first month of operations for Jessie Jane's Campus Delivery.

Remember, capital does not mean cash. The cash is shown in the cash account.

Transaction (a): Investment by owner

An Increase in an Asset Offset by an Increase in Owner's Equity. Jessica Jane opened a bank account with a deposit of $2,000 for her business. The new business now has $2,000 of the asset Cash. Since Jessie contributed the asset, the owner's equity element, Jessica Jane, Capital, increases by the same amount.

Assets (Items Owned)	=	Liabilities (Amounts Owed)	+	Owner's Equity (Owner's Investment)
Cash	=			Jessica Jane, Capital
(a) $2,000	=			$2,000

Transaction (b): Purchase of an asset for cash

An Increase in an Asset Offset by a Decrease in Another Asset. Jessie decided that the fastest and easiest way to get around campus and find parking is on a motor scooter. Thus, she bought a motor scooter (delivery equipment) for $1,200 cash. Jessie exchanged one asset, cash, for another, delivery equipment. This transaction reduces Cash and creates a new asset, Delivery Equipment.

LEARNING KEY

If transactions are entered correctly, the accounting equation always remains in balance.

	Assets (Items Owned)		=	Liabilities (Amounts Owed)	+	Owner's Equity (Owner's Investment)
	Cash	+ Delivery Equipment	=			Jessica Jane, Capital
	$2,000					$2,000
(b)	−1,200	+$1,200				
	$ 800 +	$1,200				$2,000
	$2,000		=			$2,000

Transaction (c): Purchase of an asset on account

An Increase in an Asset Offset by an Increase in a Liability. Jessie hired a friend to work for her, which meant that a second scooter would be needed. Given Jessie's limited cash, she bought the dealer's demonstration model for $900. The seller agreed to allow Jessie to spread the payments over the next three months. This transaction increased an asset, Delivery Equipment, by $900 and increased the liability, Accounts Payable, by an equal amount.

	Assets (Items Owned)		=	Liabilities (Amounts Owed)	+	Owner's Equity (Owner's Investment)
	Cash	+ Delivery Equipment	=	Accounts Payable	+	Jessica Jane, Capital
	$ 800	$1,200				$2,000
(c)		+900		+$900		
	$ 800 +	$2,100	=	$900	+	$2,000
	$2,900			$2,900		

Transaction (d): Payment on a loan

A Decrease in an Asset Offset by a Decrease in a Liability. Jessie paid the first installment on the scooter of $300 [see transaction (c)]. This payment decreased the asset, Cash, and the liability, Accounts Payable, by $300.

Assets (Items Owned)			=	Liabilities (Amounts Owed)	+	Owner's Equity (Owner's Investment)
Cash	+	Delivery Equipment	=	Accounts Payable	+	Jessica Jane, Capital
$ 800		$2,100		$900		$2,000
(d) −300				−300		
$ 500	+	$2,100	=	$600	+	$2,000
$2,600			=	$2,600		

Expanding the Accounting Equation: Revenues, Expenses, and Withdrawals

In the preceding sections, three key accounting elements of every business entity were defined and explained: assets, liabilities, and owner's equity. To complete the explanation of the accounting process, three additional elements must be added to the discussion: revenues, expenses, and withdrawals.

Revenues

Revenues represent the amount a business charges customers for products sold or services performed. Customers generally pay with cash or a credit card, or they promise to pay at a later date. Most businesses recognize revenues when earned, even if cash has not yet been received. Separate accounts are used to recognize different types of revenue. Examples include Delivery Fees; Consulting Fees; Rent Revenue, if the business rents space to others; Interest Revenue, for interest earned on bank deposits; and Sales, for sales of merchandise. *Revenues increase both assets and owner's equity.*

Expenses

Expenses represent the decrease in assets (or increase in liabilities) as a result of efforts made to produce revenues. Common examples of expenses are rent, salaries, supplies consumed, and taxes. As with revenues, separate accounts are used to maintain records for each different type of expense. Expenses are "incurred" as assets are consumed (such as supplies), cash is paid for services performed for the business, or a promise is made to pay cash at a future date for services performed for the business (such as wages). The promise to pay in the future represents a liability. *Expenses either decrease assets or increase liabilities. Expenses always reduce owner's equity.*

The main purposes of recognizing an expense are to keep track of the amount and types of expenses incurred and to show the reduction in owner's equity. Note that an expense can cause a reduction in assets or an increase in liabilities. Wages earned by employees is a good example. If paid, the expense reduces an asset, Cash. If not paid, it increases a liability, Wages Payable. Either way, owner's equity is reduced.

If total revenues exceed total expenses for the period, the excess is the **net income** or net profit for the period. On the other hand, if expenses exceed revenues for the period, the excess is a **net loss** for the period.

LEARNING KEY

It is important to remember that expenses do not always reduce cash and revenues do not always increase cash right away.

Revenues	$900	Revenues	$ 300
Expenses	500	Expenses	500
Net income	$400	Net loss	$(200)

The owner can determine the time period used in the measurement of net income or net loss. It may be a month, a quarter (three months), a year, or some other time period. The concept that income determination can be made on a periodic basis is known as the **accounting period concept**. Any accounting period of 12 months is called a **fiscal year**. The fiscal year frequently coincides with the calendar year.

LEARNING KEY

Owner's Equity	
Decrease	Increase
Expenses	Revenues
Drawing	Investments

Withdrawals

Withdrawals, or **drawing**, reduce owner's equity as a result of the owner taking cash or other assets out of the business for personal use. Since earnings are expected to offset withdrawals, this reduction is viewed as temporary.

The accounting equation is expanded to include revenues, expenses, and withdrawals. Note that revenues increase owner's equity, while expenses and drawing reduce owner's equity.

Assets (Items Owned)			=	Liabilities (Amounts Owed)	+	Owner's Equity (Owner's Investment + Earnings)					
Cash	+	Delivery Equipment	=	Accounts Payable	+	Jessica Jane, Capital	−	Jessica Jane, Drawing	+ Revenues	−	Expenses
Balance $ 500	+	$2,100	=	$600	+	$2,000					
		$2,600	=					$2,600			

Effect of Revenue, Expense, and Withdrawal Transactions on the Accounting Equation

To show the effects of revenue, expense, and withdrawal transactions, the example of Jessie Jane's Campus Delivery will be continued. Assume that the following transactions took place in Jessie's business during June 20--.

Transaction (e): Delivery revenues earned in cash

An Increase in an Asset Offset by an Increase in Owner's Equity Resulting from Revenue. Jessie received $500 cash from clients for delivery services. This transaction increased the asset, Cash, and increased owner's equity by $500. The increase in owner's equity is shown by increasing the revenue account, Delivery Fees, by $500.

Assets (Items Owned)			=	Liabilities (Amounts Owed)	+	Owner's Equity (Owner's Investment + Earnings)					
Cash	+	Delivery Equipment	=	Accounts Payable	+	Jessica Jane, Capital	−	Jessica Jane, Drawing	+ Revenues	− Expenses	Description
$ 500		$2,100		$600		$2,000					
(e) +500									+$500		Deliv. Fees
$1,000	+	$2,100	=	$600	+	$2,000			+ $500		
		$3,100	=					$3,100			

Transaction (f): Paid rent for month

A Decrease in an Asset Offset by a Decrease in Owner's Equity Resulting from an Expense. Jessie rents a small office on campus. She paid $200 for office rent for June. This transaction decreased both Cash and owner's equity by $200.

The decrease in owner's equity is shown by increasing an expense called Rent Expense by $200. An increase in an expense decreases owner's equity.

Assets (Items Owned)		=	Liabilities (Amounts Owed)	+	Owner's Equity (Owner's Investment + Earnings)					
Cash	+ Delivery Equipment	=	Accounts Payable	+	Jessica Jane, Capital	− Jessica Jane, Drawing	+ Revenues	− Expenses	Description
$1,000	$2,100		$600		$2,000		$500		
(f) −200								+$200	Rent Exp.
$ 800 +	$2,100	=	$600	+	$2,000		+ $500	− $200	
$2,900		=			$2,900				

Transaction (g): Paid telephone bill

A Decrease in an Asset Offset by a Decrease in Owner's Equity Resulting from an Expense. Jessie paid $50 in cash for telephone service. This transaction, like the previous one, decreased both Cash and owner's equity. This decrease in owner's equity is shown by increasing an expense called Telephone Expense by $50.

Assets (Items Owned)		=	Liabilities (Amounts Owed)	+	Owner's Equity (Owner's Investment + Earnings)					
Cash	+ Delivery Equipment	=	Accounts Payable	+	Jessica Jane, Capital	− Jessica Jane, Drawing	+ Revenues	− Expenses	Description
$ 800	$2,100		$600		$2,000		$500	$200	
(g) − 50								+ 50	Tele. Expense
$ 750 +	$2,100	=	$600	+	$2,000		+ $500	− $250	
$2,850		=			$2,850				

Transaction (h): Delivery revenues earned on account

An Increase in an Asset Offset by an Increase in Owner's Equity Resulting from Revenue. Jessie extends credit to regular customers. Often, delivery services are performed for which payment will be received later. Since revenues are recognized when earned, an increase in owner's equity must be reported by increasing the revenue account. Since no cash is received at this time, Cash cannot be increased. Instead, an increase is reported for another asset, Accounts Receivable. *The total of Accounts Receivable at any point in time reflects the amount owed to Jessie by her customers.* Deliveries made on account amounted to $600. Accounts Receivable and Delivery Fees are increased.

Assets (Items Owned)			=	Liabilities (Amounts Owed)	+	Owner's Equity (Owner's Investment + Earnings)					
Cash	+ Accounts Receivable	+ Delivery Equipment	=	Accounts Payable	+	Jessica Jane, Capital	− Jessica Jane, Drawing	+ Revenues	− Expenses	Description
$ 750		$2,100		$600		$2,000		$ 500	$250	
(h)	+$ 600							+ 600		Deliv. Fees
$ 750 +	$ 600 +	$2,100	=	$600	+ $2,000			+ $1,100	− $250	
$3,450			=			$3,450				

Transaction (i): Purchase of supplies

An Increase in an Asset Offset by a Decrease in an Asset. Jessie bought pens, paper, delivery envelopes, and other supplies for $80 cash. These supplies should last for several months. Since they will generate future benefits, the supplies should be recorded as an asset. The accounting equation will show an increase in an asset, Supplies, and a decrease in Cash.

Assets (Items Owned)				=	Liabilities (Amounts Owed)	+	Owner's Equity (Owner's Investment + Earnings)					
Cash	+ Accounts Receivable	+ Supplies	+ Delivery Equipment	=	Accounts Payable	+	Jessica Jane, Capital	– Jessica Jane, Drawing	+ Revenues	– Expenses	Description
$ 750	$ 600		$2,100		$600		$2,000		$1,100	$250	
(i) – 80		+$80									
$ 670 +	$ 600 +	$80 +	$2,100	=	$600	+	$2,000		+ $1,100	– $250	
		$3,450		=				$3,450			

Transaction (j): Payment of insurance premium

An Increase in an Asset Offset by a Decrease in an Asset. Since Jessie plans to graduate and sell the business next January, she paid $200 for an eight-month liability insurance policy. Insurance is paid in advance and will provide future benefits. Thus, it is treated as an asset. We must expand the equation to include another asset, Prepaid Insurance, and show that Cash has been reduced.

Assets (Items Owned)					=	Liabilities (Amounts Owed)	+	Owner's Equity (Owner's Investment + Earnings)					
Cash	+ Accounts Receivable	+ Supplies	+ Prepaid Insurance	+ Delivery Equipment	=	Accounts Payable	+	Jessica Jane, Capital	– Jessica Jane, Drawing	+ Revenues	– Expenses	Description
$ 670	$ 600	$80		$2,100		$600		$2,000		$1,100	$250	
(j) – 200			+$200									
$ 470 +	$ 600 +	$80 +	$200 +	$2,100	=	$600	+	$2,000		+ $1,100	– $250	
		$3,450			=				$3,450			

As shown in transactions (i), (j), and (k), transactions do not always affect both sides of the accounting equation.

Transaction (k): Cash receipts from prior sales on account

An Increase in an Asset Offset by a Decrease in an Asset. Jessie received $570 in cash for delivery services performed for customers earlier in the month [see transaction (h)]. Receipt of this cash increases the cash account and reduces the amount due from customers reported in the accounts receivable account. *Notice that owner's equity is not affected in this transaction. Owner's equity increased in transaction (h) when revenue was recognized as it was earned, rather than now when cash is received.*

Assets (Items Owned)					=	Liabilities (Amounts Owed)		Owner's Equity (Owner's Investment + Earnings)				
Cash +	Accounts Receivable +	Supplies +	Prepaid Insurance +	Delivery Equipment =		Accounts Payable +		Jessica Jane, Capital –	Jessica Jane, Drawing +	Revenues –	Expenses	Description
$ 470	$ 600	$80	$200	$2,100		$600		$2,000		$1,100	$250	
(k) +570	– 570											
$1,040 +	$ 30 +	$80 +	$200 +	$2,100 =		$600	+	$2,000	+	$1,100 –	$250	
		$3,450							$3,450			

Transaction (l): Purchase of an asset on account making a partial payment

An Increase in an Asset Offset by a Decrease in an Asset and an Increase in a Liability. With business increasing, Jessie hired a second employee and bought a third motor scooter. The scooter cost $1,500. Jessie paid $300 in cash and will spread the remaining payments over the next four months. The asset Delivery Equipment increases by $1,500, Cash decreases by $300, and the liability Accounts Payable increases by $1,200. *Note that this transaction changes three accounts. Even so, the accounting equation remains in balance.*

Assets (Items Owned)					=	Liabilities (Amounts Owed)		Owner's Equity (Owner's Investment + Earnings)				
Cash +	Accounts Receivable +	Supplies +	Prepaid Insurance +	Delivery Equipment =		Accounts Payable +		Jessica Jane, Capital –	Jessica Jane, Drawing +	Revenues –	Expenses	Description
$1,040	$30	$80	$200	$2,100		$ 600		$2,000		$1,100	$250	
(l) –300				+1,500		+1,200						
$ 740 +	$30 +	$80 +	$200 +	$3,600 =		$1,800	+	$2,000	+	$1,100 –	$250	
		$4,650							$4,650			

Transaction (m): Payment of wages

A Decrease in an Asset Offset by a Decrease in Owner's Equity Resulting from an Expense. Jessie paid her part-time employees $650 in wages. This represents an additional business expense. As with other expenses, Cash is reduced and owner's equity is reduced by increasing an expense.

Assets (Items Owned)					=	Liabilities (Amounts Owed)		Owner's Equity (Owner's Investment + Earnings)				
Cash +	Accounts Receivable +	Supplies +	Prepaid Insurance +	Delivery Equipment =		Accounts Payable +		Jessica Jane, Capital –	Jessica Jane, Drawing +	Revenues –	Expenses	Description
$740	$30	$80	$200	$3,600		$1,800		$2,000		$1,100	$250	
(m) – 650											+650	Wages Exp.
$ 90 +	$30 +	$80 +	$200 +	$3,600 =		$1,800	+	$2,000	+	$1,100 –	$900	
		$4,000							$4,000			

Transaction (n): Deliveries made for cash and on account

An Increase in Two Assets Offset by an Increase in Owner's Equity. Total delivery fees for the remainder of the month amounted to $1,050: $430 in cash and $620 on account. Since all of these delivery fees have been earned, the revenue account increases by $1,050. Also, Cash increases by $430 and Accounts Receivable increases by $620. Thus, revenues increase assets and owner's equity. Note, once again, that one event impacts three accounts while the equation remains in balance.

Assets (Items Owned)					=	Liabilities (Amounts Owed)	+	Owner's Equity (Owner's Investment + Earnings)				
Cash +	Accounts Receivable +	Supplies +	Prepaid Insurance +	Delivery Equipment =		Accounts Payable	+	Jessica Jane, Capital	− Jessica Jane, Drawing	+ Revenues	− Expenses	Description
$ 90 (n) + 430	$ 30 + 620	$80	$200	$3,600		$1,800		$2,000		$1,100 +1,050	$900	Deliv. Fees
$520 +	$650 +	$80 +	$200 +	$3,600 =		$1,800	+ $2,000			+ $2,150 −	$900	
$5,050					=			$5,050				

Transaction (o): Withdrawal of cash from business

LEARNING KEY

Withdrawals by the owner are reported in the drawing account. Withdrawals are the opposite of investments by the owner.

A Decrease in an Asset Offset by a Decrease in Owner's Equity Resulting from a Withdrawal by the Owner. At the end of the month, Jessie took $150 in cash from the business to purchase books for her classes. Since the books are not business related, this is a withdrawal. Withdrawals can be viewed as the opposite of investments by the owner. Both owner's equity and Cash decrease.

Assets (Items Owned)					=	Liabilities (Amounts Owed)	+	Owner's Equity (Owner's Investment + Earnings)				
Cash +	Accounts Receivable +	Supplies +	Prepaid Insurance +	Delivery Equipment =		Accounts Payable	+	Jessica Jane, Capital	− Jessica Jane, Drawing	+ Revenues	− Expenses	Description
$ 520 (o) − 150	$650	$80	$200	$3,600		$1,800		$2,000	+$150	$2,150	$900	
$370 +	$650 +	$80 +	$200 +	$3,600 =		$1,800	+ $2,000 −		$150	+ $2,150 −	$900	
$4,900					=			$4,900				

Figure 2-1 shows a summary of the transactions. Use this summary to test your understanding of transaction analysis by describing the economic event represented by each transaction. At the bottom of Figure 2-1, the asset accounts and their totals are compared with the liability and owner's equity accounts and their totals.

FIGURE 2-1 Summary of Transactions Illustrated

Trans-action	Cash +	Accounts Receivable +	Supplies +	Prepaid Insurance +	Delivery Equipment =	Accounts Payable +	Jessica Jane, Capital –	Jessica Jane, Drawing +	Revenues –	Expenses	Description
	Assets (Items Owned)					**= Liabilities + (Amounts Owed)**	**Owner's Equity (Owner's Investment + Earnings)**				
Balance (a)	2,000						2,000				
Balance (b)	2,000 (1,200)				1,200		2,000				
Balance (c)	800				1,200 900	900	2,000				
Balance (d)	800 (300)				2,100	900 (300)	2,000				
Balance (e)	500 500				2,100	600	2,000		500		Deliv. Fees
Balance (f)	1,000 (200)				2,100	600	2,000		500	200	Rent Exp.
Balance (g)	800 (50)				2,100	600	2,000		500	200 50	Tele. Exp.
Balance (h)	750	600			2,100	600	2,000		500 600	250	Deliv. Fees
Balance (i)	750 (80)	600	80		2,100	600	2,000		1,100	250	
Balance (j)	670 (200)	600	80	200	2,100	600	2,000		1,100	250	
Balance (k)	470 570	600 (570)	80	200	2,100	600	2,000		1,100	250	
Balance (l)	1,040 (300)	30	80	200	2,100 1,500	· 600 1,200	2,000		1,100	250	
Balance (m)	740 (650)	30	80	200	3,600	1,800	2,000		1,100	250 650	Wages Exp.
Balance (n)	90 430	30 620	80	200	3,600	1,800	2,000		1,100 1,050	900	Deliv. Fees
Balance (o)	520 (150)	650	80	200	3,600	1,800	2,000	150	2,150	900	
Balance	370 +	650 +	80 +	200 +	3,600 =	1,800 +	2,000 –	150 +	2,150 –	900	

Cash	$ 370	Accounts Payable	$ 1,800
Accounts Receivable	650	Jessica Jane, Capital	2,000
Supplies	80	Jessica Jane, Drawing	(150)
Prepaid Insurance	200	Delivery Fees	2,150
Delivery Equipment	3,600	Rent Expense	(200)
Total assets	$ 4,900	Telephone Expense	(50)
		Wages Expense	(650)
		Total liabilities and owner's equity	$ 4,900

Amounts in ( ) are subtracted

LEARNING KEY

As with the running totals in the table, the listing immediately below the table provides proof that the accounting equation is in balance.

FINANCIAL STATEMENTS

LO5 **Prepare and describe the purposes of a simple income statement, statement of owner's equity, and balance sheet.**

Three financial statements commonly prepared by a business entity are the income statement, statement of owner's equity, and balance sheet. The transaction information gathered and summarized in the accounting equation may be used to prepare these financial statements. Figure 2-2 shows the following:

1. A summary of the specific revenue and expense transactions and the ending totals for the asset, liability, capital, and drawing accounts from the accounting equation.

2. The financial statements and their linkages with the accounting equation and each other.

Note that each of the financial statements in Figure 2-2 has a heading consisting of:

HEADING FOR FINANCIAL STATEMENTS	
1. The name of the company	Jessie Jane's Campus Delivery
2. The title of the statement	Income Statement, Statement of Owner's Equity, or Balance Sheet
3. The time period covered or the date of the statement	For Month Ended June 30, 20--, or June 30, 20--

The income statement and statement of owner's equity provide information concerning events covering a period of time, in this case, *the month ended* June 30, 20--. The balance sheet, on the other hand, offers a picture of the business *on a specific date*, June 30, 20--.

The Income Statement

The **income statement**, sometimes called the **profit and loss statement** or **operating statement**, reports the profitability of business operations for a specific period of time. Jessie's income statement shows the revenues earned for the month of June. Next, the expenses incurred as a result of the efforts made to earn these revenues are deducted. If the revenues are greater than the expenses, net income is reported. If the expenses are greater than the revenue, a net loss is reported.

┌─ **LEARNING KEY**

Income Statement			Income Statement		
Revenues	$500		Revenues	$ 500	
Expenses	400		Expenses	700	
Net income	$100		Net loss	$(200)	

By carefully studying the income statement, it is clear that Jessie earns revenues in only one way: by making deliveries. If other types of services were offered, these revenues would also be identified on the statement. Further, the reader can see the kinds of expenses that were incurred. The reader can make a judgment as to whether these seem reasonable given the amount of revenue

FIGURE 2-2 Summary and Financial Statements

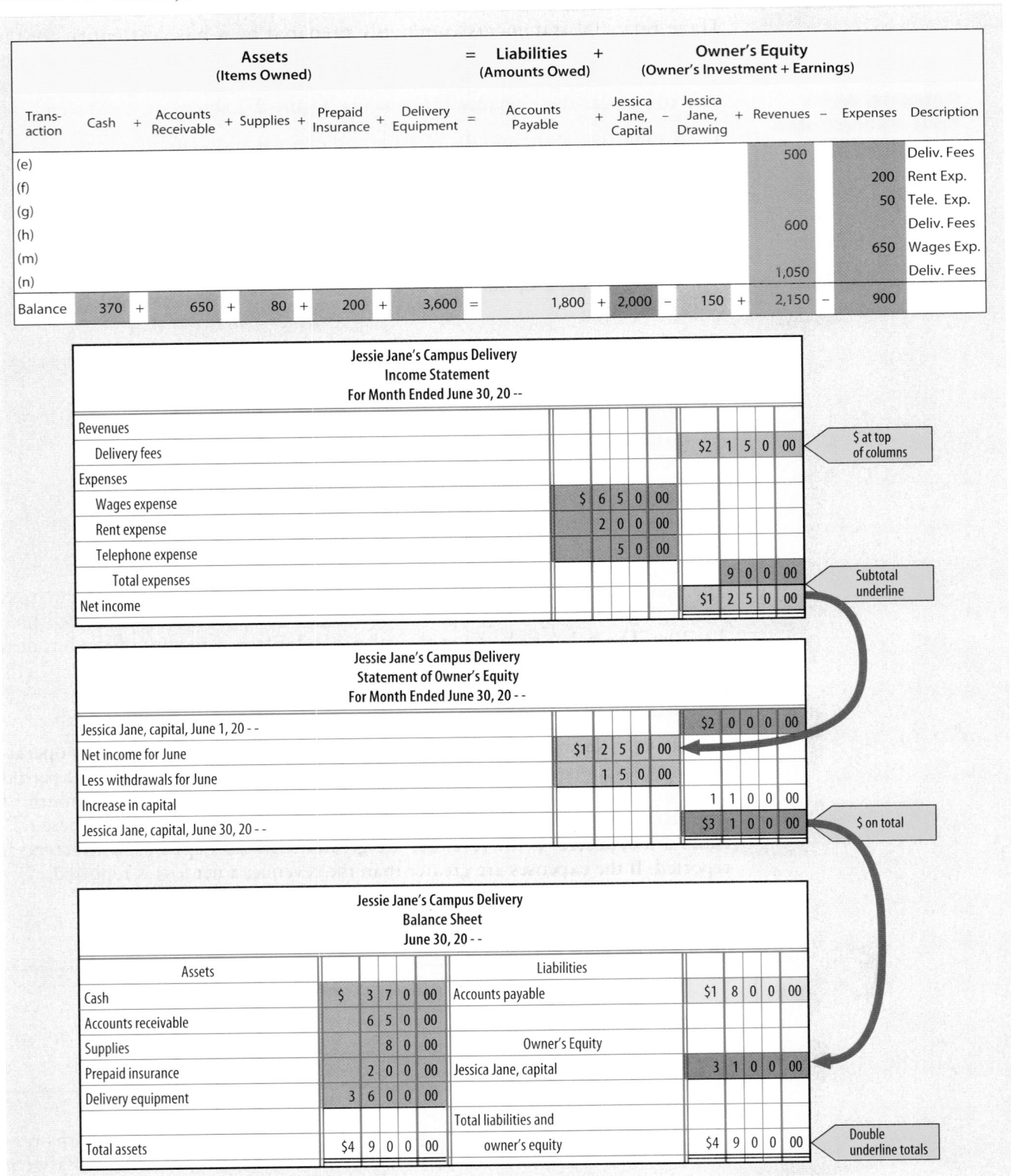

earned. Finally, the most important number on the statement is the net income. This is known as the "bottom line."

The Statement of Owner's Equity

The **statement of owner's equity** illustrated in Figure 2-2 reports on these activities for the month of June. Jessie started her business with an investment of $2,000. During the month of June, she earned $1,250 in net income and withdrew $150 for personal expenses. This resulted in a net increase in Jessie's capital of $1,100. Jessie's $2,000 original investment, plus the net increase of $1,100, results in her ending capital of $3,100.

Note that Jessie's original investment and later withdrawal are taken from the accounting equation. *The net income figure could have been computed from information in the accounting equation. However, it is easier to simply transfer net income as reported on the income statement to the statement of owner's equity.* This is an important linkage between the income statement and statement of owner's equity.

If Jessie had a net loss of $500 for the month, the statement of owner's equity would be prepared as shown in Figure 2-3.

FIGURE 2-3   Statement of Owner's Equity with Net Loss

Jessie Jane's Campus Delivery Statement of Owner's Equity For Month Ended June 30, 20 - -										
Jessica Jane, capital, June 1, 20 - -							$2	0	0	0	00
Less: Net loss for June	$	5	0	0	00					
Withdrawals for June		1	5	0	00					
Decrease in capital								6	5	0	00
Jessica Jane, capital, June 30, 20 - -							$1	3	5	0	00

The Balance Sheet

The **balance sheet** reports a firm's assets, liabilities, and owner's equity on a specific date. It is called a balance sheet because it confirms that the accounting equation has remained in balance. It is also referred to as a **statement of financial position** or **statement of financial condition**.

As illustrated in Figure 2-2, the asset and liability accounts are taken from the accounting equation and reported on the balance sheet. *The total of Jessie's capital account on June 30 could have been computed from the owner's equity accounts in the accounting equation ($2,000 − $150 + $2,150 − $900). However, it is simpler to take the June 30, 20--, capital as computed on the statement of owner's equity and transfer it to the balance sheet.* This is an important linkage between these two statements.

GUIDELINES FOR PREPARING FINANCIAL STATEMENTS

1. Financial statements are prepared primarily for users not associated with the company. To make a good impression and enhance understanding, financial statements must follow a standard form with careful attention to placement, spacing, and indentations.

2. All statements have a heading with the name of the company, name of the statement, and accounting period or date.

3. Single rules (lines) indicate that the numbers above the line have been added or subtracted. Double rules (double underlines) indicate a total.

4. Dollar signs are used at the top of columns and for the first amount entered in a column beneath a ruling.

5. On the income statement, a common practice is to list expenses from highest to lowest dollar amount, with miscellaneous expense listed last.

6. On the balance sheet, assets are listed from most liquid to least liquid. **Liquidity** measures the ease with which the asset will be converted to cash. Liabilities are listed from most current to least current.

OVERVIEW OF THE ACCOUNTING PROCESS

LO6 Define the three basic phases of the accounting process.

Figure 2-4 shows the three basic phases of the accounting process in terms of input, processing, and output.

- *Input.* Business transactions provide the necessary **input**.
- *Processing.* Recognizing the effect of these transactions on the assets, liabilities, owner's equity, revenues, and expenses of a business is the **processing** function.
- *Output.* The financial statements are the **output**.

FIGURE 2-4   Input, Processing, and Output

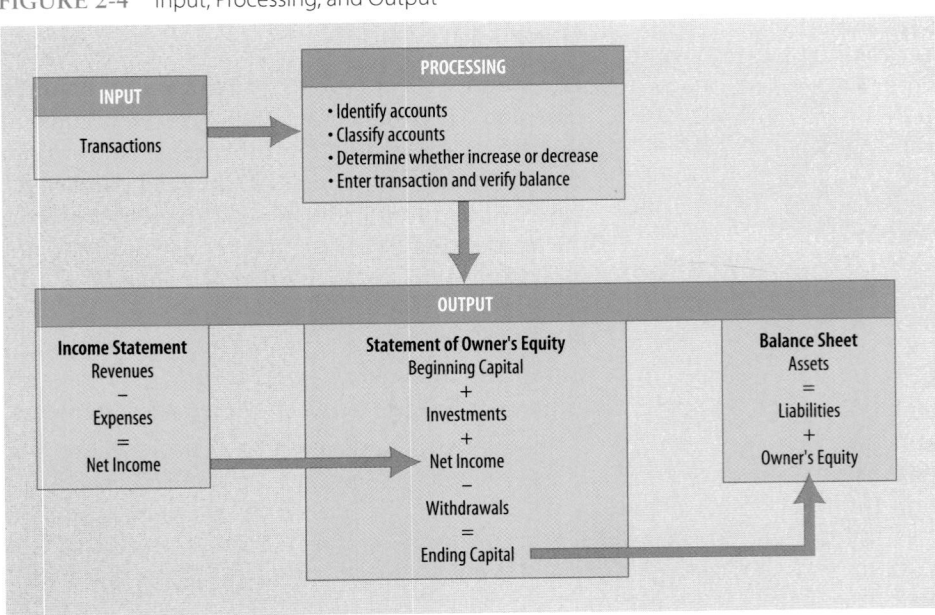

Computers and Accounting

Computer Skills for Accountants—Gary P. Schneider, University of San Diego

In recent years, accountants and others increasingly use computers in their daily work activities. Most accountants find themselves using word-processing, spreadsheet, presentation, database, e-mail, and web browser software on a regular basis. Being a skilled computer user is important for accountants who want to obtain good jobs in the field. The specific skills needed by accountants include:

- **Word-processing software.** Accountants are frequently required to prepare reports for management or outside parties. Having good writing skills is important, but knowing how to use computers to design and format interesting, informative documents is also important.

- **Spreadsheet software.** This is an important tool for accountants. Most accountants find themselves using spreadsheet software daily. Accountants use spreadsheet software to analyze the details of accounts, to project costs and revenues, to create budgets, to perform "what-if" analyses of proposed business strategies, and to calculate the likely return on invested funds. Most spreadsheet software packages include chart-building features. Accountants must know how to use these features to create informative charts and integrate them into reports and memos.

- **Presentation software.** Increasingly, accountants are called upon to deliver their results to company management, lenders, and investors in the form of personal presentations. This requires good oral communication skills and the ability to create and use effective visual aids. One of the most commonly used visual aids is the computer presentation. Accountants must know how to build an effective presentation that incorporates the results of their work. Presentation software is an important tool that can help accountants who make oral reports full of facts and figures compelling and interesting.

- **Database software.** Database software is used by all types of businesses and not-for-profit organizations to keep track of their activities. Companies often keep databases for customers, employees, suppliers, and even competitors. Accountants use database software to extract the information they need to prepare financial statements. Auditors need to know how to access their clients' databases so they can gather evidence to support their opinions on their clients' financial statements. In large organizations, most of the accounting records are stored in databases.

- **E-mail software.** A large percentage of business communication is conducted using e-mail. This is another software tool that accountants use daily to ask questions, gather information, and report the results of their work to others. Accountants must know how to attach reports, spreadsheets, presentations, and other files they have created to e-mail messages.

- **Web browser software.** The Internet and the World Wide Web (the Web) have become important resources for accountants. The Web offers accountants a way to stay current with the field of accounting by providing access to the business press, accounting journals, and information about their industry.

In addition to these six types of general office productivity software, many companies have their own software for specific functions, including accounting. Although companies usually provide training to new employees who need to use specific software products, most companies expect newly hired accountants to have basic skills in using word-processing, spreadsheet, presentation, database, e-mail, and web browser software. Many employers expect new accounting employees to have considerable skills in some of these software tools, particularly spreadsheet and database software.

Learning Objectives	Key Points to Remember
LO1 Define the accounting elements.	The three key accounting elements are assets, liabilities, and owner's equity. Owner's equity is expanded in LO4 to include revenues, expenses, and drawing.
LO2 Construct the accounting equation.	The accounting equation is: Assets = Liabilities + Owner's Equity
LO3 Analyze business transactions.	Three questions must be answered in analyzing business transactions: 1. What happened? 2. Which accounts are affected? 3. How is the accounting equation affected?
LO4 Show the effects of business transactions on the accounting equation.	Each transaction affects at least two accounts and one or more of the three basic accounting elements. The transactions described in this chapter can be classified into five groups: 1. Increase in an asset offset by an increase in owner's equity. 2. Increase in an asset offset by a decrease in another asset. 3. Increase in an asset offset by an increase in a liability. 4. Decrease in an asset offset by a decrease in a liability. 5. Decrease in an asset offset by a decrease in owner's equity.
LO5 Prepare and describe the purposes of a simple income statement, statement of owner's equity, and balance sheet.	The purposes of the income statement, statement of owner's equity, and balance sheet can be summarized as follows:

STATEMENT	PURPOSE
Income statement	Reports net income or loss Revenues − Expenses = Net Income or Loss
Statement of owner's equity	Shows changes in the owner's capital account Beginning Capital + Investments + Net Income − Withdrawals = Ending Capital
Balance sheet	Verifies balance of accounting equation Assets = Liabilities + Owner's Equity

Learning Objectives	Key Points to Remember
LO6 Define the three basic phases of the accounting process.	The three basic phases of the accounting process are shown below. • **Input.** Business transactions provide the necessary input. • **Processing.** Recognizing the effect of these transactions on the assets, liabilities, owner's equity, revenues, and expenses of a business is the processing function. • **Output.** The financial statements are the output.

DEMONSTRATION PROBLEM

Damon Young has started his own business, Home and Away Inspections. He inspects property for buyers and sellers of real estate. Young rents office space and has a part-time assistant to answer the phone and help with inspections. The transactions for the month of September are as follows:

(a)   On the first day of the month, Young invested cash by making a deposit in a bank account for the business, $15,000.

(b)   Paid rent for September, $300.

(c)   Bought a used truck for cash, $8,000.

(d)   Purchased tools on account from Crafty Tools, $3,000.

(e)   Paid electricity bill, $50.

(f)   Paid two-year premium for liability insurance on truck, $600.

(g)   Received cash from clients for services performed, $2,000.

(h)   Paid part-time assistant (wages) for first half of month, $200.

(i)   Performed inspection services for clients on account, $1,000.

(j)   Paid telephone bill, $35.

(k)   Bought office supplies costing $300. Paid $100 cash and will pay the balance next month, $200.

(l)   Received cash from clients for inspections performed on account in (i), $300.

(m)   Paid part-time assistant (wages) for last half of month, $250.

(n)   Made partial payment on tools bought in (d), $1,000.

(o)   Earned additional revenues amounting to $2,000: $1,400 in cash and $600 on account.

(p)   Young withdrew cash at the end of the month for personal expenses, $500.

REQUIRED

1.   Enter the transactions in an accounting equation similar to the one illustrated on the following page. After each transaction, show the new amount for each account.

Assets (Items Owned)						= Liabilities + (Amounts Owed)	Owner's Equity (Owner's Investment + Earnings)				
Cash +	Accounts Receivable +	Supplies +	Prepaid Insurance +	Tools +	Truck =	Accounts Payable	+ Damon Young, Capital	− Damon Young, Drawing	+ Revenues	− Expenses	Description

2. Compute the ending balances for all accounts.

3. Prepare an income statement for Home and Away Inspections for the month of September 20--.

4. Prepare a statement of owner's equity for Home and Away Inspections for the month of September 20--.

5. Prepare a balance sheet for Home and Away Inspections as of September 30, 20--.

Solution 1, 2.

Assets (Items Owned)						= Liabilities + (Amounts Owed)	Owner's Equity (Owner's Investment + Earnings)				
Cash +	Accounts Receivable +	Supplies +	Prepaid Insurance +	Tools +	Truck =	Accounts Payable	+ Damon Young, Capital	− Damon Young, Drawing	+ Revenues	− Expenses	Description
Bal.											
(a) 15,000							15,000				
Bal. 15,000							15,000				
(b) (300)										300	Rent Exp.
Bal. 14,700							15,000			300	
(c) (8,000)					8,000						
Bal. 6,700					8,000		15,000			300	
(d)				3,000		3,000					
Bal. 6,700				3,000	8,000	3,000	15,000			300	
(e) (50)										50	Utilities Exp.
Bal. 6,650				3,000	8,000	3,000	15,000			350	
(f) (600)			600								
Bal. 6,050			600	3,000	8,000	3,000	15,000			350	
(g) 2,000									2,000		Inspect. Fees
Bal. 8,050			600	3,000	8,000	3,000	15,000		2,000	350	
(h) (200)										200	Wages Exp.
Bal. 7,850			600	3,000	8,000	3,000	15,000		2,000	550	
(i)	1,000								1,000		Inspect. Fees
Bal. 7,850	1,000		600	3,000	8,000	3,000	15,000		3,000	550	
(j) (35)										35	Tele. Exp.
Bal. 7,815	1,000		600	3,000	8,000	3,000	15,000		3,000	585	
(k) (100)		300				200					
Bal. 7,715	1,000	300	600	3,000	8,000	3,200	15,000		3,000	585	
(l) 300	(300)										
Bal. 8,015	700	300	600	3,000	8,000	3,200	15,000		3,000	585	
(m) (250)										250	Wages Exp.
Bal. 7,765	700	300	600	3,000	8,000	3,200	15,000		3,000	835	
(n) (1,000)						(1,000)					
Bal. 6,765	700	300	600	3,000	8,000	2,200	15,000		3,000	835	
(o) 1,400	600								2,000		Inspect. Fees
Bal. 8,165	1,300	300	600	3,000	8,000	2,200	15,000		5,000	835	
(p) (500)								500			
Bal. 7,665 +	1,300 +	300 +	600 +	3,000 +	8,000 =	2,200	+ 15,000	− 500 +	5,000	− 835	

3.

Home and Away Inspections Income Statement For Month Ended September 30, 20 --													
Revenues													
Inspection fees									$5	0	0	0	00
Expenses													
Wages expense		$	4	5	0	00							
Rent expense			3	0	0	00							
Utilities expense				5	0	00							
Telephone expense				3	5	00							
Total expenses										8	3	5	00
Net income									$4	1	6	5	00

4.

Home and Away Inspections Statement of Owner's Equity For Month Ended September 30, 20 - -													
Damon Young, capital, September 1, 20 - -									$15	0	0	0	00
Net income for September		$4	1	6	5	00							
Less withdrawals for September			5	0	0	00							
Increase in capital									3	6	6	5	00
Damon Young, capital, September 30, 20 - -									$18	6	6	5	00

5.

Home and Away Inspections Balance Sheet September 30, 20 - -													
Assets						**Liabilities**							
Cash	$ 7	6	6	5	00	Accounts payable		$ 2	2	0	0	00	
Accounts receivable	1	3	0	0	00								
Supplies		3	0	0	00	**Owner's Equity**							
Prepaid insurance		6	0	0	00	Damon Young, capital		18	6	6	5	00	
Tools	3	0	0	0	00								
Truck	8	0	0	0	00	Total liabilities and							
Total assets	$20	8	6	5	00	owner's equity		$20	8	6	5	00	

KEY TERMS

account (22)   A separate record used to summarize changes in each asset, liability, and owner's equity of a business.

account title (22)   Provides a description of the particular type of asset, liability, owner's equity, revenue, or expense.

accounting equation (21)   The accounting equation consists of the three basic accounting elements: assets = liabilities + owner's equity.

accounting period concept (25)   The concept that income determination can be made on a periodic basis.

accounts payable (20)   An unwritten promise to pay a supplier for assets purchased or services received.

accounts receivable (20)   An amount owed to a business by its customers as a result of the sale of goods or services.

asset (20)   An item that is owned by a business and will provide future benefits.

balance sheet (33)   Reports assets, liabilities, and owner's equity on a specific date. It is called a balance sheet because it confirms that the accounting equation is in balance.

business entity (20)   An individual, association, or organization that engages in economic activities and controls specific economic resources.

business entity concept (20)   The concept that nonbusiness assets and liabilities are not included in the business entity's accounting records.

business transaction (22)   An economic event that has a direct impact on the business.

capital (20)   Another term for owner's equity, the amount by which the business assets exceed the business liabilities.

drawing (25)   Withdrawals that reduce owner's equity as a result of the owner taking cash or other assets out of the business for personal use.

expenses (24)   The decrease in assets (or increase in liabilities) as a result of efforts to produce revenues.

fiscal year (25)   Any accounting period of 12 months' duration.

income statement (31)   Reports the profitability of business operations for a specific period of time.

input (34)   Business transactions provide the necessary input for the accounting information system.

liability (20)   Something owed to another business entity.

liquidity (34)   A measure of the ease with which an asset will be converted to cash.

net income (24)   The excess of total revenues over total expenses for the period.

net loss (24)   The excess of total expenses over total revenues for the period.

net worth (20)   Another term for owner's equity, the amount by which the business assets exceed the business liabilities.

notes payable (20)   A formal written promise to pay a supplier or lender a specified sum of money at a definite future time.

operating statement (31)   Another name for the income statement, which reports the profitability of business operations for a specific period of time.

output (34)   The financial statements are the output of the accounting information system.

owner's equity (20)   The amount by which the business assets exceed the business liabilities.

processing (34)   Recognizing the effect of transactions on the assets, liabilities, owner's equity, revenues, and expenses of a business.

profit and loss statement (31)   Another name for the income statement, which reports the profitability of business operations for a specific period of time.

revenues (24)   The amount a business charges customers for products sold or services performed.

statement of financial condition (33)   Another name for the balance sheet, which reports assets, liabilities, and owner's equity on a specific date.

statement of financial position (33)   Another name for the balance sheet, which reports assets, liabilities, and owner's equity on a specific date.

statement of owner's equity (33)   Reports beginning capital plus net income less withdrawals to compute ending capital.

withdrawals (25)   Reduce owner's equity as a result of the owner taking cash or other assets out of the business for personal use.

Self-Study Test Questions

True/False

1. Assets are items that are owned by the business and are expected to provide future benefits.

2. Accounts Payable is an example of an asset account.

3. According to the business entity concept, nonbusiness assets and liabilities are not included in the business's accounting records.

4. The accounting equation (assets = liabilities + owner's equity) must always be in balance.

5. When an asset increases, a liability must also increase.

6. When total revenues exceed total expenses, the difference is called net loss.

7. Expenses represent outflows of assets or increases in liabilities as a result of efforts to produce revenues.

Multiple Choice

1. An increase to which of these accounts will increase owner's equity?

   (a) Accounts Payable
   (b) Drawing
   (c) Client Fees
   (d) Rent Expense

2. When delivery revenue is earned in cash, which accounts increase or decrease?

   (a) Cash increases; Revenue increases.
   (b) Cash decreases; Revenue increases.
   (c) Cash decreases; Revenue decreases.
   (d) Cash does not change; owner's equity increases.

3. When delivery revenue is earned on account, which accounts increase or decrease?

   (a) Cash increases; Revenue increases.
   (b) Accounts Receivable increases; Revenue increases.
   (c) Accounts Receivable increases; Revenue decreases.
   (d) Accounts Receivable decreases; Revenue decreases.

4. When payment is made on an existing debt, which accounts increase or decrease?

   (a) Cash increases; Accounts Receivable increases.
   (b) Cash decreases; Accounts Payable increases.
   (c) Cash increases; Accounts Payable increases.
   (d) Cash decreases; Accounts Payable decreases.

5. Which of the following accounts does not appear on the income statement?

   (a) Delivery Fees   (c) Drawing
   (b) Wages Expense   (d) Rent Expense

The answers to the Self-Study Test Questions are at the end of the text.

REVIEW QUESTIONS

LO1	1.	Why is it necessary to distinguish between business assets and liabilities and nonbusiness assets and liabilities of a single proprietor?
LO1/4	2.	Name and define the six major elements of the accounting equation.
LO3	3.	List the three basic questions that must be answered when analyzing the effects of a business transaction on the accounting equation.
LO5	4.	What is the function of an income statement?
LO5	5.	What is the function of a statement of owner's equity?
LO5	6.	What is the function of a balance sheet?
LO6	7.	What are the three basic phases of the accounting process?

R E V I S I T I N G   T H E   O P E N E R

In the chapter opener on page 19, you are asked to consider what kinds of questions you think Jessie should ask herself to improve her understanding of an event and its impact on the business. Please make a list of these questions.

© DIGITAL IMAGING GROUP

SERIES A EXERCISES

E 2-1A (LO1)

ACCOUNTING ELEMENTS Label each of the following accounts as an asset (A), a liability (L), or owner's equity (OE), using the following format:

Item	Account	Classification
Money in bank	Cash	
Office supplies	Supplies	
Money owed	Accounts Payable	
Office chairs	Office Furniture	
Net worth of owner	John Smith, Capital	
Money withdrawn by owner	John Smith, Drawing	
Money owed by customers	Accounts Receivable	

E 2-2A (LO2)

THE ACCOUNTING EQUATION Using the accounting equation, compute the missing elements.

Assets	=	Liabilities	+	Owner's Equity
_____	=	$24,000	+	$10,000
$25,000	=	$18,000	+	_____
$40,000	=	_____	+	$15,000

E 2-3A (LO3/4)

✓ Assets following (d): $22,000

EFFECTS OF TRANSACTIONS (BALANCE SHEET ACCOUNTS) Alice Stern started a business. During the first month (February 20--), the following transactions occurred. Show the effect of each transaction on the accounting equation: *Assets = Liabilities + Owner's Equity*. After each transaction, show the new totals.

(a) Invested cash in the business, $20,000.
(b) Bought office equipment on account, $3,500.
(c) Bought office equipment for cash, $1,200.
(d) Paid cash on account to supplier in transaction (b), $1,500.

E 2-4A (LO3/4)

✓ Assets following (k): $23,427

EFFECTS OF TRANSACTIONS (REVENUE, EXPENSE, WITHDRAWALS) This exercise is an extension of Exercise 2-3A. Assume Alice Stern completed the following additional transactions during February. Show the effect of each transaction on the basic elements of the expanded accounting equation: *Assets = Liabilities + Owner's Equity (Capital − Drawing + Revenues − Expenses)*. After each transaction, show the new balance for each accounting element.

(e) Received cash from a client for professional services, $2,500.
(f) Paid office rent for February, $900.
(g) Paid February telephone bill, $73.
(h) Withdrew cash for personal use, $500.
(i) Performed services for clients on account, $1,000.
(j) Paid wages to part-time employee, $600.
(k) Received cash for services performed on account in transaction (i), $600.

E 2-5A (LO1/4/5)

FINANCIAL STATEMENT ACCOUNTS Label each of the following accounts as an asset (A), liability (L), owner's equity (OE), revenue (R), or expense (E). Indicate the financial statement on which the account belongs—income statement (IS), statement of owner's equity (SOE), or balance sheet (BS)—in a format similar to the following.

Account	Classification	Financial Statement
Cash		
Rent Expense		
Accounts Payable		
Service Fees		
Supplies		
Wages Expense		
Ramon Martinez, Drawing		
Ramon Martinez, Capital		
Prepaid Insurance		
Accounts Receivable		

E 2-6A (LO5)

✓ Capital, 6/30: $22,000

STATEMENT OF OWNER'S EQUITY REPORTING NET INCOME Betsy Ray started an accounting service on June 1, 20--, by investing $20,000. Her net income for the month was $10,000 and she withdrew $8,000. Prepare a statement of owner's equity for the month of June.

E 2-7A (LO5)

✓ Capital, 6/30: $9,000

STATEMENT OF OWNER'S EQUITY REPORTING NET LOSS Based on the information provided in Exercise 2-6A, prepare a statement of owner's equity assuming Ray had a net loss of $3,000.

SERIES A PROBLEMS

P 2-8A (LO1/2)

✓ 3: $34,920 = $12,570 + $22,350

THE ACCOUNTING EQUATION Dr. John Schleper is a chiropractor. As of December 31, he owned the following property that related to his professional practice.

Cash	$ 4,750
Office Equipment	6,200
X-ray Equipment	11,680
Laboratory Equipment	7,920

He also owes the following business suppliers:

Chateau Gas Company	$ 2,420
Aloe Medical Supply Company	3,740

REQUIRED

1. From the preceding information, compute the accounting elements and enter them in the accounting equation shown as follows.

Assets	=	Liabilities	+	Owner's Equity
_____	=	_____	+	_____

2. During January, the assets increase by $7,290, and the liabilities increase by $4,210. Compute the resulting accounting equation.

3. During February, the assets decrease by $2,920, and the liabilities increase by $2,200. Compute the resulting accounting equation.

P 2-9A (LO3/4)

✓ Total cash following (g): $12,950

EFFECT OF TRANSACTIONS ON ACCOUNTING EQUATION Jay Pembroke started a business. During the first month (April 20--), the following transactions occurred.

(a) Invested cash in business, $18,000.
(b) Bought office supplies for $4,600: $2,000 in cash and $2,600 on account.
(c) Paid one-year insurance premium, $1,200.
(d) Earned revenues totaling $3,300: $1,300 in cash and $2,000 on account.
(e) Paid cash on account to the company that supplied the office supplies in transaction (b), $2,300.
(f) Paid office rent for the month, $750.
(g) Withdrew cash for personal use, $100.

REQUIRED

Show the effect of each transaction on the individual accounts of the expanded accounting equation: *Assets = Liabilities + Owner's Equity (Capital − Drawing + Revenues − Expenses)*. After each transaction, show the new account totals.

P 2-10A (LO5)

✓ Net income: $2,550

INCOME STATEMENT Based on Problem 2-9A, prepare an income statement for Jay Pembroke for the month of April 20--.

P 2-11A (LO5)

✓ Capital, 4/30: $20,450

STATEMENT OF OWNER'S EQUITY Based on Problem 2-9A, prepare a statement of owner's equity for Jay Pembroke for the month of April 20--.

P 2-12A (LO5)

✓ Total assets, 4/30: $20,750

BALANCE SHEET Based on Problem 2-9A, prepare a balance sheet for Jay Pembroke as of April 30, 20--.

SERIES B EXERCISES

E 2-1B (LO1)

ACCOUNTING ELEMENTS Label each of the following accounts as an asset (A), liability (L), or owner's equity (OE) using the following format.

Account	Classification
Cash	
Accounts Payable	
Supplies	
Bill Jones, Drawing	
Prepaid Insurance	
Accounts Receivable	
Bill Jones, Capital	

E 2-2B (LO2)

THE ACCOUNTING EQUATION Using the accounting equation, compute the missing elements.

Assets	=	Liabilities	+	Owner's Equity
_____	=	$20,000	+	$5,000
$30,000	=	$15,000	+	_____
$20,000	=	_____	+	$10,000

E 2-3B (LO3/4)

✓ Assets following (d): $32,500

EFFECTS OF TRANSACTIONS (BALANCE SHEET ACCOUNTS) Jon Wallace started a business. During the first month (March 20--), the following transactions occurred. Show the effect of each transaction on the accounting equation: *Assets = Liabilities + Owner's Equity*. After each transaction, show the new account totals.

(a)   Invested cash in the business, $30,000.
(b)   Bought office equipment on account, $4,500.
(c)   Bought office equipment for cash, $1,600.
(d)   Paid cash on account to supplier in transaction (b), $2,000.

E 2-4B (LO3/4)

✓ Assets following (k): $34,032

EFFECTS OF TRANSACTIONS (REVENUE, EXPENSE, WITHDRAWALS) This exercise is an extension of Exercise 2-3B. Assume Jon Wallace completed the following additional transactions during March. Show the effect of each transaction on the basic elements of the expanded accounting equation: *Assets = Liabilities + Owner's Equity (Capital − Drawing + Revenues − Expenses)*. After each transaction, show the new balance for each accounting element.

(e)   Performed services and received cash, $3,000.
(f)   Paid rent for March, $1,000.
(g)   Paid March telephone bill, $68.
(h)   Jon Wallace withdrew cash for personal use, $800.
(i)   Performed services for clients on account, $900.
(j)   Paid wages to part-time employee, $500.
(k)   Received cash for services performed on account in transaction (i), $500.

E 2-5B (LO1/4/5)

FINANCIAL STATEMENT ACCOUNTS Label each of the following accounts as an asset (A), liability (L), owner's equity (OE), revenue (R), or expense (E). Indicate the financial statement on which the account belongs—income statement (IS), statement of owner's equity (SOE), or balance sheet (BS)—in a format similar to the following.

Account	Classification	Financial Statement
Cash		
Rent Expense		
Accounts Payable		
Service Fees		
Supplies		
Wages Expense		
Amanda Wong, Drawing		
Amanda Wong, Capital		
Prepaid Insurance		
Accounts Receivable		

E 2-6B (LO5)
✓ Capital, 6/30: $14,000

STATEMENT OF OWNER'S EQUITY REPORTING NET INCOME Efran Lopez started a financial consulting service on June 1, 20--, by investing $15,000. His net income for the month was $6,000 and he withdrew $7,000 for personal use. Prepare a statement of owner's equity for the month of June.

E 2-7B (LO5)
✓ Capital, 6/30: $6,000

STATEMENT OF OWNER'S EQUITY REPORTING NET LOSS Based on the information provided in Exercise 2-6B, prepare a statement of owner's equity assuming Lopez had a net loss of $2,000.

SERIES B PROBLEMS

P 2-8B (LO1/2)
✓ 3: $25,235 = $10,165 + $15,070

THE ACCOUNTING EQUATION Dr. Patricia Parsons is a dentist. As of January 31, Parsons owned the following property that related to her professional practice:

Cash	$3,560
Office Equipment	4,600
X-ray Equipment	8,760
Laboratory Equipment	5,940

She also owes the following business suppliers:

Cupples Gas Company	$1,815
Swan Dental Lab	2,790

REQUIRED

1.   From the preceding information, compute the accounting elements and enter them in the accounting equation as shown below.

Assets	=	Liabilities	+	Owner's Equity
_____	=	_____	+	_____

2.   During February, the assets increase by $4,565, and the liabilities increase by $3,910. Compute the resulting accounting equation.

3.   During March, the assets decrease by $2,190, and the liabilities increase by $1,650. Compute the resulting accounting equation.

P 2-9B (LO3/4)

✓ Total cash following (g): $11,300

EFFECT OF TRANSACTIONS ON ACCOUNTING EQUATION David Segal started a business. During the first month (October 20--), the following transactions occurred.

(a)   Invested cash in the business, $15,000.
(b)   Bought office supplies for $3,800: $1,800 in cash and $2,000 on account.
(c)   Paid one-year insurance premium, $1,000.
(d)   Earned revenues amounting to $2,700: $1,700 in cash and $1,000 on account.
(e)   Paid cash on account to the company that supplied the office supplies in transaction (b), $1,800.
(f)   Paid office rent for the month, $650.
(g)   Withdrew cash for personal use, $150.

REQUIRED

Show the effect of each transaction on the individual accounts of the expanded accounting equation: *Assets = Liabilities + Owner's Equity (Capital − Drawing + Revenues − Expenses)*. After each transaction, show the new account totals.

P 2-10B (LO5)

✓ Net income: $2,050

INCOME STATEMENT Based on Problem 2-9B, prepare an income statement for David Segal for the month of October 20--.

P 2-11B (LO5)

✓ Capital, 10/31: $16,900

STATEMENT OF OWNER'S EQUITY Based on Problem 2-9B, prepare a statement of owner's equity for David Segal for the month of October 20--.

P 2-12B (LO5)

✓ Total assets, 10/31: $17,100

BALANCE SHEET Based on Problem 2-9B, prepare a balance sheet for David Segal as of October 31, 20--.

MANAGING YOUR WRITING

Write a brief memo that explains the differences and similarities between expenses and withdrawals.

MASTERY PROBLEM

Lisa Vozniak started her own business, We Do Windows. She offers interior and exterior window cleaning for local area residents. Lisa rents a garage to store her tools and cleaning supplies and has a part-time assistant to answer the phone and handle third-story work. (Lisa is afraid of heights.) The transactions for the month of July are as follows:

(a) On the first day of the month, Vozniak invested cash by making a deposit in a bank account for the business, $8,000.
(b) Paid rent for July, $150.
(c) Purchased a used van for cash, $5,000.
(d) Purchased tools on account from Clean Tools, $600.
(e) Purchased cleaning supplies that cost $300. Paid $200 cash and will pay the balance next month, $100.
(f) Paid part-time assistant (wages) for first half of month, $100.
(g) Paid for advertising, $75.
(h) Paid two-year premium for liability insurance on van, $480.
(i) Received cash from clients for services performed, $800.
(j) Performed cleaning services for clients on account, $500.
(k) Paid telephone bill, $40.
(l) Received cash from clients for window cleaning performed on account in transaction (j), $200.
(m) Paid part-time assistant (wages) for last half of month, $150.
(n) Made partial payment on tools purchased in transaction (d), $200.
(o) Earned additional revenues amounting to $800: $600 in cash and $200 on account.
(p) Vozniak withdrew cash at the end of the month for personal expenses, $100.

REQUIRED

1. Enter the above transactions in an accounting equation similar to the one illustrated below. After each transaction, show the new amount for each account.

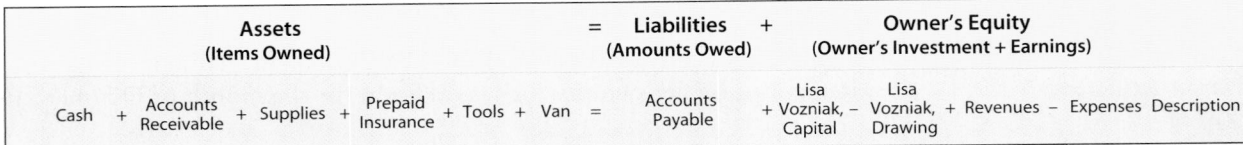

Assets (Items Owned)						=	Liabilities (Amounts Owed)	+	Owner's Equity (Owner's Investment + Earnings)				
Cash	+ Accounts Receivable	+ Supplies	+ Prepaid Insurance	+ Tools	+ Van	=	Accounts Payable	+ Lisa Vozniak Capital	– Lisa Vozniak, Drawing	+ Revenues	– Expenses	Description

2. Compute the ending balances for all accounts.

3. Prepare an income statement for We Do Windows for the month of July 20--.

4. Prepare a statement of owner's equity for We Do Windows for the month of July 20--.

5. Prepare a balance sheet for We Do Windows as of July 31, 20--.

CHALLENGE PROBLEM

This problem challenges you to apply your cumulative accounting knowledge to move a step beyond the material in the chapter.

✓ **Cash from operating activities: $2,165**

In this chapter, you learned about three important financial statements: the income statement, statement of owner's equity, and balance sheet. As mentioned in the margin note on page 34, most firms also prepare a statement of cash flows. Part of this statement reports the **cash received** from customers, and **cash paid** for goods and services.

REQUIRED

Take another look at the Demonstration Problem for Damon Young's "Home and Away Inspections." Note that when revenues are measured based on the amount earned, and expenses are measured based on the amount incurred, net income for the period was $4,165. Now, compute the difference between cash received from customers and cash paid to suppliers of goods and services by completing the form provided below. Are these measures different? Which provides a better measure of profitability?

Cash from customers

Cash paid for wages

Cash paid for rent

Cash paid for utilities

Cash paid for insurance

Cash paid for supplies

Cash paid for telephone

    Total cash paid for operating items

Difference between cash received from
    customers and cash paid for goods
    and services

Objectives

Careful study of this chapter should enable you to:

LO1
Define the parts of a T account.

LO2
Foot and balance a T account.

LO3
Describe the effects of debits and credits on specific types of accounts.

LO4
Use T accounts to analyze transactions.

LO5
Prepare a trial balance and explain its purposes and linkages with the financial statements.

The Double-Entry Framework

How do you keep track of your personal finances? Perhaps you make a list of your earnings and other cash inflows. Then you prepare a list of how the money was spent. Jessie needs to do this, too. However, since businesses earn and spend money in many different ways, and enter thousands of transactions, a systematic approach must be followed. This is called the double-entry framework. Could you use this double-entry system for your personal finances, or for a small business that you might start?

The terms asset, liability, owner's equity, revenue, and expense were explained in Chapter 2. Examples showed how individual business transactions change one or more of these basic accounting elements. Each transaction had a dual effect. An increase or decrease in any asset, liability, owner's equity, revenue, or expense was *always* accompanied by an offsetting change within the basic accounting elements. The fact that each transaction has a dual effect upon the accounting elements provides the basis for what is called **double-entry accounting**. To understand double-entry accounting, it is important to learn how T accounts work and the role of debits and credits in accounting.

THE T ACCOUNT

LO1 Define the parts of a T account.

The assets of a business may consist of a number of items, such as cash, accounts receivable, equipment, buildings, and land. The liabilities may consist of one or more items, such as accounts payable and notes payable. Similarly, owner's equity may consist of the owner's investments and various revenue and expense items. A separate account is used to record the increases and decreases in each type of asset, liability, owner's equity, revenue, and expense.

The T account gets its name from the fact that it resembles the letter T. As shown below, there are three major parts of an account:

1. the title,

2. the debit, or left side, and

3. the credit, or right side.

Title	
Debit = Left	Credit = Right

The debit side is always on the left and the credit side is always on the right. This is true for all types of asset, liability, owner's equity, revenue, and expense accounts.

LEARNING KEY

Debit means left and credit means right.

BALANCING A T ACCOUNT

LO2 Foot and balance a T account.

To determine the balance of a T account at any time, simply total the dollar amounts on the debit and credit sides. These totals are known as **footings**. The difference between the footings is called the **balance** of the account. This amount is then written on the side with the larger footing.

In Chapter 2, the accounting equation was used to analyze business transactions. This required columns in which to record the increases and decreases in various accounts. Let's compare this approach with the use of a T account for the transactions affecting cash. When a T account is used, increases in cash are recorded on the debit side and decreases are recorded on the credit side. Transactions for Jessie Jane's Campus Delivery are shown in Figure 3-1.

FIGURE 3-1   Cash T Account

COLUMNAR SUMMARY (From Chapter 2, page 30)		T ACCOUNT FORM	

COLUMNAR SUMMARY
(From Chapter 2, page 30)

Transaction	Cash
(a)	2,000
(b)	(1,200)
(d)	(300)
(e)	500
(f)	(200)
(g)	(50)
(i)	(80)
(j)	(200)
(k)	570
(l)	(300)
(m)	(650)
(n)	430
(o)	(150)
Balance	370

T ACCOUNT FORM

Cash

(a)	2,000	(b)	1,200
(e)	500	(d)	300
(k)	570	(f)	200
(n)	430	(g)	50
footing →	**3,500**	(i)	80
		(j)	200
		(l)	300
		(m)	650
Balance →	370	(o)	150
		3,130 ← footing	

DEBITS AND CREDITS

LO3 Describe the effects of debits and credits on specific types of accounts.

To **debit** an account means to enter an amount on the left or debit side of the account. To **credit** an account means to enter an amount on the right or credit side of the account. *Debits may increase or decrease the balances of specific accounts. This is also true for credits. To learn how to use debits and credits, it is best to reflect on the accounting equation.*

Abbreviations:
Often debit and credit are abbreviated as: Dr. = Debit Cr. = Credit (based on the Latin terms "debere" and "credere")

Assets		=	Liabilities		+	Owner's Equity	
Debit	Credit		Debit	Credit		Debit	Credit
+	–		–	+		–	+

Assets

Assets are on the left side of the accounting equation. Therefore, increases are entered on the left (debit) side of an asset account and decreases are entered on the right (credit) side.

Liabilities and Owner's Equity

Liabilities and owner's equity are on the right side of the equation. Therefore, increases are entered on the right (credit) side and decreases are entered on the left (debit) side.

The Owner's Equity Umbrella

Owner's equity includes four types of accounts: Owner's Capital, Revenues, Expenses, and Drawing. Expanding the accounting equation helps illustrate the use of debits and credits. Since these accounts affect owner's equity, they are shown under the "umbrella" of owner's equity in the accounting equation in Figure 3-2.

FIGURE 3-2 The Accounting Equation and the Owner's Equity Umbrella

Assets		=	Liabilities		+	Owner's Equity Jessica Jane, Capital	
Debit	**Credit**		**Debit**	**Credit**		**Debit**	**Credit**
+	–		–	+		–	+

Drawing

Debit	Credit
+	–

Revenues

Debit	Credit
–	+

Expenses

Debit	Credit
+	–

Owner's Capital

The owner's capital account, Jessica Jane, Capital, in Figure 3-2 reports the amount the owner has invested in the business. These investments increase the owner's equity and are credited to the owner's capital account.

Drawing

Withdrawals of cash and other assets by the owner for personal reasons decrease owner's equity. Withdrawals could be debited directly to the owner's capital account. However, readers of financial statements want to know the amount of withdrawals for the accounting period. Thus, as shown in Figure 3-2, withdrawals are debited to a separate account, Drawing.

Revenues

Revenues increase owner's equity. Revenues could be recorded directly on the credit side of the owner's capital account. However, readers of financial statements are interested in the specific types of revenues earned. Therefore, specific revenue accounts, like Delivery Fees, Sales, and Service Fees, are used. These specific accounts are credited when revenue is earned.

Expenses

Expenses decrease owner's equity. Expenses could be recorded on the debit side of the owner's capital account. However, readers of financial statements want to see the types of expenses incurred during the accounting period. Thus, specific expense accounts are maintained for items like rent, wages, advertising, and utilities. These specific accounts are debited as expenses are incurred.

Normal Balances

A **normal balance** is the side of an account that is used to increase the account. Thus, the normal balances for the accounts illustrated in Figure 3-2 are shown with a "+" sign. Since assets are debited for increases, these accounts normally have **debit balances**. Liability and owner's capital accounts are credited for

LEARNING KEY

You could credit the owner's capital account for revenues and debit the capital account for expenses and withdrawals. However, this is not a good idea. Using specific accounts provides additional information. Remember: An increase in an expense decreases owner's equity.

increases; thus, these accounts normally have **credit balances**. Since expense and drawing accounts are debited for increases (reducing owner's equity), these accounts normally have debit balances. Finally, revenue accounts are credited for increases (increasing owner's equity); thus, these accounts normally have credit balances. A summary of normal balances is provided in Figure 3-3.

FIGURE 3-3   Normal Balances

ACCOUNT	INCREASE	DECREASE	NORMAL BALANCE
Assets	Debit	Credit	Debit
Liabilities	Credit	Debit	Credit
Owner's Capital	Credit	Debit	Credit
Revenues	Credit	Debit	Credit
Expenses	Debit	Credit	Debit
Drawing	Debit	Credit	Debit

TRANSACTION ANALYSIS

LO4 **Use T accounts to analyze transactions.**

LEARNING KEY

If you have a debit, you must always have at least one credit. If you have a credit, you must always have at least one debit.

In Chapter 2, you learned how to analyze transactions by using the accounting equation. Here, we continue to use the accounting equation, but add debits and credits by using T accounts. As shown in Figure 3-4, the three basic questions that must be answered when analyzing a transaction are essentially the same but are expanded slightly to address the use of the owner's equity umbrella and T accounts. You must determine the location of the account within the accounting equation and/or the owner's equity umbrella. You must also determine whether the accounts should be debited or credited.

FIGURE 3-4   Steps in Transaction Analysis

1. **What happened?**
   Make certain you understand the event that has taken place.

2. **Which accounts are affected?**
   Once you have determined what happened, you must:
   • Identify the accounts that are affected.
   • Classify these accounts as assets, liabilities, owner's equity, revenues, or expenses.
   • Identify the location of the accounts in the accounting equation and/or the owner's equity umbrella—left or right.

3. **How is the accounting equation affected?**
   • Determine whether the accounts have increased or decreased.
   • Determine whether the accounts should be debited or credited.
   • Make certain that the accounting equation remains in balance after the transaction has been entered.
   (1) Assets = Liabilities + Owner's Equity.
   (2) Debits = Credits for every transaction.

Debits and Credits: Asset, Liability, and Owner's Equity Accounts

Transactions (a) through (d) from Jessie Jane's Campus Delivery (Chapter 2) demonstrate the double-entry process for transactions affecting asset, liability, and owner's equity accounts.

As you study each transaction, answer the three questions: (1) What happened? (2) Which accounts are affected? and (3) How is the accounting equation affected? The transaction statement tells you what happened. The analysis following the illustration of each transaction tells which accounts are affected. The illustration shows you how the accounting equation is affected.

Transaction (a): Investment by owner

Jessica Jane opened a bank account with a deposit of $2,000 for her business (Figure 3-5).

Analysis. As a result of this transaction, the business acquired an asset, Cash. In exchange for the asset, the business gave Jessica Jane owner's equity. The owner's equity account is called Jessica Jane, Capital. The transaction is entered as an increase in an asset and an increase in owner's equity. Debit Cash and credit Jessica Jane, Capital for $2,000.

FIGURE 3-5   Transaction (a): Investment by Owner

Assets		=	Liabilities		+	Owner's Equity	
Debit	**Credit**		**Debit**	**Credit**		**Debit**	**Credit**
+	−		−	+		−	+
Cash						Jessica Jane, Capital	
(a) 2,000							(a) 2,000
$2,000		=	$0		+	$2,000	
$2,000		=				$2,000	

Transaction (b): Purchase of an asset for cash

Jessie bought a motor scooter (delivery equipment) for $1,200 cash (Figure 3-6).

Analysis. Jessie exchanged one asset, Cash, for another, Delivery Equipment. Debit Delivery Equipment and credit Cash for $1,200. Notice that the total assets

FIGURE 3-6   Transaction (b): Purchase of an Asset for Cash

Assets		=	Liabilities		+	Owner's Equity	
Debit	**Credit**		**Debit**	**Credit**		**Debit**	**Credit**
+	−		−	+		−	+
Cash						Jessica Jane, Capital	
Bal. 2,000							Bal. 2,000
	(b) 1,200						
Bal. 800							
Delivery Equipment							
(b) 1,200							
$2,000		=	$0		+	$2,000	
$2,000		=				$2,000	

are still $2,000 as they were following transaction (a). Transaction (b) shifted assets from cash to delivery equipment, but total assets remained the same.

Transaction (c): Purchase of an asset on account

Jessie bought a second motor scooter on account for $900 (Figure 3-7).

Analysis. The asset, Delivery Equipment, increases by $900 and the liability, Accounts Payable, increases by the same amount. Thus, debit Delivery Equipment and credit Accounts Payable for $900.

FIGURE 3-7   Transaction (c): Purchase of an Asset on Account

Assets		=	Liabilities		+	Owner's Equity	
Debit	Credit		Debit	Credit		Debit	Credit
+	−		−	+		−	+
Cash			Accounts Payable			Jessica Jane, Capital	
Bal. 800				(c) 900			Bal. 2,000
Delivery Equipment							
Bal. 1,200							
(c) 900							
Bal. 2,100							
$2,900		=	$900		+	$2,000	
$2,900		=			$2,900		

Transaction (d): Payment on a loan

Jessie made the first $300 payment on the scooter purchased in transaction (c) (Figure 3-8).

Analysis. This payment decreases the asset, Cash, and decreases the liability, Accounts Payable. Debit Accounts Payable and credit Cash for $300.

FIGURE 3-8   Transaction (d): Payment on a Loan

Assets		=	Liabilities		+	Owner's Equity	
Debit	Credit		Debit	Credit		Debit	Credit
+	−		−	+		−	+
Cash			Accounts Payable			Jessica Jane, Capital	
Bal. 800				Bal. 900			Bal. 2,000
	(d) 300		(d) 300				
Bal. 500				Bal. 600			
Delivery Equipment							
Bal. 2,100							
$2,600		=	$600		+	$2,000	
$2,600		=			$2,600		

Notice that for transactions (a) through (d), the debits equal credits and the accounting equation is in balance. Review transactions (a) through (d). Again, identify the accounts that were affected and how they were classified (assets, liabilities, or owner's equity). Finally, note each account's location within the accounting equation.

LEARNING KEY

Credits increase the capital account. Revenues increase capital. Thus, revenues are shown under the credit side of the capital account. Debits decrease the capital account. Expenses and drawing reduce owner's equity. Thus, they are shown under the debit side of the capital account.

Debits and Credits: Including Revenues, Expenses, and Drawing

Transactions (a) through (d) involved only assets, liabilities, and the owner's capital account. To complete the illustration of Jessie Jane's Campus Delivery, the equation is expanded to include revenues, expenses, and drawing. Remember, revenues increase owner's equity and are shown under the credit side of the capital account. Expenses and drawing decrease owner's equity and are shown under the debit side of the capital account. The expanded equation is shown in Figure 3-9.

FIGURE 3-9   The Expanded Accounting Equation

Assets		=	Liabilities		+	Owner's Equity (Jessica Jane, Capital)	
Debit	Credit		Debit	Credit		Debit	Credit
+	–		–	+		–	+

		Drawing		Expenses		Revenues	
		Debit	Credit	Debit	Credit	Debit	Credit
		+	–	+	–	–	+

Transaction (e): Delivery revenues earned in cash

Jessie made deliveries and received $500 cash from clients (Figure 3-10).

Analysis. The asset, Cash, and the revenue, Delivery Fees, increase. Debit Cash and credit Delivery Fees for $500.

FIGURE 3-10   Transaction (e): Delivery Revenues Earned in Cash

Assets		=	Liabilities		+	Owner's Equity	
Debit	Credit		Debit	Credit		Debit	Credit
+	–		–	+		–	+

Cash			Accounts Payable			Jessica Jane, Capital	
Bal. 500				Bal. 600			Bal. 2,000
(e) 500							
Bal. 1,000							

Delivery Equipment						Drawing		Expenses		Revenues	
Bal. 2,100						Debit	Credit	Debit	Credit	Debit	Credit
						+	–	+	–	–	+

Delivery Fees
(e) 500

$3,100	=	$600	+			$2,500	
$3,100	=				$3,100		

Transaction (f): Paid rent for month

Jessie paid $200 for office rent for June (Figure 3-11).

Analysis. Rent Expense increases and Cash decreases. Debit Rent Expense and credit Cash for $200.

A debit to an expense account *increases* that expense and *decreases* owner's equity. Notice that the placement of the plus and minus signs for expenses are opposite the placement of the signs for owner's equity. Note also that expenses are located on the left (debit) side of the owner's equity umbrella.

FIGURE 3-11   Transaction (f): Paid Rent for Month

Assets		=	Liabilities		+	Owner's Equity			
Debit	**Credit**		**Debit**	**Credit**		**Debit**		**Credit**	
+	−		−	+		−		+	

Cash			Accounts Payable			Jessica Jane, Capital			
Bal. 1,000	(f) 200			Bal. 600					Bal. 2,000
Bal. 800									

Delivery Equipment			Drawing		Expenses		Revenues		
Bal. 2,100			**Debit**	**Credit**	**Debit**	**Credit**	**Debit**	**Credit**	
			+	−	+	−	−	+	

					Rent Expense		Delivery Fees	
					(f) 200			Bal. 500

$2,900	=	$600	+	$2,300
$2,900	=			$2,900

Transaction (g): Paid telephone bill

Jessie paid for telephone service, $50 (Figure 3-12).

Analysis. This transaction, like the previous one, increases an expense and decreases an asset. Debit Telephone Expense and credit Cash for $50.

FIGURE 3-12   Transaction (g): Paid Telephone Bill

Assets		=	Liabilities		+	Owner's Equity			
Debit	**Credit**		**Debit**	**Credit**		**Debit**		**Credit**	
+	−		−	+		−		+	

Cash			Accounts Payable			Jessica Jane, Capital			
Bal. 800	(g) 50			Bal. 600					Bal. 2,000
Bal. 750									

Delivery Equipment			Drawing		Expenses		Revenues		
Bal. 2,100			**Debit**	**Credit**	**Debit**	**Credit**	**Debit**	**Credit**	
			+	−	+	−	−	+	

					Rent Expense		Delivery Fees	
					Bal. 200			Bal. 500
					Telephone Expense			
					(g) 50			

$2,850	=	$600	+	$2,250
$2,850	=			$2,850

Transaction (h): Delivery revenues earned on account
Jessie made deliveries on account for $600 (Figure 3-13).

Analysis. As discussed in Chapter 2, delivery services are performed for which payment will be received later. This is called offering services "on account" or "on credit." Instead of receiving cash, Jessie receives a promise that her customers will pay cash in the future. Therefore, the asset, Accounts Receivable, increases. Since revenues are recognized when earned, the revenue account, Delivery Fees, also increases. Debit Accounts Receivable and credit Delivery Fees for $600.

FIGURE 3-13   Transaction (h): Delivery Revenues Earned on Account

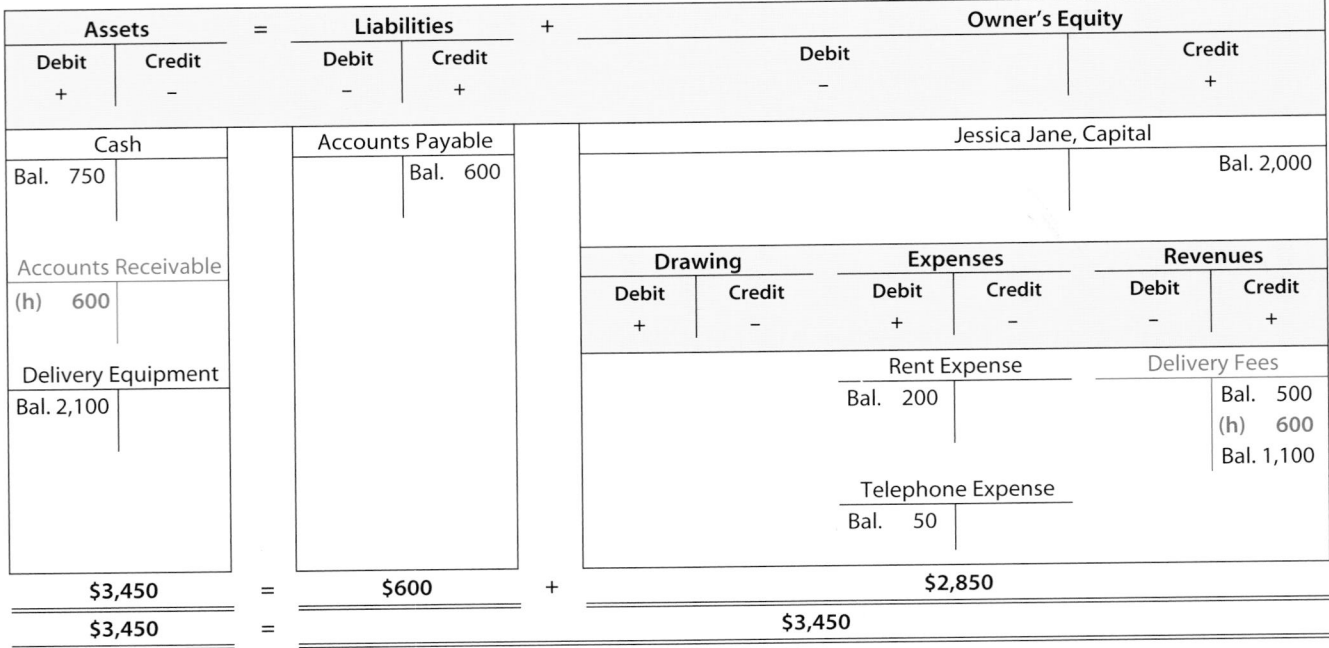

Review transactions (e) through (h). Two of these transactions are expenses and two are revenue transactions. Each of these transactions affected the owner's equity umbrella. Three transactions affected Cash and one transaction affected Accounts Receivable. Keep in mind that expense and revenue transactions do not always affect cash.

Notice that the debits equal credits and the accounting equation is in balance after each transaction. As you review transactions (e) through (h), identify the accounts that were affected and classify each account (assets, liabilities, owner's equity, revenue, or expense). Notice each account's location within the accounting equation and the owner's equity umbrella.

Upcoming transactions (i) and (j) both involve an exchange of cash for another asset. As you analyze these two transactions and answer the three questions about these transactions, you may wonder why prepaid insurance and supplies are assets while the rent and telephone bill in transactions (f) and (g) are expenses. Prepaid insurance and supplies are assets because they will provide benefits for more than one month. Jessie pays her rent and her telephone bill each month so they are classified as expenses. If Jessie paid her rent only once every three months, she would need to set up an asset account called Prepaid Rent. She would debit this account when she paid the rent.

Transaction (i): Purchase of supplies

Jessie bought pens, paper, delivery envelopes, and other supplies for $80 cash (Figure 3-14).

Analysis. These supplies will last for several months. Since they will generate future benefits, the supplies should be recorded as an asset. An asset, Supplies, increases, and an asset, Cash, decreases. Debit Supplies and credit Cash for $80.

FIGURE 3-14   Transaction (i): Purchase of Supplies

Assets		=	Liabilities		+	Owner's Equity	
Debit	Credit		Debit	Credit		Debit	Credit
+	–		–	+		–	+

Cash			Accounts Payable			Jessica Jane, Capital	
Bal. 750				Bal. 600			Bal. 2,000
	(i) 80						
Bal. 670							

Accounts Receivable	
Bal. 600	

	Drawing		Expenses		Revenues	
	Debit	Credit	Debit	Credit	Debit	Credit
	+	–	+	–	–	+

Supplies	
(i) 80	

Rent Expense		Delivery Fees	
Bal. 200			Bal. 1,100

Delivery Equipment	
Bal. 2,100	

Telephone Expense	
Bal. 50	

$3,450	=	$600	+	$2,850
$3,450	=			$3,450

A   BROADER   VIEW

Supplies—Asset or Expense?

When businesses buy office supplies from Staples or other suppliers, the supplies are initially recorded as assets. This is done because the supplies will provide future benefits. Those still remaining at the end of the accounting period are reported on the balance sheet as assets. Supplies actually used during the period are recognized as an expense on the income statement. We will discuss how to account for the expense in Chapter 5.

AP IMAGES

PROFILES IN ACCOUNTING

Jeanette Anderson, Factory Accounting Clerk

Jeanette Anderson earned a 4.0 GPA and membership in Phi Theta Kappa while completing her Associate Degree in Business at Eastern Wyoming College. While on campus, she held a work-study job as an Instructor Assistant. In this position, Jeanette demonstrated a sound work ethic, an ability to get along well with others, and competence.

After graduation, she went to work for Imperial/Holly Sugar Corp. in Torrington, Wyoming. Her duties include working with automated accounts payable, accounts receivable, and inventory control. During the annual harvest campaign, she supervises data entry clerks.

Jeanette believes the key to her success has been her understanding of double-entry accounting combined with her computer skills. Possessing problem-solving skills and being flexible are also important.

Source: Jack Kappeler, Eastern Wyoming College

Transaction (j): Payment of insurance premium

Jessie paid $200 for an eight-month liability insurance policy (Figure 3-15).

Analysis. Since insurance is paid in advance and will provide future benefits, it is treated as an asset. Therefore, one asset, Prepaid Insurance, increases and another, Cash, decreases. Debit Prepaid Insurance and credit Cash for $200.

FIGURE 3-15 Transaction (j): Payment of Insurance Premium

Assets		=	Liabilities		+	Owner's Equity		
Debit	**Credit**		**Debit**	**Credit**		**Debit**		**Credit**
+	–		–	+		–		+
Cash			Accounts Payable			Jessica Jane, Capital		
Bal. 670				Bal. 600				Bal. 2,000
	(j) 200							
Bal. 470								
Accounts Receivable						**Drawing**	**Expenses**	**Revenues**
Bal. 600						Debit | Credit	Debit | Credit	Debit | Credit
						+ | –	+ | –	– | +
Supplies							Rent Expense	Delivery Fees
Bal. 80							Bal. 200	Bal. 1,100
Prepaid Insurance							Telephone Expense	
(j) 200							Bal. 50	
Delivery Equipment								
Bal. 2,100								
$3,450		=	**$600**		+	**$2,850**		
$3,450		=				**$3,450**		

Transaction (k): Cash receipts from prior sales on account

Jessie received $570 in cash for delivery services performed for customers earlier in the month [see transaction (h)] (Figure 3-16).

Analysis. This transaction increases Cash and reduces the amount due from customers reported in Accounts Receivable. Debit Cash and credit Accounts Receivable $570.

As you analyze transaction (k), notice which accounts are affected and the location of these accounts in the accounting equation. Jessie received cash, but this transaction did not affect revenue. The revenue was recorded in transaction (h). Transaction (k) is an exchange of one asset (Accounts Receivable) for another asset (Cash).

FIGURE 3-16   Transaction (k): Cash Receipts from Prior Sales on Account

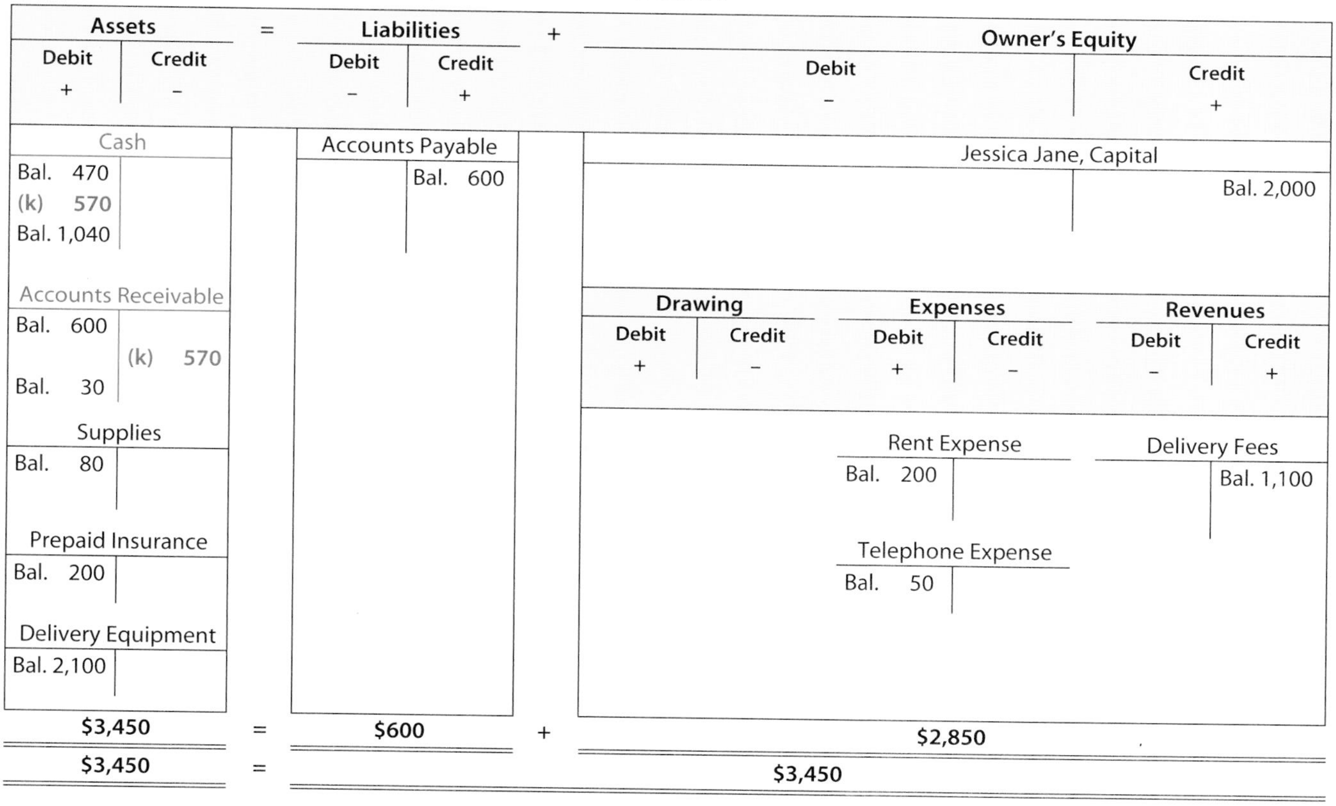

As you analyze transactions (l) through (o), make certain that you understand what has happened in each transaction. Identify the accounts that are affected and the locations of these accounts within the accounting equation. Notice that the accounting equation remains in balance after every transaction and debits equal credits for each transaction.

Transaction (I): Purchase of an asset on credit making a partial payment

Jessie bought a third motor scooter for $1,500. Jessie made a down payment of $300 and spread the remaining payments over the next four months (Figure 3-17).

Analysis. The asset, Delivery Equipment, increases by $1,500, Cash decreases by $300, and the liability, Accounts Payable, increases by $1,200. Thus, debit Delivery Equipment for $1,500, credit Cash for $300, and credit Accounts Payable for $1,200. This transaction requires one debit and two credits. Even so, total debits ($1,500) equal the total credits ($1,200 + $300) and the accounting equation remains in balance.

FIGURE 3-17 Transaction (I): Purchase of an Asset on Credit Making a Partial Payment

Assets		=	Liabilities		+	Owner's Equity		
Debit	**Credit**		**Debit**	**Credit**		**Debit**		**Credit**
+	−		−	+		−		+

Cash		Accounts Payable		Jessica Jane, Capital	
Bal. 1,040			Bal. 600		Bal. 2,000
	(I) 300		(I) 1,200		
Bal. 740			Bal. 1,800		

Accounts Receivable		Drawing		Expenses		Revenues	
Bal. 30		**Debit**	**Credit**	**Debit**	**Credit**	**Debit**	**Credit**
		+	−	+	−	−	+

Supplies		Rent Expense		Delivery Fees	
Bal. 80		Bal. 200			Bal. 1,100

Prepaid Insurance		Telephone Expense	
Bal. 200		Bal. 50	

Delivery Equipment	
Bal. 2,100	
(I) 1,500	
Bal. 3,600	

$4,650	=	$1,800	+	$2,850
$4,650	=			$4,650

Transaction (m): Payment of wages

Jessie paid her part-time employees $650 in wages (Figure 3-18).

Analysis. This is an additional business expense. Wages Expense increases and Cash decreases. Debit Wages Expense and credit Cash for $650.

FIGURE 3-18　Transaction (m): Payment of Wages

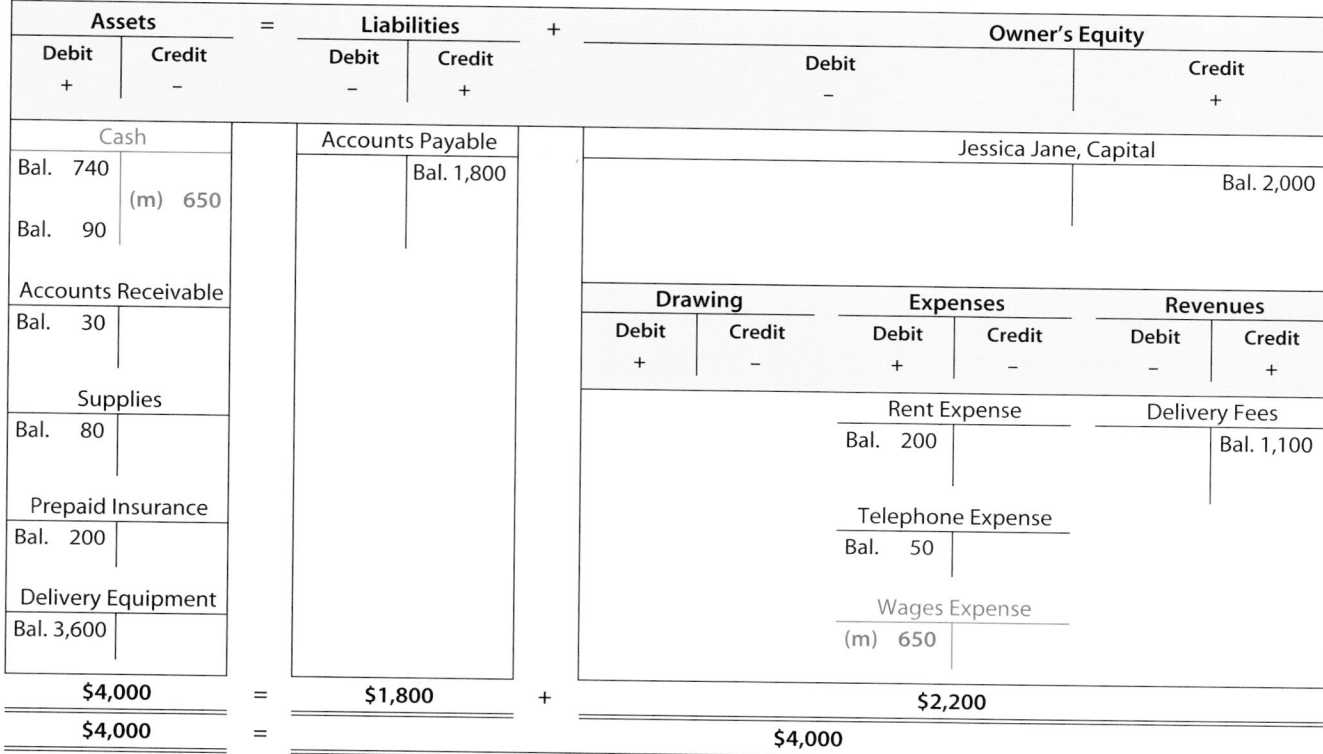

Transaction (n): Deliveries made for cash and credit

Total delivery fees for the remainder of the month amounted to $1,050: $430 in cash and $620 on account (Figure 3-19 on the next page).

Analysis. Since the delivery fees have been earned, the revenue account increases by $1,050. Also, Cash increases by $430 and Accounts Receivable increases by $620. Note once again that one event impacts three accounts. This time we have debits of $430 to Cash and $620 to Accounts Receivable, and a credit of $1,050 to Delivery Fees. As before, the total debits ($430 + $620) equal the total credits ($1,050) and the accounting equation remains in balance.

Transaction (o): Withdrawal of cash from business

At the end of the month, Jessie withdrew $150 in cash from the business to purchase books for her classes (Figure 3-20 on the next page).

Analysis. Cash withdrawals decrease owner's equity and decrease cash. Debit Jessica Jane, Drawing and credit Cash for $150.

Withdrawals are reported in the drawing account. Withdrawals by an owner are the opposite of an investment. You could debit the owner's capital account for withdrawals. However, using a specific account tells the user of the accounting information how much was withdrawn for the period.

FIGURE 3-19 Transaction (n): Deliveries Made for Cash and Credit

Assets		=	Liabilities		+	Owner's Equity	
Debit	Credit		Debit	Credit		Debit	Credit
+	−		−	+		−	+

Cash		Accounts Payable		Jessica Jane, Capital	
Bal. 90			Bal. 1,800		Bal. 2,000
(n) 430					
Bal. 520					

	Drawing		Expenses		Revenues	
	Debit	Credit	Debit	Credit	Debit	Credit
	+	−	+	−	−	+

Accounts Receivable	
Bal. 30	
(n) 620	
Bal. 650	

Rent Expense		Delivery Fees	
Bal. 200			Bal. 1,100
			(n) 1,050
			Bal. 2,150

Supplies	
Bal. 80	

Prepaid Insurance	
Bal. 200	

Telephone Expense	
Bal. 50	

Delivery Equipment	
Bal. 3,600	

Wages Expense	
Bal. 650	

$5,050	=	$1,800	+	$3,250
$5,050	=			$5,050

FIGURE 3-20 Transaction (o): Withdrawal of Cash from Business

Assets		=	Liabilities		+	Owner's Equity	
Debit	Credit		Debit	Credit		Debit	Credit
+	−		−	+		−	+

Cash		Accounts Payable		Jessica Jane, Capital	
Bal. 520			Bal. 1,800		Bal. 2,000
	(o) 150				
Bal. 370					

	Drawing		Expenses		Revenues	
	Debit	Credit	Debit	Credit	Debit	Credit
	+	−	+	−	−	+

Accounts Receivable	
Bal. 650	

Jessica Jane, Drawing		Rent Expense		Delivery Fees	
(o) 150		Bal. 200			Bal. 2,150

Supplies	
Bal. 80	

Prepaid Insurance	
Bal. 200	

Telephone Expense	
Bal. 50	

Delivery Equipment	
Bal. 3,600	

Wages Expense	
Bal. 650	

$4,900	=	$1,800	+	$3,100
$4,900	=			$4,900

Summary of Transactions

In illustrating transactions (a) through (o), each T account for Jessie Jane's Campus Delivery shows a balance before and after each transaction. To focus your attention on the transaction being explained, only a single entry was shown. In practice, this is not done. Instead, each account gathers all transactions for a period. Jessie's accounts, with all transactions listed, are shown in Figure 3-21. Note the following four items.

1. The footings are directly under the debit (left) and credit (right) sides of the T account for those accounts with more than one debit or credit.

2. The balance is shown on the side with the larger footing.

FIGURE 3-21   Summary of Transactions (a) Through (o)

3. The footing serves as the balance for accounts with entries on only one side of the account.

4. If an account has only a single entry, it is not necessary to enter a footing or balance.

THE TRIAL BALANCE

LO5 Prepare a trial balance and explain its purposes and linkages with the financial statements.

Recall the two very important rules in double-entry accounting:

1. The sum of the debits must equal the sum of the credits. This means that at least two accounts are affected by each transaction. This rule is so important that many computer accounting programs will not permit a transaction to be entered into the accounting system unless the debits equal the credits.

2. The accounting equation must remain in balance.

In illustrating the transactions for Jessie Jane's Campus Delivery, the equality of the accounting equation was verified after each transaction. Because of the large number of transactions entered each day, this is not done in practice. Instead, a trial balance is prepared periodically to determine the equality of the debits and credits. A **trial balance** is a list of all accounts showing the title and balance of each account. By totaling the debits and credits, their equality can be tested.

A trial balance of Jessie's accounts, taken on June 30, 20--, is shown in Figure 3-22. This date is shown on the third line of the heading. The trial balance shows that the debit and credit totals are equal in amount. This is proof that (1) in entering transactions (a) through (o), the total of the debits was equal to the total of the credits, and (2) the accounting equation has remained in balance.

A trial balance is not a formal statement or report. Normally, only the accountant sees it. As shown in Figure 3-23, a trial balance can be used as an aid in preparing the financial statements.

LEARNING KEY

A trial balance provides proof that total debits equal total credits and shows that the accounting equation is in balance.

Since a trial balance is not a formal statement, dollar signs are not used.

FIGURE 3-22 Trial Balance

<table>
<tr><td colspan="3" align="center">Jessie Jane's Campus Delivery
Trial Balance
June 30, 20 - -</td></tr>
<tr><th>ACCOUNT TITLE</th><th>DEBIT BALANCE</th><th>CREDIT BALANCE</th></tr>
<tr><td>Cash</td><td>3 7 0 00</td><td></td></tr>
<tr><td>Accounts Receivable</td><td>6 5 0 00</td><td></td></tr>
<tr><td>Supplies</td><td>8 0 00</td><td></td></tr>
<tr><td>Prepaid Insurance</td><td>2 0 0 00</td><td></td></tr>
<tr><td>Delivery Equipment</td><td>3 6 0 0 00</td><td></td></tr>
<tr><td>Accounts Payable</td><td></td><td>1 8 0 0 00</td></tr>
<tr><td>Jessica Jane, Capital</td><td></td><td>2 0 0 0 00</td></tr>
<tr><td>Jessica Jane, Drawing</td><td>1 5 0 00</td><td></td></tr>
<tr><td>Delivery Fees</td><td></td><td>2 1 5 0 00</td></tr>
<tr><td>Rent Expense</td><td>2 0 0 00</td><td></td></tr>
<tr><td>Telephone Expense</td><td>5 0 00</td><td></td></tr>
<tr><td>Wages Expense</td><td>6 5 0 00</td><td></td></tr>
<tr><td></td><td>5 9 5 0 00</td><td>5 9 5 0 00</td></tr>
</table>

FIGURE 3-23   Linkages Between the Trial Balance and Financial Statements

Jessie Jane's Campus Delivery
Trial Balance
June 30, 20 - -

ACCOUNT TITLE	DEBIT BALANCE	CREDIT BALANCE
Cash	3 7 0 00	
Accounts Receivable	6 5 0 00	
Supplies	8 0 00	
Prepaid Insurance	2 0 0 00	
Delivery Equipment	3 6 0 0 00	
Accounts Payable		1 8 0 0 00
Jessica Jane, Capital		2 0 0 0 00
Jessica Jane, Drawing	1 5 0 00	
Delivery Fees		2 1 5 0 00
Rent Expense	2 0 0 00	
Telephone Expense	5 0 00	
Wages Expense	6 5 0 00	
	5 9 5 0 00	5 9 5 0 00

Jessie Jane's Campus Delivery
Income Statement
For Month Ended June 30, 20 --

Revenue:		
Delivery fees		$2 1 5 0 00
Expenses:		
Wages expense	$ 6 5 0 00	
Rent expense	2 0 0 00	
Telephone expense	5 0 00	
Total expenses		9 0 0 00
Net income		$1 2 5 0 00

Jessie Jane's Campus Delivery
Statement of Owner's Equity
For Month Ended June 30, 20 - -

Jessica Jane, capital, June 1, 20 -		$2 0 0 0 00
Net income for June	$1 2 5 0 00	
Less withdrawals for June	1 5 0 00	
Increase in capital		1 1 0 0 00
Jessica Jane, capital, June 30, 20 -		$3 1 0 0 00

Jessie Jane's Campus Delivery
Balance Sheet
June 30, 20 - -

Assets		Liabilities	
Cash	$ 3 7 0 00	Accounts payable	$1 8 0 0 00
Accounts receivable	6 5 0 00		
Supplies	8 0 00	Owner's Equity	
Prepaid insurance	2 0 0 00	Jessica Jane, capital	3 1 0 0 00
Delivery equipment	3 6 0 0 00		
Total assets	$4 9 0 0 00	Total liabilities and owner's equity	$4 9 0 0 00

Learning Objectives	Key Points to Remember
LO1 Define the parts of a T account.	The parts of a T account are: 1. the title, 2. the debit or left side, and 3. the credit or right side.

Title

Debit = Left	Credit = Right

Learning Objectives	Key Points to Remember
LO2 Foot and balance a T account.	Rules for footing and balancing T accounts are: 1. The footings are directly under the debit (left) and credit (right) sides of the T account for those accounts with more than one debit or credit. 2. The balance is shown on the side with the larger footing. 3. The footing serves as the balance for accounts with entries on only one side of the account. 4. If an account has only a single entry, it is not necessary to enter a footing or balance.
LO3 Describe the effects of debits and credits on specific types of accounts.	Rules for debits and credits. (See illustration below.) 1. Assets are on the left side of the accounting equation. Therefore, increases are entered on the left (debit) side of an asset account and decreases are entered on the right (credit) side. 2. Liabilities and owner's equity are on the right side of the accounting equation. Therefore, increases are entered on the right (credit) side and decreases are entered on the left (debit) side. 3. Revenues increase owner's equity. Therefore, increases are entered on the right (credit) side and decreases are entered on the left (debit) side. 4. Expenses and drawing decrease owner's equity. Therefore, increases are entered on the left (debit) side and decreases are entered on the right (credit) side.

Accounting Equation with Owner's Equity Umbrella

Assets		=	Liabilities		+	Owner's Equity Jessica Jane, Capital	
Debit	Credit		Debit	Credit		Debit	Credit
+	−		−	+		−	+

Drawing		Revenues	
Debit	Credit	Debit	Credit
+	−	−	+

Expenses	
Debit	Credit
+	−

Learning Objectives	Key Points to Remember
LO4 Use T accounts to analyze transactions.	Picture the accounting equation in your mind as you analyze transactions. When entering transactions in T accounts: 1. The sum of the debits must equal the sum of the credits. 2. At least two accounts are affected by each transaction. 3. When finished, the accounting equation must remain in balance.
LO5 Prepare a trial balance and explain its purposes and linkages with the financial statements.	A trial balance shows that the debit and credit totals are equal. A trial balance also can be used in preparing the financial statements.

DEMONSTRATION PROBLEM

Celia Pints opened We-Buy, You-Pay Shopping Services. For a fee that is based on the amount of research and shopping time required, Pints and her associates will shop for almost anything from groceries to home furnishings. Business is particularly heavy around Christmas and in early summer. The business operates from a rented store front. The associates receive a commission based on the revenues they produce and a mileage reimbursement for the use of their personal automobiles for shopping trips. Pints decided to use the following accounts to record transactions.

Assets
    Cash
    Accounts Receivable
    Office Equipment
    Computer Equipment
Liabilities
    Accounts Payable
    Notes Payable

Owner's Equity
    Celia Pints, Capital
    Celia Pints, Drawing
Revenue
    Shopping Fees
Expenses
    Rent Expense
    Telephone Expense
    Commissions Expense
    Utilities Expense
    Travel Expense

The following transactions are for the month of December 20--.

(a) Pints invested cash in the business, $30,000.

(b) Bought office equipment for $10,000. Paid $2,000 in cash and promised to pay the balance over the next four months.

(c) Paid rent for December, $500.

(d) Provided shopping services for customers on account, $5,200.

(e) Paid telephone bill, $90.

(f) Borrowed cash from the bank by signing a note payable, $5,000.

(g) Bought a computer and printer, $4,800.

(h) Collected cash from customers for services performed on account, $4,000.

(i) Paid commissions to associates for revenues generated during the first half of the month, $3,500.

(j) Paid utility bill, $600.

(k) Paid cash on account for the office equipment purchased in transaction (b), $2,000.

(l) Earned shopping fees of $13,200: $6,000 in cash and $7,200 on account.

(m) Paid commissions to associates for last half of month, $7,000.

(n) Paid mileage reimbursements for the month, $1,500.

(o) Paid cash on note payable to bank, $1,000.

(p) Pints withdrew cash for personal use, $2,000.

(continued)

REQUIRED

1. Enter the transactions for December in T accounts. Use the accounting equation as a guide for setting up the T accounts.

2. Foot the T accounts and determine their balances as necessary.

3. Prepare a trial balance of the accounts as of December 31 of the current year.

4. Prepare an income statement for the month ended December 31 of the current year.

5. Prepare a statement of owner's equity for the month ended December 31 of the current year.

6. Prepare a balance sheet as of December 31 of the current year.

Solution 1, 2.

Assets		=	Liabilities		+	Owner's Equity		
Debit	Credit		Debit	Credit		Debit		Credit
+	−		−	+		−		+

Cash

(a) 30,000	(b) 2,000
(f) 5,000	(c) 500
(h) 4,000	(e) 90
(l) 6,000	(g) 4,800
45,000	(i) 3,500
	(j) 600
	(k) 2,000
	(m) 7,000
	(n) 1,500
	(o) 1,000
	(p) 2,000
	24,990
Bal. 20,010	

Accounts Receivable

(d) 5,200	(h) 4,000
(l) 7,200	
12,400	
Bal. 8,400	

Office Equipment

(b) 10,000	

Computer Equipment

(g) 4,800	

Accounts Payable

(k) 2,000	(b) 8,000
	Bal. 6,000

Notes Payable

(o) 1,000	(f) 5,000
	Bal. 4,000

Celia Pints, Capital

	(a) 30,000

Drawing		Expenses		Revenues	
Debit	Credit	Debit	Credit	Debit	Credit
+	−	+	−	−	+

Celia Pints, Drawing

(p) 2,000	

Rent Expense

(c) 500	

Shopping Fees

	(d) 5,200
	(l) 13,200
	Bal. 18,400

Telephone Expense

(e) 90	

Commissions Expense

(i) 3,500	
(m) 7,000	
Bal. 10,500	

Utilities Expense

(j) 600	

Travel Expense

(n) 1,500	

$43,210	=	$10,000	+	$33,210
$43,210	=			$43,210

3.

We-Buy, You-Pay Shopping Services Trial Balance December 31, 20 - -										
ACCOUNT TITLE	DEBIT BALANCE					CREDIT BALANCE				
Cash	20	0	1	0	00					
Accounts Receivable	8	4	0	0	00					
Office Equipment	10	0	0	0	00					
Computer Equipment	4	8	0	0	00					
Accounts Payable						6	0	0	0	00
Notes Payable						4	0	0	0	00
Celia Pints, Capital						30	0	0	0	00
Celia Pints, Drawing	2	0	0	0	00					
Shopping Fees						18	4	0	0	00
Rent Expense		5	0	0	00					
Telephone Expense			9	0	00					
Commissions Expense	10	5	0	0	00					
Utilities Expense		6	0	0	00					
Travel Expense	1	5	0	0	00					
	58	4	0	0	00	58	4	0	0	00

4.

We-Buy, You-Pay Shopping Services Income Statement For Month Ended December 31, 20 - -										
Revenue:										
Shopping fees						$18	4	0	0	00
Expenses:										
Commissions expense	$10	5	0	0	00					
Travel expense	1	5	0	0	00					
Utilities expense		6	0	0	00					
Rent expense		5	0	0	00					
Telephone expense			9	0	00					
Total expenses						13	1	9	0	00
Net income						$ 5	2	1	0	00

5.

We-Buy, You-Pay Shopping Services Statement of Owner's Equity For Month Ended December 31, 20 - -										
Celia Pints, capital, December 1, 20 - -						$30	0	0	0	00
Net income for December	$5	2	1	0	00					
Less withdrawals for December	2	0	0	0	00					
Increase in capital						3	2	1	0	00
Celia Pints, capital, December 31, 20 - -						$33	2	1	0	00

(continued)

6.

We-Buy, You-Pay Shopping Services											
Balance Sheet											
December 31, 20 - -											
Assets						Liabilities					
Cash	$ 20	0	1	0	00	Accounts payable	$ 6	0	0	0	00
Accounts receivable	8	4	0	0	00	Notes payable	4	0	0	0	00
Office equipment	10	0	0	0	00	Total liabilities	$10	0	0	0	00
Computer equipment	4	8	0	0	00						
						Owner's Equity					
						Celia Pints, capital	33	2	1	0	00
Total assets	$43	2	1	0	00	Total liabilities and owner's equity	$43	2	1	0	00

KEY TERMS

balance (54)   The difference between the footings of an account.

credit (55)   To enter an amount on the right side of an account.

credit balance (57)   The normal balance of liability, owner's equity, and revenue accounts.

debit (55)   To enter an amount on the left side of an account.

debit balance (56)   The normal balance of asset, expense, and drawing accounts.

double-entry accounting (54)   A system in which each transaction has a dual effect on the accounting elements.

footings (54)   The total dollar amounts on the debit and credit sides of an account.

normal balance (56)   The side of an account that is increased.

trial balance (70)   A list of all accounts, showing the title and balance of each account, used to prove that the sum of the debits equals the sum of the credits.

Self-Study Test Questions

True/False

1.   To debit an account is to enter an amount on the left side of the account.

2.   Liability accounts normally have debit balances.

3.   Increases in owner's equity are entered as credits.

4.   Revenue accounts normally have debit balances.

5.   To credit an account is to enter an amount on the right side of the account.

6.   A debit to an asset account will decrease it.

Multiple Choice

1. A common example of an asset is

    (a) Professional Fees.
    (b) Rent Expense.
    (c) Accounts Receivable.
    (d) Accounts Payable.

2. To record the payment of rent expense, an accountant would

    (a) debit Cash; credit Rent Expense.
    (b) debit Rent Expense; debit Cash.
    (c) debit Rent Expense; credit Cash.
    (d) credit Rent Expense; credit Cash.

3. The accounting equation may be expressed as

    (a) Assets = Liabilities − Owner's Equity.
    (b) Assets = Liabilities + Owner's Equity.
    (c) Liabilities = Owner's Equity − Assets.
    (d) all of the above.

4. Liability, owner's equity, and revenue accounts normally have

    (a) debit balances.
    (b) large balances.
    (c) negative balances.
    (d) credit balances.

5. An investment of cash by the owner will

    (a) increase assets and owner's equity.
    (b) increase assets and liabilities.
    (c) increase liabilities and owner's equity.
    (d) increase owner's equity; decrease liabilities.

The answers to the Self-Study Test Questions are at the end of the text.

REVIEW QUESTIONS

LO1   1.   What are the three major parts of a T account?

LO1   2.   What is the left side of the T account called? the right side?

LO2   3.   What is a footing?

LO3   4.   What is the relationship between the revenue and expense accounts and the owner's equity account?

LO5   5.   What is the function of the trial balance?

© DIGITAL IMAGING GROUP

REVISITING THE OPENER

In the chapter opener on page 53, you are asked to consider whether you could use the double-entry bookkeeping system illustrated in this chapter for your personal finances. Reflect for a moment on your financial transactions over the past week or month. To refresh your memory, review your checkbook for checks written and deposits made. Further, review your credit card statements to help you remember how you spent your money. After you have gathered your transactions, set up T accounts for your different types of transactions. Then, enter these transactions in the T accounts, compute ending balances, and prepare an income statement.

SERIES A EXERCISES

E 3-1A (LO2)

✓ Cash bal.: $1,200 (Dr.)

FOOT AND BALANCE A T ACCOUNT Foot and balance the cash T account shown.

Cash	
500	100
400	200
600	

E 3-2A (LO3)

DEBIT AND CREDIT ANALYSIS Complete the following questions using either "debit" or "credit":

(a)   The cash account is increased with a _____.
(b)   The owner's capital account is increased with a _____.
(c)   The delivery equipment account is increased with a _____.
(d)   The cash account is decreased with a _____.
(e)   The liability account Accounts Payable is increased with a _____.
(f)   The revenue account Delivery Fees is increased with a _____.
(g)   The asset account Accounts Receivable is increased with a _____.
(h)   The rent expense account is increased with a _____.
(i)   The owner's drawing account is increased with a _____.

E 3-3A (LO2/3/4)
✓ Cash bal. after (c): $2,700 (Dr.)

ANALYSIS OF T ACCOUNTS Jim Arnold began a business called Arnold's Shoe Repair.

1. Create T accounts for Cash; Supplies; Jim Arnold, Capital; and Utilities Expense. Identify the following transactions by letter and place them on the proper side of the T accounts:

    (a) Invested cash in the business, $5,000.
    (b) Purchased supplies for cash, $800.
    (c) Paid utility bill, $1,500.

2. Foot the T account for cash and enter the ending balance.

E 3-4A (LO3)

NORMAL BALANCE OF ACCOUNT Indicate the normal balance (debit or credit) for each of the following accounts:

1. Cash
2. Wages Expense
3. Accounts Payable
4. Owner's Drawing
5. Supplies
6. Owner's Capital
7. Equipment

E 3-5A (LO4)

TRANSACTION ANALYSIS Sheryl Hansen started a business on May 1, 20--. Analyze the following transactions for the first month of business using T accounts. Label each T account with the title of the account affected and then place the transaction letter and the dollar amount on the debit or credit side.

(a) Invested cash in the business, $4,000.
(b) Bought equipment for cash, $500.
(c) Bought equipment on account, $800.
(d) Paid cash on account for equipment purchased in transaction (c), $300.
(e) Withdrew cash for personal use, $700.

E 3-6A (LO2)
✓ Cash bal. after (e): $2,500 (Dr.)

FOOT AND BALANCE T ACCOUNTS Foot and balance the T accounts prepared in Exercise 3-5A if necessary.

E 3-7A (LO2/4)
✓ Cash bal. after (k): $24,400 (Dr.)

ANALYSIS OF TRANSACTIONS Charles Chadwick opened a business called Charlie's Detective Service in January 20--. Set up T accounts for the following accounts: Cash; Accounts Receivable; Office Supplies; Computer Equipment; Office Furniture; Accounts Payable; Charles Chadwick, Capital; Charles Chadwick, Drawing; Professional Fees; Rent Expense; and Utilities Expense.

The following transactions occurred during the first month of business. Record these transactions in T accounts. After all transactions are recorded, foot and balance the accounts if necessary.

(a) Invested cash in the business, $30,000.
(b) Bought office supplies for cash, $300.
(c) Bought office furniture for cash, $5,000.
(d) Purchased computer and printer on account, $8,000.
(e) Received cash from clients for services, $3,000.
(f) Paid cash on account for computer and printer purchased in transaction (d), $4,000.

(continued)

(g) Earned professional fees on account during the month, $9,000.
(h) Paid cash for office rent for January, $1,500.
(i) Paid utility bills for the month, $800.
(j) Received cash from clients billed in transaction (g), $6,000.
(k) Withdrew cash for personal use, $3,000.

E 3-8A (LO5)
✓ Trial bal. total debits: $46,000

TRIAL BALANCE Based on the transactions recorded in Exercise 3-7A, prepare a trial balance for Charlie's Detective Service as of January 31, 20--.

E 3-9A (LO5)
✓ Trial bal. total debits: $21,400

TRIAL BALANCE The following accounts have normal balances. Prepare a trial balance for Juanita's Delivery Service as of September 30, 20--.

Cash	$ 5,000
Accounts Receivable	3,000
Supplies	800
Prepaid Insurance	600
Delivery Equipment	8,000
Accounts Payable	2,000
Juanita Raye, Capital	10,000
Juanita Raye, Drawing	1,000
Delivery Fees	9,400
Wages Expense	2,100
Rent Expense	900

E 3-10A (LO5)
✓ Net income: $6,400

INCOME STATEMENT From the information in Exercise 3-9A, prepare an income statement for Juanita's Delivery Service for the month ended September 30, 20--.

E 3-11A (LO5)
✓ Capital, 9/30: $15,400

STATEMENT OF OWNER'S EQUITY From the information in Exercise 3-9A, prepare a statement of owner's equity for Juanita's Delivery Service for the month ended September 30, 20--.

E 3-12A (LO5)
✓ Total assets, 9/30: $17,400

BALANCE SHEET From the information in Exercise 3-9A, prepare a balance sheet for Juanita's Delivery Service as of September 30, 20--.

SERIES A PROBLEMS

P 3-13A (LO2/4/5)
✓ Cash bal. after (p): $14,820 (Dr.);
Trial bal. total debits: $38,200

T ACCOUNTS AND TRIAL BALANCE Harold Long started a business in May 20-- called Harold's Home Repair. Long hired a part-time college student as an assistant. Long has decided to use the following accounts for recording transactions:

Assets	Owner's Equity
Cash	Harold Long, Capital
Accounts Receivable	Harold Long, Drawing
Office Supplies	Revenue
Prepaid Insurance	Service Fees
Equipment	Expenses
Van	Rent Expense
Liabilities	Wages Expense
Accounts Payable	Telephone Expense
	Gas and Oil Expense

The following transactions occurred during May:

(a) Invested cash in the business, $20,000.
(b) Purchased a used van for cash, $7,000.
(c) Purchased equipment on account, $5,000.
(d) Received cash for services rendered, $6,000.
(e) Paid cash on account owed from transaction (c), $2,000.
(f) Paid rent for the month, $900.
(g) Paid telephone bill, $200.
(h) Earned revenue on account, $4,000.
(i) Purchased office supplies for cash, $120.
(j) Paid wages to student, $600.
(k) Purchased a one-year insurance policy, $1,200.
(l) Received cash from services performed in transaction (h), $3,000.
(m) Paid cash for gas and oil expense on the van, $160.
(n) Purchased additional equipment for $3,000, paying $1,000 cash and spreading the remaining payments over the next 10 months.
(o) Earned service fees for the remainder of the month of $3,200: $1,800 in cash and $1,400 on account.
(p) Withdrew cash at the end of the month, $2,800.

REQUIRED

1. Enter the transactions in T accounts, identifying each transaction with its corresponding letter.

2. Foot and balance the accounts where necessary.

3. Prepare a trial balance as of May 31, 20--.

P 3-14A (LO5)

✓ Net income: $11,340

✓ Owner's equity, 5/31: $28,540

✓ Total assets, 5/31: $33,540

NET INCOME AND CHANGE IN OWNER'S EQUITY Refer to the trial balance of Harold's Home Repair in Problem 3-13A to determine the following information. Use the format provided below.

1. a. Total revenue for the month   _____

    b. Total expenses for the month   _____

    c. Net income for the month   _____

2. a. Harold Long's original investment   _____
        in the business

            + The net income for the month   _____

            − Owner's drawing   _____

            Increase (decrease) in capital   _____

            = Ending owner's equity   _____

    b. End of month accounting equation:

Assets	=	Liabilities	+	Owner's Equity
_____	=	_____	+	_____

P 3-15A (LO5)

✓ NI: $11,340; Capital, 5/31/20--:

$28,540; Total assets: $33,540

FINANCIAL STATEMENTS Refer to the trial balance in Problem 3-13A and to the analysis of the change in owner's equity in Problem 3-14A.

1. Prepare an income statement for Harold's Home Repair for the month ended May 31, 20--.

2. Prepare a statement of owner's equity for Harold's Home Repair for the month ended May 31, 20--.

3. Prepare a balance sheet for Harold's Home Repair as of May 31, 20--.

SERIES B EXERCISES

E 3-1B (LO2)
✓ Accts. Pay: $400 (Cr.)

FOOT AND BALANCE A T ACCOUNT Foot and balance the accounts payable T account shown.

Accounts Payable	
300	450
250	350
	150

E 3-2B (LO3)

DEBIT AND CREDIT ANALYSIS Complete the following questions using either "debit" or "credit":

(a) The asset account Prepaid Insurance is increased with a _____.
(b) The owner's drawing account is increased with a _____.
(c) The asset account Accounts Receivable is decreased with a _____.
(d) The liability account Accounts Payable is decreased with a _____.
(e) The owner's capital account is increased with a _____.
(f) The revenue account Professional Fees is increased with a _____.
(g) The expense account Repair Expense is increased with a _____.
(h) The asset account Cash is decreased with a _____.
(i) The asset account Delivery Equipment is decreased with a _____.

E 3-3B (LO2/3/4)
✓ Cash bal. after (c): $3,900 (Dr.)

ANALYSIS OF T ACCOUNTS Roberto Alvarez began a business called Roberto's Fix-It Shop.

1. Create T accounts for Cash; Supplies; Roberto Alvarez, Capital; and Utilities Expense. Identify the following transactions by letter and place them on the proper side of the T accounts:

   (a) Invested cash in the business, $6,000.
   (b) Purchased supplies for cash, $1,200.
   (c) Paid utility bill, $900.

2. Foot the T account for cash and enter the ending balance.

E 3-4B (LO3)

NORMAL BALANCE OF ACCOUNT Indicate the normal balance (debit or credit) for each of the following accounts:

1. Cash
2. Rent Expense
3. Notes Payable
4. Owner's Drawing
5. Accounts Receivable
6. Owner's Capital
7. Tools

E 3-5B (LO4)

TRANSACTION ANALYSIS George Atlas started a business on June 1, 20--. Analyze the following transactions for the first month of business using T accounts. Label each T account with the title of the account affected and then place the transaction letter and the dollar amount on the debit or credit side.

(a)   Invested cash in the business, $7,000.
(b)   Purchased equipment for cash, $900.
(c)   Purchased equipment on account, $1,500.
(d)   Paid cash on account for equipment purchased in transaction (c), $800.
(e)   Withdrew cash for personal use, $1,100.

E 3-6B (LO2)

✓ Cash bal. after (e): $4,200 (Dr.)

FOOT AND BALANCE T ACCOUNTS Foot and balance the T accounts prepared in Exercise 3-5B if necessary.

E 3-7B (LO2/4)

✓ Cash bal. after (k): $9,000 (Dr.)

ANALYSIS OF TRANSACTIONS Nicole Lawrence opened a business called Nickie's Neat Ideas in January 20--. Set up T accounts for the following accounts: Cash; Accounts Receivable; Office Supplies; Computer Equipment; Office Furniture; Accounts Payable; Nicole Lawrence, Capital; Nicole Lawrence, Drawing; Professional Fees; Rent Expense; and Utilities Expense.

The following transactions occurred during the first month of business. Record these transactions in T accounts. After all transactions have been recorded, foot and balance the accounts if necessary.

(a)   Invested cash in the business, $18,000.
(b)   Purchased office supplies for cash, $500.
(c)   Purchased office furniture for cash, $8,000.
(d)   Purchased computer and printer on account, $5,000.
(e)   Received cash from clients for services, $4,000.
(f)   Paid cash on account for computer and printer purchased in transaction (d), $2,000.
(g)   Earned professional fees on account during the month, $7,000.
(h)   Paid office rent for January, $900.
(i)   Paid utility bills for the month, $600.
(j)   Received cash from clients that were billed previously in transaction (g), $3,000.
(k)   Withdrew cash for personal use, $4,000.

E 3-8B (LO5)

✓ Trial bal. total debits: $32,000

TRIAL BALANCE Based on the transactions recorded in Exercise 3-7B, prepare a trial balance for Nickie's Neat Ideas as of January 31, 20--.

E 3-9B (LO5)

✓ Trial bal. total debits: $27,500

TRIAL BALANCE The following accounts have normal balances. Prepare a trial balance for Bill's Delivery Service as of September 30, 20--.

Cash	$ 7,000	Bill Swift, Capital	$12,000
Accounts Receivable	4,000	Bill Swift, Drawing	2,000
Supplies	600	Delivery Fees	12,500
Prepaid Insurance	900	Wages Expense	3,000
Delivery Equipment	9,000	Rent Expense	1,000
Accounts Payable	3,000		

E 3-10B (LO5)

✓ Net income: $8,500

INCOME STATEMENT From the information in Exercise 3-9B, prepare an income statement for Bill's Delivery Service for the month ended September 30, 20--.

E 3-11B (LO5)

✓ Capital, 9/30: $18,500

STATEMENT OF OWNER'S EQUITY From the information in Exercise 3-9B, prepare a statement of owner's equity for Bill's Delivery Service for the month ended September 30, 20--.

E 3-12B (LO5)

✓ Total assets, 9/30: $21,500

BALANCE SHEET From the information in Exercise 3-9B, prepare a balance sheet for Bill's Delivery Service as of September 30, 20--.

SERIES B PROBLEMS

P 3-13B (LO2/4/5)

✓ Cash bal. after (p): $20,200 (Dr.);
Trial bal. total debits: $44,300

T ACCOUNTS AND TRIAL BALANCE Sue Jantz started a business in August 20-- called Jantz Plumbing Service. Jantz hired a part-time college student as an administrative assistant. Jantz has decided to use the following accounts:

Assets
    Cash
    Accounts Receivable
    Office Supplies
    Prepaid Insurance
    Plumbing Equipment
    Van
Liabilities
    Accounts Payable

Owner's Equity
    Sue Jantz, Capital
    Sue Jantz, Drawing
Revenue
    Service Fees
Expenses
    Rent Expense
    Wages Expense
    Telephone Expense
    Advertising Expense

The following transactions occurred during August.

(a)   Invested cash in the business, $30,000.
(b)   Purchased a used van for cash, $8,000.
(c)   Purchased plumbing equipment on account, $4,000.
(d)   Received cash for services rendered, $3,000.
(e)   Paid cash on account owed from transaction (c), $1,000.
(f)   Paid rent for the month, $700.
(g)   Paid telephone bill, $100.
(h)   Earned revenue on account, $4,000.
(i)   Purchased office supplies for cash, $300.
(j)   Paid wages to student, $500.
(k)   Purchased a one-year insurance policy, $800.
(l)   Received cash from services performed in transaction (h), $3,000.
(m)   Paid cash for advertising expense, $2,000.
(n)   Purchased additional plumbing equipment for $2,000, paying $500 cash and spreading the remaining payments over the next six months.

(o) Earned revenue from services for the remainder of the month of $2,800: $1,100 in cash and $1,700 on account.

(p) Withdrew cash at the end of the month, $3,000.

REQUIRED

1. Enter the transactions in T accounts, identifying each transaction with its corresponding letter.

2. Foot and balance the accounts where necessary.

3. Prepare a trial balance as of August 31, 20--.

P 3-14B (LO5)

✓ Net income: $6,500

✓ Owner's equity, 8/31: $33,500

✓ Total assets, 8/31: $38,000

NET INCOME AND CHANGE IN OWNER'S EQUITY Refer to the trial balance of Jantz Plumbing Service in Problem 3-13B to determine the following information. Use the format provided below.

1. a. Total revenue for the month   _____

    b. Total expenses for the month   _____

    c. Net income for the month   _____

2. a. Sue Jantz's original investment   _____
        in the business

        + The net income for the month   _____

        − Owner's drawing   _____

        Increase (decrease) in capital   _____

        = Ending owner's equity   _____

    b. End of month accounting equation:

Assets	=	Liabilities	+	Owner's Equity
_____	=	_____	+	_____

P 3-15B (LO5)

✓ NI: $6,500; Capital, 8/31/20--: $33,500; Total assets: $38,000

FINANCIAL STATEMENTS Refer to the trial balance in Problem 3-13B and to the analysis of the change in owner's equity in Problem 3-14B.

REQUIRED

1. Prepare an income statement for Jantz Plumbing Service for the month ended August 31, 20--.

2. Prepare a statement of owner's equity for Jantz Plumbing Service for the month ended August 31, 20--.

3. Prepare a balance sheet for Jantz Plumbing Service as of August 31, 20--.

MANAGING YOUR WRITING

Write a one-page memo to your instructor explaining how you could use the double-entry system to maintain records of your personal finances. What types of accounts would you use for the accounting elements?

MASTERY PROBLEM

✓ Cash bal. after (p): $1,980;
Trial bal. debit total: $5,840;
Net income: $500;
Total assets: $4,300

Craig Fisher started a lawn service called Craig's Quick Cut to earn money over the summer months. Fisher has decided to use the following accounts for recording transactions:

Assets
    Cash
    Accounts Receivable
    Mowing Equipment
    Lawn Tools
Liabilities
    Accounts Payable
    Notes Payable
Owner's Equity
    Craig Fisher, Capital
    Craig Fisher, Drawing

Revenue
    Lawn Fees
Expenses
    Rent Expense
    Wages Expense
    Telephone Expense
    Gas and Oil Expense
    Transportation Expense

Transactions for the month of June are listed below.

(a)   Invested cash in the business, $3,000.
(b)   Bought mowing equipment for $1,000: paid $200 in cash and promised to pay the balance over the next four months.
(c)   Paid garage rent for June, $50.
(d)   Provided lawn services for customers on account, $520.
(e)   Paid telephone bill, $30.
(f)   Borrowed cash from the bank by signing a note payable, $500.
(g)   Bought lawn tools, $480.
(h)   Collected cash from customers for services performed on account in transaction (d), $400.
(i)   Paid associates for lawn work done during the first half of the month, $350.
(j)   Paid for gas and oil for the equipment, $60.
(k)   Paid cash on account for the mowing equipment purchased in transaction (b), $200.
(l)   Earned lawn fees of $1,320: $600 in cash and $720 on account.
(m)   Paid associates for last half of month, $700.
(n)   Reimbursed associates for costs incurred using their own vehicles for transportation, $150.
(o)   Paid on note payable to bank, $100.
(p)   Withdrew cash for personal use, $200.

REQUIRED

1.   Enter the transactions for June in T accounts. Use the accounting equation as a guide for setting up the T accounts.

2.   Foot and balance the T accounts where necessary.

3.   Prepare a trial balance of the accounts as of June 30, 20--.

4.   Prepare an income statement for the month ended June 30, 20--.

5.   Prepare a statement of owner's equity for the month ended June 30, 20--.

6.   Prepare a balance sheet as of June 30, 20--.

CHALLENGE PROBLEM

✓ Capital, 8/31/20--: $600

Your friend Chris Stevick started a part-time business in June and has been keeping her own accounting records. She has been preparing monthly financial statements. At the end of August, she stopped by to show you her performance for the most recent month. She prepared the following income statement and balance sheet.

Income Statement		Balance Sheet	End of Month	Beginning of Month
Revenues	$500	Cash	$600	$400
Expenses	200	Capital	600	400
Net Income	$300			

Chris has also heard that there is a statement of owner's equity, but she is not familiar with that statement. She asks if you can help her prepare one. After confirming that she has no assets other than cash, no liabilities, and made no additional investments in the business in August, you agree.

REQUIRED

1. Prepare the statement of owner's equity for your friend's most recent month.

2. What suggestions might you make to Chris that would make her income statement more useful?

Objectives
Careful study of this chapter should enable you to:

LO1
Describe the flow of data from source documents through the trial balance.

LO2
Describe the chart of accounts as a means of classifying financial information.

LO3
Describe and explain the purpose of source documents.

LO4
Journalize transactions.

LO5
Post to the general ledger and prepare a trial balance.

LO6
Explain how to find and correct errors.

Journalizing and Posting Transactions

With business picking up, Jessie realized that she needed help maintaining records of her business transactions. Since she has not studied accounting and prefers to spend her time making deliveries and meeting with new clients, she hired an accounting student, Mitch, to help her "keep the books." After a few days on the job, Mitch and Jessie sat down to discuss the business events that had taken place and the entries made by Mitch. As might be expected, Mitch had misunderstood a few transactions and had entered them improperly. Jessie suggested that they go through the journal and ledger to erase the errors and make the corrections. Is this the best way to make corrections?

The double-entry framework of accounting was explained and illustrated in Chapter 3. To demonstrate the use of debits and credits, business transactions were entered directly into T accounts. Now we will take a more detailed look at the procedures used to account for business transactions.

FLOW OF DATA

LO1 Describe the flow of data from source documents through the trial balance.

This chapter traces the flow of financial data from the source documents through the accounting information system. This process includes the following steps:

1. Analyze what happened by using information from source documents and the firm's chart of accounts.

2. Enter business transactions in the general journal in the form of journal entries.

3. Post these journal entries to the accounts in the general ledger.

4. Prepare a trial balance.

The flow of data from the source documents through the preparation of a trial balance is shown in Figure 4-1.

FIGURE 4-1   Flow of Data from Source Documents through Trial Balance

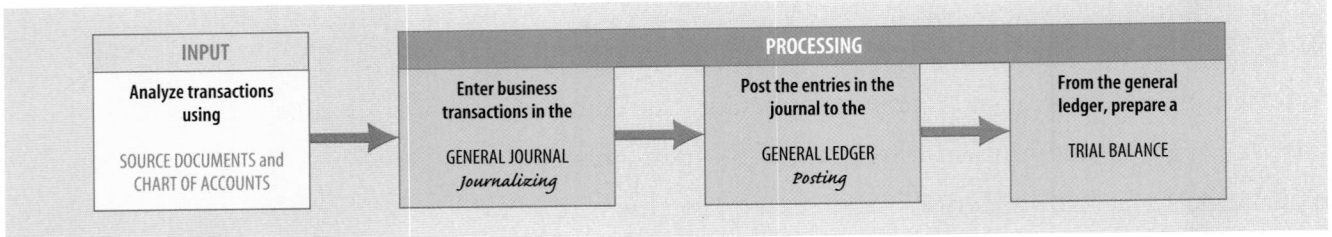

THE CHART OF ACCOUNTS

LO2 Describe the chart of accounts as a means of classifying financial information.

You learned in Chapters 2 and 3 that there are three basic questions that must be answered when analyzing transactions:

1. What happened?

2. Which accounts are affected?

3. How is the accounting equation affected?

To determine which accounts are affected (step 2), the accountant must know the accounts being used by the business. A list of all accounts used by a business is called a **chart of accounts**.

The chart of accounts includes the account titles in numeric order for all assets, liabilities, owner's equity, revenues, and expenses. The numbering should follow a consistent pattern. In Jessie Jane's Campus Delivery, asset accounts begin with "1," liability accounts begin with "2," owner's equity accounts begin with "3," revenue accounts begin with "4," and expense accounts begin with "5." Jessie uses three-digit numbers for all accounts.

A chart of accounts for Jessie Jane's Campus Delivery is shown in Figure 4-2. Jessie would not need many accounts initially because the business is new. Additional accounts can easily be added as needed. Note that the accounts are arranged according to the accounting equation.

FIGURE 4-2   Chart of Accounts

JESSIE JANE'S CAMPUS DELIVERY CHART OF ACCOUNTS			
Assets (100–199)		**Revenues** (400–499)	
101	Cash	401	Delivery Fees
122	Accounts Receivable		
141	Supplies	**Expenses** (500–599)	
145	Prepaid Insurance	511	Wages Expense
185	Delivery Equipment	521	Rent Expense
		525	Telephone Expense
Liabilities (200–299)			
202	Accounts Payable		
Owner's Equity (300–399)			
311	Jessica Jane, Capital		
312	Jessica Jane, Drawing		

SOURCE DOCUMENTS

L03 Describe and explain the purpose of source documents.

Almost any document that provides information about a business transaction can be called a **source document**. A source document triggers the analysis of what happened. It begins the process of entering transactions in the accounting system. Examples of source documents are shown in Figure 4-3. These source documents provide information that is useful in determining the effect of business transactions on specific accounts.

In addition to serving as input for transaction analysis, source documents serve as objective evidence of business transactions. If anyone questions the accounting records, these documents may be used as objective, verifiable evidence of the accuracy of the accounting records. For this reason, source documents are filed for possible future reference. *Having objective, verifiable evidence that a transaction occurred is an important accounting concept.*

FIGURE 4-3 Source Documents

1

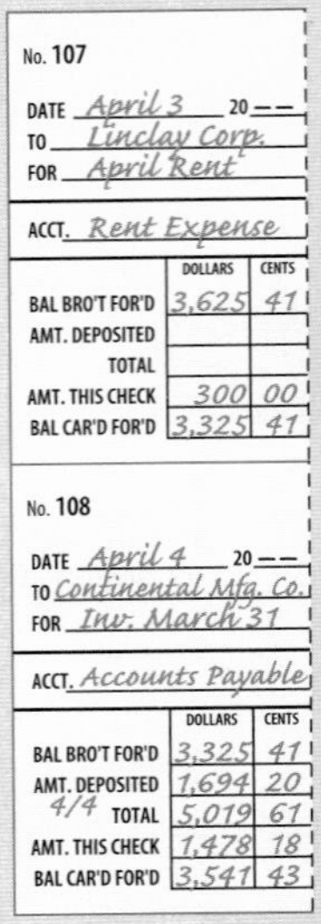
No. 107
DATE April 3 20--
TO Linclay Corp.
FOR April Rent
ACCT. Rent Expense
DOLLARS CENTS
BAL BRO'T FOR'D 3,625 41
AMT. DEPOSITED
TOTAL
AMT. THIS CHECK 300 00
BAL CAR'D FOR'D 3,325 41
No. 108
DATE April 4 20--
TO Continental Mfg. Co.
FOR Inv. March 31
ACCT. Accounts Payable
DOLLARS CENTS
BAL BRO'T FOR'D 3,325 41
AMT. DEPOSITED 1,694 20
4/4 TOTAL 5,019 61
AMT. THIS CHECK 1,478 18
BAL CAR'D FOR'D 3,541 43

Check Stubs

2

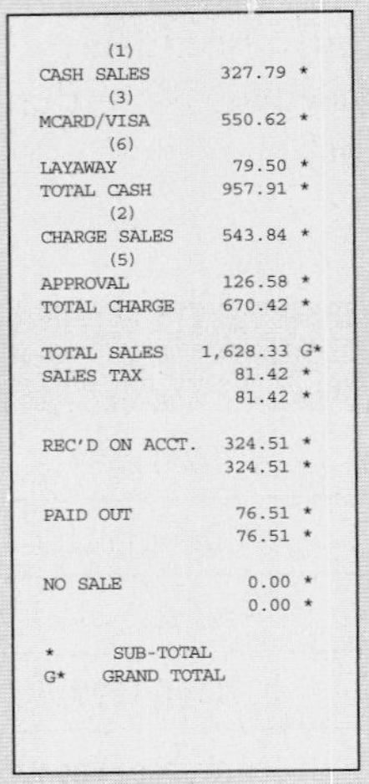
(1)
CASH SALES 327.79 *
(3)
MCARD/VISA 550.62 *
(6)
LAYAWAY 79.50 *
TOTAL CASH 957.91 *
(2)
CHARGE SALES 543.84 *
(5)
APPROVAL 126.58 *
TOTAL CHARGE 670.42 *
TOTAL SALES 1,628.33 G*
SALES TAX 81.42 *
81.42 *
REC'D ON ACCT. 324.51 *
324.51 *
PAID OUT 76.51 *
76.51 *
NO SALE 0.00 *
0.00 *
* SUB-TOTAL
G* GRAND TOTAL

Cash Register Tape Summary

3

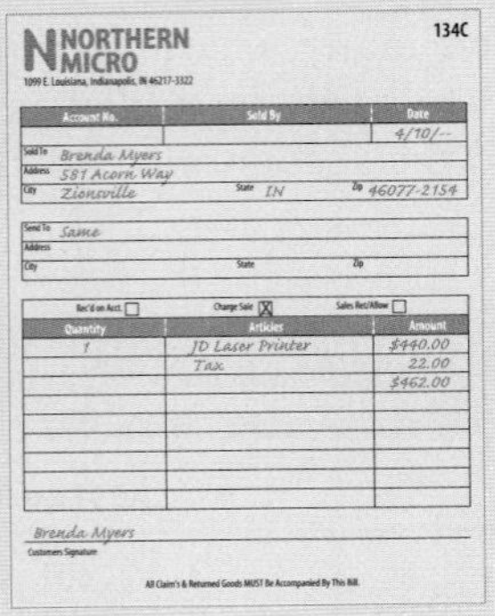
NORTHERN MICRO
134C
4/10/--
Brenda Myers
581 Acorn Way
Zionsville
IN
46077-2154
Same
JD Laser Printer
Tax
$440.00
22.00
$462.00
Brenda Myers

Sales Ticket

4

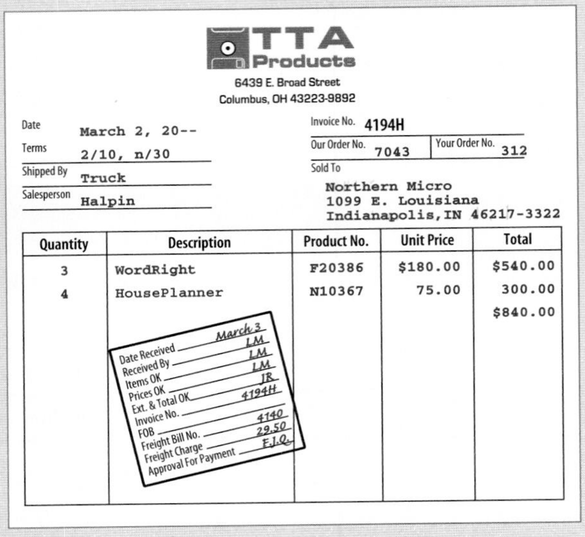
TTA Products
6439 E. Broad Street
Columbus, OH 43223-9892
Date March 2, 20--
Terms 2/10, n/30
Shipped By Truck
Salesperson Halpin
Invoice No. 4194H
Our Order No. 7043
Your Order No. 312
Sold To
Northern Micro
1099 E. Louisiana
Indianapolis, IN 46217-3322
Quantity
Description
Product No.
Unit Price
Total
3 WordRight F20386 $180.00 $540.00
4 HousePlanner N10367 75.00 300.00
$840.00
Date Received March 3
Received By LM
Items OK LM
Prices OK LM
Ext. & Total OK JR
Invoice No. 4194H
FOB
Freight Bill No. 4140
Freight Charge 29.50
Approval For Payment FJQ

Purchase Invoice

SOURCE DOCUMENTS	
Example	**Provides Information About**
1. Check stubs or copies of checks	Cash payments
2. Receipt stubs, copies of receipts, cash register tapes, or memos of cash register totals	Cash receipts
3. Copies of sales tickets or sales invoices issued to customers or clients	Sales of goods or services
4. Purchase invoices received from suppliers	Purchases of goods or services

A BROADER VIEW

© ED BOCK/CORBIS

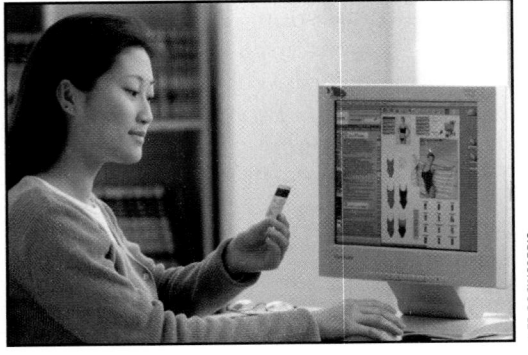

Electronic Source Documents

With the ability to go shopping in cyberspace, more transactions are being initiated electronically. Even Sears, known for its low prices and excellent in-store service, has "online" shopping at http://www.sears.com. Customers can place orders and these orders can be filled, all based on electronic communications. This means that more and more "source documents" will be in an electronic form.

THE GENERAL JOURNAL

LO4 Journalize transactions.

LEARNING KEY

A journal provides a day-by-day listing of all transactions completed by the business.

A day-by-day listing of the transactions of a business is called a **journal**. The purpose of a journal is to provide a record of all transactions completed by the business. The journal shows the date of each transaction, titles of the accounts to be debited and credited, and the amounts of the debits and credits.

A journal is commonly referred to as a **book of original entry** because it is here that the first formal accounting record of a transaction is made. Although many types of journals are used in business, the simplest journal form is a two-column general journal (Figure 4-4). Any kind of business transaction may be entered into a general journal.

A **two-column general journal** is so-named because it has only two amount columns, one for debit amounts and one for credit amounts. Journal pages are numbered in the upper right-hand corner. The five column numbers in Figure 4-4 are explained in Figure 4-5.

FIGURE 4-4   Two-Column General Journal

	DATE	DESCRIPTION	POST. REF.	DEBIT	CREDIT	
1	20-- **1**	**2**	**3**	**4**	**5**	1
2						2
3						3

GENERAL JOURNAL   PAGE **1**

FIGURE 4-5   The Columns in a Two-Column General Journal

Column **1** Date	The year is entered in small figures at the top of the column immediately below the column heading. The year is repeated only at the top of each new page. The month is entered for the first entry on the page and for the first transaction of the month. The day of the month is recorded for every transaction, even if it is the same as the prior entry.
Column **2** Description	The *Description* or *Explanation* column is used to enter the titles of the accounts affected by each transaction, and to provide a very brief description of the transaction. Each transaction affects two or more accounts. The account(s) to be debited are entered first at the extreme left of the column. The account(s) to be credited are listed after the debits and indented. The description should be entered immediately following the last credit entry with an additional indentation.
Column **3** Posting Reference	No entries are made in the *Posting Reference* column during journalizing. Entries are made in this column when the debits and credits are copied to the proper accounts in the ledger. This process will be explained in detail later in this chapter.
Column **4** Debit Amount	The *Debit amount column* is used to enter the amount to be debited to an account. The amount should be entered on the same line as the title of that account.
Column **5** Credit Amount	The *Credit amount column* is used to enter the amount to be credited to an account. The amount should be entered on the same line as the title of that account.

Journalizing

Entering the transactions in a journal is called **journalizing**. For every transaction, the entry should include the date, the title of each account affected, the amounts, and a brief description.

To illustrate the journalizing process, transactions for the first month of operations of Jessie Jane's Campus Delivery will be journalized. The transactions are listed in Figure 4-6. Since you analyzed these transactions in Chapters 2 and 3, the journalizing process should be easier to understand. Let's start with a close look at the steps followed when journalizing the first transaction, Jessie's initial investment of $2,000.

FIGURE 4-6   Summary of Transactions

SUMMARY OF TRANSACTIONS JESSIE JANE'S CAMPUS DELIVERY		
Transaction		
(a)	June 1	Jessica Jane invested cash in her business, $2,000.
(b)	3	Bought delivery equipment for cash, $1,200.
(c)	5	Bought delivery equipment on account from Big Red Scooters, $900.
(d)	6	Paid first installment from transaction (c) to Big Red Scooters, $300.
(e)	6	Received cash for delivery services rendered, $500.
(f)	7	Paid cash for June office rent, $200.
(g)	15	Paid telephone bill, $50.
(h)	15	Made deliveries on account for a total of $600: Accounting Department ($400) and the School of Music ($200).
(i)	16	Bought supplies for cash, $80.
(j)	18	Paid cash for an eight-month liability insurance policy, $200. Coverage began on June 1.
(k)	20	Received $570 in cash for services performed in transaction (h): $400 from the Accounting Department and $170 from the School of Music.
(l)	25	Bought a third scooter from Big Red Scooters, $1,500. Paid $300 cash, with the remaining payments expected over the next four months.
(m)	27	Paid wages of part-time employees, $650.
(n)	30	Earned delivery fees for the remainder of the month amounting to $1,050: $430 in cash and $620 on account. Deliveries on account: Accounting Department ($250) and Athletic Ticket Office ($370).
(o)	30	Jessie withdrew cash for personal use, $150.

Transaction (a)

June 1   Jessica Jane opened a bank account with a deposit of $2,000 for her business.

STEP 1   **Enter the date.** Since this is the first entry on the journal page, the year is entered on the first line of the Date column (in small print at the top of the line). The month and day are entered on the same line, below the year, in the Date column.

		GENERAL JOURNAL				PAGE 1	
	DATE	DESCRIPTION	POST. REF.	DEBIT	CREDIT		
1	20-- June 1						1
2							2

STEP 2   **Enter the debit.** Cash is entered on the first line at the extreme left of the Description column. The amount of the debit, $2,000, is entered on the same line in the Debit column. Since this is not a formal financial statement, dollar signs are not used.

In Chapter 3, we simply debited the T account.

Cash	
(a) 2,000	

		GENERAL JOURNAL						PAGE 1	
	DATE	DESCRIPTION	POST. REF.	DEBIT		CREDIT		
1	20-- June 1	Cash		2 0 0 0 00				1
2								2

STEP 3   **Enter the credit.** The title of the account to be credited, Jessica Jane, Capital, is entered on the second line, indented one-half inch from the left side of the Description column. The amount of the credit, $2,000, is entered on the same line in the Credit column.

In Chapter 3, we simply credited the T account.

Jessica Jane, Capital	
	(a) 2,000

		GENERAL JOURNAL					PAGE 1	
	DATE	DESCRIPTION	POST. REF.	DEBIT		CREDIT		
1	20-- June 1	Cash		2 0 0 0 00				1
2		Jessica Jane, Capital				2 0 0 0 00		2

STEP 4   **Enter the explanation.** The explanation of the entry is entered on the next line, indented an additional one-half inch. The second line of the explanation, if needed, is also indented the same distance as the first.

		GENERAL JOURNAL					PAGE 1	
	DATE	DESCRIPTION	POST. REF.	DEBIT		CREDIT		
1	20-- June 1	Cash		2 0 0 0 00				1
2		Jessica Jane, Capital				2 0 0 0 00		2
3		Owner's original investment in						3
4		delivery business						4

To enter transaction (b), the purchase of a motor scooter for $1,200 cash, we skip a line and follow the same four steps. Note that the month and year do not need to be repeated. The day of the month must, however, be entered.

GENERAL JOURNAL   PAGE 1

	DATE		DESCRIPTION	POST. REF.	DEBIT	CREDIT	
1	20-- June	1	Cash		2 0 0 0 00		1
2			Jessica Jane, Capital			2 0 0 0 00	2
3			Owner's original investment in				3
4			delivery business				4
5							5
6		3	Delivery Equipment		1 2 0 0 00		6
7			Cash			1 2 0 0 00	7
8			Purchased delivery equipment for cash				8

Skip a line

The journal entries for the month of June are shown in Figure 4-7. Note that the entries on June 25 and June 30 affect more than two accounts. Entries requiring more than one debit and/or one credit are called **compound entries**. The entry on June 25 has two credits. The credits are listed after the debit, indented and listed one under the other. The entry on June 30 has two debits. They are aligned with the left margin of the Description column and listed one under the other. In both cases, the debits equal the credits.

FIGURE 4-7   General Journal Entries

GENERAL JOURNAL   PAGE 1

	DATE		DESCRIPTION	POST. REF.	DEBIT	CREDIT	
1	20-- June	1	Cash		2 0 0 0 00		1
2			Jessica Jane, Capital			2 0 0 0 00	2
3			Owner's original investment in				3
4			delivery business				4
5							5
6			Delivery Equipment		1 2 0 0 00		6
7			Cash			1 2 0 0 00	7
8			Purchased delivery equipment for cash				8
9							9
10		5	Delivery Equipment		9 0 0 00		10
11			Accounts Payable			9 0 0 00	11
12			Purchased delivery equipment on account				12
13			from Big Red Scooters				13
14							14
15		6	Accounts Payable		3 0 0 00		15
16			Cash			3 0 0 00	16
17			Made partial payment to Big Red Scooters				17
18							18
19		6	Cash		5 0 0 00		19
20			Delivery Fees			5 0 0 00	20
21			Received cash for delivery services				21
22							22
23		7	Rent Expense		2 0 0 00		23
24			Cash			2 0 0 00	24
25			Paid office rent for June				25
26							26

(List debits first.)
(List credits second and indented.)
(Explanation is third and indented.)
(Space to make entries easier to read. To prevent improper changes to entries, the extra spacing might not be used in practice.)

FIGURE 4-7   General Journal Entries *(continued)*

GENERAL JOURNAL   PAGE 1

	DATE		DESCRIPTION	POST. REF.	DEBIT	CREDIT	
27		15	Telephone Expense		5 0 00		27
28			Cash			5 0 00	28
29			Paid telephone bill for June				29
30							30
31		15	Accounts Receivable		6 0 0 00		31
32			Delivery Fees			6 0 0 00	32
33			Deliveries made on account for Accounting				33
34			Department ($400) and School of Music ($200)				34
35							35

GENERAL JOURNAL   PAGE 2

	DATE		DESCRIPTION	POST. REF.	DEBIT	CREDIT	
1	20-- June	16	Supplies		8 0 00		1
2			Cash			8 0 00	2
3			Purchased supplies for cash				3
4							4
5		18	Prepaid Insurance		2 0 0 00		5
6			Cash			2 0 0 00	6
7			Paid premium for eight-month				7
8			insurance policy				8
9							9
10		20	Cash		5 7 0 00		10
11			Accounts Receivable			5 7 0 00	11
12			Received cash on account from Accounting				12
13			Department ($400) and School of Music ($170)				13
14							14
15		25	Delivery Equipment		1 5 0 0 00		15
16	*Line up credits*		Accounts Payable *Compound entry*			1 2 0 0 00	16
17			Cash			3 0 0 00	17
18			Purchased scooter with down payment;				18
19			balance on account with Big Red Scooters				19
20							20
21		27	Wages Expense		6 5 0 00		21
22			Cash			6 5 0 00	22
23			Paid employees				23
24							24
25		30	Cash *Compound entry*		4 3 0 00		25
26	*Line up debits*		Accounts Receivable		6 2 0 00		26
27			Delivery Fees			1 0 5 0 00	27
28			Deliveries made for cash and on account to				28
29			Accounting Department ($250) and				29
30			Athletic Ticket Office ($370)				30
31							31
32		30	Jessica Jane, Drawing		1 5 0 00		32
33			Cash			1 5 0 00	33
34			Owner's withdrawal				34

Debits = Credits

Debits = Credits

THE GENERAL LEDGER

LO5 **Post to the general ledger and prepare a trial balance.**

LEARNING KEY

While the journal provides a day-by-day record of business transactions, the ledger provides a record of the transactions entered in each account.

A three-column account with just one column for the normal balance also may be used for some purposes.

The journal provides a day-by-day record of business transactions. To determine the current balance of specific accounts, however, the information in the journal must be transferred to accounts similar to the T accounts illustrated in Chapter 3. This process is called posting.

A complete set of all the accounts used by a business is known as the **general ledger.** The general ledger accumulates a complete record of the debits and credits made to each account as a result of entries made in the journal. The accounts are numbered and arranged in the same order as the chart of accounts. That is, accounts are numbered and grouped by classification: assets, liabilities, owner's equity, revenues, and expenses.

General Ledger Account

For purposes of illustration, the T account was introduced in Chapter 3. In practice, businesses are more likely to use a version of the account called the **general ledger account.** Figure 4-8 compares the Cash T account from Chapter 3 for Jessie Jane's Campus Delivery and a general ledger account summarizing the same cash transactions. A four-column general ledger account contains columns for the debit or credit transaction and columns for the debit or credit running balance. In addition, there are columns for the date, description of the item, and posting reference. The Item column is used to provide descriptions of special entries. For example, "Balance" is written in this column when the balance of an account is transferred to a new page. In addition, "Correcting," "Adjusting," "Closing," or "Reversing" may be written in this column when these types of entries are made. Correcting entries are addressed later in the chapter. Adjusting, closing, and reversing entries are addressed in Chapters 5, 6, and 15, respectively. The Posting Reference (Post. Ref.) column is used to indicate the journal page from which an entry was posted, or a check mark (✓) is inserted to indicate that no posting was required.

FIGURE 4-8   Comparison of T Account and General Ledger Account

As shown in Figure 4-8, the primary advantage of the T account is that the debit and credit sides of the account are easier to identify. Thus, for demonstration purposes and analyzing what happened, T accounts are very helpful. However, computing the balance of a T account is cumbersome. The primary advantage of the general ledger account is that it maintains a running balance.

Note that the heading for the general ledger account has the account title and an account number. The account number is taken from the chart of accounts and is used in the posting process.

Posting to the General Ledger

The process of copying the debits and credits from the journal to the ledger accounts is known as **posting**. All amounts entered in the journal must be posted to the general ledger accounts. Posting from the journal to the ledger is done daily or at frequent intervals.

To illustrate the posting process, the first journal entry for Jessie Jane's Campus Delivery will be posted step by step. There are five steps in the process of posting each debit and credit. First, let's post the debit to Cash (Figure 4-9).

FIGURE 4-9   Posting a Debit

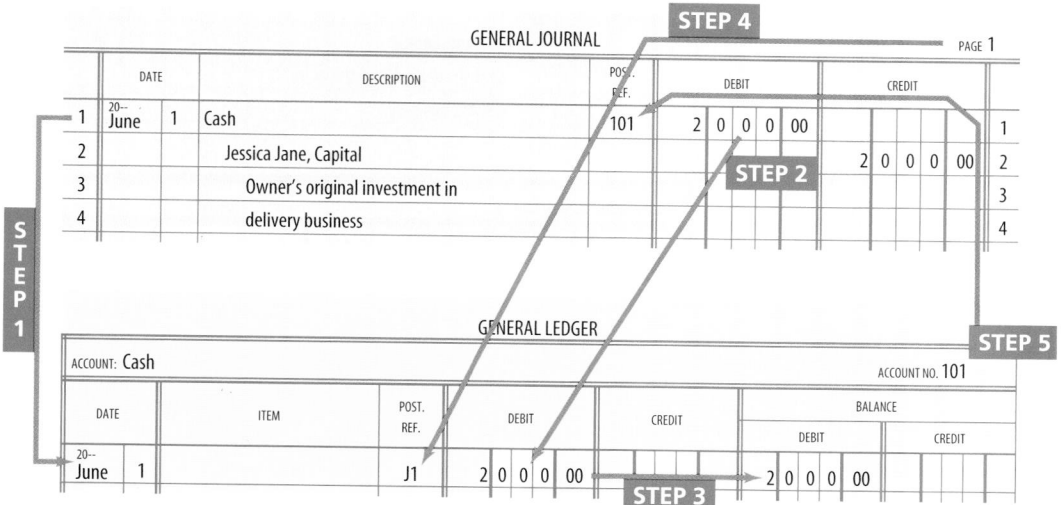

In the ledger account:

STEP 1   **Enter the date of the transaction in the Date column.** Enter the year, "20--," the month, "June," and the day, "1," in the Date column of the cash account.

STEP 2   **Enter the debit.** Copy the $2,000 debit to Cash in the journal to the Debit column of the ledger. Since this is not a formal financial statement, dollar signs are not used.

STEP 3   **Enter the balance of the account.** Enter the $2,000 balance in the Balance columns under Debit. (If the balance of the account is zero, draw a line through the Debit and Credit columns.)

STEP 4   **Enter the journal page in the Posting Reference column.** Enter "J1" in the Posting Reference column since the posting came from page 1 of the journal.

The Item column is left blank, except for special reasons such as indicating the beginning balance, adjusting, correcting, closing, or reversing entries.

In the journal:

STEP 5 **Enter the ledger account number in the Posting Reference column.** Enter the account number for Cash, 101 (see chart of accounts in Figure 4-2 on page 91), in the Posting Reference column of the journal on the same line as the debit to Cash for $2,000.

Step 5 is the last step in the posting process. After this step is completed, the posting references will indicate which journal entries have been posted to the ledger accounts. This is very helpful, particularly if you are interrupted during the posting process. The information in the Posting Reference columns of the journal and ledger provides a link between the journal and ledger known as a **cross-reference**.

Now let's post the credit portion of the first entry (Figure 4-10).

FIGURE 4-10   Posting a Credit

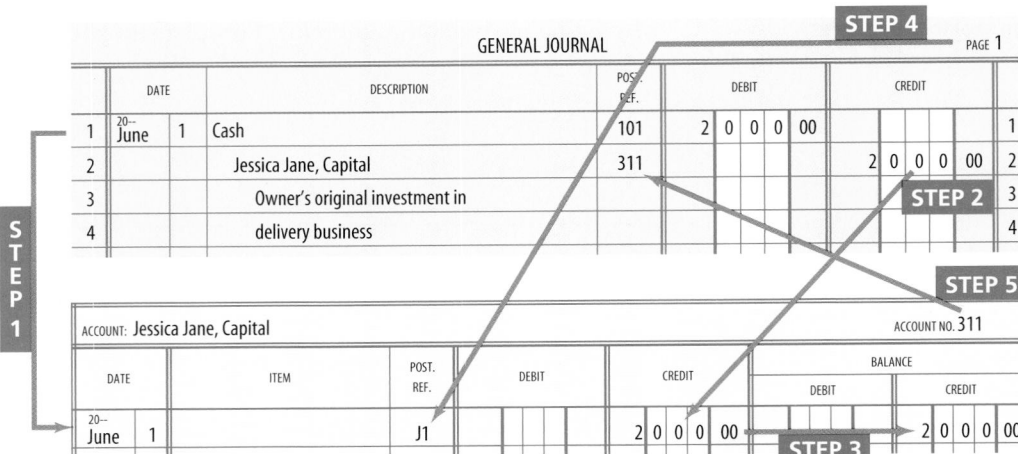

In the ledger account:

STEP 1 **Enter the date of the transaction in the Date column.** Enter the year, "20--," the month, "June," and the day, "1," in the Date column of the account Jessica Jane, Capital.

STEP 2 **Enter the credit.** Copy the $2,000 credit to Jessica Jane, Capital in the journal to the Credit column in the ledger.

STEP 3 **Enter the balance of the account.** Enter the $2,000 balance in the Balance columns under Credit. (If the balance of the account is zero, draw a line through the Debit and Credit columns.)

STEP 4 **Enter the journal page in the Posting Reference column.** Enter "J1" in the Posting Reference column since the posting came from page 1 of the journal.

In the journal:

STEP 5 **Enter the ledger account number in the Posting Reference column.** Enter the account number for Jessica Jane, Capital, 311, in the Posting Reference column. Again, this last step indicates that the credit has been posted to the general ledger.

After posting the journal entries for Jessie Jane's Campus Delivery for the month of June, the general journal and general ledger should appear as illustrated in Figures 4-11 and 4-12 on pages 101–104. *Note that the Posting Reference column of the journal has been filled in because the entries have been posted.*

FIGURE 4-11   General Journal After Posting

GENERAL JOURNAL   PAGE 1

	DATE		DESCRIPTION	POST. REF.	DEBIT					CREDIT					
1	20-- June	1	Cash	101	2	0	0	0	00						1
2			Jessica Jane, Capital	311						2	0	0	0	00	2
3			Owner's original investment in												3
4			delivery business												4
5															5
6		3	Delivery Equipment	185	1	2	0	0	00						6
7			Cash	101						1	2	0	0	00	7
8			Purchased delivery equipment for cash												8
9															9
10		5	Delivery Equipment	185		9	0	0	00						10
11			Accounts Payable	202							9	0	0	00	11
12			Purchased delivery equipment on account												12
13			from Big Red Scooters												13
14															14
15		6	Accounts Payable	202		3	0	0	00						15
16			Cash	101							3	0	0	00	16
17			Made partial payment to Big Red Scooters												17
18															18
19		6	Cash	101		5	0	0	00						19
20			Delivery Fees	401							5	0	0	00	20
21			Received cash for delivery services												21
22															22
23		7	Rent Expense	521		2	0	0	00						23
24			Cash	101							2	0	0	00	24
25			Paid office rent for June												25
26															26
27		15	Telephone Expense	525			5	0	00						27
28			Cash	101								5	0	00	28
29			Paid telephone bill for June												29
30															30
31		15	Accounts Receivable	122		6	0	0	00						31
32			Delivery Fees	401							6	0	0	00	32
33			Deliveries made on account for Accounting												33
34			Department ($400) and School of Music ($200)												34
35															35

(continued)

FIGURE 4-11   General Journal After Posting *(continued)*

	DATE		DESCRIPTION	POST. REF.	DEBIT				CREDIT				
1	20-- June	16	Supplies	141		8	0	00					1
2			Cash	101						8	0	00	2
3			Purchased supplies for cash										3
4													4
5		18	Prepaid Insurance	145	2	0	0	00					5
6			Cash	101					2	0	0	00	6
7			Paid premium for eight-month										7
8			insurance policy										8
9													9
10		20	Cash	101	5	7	0	00					10
11			Accounts Receivable	122					5	7	0	00	11
12			Received cash on account from Accounting										12
13			Department ($400) and School of Music ($170)										13
14													14
15		25	Delivery Equipment	185	1 5	0	0	00					15
16			Accounts Payable	202					1 2	0	0	00	16
17			Cash	101					3	0	0	00	17
18			Purchased scooter with down payment;										18
19			balance on account with Big Red Scooters										19
20													20
21		27	Wages Expense	511	6	5	0	00					21
22			Cash	101					6	5	0	00	22
23			Paid employees										23
24													24
25		30	Cash	101	4	3	0	00					25
26			Accounts Receivable	122	6	2	0	00					26
27			Delivery Fees	401					1 0	5	0	00	27
28			Deliveries made for cash and on account to										28
29			Accounting Department ($250) and										29
30			Athletic Ticket Office ($370)										30
31													31
32		30	Jessica Jane, Drawing	312	1	5	0	00					32
33			Cash	101					1	5	0	00	33
34			Owner's withdrawal										34
35													35

GENERAL JOURNAL — PAGE 2

FIGURE 4-12   General Ledger After Posting

GENERAL LEDGER

ACCOUNT: Cash   ACCOUNT NO. 101

DATE		ITEM	POST. REF.	DEBIT	CREDIT	BALANCE DEBIT	BALANCE CREDIT
20-- June	1		J1	2 0 0 0 00		2 0 0 0 00	
	3		J1		1 2 0 0 00	8 0 0 00	
	6		J1		3 0 0 00	5 0 0 00	
	6		J1	5 0 0 00		1 0 0 0 00	
	7		J1		2 0 0 00	8 0 0 00	
	15		J1		5 0 00	7 5 0 00	
	16		J2		8 0 00	6 7 0 00	
	18		J2		2 0 0 00	4 7 0 00	
	20		J2	5 7 0 00		1 0 4 0 00	
	25		J2		3 0 0 00	7 4 0 00	
	27		J2		6 5 0 00	9 0 00	
	30		J2	4 3 0 00		5 2 0 00	
	30		J2		1 5 0 00	3 7 0 00	

ACCOUNT: Accounts Receivable   ACCOUNT NO. 122

DATE		ITEM	POST. REF.	DEBIT	CREDIT	BALANCE DEBIT	BALANCE CREDIT
20-- June	15		J1	6 0 0 00		6 0 0 00	
	20		J2		5 7 0 00	3 0 00	
	30		J2	6 2 0 00		6 5 0 00	

ACCOUNT: Supplies   ACCOUNT NO. 141

DATE		ITEM	POST. REF.	DEBIT	CREDIT	BALANCE DEBIT	BALANCE CREDIT
20-- June	16		J2	8 0 00		8 0 00	

ACCOUNT: Prepaid Insurance   ACCOUNT NO. 145

DATE		ITEM	POST. REF.	DEBIT	CREDIT	BALANCE DEBIT	BALANCE CREDIT
20-- June	18		J2	2 0 0 00		2 0 0 00	

ACCOUNT: Delivery Equipment   ACCOUNT NO. 185

DATE		ITEM	POST. REF.	DEBIT	CREDIT	BALANCE DEBIT	BALANCE CREDIT
20-- June	3		J1	1 2 0 0 00		1 2 0 0 00	
	5		J1	9 0 0 00		2 1 0 0 00	
	25		J2	1 5 0 0 00		3 6 0 0 00	

(continued)

FIGURE 4-12 General Ledger After Posting (continued)

ACCOUNT: Accounts Payable — ACCOUNT NO. 202

DATE	ITEM	POST. REF.	DEBIT	CREDIT	BALANCE DEBIT	BALANCE CREDIT
20-- June 5		J1		9 0 0 00		9 0 0 00
6		J1	3 0 0 00			6 0 0 00
25		J2		1 2 0 0 00		1 8 0 0 00

ACCOUNT: Jessica Jane, Capital — ACCOUNT NO. 311

DATE	ITEM	POST. REF.	DEBIT	CREDIT	BALANCE DEBIT	BALANCE CREDIT
20-- June 1		J1		2 0 0 0 00		2 0 0 0 00

ACCOUNT: Jessica Jane, Drawing — ACCOUNT NO. 312

DATE	ITEM	POST. REF.	DEBIT	CREDIT	BALANCE DEBIT	BALANCE CREDIT
20-- June 30		J2	1 5 0 00		1 5 0 00	

ACCOUNT: Delivery Fees — ACCOUNT NO. 401

DATE	ITEM	POST. REF.	DEBIT	CREDIT	BALANCE DEBIT	BALANCE CREDIT
20-- June 6		J1		5 0 0 00		5 0 0 00
15		J1		6 0 0 00		1 1 0 0 00
30		J2		1 0 5 0 00		2 1 5 0 00

ACCOUNT: Wages Expense — ACCOUNT NO. 511

DATE	ITEM	POST. REF.	DEBIT	CREDIT	BALANCE DEBIT	BALANCE CREDIT
20-- June 27		J2	6 5 0 00		6 5 0 00	

ACCOUNT: Rent Expense — ACCOUNT NO. 521

DATE	ITEM	POST. REF.	DEBIT	CREDIT	BALANCE DEBIT	BALANCE CREDIT
20-- June 7		J1	2 0 0 00		2 0 0 00	

ACCOUNT: Telephone Expense — ACCOUNT NO. 525

DATE	ITEM	POST. REF.	DEBIT	CREDIT	BALANCE DEBIT	BALANCE CREDIT
20-- June 15		J1	5 0 00		5 0 00	

The Trial Balance

In Chapter 3, a **trial balance** was used to prove that the totals of the debit and credit balances in the T accounts were equal. In this chapter, a trial balance is used to prove the equality of the debits and credits in the ledger accounts. A trial balance can be prepared daily, weekly, monthly, or whenever desired. Before preparing a trial balance, all transactions should be journalized and posted so that the effect of all transactions will be reflected in the ledger accounts.

The trial balance for Jessie Jane's Campus Delivery shown in Figure 4-13 was prepared from the balances in the general ledger in Figure 4-12. The accounts are listed in the order used in the chart of accounts. This order is also often used when preparing financial statements. In Chapter 2, we pointed out that many firms list expenses from highest to lowest amounts. Some firms list expenses according to the chart of accounts, which is the method we will follow.

LEARNING KEY

The chart of accounts determines the order for listing accounts in the general ledger and trial balance. This order may also be used when preparing financial statements.

FIGURE 4-13   Trial Balance

ACCOUNT TITLE	ACCOUNT NO.	DEBIT BALANCE				CREDIT BALANCE			
Jessie Jane's Campus Delivery **Trial Balance** **June 30, 20 - -**									
Cash	101		3	7	0	00				
Accounts Receivable	122		6	5	0	00				
Supplies	141			8	0	00				
Prepaid Insurance	145		2	0	0	00				
Delivery Equipment	185	3	6	0	0	00				
Accounts Payable	202						1	8	0	0	00
Jessica Jane, Capital	311						2	0	0	0	00
Jessica Jane, Drawing	312		1	5	0	00				
Delivery Fees	401						2	1	5	0	00
Wages Expense	511		6	5	0	00				
Rent Expense	521		2	0	0	00				
Telephone Expense	525			5	0	00				
		5	9	5	0	00	5	9	5	0	00

Even though the trial balance indicates that the ledger is in balance, the ledger can still contain errors. For example, if a journal entry was made debiting or crediting the wrong accounts, or if an item was posted to the wrong account, the ledger will still be in balance. It is important, therefore, to be very careful in preparing the journal entries and in posting them to the ledger accounts.

FINDING AND CORRECTING ERRORS IN THE TRIAL BALANCE

LO6 Explain how to find and correct errors.

Tips are available to help if your trial balance has an error. Figure 4-14 offers hints for finding the error when your trial balance does not balance.

FIGURE 4-14   Tips for Finding Errors in the Trial Balance

1. Double check your addition. Review balances to see if they are too large or small, relative to other accounts, or entered in the wrong column.

2. Find the difference between the debits and the credits.

    a. If the difference is equal to the amount of a specific transaction, perhaps you forgot to post the debit or credit portion of this transaction.

    b. Divide the difference by 2. If the difference is evenly divisible by 2, you may have posted two debits or two credits for a transaction. If a debit was posted as a credit, it would mean that one transaction had two credits and no debits. The difference between the total debits and credits would be twice the amount of the debit that was posted as a credit.

    c. Divide the difference by 9. If the difference is evenly divisible by 9, you may have committed a **slide error** or a **transposition error**. A slide occurs when debit or credit amounts "slide" a digit or two to the left or right when entered. For example, if *$250* was entered as *$25*:

$$\$250 \quad - \quad \$25 \quad = \quad \$225$$
$$\$225 \quad \div \quad \$9 \quad = \quad \$25$$

The difference is evenly divisible by 9.

A transposition occurs when two digits are reversed. For example, if *$250* was entered as *$520*:

$$\$520 \quad - \quad \$250 \quad = \quad \$270$$
$$\$270 \quad \div \quad \$9 \quad = \quad \$30$$

Again, the difference is evenly divisible by 9.

If the tips in Figure 4-14 don't work, you must retrace your steps through the accounting process. Double check your addition for the ledger accounts. Also trace all postings. Be patient as you search for your error. Use this process as an opportunity to reinforce your understanding of the flow of information through the accounting system. Much can be learned while looking for an error.

Once you have found an error, there are two methods of making the correction. Although you may want to erase when correcting your homework, this is not acceptable in practice. An erasure may suggest that you are trying to hide something. You should use the ruling method or make a correcting entry instead.

Ruling Method

The **ruling method** should be used to correct two types of errors:

1. When an incorrect journal entry has been made, but not yet posted.

2. When a proper entry has been made but posted to the wrong account or for the wrong amount.

When using the ruling method, draw a single line through the incorrect account title or amount and write the correct information directly above the line. Corrections should be initialed by someone authorized to make such changes. This is done so the source and reason for the correction can be traced. This type of correction may be made in the journal or ledger accounts, as shown in Figure 4-15.

FIGURE 4-15   Ruling Method of Making a Correction

GENERAL JOURNAL   PAGE 2

	DATE		DESCRIPTION	POST. REF.	DEBIT	CREDIT	
1	20-- Sept.	17	*Wages Expense MP* ~~Entertainment Expense~~		6 5 0 00		1
2			Cash			6 5 0 00	2
3			Paid employees				3
4							4
5		18	Prepaid Insurance		*MP 2 0 0 00* ~~2 0 00~~		5
6			Cash			*MP 2 0 0 00* ~~2 0 00~~	6
7			Paid premium for eight-month				7
8			insurance policy				8
9							9

Slide

GENERAL LEDGER

ACCOUNT: Accounts Payable   ACCOUNT NO. 202

DATE		ITEM	POST. REF.	DEBIT	CREDIT	BALANCE	
						DEBIT	CREDIT
20-- Sept.	8		J1		7 0 0 00		7 0 0 00
	15		J1	2 0 0 00			5 0 0 00
	25		J2		*1 2 0 0 00 MP* ~~2 1 0 0 00~~		*MP 1 7 0 0 00* ~~2 6 0 0 00~~

Transposition

Correcting Entry Method

If an incorrect entry has been journalized and posted to the wrong account, a **correcting entry** should be made. For example, assume that a $400 payment for Rent Expense was incorrectly debited to Repair Expense and correctly credited to Cash. This requires a correcting entry and explanation as shown in Figure 4-16. Figure 4-17 shows the effects of the correcting entry on the ledger accounts. Generally, "Correcting" is written in the Item column of the general ledger account.

FIGURE 4-16   Correcting Entry Method

	DATE		DESCRIPTION	POST. REF.	DEBIT	CREDIT	
1	20-- Sept.	25	Rent Expense	521	4 0 0 00		1
2			Repair Expense	537		4 0 0 00	2
3			To correct error in which payment for rent				3
4			was debited to Repair Expense				4
5							5

GENERAL JOURNAL — PAGE 6

FIGURE 4-17   Effects of Correcting Entry on Ledger Accounts

GENERAL LEDGER

ACCOUNT: Rent Expense — ACCOUNT NO. 521

DATE		ITEM	POST. REF.	DEBIT	CREDIT	BALANCE DEBIT	BALANCE CREDIT
20-- Sept.	25	Correcting	J6	4 0 0 00		4 0 0 00	

ACCOUNT: Repair Expense — ACCOUNT NO. 537

DATE		ITEM	POST. REF.	DEBIT	CREDIT	BALANCE DEBIT	BALANCE CREDIT
20-- Sept.	10		J5	5 0 00		5 0 00	
	15		J5	4 0 0 00		4 5 0 00	
	25	Correcting	J6		4 0 0 00	5 0 00	

Learning Objectives	Key Points to Remember
LO1 Describe the flow of data from source documents through the trial balance.	The flow of data from the source documents through the trial balance is: 1. Analyze business transactions. 2. Journalize transactions in the general journal. 3. Post journal entries to the general ledger. 4. Prepare a trial balance. **INPUT** — Analyze transactions using SOURCE DOCUMENTS and CHART OF ACCOUNTS → **PROCESSING**: Enter business transactions in the GENERAL JOURNAL *Journalizing* → Post the entries in the journal to the GENERAL LEDGER *Posting* → From the general ledger, prepare a TRIAL BALANCE
LO2 Describe the chart of accounts as a means of classifying financial information.	The chart of accounts includes the account titles in numerical order for all assets, liabilities, owner's equity, revenues, and expenses. The chart of accounts is used in classifying information about transactions.
LO3 Describe and explain the purpose of source documents.	Source documents trigger the analysis of business transactions and the entries into the accounting system.
LO4 Journalize transactions.	A journal provides a day-by-day listing of transactions. The journal shows the date, titles of the accounts to be debited or credited, and the amounts of the debits and credits. The steps in the journalizing process are: 1. Enter the date. 2. Enter the debit. Accounts to be debited are entered first. 3. Enter the credit. Accounts to be credited are entered after the debits and are indented one-half inch. 4. Enter the explanation. A brief explanation of the transaction should be entered in the description column on the line following the last credit. The explanation should be indented an additional one-half inch.
LO5 Post to the general ledger and prepare a trial balance.	The general ledger is a complete set of all accounts used by the business. The steps in posting from the general journal to the general ledger are: In the general ledger: 1. Enter the date of each transaction. 2. Enter the amount of each debit or credit in the Debit or Credit column. 3. Enter the new balance. 4. Enter the journal page number from which each transaction is posted in the Posting Reference column. In the journal: 5. Enter the account number to which each transaction is posted in the Posting Reference column. The trial balance provides a check to make sure the total of all debit balances in the ledger accounts equals the total of all credit balances in the ledger accounts.
LO6 Explain how to find and correct errors.	Errors may be found by verifying your addition, by dividing the difference between the debits and credits by 2 or 9, and by retracing your steps through the accounting process. Use the ruling method or the correcting entry method to correct the error.

DEMONSTRATION PROBLEM

George Fielding is a financial planning consultant. He provides budgeting, estate planning, tax planning, and investing advice for professional golfers. He developed the following chart of accounts for his business.

Assets
101   Cash
142   Office Supplies

Liabilities
202   Accounts Payable

Owner's Equity
311   George Fielding, Capital
312   George Fielding, Drawing

Revenues
401   Professional Fees

Expenses
511   Wages Expense
521   Rent Expense
525   Telephone Expense
533   Utilities Expense
534   Charitable Contributions Expense
538   Automobile Expense

The following transactions took place during the month of December of the current year.

Dec. 1   Fielding invested cash to start the business, $20,000.

3   Paid Bollhorst Real Estate for December office rent, $1,000.

4   Received cash from Aaron Patton, a client, for services, $2,500.

6   Paid T. Z. Anderson Electric for December heating and light, $75.

7   Received cash from Andrew Conder, a client, for services, $2,000.

12   Paid Fichter's Super Service for gasoline and oil purchases for the company car, $60.

14   Paid Hillenburg Staffing for temporary secretarial services during the past two weeks, $600.

17   Bought office supplies from Bowers Office Supply on account, $280.

20   Paid Mitchell Telephone Co. for business calls during the past month, $100.

21   Fielding withdrew cash for personal use, $1,100.

24   Made donation to the National Multiple Sclerosis Society, $100.

27   Received cash from Billy Walters, a client, for services, $2,000.

28   Paid Hillenburg Staffing for temporary secretarial services during the past two weeks, $600.

29   Made payment on account to Bowers Office Supply, $100.

REQUIRED

1.   Record the preceding transactions in a general journal.

2.   Post the entries to the general ledger.

3.   Prepare a trial balance.

Solution 1, 2.

	DATE		DESCRIPTION	POST. REF.	DEBIT					CREDIT					
1	20-- Dec.	1	Cash	101	20	0	0	0	00						1
2			George Fielding, Capital	311						20	0	0	0	00	2
3			Owner's original investment in												3
4			consulting business												4
5															5
6		3	Rent Expense	521	1	0	0	0	00						6
7			Cash	101						1	0	0	0	00	7
8			Paid rent for December												8
9															9
10		4	Cash	101	2	5	0	0	00						10
11			Professional Fees	401						2	5	0	0	00	11
12			Received cash for services rendered												12
13															13
14		6	Utilities Expense	533			7	5	00						14
15			Cash	101								7	5	00	15
16			Paid utilities												16
17															17
18		7	Cash	101	2	0	0	0	00						18
19			Professional Fees	401						2	0	0	0	00	19
20			Received cash for services rendered												20
21															21
22		12	Automobile Expense	538			6	0	00						22
23			Cash	101								6	0	00	23
24			Paid for gas and oil												24
25															25
26		14	Wages Expense	511		6	0	0	00						26
27			Cash	101							6	0	0	00	27
28			Paid temporary secretaries												28
29															29
30		17	Office Supplies	142		2	8	0	00						30
31			Accounts Payable	202							2	8	0	00	31
32			Purchased office supplies on account from												32
33			Bowers Office Supply												33
34															34
35															35

GENERAL JOURNAL   PAGE 1

(continued)

GENERAL JOURNAL

PAGE 2

	DATE		DESCRIPTION	POST. REF.	DEBIT	CREDIT	
1	20-- Dec.	20	Telephone Expense	525	1 0 0 00		1
2			Cash	101		1 0 0 00	2
3			Paid telephone bill				3
4							4
5		21	George Fielding, Drawing	312	1 1 0 0 00		5
6			Cash	101		1 1 0 0 00	6
7			Owner's withdrawal				7
8							8
9		24	Charitable Contributions Expense	534	1 0 0 00		9
10			Cash	101		1 0 0 00	10
11			Contribution to National Multiple				11
12			Sclerosis Society				12
13							13
14		27	Cash	101	2 0 0 0 00		14
15			Professional Fees	401		2 0 0 0 00	15
16			Received cash for services rendered				16
17							17
18		28	Wages Expense	511	6 0 0 00		18
19			Cash	101		6 0 0 00	19
20			Paid temporary secretaries				20
21							21
22		29	Accounts Payable	202	1 0 0 00		22
23			Cash	101		1 0 0 00	23
24			Payment on account to Bowers Office Supply				24

2.

GENERAL LEDGER

ACCOUNT: Cash   ACCOUNT NO. 101

DATE		ITEM	POST. REF.	DEBIT	CREDIT	BALANCE DEBIT	BALANCE CREDIT
20-- Dec.	1		J1	20 0 0 0 00		20 0 0 0 00	
	3		J1		1 0 0 0 00	19 0 0 0 00	
	4		J1	2 5 0 0 00		21 5 0 0 00	
	6		J1		7 5 00	21 4 2 5 00	
	7		J1	2 0 0 0 00		23 4 2 5 00	
	12		J1		6 0 00	23 3 6 5 00	
	14		J1		6 0 0 00	22 7 6 5 00	
	20		J2		1 0 0 00	22 6 6 5 00	
	21		J2		1 1 0 0 00	21 5 6 5 00	
	24		J2		1 0 0 00	21 4 6 5 00	
	27		J2	2 0 0 0 00		23 4 6 5 00	
	28		J2		6 0 0 00	22 8 6 5 00	
	29		J2		1 0 0 00	22 7 6 5 00	

ACCOUNT: Office Supplies   ACCOUNT NO. 142

DATE		ITEM	POST. REF.	DEBIT	CREDIT	BALANCE	
						DEBIT	CREDIT
20-- Dec.	17		J1	2 8 0 00		2 8 0 00	

ACCOUNT: Accounts Payable   ACCOUNT NO. 202

DATE		ITEM	POST. REF.	DEBIT	CREDIT	BALANCE	
						DEBIT	CREDIT
20-- Dec.	17		J1		2 8 0 00		2 8 0 00
	29		J2	1 0 0 00			1 8 0 00

ACCOUNT: George Fielding, Capital   ACCOUNT NO. 311

DATE		ITEM	POST. REF.	DEBIT	CREDIT	BALANCE	
						DEBIT	CREDIT
20-- Dec.	1		J1		20 0 0 0 00		20 0 0 0 00

ACCOUNT: George Fielding, Drawing   ACCOUNT NO. 312

DATE		ITEM	POST. REF.	DEBIT	CREDIT	BALANCE	
						DEBIT	CREDIT
20-- Dec.	21		J2	1 1 0 0 00		1 1 0 0 00	

ACCOUNT: Professional Fees   ACCOUNT NO. 401

DATE		ITEM	POST. REF.	DEBIT	CREDIT	BALANCE	
						DEBIT	CREDIT
20-- Dec.	4		J1		2 5 0 0 00		2 5 0 0 00
	7		J1		2 0 0 0 00		4 5 0 0 00
	27		J2		2 0 0 0 00		6 5 0 0 00

ACCOUNT: Wages Expense   ACCOUNT NO. 511

DATE		ITEM	POST. REF.	DEBIT	CREDIT	BALANCE	
						DEBIT	CREDIT
20-- Dec.	14		J1	6 0 0 00		6 0 0 00	
	28		J2	6 0 0 00		1 2 0 0 00	

ACCOUNT: Rent Expense   ACCOUNT NO. 521

DATE		ITEM	POST. REF.	DEBIT	CREDIT	BALANCE	
						DEBIT	CREDIT
20-- Dec.	3		J1	1 0 0 0 00		1 0 0 0 00	

(continued)

ACCOUNT: Telephone Expense — ACCOUNT NO. 525

DATE	ITEM	POST. REF.	DEBIT	CREDIT	BALANCE DEBIT	BALANCE CREDIT
20-- Dec. 20		J2	1 0 0 00		1 0 0 00	

ACCOUNT: Utilities Expense — ACCOUNT NO. 533

DATE	ITEM	POST. REF.	DEBIT	CREDIT	BALANCE DEBIT	BALANCE CREDIT
20-- Dec. 6		J1	7 5 00		7 5 00	

ACCOUNT: Charitable Contributions Expense — ACCOUNT NO. 534

DATE	ITEM	POST. REF.	DEBIT	CREDIT	BALANCE DEBIT	BALANCE CREDIT
20-- Dec. 24		J2	1 0 0 00		1 0 0 00	

ACCOUNT: Automobile Expense — ACCOUNT NO. 538

DATE	ITEM	POST. REF.	DEBIT	CREDIT	BALANCE DEBIT	BALANCE CREDIT
20-- Dec. 12		J1	6 0 00		6 0 00	

3.

George Fielding, Financial Planning Consultant
Trial Balance
December 31, 20 - -

ACCOUNT TITLE	ACCOUNT NO.	DEBIT BALANCE	CREDIT BALANCE
Cash	101	22 7 6 5 00	
Office Supplies	142	2 8 0 00	
Accounts Payable	202		1 8 0 00
George Fielding, Capital	311		20 0 0 0 00
George Fielding, Drawing	312	1 1 0 0 00	
Professional Fees	401		6 5 0 0 00
Wages Expense	511	1 2 0 0 00	
Rent Expense	521	1 0 0 0 00	
Telephone Expense	525	1 0 0 00	
Utilities Expense	533	7 5 00	
Charitable Contributions Expense	534	1 0 0 00	
Automobile Expense	538	6 0 00	
		26 6 8 0 00	26 6 8 0 00

KEY TERMS

book of original entry (93)   The journal or the first formal accounting record of a transaction.

chart of accounts (90)   A list of all accounts used by a business.

compound entry (96)   A general journal entry that affects more than two accounts.

correcting entry (108)   An entry to correct an incorrect entry that has been journalized and posted to the wrong account.

cross-reference (100)   The information in the Posting Reference columns of the journal and ledger that provides a link between the journal and ledger.

general ledger (98)   A complete set of all the accounts used by a business. The general ledger accumulates a complete record of the debits and credits made to each account as a result of entries made in the journal.

general ledger account (98)   An account with columns for the debit or credit transaction and columns for the debit or credit running balance.

Chronological

journal (93)   A day-by-day listing of the transactions of a business.

journalizing (93)   Entering the transactions in a journal.

posting (99)   Copying the debits and credits from the journal to the ledger accounts.

ruling method (107)   A method of correcting an entry in which a line is drawn through the error and the correct information is placed above it.

slide error (106)   An error that occurs when debit or credit amounts "slide" a digit or two to the left or right.

source document (91)   Any document that provides information about a business transaction.

transposition error (106)   An error that occurs when two digits are reversed.

trial balance (105)   A list used to prove that the totals of the debit and credit balances in the ledger accounts are equal.

two-column general journal (93)   A journal with only two amount columns, one for debit amounts and one for credit amounts.

Self-Study Test Questions

True/False

1. Source documents serve as historical evidence of business transactions.

2. No entries are made in the Posting Reference column at the time of journalizing.

3. When entering the credit item in a general journal, it should be listed after all debits and indented.

4. The chart of accounts lists capital accounts first, followed by liabilities, assets, expenses, and revenue.

5. When an incorrect entry has been journalized and posted to the wrong account, a correcting entry should be made.

Multiple Choice

1. The process of copying debits and credits from the journal to the ledger is called

   (a) journalizing.
   (b) posting.

   (c) cross-referencing.
   (d) sliding.

2. To purchase an asset such as office equipment on account, you would credit which account?

   (a) Cash
   (b) Accounts Receivable

   (c) Accounts Payable
   (d) Capital

3. When fees are earned but will be paid later, which account is debited?

   (a) Cash
   (b) Accounts Receivable

   (c) Accounts Payable
   (d) Capital

4. When the correct numbers are used but are in the wrong order, the error is called a

   (a) transposition.
   (b) slide.

   (c) ruling.
   (d) correcting entry.

5. A revenue account will begin with the number _____ in the chart of accounts.

   (a) 1
   (b) 2

   (c) 3
   (d) 4

The answers to the Self-Study Test Questions are at the end of the text.

REVIEW QUESTIONS

LO1   1. Trace the flow of accounting information through the accounting system.

LO2   2. Explain the purpose of a chart of accounts.

LO2   3. Name the five types of financial statement classifications for which it is ordinarily desirable to keep separate accounts.

LO3   4. Name a source document that provides information about each of the following types of business transactions:
      a. Cash payment
      b. Cash receipt
      c. Sale of goods or services
      d. Purchase of goods or services

LO4   5. Where is the first formal accounting record of a business transaction usually made?

LO4   6. Describe the four steps required to journalize a business transaction in a general journal.

LO5   7. In what order are the accounts customarily placed in the ledger?

LO5   8. Explain the primary advantage of a general ledger account.

LO5   9. Explain the five steps required when posting the journal to the ledger.

LO5   10. What information is entered in the Posting Reference column of the journal as an amount is posted to the proper account in the ledger?

LO6   11. Explain why the ledger can still contain errors even though the trial balance is in balance. Give examples of two such types of errors.

LO6   12. What is a slide error?

LO6   13. What is a transposition error?

LO6   14. What is the ruling method of correcting an error?

LO6   15. What is the correcting entry method?

REVISITING THE OPENER

In the chapter opener on page 89, you are asked to consider the best method for correcting errors. Is it appropriate to erase entries when making corrections? Let's assume that Mitch made the following entries:

(1) Cash	100	
Sales		100
(2) Rent Expense	50	
Cash		50

Entry (1) has been posted to the general ledger. It is correct, but the amount of the sale was actually $80. Prepare the proper correction.

    Entry (2) has not been posted to the general ledger. Cash of $50 was paid for rent, but the debit should have been made to Prepaid Rent, not Rent Expense. Prepare the proper correction.

SERIES A EXERCISES

E 4-1A (LO3)

SOURCE DOCUMENTS Source documents trigger the analysis of events requiring an accounting entry. Match the following source documents with the type of information they provide.

1. Check stubs or check register
2. Purchase invoice from suppliers (vendors)
3. Sales tickets or invoices to customers
4. Receipts or cash register tapes

a. A good or service has been sold.
b. Cash has been received by the business.
c. Cash has been paid by the business.
d. Goods or services have been purchased by the business.

E 4-2A (LO4)

GENERAL JOURNAL ENTRIES For each of the following transactions, list the account to be debited and the account to be credited in the general journal.

1. Invested cash in the business, $5,000.
2. Paid office rent, $500.
3. Purchased office supplies on account, $300.
4. Received cash for services rendered (fees), $400.
5. Paid cash on account, $50.
6. Rendered services on account, $300.
7. Received cash for an amount owed by a customer, $100.

E 4-3A (LO5)
✓ Final cash bal.: $4,950

GENERAL LEDGER ACCOUNTS Set up T accounts for each of the general ledger accounts needed for Exercise 4-2A and post debits and credits to the accounts. Foot the accounts and enter the balances. Prove that total debits equal total credits.

E 4-4A (LO4)

GENERAL JOURNAL ENTRIES Jean Jones has opened Jones Consulting. Journalize the following transactions that occurred during January of the current year. Use the following journal pages: January 1–10, page 1, and January 11–29, page 2. Use the following chart of accounts.

Chart of Accounts

Assets
101 Cash
142 Office Supplies
181 Office Equipment

Liabilities
202 Accounts Payable

Owner's Equity
311 Jean Jones, Capital
312 Jean Jones, Drawing

Revenues
401 Consulting Fees

Expenses
511 Wages Expense
521 Rent Expense
525 Telephone Expense
533 Utilities Expense
549 Miscellaneous Expense

Jan. 1   Jones invested cash in the business, $10,000.

2   Paid office rent, $500.

3   Purchased office equipment on account, $1,500.

5   Received cash for services rendered, $750.

8   Paid telephone bill, $65.

10   Paid for a magazine subscription (miscellaneous expense), $15.

11   Purchased office supplies on account, $300.

15   Made a payment on account (see Jan. 3 transaction), $150.

18   Paid part-time employee, $500.

21   Received cash for services rendered, $350.

25   Paid utilities bill, $85.

27   Jones withdrew cash for personal use, $100.

29   Paid part-time employee, $500.

E 4-5A (LO5)

✓ Final cash bal.: $9,185;
Trial Bal. total debits: $12,750

GENERAL LEDGER ACCOUNTS; TRIAL BALANCE Set up general ledger accounts using the chart of accounts provided in Exercise 4-4A. Post the transactions from Exercise 4-4A to the general ledger accounts and prepare a trial balance.

E 4-6A (LO5)

✓ Total assets, Jan. 31: $10,985

FINANCIAL STATEMENTS From the information in Exercises 4-4A and 4-5A, prepare an income statement, a statement of owner's equity, and a balance sheet.

E 4-7A (LO5)

✓ Total assets. July 31: $7,100

FINANCIAL STATEMENTS From the following trial balance taken after one month of operation, prepare an income statement, a statement of owner's equity, and a balance sheet.

TJ's Paint Service
Trial Balance
July 31, 20 - -

ACCOUNT TITLE	ACCOUNT NO.	DEBIT BALANCE	CREDIT BALANCE
Cash	101	4 3 0 0 00	
Accounts Receivable	122	1 1 0 0 00	
Supplies	141	8 0 0 00	
Paint Equipment	183	9 0 0 00	
Accounts Payable	202		2 1 5 0 00
TJ Ulza, Capital	311		3 2 0 5 00
TJ Ulza, Drawing	312	5 0 0 00	
Painting Fees	401		3 6 0 0 00
Wages Expense	511	9 0 0 00	
Rent Expense	521	2 5 0 00	
Telephone Expense	525	5 0 00	
Transportation Expense	526	6 0 00	
Utilities Expense	533	7 0 00	
Miscellaneous Expense	549	2 5 00	
		8 9 5 5 00	8 9 5 5 00

E 4-8A (LO6)

FINDING AND CORRECTING ERRORS Joe Adams bought $500 worth of office supplies on account. The following entry was recorded on May 17. Find the error(s) and correct it (them) using the ruling method.

14															14
15	20-- May	17	Office Equipment					4	0	0	00				15
16			Cash									4	0	0	00	16
17			Purchased copy paper												17

On May 25, after the transactions had been posted, Adams discovered that the following entry contains an error. The cash received represents a collection on account, rather than new service fees. Correct the error in the general journal using the correcting entry method.

22															22
23	20-- May	23	Cash	101	1	0	0	0	00						23
24			Service Fees	401							1	0	0	0	00	24
25			Received cash for services previously earned												25

SERIES A PROBLEMS

P 4-9A (LO4/5)

✓ Cash bal., Jan. 31: $10,021

Trial Bal. total debits: $13,460

JOURNALIZING AND POSTING TRANSACTIONS Annette Creighton opened Creighton Consulting. She rented a small office and paid a part-time worker to answer the telephone and make deliveries. Her chart of accounts is as follows:

Chart of Accounts

Assets		Revenues	
101	Cash	401	Consulting Fees
142	Office Supplies		
181	Office Equipment	**Expenses**	
		511	Wages Expense
Liabilities		512	Advertising Expense
202	Accounts Payable	521	Rent Expense
		525	Telephone Expense
		526	Transportation Expense
Owner's Equity		533	Utilities Expense
311	Annette Creighton, Capital	549	Miscellaneous Expense
312	Annette Creighton, Drawing		

Creighton's transactions for the first month of business are as follows:

Jan. 1	Creighton invested cash in the business, $10,000.
1	Paid rent, $500.
2	Purchased office supplies on account, $300.
4	Purchased office equipment on account, $1,500.
6	Received cash for services rendered, $580.
7	Paid telephone bill, $42.
8	Paid utilities bill, $38.

Jan. 10	Received cash for services rendered, $360.
12	Made payment on account, $50.
13	Paid for car rental while visiting an out-of-town client (transportation expense), $150.
15	Paid part-time worker, $360.
17	Received cash for services rendered, $420.
18	Creighton withdrew cash for personal use, $100.
20	Paid for a newspaper ad, $26.
22	Reimbursed part-time employee for cab fare incurred delivering materials to clients (transportation expense), $35.
24	Paid for books on consulting practices (miscellaneous expense), $28.
25	Received cash for services rendered, $320.
27	Made payment on account for office equipment purchased, $150.
29	Paid part-time worker, $360.
30	Received cash for services rendered, $180.

REQUIRED

1. Set up general ledger accounts from the chart of accounts.

2. Journalize the transactions for January in a two-column general journal. Use the following journal page numbers: January 1–10, page 1; January 12–24, page 2; January 25–30, page 3.

3. Post the transactions from the general journal.

4. Prepare a trial balance.

5. Prepare an income statement and a statement of owner's equity for the month of January, and a balance sheet as of January 31, 20--.

P 4-10A (LO4/5)

✓ Cash bal., June 30: $3,958

Trial Bal. total debits: $22,358

JOURNALIZING AND POSTING TRANSACTIONS Jim Andrews opened a delivery business in March. He rented a small office and has a part-time assistant. His trial balance shows accounts for the first three months of business.

Jim's Quick Delivery Trial Balance May 31, 20 - -													
ACCOUNT TITLE	ACCOUNT NO.	DEBIT BALANCE					CREDIT BALANCE					
Cash	101	3	8	2	6	00						
Accounts Receivable	122	1	2	1	2	00						
Office Supplies	142		6	4	8	00						
Office Equipment	181	2	1	0	0	00						
Delivery Truck	185	8	0	0	0	00						
Accounts Payable	202						6	0	0	0	00	
Jim Andrews, Capital	311						4	4	7	8	00	
Jim Andrews, Drawing	312	1	8	0	0	00						
Delivery Fees	401						9	8	8	0	00	
Wages Expense	511	1	2	0	0	00						
Advertising Expense	512			9	0	00						
Rent Expense	521		9	0	0	00						
Telephone Expense	525		1	2	6	00						
Electricity Expense	533			9	8	00						
Charitable Contributions Expense	534			6	0	00						
Gas and Oil Expense	538		1	8	6	00						
Miscellaneous Expense	549		1	1	2	00						
		20	3	5	8	00	20	3	5	8	00	

Andrews' transactions for the month of June are as follows:

June 1   Paid rent, $300.

2   Performed delivery services for $300: $100 in cash and $200 on account.

4   Paid for newspaper advertising, $15.

6   Purchased office supplies on account, $180.

7   Received cash for delivery services rendered, $260.

9   Paid cash on account (truck payment), $200.

10   Purchased a copier (office equipment) for $700: paid $100 in cash and put $600 on account.

11   Made a contribution to the Red Cross (charitable contributions), $20.

12   Received cash for delivery services rendered, $380.

13   Received cash on account for services previously rendered, $100.

15   Paid a part-time worker, $200.

16   Paid electric bill, $36.

18   Paid telephone bill, $46.

19   Received cash on account for services previously rendered, $100.

20   Andrews withdrew cash for personal use, $200.

21   Paid for gas and oil, $32.

22   Made payment on account (for office supplies), $40.

24   Received cash for services rendered, $340.

June 26   Paid for a magazine subscription (miscellaneous expense), $15.

27   Received cash for services rendered, $180.

27   Received cash on account for services previously rendered, $100.

29   Paid for gasoline, $24.

30   Paid a part-time worker, $200.

REQUIRED

1.   Set up general ledger accounts by entering the balances as of June 1.

2.   Journalize the transactions for June in a two-column general journal. Use the following journal pages: June 1–10, page 7; June 11–20, page 8; June 21–30, page 9.

3.   Post the entries from the general journal.

4.   Prepare a trial balance.

P 4-11A (LO6)

CORRECTING ERRORS Assuming that all entries have been posted, prepare correcting entries for each of the following errors.

1.   The following entry was made to record the purchase of $500 in supplies on account:

Supplies	142	500	
Cash	101		500

2.   The following entry was made to record the payment of $300 in wages:

Rent Expense	521	300	
Cash	101		300

3.   The following entry was made to record a $200 payment to a supplier on account:

Supplies	142	100	
Cash	101		100

SERIES B EXERCISES

E 4-1B (LO3)

SOURCE DOCUMENTS What type of information is found on each of the following source documents?

1.   Cash register tape

2.   Sales ticket (issued to customer)

3.   Purchase invoice (received from supplier or vendor)

4.   Check stub

E 4-2B (LO4)

GENERAL JOURNAL ENTRIES For each of the following transactions, list the account to be debited and the account to be credited in the general journal.

1.   Invested cash in the business, $1,000.

2.   Performed services on account, $200.

(continued)

3.   Purchased office equipment on account, $500.

4.   Received cash on account for services previously rendered, $200.

5.   Made a payment on account, $100.

E 4-3B (LO5)

✓ Final cash bal.: $1,100

GENERAL LEDGER ACCOUNTS Set up T accounts for each of the general ledger accounts needed for Exercise 4-2B and post debits and credits to the accounts. Foot the accounts and enter the balances. Prove that total debits equal total credits.

E 4-4B (LO4)

GENERAL JOURNAL ENTRIES Sengel Moon opened The Bike Doctor. Journalize the following transactions that occurred during the month of October of the current year. Use the following journal pages: October 1–12, page 1, and October 14–29, page 2. Use the following chart of accounts.

Chart of Accounts

Assets
101   Cash
141   Bicycle Parts
142   Office Supplies

Liabilities
202   Accounts Payable

Owner's Equity
311   Sengel Moon, Capital
312   Sengel Moon, Drawing

Revenues
401   Repair Fees

Expenses
511   Wages Expense
521   Rent Expense
525   Telephone Expense
533   Utilities Expense
549   Miscellaneous Expense

Oct. 1   Moon invested cash in the business, $15,000.

2   Paid shop rental for the month, $300.

3   Purchased bicycle parts on account, $2,000.

5   Purchased office supplies on account, $250.

8   Paid telephone bill, $38.

9   Received cash for services, $140.

11   Paid a sports magazine subscription (miscellaneous expense), $15.

12   Made payment on account (see Oct. 3 transaction), $100.

14   Paid part-time employee, $300.

15   Received cash for services, $350.

16   Paid utilities bill, $48.

19   Received cash for services, $250.

23   Moon withdrew cash for personal use, $50.

25   Made payment on account (see Oct. 5 transaction), $50.

29   Paid part-time employee, $300.

E 4-5B (LO5)

✓ Final cash bal.: $14,539;
Trial Bal. total debits: $17,840

GENERAL LEDGER ACCOUNTS; TRIAL BALANCE Set up general ledger accounts using the chart of accounts provided in Exercise 4-4B. Post the transactions from Exercise 4-4B to the general ledger accounts and prepare a trial balance.

E 4-6B (LO5)

✓ Total assets, Oct. 31: $16,789

FINANCIAL STATEMENTS From the information in Exercises 4-4B and 4-5B, prepare an income statement, a statement of owner's equity, and a balance sheet.

E 4-7B (LO5)

✓ Total assets, Mar. 31: $11,900

FINANCIAL STATEMENTS From the following trial balance taken after one month of operation, prepare an income statement, a statement of owner's equity, and a balance sheet.

AT Speaker's Bureau Trial Balance March 31, 20 - -			
ACCOUNT TITLE	ACCOUNT NO.	DEBIT BALANCE	CREDIT BALANCE
Cash	101	6 6 0 0 00	
Accounts Receivable	122	2 8 0 0 00	
Office Supplies	142	1 0 0 0 00	
Office Equipment	181	1 5 0 0 00	
Accounts Payable	202		3 0 0 0 00
AT Speaker, Capital	311		6 0 9 8 00
AT Speaker, Drawing	312	8 0 0 00	
Speaking Fees	401		4 8 0 0 00
Wages Expense	511	4 0 0 00	
Rent Expense	521	2 0 0 00	
Telephone Expense	525	3 5 00	
Travel Expense	526	4 5 0 00	
Utilities Expense	533	8 8 00	
Miscellaneous Expense	549	2 5 00	
		13 8 9 8 00	13 8 9 8 00

E 4-8B (LO6)

FINDING AND CORRECTING ERRORS Mary Smith purchased $350 worth of office equipment on account. The following entry was recorded on April 6. Find the error(s) and correct it (them) using the ruling method.

7						7
8	20-- Apr.	6	Office Supplies	5 3 0 00		8
9			Cash		5 3 0 00	9
10			Purchased office equipment			10

On April 25, after the transactions had been posted, Smith discovered the following entry contains an error. When her customer received services, Cash was debited, but no cash was received. Correct the error in the journal using the correcting entry method.

27						27
28	20-- Apr.	21	Cash	101	3 0 0 00	28
29			Service Fees	401	3 0 0 00	29
30			Revenue earned from services			30
31			previously rendered			31

SERIES B PROBLEMS

P 4-9B (LO4/5)

✓ Cash bal., May 31: $4,500;
Trial Bal. total debits: $8,790

JOURNALIZING AND POSTING TRANSACTIONS Benito Mendez opened Mendez Appraisals. He rented office space and has a part-time secretary to answer the telephone and make appraisal appointments. His chart of accounts is as follows:

Chart of Accounts

Assets
101   Cash
122   Accounts Receivable
142   Office Supplies
181   Office Equipment

Liabilities
202   Accounts Payable

Owner's Equity
311   Benito Mendez, Capital
312   Benito Mendez, Drawing

Revenues
401   Appraisal Fees

Expenses
511   Wages Expense
512   Advertising Expense
521   Rent Expense
525   Telephone Expense
526   Transportation Expense
533   Electricity Expense
549   Miscellaneous Expense

Mendez's transactions for the first month of business are as follows:

May 1	Mendez invested cash in the business, $5,000.
2	Paid rent, $500.
3	Purchased office supplies, $100.
4	Purchased office equipment on account, $2,000.
5	Received cash for services rendered, $280.
8	Paid telephone bill, $38.
9	Paid electric bill, $42.
10	Received cash for services rendered, $310.
13	Paid part-time employee, $500.
14	Paid car rental for out-of-town trip, $200.
15	Paid for newspaper ad, $30.
18	Received cash for services rendered, $620.
19	Paid mileage reimbursement for part-time employee's use of personal car for business deliveries (transportation expense), $22.
21	Mendez withdrew cash for personal use, $50.
23	Made payment on account for office equipment purchased earlier, $200.
24	Earned appraisal fee, which will be paid in a week, $500.
26	Paid for newspaper ad, $30.
27	Paid for local softball team sponsorship (miscellaneous expense), $15.
28	Paid part-time employee, $500.

May 29   Received cash on account, $250.

30   Received cash for services rendered, $280.

31   Paid cab fare (transportation expense), $13.

REQUIRED

1.   Set up general ledger accounts from the chart of accounts.

2.   Journalize the transactions for May in a two-column general journal. Use the following journal page numbers: May 1–10, page 1; May 13–24, page 2; May 26–31, page 3.

3.   Post the transactions from the general journal.

4.   Prepare a trial balance.

5.   Prepare an income statement and a statement of owner's equity for the month of May, and a balance sheet as of May 31, 20--.

P 4-10B (LO4/5)

✓ Cash bal., Nov. 30: $7,012;
Trial Bal. total debits: $16,105

JOURNALIZING AND POSTING TRANSACTIONS Ann Taylor owns a suit tailoring shop. She opened business in September. She rented a small work space and has an assistant to receive job orders and process claim tickets. Her trial balance shows her account balances for the first two months of business.

Taylor Tailoring Trial Balance October 31, 20 - -				
ACCOUNT TITLE	ACCOUNT NO.	DEBIT BALANCE	CREDIT BALANCE	
Cash	101	6 2 1 1 00		
Accounts Receivable	122	4 8 4 00		
Tailoring Supplies	141	1 0 0 0 00		
Tailoring Equipment	183	3 8 0 0 00		
Accounts Payable	202		4 1 2 5 00	
Ann Taylor, Capital	311		6 1 3 0 00	
Ann Taylor, Drawing	312	8 0 0 00		
Tailoring Fees	401		3 6 0 0 00	
Wages Expense	511	8 0 0 00		
Advertising Expense	512	3 4 00		
Rent Expense	521	6 0 0 00		
Telephone Expense	525	6 0 00		
Electricity Expense	533	4 4 00		
Miscellaneous Expense	549	2 2 00		
		13 8 5 5 00	13 8 5 5 00	

Taylor's transactions for November are as follows:

Nov. 1   Paid rent, $300.

2   Purchased tailoring supplies on account, $150.

3   Purchased a new button hole machine on account, $300.

5   Earned first week's revenue, $400: $100 in cash and $300 on account.

8   Paid for newspaper advertising, $13.

(continued)

Nov. 9 Paid telephone bill, $28.

10 Paid electric bill, $21.

11 Received cash on account from customers, $200.

12 Earned second week's revenue, $450: $200 in cash and $250 on account.

15 Paid assistant, $400.

16 Made payment on account, $100.

17 Paid for magazine subscription (miscellaneous expense), $12.

19 Earned third week's revenue, $450: $300 in cash, $150 on account.

23 Received cash on account from customers, $300.

24 Paid for newspaper advertising, $13.

26 Paid for postage (miscellaneous expense), $12.

27 Earned fourth week's revenue, $600: $200 in cash and $400 on account.

30 Received cash on account from customers, $400.

REQUIRED

1. Set up general ledger accounts by entering the balances as of November 1, 20--.

2. Journalize the transactions for November in a two-column general journal. Use the following journal page numbers: November 1–11, page 7; November 12–24, page 8; November 26–30, page 9.

3. Post the entries from the general journal.

4. Prepare a trial balance.

P 4-11B (L06)   **CORRECTING ERRORS** Assuming that all entries have been posted, prepare correcting entries for each of the following errors.

1. The following entry was made to record the purchase of $400 in equipment on account.

Supplies	142	400	
Cash	101		400

2. The following entry was made to record the payment of $200 for advertising.

Repair Expense	537	200	
Cash	101		200

3. The following entry was made to record a $600 payment to a supplier on account.

Prepaid Insurance	145	400	
Cash	101		400

MANAGING YOUR WRITING

You are a public accountant with many small business clients. During a recent visit to a client's business, the bookkeeper approached you with a problem. The columns of the trial balance were not equal. You helped the bookkeeper find and correct the error, but believe you should go one step further. Write a memo to all of your clients that explains the purpose of the double-entry framework, the importance of maintaining the equality of the accounting equation, the errors that might cause an inequality, and suggestions for finding the errors.

MASTERY PROBLEM

✓ Cash bal., June 30: $45,495;
Trial Bal. total debits: $96,200

Barry Bird opened the Barry Bird Basketball Camp for children ages 10 through 18. Campers typically register for one week in June or July, arriving on Sunday and returning home the following Saturday. College players serve as cabin counselors and assist the local college and high school coaches who run the practice sessions. The registration fee includes a room, meals at a nearby restaurant, and basketball instruction. In the off-season, the facilities are used for weekend retreats and coaching clinics. Bird developed the following chart of accounts for his service business.

Chart of Accounts

Assets		Revenues	
101	Cash	401	Registration Fees
142	Office Supplies		
183	Athletic Equipment	Expenses	
184	Basketball Facilities	511	Wages Expense
		512	Advertising Expense
Liabilities		524	Food Expense
202	Accounts Payable	525	Telephone Expense
		533	Utilities Expense
Owner's Equity		536	Postage Expense
311	Barry Bird, Capital		
312	Barry Bird, Drawing		

The following transactions took place during the month of June.

June 1   Bird invested cash in the business, $10,000.

1   Purchased basketballs and other athletic equipment, $3,000.

2   Paid Hite Advertising for flyers that had been mailed to prospective campers, $5,000.

2   Collected registration fees, $15,000.

2   Rogers Construction completed work on a new basketball court that cost $12,000. Arrangements were made to pay the bill in July.

5   Purchased office supplies on account from Gordon Office Supplies, $300.

6   Received bill from Magic's Restaurant for meals served to campers on account, $5,800.

7   Collected registration fees, $16,200.

(continued)

June 10   Paid wages to camp counselors, $500.

14   Collected registration fees, $13,500.

14   Received bill from Magic's Restaurant for meals served to campers on account, $6,200.

17   Paid wages to camp counselors, $500.

18   Paid postage, $85.

21   Collected registration fees, $15,200.

22   Received bill from Magic's Restaurant for meals served to campers on account, $6,500.

24   Paid wages to camp counselors, $500.

28   Collected registration fees, $14,000.

30   Received bill from Magic's Restaurant for meals served to campers on account, $7,200.

30   Paid wages to camp counselors, $500.

30   Paid Magic's Restaurant on account, $25,700.

30   Paid utility bill, $500.

30   Paid telephone bill, $120.

30   Bird withdrew cash for personal use, $2,000.

REQUIRED

1.   Enter the transactions in a general journal. Use the following journal pages: June 1–6, page 1; June 7–22, page 2; June 24–30, page 3.

2.   Post the entries to the general ledger.

3.   Prepare a trial balance.

CHALLENGE PROBLEM

This problem challenges you to apply your cumulative accounting knowledge to move a step beyond the material in the chapter.

✓ **Total debits: $19,150**

Journal entries and a trial balance for Fred Phaler Consulting follow. As you will note, the trial balance does not balance, suggesting that there are errors. Recall that the chapter offers tips on identifying individual posting errors. These techniques are not as effective when there are two or more errors. Thus, you will need to first carefully inspect the trial balance to see if you can identify any obvious errors due to amounts that either look out of proportion or are simply reported in the wrong place. Then, you will need to carefully evaluate the other amounts by using the techniques offered in the text, or tracing the journal entries to the amounts reported on the trial balance. (Hint: Four errors were made in the posting process and preparation of the trial balance.)

GENERAL JOURNAL

PAGE 1

	DATE		DESCRIPTION	POST. REF.	DEBIT					CREDIT					
1	20-- June	1	Cash	101	10	0	0	0	00						1
2			Fred Phaler, Capital	311						10	0	0	0	00	2
3															3
4		2	Rent Expense	521		5	0	0	00						4
5			Cash	101							5	0	0	00	5
6															6
7		3	Cash	101	4	0	0	0	00						7
8			Professional Fees	401						4	0	0	0	00	8
9															9
10		4	Utilities Expense	533		1	0	0	00						10
11			Cash	101							1	0	0	00	11
12															12
13		7	Cash	101	3	0	0	0	00						13
14			Professional Fees	401						3	0	0	0	00	14
15															15
16		12	Automobile Expense	526			5	0	00						16
17			Cash	101								5	0	00	17
18															18
19		14	Wages Expense	511		5	0	0	00						19
20			Cash	101							5	0	0	00	20
21															21
22		14	Office Supplies	142		2	5	0	00						22
23			Accounts Payable	202							2	5	0	00	23
24															24
25		20	Telephone Expense	525		1	0	0	00						25
26			Cash	101							1	0	0	00	26
27															27
28		21	Fred Phaler, Drawing	312	1	2	0	0	00						28
29			Cash	101						1	2	0	0	00	29
30															30
31		24	Accounts Receivable	122	2	0	0	0	00						31
32			Professional Fees	401						2	0	0	0	00	32
33															33
34		25	Accounts Payable	202		1	0	0	00						34
35			Cash	101							1	0	0	00	35
36															36
37		30	Wages Expense	511		3	0	0	00						37
38			Cash	101							3	0	0	00	38

(continued)

Fred Phaler Consulting Trial Balance June 30, 20 - -												
ACCOUNT TITLE	ACCOUNT NO.	DEBIT BALANCE						CREDIT BALANCE				
Cash	101							13	9	0	0	00
Accounts Receivable	122	2	0	0	0	00						
Office Supplies	142		2	5	0	00						
Accounts Payable	202		1	0	0	00						
Fred Phaler, Capital	311							10	0	0	0	00
Fred Phaler, Drawing	312	2	1	0	0	00						
Professional Fees	401							9	0	0	0	00
Wages Expense	511		8	0	0	00						
Rent Expense	521		5	0	0	00						
Telephone Expense	525		1	0	0	00						
Automobile Expense	526	50	0	0	0	00						
Utilities Expense	533		1	0	0	00						
		55	9	5	0	00		32	9	0	0	00

REQUIRED

1. Find the errors.

2. Explain what caused the errors.

3. Prepare a corrected trial balance.

Objectives
Careful study of this chapter should enable you to:

LO1
Prepare end-of-period adjustments.

LO2
Prepare a work sheet.

LO3
Describe methods for finding errors on the work sheet.

LO4
Journalize adjusting entries.

LO5
Post adjusting entries to the general ledger.

LO6
Explain the cash, modified cash, and accrual bases of accounting.

Adjusting Entries and the Work Sheet

At the end of the first month of operations, Jessie and Mitch were looking over the trial balance. "These accounts don't look right," said Jessie. "Don't worry, I just need to make a few adjustments before we prepare the financial statements," replied Mitch. Does it seem appropriate to make adjustments prior to issuing financial statements?

Up to this point, you have learned how to journalize business transactions, post to the ledger, and prepare a trial balance. Now it is time to learn how to make end-of-period adjustments to the accounts listed in the trial balance. This chapter explains the need for adjustments and illustrates how they are made using a work sheet.

END-OF-PERIOD ADJUSTMENTS

LO1 Prepare end-of-period adjustments.

Transactions are entered as they occur throughout the year. Adjustments are made at the end of the accounting period for items that do not involve exchanges with an outside party.

Throughout the accounting period, business transactions are entered in the accounting system. These transactions are based on exchanges between the business and other companies and individuals. During the accounting period, other changes occur that affect the business's financial condition. For example, equipment is wearing out, prepaid insurance and supplies are being used up, and employees are earning wages that have not yet been paid. Since these events have not been entered into the accounting system, **adjusting entries** must be made prior to the preparation of financial statements.

The **matching principle** in accounting requires the matching of revenues earned during an accounting period with the expenses incurred to produce the revenues. This approach offers the best measure of net income. The income statement reports earnings for a specific period of time and the balance sheet reports the assets, liabilities, and owner's equity on a specific date. Thus, to follow the matching principle, the accounts must be brought up to date before financial statements are prepared. This requires adjusting some of the accounts listed in the trial balance. Figure 5-1 lists reasons to adjust the trial balance.

LEARNING KEY

Matching revenues earned with expenses incurred to produce those revenues offers the best measure of net income.

FIGURE 5-1   Reasons to Adjust the Trial Balance

1. To report all revenues earned during the accounting period.
2. To report all expenses incurred to produce the revenues earned in this accounting period.
3. To accurately report the assets on the balance sheet date. Some assets may have been used up during the accounting period.
4. To accurately report the liabilities on the balance sheet date. Expenses may have been incurred but not yet paid.

Generally, adjustments are made and financial statements prepared at the end of a 12-month period called a **fiscal year**. This period does not need to be the same as a calendar year. In fact, many businesses schedule their fiscal year-end for a time when business is slow. In this chapter, we continue the illustration of Jessie Jane's Campus Delivery and will prepare adjustments at the end of the first month of operations. We will focus on the following accounts: Supplies, Prepaid Insurance, Delivery Equipment, and Wages Expense.

A BROADER VIEW

© TIM BOYLE / GETTY IMAGES

Adjusting Entries

Are adjusting entries important? The Walt Disney Company and Mattel, Inc., probably think so. The Walt Disney Company granted Mattel, Inc., the right to make and sell toys based on Disney characters. In return, Mattel agreed to make payments to Disney as the toys were sold. One of the issues in a court case was whether Mattel should have made an adjusting entry when it fell behind on these payments. The entry would have been:

Royalty Expense	17,000,000	
Accounts Payable (Disney)		17,000,000

This adjusting entry would have reduced Mattel's fourth-quarter earnings for that year by more than 15%. Following an investigation by the Securities and Exchange Commission, Mattel eventually agreed to make an adjustment to later financial statements.

Supplies

During June, Jessie purchased supplies consisting of paper, pens, and delivery envelopes for $80. *Since these supplies were expected to provide future benefits, Supplies, an asset, was debited at the time of the purchase.* No other entries were made to the supplies account during June. As reported on the trial balance in Figure 5-2, the $80 balance remains in the supplies account at the end of the month.

FIGURE 5-2   Trial Balance

Jessie Jane's Campus Delivery
Trial Balance
June 30, 20 - -

ACCOUNT TITLE	ACCOUNT NO.	DEBIT BALANCE	CREDIT BALANCE
Cash	101	3 7 0 00	
Accounts Receivable	122	6 5 0 00	
Supplies	141	8 0 00	
Prepaid Insurance	145	2 0 0 00	
Delivery Equipment	185	3 6 0 0 00	
Accounts Payable	202		1 8 0 0 00
Jessica Jane, Capital	311		2 0 0 0 00
Jessica Jane, Drawing	312	1 5 0 00	
Delivery Fees	401		2 1 5 0 00
Wages Expense	511	6 5 0 00	
Rent Expense	521	2 0 0 00	
Telephone Expense	525	5 0 00	
		5 9 5 0 00	5 9 5 0 00

As supplies are used, an expense is incurred. However, it is not practical to make a journal entry to recognize this expense and the reduction in the supplies account every time someone uses an envelope. It is more efficient to wait until the end of the accounting period to make one adjusting entry to reflect the expense incurred for the use of supplies for the entire month.

At the end of the month, an inventory, or physical count, of the remaining supplies is taken. The inventory shows that supplies costing $20 were still unused at the end of June. Since Jessie bought supplies costing $80, and only $20 worth remain, supplies costing $60 must have been used ($80 − $20 = $60). Thus, supplies expense for the month is $60. (Trial balance is abbreviated as TB in Figure 5-3 and other T account illustrations.)

Since $60 worth of supplies have been used, Supplies Expense is debited and Supplies (asset) is credited for $60 (Figure 5-3). Thus, as shown in Figure 5-4, supplies with a cost of $20 will be reported as an asset on the balance sheet and a supplies expense of $60 will be reported on the income statement. The adjusting entry affected an income statement account (Supplies Expense) and a balance sheet account (Supplies).

LEARNING KEY

Since it is not practical to make a journal entry for supplies expense each time supplies are used, one adjusting entry is made at the end of the accounting period.

FIGURE 5-3   Adjustment for Supplies

Assets		=	Liabilities		+	Owner's Equity					
Debit	**Credit**		**Debit**	**Credit**		**Debit**				**Credit**	
+	−		−	+		−				+	

		Drawing		Expenses		Revenues	
		Debit	**Credit**	**Debit**	**Credit**	**Debit**	**Credit**
		+	−	+	−	−	+

Supplies				Supplies Expense	
TB 80				Adj. 60	
	Adj. 60				
Bal. 20					

FIGURE 5-4   Effect of Adjusting Entry for Supplies on Financial Statements

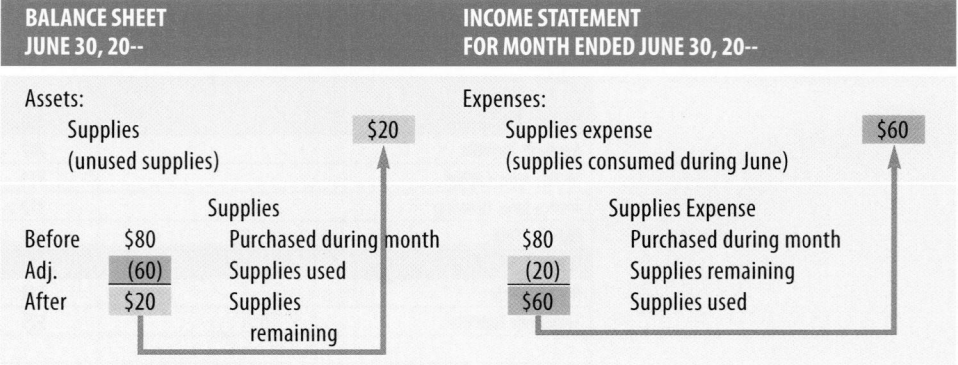

LEARNING KEY

By making an adjusting entry that debits Supplies Expense and credits Supplies, you are taking the amount of supplies used out of Supplies and putting it in Supplies Expense.

Prepaid Insurance

On June 18, Jessie paid $200 for an eight-month liability insurance policy with coverage beginning on June 1. *Prepaid Insurance, an asset, was debited because the insurance policy is expected to provide future benefits.* The $200 balance is reported on the trial balance. As the insurance policy expires with the passage of time, the asset should be reduced and an expense recognized.

Since the $200 premium covers eight months, the cost of the expired coverage for June is $25 ($200 ÷ 8 months). As shown in Figure 5-5, the adjusting entry is to debit Insurance Expense for $25 and credit Prepaid Insurance for $25. Figure 5-6 shows that the unexpired portion of the insurance premium will be reported on the balance sheet as Prepaid Insurance of $175. The expired portion will be reported on the income statement as Insurance Expense of $25.

FIGURE 5-5   Adjustment for Expired Insurance

Assets		=	Liabilities		+	Owner's Equity			
Debit	**Credit**		**Debit**	**Credit**		**Debit**		**Credit**	
+	–		–	+		–		+	

		Drawing		Expenses		Revenues	
		Debit	**Credit**	**Debit**	**Credit**	**Debit**	**Credit**
		+	–	+	–	–	+

Prepaid Insurance
TB 200
　　　　Adj. 25
Bal. 175

Insurance Expense
Adj.   25

FIGURE 5-6   Effect of Adjusting Entry for Prepaid Insurance on Financial Statements

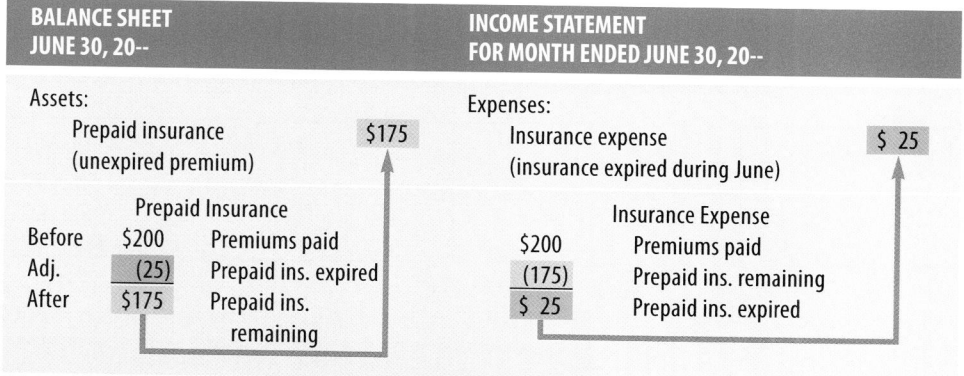

BALANCE SHEET JUNE 30, 20--			INCOME STATEMENT FOR MONTH ENDED JUNE 30, 20--		
Assets:			Expenses:		
Prepaid insurance (unexpired premium)		$175	Insurance expense (insurance expired during June)		$ 25

	Prepaid Insurance			Insurance Expense	
Before	$200	Premiums paid	$200	Premiums paid
Adj.	(25)	Prepaid ins. expired	(175)	Prepaid ins. remaining
After	$175	Prepaid ins. remaining	$ 25	Prepaid ins. expired

PROFILES IN ACCOUNTING

Jeff Clifton, Account Supervisor

Jeff Clifton maintained a 4.0 GPA with nearly perfect attendance while earning an Associate Degree in Accounting Automation. He performed an externship with Brooke County Taxing Authority and then began working as an accounts receivable clerk with the DeBartolo Properties Management, Inc., in Youngstown, Ohio.

He was promoted and is now an account supervisor. His duties include managing accounts receivable for 20 development properties across the United States, supervising five employees, and interviewing prospective employees.

According to Jeff, being self-motivated is the main key to success. You need to work hard and success will come. Accounting interested Jeff because he enjoys working with numbers and considers himself to be very analytical.

Wages Expense

Jessie paid her part-time employees $650 on June 27. Since then, they have earned an additional $50, but have not yet been paid. The additional wages expense must be recognized.

Since the employees have not been paid, Wages Payable, a liability, should be established. Thus, Wages Expense is debited and Wages Payable is credited for $50 in Figure 5-7. Note in Figure 5-8 that Wages Expense of $700 is reported on the income statement and Wages Payable of $50 is reported on the balance sheet.

FIGURE 5-7 Adjustment for Unpaid Wages

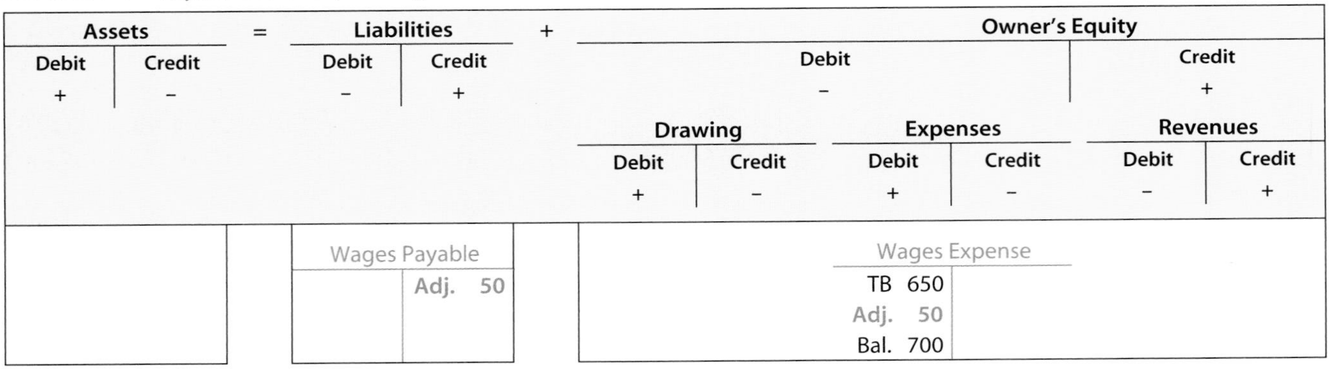

FIGURE 5-8 Effect of Adjusting Entry for Wages on Financial Statements

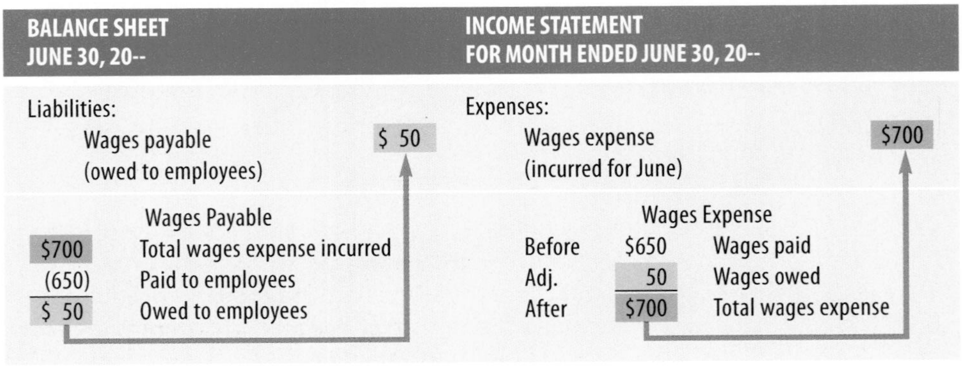

Depreciation Expense

During the month of June, Jessie purchased three motor scooters. Since the scooters will provide future benefits, they were recorded as assets in the delivery equipment account. Under the **historical cost principle**, assets are recorded at their actual cost, in this case $3,600. This cost remains on the books as long as the business owns the asset. No adjustments are made for changes in the market value of the asset. It does not matter whether the firm got a "good buy" or paid "too much" when the asset was purchased.

> ## LEARNING KEY
>
> The historical cost principle is an important accounting concept. Assets are recorded at their actual cost. This historical cost is not adjusted for changes in market values.

To learn about other depreciation methods, see the appendix to this chapter.

The period of time that an asset is expected to help produce revenues is called its **useful life**. The asset's useful life expires as a result of wear and tear or because it no longer satisfies the needs of the business. For example, as Jessie adds miles to her scooters, they will become less reliable and will eventually fail to run. As this happens, depreciation expense should be recognized and the value of the asset should be reduced. **Depreciation** is a method of *matching* an asset's original cost against the revenues produced over its useful life. There are many depreciation methods. In our example, we will use the **straight-line method**.

Depreciation expense is based on estimates of useful lives and salvage values.

Let's assume that Jessie's motor scooters have estimated useful lives of three years and will have no salvage value at the end of that time period. **Salvage value** (also called scrap value, or residual value) is the expected **market value** or selling price of the asset at the end of its useful life. The **depreciable cost** of these scooters is the original cost, less salvage value, or $3,600. It is this amount that is subject to depreciation. Let's also assume that a full month's depreciation is recognized in the month in which an asset is purchased.

The depreciable cost is spread over 36 months (3 years × 12 months). Thus, the straight-line depreciation expense for the month of June is $100 ($3,600 ÷ 36 months).

STRAIGHT-LINE DEPRECIATION				
Original Cost	−	Salvage Value	=	Depreciable Cost
$\dfrac{\text{Depreciable Cost}}{\text{Estimated Useful Life}}$	=	$\dfrac{\$3,600}{36\ \text{months}}$	=	$100 per month

When we made adjustments for supplies and prepaid insurance, the asset accounts were credited to show that they had been consumed. Assets of a durable nature that are expected to provide benefits over several years or more, called **plant assets**, require a different approach. The business maintains a record of the original cost and the amount of depreciation taken since the asset was acquired. By comparing these two amounts, the reader can estimate the relative age of the assets. Thus, instead of crediting Delivery Equipment for the amount of depreciation, a contra-asset account, Accumulated Depreciation—Delivery Equipment, is credited. "Contra" means opposite or against. Thus, a **contra-asset** has a credit balance (the opposite of an asset) and is deducted from the related asset account on the balance sheet.

LEARNING KEY

Depreciable assets provide benefits over more than one year. Therefore, the historical cost of the asset remains in the asset account. To show that it has been depreciated, a *contra-asset* account is used.

As shown in Figure 5-9, the appropriate adjusting entry consists of a debit to Depreciation Expense—Delivery Equipment and a credit to Accumulated Depreciation—Delivery Equipment. Note the position of the accumulated depreciation account in the accounting equation. It is shown in the assets section, directly beneath Delivery Equipment. Contra-asset accounts should always be shown along with the related asset account. Therefore, Delivery Equipment and Accumulated Depreciation—Delivery Equipment are shown together.

FIGURE 5-9 Adjustment for Depreciation of Delivery Equipment

Assets		=	Liabilities		+	Owner's Equity					
Debit	**Credit**		**Debit**	**Credit**		**Debit**				**Credit**	
+	–		–	+		–				+	
Delivery Equipment						**Drawing**		**Expenses**		**Revenues**	
TB 3,600						**Debit**	**Credit**	**Debit**	**Credit**	**Debit**	**Credit**
						+	–	+	–	–	+
Accumulated Depreciation— Delivery Equipment						Depreciation Expense— Delivery Equipment					
	Adj. 100					Adj. 100					

The same concept is used on the balance sheet. Note in Figure 5-10 that Accumulated Depreciation is reported immediately beneath Delivery Equipment as a deduction. The difference between these accounts is known as the **book value,** or **undepreciated cost,** of the delivery equipment. Book value simply means the value carried on the books or in the accounting records. It does *not* represent the market value, or selling price, of the asset.

LEARNING KEY

Book value = Cost of Plant Assets – Accumulated Depreciation

There is no individual account that reports book value. It must be computed.

FIGURE 5-10   Effect of Adjusting Entry for Depreciation on Financial Statements for June

BALANCE SHEET **JUNE 30, 20--**			**INCOME STATEMENT** **FOR MONTH ENDED JUNE 30, 20--**	
Assets:			Expenses:	
Delivery equipment	$3,600		Depreciation expense	$100
Less: Accumulated			(Expired cost for June)	
depreciation	100	$3,500		
		(Book value)		

If no delivery equipment is bought or sold during the next month, the same adjusting entry would be made at the end of July. If an income statement for the month of July and a balance sheet as of July 31 were prepared, the amounts shown in Figure 5-11 would be reported for the delivery equipment.

FIGURE 5-11   Effect of Adjusting Entry for Depreciation on Financial Statements for July

BALANCE SHEET **JULY 31, 20--**			**INCOME STATEMENT** **FOR MONTH ENDED JULY 31, 20--**	
Assets:			Expenses:	
Delivery equipment	$3,600		Depreciation expense	$100
Less: Accumulated			(Expired cost for July)	
depreciation	200	$3,400		
		(Book value)		

The cost ($3,600) remains unchanged, but the accumulated depreciation has increased to $200. This represents *the depreciation that has accumulated* since the delivery equipment was purchased ($100 in June and $100 in July). The depreciation expense for July is $100, the same as reported for June. Depreciation expense is reported for a specific time period. It does not accumulate across reporting periods.

Expanded Chart of Accounts

Several new accounts were needed to make the adjusting entries. New accounts are easily added to the chart of accounts, as shown in Figure 5-12. Note the close relationship between assets and contra-assets in the numbering of the accounts. Contra-accounts carry the same number as the related asset account with a ".1" suffix. For example, Delivery Equipment is account number 185 and the contra-asset account, Accumulated Depreciation—Delivery Equipment, is account number 185.1.

FIGURE 5-12   Expanded Chart of Accounts

JESSIE JANE'S CAMPUS DELIVERY CHART OF ACCOUNTS			
Assets		**Revenues**	
101	Cash	401	Delivery Fees
122	Accounts Receivable		
141	Supplies	**Expenses**	
145	Prepaid Insurance	511	Wages Expense
185	Delivery Equipment	521	Rent Expense
185.1	Accumulated Depr.—	523	Supplies Expense
	Delivery Equipment	525	Telephone Expense
		535	Insurance Expense
Liabilities		541	Depr. Expense—
202	Accounts Payable		Delivery Equipment
219	Wages Payable		
Owner's Equity			
311	Jessica Jane, Capital		
312	Jessica Jane, Drawing		

THE WORK SHEET

LO2   Prepare a work sheet.

A **work sheet** pulls together all of the information needed to enter adjusting entries and prepare the financial statements. Work sheets are not financial statements and are not a formal part of the accounting system. Ordinarily, only the accountant uses a work sheet. For this reason, a work sheet is usually prepared in pencil or as a spreadsheet on a computer.

The 10-Column Work Sheet

Although a work sheet can take several forms, a common format has a column for account titles and 10 amount columns grouped into five pairs. The work sheet format and the five steps in preparing the work sheet are illustrated in Figure 5-13. As with financial statements, the work sheet has a heading consisting of the name of the company, name of the working paper, and the date of the accounting period just ended. The five major column headings for the work sheet are Trial Balance, Adjustments, Adjusted Trial Balance, Income Statement, and Balance Sheet.

Preparing the Work Sheet

Let's apply the five steps required for the preparation of a work sheet to Jessie Jane's Campus Delivery.

STEP 1 **Prepare the Trial Balance.** As shown in Figure 5-14, the first pair of amount columns is for the trial balance. The trial balance assures the equality of the debits and credits before the adjustment process begins. The columns should be double ruled to show that they are equal.

Note that all accounts listed in the expanded chart of accounts are included in the Trial Balance columns of the work sheet. This is done even though some accounts have zero balances. The accounts with zero balances could be added to the bottom of the list as they are needed for adjusting entries. However, it is easier to include them now, especially if preparing the work sheet on an electronic spreadsheet. Listing the accounts within their proper classifications (assets, liabilities, etc.) also makes it easier to extend the amounts to the proper columns.

STEP 2 **Prepare the Adjustments.** As shown in Figure 5-15, the second pair of amount columns is used to prepare the adjusting entries. Enter the adjustments directly in these columns. When an account is debited or credited, the amount is entered on the same line as the name of the account and in the appropriate Adjustments Debit or Credit column. A small letter in parentheses identifies each adjusting entry made on the work sheet.

LEARNING KEY

For adjustments (a), (b), and (d), we are simply recognizing that assets have been used. When this happens, the asset must be decreased and an expense recognized. Note that the reported amount for delivery equipment is reduced by crediting a contra-asset.

ADJUSTMENT (a):
Supplies costing $60 were used during June.

	Debit	Credit
Supplies Expense	60	
Supplies		60

ADJUSTMENT (b):
One month's insurance premium has expired.

	Debit	Credit
Insurance Expense	25	
Prepaid Insurance		25

ADJUSTMENT (c):
Employees earned $50 that has not yet been paid.

	Debit	Credit
Wages Expense	50	
Wages Payable		50

LEARNING KEY

Adjustment (c) recognizes an economic event that has not required an actual transaction yet. Employees earned wages, but have not been paid. The adjustment recognizes an expense and a liability.

ADJUSTMENT (d):
Depreciation on the motor scooters is recognized.

	Debit	Credit
Depreciation Expense—Delivery Equipment	100	
Accumulated Depreciation—Delivery Equipment		100

When all adjustments have been entered on the work sheet, each column should be totaled to assure that the debits equal the credits for all entries. After balancing the columns, they should be double ruled.

STEP 3   **Prepare the Adjusted Trial Balance.** As shown in Figure 5-16, the third pair of amount columns on the work sheet are the **Adjusted Trial Balance columns.** When an account balance is not affected by entries in the Adjustments columns, the amount in the Trial Balance columns is extended directly to the Adjusted Trial Balance columns. *When affected by an entry in the Adjustments columns, the balance to be entered in the Adjusted Trial Balance columns increases or decreases by the amount of the adjusting entry.*

For example, in Jessica Jane's business, Supplies is listed in the Trial Balance Debit column as $80. Since the entry of $60 is in the Adjustments Credit column, the amount extended to the Adjusted Trial Balance Debit column is $20 ($80 − $60).

Wages Expense is listed in the Trial Balance Debit column as $650. Since $50 is in the Adjustments Debit column, the amount extended to the Adjusted Trial Balance Debit column is $700 ($650 + $50).

After all extensions have been made, the Adjusted Trial Balance columns are totaled to prove the equality of the debits and the credits. Once balanced, the columns are double ruled.

STEP 4   **Extend Adjusted Balances to the Income Statement and Balance Sheet Columns.** As shown in Figure 5-17, each account listed in the Adjusted Trial Balance must be extended to either the Income Statement or Balance Sheet columns. The **Income Statement columns** show the amounts that will be reported in the income statement. All revenue accounts are extended to the Income Statement Credit column and expense accounts are extended to the Income Statement Debit column.

The asset, liability, drawing, and capital accounts are extended to the **Balance Sheet columns.** Although called the Balance Sheet columns, these columns of the work sheet show the amounts that will be reported in the balance sheet and the statement of owner's equity. The asset and drawing accounts are extended to the Balance Sheet Debit column. The liability and owner's capital accounts are extended to the Balance Sheet Credit column.

LEARNING KEY

The Balance Sheet columns show the amounts for both the balance sheet and the statement of owner's equity.

FIGURE 5-13   Steps in Preparing the Work Sheet

Name of Company
Work Sheet
For Month Ended June 30, 20 - -

ACCOUNT TITLE	TRIAL BALANCE		ADJUSTMENTS		ADJUSTED TRIAL BALANCE		INCOME STATEMENT		BALANCE SHEET		
	DEBIT	CREDIT	DEBIT	CREDIT	DEBIT	CREDIT	DEBIT	CREDIT	DEBIT	CREDIT	
Insert ledger account titles	STEP 1 Prepare the trial balance		STEP 2 Prepare the adjustments		STEP 3 Prepare the adjusted trial balance		STEP 4 Extend adjusted account balances				1
											2
											3
											4
											5
											6
	Assets				Assets				Assets		7
		Liabilities				Liabilities				Liabilities	8
		Capital				Capital				Capital	9
	Drawing				Drawing				Drawing		10
		Revenues				Revenues		Revenues			11
	Expenses				Expenses		Expenses				12
											13
											14
											15
											16
											17
											18
											19
							STEP 5 Complete the work sheet				20
							1. Sum columns				21
							2. Compute net income (loss)				22
											23
											24
											25
							Net Income	Net Loss	Net Loss	Net Income	26
											27
											28
											29
											30

FIGURE 5-14   Step 1—Prepare the Trial Balance

Jessica Jane's Campus Delivery
Work Sheet
For Month Ended June 30, 20 - -

	ACCOUNT TITLE	TRIAL BALANCE DEBIT	TRIAL BALANCE CREDIT	ADJUSTMENTS DEBIT	ADJUSTMENTS CREDIT	ADJUSTED TRIAL BALANCE DEBIT	ADJUSTED TRIAL BALANCE CREDIT	INCOME STATEMENT DEBIT	INCOME STATEMENT CREDIT	BALANCE SHEET DEBIT	BALANCE SHEET CREDIT	
1	Cash	3 7 0 00										1
2	Accounts Receivable	6 5 0 00										2
3	Supplies	8 0 00										3
4	Prepaid Insurance	2 0 0 00										4
5	Delivery Equipment	3 6 0 0 00										5
6	Accum. Depr.—Delivery Equipment											6
7	Accounts Payable		1 8 0 0 00									7
8	Wages Payable											8
9	Jessica Jane, Capital		2 0 0 0 00									9
10	Jessica Jane, Drawing	1 5 0 00										10
11	Delivery Fees		2 1 5 0 00									11
12	Wages Expense	6 5 0 00										12
13	Rent Expense	2 0 0 00										13
14	Supplies Expense											14
15	Telephone Expense	5 0 00										15
16	Insurance Expense											16
17	Depr. Expense—Delivery Equipment											17
18		5 9 5 0 00	5 9 5 0 00									18
19												19
20												20
21												21
22												22
23												23
24												24
25												25
26												26
27												27
28												28
29												29
30												30

STEP 1

Preparing the Work Sheet

STEP 1   Prepare the Trial Balance.

- Write the heading, account titles, and the debit and credit amounts from the general ledger.
- Place a single rule across the Trial Balance columns and total the debit and credit amounts.
- Place a double rule under the totals for each column.
- Total debits must equal total credits.

STEP 2   Prepare the Adjustments.

- Record the adjustments.

    Hint: Make certain that each adjustment is on the same line as the account name and in the appropriate column.

    Hint: Identify each adjusting entry by a letter in parentheses.

- Rule the Adjusted Trial Balance columns.
- Total the debit and credit columns and double rule the columns.
- Total debits must equal total credits.

STEP 3   Prepare the Adjusted Trial Balance.

- Extend those debits and credits that are not adjusted directly to the appropriate Adjusted Trial Balance column.
- Enter the adjusted balances in the appropriate Adjusted Trial Balance column.

    Hint: If an account has a debit and a credit, subtract the adjustment. If an account has two debits or two credits, add the adjustment.

- Single rule the Adjusted Trial Balance columns. Total and double rule the debit and credit columns.
- Total debits must equal total credits.

STEP 4   Extend Adjusted Balances to the Income Statement and Balance Sheet Columns.

- Extend all revenue accounts to the Income Statement Credit column.
- Extend all expense accounts to the Income Statement Debit column.
- Extend the asset and drawing accounts to the Balance Sheet Debit column.
- Extend the liability and owner's capital accounts to the Balance Sheet Credit column.

STEP 5   Complete the Work Sheet.

- Rule and total the Income Statement and Balance Sheet columns.
- Calculate the difference between the Income Statement Debit and Credit columns.
- Calculate the difference between the Balance Sheet Debit and Credit columns.

    Hint: If the Income Statement credits exceed debits, net income has occurred; otherwise, a net loss has occurred. If the Balance Sheet debits exceed the credits, the difference is net income; otherwise, a net loss has occurred.

    Hint: The difference between the Balance Sheet columns should be the same as the difference between the Income Statement columns.

- Add the net income to the Income Statement Debit column or add the net loss to the Income Statement Credit column. Add the net income to the Balance Sheet Credit column or the net loss to the Balance Sheet Debit column.
- Total and double rule the columns.

STEP 5 **Complete the Work Sheet.** To complete the work sheet, first total the Income Statement columns. If the total of the credits (revenues) exceeds the total of the debits (expenses), the difference represents net income. If the total of the debits exceeds the total of the credits, the difference represents a net loss.

The Income Statement columns of Jessie's work sheet in Figure 5-18 show total credits of $2,150 and total debits of $1,135. The difference, $1,015, is the net income for the month of June. This amount should be added to the Debit column to balance the Income Statement columns. "Net Income" should be written on the same line in the Account Title column. If the business had a net loss, the amount of the loss would be added to the Income Statement Credit column and the words "Net Loss" would be written in the Account Title column. Once balanced, the columns should be double ruled.

Finally, the Balance Sheet columns are totaled. The difference between the totals of these columns also is the amount of net income or net loss for the accounting period. If the total debits exceed the total credits, the difference is net income. If the total credits exceed the total debits, the difference is a net loss. This difference should be the same as the difference we found for the Income Statement columns.

LEARNING KEY

In the Balance Sheet columns of the work sheet, total debits minus total credits equals net income if greater than zero and equals net loss if less than zero.

The Balance Sheet columns of Jessie's work sheet show total debits of $4,965 and total credits of $3,950. The difference of $1,015 represents the amount of net income for the month. This amount is added to the Credit column to balance the Balance Sheet columns. If the business had a net loss, this amount would be added to the Balance Sheet Debit column. Once balanced, the columns should be double ruled.

A trick for remembering the appropriate placement of the net income and net loss is the following: Net Income *apart*; Net Loss *together*. Figure 5-19 illustrates this learning aid.

FIGURE 5-19 Net Income Apart, Net Loss Together

Net Income

	INCOME STATEMENT		BALANCE SHEET	
	DEBIT	CREDIT	DEBIT	CREDIT
	1135 00	2000 00	4815 00	3950 00
Net Income	865 00			865 00
	2000 00	2000 00	4815 00	4815 00

Apart

Net Loss

	INCOME STATEMENT		BALANCE SHEET	
	DEBIT	CREDIT	DEBIT	CREDIT
	2500 00	2000 00	5015 00	5515 00
Net Loss		500 00	500 00	
	2500 00	2500 00	5515 00	5515 00

Together

FINDING ERRORS ON THE WORK SHEET

LO3   Describe methods for finding errors on the work sheet.

If any of the columns on the work sheet do not balance, you must find the error before you continue. Once you are confident that the work sheet is accurate, you are ready to journalize the adjusting entries and prepare financial statements. Figure 5-20 offers tips for finding errors on the work sheet.

FIGURE 5-20   Finding Errors on the Work Sheet

TIPS FOR FINDING ERRORS ON THE WORK SHEET

1. Check the addition of all columns.

2. Check the addition and subtraction required when extending to the Adjusted Trial Balance columns.

3. Make sure the adjusted account balances have been extended to the appropriate columns.

4. Make sure that the net income or net loss has been added to the appropriate columns.

JOURNALIZING ADJUSTING ENTRIES

LO4   Journalize adjusting entries.

Keep in mind that the work sheet simply helps the accountant organize the end-of-period work. *Writing the adjustments on the work sheet has no effect on the ledger accounts in the accounting system. The only way to change the balance of a ledger account is to make a journal entry.* Once the adjustments have been entered on the work sheet, simply copy the adjustments from the work sheet to the journal.

Jessie's adjusting entries are illustrated in Figure 5-21 as they would appear in a general journal. Note that the last day of the accounting period, June 30, has been entered in the date column and *"Adjusting Entries"* is written in the Description column prior to the first adjusting entry. No explanation is required in the Description column for individual adjusting entries. We simply label them as adjusting entries.

FIGURE 5-21   Adjusting Entries

GENERAL JOURNAL   PAGE 3

		DATE		DESCRIPTION	POST. REF.	DEBIT			CREDIT			
	1			Adjusting Entries								1
1	2	20-- June	30	Supplies Expense	523	6	0	00				2
	3			Supplies	141				6	0	00	3
	4											4
2	5		30	Insurance Expense	535	2	5	00				5
	6			Prepaid Insurance	145				2	5	00	6
	7											7
3	8		30	Wages Expense	511	5	0	00				8
	9			Wages Payable	219				5	0	00	9
	10											10
4	11		30	Depr. Expense — Delivery Equipment	541	1	0	0	00			11
	12			Accum. Depr. — Delivery Equipment	185.1				1	0	0	00	12

POSTING ADJUSTING ENTRIES

LO5 Post adjusting entries to the general ledger.

Adjusting entries are posted to the general ledger in the same manner as all other entries, except that "*Adjusting*" is written in the Item column of the general ledger. Figure 5-22 shows the posting of the adjusting entries. The posting reference numbers are inserted as each entry is posted.

METHODS OF ACCOUNTING: CASH, MODIFIED CASH, AND ACCRUAL

LO6 Explain the cash, modified cash, and accrual bases of accounting.

The accrual basis of accounting offers the best matching of revenues and expenses and is required under generally accepted accounting principles. GAAP financial statements prepared using the accrual method are particularly important when major businesses want to raise large amounts of money. Investors and creditors expect GAAP financial statements and generally will not invest or make loans without them. However, many small professional service organizations are not concerned with raising large amounts of money from investors and creditors. These organizations include CPAs, doctors, dentists, lawyers, engineers, and architects. Since these organizations do not need to prepare GAAP financial statements, they often use the cash or modified cash basis. If one of these organizations needs to borrow money from a bank that requires GAAP financial statements, an accountant can convert the financial statements to the accrual basis.

Under the **accrual basis of accounting**, revenues are recorded when earned. Revenues are considered earned when a service is provided or a product sold, regardless of whether cash is received. If cash is not received, a receivable is set up. The accrual basis also assumes that expenses are recorded when incurred. Expenses are incurred when a service is received or an asset consumed, regardless of when cash is paid. If cash is not paid when a service is received, a payable is set up. When assets are consumed, prepaid assets are decreased or long-term assets are depreciated. Since the accrual basis accounts for long-term assets, prepaid assets, receivables, and payables, it is the most comprehensive system and best method of measuring income for the vast majority of businesses.

FIGURE 5-22   Posting the Adjusting Entries

GENERAL LEDGER

1

ACCOUNT: **Supplies**   ACCOUNT NO. 141

DATE		ITEM	POST. REF.	DEBIT	CREDIT	BALANCE	
						DEBIT	CREDIT
20-- June	16		J1	8 0 00		8 0 00	
	30	Adjusting	J3		6 0 00	2 0 00	

ACCOUNT: **Supplies Expense**   ACCOUNT NO. 523

DATE		ITEM	POST. REF.	DEBIT	CREDIT	BALANCE	
						DEBIT	CREDIT
20-- June	30	Adjusting	J3	6 0 00		6 0 00	

2

ACCOUNT: **Prepaid Insurance**   ACCOUNT NO. 145

DATE		ITEM	POST. REF.	DEBIT	CREDIT	BALANCE	
						DEBIT	CREDIT
20-- June	18		J1	2 0 0 00		2 0 0 00	
	30	Adjusting	J3		2 5 00	1 7 5 00	

ACCOUNT: **Insurance Expense**   ACCOUNT NO. 535

DATE		ITEM	POST. REF.	DEBIT	CREDIT	BALANCE	
						DEBIT	CREDIT
20-- June	30	Adjusting	J3	2 5 00		2 5 00	

3

ACCOUNT: **Wages Payable**   ACCOUNT NO. 219

DATE		ITEM	POST. REF.	DEBIT	CREDIT	BALANCE	
						DEBIT	CREDIT
20-- June	30	Adjusting	J3		5 0 00		5 0 00

ACCOUNT: **Wages Expense**   ACCOUNT NO. 511

DATE		ITEM	POST. REF.	DEBIT	CREDIT	BALANCE	
						DEBIT	CREDIT
20-- June	27		J1	6 5 0 00		6 5 0 00	
	30	Adjusting	J3	5 0 00		7 0 0 00	

4

ACCOUNT: **Accumulated Depreciation—Delivery Equipment**   ACCOUNT NO. 185.1

DATE		ITEM	POST. REF.	DEBIT	CREDIT	BALANCE	
						DEBIT	CREDIT
20-- June	30	Adjusting	J3		1 0 0 00		1 0 0 00

ACCOUNT: **Depreciation Expense—Delivery Equipment**   ACCOUNT NO. 541

DATE		ITEM	POST. REF.	DEBIT	CREDIT	BALANCE	
						DEBIT	CREDIT
20-- June	30	Adjusting	J3	1 0 0 00		1 0 0 00	

LEARNING KEY

Accrual Basis

Accounting for:

Revenues and Expenses	**Assets and Liabilities**	
Record revenue when earned.	Accounts receivable:	Yes
Record expenses when incurred.	Accounts payable:	Yes
	Prepaid assets:	Yes
	Long-term assets:	Yes

Under the **cash basis of accounting,** revenues are recorded when cash is received and expenses are recorded when cash is paid. This method will provide results that are similar to the accrual basis if there are few receivables, payables, and assets. However, as shown in Figure 5-23, the cash and accrual bases can result in very different measures of net income if a business has significant amounts of receivables, payables, and assets.

LEARNING KEY

Cash Basis

Accounting for:

Revenues and Expenses	**Assets and Liabilities**	
Record revenue when cash is received.	Accounts receivable:	No
Record expenses when cash is paid.	Accounts payable:	No
	Prepaid assets:	No
	Long-term assets:	No

FIGURE 5-23   Cash versus Accrual Accounting

RECOGNITION OF REVENUES AND EXPENSES: ACCRUAL BASIS VS. CASH BASIS

	Transaction	Method of Accounting			
		Accrual Basis		**Cash Basis**	
		Expense	**Revenue**	**Expense**	**Revenue**
(a)	Provided services on account, $600.		$600		
(b)	Paid wages, $300.	$300		$300	
(c)	Received cash for services performed on account last month, $200.				$200
(d)	Received cleaning bill for month, $250.	250			
(e)	Paid on account for last month's advertising, $100.			100	
(f)	Purchase of supplies, $50.			50	
(g)	Supplies used during month, $40.	40			
		$590	$600	$450	$200

	Accrual Basis	Cash Basis
Revenue	$600	$200
Expense	590	450
Net Income (Loss)	$ 10	($250)
Revenues are recognized when:	earned	cash is received
Expenses are recognized when:	incurred	cash is paid

The modified cash basis is the same as the accrual basis, except receivables and payables are not recognized for revenues and operating expenses.

A third method of accounting combines aspects of the cash and accrual methods. With the **modified cash basis**, a business uses the cash basis for recording revenues and most expenses. Exceptions are made when cash is paid for assets with useful lives greater than one accounting period. For example, under a strict cash basis, if cash is paid for equipment, buildings, supplies, or insurance, the amount is immediately recorded as an expense. This approach could cause major distortions when measuring net income. Under the modified cash basis, cash payments like these are recorded as assets, and adjustments are made each period as under the accrual basis. Liabilities associated with the acquisition of these assets are also recognized.

Although similar to the accrual basis, the modified cash basis does not account for receivables or for payables for services received. Thus, the modified cash basis is a combination of the cash and accrual methods of accounting. The differences and similarities among the cash, modified cash, and accrual methods of accounting are demonstrated in Figure 5-24.

LEARNING KEY

Modified Cash Basis

Accounting for:

Revenues and Expenses

Record revenue when cash is received.

Record expenses when cash is paid, except for assets with useful lives greater than one accounting period. Accrual accounting is used for prepaid assets (insurance and supplies) and long-term assets.

Assets and Liabilities

Accounts receivable:	No
Accounts payable	
for purchase of assets:	Yes
for services received:	No
Prepaid assets:	Yes
Long-term assets:	Yes

If all businesses were the same, only one method of accounting would be needed. However, businesses vary in their need for major assets like buildings and equipment, the amount of customer receivables, and payables to suppliers. For example, if a business were rather small with no major assets, receivables, or payables, it would be simpler to use the cash basis of accounting. In addition, under these circumstances, the difference in net income under the accrual and cash bases of accounting would be small. Most individuals fit this description and use the cash basis on their tax returns.

Businesses with buildings and equipment, but few receivables and payables, might use the modified cash basis. Again, the accounting would be a little simpler and differences between net income computed under the modified cash and accrual bases would be small. Finally, businesses with buildings and equipment, and receivables and payables, should use the accrual basis of accounting to achieve the best matching of revenues and expenses.

LEARNING KEY

The shaded areas show that sometimes the modified cash basis is the same as the cash basis and sometimes it is the same as the accrual basis. For some transactions, all methods are the same.

FIGURE 5-24 Comparison of Cash, Modified Cash, and Accrual Methods

ENTRIES MADE UNDER EACH ACCOUNTING METHOD

Event	Cash	Modified Cash	Accrual
Revenues: Perform services for cash	Cash 　Professional Fees	Cash 　Professional Fees	Cash 　Professional Fees
Perform services on account	No entry	No entry	Accounts Receivable 　Professional Fees
Expenses: Pay cash for operating expenses: wages, advertising, rent, telephone, etc.	Expense 　Cash	Expense 　Cash	Expense 　Cash
Pay cash for prepaid items: insurance, supplies, etc.	Expense 　Cash	Prepaid Asset 　Cash	Prepaid Asset 　Cash
Pay cash for property, plant, and equipment (PP&E)	Expense 　Cash	PP&E Asset 　Cash	PP&E Asset 　Cash
Receive bill for services received	No entry	No entry	Expense 　Accounts Payable
End-of-period adjustments: Wages earned by employees but not paid	No entry	No entry	Wages Expense 　Wages Payable
Prepaid items used	No entry	Expense 　Prepaid Asset	Expense 　Prepaid Asset
Depreciation on property, plant, and equipment	No entry	Depreciation Expense 　Accumulated Depreciation	Depreciation Expense 　Accumulated Depreciation
Other: Purchase of assets on account	No entry	Asset 　Accounts Payable	Asset 　Accounts Payable
Payments for assets purchased on account	Expense 　Cash	Accounts Payable 　Cash	Accounts Payable 　Cash

Learning Objectives	Key Points to Remember
LO1 Prepare end-of-period adjustments.	End-of-period adjustments are necessary to bring the general ledger accounts up to date prior to preparing financial statements. Reasons to adjust the trial balance are: 1. To report all revenues earned during the accounting period. 2. To report all expenses incurred to produce the revenues during the accounting period. 3. To accurately report the assets on the balance sheet. Some assets may have expired, depreciated, or been used up during the accounting period. 4. To accurately report the liabilities on the balance sheet date. Expenses may have been incurred, but not yet paid.
LO2 Prepare a work sheet.	Steps in preparing the work sheet are: 1. Prepare the trial balance. 2. Prepare the adjustments. 3. Prepare the adjusted trial balance. 4. Extend the adjusted account balances to the Income Statement and Balance Sheet columns. 5. Total the Income Statement and Balance Sheet columns to compute the net income or net loss.
LO3 Describe methods for finding errors on the work sheet.	Tips for finding errors on the work sheet include: 1. Check the addition of all columns. 2. Check the addition and subtraction required when extending to the Adjusted Trial Balance columns. 3. Make sure the adjusted account balances have been extended to the appropriate columns. 4. Make sure that the net income or net loss has been added to the appropriate columns.
LO4 Journalize adjusting entries.	The adjustments are copied from the work sheet to the journal. The last day of the accounting period is entered in the Date column and "Adjusting Entries" is written in the Description column.
LO5 Post adjusting entries to the general ledger.	Adjusting entries are posted to the general ledger in the same manner as all other entries, except that "Adjusting" is written in the Item column of the general ledger.
LO6 Explain the cash, modified cash, and accrual bases of accounting.	Cash Basis—Record revenues when cash is received and expenses when cash is paid. Accrual Basis—Record revenues when earned and expenses as incurred. Modified Cash Basis—Same as accrual, except no accounts receivable and no accounts payable for operating expenses.

DEMONSTRATION PROBLEM

Justin Park is a lawyer specializing in corporate tax law. He began his practice on January 1. A chart of accounts and trial balance taken on December 31, 20--, are provided below.

Information for year-end adjustments:

(a)   Office supplies on hand at year-end amounted to $300.

(b)   On January 1, 20--, Park purchased office equipment costing $15,000 with an expected life of five years and no salvage value.

(c)   Computer equipment costing $6,000 with an expected life of three years and no salvage value was purchased on July 1, 20--. Assume that Park computes depreciation to the nearest full month.

(d)   A premium of $1,200 for a one-year insurance policy was paid on December 1, 20--.

(e)   Wages earned by Park's part-time secretary, which have not yet been paid, amount to $300.

REQUIRED

1.   Prepare the work sheet for the year ended December 31, 20--.

2.   Prepare adjusting entries in a general journal.

JUSTIN PARK LEGAL SERVICES CHART OF ACCOUNTS			
Assets		**Revenue**	
101	Cash	401	Client Fees
142	Office Supplies		
145	Prepaid Insurance	**Expenses**	
181	Office Equipment	511	Wages Expense
181.1	Accumulated Depr.—	521	Rent Expense
	Office Equipment	523	Office Supplies Expense
187	Computer Equipment	525	Telephone Expense
187.1	Accumulated Depr.—	533	Utilities Expense
	Computer Equipment	535	Insurance Expense
Liabilities		541	Depr. Expense—
201	Notes Payable		Office Equipment
202	Accounts Payable	542	Depr. Expense—
219	Wages Payable		Computer Equipment
Owner's Equity			
311	Justin Park, Capital		
312	Justin Park, Drawing		

Justin Park Legal Services Trial Balance December 31, 20 - -											
ACCOUNT TITLE	ACCOUNT NO.	DEBIT BALANCE					CREDIT BALANCE				
Cash	101	7	0	0	0	00					
Office Supplies	142		8	0	0	00					
Prepaid Insurance	145	1	2	0	0	00					
Office Equipment	181	15	0	0	0	00					
Computer Equipment	187	6	0	0	0	00					
Notes Payable	201						5	0	0	0	00
Accounts Payable	202							5	0	0	00
Justin Park, Capital	311						11	4	0	0	00
Justin Park, Drawing	312	5	0	0	0	00					
Client Fees	401						40	0	0	0	00
Wages Expense	511	12	0	0	0	00					
Rent Expense	521	5	0	0	0	00					
Telephone Expense	525	1	0	0	0	00					
Utilities Expense	533	3	9	0	0	00					
		56	9	0	0	00	56	9	0	0	00

The solution to part (1) is found on p. 154.

2.

		GENERAL JOURNAL					PAGE 11			
	DATE	DESCRIPTION	POST. REF.	DEBIT				CREDIT		
1		Adjusting Entries								1
2	20-- Dec. 31	Office Supplies Expense			5	0	0	00		2
3		Office Supplies				5	0	0	00	3
4										4
5	31	Depr. Expense—Office Equipment		3	0	0	0	00		5
6		Accum. Depr.—Office Equipment				3	0	0	0	00	6
7										7
8	31	Depr. Expense—Computer Equipment		1	0	0	0	00		8
9		Accum. Depr.—Computer Equipment				1	0	0	0	00	9
10										10
11	31	Insurance Expense			1	0	0	00		11
12		Prepaid Insurance				1	0	0	00	12
13										13
14	31	Wages Expense			3	0	0	00		14
15		Wages Payable				3	0	0	00	15

(continued)

Solution

1.

Justin Park Legal Services
Work Sheet
For Year Ended December 31, 20--

Account Title	Trial Balance Debit	Trial Balance Credit	Adjustments Debit	Adjustments Credit	Adjusted Trial Balance Debit	Adjusted Trial Balance Credit	Income Statement Debit	Income Statement Credit	Balance Sheet Debit	Balance Sheet Credit
1 Cash	7 0 0 0 00				7 0 0 0 00				7 0 0 0 00	
2 Office Supplies	8 0 0 00			(a) 5 0 0 00	3 0 0 00				3 0 0 00	
3 Prepaid Insurance	1 2 0 0 00			(d) 1 0 0 00	1 1 0 0 00				1 1 0 0 00	
4 Office Equipment	15 0 0 0 00				15 0 0 0 00				15 0 0 0 00	
5 Accum. Depr.—Office Equip.				(b) 3 0 0 0 00		3 0 0 0 00				3 0 0 0 00
6 Computer Equipment	6 0 0 0 00				6 0 0 0 00				6 0 0 0 00	
7 Accum. Depr.—Computer Equip.				(c) 1 0 0 0 00		1 0 0 0 00				1 0 0 0 00
8 Notes Payable		5 0 0 0 00				5 0 0 0 00				5 0 0 0 00
9 Accounts Payable		5 0 0 0 00				5 0 0 0 00				5 0 0 0 00
10 Wages Payable				(e) 3 0 0 00		3 0 0 00				3 0 0 00
11 Justin Park, Capital		6 9 0 0 00				6 9 0 0 00				6 9 0 0 00
12 Justin Park, Drawing	5 0 0 0 00				5 0 0 0 00				5 0 0 0 00	
13 Client Fees		40 0 0 0 00				40 0 0 0 00		40 0 0 0 00		
14 Wages Expense	12 0 0 0 00		(e) 3 0 0 00		12 3 0 0 00		12 3 0 0 00			
15 Rent Expense	5 0 0 0 00				5 0 0 0 00		5 0 0 0 00			
16 Office Supplies Expense			(a) 5 0 0 00		5 0 0 00		5 0 0 00			
17 Telephone Expense	1 0 0 0 00				1 0 0 0 00		1 0 0 0 00			
18 Utilities Expense	3 9 0 0 00				3 9 0 0 00		3 9 0 0 00			
19 Insurance Expense			(d) 1 0 0 00		1 0 0 00		1 0 0 00			
20 Depr. Expense—Office Equip.			(b) 3 0 0 0 00		3 0 0 0 00		3 0 0 0 00			
21 Depr. Expense—Computer Equip.			(c) 1 0 0 0 00		1 0 0 0 00		1 0 0 0 00			
22	56 9 0 0 00	56 9 0 0 00	4 9 0 0 00	4 9 0 0 00	61 2 0 0 00	61 2 0 0 00	26 8 0 0 00	40 0 0 0 00	34 4 0 0 00	21 2 0 0 00
23 Net Income							13 2 0 0 00			13 2 0 0 00
24							40 0 0 0 00	40 0 0 0 00	34 4 0 0 00	34 4 0 0 00

KEY TERMS

accrual basis of accounting (146)   A method of accounting under which revenues are recorded when earned and expenses are recorded when incurred.

Adjusted Trial Balance columns (144)   The third pair of amount columns on the work sheet. They are used to prove the equality of the debits and credits in the general ledger accounts after making all end-of-period adjustments.

adjusting entries (134)   Journal entries made at the end of an accounting period to reflect changes in account balances that are not the direct result of an exchange with an outside party.

Balance Sheet columns (144)   The work sheet columns that show the amounts that will be reported in the balance sheet and the statement of owner's equity.

book value (140)   The difference between the asset account and its related accumulated depreciation account. The value reflected by the accounting records.

cash basis of accounting (148)   A method of accounting under which revenues are recorded when cash is received and expenses are recorded when cash is paid.

contra-asset (140)   An account with a credit balance that is deducted from the related asset account on the balance sheet.

depreciable cost (139)   The cost of an asset that is subject to depreciation.

depreciation (139)   A method of matching an asset's original cost against the revenues produced over its useful life.

fiscal year (134)   A 12-month period for which financial reports are prepared.

historical cost principle (139)   A principle that requires assets to be recorded at their actual cost.

Income Statement columns (144)   The work sheet columns that show the amounts that will be reported in the income statement.

market value (139)   The amount an item can be sold for under normal economic conditions.

matching principle (134)   A principle that requires the matching of revenues earned during an accounting period with the expenses incurred to produce the revenues.

modified cash basis (149)   A method of accounting that combines aspects of the cash and accrual methods. It uses the cash basis for recording revenues and most expenses. Exceptions are made when cash is paid for assets with useful lives greater than one accounting period.

plant assets (139)   Assets of a durable nature that will be used for operations over several years. Examples include buildings and equipment.

salvage value (139)   The expected market value of an asset at the end of its useful life.

straight-line method (138)   A depreciation method in which the depreciable cost is divided by the estimated useful life.

undepreciated cost (140)   The difference between the asset account and its related accumulated depreciation account. Also known as book value.

useful life (139)   The period of time that an asset is expected to help produce revenues.

work sheet (142)   A form used to pull together all of the information needed to enter adjusting entries and prepare the financial statements.

Self-Study Test Questions

True/False

1. The matching principle in accounting requires the matching of debits and credits.

2. Adjusting entries are required at the end of the accounting period because of mistakes in the journal and ledger.

3. As part of the adjustment of supplies, an expense account is debited and Supplies is credited for the amount of supplies used during the accounting period.

4. Depreciable cost is the difference between the original cost of the asset and its accumulated depreciation.

5. The purpose of depreciation is to record the asset's market value in the accounting records.

Multiple Choice

1. The purpose of depreciation is to

   (a) spread the cost of an asset over its useful life.
   (b) show the current market value of an asset.
   (c) set up a reserve fund to purchase a new asset.
   (d) expense the asset in the year it was purchased.

2. Depreciable cost is the

   (a) difference between original cost and accumulated depreciation.
   (b) difference in actual cost and true market value.
   (c) difference between original cost and estimated salvage value.
   (d) difference between estimated salvage value and the actual salvage value.

3. Book value is the

   (a) difference between market value and estimated value.
   (b) difference between market value and historical cost.
   (c) difference between original cost and salvage value.
   (d) difference between original cost and accumulated depreciation.

4. The adjustment for wages earned but not yet paid is

   (a) debit Wages Payable and credit Wages Expense.
   (b) debit Wages Expense and credit Cash.
   (c) debit Wages Expense and credit Wages Payable.
   (d) debit Wages Expense and credit Accounts Receivable.

5. The first step in preparing a work sheet is to

   (a) prepare the trial balance.
   (b) prepare the adjustments.
   (c) prepare the adjusted trial balance.
   (d) extend the amounts from the Adjusted Trial Balance to the Income Statement and Balance Sheet columns.

The answers to the Self-Study Test Questions are at the end of the text.

REVIEW QUESTIONS

LO1   1. Explain the matching principle.

LO1   2. Explain the historical cost principle.

LO1   3. Describe a plant asset.

LO1   4. What is a contra-asset?

LO1   5. What is the useful life of an asset?

LO1   6. What is the purpose of depreciation?

LO1   7. What is an asset's depreciable cost?

LO1   8. What is the book value of an asset?

LO2   9. Explain the purpose of the work sheet.

LO2   10. Identify the five major column headings on a work sheet.

LO2   11. List the five steps taken in preparing a work sheet.

LO3   12. Describe four tips for finding errors on the work sheet.

LO6   13. Explain when revenues are recorded under the cash basis, modified cash basis, and accrual basis of accounting.

LO6   14. Explain when expenses are recorded under the cash basis, modified cash basis, and accrual basis of accounting.

© DIGITAL IMAGING GROUP

REVISITING THE OPENER

In the chapter opener on page 133, you are asked to consider whether it is appropriate to make adjustments to selected trial balance accounts before preparing the financial statements. Please draft a brief memo explaining whether adjustments are necessary and, if so, the types of adjustments that should be made.

SERIES A EXERCISES

E 5-1A (LO1)

ADJUSTMENT FOR SUPPLIES On December 31, the trial balance indicates that the supplies account has a balance, prior to the adjusting entry, of $320. A physical count of the supplies inventory shows that $90 of supplies remain. Analyze this adjustment for supplies using T accounts, and then formally enter this adjustment in the general journal.

E 5-2A (LO1)

ADJUSTMENT FOR INSURANCE On December 1, a six-month liability insurance policy was purchased for $900. Analyze the required adjustment as of December 31 using T accounts, and then formally enter this adjustment in the general journal.

E 5-3A (LO1)

ADJUSTMENT FOR WAGES On December 31, the trial balance shows wages expense of $600. An additional $200 of wages was earned by the employees, but has not yet been paid. Analyze this adjustment for wages using T accounts, and then formally enter this adjustment in the general journal.

E 5-4A (LO1)

ADJUSTMENT FOR DEPRECIATION OF ASSET On December 1, delivery equipment was purchased for $7,200. The delivery equipment has an estimated useful life of four years (48 months) and no salvage value. Using the straight-line depreciation method, analyze the necessary adjusting entry as of December 31 (one month) using T accounts, and then formally enter this adjustment in the general journal.

E 5-5A (LO1)

CALCULATION OF BOOK VALUE On June 1, 20--, a depreciable asset was acquired for $5,400. The asset has an estimated useful life of five years (60 months) and no salvage value. Using the straight-line depreciation method, calculate the book value as of December 31, 20--.

E 5-6A (LO1)

ANALYSIS OF ADJUSTING ENTRY FOR SUPPLIES Analyze each situation and indicate the correct dollar amount for the adjusting entry. (Trial balance is abbreviated as TB.)

1. Ending inventory of supplies is $130.

(Balance Sheet) Supplies		(Income Statement) Supplies Expense	
TB	460		
	Adj. _____	Adj. _____	
Bal. _____			

2. Amount of supplies used is $320.

(Balance Sheet) Supplies		(Income Statement) Supplies Expense	
TB	545		
	Adj. _____	Adj. _____	
Bal. _____			

E 5-7A (LO1)

ANALYSIS OF ADJUSTING ENTRY FOR INSURANCE Analyze each situation and indicate the correct dollar amount for the adjusting entry.

1. Amount of insurance expired is $900.

(Balance Sheet) Prepaid Insurance		(Income Statement) Insurance Expense	
TB	1,300		
	Adj. _____	Adj. _____	
Bal. _____			

2. Amount of unexpired insurance is $185.

(Balance Sheet) Prepaid Insurance		(Income Statement) Insurance Expense	
TB	860		
	Adj. _____	Adj. _____	
Bal. _____			

E 5-8A (LO2)

✓ Adjustments col. total: $1,550

WORK SHEET AND ADJUSTING ENTRIES A partial work sheet for Jim Jacobs' Furniture Repair is shown as follows. Indicate by letters (a) through (d) the four adjustments in the Adjustments columns of the work sheet, properly matching each debit and credit. Complete the Adjustments columns.

Jim Jacobs' Furniture Repair
Work Sheet (Partial)
For Year Ended December 31, 20 - -

	ACCOUNT TITLE	TRIAL BALANCE		ADJUSTMENTS		ADJUSTED TRIAL BALANCE		
		DEBIT	CREDIT	DEBIT	CREDIT	DEBIT	CREDIT	
1	Cash	1 0 0 00				1 0 0 00		1
2	Supplies	8 5 0 00				2 0 0 00		2
3	Prepaid Insurance	9 0 0 00				3 0 0 00		3
4	Delivery Equipment	3 6 0 0 00				3 6 0 0 00		4
5	Accum. Depr.—Delivery Equipment		6 0 0 00				8 0 0 00	5
6	Wages Payable						1 0 0 00	6
7	Jim Jacobs, Capital		4 0 0 0 00				4 0 0 0 00	7
8	Repair Fees		1 6 5 0 00				1 6 5 0 00	8
9	Wages Expense	6 0 0 00				7 0 0 00		9
10	Advertising Expense	2 0 0 00				2 0 0 00		10
11	Supplies Expense					6 5 0 00		11
12	Insurance Expense					6 0 0 00		12
13	Depr. Expense—Delivery Equipment					2 0 0 00		13
14		6 2 5 0 00	6 2 5 0 00			6 5 5 0 00	6 5 5 0 00	14

E 5-9A (LO4)

JOURNALIZING ADJUSTING ENTRIES From the adjustments columns in Exercise 5-8A, journalize the four adjusting entries, as of December 31, in proper general journal format.

E 5-10A (LO2)

EXTENDING ADJUSTED BALANCES TO THE INCOME STATEMENT AND BALANCE SHEET COLUMNS Indicate with an "x" whether each account total should be extended to the Income Statement Debit or Credit or to the Balance Sheet Debit or Credit columns on the work sheet.

	Income Statement		Balance Sheet	
	Debit	Credit	Debit	Credit
Cash				
Accounts Receivable				
Supplies				
Prepaid Insurance				
Delivery Equipment				
Accum. Depr.—Delivery Equipment				
Accounts Payable				
Wages Payable				
Owner, Capital				
Owner, Drawing				
Delivery Fees				
Wages Expense				
Rent Expense				
Supplies Expense				
Insurance Expense				
Depr. Exp.—Delivery Equipment				

E 5-11A (L02)

ANALYSIS OF NET INCOME OR NET LOSS ON THE WORK SHEET
Indicate with an "x" in which columns, Income Statement Debit or Credit or Balance Sheet Debit or Credit, a net income or a net loss would appear on a work sheet.

	Income Statement		Balance Sheet	
	Debit	Credit	Debit	Credit
Net Income	_____	_____	_____	_____
Net Loss	_____	_____	_____	_____

E 5-12A (L05)

POSTING ADJUSTING ENTRIES Two adjusting entries are in the following general journal. Post these adjusting entries to the four general ledger accounts. The following account numbers were taken from the chart of accounts: 141, Supplies; 219, Wages Payable; 511, Wages Expense; and 523, Supplies Expense. If you are not using the working papers that accompany this text, enter the following balances before posting the entries: Supplies, $200 Dr.; Wages Expense, $1,200 Dr.

GENERAL JOURNAL PAGE 9

	DATE		DESCRIPTION	POST. REF.	DEBIT	CREDIT	
1			Adjusting Entries				1
2	20-- Dec.	31	Supplies Expense		8 5 00		2
3			Supplies			8 5 00	3
4							4
5		31	Wages Expense		2 2 0 00		5
6			Wages Payable			2 2 0 00	6

E 5-13A (L06)
✓ See Figure 5-24 in text

CASH, MODIFIED CASH, AND ACCRUAL BASES OF ACCOUNTING
Prepare the entry for each of the following transactions, using the (a) cash basis, (b) modified cash basis, and (c) accrual basis of accounting.

1. Purchase supplies on account.
2. Make payment on asset previously purchased.
3. Purchase supplies for cash.
4. Purchase insurance for cash.
5. Pay cash for wages.
6. Pay cash for telephone expense.
7. Pay cash for new equipment.

End-of-Period Adjusting Entries:

8. Wages earned but not paid.
9. Prepaid item purchased, partly used.
10. Depreciation on long-term assets.

SERIES A PROBLEMS

P 5-14A (LO1/2)

✓ Adjustments col. total: $1,895;
Net income: $1,060

ADJUSTMENTS AND WORK SHEET SHOWING NET INCOME The trial balance after one month of operation for Mason's Delivery Service as of September 30, 20--, is shown below. Data to complete the adjustments are as follows:

(a)   Supplies inventory as of September 30, $165.
(b)   Insurance expired (used), $800.
(c)   Depreciation on delivery equipment, $400.
(d)   Wages earned by employees but not paid as of September 30, $225.

REQUIRED

1.   Enter the adjustments in the Adjustments columns of the work sheet.

2.   Complete the work sheet.

Mason's Delivery Service
Work Sheet
For Month Ended September 30, 20 - -

	ACCOUNT TITLE	TRIAL BALANCE DEBIT	TRIAL BALANCE CREDIT	ADJUSTMENTS DEBIT	ADJUSTMENTS CREDIT	
1	Cash	1 6 0 0 00				1
2	Accounts Receivable	9 4 0 00				2
3	Supplies	6 3 5 00				3
4	Prepaid Insurance	1 2 0 0 00				4
5	Delivery Equipment	6 4 0 0 00				5
6	Accum. Depr.—Delivery Equipment					6
7	Accounts Payable		1 2 2 0 00			7
8	Wages Payable					8
9	Jill Mason, Capital		8 0 0 0 00			9
10	Jill Mason, Drawing	1 4 0 0 00				10
11	Delivery Fees		6 2 0 0 00			11
12	Wages Expense	1 5 0 0 00				12
13	Advertising Expense	4 6 0 00				13
14	Rent Expense	8 0 0 00				14
15	Supplies Expense					15
16	Telephone Expense	1 6 5 00				16
17	Insurance Expense					17
18	Repair Expense	2 3 0 00				18
19	Oil and Gas Expense	9 0 00				19
20	Depr. Expense—Delivery Equipment					20
21		15 4 2 0 00	15 4 2 0 00			21

P 5-15A (LO1/2)

✓ Adjustments col. Total: $1,380;
Net loss: $2,495

ADJUSTMENTS AND WORK SHEET SHOWING A NET LOSS Jason Armstrong started a business called Campus Delivery Service. After the first month of operations, the trial balance as of November 30, 20--, is as shown on the next page.

(continued)

REQUIRED

1. Analyze the following adjustments and enter them on the work sheet.

    (a) Ending inventory of supplies on November 30, $185.
    (b) Unexpired (remaining) insurance as of November 30, $800.
    (c) Depreciation expense on van, $300.
    (d) Wages earned but not paid as of November 30, $190.

2. Complete the work sheet.

Campus Delivery Service
Work Sheet
For Month Ended November 30, 20 - -

	ACCOUNT TITLE	TRIAL BALANCE				ADJUSTMENTS				
		DEBIT		CREDIT		DEBIT		CREDIT		
1	Cash	9 8 0 00								1
2	Accounts Receivable	5 9 0 00								2
3	Supplies	5 7 5 00								3
4	Prepaid Insurance	1 3 0 0 00								4
5	Van	5 8 0 0 00								5
6	Accum. Depr.—Van									6
7	Accounts Payable			9 6 0 00						7
8	Wages Payable									8
9	Jason Armstrong, Capital			10 0 0 0 00						9
10	Jason Armstrong, Drawing	6 0 0 00								10
11	Delivery Fees			2 6 0 0 00						11
12	Wages Expense	1 8 0 0 00								12
13	Advertising Expense	3 8 0 00								13
14	Rent Expense	9 0 0 00								14
15	Supplies Expense									15
16	Telephone Expense	2 2 0 00								16
17	Insurance Expense									17
18	Repair Expense	3 1 5 00								18
19	Oil and Gas Expense	1 0 0 00								19
20	Depr. Expense—Van									20
21		13 5 6 0 00		13 5 6 0 00						21

P 5-16A (LO4/5)

JOURNALIZE AND POST ADJUSTING ENTRIES FROM THE WORK SHEET Refer to Problem 5-15A and the following additional information.

Account Name	Account Number	Balance in Account Before Adjusting Entry
Supplies	141	$ 575
Prepaid Insurance	145	1,300
Accum. Depr.—Van	185.1	0
Wages Payable	219	0
Wages Expense	511	1,800
Supplies Expense	523	0
Insurance Expense	535	0
Depr. Expense—Van	541	0

REQUIRED

1.   Journalize the adjusting entries on page 5 of the general journal.

2.   Post the adjusting entries to the general ledger. (If you are not using the working papers that accompany this text, enter the balances provided in this problem before posting the adjusting entries.)

P 5-17A (LO3)

✓Adjustments col. total: $1,160; Net income: $1,575

CORRECTING WORK SHEET WITH ERRORS A beginning accounting student tried to complete a work sheet for Joyce Lee's Tax Service. The following adjusting entries were to have been analyzed and entered onto the work sheet. The work sheet is shown on page 164.

(a)   Ending inventory of supplies as of March 31, $160.
(b)   Unexpired insurance as of March 31, $520.
(c)   Depreciation of office equipment, $275.
(d)   Wages earned, but not paid as of March 31, $110.

REQUIRED

The accounting student made a number of errors. Review the work sheet for addition mistakes, transpositions, and other errors and make all necessary corrections.

SERIES B EXERCISES

E 5-1B (LO1)

ADJUSTMENT FOR SUPPLIES On July 31, the trial balance indicates that the supplies account has a balance, prior to the adjusting entry, of $430. A physical count of the supplies inventory shows that $120 of supplies remain. Analyze the adjustment for supplies using T accounts, and then formally enter this adjustment in the general journal.

E 5-2B (LO1)

ADJUSTMENT FOR INSURANCE On July 1, a six-month liability insurance policy was purchased for $750. Analyze the required adjustment as of July 31 using T accounts, and then formally enter this adjustment in the general journal.

E 5-3B (LO1)

ADJUSTMENT FOR WAGES On July 31, the trial balance shows wages expense of $800. An additional $150 of wages was earned by the employees but has not yet been paid. Analyze the required adjustment using T accounts, and then formally enter this adjustment in the general journal.

E 5-4B (LO1)

ADJUSTMENT FOR DEPRECIATION OF ASSET On July 1, delivery equipment was purchased for $4,320. The delivery equipment has an estimated useful life of three years (36 months) and no salvage value. Using the straight-line depreciation method, analyze the necessary adjusting entry as of July 31 (one month) using T accounts, and then formally enter this adjustment in the general journal.

E 5-5B (LO1)

CALCULATION OF BOOK VALUE On January 1, 20--, a depreciable asset was acquired for $5,760. The asset has an estimated useful life of four years (48 months) and no salvage value. Use the straight-line depreciation method to calculate the book value as of July 1, 20--.

PROBLEM 5-17A

Joyce Lee's Tax Service
Work Sheet
For Month Ended March 31, 20--

#	ACCOUNT TITLE	TRIAL BALANCE DEBIT	TRIAL BALANCE CREDIT	ADJUSTMENTS DEBIT	ADJUSTMENTS CREDIT	ADJUSTED TRIAL BALANCE DEBIT	ADJUSTED TRIAL BALANCE CREDIT	INCOME STATEMENT DEBIT	INCOME STATEMENT CREDIT	BALANCE SHEET DEBIT	BALANCE SHEET CREDIT
1	Cash	1 7 2 5 00				1 7 2 5 00				1 7 5 2 00	
2	Accounts Receivable	9 6 0 00				9 6 0 00				9 6 0 00	
3	Supplies	5 2 5 00			(a) 1 6 0 00	3 6 5 00				3 6 5 00	
4	Prepaid Insurance	9 3 0 00			(b) 4 1 0 00	5 4 0 00				5 4 0 00	
5	Office Equipment	5 4 5 0 00			(c) 2 7 5 00	5 1 7 5 00				5 1 7 5 00	
6	Accum. Depr.—Office Equipment										
7	Accounts Payable		4 8 0 00				4 8 0 00				4 8 0 00
8	Wages Payable				(d) 1 1 0 00		1 1 0 00		1 1 0 00		
9	Joyce Lee, Capital		7 5 0 0 00				7 5 0 0 00				7 5 0 0 00
10	Joyce Lee, Drawing	1 1 2 5 00				1 1 2 5 00		1 1 2 5 00			
11	Professional Fees		5 7 0 0 00				5 7 0 0 00		5 7 0 0 00		
12	Wages Expense	1 4 2 0 00		(d) 1 1 0 00		1 4 2 0 00		1 4 2 0 00			1 5 8 0 00
13	Advertising Expense	3 5 0 00				3 5 0 00		3 5 0 00			
14	Rent Expense	7 0 0 00				7 0 0 00		7 0 0 00			
15	Supplies Expense			(a) 1 6 0 00		1 6 0 00		1 6 0 00			
16	Telephone Expense	1 3 0 00				1 3 0 00		1 3 0 00			
17	Utilities Expense	1 9 0 00				1 9 0 00		1 9 0 00			
18	Insurance Expense			(b) 4 1 0 00		4 1 0 00		4 1 0 00			
19	Depr. Expense—Office Equipment			(c) 2 7 5 00		2 7 5 00		2 7 5 00			
20	Miscellaneous Expense	1 7 5 00				1 7 5 00		1 7 5 00			
21											
22		13 6 8 0 00	13 6 8 0 00	9 5 5 00	9 5 5 00	13 1 6 0 00	13 7 9 0 00	4 5 6 6 00	5 8 1 0 00	9 5 0 8 00	7 9 8 0 00
23								1 2 4 4 00			1 5 2 8 00
24								5 8 1 0 00	5 8 1 0 00	9 5 0 8 00	9 5 0 8 00
25											

This work sheet contains errors.

E 5-6B (L01)

ANALYSIS OF ADJUSTING ENTRY FOR SUPPLIES Analyze each situation and indicate the correct dollar amount for the adjusting entry.

1. Ending inventory of supplies is $95.

(Balance Sheet) Supplies		(Income Statement) Supplies Expense	
TB 540			
	Adj. _____	Adj. _____	
Bal. _____			

2. Amount of supplies used is $280.

(Balance Sheet) Supplies		(Income Statement) Supplies Expense	
TB 330			
	Adj. _____	Adj. _____	
Bal. _____			

E 5-7B (L01)

ANALYSIS OF ADJUSTING ENTRY FOR INSURANCE Analyze each situation and indicate the correct dollar amount for the adjusting entry.

1. Amount of insurance expired (used) is $830.

(Balance Sheet) Prepaid Insurance		(Income Statement) Insurance Expense	
TB 960			
	Adj. _____	Adj. _____	
Bal. _____			

2. Amount of unexpired (remaining) insurance is $340.

(Balance Sheet) Prepaid Insurance		(Income Statement) Insurance Expense	
TB 1,135			
	Adj. _____	Adj. _____	
Bal. _____			

E 5-8B (L02)

✓ Adjustments col. total: $1,530

WORK SHEET AND ADJUSTING ENTRIES Page 166 shows a partial work sheet for Jasmine Kah's Auto Detailing. Indicate by letters (a) through (d) the four adjustments in the Adjustments columns of the work sheet, properly matching each debit and credit. Complete the Adjustments columns.

(continued)

Jasmine Kah's Auto Detailing
Work Sheet (Partial)
For Month Ended June 30, 20 - -

	ACCOUNT TITLE	TRIAL BALANCE DEBIT	TRIAL BALANCE CREDIT	ADJUSTMENTS DEBIT	ADJUSTMENTS CREDIT	ADJUSTED TRIAL BALANCE DEBIT	ADJUSTED TRIAL BALANCE CREDIT	
1	Cash	1 5 0 0 00				1 5 0 0 00		1
2	Supplies	5 2 0 0 00				9 0 0 00		2
3	Prepaid Insurance	7 5 0 0 00				2 0 0 00		3
4	Cleaning Equipment	5 4 0 0 0 00				5 4 0 0 0 00		4
5	Accum. Depr.— Cleaning Equipment		8 5 0 0 00				1 1 5 0 0 00	5
6	Wages Payable						2 5 0 00	6
7	Jasmine Kah, Capital		4 6 0 0 0 00				4 6 0 0 0 00	7
8	Detailing Fees		2 2 2 0 0 00				2 2 2 0 0 00	8
9	Wages Expense	7 0 0 0 00				9 5 0 0 00		9
10	Advertising Expense	1 5 0 0 00				1 5 0 0 00		10
11	Supplies Expense					4 3 0 0 00		11
12	Insurance Expense					5 5 0 0 00		12
13	Depr. Expense—Cleaning Equipment					3 0 0 0 00		13
14		7 6 7 0 0 00	7 6 7 0 0 00			8 2 2 0 0 00	8 2 2 0 0 00	14

E 5-9B (LO4)   **JOURNALIZING ADJUSTING ENTRIES** From the Adjustments columns in Exercise 5-8B, journalize the four adjusting entries as of June 30, in proper general journal format.

E 5-10B (LO2)   **EXTENDING ADJUSTED BALANCES TO THE INCOME STATEMENT AND BALANCE SHEET COLUMNS** Indicate with an "x" whether each account total should be extended to the Income Statement Debit or Credit or to the Balance Sheet Debit or Credit columns on the work sheet.

	Income Statement Debit	Income Statement Credit	Balance Sheet Debit	Balance Sheet Credit
Cash	_____	_____	_____	_____
Accounts Receivable	_____	_____	_____	_____
Supplies	_____	_____	_____	_____
Prepaid Insurance	_____	_____	_____	_____
Automobile	_____	_____	_____	_____
Accum. Depr.—Automobile	_____	_____	_____	_____
Accounts Payable	_____	_____	_____	_____
Wages Payable	_____	_____	_____	_____
Owner, Capital	_____	_____	_____	_____
Owner, Drawing	_____	_____	_____	_____
Service Fees	_____	_____	_____	_____
Wages Expense	_____	_____	_____	_____
Supplies Expense	_____	_____	_____	_____
Utilities Expense	_____	_____	_____	_____
Insurance Expense	_____	_____	_____	_____
Depr. Exp.—Automobile	_____	_____	_____	_____

E 5-11B (LO2)

ANALYSIS OF NET INCOME OR NET LOSS ON THE WORK SHEET
Insert the dollar amounts where the net income or net loss would appear on the
work sheet.

	Income Statement		Balance Sheet	
	Debit	Credit	Debit	Credit
Net Income: $2,500	_____	_____	_____	_____
Net Loss: $1,900	_____	_____	_____	_____

E 5-12B (LO5)

POSTING ADJUSTING ENTRIES Two adjusting entries are shown in the following general journal. Post these adjusting entries to the four general ledger accounts. The following account numbers were taken from the chart of accounts: 145, Prepaid Insurance; 183.1, Accumulated Depreciation—Cleaning Equipment; 541, Depreciation Expense—Cleaning Equipment; and 535, Insurance Expense. If you are not using the working papers that accompany this text, enter the following balances before posting the entries: Prepaid Insurance, $960 Dr.; Accumulated Depr.—Cleaning Equip., $870 Cr.

GENERAL JOURNAL   PAGE 7

	DATE		DESCRIPTION	POST. REF.	DEBIT	CREDIT	
1			Adjusting Entries				1
2	20-- July	31	Insurance Expense		3 2 0 00		2
3			Prepaid Insurance			3 2 0 00	3
4							4
5		31	Depr. Expense—Cleaning Equipment		1 4 5 00		5
6			Accum. Depr.—Cleaning Equipment			1 4 5 00	6

E 5-13B (LO6)

✓ See Figure 5-24 in text

CASH, MODIFIED CASH, AND ACCRUAL BASES OF ACCOUNTING For each journal entry shown below, indicate the accounting method(s) for which the entry would be appropriate. If the journal entry is not appropriate for a particular accounting method, explain the proper accounting treatment for that method.

1. Office Equipment
        Cash
            Purchased equipment for cash

2. Office Equipment
        Accounts Payable
            Purchased equipment on account

3. Cash
        Revenue
            Cash receipts for week

4. Accounts Receivable
        Revenue
            Services performed on account

5. Prepaid Insurance
        Cash
            Purchased prepaid asset

6. Supplies
        Accounts Payable
            Purchased prepaid asset

(continued)

7. Telephone Expense
     Cash
          Paid telephone bill

8. Wages Expense
     Cash
          Paid wages for month

9. Accounts Payable
     Cash
          Made payment on account

Adjusting Entries:

10. Supplies Expense
      Supplies

11. Wages Expense
      Wages Payable

12. Depreciation Expense—Office Equipment
      Accumulated Depreciation—Office Equipment

SERIES B PROBLEMS

P 5-14B (LO1/2)

✓ Adjustments col. total: $805;
Net income: $2,410

ADJUSTMENTS AND WORK SHEET SHOWING NET INCOME Louie Long started a business called Louie's Lawn Service. The trial balance as of March 31, after the first month of operation, is as follows:

Louie's Lawn Service
Work Sheet
For Month Ended March 31, 20 - -

	ACCOUNT TITLE	TRIAL BALANCE DEBIT	TRIAL BALANCE CREDIT	ADJUSTMENTS DEBIT	ADJUSTMENTS CREDIT	
1	Cash	1 3 7 5 00				1
2	Accounts Receivable	8 8 0 00				2
3	Supplies	4 9 0 00				3
4	Prepaid Insurance	8 0 0 00				4
5	Lawn Equipment	5 7 0 0 00				5
6	Accum. Depr.—Lawn Equipment					6
7	Accounts Payable		7 8 0 00			7
8	Wages Payable					8
9	Louie Long, Capital		6 5 0 0 00			9
10	Louie Long, Drawing	1 2 5 0 00				10
11	Lawn Service Fees		6 1 0 0 00			11
12	Wages Expense	1 1 4 5 00				12
13	Advertising Expense	5 4 0 00				13
14	Rent Expense	7 2 5 00				14
15	Supplies Expense					15
16	Telephone Expense	1 6 0 00				16
17	Insurance Expense					17
18	Repair Expense	2 5 0 00				18
19	Depr. Expense—Lawn Equipment					19
20	Miscellaneous Expense	6 5 00				20
21		13 3 8 0 00	13 3 8 0 00			21

REQUIRED

1.   Analyze the following adjustments and enter them on a work sheet.

    (a)   Ending supplies inventory as of March 31, $165.
    (b)   Insurance expired (used), $100.
    (c)   Depreciation of lawn equipment, $200.
    (d)   Wages earned but not paid as of March 31, $180.

2.   Complete the work sheet.

P 5-15B (LO1/2)

✓Adjustments col. total: $990;
Net loss: $1,625

ADJUSTMENTS AND WORK SHEET SHOWING A NET LOSS Val Nolan started a business called Nolan's Home Appraisals. The trial balance as of October 31, after the first month of operations, is as follows:

Nolan's Home Appraisals
Work Sheet
For Month Ended October 31, 20 - -

	ACCOUNT TITLE	TRIAL BALANCE DEBIT	TRIAL BALANCE CREDIT	ADJUSTMENTS DEBIT	ADJUSTMENTS CREDIT	
1	Cash	8 3 0 00				1
2	Accounts Receivable	7 6 0 00				2
3	Supplies	6 2 5 00				3
4	Prepaid Insurance	9 5 0 00				4
5	Automobile	6 5 0 0 00				5
6	Accum. Depr.—Automobile					6
7	Accounts Payable		1 5 0 0 00			7
8	Wages Payable					8
9	Val Nolan, Capital		9 9 0 0 00			9
10	Val Nolan, Drawing	1 1 0 0 00				10
11	Appraisal Fees		3 0 0 0 00			11
12	Wages Expense	1 5 6 0 00				12
13	Advertising Expense	4 2 0 00				13
14	Rent Expense	1 0 5 0 00				14
15	Supplies Expense					15
16	Telephone Expense	2 5 5 00				16
17	Insurance Expense					17
18	Repair Expense	2 7 0 00				18
19	Oil and Gas Expense	8 0 00				19
20	Depr. Expense—Automobile					20
21		14 4 0 0 00	14 4 0 0 00			21

REQUIRED

1.   Analyze the following adjustments and enter them on the work sheet.

    (a)   Supplies inventory as of October 31, $210.
    (b)   Unexpired (remaining) insurance as of October 31, $800.
    (c)   Depreciation of automobile, $250.
    (d)   Wages earned but not paid as of October 31, $175.

2.   Complete the work sheet.

P 5-16B (LO4/5)

JOURNALIZE AND POST ADJUSTING ENTRIES FROM THE WORK SHEET Refer to Problem 5-15B and the following additional information.

Account Name	Account Number	Balance in Account Before Adjusting Entry
Supplies	141	$ 625
Prepaid Insurance	145	950
Accum. Depr.—Automobile	185.1	0
Wages Payable	219	0
Wages Expense	511	1,560
Supplies Expense	523	0
Insurance Expense	535	0
Depr. Expense—Automobile	541	0

REQUIRED

1. Journalize the adjusting entries on page 3 of the general journal.

2. Post the adjusting entries to the general ledger. (If you are not using the working papers that accompany this text, enter the balances provided in this problem before posting the adjusting entries.)

P 5-17B (LO3)

✓Adjustments col. total: $1,640;
Net income: $1,405

CORRECTING WORK SHEET WITH ERRORS A beginning accounting student tried to complete a work sheet for Dick Ady's Bookkeeping Service. The following adjusting entries were to have been analyzed and entered in the work sheet:

(a) Ending inventory of supplies on July 31, $130.
(b) Unexpired insurance on July 31, $420.
(c) Depreciation of office equipment, $325.
(d) Wages earned, but not paid as of July 31, $95.

REQUIRED

Review the work sheet shown on page 171 for addition mistakes, transpositions, and other errors and make all necessary corrections.

MANAGING YOUR WRITING

Delia Alvarez, owner of Delia's Lawn Service, wants to borrow money to buy new lawn equipment. A local bank has asked for financial statements. Alvarez has asked you to prepare financial statements for the year ended December 31, 20--. You have been given the unadjusted trial balance on page 172 and suspect that Alvarez expects you to base your statements on this information. You are concerned, however, that some of the account balances may need to be adjusted. Write a memo to Alvarez explaining what additional information you need before you can prepare the financial statements. Alvarez is not familiar with accounting issues. Therefore, explain in your memo why you need this information, the potential impact of this information on the financial statements, and the importance of making these adjustments before approaching the bank for a loan.

PROBLEM 5-17B

Dick Ady's Bookkeeping Service
Work Sheet
For Month Ended July 31, 20 - -

#	ACCOUNT TITLE	TRIAL BALANCE DEBIT	TRIAL BALANCE CREDIT	ADJUSTMENTS DEBIT	ADJUSTMENTS CREDIT	ADJUSTED TRIAL BALANCE DEBIT	ADJUSTED TRIAL BALANCE CREDIT	INCOME STATEMENT DEBIT	INCOME STATEMENT CREDIT	BALANCE SHEET DEBIT	BALANCE SHEET CREDIT
1	Cash	1 3 6 5 00				1 3 6 5 00				1 3 5 6 00	
2	Accounts Receivable	8 4 5 00				8 4 5 00			8 4 5 00		
3	Supplies	6 2 0 00			(a) 4 9 0 00	1 3 0 00				1 3 0 00	
4	Prepaid Insurance	1 1 5 0 00			(b) 4 2 0 00	7 3 0 00				7 3 0 00	
5	Office Equipment	6 4 0 0 00			(c) 3 2 5 00	6 7 2 5 00				6 7 2 5 00	
6	Accum. Depr.—Office Equipment										
7	Accounts Payable		7 3 5 00				7 3 5 00				7 3 5 00
8	Wages Payable				(d) 9 5 00		9 5 00				5 9 00
9	Dick Ady, Capital		7 8 0 0 00				7 8 0 0 00				7 8 0 0 00
10	Dick Ady, Drawing	1 2 0 0 00				1 2 0 0 00				1 2 0 0 00	
11	Professional Fees		6 3 5 0 00				6 3 5 0 00		6 3 5 0 00		
12	Wages Expense	1 4 9 5 00		(d) 9 5 00		1 5 9 0 00		1 5 9 0 00			
13	Advertising Expense	3 8 0 00				3 8 0 00		3 8 0 00			
14	Rent Expense	8 5 0 00				8 5 0 00		8 5 0 00			
15	Supplies Expense			(a) 4 9 0 00		4 9 0 00		4 9 0 00			
16	Telephone Expense	2 0 5 00				2 0 5 00		2 5 0 00			
17	Utilities Expense	2 8 5 00				2 8 5 00		2 8 5 00			
18	Insurance Expense			(b) 4 2 0 00		4 2 0 00		4 2 0 00			
19	Depr. Expense—Office Equipment			(c) 3 2 5 00		3 2 5 00		3 2 5 00			
20	Miscellaneous Expense	9 0 00				9 0 00		9 0 00			
21		14 8 8 5 00	14 8 8 5 00	1 3 3 0 00	1 3 3 0 00	15 6 3 0 00	14 9 8 0 00	4 8 8 0 00	7 1 9 5 00	10 1 4 1 00	8 5 9 4 00
22	Net Income							2 3 1 5 00			1 5 4 7 00
23								7 1 9 5 00	7 1 9 5 00	10 1 4 1 00	10 1 4 1 00

This work sheet contains errors.

Delia's Lawn Service Trial Balance December 31, 20 - -											
ACCOUNT TITLE	ACCOUNT NO.	\multicolumn{4}{c	}{DEBIT BALANCE}				\multicolumn{4}{c}{CREDIT BALANCE}			
Cash	101		7	7	0	00					
Accounts Receivable	122	1	7	0	0	00					
Supplies	142		2	8	0	00					
Prepaid Insurance	145		4	0	0	00					
Lawn Equipment	183	13	8	0	0	00					
Accounts Payable	202							2	2	0	0	00
Delia Alvarez, Capital	311							3	0	0	0	00
Delia Alvarez, Drawing	312		3	5	0	00					
Lawn Cutting Fees	401						52	4	0	0	00
Wages Expense	511	35	8	5	0	00					
Rent Expense	521	1	2	0	0	00					
Gas and Oil Expense	538	3	2	5	0	00					
		57	6	0	0	00	57	6	0	0	00

MASTERY PROBLEM

✓ **Adjusted Trial Bal. total: $58,500; Net income: $13,630**

Kristi Williams offers family counseling services specializing in financial and marital problems. A chart of accounts and a trial balance taken on December 31, 20--, follow.

KRISTI WILLIAMS FAMILY COUNSELING SERVICES CHART OF ACCOUNTS			
Assets		**Revenue**	
101	Cash	401	Client Fees
142	Office Supplies		
145	Prepaid Insurance	**Expenses**	
181	Office Equipment	511	Wages Expense
181.1	Accumulated Depr.—	521	Rent Expense
	Office Equipment	523	Office Supplies Expense
187	Computer Equipment	533	Utilities Expense
187.1	Accumulated Depr.—	535	Insurance Expense
	Computer Equipment	541	Depr. Expense—
			Office Equipment
Liabilities		542	Depr. Expense—
201	Notes Payable		Computer Equipment
202	Accounts Payable	549	Miscellaneous Expense
Owner's Equity			
311	Kristi Williams, Capital		
312	Kristi Williams, Drawing		

ACCOUNT TITLE	ACCOUNT NO.	DEBIT BALANCE						CREDIT BALANCE					
Kristi Williams Family Counseling Services **Trial Balance** **December 31, 20 - -**													
Cash	101	8	7	3	0	00							
Office Supplies	142		7	0	0	00							
Prepaid Insurance	145		6	0	0	00							
Office Equipment	181	18	0	0	0	00							
Computer Equipment	187	6	0	0	0	00							
Notes Payable	201							8	0	0	0	00	
Accounts Payable	202							5	0	0	00		
Kristi Williams, Capital	311							11	4	0	0	00	
Kristi Williams, Drawing	312	3	0	0	0	00							
Client Fees	401							35	8	0	0	00	
Wages Expense	511	9	5	0	0	00							
Rent Expense	521	6	0	0	0	00							
Utilities Expense	533	2	1	7	0	00							
Miscellaneous Expense	549	1	0	0	0	00							
		55	7	0	0	00		55	7	0	0	00	

Information for year-end adjustments:

(a) Office supplies on hand at year-end amounted to $100.
(b) On January 1, 20--, Williams purchased office equipment that cost $18,000. It has an expected useful life of 10 years and no salvage value.
(c) On July 1, 20--, Williams purchased computer equipment costing $6,000. It has an expected useful life of three years and no salvage value. Assume that Williams computes depreciation to the nearest full month.
(d) On December 1, 20--, Williams paid a premium of $600 for a six-month insurance policy.

REQUIRED

1. Prepare the work sheet for the year ended December 31, 20--.

2. Prepare adjusting entries in a general journal.

CHALLENGE PROBLEM

This problem challenges you to apply your cumulative accounting knowledge to move a step beyond the material in the chapter.

Your friend, Diane Kiefner, teaches elementary school and operates her own wilderness kayaking tours in the summers. She thinks she has been doing fine financially, but has never really measured her profits. Until this year, her business has always had more money at the end of the summer than at the beginning. She enjoys kayaking and as long as she came out a little ahead, that was fine. Unfortunately, Diane had to dip into her savings to make up for "losses" on her kayaking tours this past summer. Hearing that you have been studying accounting, she brought a list of cash receipts and expenditures and would like you to try to figure out what happened.

(continued)

Cash balance beginning of summer	$15,000
Cash receipts from kayakers over the summer	$10,000
Cash expenditures over the summer	13,500
Amount taken from savings	(3,500)
Cash balance end of summer	$11,500

When asked for more details on the expenditures and the kayaking gear that you saw in her garage, Diane provided the following information:

Expenditures were made on the following items:

Brochures used to advertise her services (Diane only used about 1/4 of them and plans to use the remainder over the next three summers.)	$1,000
Food for trips (nothing left)	2,000
Rent on equipment used by kayakers on trips	3,000
Travel expenses	4,000
A new kayak and paddles (At the beginning of the summer, Diane bought a new kayak and paddles. Up to this time, she had always borrowed her father's. Diane expects to use the equipment for about five years. At that time, she expects it to have no value.)	3,500

A trial balance based on this information follows. As you will note, Diane's trial balance is not consistent with some of the concepts discussed in this chapter.

Diane Kiefner's Wilderness Kayaking Tours
Work Sheet
For Summer Ended 20 - -

	ACCOUNT TITLE	TRIAL BALANCE		ADJUSTMENTS		ADJUSTED TRIAL BALANCE		INCOME STATEMENT		BALANCE SHEET		
		DEBIT	CREDIT	DEBIT	CREDIT	DEBIT	CREDIT	DEBIT	CREDIT	DEBIT	CREDIT	
1	Cash	11 5 0 0 00										1
2	Diane Kiefner, Capital		15 0 0 0 00									2
3	Tour Revenue		10 0 0 0 00									3
4	Advertising Supplies Expense	1 0 0 0 00										4
5	Food Expense	2 0 0 0 00										5
6	Equipment Rental Expense	3 0 0 0 00										6
7	Travel Expense	4 0 0 0 00										7
8	Kayak Expense	3 5 0 0 00										8
9		25 0 0 0 00	25 0 0 0 00									9

REQUIRED

1. Complete Diane's work sheet by making appropriate adjustments and extensions. Note: (a) You may need to add new accounts. (b) Some of the adjustments you need to make are actually "corrections of errors" Diane has made in classifying certain items.

2. What is your best measure of Diane's net income for the summer of 20--?

Chapter 5 Appendix
Depreciation Methods

Objectives

Careful study of this appendix should enable you to:

LO1 Prepare a depreciation schedule using the straight-line method.

LO2 Prepare a depreciation schedule using the sum-of-the-years'-digits method.

LO3 Prepare a depreciation schedule using the double-declining-balance method.

LO4 Prepare a depreciation schedule for tax purposes using the Modified Accelerated Cost Recovery System.

In Chapter 5, we introduced the straight-line method of depreciation. Here, we will review this method and illustrate three others: sum-of-the-years'-digits; double-declining-balance; and, for tax purposes, the Modified Accelerated Cost Recovery System. For all illustrations, we will assume that a delivery van was purchased for $40,000. It has a five-year useful life and salvage value of $4,000.

STRAIGHT-LINE METHOD

LO1 Prepare a depreciation schedule using the straight-line method.

Under the **straight-line depreciation method**, an equal amount of depreciation will be taken each period. First, compute the depreciable cost by subtracting the salvage value from the cost of the asset. This is done because we expect to sell the asset for $4,000 at the end of its useful life. Thus, the total cost to be recognized as an expense over the five years is $36,000, not $40,000.

Cost	–	Salvage Value	=	Depreciable Cost
$40,000	–	$4,000	=	$36,000

Next, we divide the depreciable cost by the expected life of the asset, five years.

$$\text{Depreciation Expense per Year} = \frac{\text{Depreciable Cost}}{\text{Years of Life}}$$

$$\$7,200 \text{ per year} = \frac{\$36,000}{5 \text{ years}}$$

When preparing a depreciation schedule, it is often convenient to use a depreciation rate per year. In this case, it would be 20% (100% ÷ 5 years of life). Figure 5A-1 shows the depreciation expense, accumulated depreciation, and book value for each of the five years.

FIGURE 5A-1   Depreciation Schedule Using Straight-Line Method

STRAIGHT-LINE DEPRECIATION					
Year	Depreciable Cost[a]	× Rate[b] =	Depreciation Expense	Accumulated Depreciation (End of Year)	Book Value[c] (End of Year)
1	$36,000	20%	$7,200	$ 7,200	$32,800
2	36,000	20%	7,200	14,400	25,600
3	36,000	20%	7,200	21,600	18,400
4	36,000	20%	7,200	28,800	11,200
5	36,000	20%	7,200	36,000	4,000

[a]Depreciable Cost = Cost − Salvage Value ($40,000 − $4,000 = $36,000)
[b]Rate = 1 year ÷ 5 years of life × 100 = 20%
[c]Book Value = Cost ($40,000) − Accumulated Depreciation

SUM-OF-THE-YEARS'-DIGITS

LO2 Prepare a depreciation schedule using the sum-of-the-years'-digits method.

Under the **sum-of-the-years'-digits depreciation method**, depreciation is determined by multiplying the depreciable cost by a schedule of fractions. The numerator of the fraction for a specific year is the number of years of remaining useful life for the asset, measured from the beginning of the year. The denominator for all fractions is determined by adding the digits that represent the years of the estimated life of the asset. The calculation of the **sum-of-the-years'-digits** for our delivery van with a five-year useful life is shown below.

Sum-of-the-Years'-Digits = 5 + 4 + 3 + 2 + 1 = 15

A depreciation schedule using these fractions is shown in Figure 5A-2.

FIGURE 5A-2   Depreciation Schedule Using Sum-of-the-Years'-Digits Method

SUM-OF-THE-YEARS'-DIGITS					
Year	Depreciable Cost[a]	× Rate[b] =	Depreciation Expense	Accumulated Depreciation (End of Year)	Book Value[c] (End of Year)
1	$36,000	5/15	$12,000	$12,000	$28,000
2	36,000	4/15	9,600	21,600	18,400
3	36,000	3/15	7,200	28,800	11,200
4	36,000	2/15	4,800	33,600	6,400
5	36,000	1/15	2,400	36,000	4,000

[a]Depreciable Cost = Cost − Salvage Value ($40,000 − $4,000 = $36,000)
[b]Rate = Number of Years of Remaining Useful Life ÷ Sum-of-the-Years'-Digits
[c]Book Value = Cost ($40,000) − Accumulated Depreciation

DOUBLE-DECLINING-BALANCE METHOD

LO3 Prepare a depreciation schedule using the double-declining-balance method.

Under the **double-declining-balance depreciation method**, the book value is multiplied by a fixed rate, often double the straight-line rate. The van has a five-year life, so the straight-line rate is 1 ÷ 5, or 20%. Double the straight-line rate is 2 × 20%, or 40%. The double-declining-balance depreciation schedule is shown in Figure 5A-3. Note that the rate is applied to the book value of the asset. Once the book value is reduced to the expected salvage value, $4,000, no more depreciation may be recognized.

FIGURE 5A-3   Depreciation Schedule Using Double-Declining-Balance Method

DOUBLE-DECLINING-BALANCE METHOD

Year	Book Value[a] (Beginning of Year)	× Rate[b] =	Depreciation Expense	Accumulated Depreciation (End of Year)	Book Value[a] (End of Year)
1	$40,000	40%	$16,000	$16,000	$24,000
2	24,000	40%	9,600	25,600	14,400
3	14,400	40%	5,760	31,360	8,640
4	8,640	40%	3,456	34,816	5,184
5	5,184		1,184	36,000	4,000

[a]Book Value = Cost ($40,000) − Accumulated Depreciation
[b]Rate = Double the straight-line rate (1/5 × 2 = 2/5, or 40%)

MODIFIED ACCELERATED COST RECOVERY SYSTEM

For assets purchased since 1986, many firms use the **Modified Accelerated Cost Recovery System (MACRS)** for tax purposes. Under this method, the Internal Revenue Service (IRS) classifies various assets according to useful life and sets depreciation rates for each year of the asset's life. These rates are then multiplied by the cost of the asset. Even though the van is expected to have a useful life of five years, and a salvage value of $4,000, the IRS schedule, shown in Figure 5A-4, spreads the depreciation over a six-year period and assumes no salvage value.

FIGURE 5A-4   Depreciation Schedule Using Modified Accelerated Cost Recovery System

MODIFIED ACCELERATED COST RECOVERY SYSTEM

Year	Cost	× Rate[a] =	Depreciation Expense	Accumulated Depreciation (End of Year)	Book Value[b] (End of Year)
1	$40,000	20.00%	$ 8,000	$ 8,000	$32,000
2	40,000	32.00%	12,800	20,800	19,200
3	40,000	19.20%	7,680	28,480	11,520
4	40,000	11.52%	4,608	33,088	6,912
5	40,000	11.52%	4,608	37,696	2,304
6	40,000	5.76%	2,304	40,000	0

[a]Rates set by IRS
[b]Book Value = Cost ($40,000) − Accumulated Depreciation

Learning Objectives	Key Points to Remember
LO1 **Prepare a depreciation schedule using the straight-line method.**	Under straight-line depreciation, an equal amount of depreciation is taken each period. Depreciation expense for each year is computed as follows: Cost − Salvage Value = Depreciable Cost/Expected Years of Life = Depreciation Expense per Year
LO2 **Prepare a depreciation schedule using the sum-of-the-years'-digits method.**	Under the sum-of-the-years'-digits method, the depreciable cost is multiplied by a fraction. The fraction consists of the following: $$\frac{\text{Remaining Years of Life Measured from the Beginning of the Current Year}}{\text{Sum-of-the-Years'-Digits}}$$ If an asset has a life of three years, the sum-of-the-years'-digits is equal to: $$3 + 2 + 1 = 6$$ Depreciation would be computed as follows: Year 1: 3/6 × Depreciable Cost Year 2: 2/6 × Depreciable Cost Year 3: 1/6 × Depreciable Cost
LO3 **Prepare a depreciation schedule using the double-declining-balance method.**	Under this method, the book value (the declining balance) is multiplied by a fixed rate, often double the straight-line rate.
LO4 **Prepare a depreciation schedule for tax purposes using the Modified Accelerated Cost Recovery System.**	Under this method, the IRS provides the tax rates to be applied to the cost of the asset. Simply multiply the rate provided by the IRS by the cost of the asset.

KEY TERMS

double-declining-balance depreciation method (176)   A depreciation method that recognizes depreciation each year by multiplying a rate (typically double the straight-line rate) by the book value of the asset.

Modified Accelerated Cost Recovery System (MACRS) (177)   A depreciation method in which rates determined by the IRS are multiplied by the cost of the asset to determine depreciation expense for the year.

straight-line depreciation method (175)   A depreciation method that recognizes an equal amount of depreciation each year.

sum-of-the-years'-digits (176)   If an asset has a five-year life, the sum-of-the-years'-digits is computed as follows: 5 + 4 + 3 + 2 + 1 = 15.

sum-of-the-years'-digits depreciation method (176)   A depreciation method that recognizes depreciation each year by multiplying a fraction by the depreciable cost. The numerator of the fraction is the remaining life of the asset, measured from the beginning of the year. The denominator is the sum-of-the-years'-digits.

REVIEW QUESTIONS

1. List three depreciation methods used for financial reporting.
2. Which depreciation method is used for tax purposes?

SERIES A EXERCISES

E 5Apx-1A (LO1)
✓ Accum. depr. end of Yr. 2: $10,000

STRAIGHT-LINE DEPRECIATION A small delivery truck was purchased on January 1 at a cost of $25,000. It has an estimated useful life of four years and an estimated salvage value of $5,000. Prepare a depreciation schedule showing the depreciation expense, accumulated depreciation, and book value for each year under the straight-line method.

E 5Apx-2A (LO2)
✓ Accum. depr. end of Yr. 2: $14,000

SUM-OF-THE-YEARS'-DIGITS DEPRECIATION Using the information given in Exercise 5Apx-1A, prepare a depreciation schedule showing the depreciation expense, accumulated depreciation, and book value for each year under the sum-of-the-years'-digits method.

E 5Apx-3A (LO3)
✓ Accum. depr. end of Yr. 2: $18,750

DOUBLE-DECLINING-BALANCE DEPRECIATION Using the information given in Exercise 5Apx-1A, prepare a depreciation schedule showing the depreciation expense, accumulated depreciation, and book value for each year under the double-declining-balance method.

E 5Apx-4A (LO4)
✓ Accum. depr. end of Yr. 2: $13,000

MODIFIED ACCELERATED COST RECOVERY SYSTEM Using the information given in Exercise 5Apx-1A and the rates shown in Figure 5A-4, prepare a depreciation schedule showing the depreciation expense, accumulated depreciation, and book value for each year under the Modified Accelerated Cost Recovery System. For tax purposes, assume that the truck has a useful life of five years. (The IRS schedule will spread depreciation over six years.)

SERIES B EXERCISES

E 5Apx-1B (LO1)
✓Accum. depr. end of Yr. 2: $1,800

STRAIGHT-LINE DEPRECIATION A computer was purchased on January 1 at a cost of $5,000. It has an estimated useful life of five years and an estimated salvage value of $500. Prepare a depreciation schedule showing the depreciation expense, accumulated depreciation, and book value for each year under the straight-line method.

E 5Apx-2B (LO2)
✓Accum. depr. end of Yr. 2: $2,700

SUM-OF-THE-YEARS'-DIGITS DEPRECIATION Using the information given in Exercise 5Apx-1B, prepare a depreciation schedule showing the depreciation expense, accumulated depreciation, and book value for each year under the sum-of-the-years'-digits method.

E 5Apx-3B (LO3)
✓Accum. depr. end of Yr. 2: $3,200

DOUBLE-DECLINING-BALANCE DEPRECIATION Using the information given in Exercise 5Apx-1B, prepare a depreciation schedule showing the depreciation expense, accumulated depreciation, and book value for each year under the double-declining-balance method.

E 5Apx-4B (LO4)
✓Accum. depr. end of Yr. 2: $2,600

MODIFIED ACCELERATED COST RECOVERY SYSTEM Using the information given in Exercise 5Apx-1B and the rates shown in Figure 5A-4, prepare a depreciation schedule showing the depreciation expense, accumulated depreciation, and book value for each year under the Modified Accelerated Cost Recovery System. For tax purposes, assume that the computer has a useful life of five years. (The IRS schedule will spread depreciation over six years.)

Objectives

Careful study of this chapter should enable you to:

LO1
Prepare financial statements with the aid of a work sheet.

LO2
Journalize and post closing entries.

LO3
Prepare a post-closing trial balance.

LO4
List and describe the steps in the accounting cycle.

Financial Statements and the Closing Process

"Come on Jessie, let's get busy. We have to close the books before we go to the New Year's Eve party," said Mitch. But after seeing the disappointed look on Jessie's face, Mitch changed his mind. "What the heck. Let's do it next week, while we recover from watching all of those bowl games." "Great," said Jessie, "let's get out of here." Will Mitch and Jessie be in trouble for not closing the books before the end of the year?

The work sheet, introduced in Chapter 5, is used for three major end-of-period activities:

1. journalizing adjusting entries,
2. preparing financial statements, and
3. journalizing closing entries.

This chapter illustrates the use of the work sheet for preparing financial statements and closing entries. In addition, the post-closing trial balance is explained and illustrated. All of these activities take place at the end of the firm's fiscal year. However, to continue our illustration of Jessie Jane's Campus Delivery, we demonstrate these activities at the end of the first month of operations.

THE FINANCIAL STATEMENTS

LO1 Prepare financial statements with the aid of a work sheet.

Since Jessie made no additional investments during the month, the work sheet prepared in Chapter 5 supplies all of the information needed to prepare an income statement, a statement of owner's equity, and a balance sheet. The statements and work sheet columns from which they are derived for Jessie Jane's Campus Delivery are shown in Figures 6-1 and 6-2.

As you refer to the financial statements in Figures 6-1 and 6-2, notice the placement of dollar signs, single rulings, and double rulings. Dollar signs are placed at the top of each column and beneath rulings. Single rulings indicate addition or subtraction, and double rulings are placed under totals. Notice that each statement heading contains three lines: (1) company name, (2) statement title, and (3) period ended or date.

The Income Statement

Figure 6-1 shows how the Income Statement columns of the work sheet provide the information needed to prepare an income statement. Revenue is shown first, followed by an itemized and totaled list of expenses. Then, net income is calculated to double check the accuracy of the work sheet. It is presented with a double ruling as the last item in the statement.

The expenses could be listed in the same order that they appear in the chart of accounts or in descending order by dollar amount. The second approach helps the reader identify the most important expenses.

The Statement of Owner's Equity

Figure 6-2 shows that the Balance Sheet columns of the work sheet provide the information needed to prepare a statement of owner's equity. Jessie's capital account balance and the drawing account balance are in the Balance Sheet columns of the work sheet. The net income for the year can be found either on the work sheet at the bottom of the Income Statement (see Figure 6-1) and Balance Sheet columns or on the income statement. With these three items of information, the statement of owner's equity can be prepared.

Be careful when using the capital account balance reported in the Balance Sheet columns of the work sheet. This account balance is the beginning balance *plus any additional investments made during the period.* Since Jessie made no additional investments during June, the $2,000 balance may be used as the beginning balance on the statement of owner's equity.

Multiple columns are used on the financial statements to make them easier to read. There are no debit or credit columns on the financial statements.

LEARNING KEY

The owner's capital account in the general ledger must be reviewed to determine if additional investments were made during the accounting period.

FIGURE 6-1   Linkages Between the Work Sheet and Income Statement

Jessie Jane's Campus Delivery
Work Sheet (Partial)
For Month Ended June 30, 20 --

| | ACCOUNT TITLE | INCOME STATEMENT | |
		DEBIT	CREDIT
1	Cash		
2	Accounts Receivable		
3	Supplies		
4	Prepaid Insurance		
5	Delivery Equipment		
6	Accum. Depr.—Delivery Equipment		
7	Accounts Payable		
8	Wages Payable		
9	Jessica Jane, Capital		
10	Jessica Jane, Drawing		
11	Delivery Fees		2 1 5 0 00
12	Wages Expense	7 0 0 00	
13	Rent Expense	2 0 0 00	
14	Supplies Expense	6 0 00	
15	Telephone Expense	5 0 00	
16	Insurance Expense	2 5 00	
17	Depr. Expense—Delivery Equipment	1 0 0 00	
18		1 1 3 5 00	2 1 5 0 00
19	Net Income	1 0 1 5 00	
20		2 1 5 0 00	2 1 5 0 00
21			
22			
23			
24			
25			
26			
27			
28			
29			

Prepare 1st

Jessie Jane's Campus Delivery
Income Statement
For Month Ended June 30, 20 --

Revenue:			
Delivery fees			$ 2 1 5 0 00
Expenses:			
Wages expense	$ 7 0 0 00		
Rent expense	2 0 0 00		
Supplies expense	6 0 00		
Telephone expense	5 0 00		
Insurance expense	2 5 00		
Depr. expense—delivery equip.	1 0 0 00		
Total expenses			1 1 3 5 00
Net income			$ 1 0 1 5 00

Name of company
Title of statement
Accounting period ended

Revenues listed first

Expenses listed second by amount (largest to smallest), or in chart of accounts order. Amounts are itemized in left column, subtotaled in right column.

Dollar signs used at top of columns and under rulings.

Single rulings indicate addition or subtraction.

Double rulings indicate totals.

FIGURE 6-2 Linkages Between the Work Sheet, Statement of Owner's Equity, and Balance Sheet

Note: The statement of owner's equity is prepared before the balance sheet. The S.O.E. is shown below the B.S. to enhance the illustration of the linkages between the work sheet and financial statements.

Jessie Jane's Campus Delivery
Work Sheet (Partial)
For Month Ended June 30, 20 - -

	ACCOUNT TITLE	BALANCE SHEET DEBIT	BALANCE SHEET CREDIT
1	Cash	370 00	
2	Accounts Receivable	650 00	
3	Supplies	20 00	
4	Prepaid Insurance	175 00	
5	Delivery Equipment	3600 00	
6	Accum. Depr.—Delivery Equip.		100 00
7	Accounts Payable		1800 00
8	Wages Payable		50 00
9	Jessica Jane, Capital		2000 00
10	Jessica Jane, Drawing	150 00	
11	Delivery Fees		
12	Wages Expense		
13	Rent Expense		
14	Supplies Expense		
15	Telephone Expense		
16	Insurance Expense		
17	Depr. Expense—Delivery Equip.		
18		4965 00	3950 00
19	Net Income		1015 00
20		4965 00	4965 00
21			

Prepare 3rd

Jessie Jane's Campus Delivery
Balance Sheet
June 30, 20 --

Assets		
Current assets:		
Cash	$ 370 00	
Accounts receivable	650 00	
Supplies	20 00	
Prepaid insurance	175 00	
Total current assets		$ 1215 00
Property, plant, and equipment:		
Delivery equipment	$3600 00	
Less accumulated depreciation	100 00	3500 00
Total assets		$ 4715 00
Liabilities		
Current liabilities:		
Accounts payable	$1800 00	
Wages payable	50 00	
Total current liabilities		$ 1850 00
Owner's Equity		
Jessica Jane, capital		2865 00
Total liabilities and owner's equity		$ 4715 00

Prepare 2nd

Jessie Jane's Campus Delivery
Statement of Owner's Equity
For Month Ended June 30, 20 --

Jessica Jane, capital, June 1, 20--		$ 2000 00
Net income for June	$ 1015 00	
Less withdrawals for June	150 00	
Increase in capital		865 00
Jessica Jane, capital, June 30, 20--		$ 2865 00

Name of company
Title of statement
Accounting period ended

Current assets: cash and items that will be converted to cash or consumed within a year.

Property, plant, and equipment: durable assets that will help produce revenues for several years.

Current liabilities: amounts owed that will be paid within a year (will require the use of current assets).

Ending capital is not taken from the work sheet. It is computed on the statement of owner's equity.

Dollar signs used at top of columns and beneath rulings.

Single rulings indicate addition or subtraction.

Double rulings indicate totals.

The Balance Sheet

As shown in Figure 6-2, the work sheet and the statement of owner's equity are used to prepare Jessie's balance sheet. The asset and liability amounts can be found in the Balance Sheet columns of the work sheet. The ending balance in Jessica Jane, Capital has been computed on the statement of owner's equity. This amount should be copied from the statement of owner's equity to the balance sheet.

Two important features of the balance sheet in Figure 6-2 should be noted. First, it is a **report form of balance sheet**, which means that the liabilities and owner's equity sections are shown below the assets section. It differs from an **account form of balance sheet** in which the assets are on the left and the liabilities and owner's equity sections are on the right. (See Jessie's balance sheet illustrated in Figure 2-2 on page 32 in Chapter 2.)

Second, it is a **classified balance sheet**, which means that similar items are grouped together on the balance sheet. Assets are classified as current assets and property, plant, and equipment. Similarly, liabilities are broken down into current and long-term sections. The following major balance sheet classifications are generally used.

Current Assets

Current assets include cash and assets that will be converted into cash or consumed within either one year or the normal operating cycle of the business, whichever is longer. Examples include cash, accounts receivable, supplies, and prepaid insurance. An **operating cycle** is the period of time required to purchase supplies and services and convert them back into cash.

Property, Plant, and Equipment

Property, plant, and equipment, also called **plant assets** or **long-term assets**, represent assets that are expected to serve the business for many years. Examples include land, buildings, and equipment.

Current Liabilities

Current liabilities are due within either one year or the normal operating cycle of the business, whichever is longer. They will be paid out of current assets. Accounts payable and wages payable are classified as current liabilities.

Long-Term Liabilities

Long-term liabilities, or **long-term debt**, are obligations that are not expected to be paid within a year and do not require the use of current assets. A mortgage on an office building is an example of a long-term liability. Jessie has no long-term debts. If she did, they would be listed on the balance sheet in the long-term liabilities section immediately following the current liabilities.

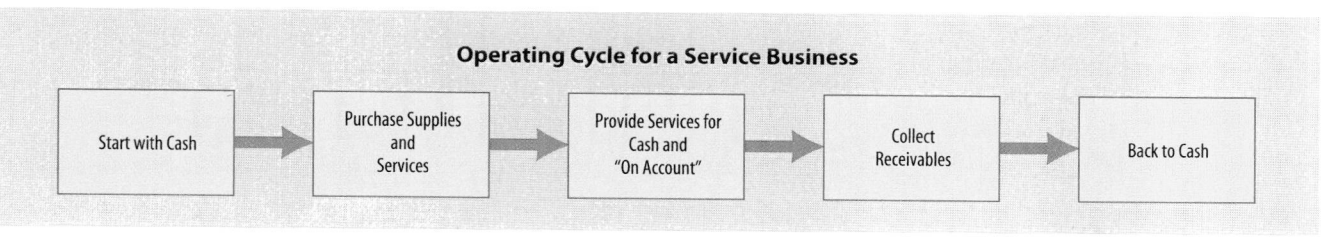

Operating Cycle for a Service Business

Start with Cash → Purchase Supplies and Services → Provide Services for Cash and "On Account" → Collect Receivables → Back to Cash

Additional Investments by the Owner

If the owner of a business made additional investments during the accounting period, the owner's capital reported in the Balance Sheet columns of the work sheet would represent the beginning balance plus any additional investments made during the accounting period. If this amount were used as the beginning balance on the statement of owner's equity, it would not equal the ending balance from last period and would create confusion for those comparing the two statements. In addition, the statement would not reflect all of the activities affecting the owner's capital account during the period.

Thus, we must also review the owner's capital account in the general ledger to get the information needed to prepare the statement of owner's equity. Figure 6-3 illustrates this situation for another business, Ramon's Shopping Service. The $5,000 balance of July 1, 20--, in Ramon Balboa's general ledger capital account is used as the beginning balance on the statement of owner's equity. Note that this is also the ending balance on June 30, 20--. The additional investment of $3,000 made on July 5 and posted to Balboa's general ledger capital account is reported by writing "add additional investments" on the line immediately after the beginning balance. The beginning balance plus the additional investment equals the total investment by the owner in the business and is the amount reported in the Balance Sheet columns of the work sheet. From this point, the preparation of the statement is the same as for businesses without additional investments.

FIGURE 6-3 Statement of Owner's Equity with Additional Investment

GENERAL LEDGER

ACCOUNT: Ramon Balboa, Capital — ACCOUNT NO. 311

DATE		ITEM	POST. REF.	DEBIT	CREDIT	BALANCE DEBIT	BALANCE CREDIT
20-- July	1		J5		5,000.00		5,000.00
	5		J5		3,000.00		8,000.00

Amount invested July 1

Additional investment

Amount reported on work sheet

Ramon's Shopping Service
Statement of Owner's Equity
For Months Ended June 30 and July 31, 20 - -

	June		July	
Ramon Balboa, beginning capital		$ 4,000.00		$ 5,000.00
Add additional investments				3,000.00
Total investment				$ 8,000.00
Net income for the month	$ 1,500.00		$ 2,100.00	
Less withdrawals for the month	500.00		250.00	
Increase in capital		1,000.00		1,850.00
Ramon Balboa, ending capital		$ 5,000.00		$ 9,850.00

From general ledger

From work sheet

THE CLOSING PROCESS

LEARNING KEY

Permanent accounts contain the results of all transactions since the business started. Their balances are carried forward to each new accounting period.

LEARNING KEY

Temporary accounts contain information for one accounting period. These accounts are closed at the end of each accounting period.

The income summary account is not really needed for the closing process. Revenue and expense accounts can be closed to the owner's capital account. One benefit of using the income summary account is that its balance

before closing to the capital account equals the net income or net loss for the period. Thus, it can serve as a check of the accuracy of the closing entries for revenues and expenses.

Computer programs post the closing entries to the owner's capital account automatically.

Assets, liabilities, and the owner's capital account accumulate information across accounting periods. Their balances are brought forward for each new period. For example, the amount of cash at the end of one accounting period must be the same as the amount of cash at the beginning of the next period. Thus, the balance reported for Cash is a result of all cash transactions since the business first opened. This is true for all accounts reported on the balance sheet. For this reason, they are called **permanent accounts**.

Revenue, expense, and drawing accounts accumulate information *for a specific accounting period*. At the end of the fiscal year, these accounts must be *closed*. The **closing process** gives these accounts zero balances so they are prepared to accumulate new information for the next accounting period. Since these accounts do not accumulate information across accounting periods, they are called **temporary accounts**. The drawing account and all accounts reported in the income statement are temporary accounts and must be closed at the end of each accounting period.

The accounting records are closed "as of" December 31, or another fiscal year-end chosen by the business. The actual adjusting entries, closing entries, and financial statements are generally prepared several weeks after the official closing date. However, it is important to include all transactions occurring prior to year-end in the *current* year's financial statements. Similarly, transactions taking place after year-end must be included in the *next* year's financial statements. Improper timing of the recognition of transactions taking place around the end of the year can have major effects on the reported profits. For example, some businesses have been found to "leave the books open" for a few days to include a major sale, or other profitable transactions, that actually took place after the end of the fiscal year. If undetected, the good news could be reported on the current year's statements, rather than in the following year. Similarly, a business could be tempted to "close early" to avoid recognizing unprofitable events occurring during the last few days of the year. Thus, proper treatment of transactions taking place around the end of the year is carefully monitored by auditors.

The closing process is most clearly demonstrated by returning to the accounting equation and T accounts. As shown in Figure 6-4, revenue, expense, and drawing accounts impact owner's equity and should be considered "under the umbrella" of the capital account. The effect of these accounts on owner's equity is formalized at the end of the accounting period when the balances of the temporary accounts are transferred to the owner's capital account (a permanent account) during the closing process.

The four basic steps in the closing process are illustrated in Figure 6-4. As you can see, a new account, **Income Summary**, is used in the closing process. This account may also be called *Expense and Revenue Summary*. This temporary account is used to close the revenue and expense accounts. After closing the revenues and expenses to Income Summary, the balance of this account is equal to the net income. This is why it is called Income Summary. Income Summary is opened during the closing process. Then it is closed to the owner's capital account. It does not appear on any financial statement. The four steps in the closing process are explained on page 188.

FIGURE 6-4   The Closing Process

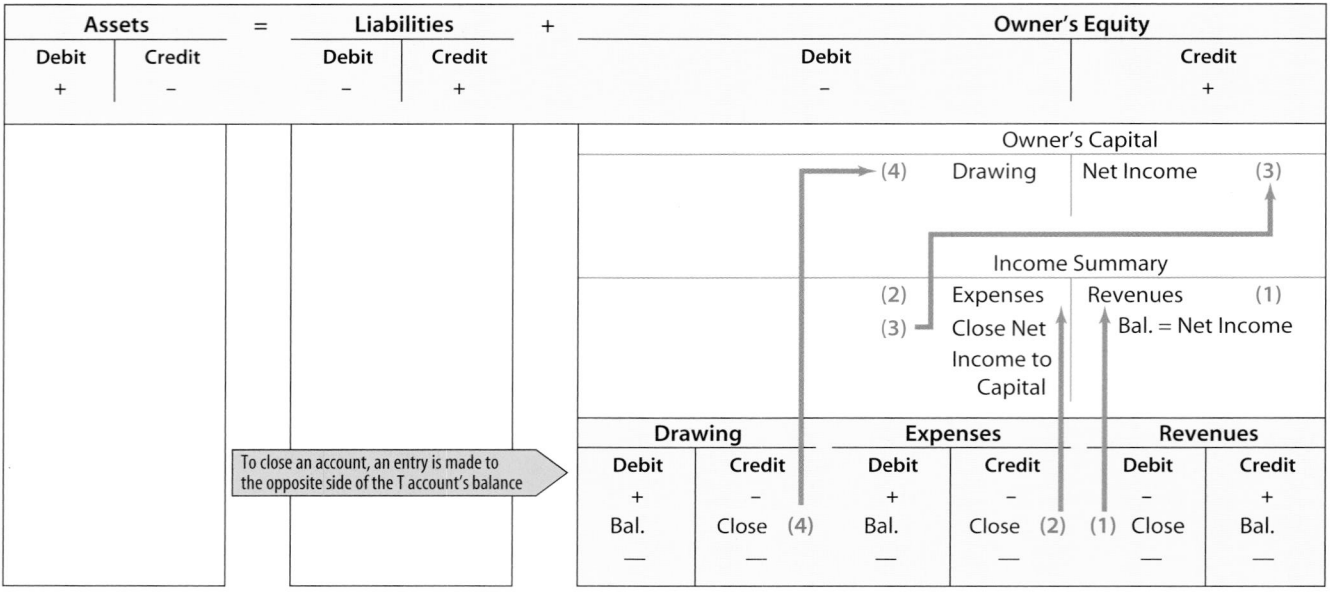

STEPS IN THE CLOSING PROCESS

STEP 1 **Close Revenue Accounts to Income Summary.** Revenues have credit balances and increase owner's equity. Therefore, the revenue account is debited to create a zero balance. Income Summary is credited for the same amount.

STEP 2 **Close Expense Accounts to Income Summary.** Expenses have debit balances and reduce owner's equity. Therefore, the expense accounts are credited to create a zero balance. Income Summary must be debited for the total of the expenses.

STEP 3 **Close Income Summary to the Owner's Capital Account.** The balance in Income Summary represents the net income (credit balance) or net loss (debit balance) for the period. This balance is transferred to the owner's capital account. If net income has been earned, Income Summary is debited to create a zero balance, and the owner's capital account is credited. If a net loss has been incurred, the owner's capital account is debited and Income Summary is credited to create a zero balance. Figure 6-5 shows examples for closing net income and net loss.

STEP 4 **Close Drawing to the Owner's Capital Account.** Drawing has a debit balance and reduces owner's equity. Therefore, it is credited to create a zero balance. The owner's capital account is debited.

LEARNING KEY

The owner can make withdrawals from the business at any time, as long as the assets are available. These withdrawals have nothing to do with measuring the profitability of the firm. Thus, they are closed directly to the owner's capital account.

Upon completion of these four steps, all temporary accounts have zero balances. The earnings and withdrawals for the period have been transferred to the owner's capital account. Closing entries for Jessie Jane's Campus Delivery, in T account form, are illustrated in Figure 6-6.

FIGURE 6-5   Step 3: Closing Net Income and Closing Net Loss

NET INCOME

Capital

	1,000	STEP 3
	(Net Income)	

Income Summary

(Expenses)	4,000	5,000	(Revenues)
STEP 3 to close	1,000	1,000	(Bal. before closing)
	—	—	

NET LOSS

Capital

STEP 3	2,000	
(Net Loss)		

Income Summary

(Expenses)	6,000	4,000	(Revenues)
(Bal. before closing)	2,000	2,000	STEP 3 to close
	—	—	

FIGURE 6-6   Closing Entries in T Account Form

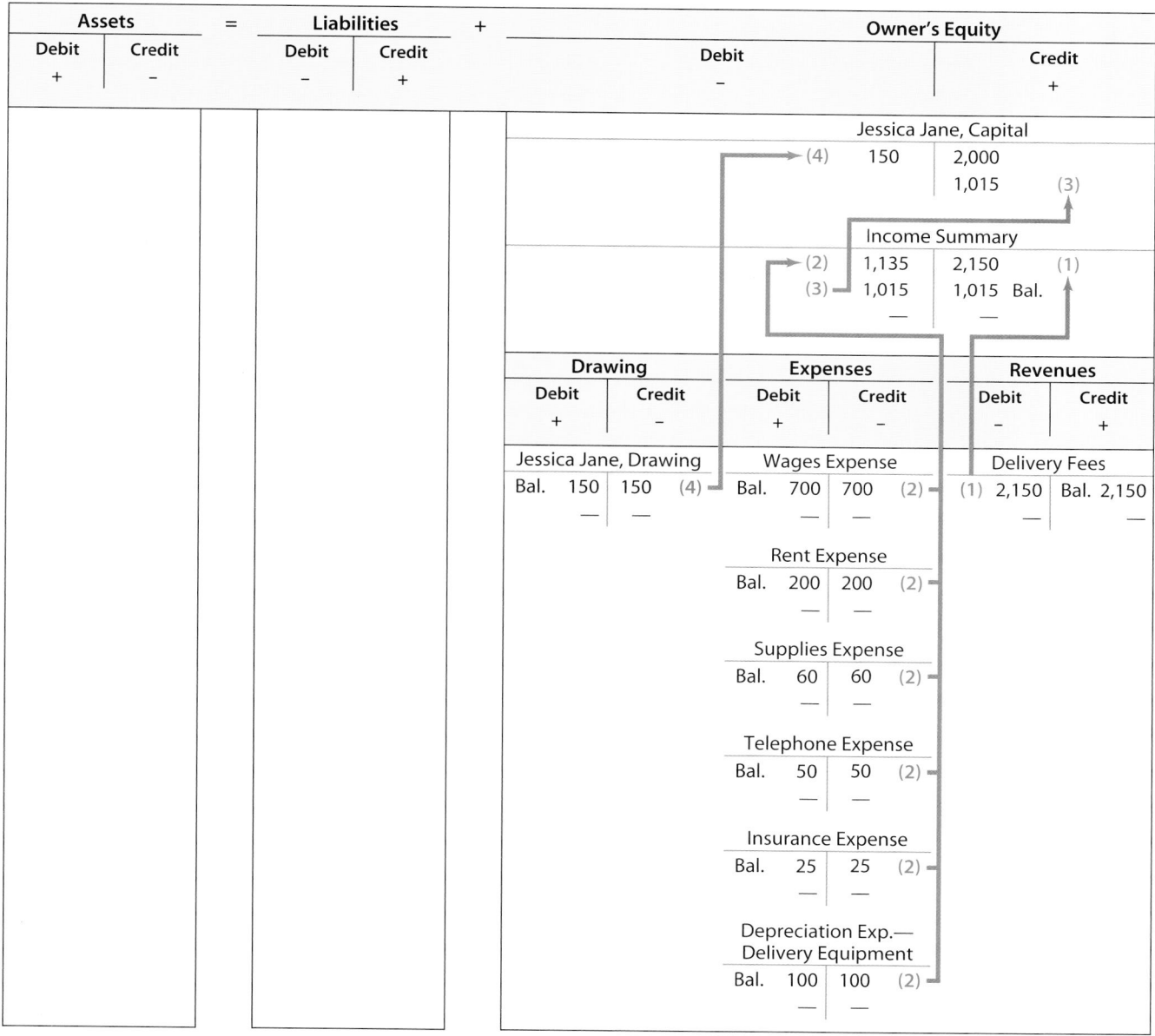

Dashes (—) in the T Accounts indicate zero balances

A BROADER VIEW

©STAN HONDA/AFP/GETTY IMAGES

Importance of Earnings to the Stock Market

Investors in the stock market pay close attention to earnings reported on the income statement. This information is so important that corporate officials often announce expected earnings before the financial statements are actually distributed to the public. If the announcement is different from what investors are expecting, the price of the stock may go up or down. For example, when Aetna, a leader in the managed health care industry, warned that earnings would be about 27 percent lower than expected by stock analysts, its stock price fell more than 10 percent.

Journalize Closing Entries

Of course, to actually change the ledger accounts, the closing entries must be journalized and posted to the general ledger. As shown in Figure 6-7, the balances of the accounts to be closed are readily available from the Income Statement and Balance Sheet columns of the work sheet. These balances are used to illustrate the closing entries for Jessie Jane's Campus Delivery, in general journal form. Remember: Closing entries are made at the end of the *fiscal year*. Closing entries made at the end of June are illustrated here so you can see the completion of the accounting cycle for Jessie Jane's Campus Delivery. Like adjusting entries, the closing entries are made on the last day of the accounting period. "Closing Entries" is written in the Description column before the first entry and no explanations are required. Note that it is best to make one compound entry to close the expense accounts.

Post the Closing Entries

The account numbers have been entered in the Posting Reference column of the journal to show that the entries have been posted to the ledger accounts illustrated in Figure 6-8. Note that "Closing" has been written in the Item column of each account to identify the closing entries. Zero account balances are recorded by drawing a line in both the Balance Debit and Credit columns.

FIGURE 6-7 Closing Entries in Journal Form

Jessie Jane's Campus Delivery
Work Sheet (Partial)
For Month Ended June 30, 20 - -

ACCOUNT TITLE	INCOME STATEMENT DEBIT	INCOME STATEMENT CREDIT	BALANCE SHEET DEBIT	BALANCE SHEET CREDIT	
1 Cash			3 7 0 00		1
2 Accounts Receivable			6 5 0 00		2
3 Supplies			2 0 00		3
4 Prepaid Insurance			1 7 5 00		4
5 Delivery Equipment			3 6 0 0 00		5
6 Accum. Depr.—Delivery Equipment				1 0 0 00	6
7 Accounts Payable				1 8 0 0 00	7
8 Wages Payable				5 0 00	8
9 Jessica Jane, Capital				2 0 0 0 00	9
10 Jessica Jane, Drawing			1 5 0 00		10
11 Delivery Fees		2 1 5 0 00			11
12 Wages Expense	7 0 0 00				12
13 Rent Expense	2 0 0 00				13
14 Supplies Expense	6 0 00				14
15 Telephone Expense	5 0 00				15
16 Insurance Expense	2 5 00				16
17 Depr. Expense—Delivery Equipment	1 0 00				17
18	1 1 3 5 00	2 1 5 0 00	4 9 6 5 00	3 9 5 0 00	18
19 Net Income	1 0 1 5 00			1 0 1 5 00	19
20	2 1 5 0 00	2 1 5 0 00	4 9 6 5 00	4 9 6 5 00	20

STEP 2

STEP 1 Close revenue accounts to Income Summary.

STEP 2 Close expense accounts to Income Summary.

STEP 3 Close Income Summary to the owner's capital account.

STEP 4 Close Drawing to the owner's capital account.

GENERAL JOURNAL   PAGE 4

DATE	DESCRIPTION	POST. REF.	DEBIT	CREDIT	
	Closing Entries				1
20--					
June 30	Delivery Fees	401	2 1 5 0 00		2
	Income Summary	313		2 1 5 0 00	3
					4
30	Income Summary	313	1 1 3 5 00		5
	Wages Expense	511		7 0 0 00	6
	Rent Expense	521		2 0 0 00	7
	Supplies Expense	523		6 0 00	8
	Telephone Expense	525		5 0 00	9
	Insurance Expense	535		2 5 00	10
	Depr. Expense—Delivery Equipment	541		1 0 00	11
					12
30	Income Summary	313	1 0 1 5 00		13
	Jessica Jane, Capital	311		1 0 1 5 00	14
					15
30	Jessica Jane, Capital	311	1 5 0 00		16
	Jessica Jane, Drawing	312		1 5 0 00	17
					18
					19

STEP 1

Compound Entry

STEP 3

STEP 4

No explanations are necessary

LEARNING KEY

Each individual revenue, expense, and drawing account must be closed.

FIGURE 6-8   Closing Entries Posted to the General Ledger

GENERAL LEDGER

ACCOUNT: Jessica Jane, Capital　　　　　　　　　　　　　　　　ACCOUNT NO. 311

DATE		ITEM	POST. REF.	DEBIT	CREDIT	BALANCE DEBIT	BALANCE CREDIT
20-- June	1		J1		2 0 0 0 00		2 0 0 0 00
	30	Closing	J4		1 0 1 5 00		3 0 1 5 00
	30	Closing	J4	1 5 0 00			2 8 6 5 00

ACCOUNT: Jessica Jane, Drawing　　　　　　　　　　　　　　　　ACCOUNT NO. 312

DATE		ITEM	POST. REF.	DEBIT	CREDIT	BALANCE DEBIT	BALANCE CREDIT
20-- June	30		J2	1 5 0 00		1 5 0 00	
	30	Closing	J4		1 5 0 00		

ACCOUNT: Income Summary　　　　　　　　　　　　　　　　ACCOUNT NO. 313

DATE		ITEM	POST. REF.	DEBIT	CREDIT	BALANCE DEBIT	BALANCE CREDIT
20-- June	30	Closing	J4		2 1 5 0 00		2 1 5 0 00
	30	Closing	J4	1 1 3 5 00			1 0 1 5 00
	30	Closing	J4	1 0 1 5 00			

ACCOUNT: Delivery Fees　　　　　　　　　　　　　　　　ACCOUNT NO. 401

DATE		ITEM	POST. REF.	DEBIT	CREDIT	BALANCE DEBIT	BALANCE CREDIT
20-- June	6		J1		5 0 0 00		5 0 0 00
	15		J1		6 0 0 00		1 1 0 0 00
	30		J2		1 0 5 0 00		2 1 5 0 00
	30	Closing	J4	2 1 5 0 00			

ACCOUNT: Wages Expense　　　　　　　　　　　　　　　　ACCOUNT NO. 511

DATE		ITEM	POST. REF.	DEBIT	CREDIT	BALANCE DEBIT	BALANCE CREDIT
20-- June	27		J2	6 5 0 00		6 5 0 00	
	30	Adjusting	J3	5 0 00		7 0 0 00	
	30	Closing	J4		7 0 0 00		

ACCOUNT: Rent Expense　　　　　　　　　　　　　　　　ACCOUNT NO. 521

DATE		ITEM	POST. REF.	DEBIT	CREDIT	BALANCE DEBIT	BALANCE CREDIT
20-- June	7		J1	2 0 0 00		2 0 0 00	
	30	Closing	J4		2 0 0 00		

ACCOUNT: Supplies Expense　　　　　　　　　　　　　　　　ACCOUNT NO. 523

DATE		ITEM	POST. REF.	DEBIT	CREDIT	BALANCE DEBIT	BALANCE CREDIT
20-- June	30	Adjusting	J3	6 0 00		6 0 00	
	30	Closing	J4		6 0 00		

FIGURE 6-8   Closing Entries Posted to the General Ledger (*continued*)

ACCOUNT: Telephone Expense   ACCOUNT NO. 525

DATE		ITEM	POST. REF.	DEBIT	CREDIT	BALANCE DEBIT	BALANCE CREDIT
20-- June	15		J1	5 0 00		5 0 00	
	30	Closing	J4		5 0 00		

ACCOUNT: Insurance Expense   ACCOUNT NO. 535

DATE		ITEM	POST. REF.	DEBIT	CREDIT	BALANCE DEBIT	BALANCE CREDIT
20-- June	30	Adjusting	J3	2 5 00		2 5 00	
	30	Closing	J4		2 5 00		

ACCOUNT: Depreciation Expense—Delivery Equipment   ACCOUNT NO. 541

DATE		ITEM	POST. REF.	DEBIT	CREDIT	BALANCE DEBIT	BALANCE CREDIT
20-- June	30	Adjusting	J3	1 0 0 00		1 0 0 00	
	30	Closing	J4		1 0 0 00		

POST-CLOSING TRIAL BALANCE

LO3 Prepare a post-closing trial balance.

After posting the closing entries, a **post-closing trial balance** should be prepared to prove the equality of the debit and credit balances in the general ledger accounts. The ending balance of each general ledger account that remains open at the end of the year is listed. Remember: Only the permanent accounts remain open after the closing process is completed. Figure 6-9 shows the post-closing trial balance for Jessie's ledger.

FIGURE 6-9   Post-Closing Trial Balance

Jessie Jane's Campus Delivery
Post-Closing Trial Balance
June 30, 20 - -

ACCOUNT TITLE	ACCOUNT NO.	DEBIT BALANCE	CREDIT BALANCE
Cash	101	3 7 0 00	
Accounts Receivable	122	6 5 0 00	
Supplies	141	2 0 00	
Prepaid Insurance	145	1 7 5 00	
Delivery Equipment	185	3 6 0 0 00	
Accumulated Depreciation—Delivery Equipment	185.1		1 0 0 00
Accounts Payable	202		1 8 0 0 00
Wages Payable	219		5 0 00
Jessica Jane, Capital	311		2 8 6 5 00
		4 8 1 5 00	4 8 1 5 00

LO4 List and describe the steps in the accounting cycle.

Note that all amounts reflected on the post-closing trial balance are the same as reported in the Balance Sheet columns of the work sheet except Drawing and Owner's Capital. Drawing was closed. Owner's Capital was updated to reflect revenues, expenses, and drawing for the accounting period.

THE ACCOUNTING CYCLE

The steps involved in accounting for all of the business activities during an accounting period are called the **accounting cycle**. The cycle begins with the analysis of source documents and ends with a post-closing trial balance. A brief summary of the steps in the cycle follows.

STEPS IN THE ACCOUNTING CYCLE

During Accounting Period

STEP 1   Analyze source documents.

STEP 2   Journalize the transactions.

STEP 3   Post to the general ledger accounts.

End of Accounting Period

STEP 4   Prepare a trial balance.

STEP 5   Determine and prepare the needed adjustments on the work sheet.

STEP 6   Complete an end-of-period work sheet.

STEP 7   Journalize and post the adjusting entries.

STEP 8   Prepare an income statement, a statement of owner's equity, and a balance sheet.

STEP 9   Journalize and post the closing entries.

STEP 10   Prepare a post-closing trial balance.

Steps 4 through 10 in the preceding list are performed *as of* the last day of the accounting period. This does not mean that they are actually done on the last day. The accountant may not be able to do any of these things until the first few days (sometimes weeks) of the next period. Nevertheless, the work sheet, statements, and entries are prepared as of the closing date.

Computers and Accounting

Accounting Software—Gary P. Schneider, University of San Diego, and Toni Hartley, Laurel Business Institute

People use computers to help them do many common tasks in business, at school, and in everyday life. For example, instead of writing a homework assignment using pen and paper or a typewriter, many students use software on a personal computer to create the homework assignment. If the homework requires calculations, students might use spreadsheet software to perform those calculations and paste the results into the document. If the homework requires a figure or other artwork, students might use a graphics program to create the art and, again, paste the results into the document. Some students will print the assignment and carry it to class. Other students may use the computer to handle the delivery chore. They can use their e-mail software to attach the document file to an e-mail message and send it to their instructor's e-mail account.

Similarly, accountants use computers to make their jobs easier. They use the types of software that other office workers use: word processing, spreadsheet, presentation, database, e-mail, and web browser software. Although it is possible to create journals and ledgers for a small business using spreadsheet software, most accountants use software that is designed to help them perform the accounting tasks you have learned about thus far in this book. Most of these accounting software packages include databases or are built on database software.

Many different companies develop accounting software. Some companies develop more than one accounting software package. The needs of a small business are quite different from the needs of a major international company. Thus, different accounting software products are available for businesses of different sizes. Although the accounting software used by larger companies is often more complex and can do more things than the software used by smaller companies, remember that the basic accounting tasks that the software must accomplish are very much the same in any size company. Also, keep in mind that accounting software does not change any of the fundamental principles that you have learned in this book. It just makes the work easier for accountants. Larger companies often write their own accounting software. In the past, this software was written in a procedural language, such as COBOL. Today, most custom-written accounting software is built using the tools and features that are a part of large database software products sold by companies such as IBM, Microsoft, and Oracle.

Good software can make accountants' jobs easier in two ways: (1) The software can do some tasks automatically, and (2) it can reduce the likelihood of errors in tasks that accountants must still do themselves, for example, making adjusting journal entries such as those you learned about in Chapter 5. At the end of the accounting period, the accountant must adjust the amount of prepaid insurance to reflect the insurance expense that has expired during the period. In a manual bookkeeping system, the accountant would debit Insurance Expense and credit Prepaid Insurance for the amount of the prepaid insurance that is used up in the period. The accountant would

(continued)

Figure A

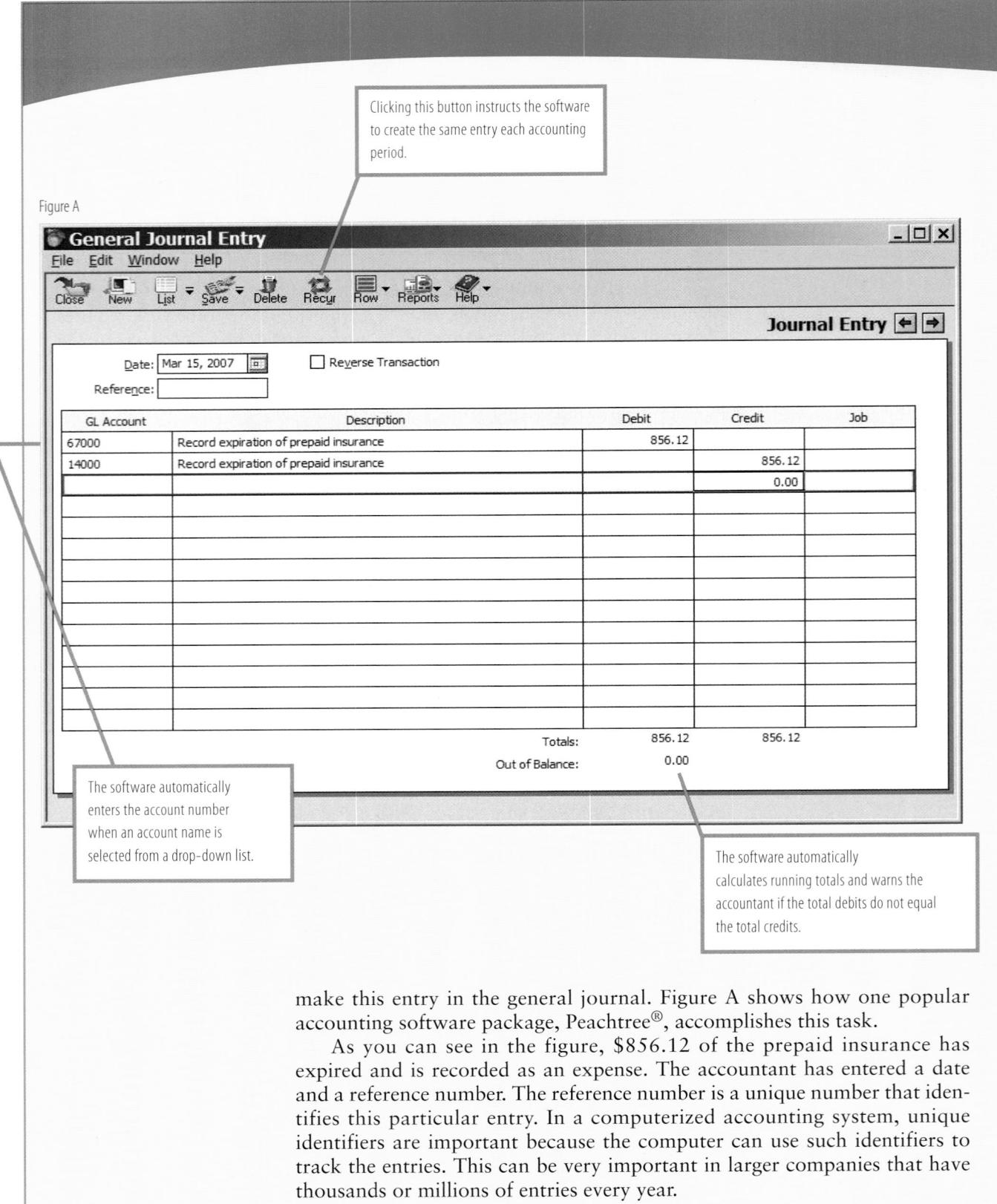

Clicking this button instructs the software to create the same entry each accounting period.

The software automatically enters the account number when an account name is selected from a drop-down list.

The software automatically calculates running totals and warns the accountant if the total debits do not equal the total credits.

make this entry in the general journal. Figure A shows how one popular accounting software package, Peachtree®, accomplishes this task.

As you can see in the figure, $856.12 of the prepaid insurance has expired and is recorded as an expense. The accountant has entered a date and a reference number. The reference number is a unique number that identifies this particular entry. In a computerized accounting system, unique identifiers are important because the computer can use such identifiers to track the entries. This can be very important in larger companies that have thousands or millions of entries every year.

Next, the accountant has entered account numbers for Insurance Expense and Prepaid Insurance. When an account name is selected from a drop-down list, the computer displays and enters the corresponding account number. This is an important error-reduction feature. It can help the accountant catch a mistaken account number entry. Finally, the accountant enters the amounts of the debit and credit for the two accounts. The software keeps a running total of the debits and credits entered and displays an Out of Balance amount if the debits and credits do not equal. Once again, the software helps prevent errors.

If an entry is one that occurs regularly, such as a monthly depreciation expense entry, the accountant can click the Recur button near the top of the form to have the software create the entry automatically every period. When the accountant has reviewed the entry and made sure that the accounts are correct and the debits and credits balance, he or she can click the Save button to record the debits and credits in the general ledger.

Figure B

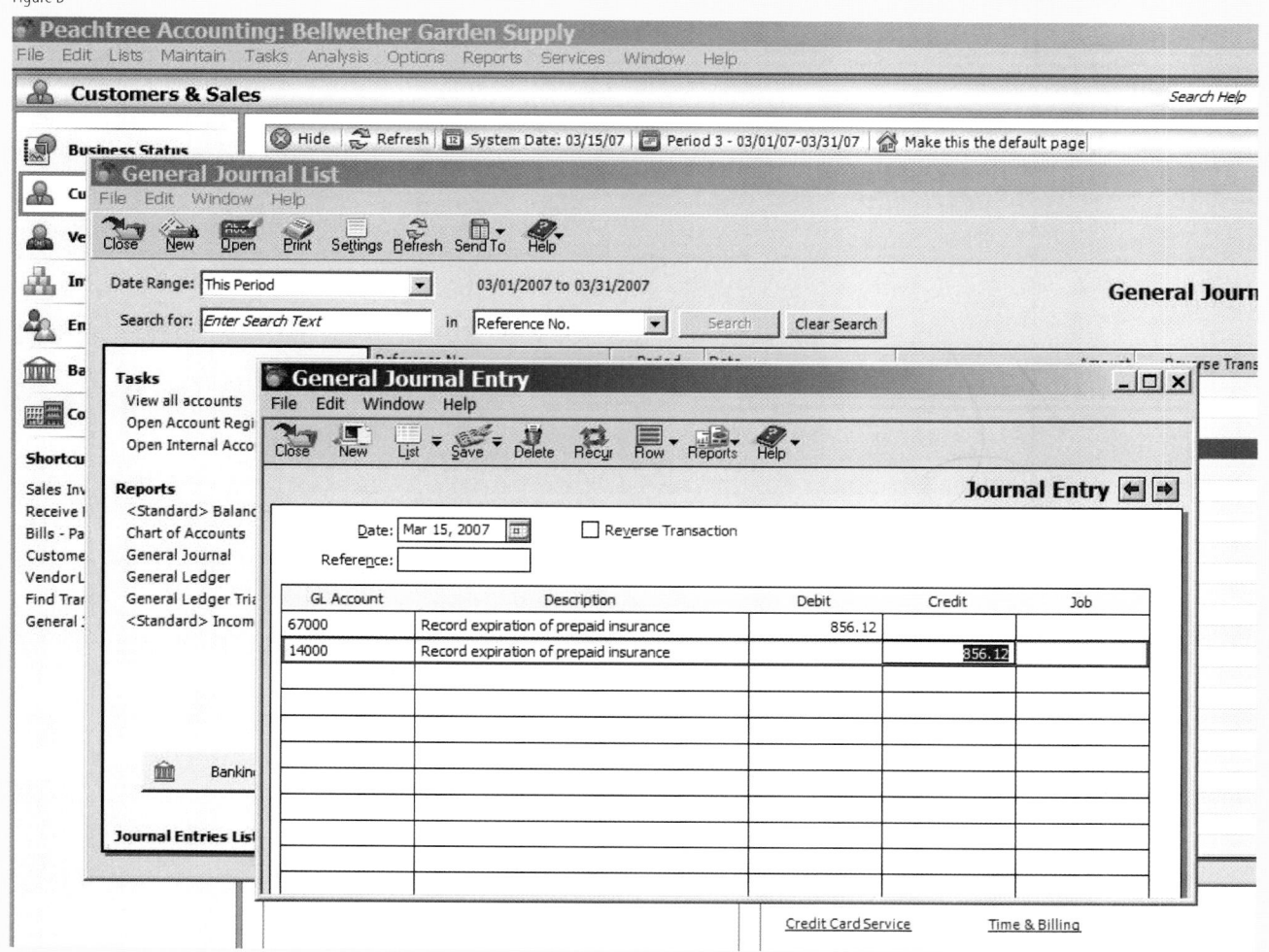

(continued)

Accountants can use the software to perform the same kinds of tasks that are necessary in any accounting system, manual or computerized. In every accounting system, someone must create and maintain the chart of accounts and make entries in the general journal. Although accountants rarely change the accounting periods of their companies, it is something that the software must be capable of doing. Finally, the reports that the software can produce include printouts of the general journal and the general ledger, along with the standard financial statements.

Learning Objectives	Key Points to Remember
LO1 Prepare financial statements with the aid of a work sheet.	The work sheet is used as an aid in preparing: 1. adjusting entries, 2. financial statements, and 3. closing entries. The following classifications are used for accounts reported on the balance sheet. • *Current assets* include cash and assets that will be converted into cash or consumed within either one year or the normal operating cycle of the business, whichever is longer. An *operating cycle* is the time required to purchase supplies and services and convert them back into cash. • *Property, plant, and equipment*, also called *plant assets* or *long-term assets*, represent assets that are expected to serve the business for many years. • *Current liabilities* are liabilities that are due within either one year or the normal operating cycle of the business, whichever is longer, and that are to be paid out of current assets. • *Long-term liabilities*, or *long-term debt*, are obligations that are not expected to be paid within a year and do not require the use of current assets.
LO2 Journalize and post closing entries.	Steps in the closing process are: 1. Close revenue accounts to Income Summary. 2. Close expense accounts to Income Summary. 3. Close Income Summary to the owner's capital account. 4. Close Drawing to the owner's capital account.

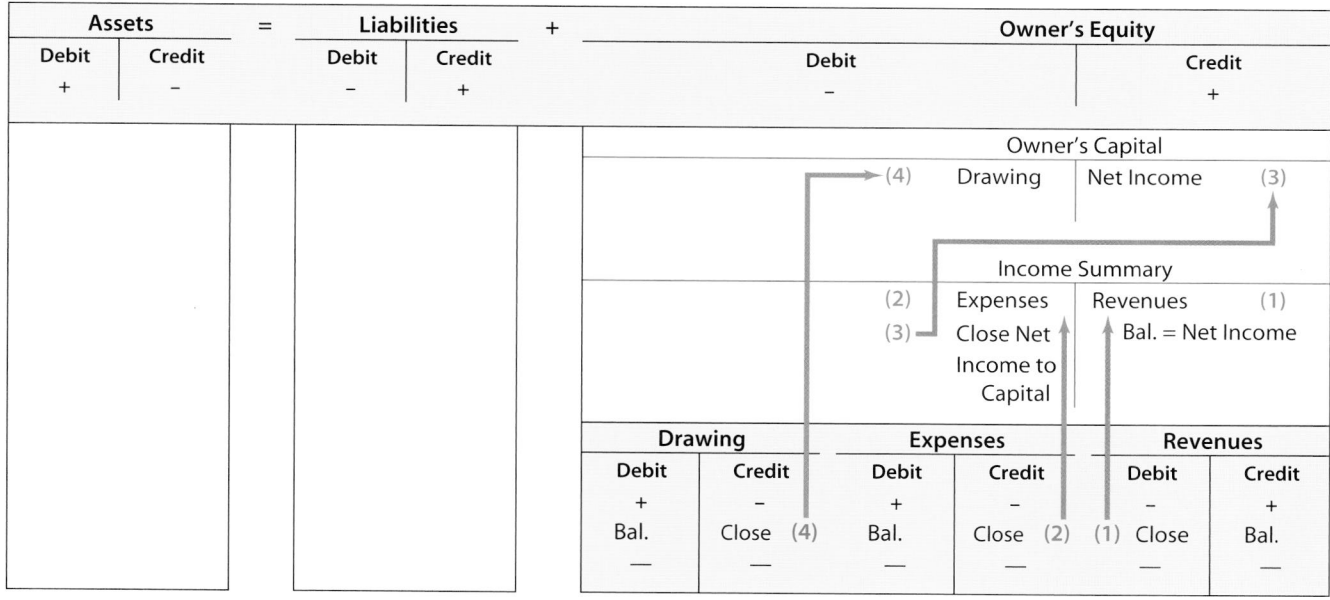

Learning Objectives	Key Points to Remember
LO3 Prepare a post-closing trial balance.	After posting the closing entries, a post-closing trial balance should be prepared to prove the equality of the debit and credit balances in the general ledger accounts. The accounts shown in the post-closing trial balance are the permanent accounts.
LO4 List and describe the steps in the accounting cycle.	Steps in the accounting cycle are: *During Accounting Period* 1. Analyze source documents. 2. Journalize the transactions. 3. Post to the general ledger accounts. *End of Accounting Period* 4. Prepare a trial balance. 5. Determine and prepare the needed adjustments on the work sheet. 6. Complete an end-of-period work sheet. 7. Journalize and post the adjusting entries. 8. Prepare an income statement, a statement of owner's equity, and a balance sheet. 9. Journalize and post the closing entries. 10. Prepare a post-closing trial balance.

DEMONSTRATION PROBLEM

Timothy Chang owns and operates Hard Copy Printers. A work sheet for the year ended December 31, 20--, is provided on the next page. Chang made no additional investments during the year.

REQUIRED

1.   Prepare financial statements.

2.   Prepare closing entries.

Hard Copy Printers
Work Sheet
For Year Ended December 31, 20 - -

	Account Title	Trial Balance Debit	Trial Balance Credit	Adjustments Debit	Adjustments Credit	Adjusted Trial Balance Debit	Adjusted Trial Balance Credit	Income Statement Debit	Income Statement Credit	Balance Sheet Debit	Balance Sheet Credit	
1	Cash	11 8 0 0 00				11 8 0 0 00				11 8 0 0 00		1
2	Paper Supplies	3 6 0 0 00			(a) 3 5 5 0 00	5 0 00				5 0 00		2
3	Prepaid Insurance	1 0 0 0 00			(b) 5 0 5 00	4 9 5 00				4 9 5 00		3
4	Printing Equipment	5 8 0 0 00				5 8 0 0 00				5 8 0 0 00		4
5	Accum. Depr.—Printing Equipment				(d) 1 2 0 0 00		1 2 0 0 00				1 2 0 0 00	5
6	Accounts Payable		5 0 0 0 00				5 0 0 0 00				5 0 0 0 00	6
7	Wages Payable				(c) 3 0 00		3 0 00				3 0 00	7
8	Timothy Chang, Capital		10 0 0 0 00				10 0 0 0 00				10 0 0 0 00	8
9	Timothy Chang, Drawing	13 0 0 0 00				13 0 0 0 00				13 0 0 0 00		9
10	Printing Fees		35 1 0 0 00				35 1 0 0 00		35 1 0 0 00			10
11	Wages Expense	11 9 7 0 00		(c) 3 0 00		12 0 0 0 00		12 0 0 0 00				11
12	Rent Expense	7 5 0 0 00				7 5 0 0 00		7 5 0 0 00				12
13	Paper Supplies Expense			(a) 3 5 5 0 00		3 5 5 0 00		3 5 5 0 00				13
14	Telephone Expense	5 5 0 00				5 5 0 00		5 5 0 00				14
15	Utilities Expense	1 0 0 0 00				1 0 0 0 00		1 0 0 0 00				15
16	Insurance Expense			(b) 5 0 5 00		5 0 5 00		5 0 5 00				16
17	Depr. Expense—Printing Equipment			(d) 1 2 0 0 00		1 2 0 0 00		1 2 0 0 00				17
18		45 6 0 0 00	45 6 0 0 00	5 2 8 5 00	5 2 8 5 00	46 8 3 0 00	46 8 3 0 00	26 3 0 5 00	35 1 0 0 00	20 5 2 5 00	11 7 3 0 00	18
19	Net Income							8 7 9 5 00			8 7 9 5 00	19
20								35 1 0 0 00	35 1 0 0 00	20 5 2 5 00	20 5 2 5 00	20

(continued)

Solution 1.

Hard Copy Printers Income Statement For Year Ended December 31, 20 - -										
Revenue:										
Printing fees						$ 35	1	0	0	00
Expenses:										
Wages expense	$ 12	0	0	0	00					
Rent expense	7	5	0	0	00					
Paper supplies expense	3	5	5	0	00					
Telephone expense		5	5	0	00					
Utilities expense	1	0	0	0	00					
Insurance expense		5	0	5	00					
Depreciation expense—printing equipment	1	2	0	0	00					
Total expenses						26	3	0	5	00
Net income						$ 8	7	9	5	00

Hard Copy Printers Statement of Owner's Equity For Year Ended December 31, 20 - -										
Timothy Chang, capital, January 1, 20 - -						$ 10	0	0	0	00
Net income for 20 - -	$ 8	7	9	5	00					
Less withdrawals for 20 - -	13	0	0	0	00					
Decrease in capital						(4	2	0	5	00)
Timothy Chang, capital, December 31, 20 - -						$ 5	7	9	5	00

Hard Copy Printers Balance Sheet December 31, 20 - -										
Assets										
Current assets:										
Cash	$ 1	1	8	0	00					
Paper supplies			5	0	00					
Prepaid insurance		4	9	5	00					
Total current assets						$ 1	7	2	5	00
Property, plant, and equipment:										
Printing equipment	$ 5	8	0	0	00					
Less accumulated depreciation	1	2	0	0	00	4	6	0	0	00
Total assets						$ 6	3	2	5	00
Liabilities										
Current liabilities:										
Accounts payable	$	5	0	0	00					
Wages payable			3	0	00					
Total current liabilities						$	5	3	0	00
Owner's Equity										
Timothy Chang, capital							5	7	9	5	00
Total liabilities and owner's equity						$ 6	3	2	5	00

2.   *from worksheet pg. 201*

	DATE		DESCRIPTION	POST. REF.	DEBIT					CREDIT					
			GENERAL JOURNAL										PAGE 4		
1			Closing Entries												1
2	20-- Dec.	31	Printing Fees		35	1	0	0	00						2
3			Income Summary							35	1	0	0	00	3
4															4
5		31	Income Summary *(not Income)*		26	3	0	5	00						5
6			Wages Expense							12	0	0	0	00	6
7			Rent Expense							7	5	0	0	00	7
8			Paper Supplies Expense							3	5	5	0	00	8
9			Telephone Expense								5	5	0	00	9
10			Utilities Expense							1	0	0	0	00	10
11			Insurance Expense								5	0	5	00	11
12			Depr. Expense—Printing Equipment							1	2	0	0	00	12
13															13
14		31	Income Summary		8	7	9	5	00						14
15			Timothy Chang, Capital							8	7	9	5	00	15
16															16
17		31	Timothy Chang, Capital		13	0	0	0	00						17
18			Timothy Chang, Drawing							13	0	0	0	00	18
19															19

KEY TERMS

account form of balance sheet (185)   A balance sheet in which the assets are on the left and the liabilities and the owner's equity sections are on the right.

accounting cycle (194)   The steps involved in accounting for all of the business activities during an accounting period.

classified balance sheet (185)   A balance sheet with separate categories for current assets; property, plant, and equipment; current liabilities; and long-term liabilities.

closing process (187)   The process of giving zero balances to the temporary accounts so that they can accumulate information for the next accounting period.

current assets (185)   Cash and assets that will be converted into cash or consumed within either one year or the normal operating cycle of the business, whichever is longer.

current liabilities (185)   Liabilities that are due within either one year or the normal operating cycle of the business, whichever is longer, and that are to be paid out of current assets.

Income Summary (187)   A temporary account used in the closing process to summarize the effects of all revenue and expense accounts.

long-term assets (185)   See property, plant, and equipment.

long-term debt (185)   See long-term liabilities.

long-term liabilities (185)   Obligations that are not expected to be paid within a year and do not require the use of current assets. Also called long-term debt.

operating cycle (185)   The period of time required to purchase supplies and services and convert them back into cash.

permanent accounts (187)   Accounts that accumulate information across accounting periods; all accounts reported on the balance sheet.

plant assets (185)   See property, plant, and equipment.

post-closing trial balance (193)   Prepared after posting the closing entries to prove the equality of the debit and credit balances in the general ledger accounts.

property, plant, and equipment (185)   Assets that are expected to serve the business for many years. Also called plant assets or long-term assets.

report form of balance sheet (185)   A balance sheet in which the liabilities and the owner's equity sections are shown below the assets section.

temporary accounts (187)   Accounts that do not accumulate information across accounting periods but are closed, such as the drawing account and all income statement accounts.

Self-Study Test Questions

True/False

1. Expenses are listed on the income statement as they appear in the chart of accounts or in descending order (by dollar amount).

2. Additional investments of capital during the month are not reported on the statement of owner's equity.

3. The income statement cannot be prepared using the work sheet alone.

4. A classified balance sheet groups similar items together such as current assets.

5. Temporary accounts are closed at the end of each accounting period.

Multiple Choice

1. Which of these types of accounts is considered a "permanent" account?

   (a) Revenue
   (b) Asset ✓
   (c) Drawing
   (d) Expense

2. Which of these accounts is considered a "temporary" account?

   (a) Cash
   (b) Accounts Payable
   (c) J. Jones, Capital
   (d) J. Jones, Drawing ✓

3. Which of these is the first step in the closing process?

   (a) Close revenue account(s). ✓
   (b) Close expense accounts. ✗
   (c) Close the income summary account. add. to capital
   (d) Close the drawing account. Close

4. The _____ is prepared after closing entries are posted to prove the equality of debit and credit balances.

   (a) balance sheet
   (b) income statement
   (c) post-closing trial balance ✓
   (d) statement of owner's equity

5. Steps that begin with analyzing source documents and conclude with the post-closing trial balance are called the

   (a) closing process.
   (b) accounting cycle. ✓
   (c) adjusting entries.
   (d) posting process.

The answers to the Self-Study Test Questions are at the end of the text.

REVIEW QUESTIONS

LO1   1. Identify the source of the information needed to prepare the income statement.

LO1   2. Describe two approaches to listing the expenses in the income statement.

LO1   3. Identify the sources of the information needed to prepare the statement of owner's equity.

LO1   4. If additional investments were made during the year, what information in addition to the work sheet would be needed to prepare the statement of owner's equity?

LO1   5. Identify the sources of the information needed to prepare the balance sheet.

LO2   6. What is a permanent account? On which financial statement are permanent accounts reported?

LO2   7. Name three types of temporary accounts.

LO2   8. List the four steps for closing the temporary accounts.

LO2   9. Describe the net effect of the four closing entries on the balance of the owner's capital account. Where else is this same amount calculated?

LO3   10. What is the purpose of the post-closing trial balance?

LO4   11. List the 10 steps in the accounting cycle.

REVISITING THE OPENER

In the chapter opener on page 181, you are asked to consider whether Jessie and Mitch must prepare the closing entries on New Year's Eve. Please draft a memo to address the following questions:

(1) What is the purpose of the closing entries?

(2) Must the closing entries actually be made on the last day of the accounting period?

(3) Why is the closing date important?

SERIES A EXERCISES   Do as Homework

E 6-1A (LO1)
✓ Net income: $1,990

INCOME STATEMENT From the partial work sheet for Case Advising, prepare an income statement.

Case Advising
Work Sheet (Partial)
For Month Ended January 31, 20 - -

	ACCOUNT TITLE	INCOME STATEMENT DEBIT				INCOME STATEMENT CREDIT				BALANCE SHEET DEBIT				BALANCE SHEET CREDIT				
1	Cash									1	2	1	2	00				1
2	Accounts Receivable										8	9	6	00				2
3	Supplies										4	8	2	00				3
4	Prepaid Insurance										9	0	0	00				4
5	Office Equipment									3	0	0	0	00				5
6	Accum. Depr.—Office Equipment														1	0	0	00	6
7	Accounts Payable													1	0	0	0	00	7
8	Wages Payable														2	0	0	00	8
9	Bill Case, Capital													4	0	0	0	00	9
10	Bill Case, Drawing										8	0	0	00				10
11	Advising Fees					3	7	9	3	00								11
12	Wages Expense	8	0	0	00													12
13	Advertising Expense		8	0	00													13
14	Rent Expense	5	0	0	00													14
15	Supplies Expense	1	2	0	00													15
16	Telephone Expense		5	8	00													16
17	Electricity Expense		4	4	00													17
18	Insurance Expense		3	0	00													18
19	Gas and Oil Expense		3	8	00													19
20	Depr. Expense—Office Equipment	1	0	0	00													20
21	Miscellaneous Expense		3	3	00													21
22		1	8	0	3	00	3	7	9	3	00	7	2	9	0	00	5	3	0	0	00	22
23	Net Income	1	9	9	0	00											1	9	9	0	00	23
24		3	7	9	3	00	3	7	9	3	00	7	2	9	0	00	7	2	9	0	00	24

E 6-2A (LO1)
✓ Capital 1/31: $5,190

STATEMENT OF OWNER'S EQUITY From the partial work sheet in Exercise 6-1A, prepare a statement of owner's equity, assuming no additional investment was made by the owner.

E 6-3A (LO1)
✓ Total assets: $6,390

BALANCE SHEET From the partial work sheet in Exercise 6-1A, prepare a balance sheet.

E 6-4A (LO2)
✓ Capital 1/31: $5,190

CLOSING ENTRIES (NET INCOME) Set up T accounts for Case Advising based on the work sheet in Exercise 6-1A and the chart of accounts provided below. Enter the existing balance for each account. Prepare closing entries in general journal form. Then post the closing entries to the T accounts.

(continued)

Chart of Accounts

Assets
101   Cash
122   Accounts Receivable
141   Supplies
145   Prepaid Insurance
181   Office Equipment
181.1 Accum. Depr.—Office Equip.

Liabilities
202   Accounts Payable
219   Wages Payable

Owner's Equity
311   Bill Case, Capital
312   Bill Case, Drawing
313   Income Summary

Revenues
401   Advising Fees

Expenses
511   Wages Expense
512   Advertising Expense
521   Rent Expense
524   Supplies Expense
525   Telephone Expense
533   Electricity Expense
535   Insurance Expense
538   Gas and Oil Expense
541   Depr. Exp.—Office Equip.
549   Miscellaneous Expense

E 6-5A (LO2)

✓ Capital 1/31: $2,597

CLOSING ENTRIES (NET LOSS) Using the following T accounts, prepare closing entries in general journal form dated January 31, 20--. Then post the closing entries to the T accounts.

Accum. Depr.— Del. Equip. 185.1	Wages Expense 511	Electricity Expense 533
Bal. 100	Bal. 1,800	Bal. 44

Wages Payable 219	Advertising Expense 512	Insurance Expense 535
Bal. 200	Bal. 80	Bal. 30

Saburo Goto, Capital 311	Rent Expense 521	Gas and Oil Expense 538
Bal. 4,000	Bal. 500	Bal. 38

Saburo Goto, Drawing 312	Supplies Expense 523	Depr. Exp.— Del. Equip. 541
Bal. 800	Bal. 120	Bal. 100

Income Summary 313	Telephone Expense 525	Miscellaneous Expense 549
	Bal. 58	Bal. 33

Delivery Fees   401
Bal.   2,200

SERIES A PROBLEMS

P 6-6A (LO1)

✓ Net income: $1,400;
Capital 1/31: $7,400;
Total assets: $8,650

FINANCIAL STATEMENTS Page 210 shows a work sheet for Monte's Repairs. No additional investments were made by the owner during the month.

REQUIRED

1. Prepare an income statement.

2. Prepare a statement of owner's equity.

3. Prepare a balance sheet.

P 6-7A (LO1)

✓ Capital 1/31: $6,820

STATEMENT OF OWNER'S EQUITY The capital account for Autumn Chou, including an additional investment, and a partial work sheet are shown below.

REQUIRED

Prepare a statement of owner's equity.

GENERAL LEDGER

ACCOUNT: Autumn Chou, Capital   ACCOUNT NO. 311

DATE		ITEM	POST. REF.	DEBIT	CREDIT	BALANCE DEBIT	BALANCE CREDIT
20-- Jan.	1	Balance	✔				4 8 0 0 00
	18		J 1		1 2 0 0 00		6 0 0 0 00

from pg. 210

Autumn's Home Designs
Work Sheet (Partial)
For Month Ended January 31, 20 - -

	ACCOUNT TITLE	INCOME STATEMENT DEBIT	INCOME STATEMENT CREDIT	BALANCE SHEET DEBIT	BALANCE SHEET CREDIT	
1	Cash			3 2 0 0 00		1
2	Accounts Receivable			1 6 0 0 00		2
3	Supplies			8 0 0 00		3
4	Prepaid Insurance			9 0 0 00		4
5	Office Equipment			2 5 0 0 00		5
6	Accum. Depr.—Office Equipment				5 0 00	6
7	Accounts Payable				1 9 5 0 00	7
8	Wages Payable				1 8 0 00	8
9	Autumn Chou, Capital				6 0 0 0 00	9
10	Autumn Chou, Drawing			1 0 0 0 00		10
11	Design Fees		4 8 6 6 00			11
12	Wages Expense	1 9 0 0 00				12
13	Advertising Expense	2 1 00				13
14	Rent Expense	6 0 0 00				14
15	Supplies Expense	2 0 0 00				15
16	Telephone Expense	8 5 00				16
17	Electricity Expense	4 8 00				17
18	Insurance Expense	6 0 00				18
19	Gas and Oil Expense	3 2 00				19
20	Depr. Expense—Office Equipment	5 0 00				20
21	Miscellaneous Expense	5 0 00				21
22		3 0 4 6 00	4 8 6 6 00	10 0 0 0 00	8 1 8 0 00	22
23	Net Income	1 8 2 0 00			1 8 2 0 00	23
24		4 8 6 6 00	4 8 6 6 00	10 0 0 0 00	10 0 0 0 00	24

(continued)

(PROBLEM 6-6A)

Monte's Repairs
Work Sheet
For Month Ended January 31, 20 - -

	ACCOUNT TITLE	TRIAL BALANCE		ADJUSTMENTS		ADJUSTED TRIAL BALANCE		INCOME STATEMENT		BALANCE SHEET	
		DEBIT	CREDIT	DEBIT	CREDIT	DEBIT	CREDIT	DEBIT	CREDIT	DEBIT	CREDIT
1	Cash	3 0 8 0 00				3 0 8 0 00				3 0 8 0 00	
2	Accounts Receivable	1 2 0 0 00				1 2 0 0 00				1 2 0 0 00	
3	Supplies	8 0 0 00			(a) 2 0 0 00	6 0 0 00				6 0 0 00	
4	Prepaid Insurance	9 0 0 00			(b) 1 0 0 00	8 0 0 00				8 0 0 00	
5	Delivery Equipment	3 0 0 0 00				3 0 0 0 00				3 0 0 0 00	
6	Accum. Depr.—Delivery Equipment				(d) 3 0 00		3 0 00				3 0 00
7	Accounts Payable		1 1 0 0 00				1 1 0 0 00				1 1 0 0 00
8	Wages Payable				(c) 1 5 0 00		1 5 0 00				1 5 0 00
9	Monte Eli, Capital		7 0 0 0 00				7 0 0 0 00				7 0 0 0 00
10	Monte Eli, Drawing	1 0 0 0 00				1 0 0 0 00				1 0 0 0 00	
11	Repair Fees		4 2 3 0 00				4 2 3 0 00		4 2 3 0 00		
12	Wages Expense	1 6 5 0 00		(c) 1 5 0 00		1 8 0 0 00		1 8 0 0 00			
13	Advertising Expense	1 7 0 00				1 7 0 00		1 7 0 00			
14	Rent Expense	4 2 0 00				4 2 0 00		4 2 0 00			
15	Supplies Expense			(a) 2 0 0 00		2 0 0 00		2 0 0 00			
16	Telephone Expense	4 9 00				4 9 00		4 9 00			
17	Insurance Expense			(b) 1 0 0 00		1 0 0 00		1 0 0 00			
18	Gas and Oil Expense	3 3 00				3 3 00		3 3 00			
19	Depr. Expense—Delivery Equipment			(d) 3 0 00		3 0 00		3 0 00			
20	Miscellaneous Expense	2 8 00				2 8 00		2 8 00			
21		12 3 3 0 00	12 3 3 0 00	4 8 0 00	4 8 0 00	12 5 1 0 00	12 5 1 0 00	2 8 3 0 00	4 2 3 0 00	9 6 8 0 00	8 2 8 0 00
22	Net Income							1 4 0 0 00			1 4 0 0 00
23								4 2 3 0 00	4 2 3 0 00	9 6 8 0 00	9 6 8 0 00
24											
25											
26											
27											
28											
29											
30											

P 6-8A (LO2/3)

✓ Capital 1/31:$7,400;
Post-closing Trial Bal.
total debits: $8,680

KLOOSTER & ALLEN

CLOSING ENTRIES AND POST-CLOSING TRIAL BALANCE Refer to the work sheet in Problem 6-6A for Monte's Repairs. The trial balance amounts (before adjustments) have been entered in the ledger accounts provided in the working papers. If you are not using the working papers that accompany this book, set up ledger accounts and enter these balances as of January 31, 20--. A chart of accounts is provided below.

Monte's Repairs
Chart of Accounts

Assets
101   Cash
122   Accounts Receivable
141   Supplies
145   Prepaid Insurance
185   Delivery Equipment
185.1 Accum. Depr.—Delivery Equip.

Liabilities
202   Accounts Payable
219   Wages Payable

Owner's Equity
311   Monte Eli, Capital   *Credits* *Debit*
312   Monte Eli, Drawing
313   Income Summary

Revenues
401   Repair Fees   *Debit, credit Capital*

Expenses   *Credits*
511   Wages Expense
512   Advertising Expense
521   Rent Expense
523   Supplies Expense
525   Telephone Expense
535   Insurance Expense
538   Gas and Oil Expense
541   Depr. Exp.—Delivery Equip.
549   Miscellaneous Expense

2830 - Debit to Capital

REQUIRED

1.   Journalize (page 10) and post the adjusting entries

2.   Journalize (page 11) and post the closing entries.

3.   Prepare a post-closing trial balance.

SERIES B EXERCISES

E 6-1B (LO1)

✓ Net income: $1,826

INCOME STATEMENT From the partial work sheet for Adams' Shoe Shine on the next page, prepare an income statement.

E 6-2B (LO1)

✓ Capital 6/30: $5,826

STATEMENT OF OWNER'S EQUITY From the partial work sheet in Exercise 6-1B, prepare a statement of owner's equity, assuming no additional investment was made by the owner.

E 6-3B (LO1)

✓ Total assets: $7,936

BALANCE SHEET From the partial work sheet in Exercise 6-1B, prepare a balance sheet for Adams' Shoe Shine.

(continued)

(EXERCISE 6-1B)

Adams' Shoe Shine
Work Sheet (Partial)
For Month Ended June 30, 20 - -

	ACCOUNT TITLE	INCOME STATEMENT		BALANCE SHEET		
		DEBIT	CREDIT	DEBIT	CREDIT	
1	Cash			3 2 6 2 00		1
2	Accounts Receivable			1 2 4 4 00		2
3	Supplies			8 0 0 00		3
4	Prepaid Insurance			6 4 0 00		4
5	Office Equipment			2 1 0 0 00		5
6	Accum. Depr.—Office Equipment				1 1 0 00	6
7	Accounts Payable				1 8 5 0 00	7
8	Wages Payable				2 6 0 00	8
9	Mary Adams, Capital				6 0 0 0 00	9
10	Mary Adams, Drawing			2 0 0 0 00		10
11	Service Fees		4 8 1 3 00			11
12	Wages Expense	1 0 8 0 00				12
13	Advertising Expense	3 4 00				13
14	Rent Expense	9 0 0 00				14
15	Supplies Expense	3 2 2 00				15
16	Telephone Expense	1 3 3 00				16
17	Utilities Expense	1 0 2 00				17
18	Insurance Expense	1 2 0 00				18
19	Gas and Oil Expense	8 8 00				19
20	Depr. Expense—Office Equipment	1 1 0 00				20
21	Miscellaneous Expense	9 8 00				21
22		2 9 8 7 00	4 8 1 3 00	10 0 4 6 00	8 2 2 0 00	22
23	Net Income	1 8 2 6 00			1 8 2 6 00	23
24		4 8 1 3 00	4 8 1 3 00	10 0 4 6 00	10 0 4 6 00	24

E 6-4B (LO2)

✓ Capital 6/30: $5,826

CLOSING ENTRIES (NET INCOME) Set up T accounts for Adams' Shoe Shine based on the work sheet in Exercise 6-1B and the chart of accounts provided below. Enter the existing balance for each account. Prepare closing entries in general journal form. Then, post the closing entries to the T accounts.

Chart of Accounts

Assets
101   Cash
122   Accounts Receivable
141   Supplies
145   Prepaid Insurance
181   Office Equipment
181.1   Accum. Depr.—Office Equip.

Liabilities
202   Accounts Payable
219   Wages Payable

Owner's Equity
311   Mary Adams, Capital
312   Mary Adams, Drawing
313   Income Summary

Revenues
401   Service Fees

Expenses
511   Wages Expense
512   Advertising Expense
521   Rent Expense
523   Supplies Expense
525   Telephone Expense
533   Utilities Expense
535   Insurance Expense
538   Gas and Oil Expense
542   Depr. Exp.—Office Equip.
549   Miscellaneous Expense

E 6-5B (LO2)

✓ Capital 6/30: $3,826

CLOSING ENTRIES (NET LOSS) Using the following T accounts, prepare closing entries in general journal form dated June 30, 20--. Then post the closing entries to the T accounts.

Accum. Depr.— Office Equip.		181.1
	Bal.	110

Wages Payable		219
	Bal.	260

Raquel Zapata, Capital		311
	Bal.	6,000

Raquel Zapata, Drawing		312
Bal.	2,000	

Income Summary		313

Referral Fees		401
	Bal.	2,813

Wages Expense		511
Bal.	1,080	

Advertising Expense		512
Bal.	34	

Rent Expense		521
Bal.	900	

Supplies Expense		523
Bal.	322	

Telephone Expense		525
Bal.	133	

Utilities Expense		533
Bal.	102	

Insurance Expense		535
Bal.	120	

Gas and Oil Expense		538
Bal.	88	

Depr. Exp.— Office Equip.		541
Bal.	110	

Miscellaneous Expense		549
Bal.	98	

SERIES B PROBLEMS

P 6-6B (LO1)

✓ Net income: $1,450;
Capital 6/30: $7,650;
Total assets: $9,350

FINANCIAL STATEMENTS A work sheet for Juanita's Consulting is shown on the following page. There were no additional investments made by the owner during the month.

REQUIRED

1. Prepare an income statement.

2. Prepare a statement of owner's equity.

3. Prepare a balance sheet.

(continued)

(PROBLEM 6-6B)

Juanita's Consulting
Work Sheet
For Month Ended June 30, 20 - -

	ACCOUNT TITLE	TRIAL BALANCE DEBIT	TRIAL BALANCE CREDIT	ADJUSTMENTS DEBIT	ADJUSTMENTS CREDIT	ADJUSTED TRIAL BALANCE DEBIT	ADJUSTED TRIAL BALANCE CREDIT	INCOME STATEMENT DEBIT	INCOME STATEMENT CREDIT	BALANCE SHEET DEBIT	BALANCE SHEET CREDIT	
1	Cash	5 2 8 5 00				5 2 8 5 00				5 2 8 5 00		1
2	Accounts Receivable	1 0 7 5 00				1 0 7 5 00				1 0 7 5 00		2
3	Supplies	7 5 0 00			(a) 2 5 0 00	5 0 0 00				5 0 0 00		3
4	Prepaid Insurance	5 0 0 00			(b) 1 0 0 00	4 0 0 00				4 0 0 00		4
5	Office Equipment	2 2 0 0 00				2 2 0 0 00				2 2 0 0 00		5
6	Accum. Depr.—Office Equipment				(d) 1 1 0 00		1 1 0 00				1 1 0 00	6
7	Accounts Payable		1 5 0 0 00				1 5 0 0 00				1 5 0 0 00	7
8	Wages Payable				(c) 2 0 0 00		2 0 0 00				2 0 0 00	8
9	Juanita Alvarez, Capital		7 0 0 0 00				7 0 0 0 00				7 0 0 0 00	9
10	Juanita Alvarez, Drawing	8 0 0 00				8 0 0 00				8 0 0 00		10
11	Consulting Fees		4 2 0 4 00				4 2 0 4 00		4 2 0 4 00			11
12	Wages Expense	1 4 0 0 00		(c) 2 0 0 00		1 6 0 0 00		1 6 0 0 00				12
13	Advertising Expense	6 0 00				6 0 00		6 0 00				13
14	Rent Expense	5 0 0 00				5 0 0 00		5 0 0 00				14
15	Supplies Expense			(a) 2 5 0 00		2 5 0 00		2 5 0 00				15
16	Telephone Expense	4 6 00				4 6 00		4 6 00				16
17	Electricity Expense	3 9 00				3 9 00		3 9 00				17
18	Insurance Expense			(b) 1 0 0 00		1 0 0 00		1 0 0 00				18
19	Gas and Oil Expense	2 8 00				2 8 00		2 8 00				19
20	Depr. Expense—Office Equipment			(d) 1 1 0 00		1 1 0 00		1 1 0 00				20
21	Miscellaneous Expense	2 1 00				2 1 00		2 1 00				21
22		12 7 0 4 00	12 7 0 4 00	6 6 0 00	6 6 0 00	13 0 1 4 00	13 0 1 4 00	2 7 5 4 00	4 2 0 4 00	10 2 6 0 00	8 8 1 0 00	22
23	Net Income							1 4 5 0 00			1 4 5 0 00	23
24								4 2 0 4 00	4 2 0 4 00	10 2 6 0 00	10 2 6 0 00	24
25												25
26												26
27												27
28												28
29												29
30												30

P 6-7B (LO1)

✓ Capital 1/31: $9,975

STATEMENT OF OWNER'S EQUITY The capital account for Minta's Editorial Services, including an additional investment, and a partial work sheet are shown below.

GENERAL LEDGER

ACCOUNT: Minta Berry, Capital   ACCOUNT NO. 311

DATE		ITEM	POST. REF.	DEBIT	CREDIT	BALANCE DEBIT	BALANCE CREDIT
20-- Jan.	1	Balance	✔				3 6 0 0 00
	22		J 1		2 9 0 0 00		6 5 0 0 00

Minta's Editorial Services
Work Sheet (Partial)
For Month Ended January 31, 20 - -

	ACCOUNT TITLE	INCOME STATEMENT DEBIT	INCOME STATEMENT CREDIT	BALANCE SHEET DEBIT	BALANCE SHEET CREDIT	
1	Cash			3 8 0 0 00		1
2	Accounts Receivable			2 2 0 0 00		2
3	Supplies			1 0 0 0 00		3
4	Prepaid Insurance			9 5 0 00		4
5	Computer Equipment			4 5 0 0 00		5
6	Accum. Depr.—Computer Equipment				2 2 5 00	6
7	Accounts Payable				2 1 0 0 00	7
8	Wages Payable				1 5 0 00	8
9	Minta Berry, Capital				6 5 0 0 00	9
10	Minta Berry, Drawing			1 7 0 0 00		10
11	Editing Fees		7 0 1 2 00			11
12	Wages Expense	6 0 0 00				12
13	Advertising Expense	4 9 00				13
14	Rent Expense	4 5 0 00				14
15	Supplies Expense	2 8 8 00				15
16	Telephone Expense	4 4 00				16
17	Utilities Expense	3 8 00				17
18	Insurance Expense	1 2 5 00				18
19	Depr. Expense—Computer Equipment	2 2 5 00				19
20	Miscellaneous Expense	1 8 00				20
21		1 8 3 7 00	7 0 1 2 00	14 1 5 0 00	8 9 7 5 00	21
22	Net Income	5 1 7 5 00			5 1 7 5 00	22
23		7 0 1 2 00	7 0 1 2 00	14 1 5 0 00	14 1 5 0 00	23

REQUIRED

Prepare a statement of owner's equity.

P 6-8B (LO2/3)

✓ Capital 6/30: $7,650;
Post-closing Trial Bal.
total debits: $9,460

CLOSING ENTRIES AND POST-CLOSING TRIAL BALANCE Refer to the work sheet for Juanita's Consulting in Problem 6-6B. The trial balance amounts (before adjustments) have been entered in the ledger accounts provided in the working papers. If you are not using the working papers that accompany this book, set up ledger accounts and enter these balances as of June 30, 20--. A chart of accounts is provided below.

Juanita's Consulting
Chart of Accounts

Assets
101   Cash
122   Accounts Receivable
141   Supplies
145   Prepaid Insurance
181   Office Equipment
181.1 Accum. Depr.—Office Equip.

Liabilities
202   Accounts Payable
219   Wages Payable

Owner's Equity
311   Juanita Alvarez, Capital
312   Juanita Alvarez, Drawing
313   Income Summary

Revenues
401   Consulting Fees

Expenses
511   Wages Expense
512   Advertising Expense
521   Rent Expense
523   Supplies Expense
525   Telephone Expense
533   Electricity Expense
535   Insurance Expense
538   Gas and Oil Expense
541   Depr. Exp.—Office Equip.
549   Miscellaneous Expense

REQUIRED

1. Journalize (page 10) and post the adjusting entries.

2. Journalize (page 11) and post the closing entries.

3. Prepare a post-closing trial balance.

MANAGING YOUR WRITING

At lunch, two bookkeepers got into a heated discussion about whether closing entries should be made before or after preparing the financial statements. They have come to you to resolve this issue and have agreed to accept your position. Write a memo explaining the purpose of closing entries and whether they should be made before or after preparing the financial statements.

MASTERY PROBLEM

✓ Total assets: $4,740;
E. Soltis, capital, Dec. 31: $4,475

Elizabeth Soltis owns and operates Aunt Ibby's Styling Salon. A year-end work sheet is provided on the next page. Using this information, prepare adjusting entries, financial statements, and closing entries. Soltis made no additional investments during the year.

Aunt Ibby's Styling Salon
Work Sheet
For Year Ended December 31, 20 - -

	ACCOUNT TITLE	TRIAL BALANCE DEBIT	TRIAL BALANCE CREDIT	ADJUSTMENTS DEBIT	ADJUSTMENTS CREDIT	ADJUSTED TRIAL BALANCE DEBIT	ADJUSTED TRIAL BALANCE CREDIT	INCOME STATEMENT DEBIT	INCOME STATEMENT CREDIT	BALANCE SHEET DEBIT	BALANCE SHEET CREDIT	
1	Cash	9 4 0 00				9 4 0 00				9 4 0 00		1
2	Styling Supplies	1 5 0 0 00			(a) 1 4 5 0 00	5 0 00				5 0 00		2
3	Prepaid Insurance	8 0 0 00			(b) 6 5 0 00	1 5 0 00				1 5 0 00		3
4	Salon Equipment	4 5 0 0 00				4 5 0 0 00				4 5 0 0 00		4
5	Accum. Depr.—Salon Equipment				(d) 9 0 0 00		9 0 0 00				9 0 0 00	5
6	Accounts Payable		2 2 5 00				2 2 5 00				2 2 5 00	6
7	Wages Payable				(c) 4 0 00		4 0 00				4 0 00	7
8	Elizabeth Soltis, Capital		2 7 6 5 00				2 7 6 5 00				2 7 6 5 00	8
9	Elizabeth Soltis, Drawing	1 2 0 0 0 00				1 2 0 0 0 00				1 2 0 0 0 00		9
10	Styling Fees		3 2 0 0 0 00				3 2 0 0 0 00		3 2 0 0 0 00			10
11	Wages Expense	8 0 0 0 00		(c) 4 0 00		8 0 4 0 00		8 0 4 0 00				11
12	Rent Expense	6 0 0 0 00				6 0 0 0 00		6 0 0 0 00				12
13	Styling Supplies Expense			(a) 1 4 5 0 00		1 4 5 0 00		1 4 5 0 00				13
14	Telephone Expense	4 5 0 00				4 5 0 00		4 5 0 00				14
15	Utilities Expense	8 0 0 00				8 0 0 00		8 0 0 00				15
16	Insurance Expense			(b) 6 5 0 00		6 5 0 00		6 5 0 00				16
17	Depr. Expense—Salon Equipment			(d) 9 0 0 00		9 0 0 00		9 0 0 00				17
18		34 9 9 0 00	34 9 9 0 00	3 0 4 0 00	3 0 4 0 00	35 9 3 0 00	35 9 3 0 00	18 2 9 0 00	32 0 0 0 00	17 6 4 0 00	3 9 3 0 00	18
19	Net Income							13 7 1 0 00			13 7 1 0 00	19
20								32 0 0 0 00	32 0 0 0 00	17 6 4 0 00	17 6 4 0 00	20
21												21
22												22
23												23
24												24
25												25
26												26
27												27
28												28
29												29
30												30

CHALLENGE PROBLEM

This problem challenges you to apply your cumulative accounting knowledge to move a step beyond the material in the chapter.

✓ Net loss: $2,100;

Capital, 1/31/20--: ($700)

Provided below is a partial work sheet for Ardery Advising.

Ardery Advising
Work Sheet (Partial)
For Month Ended January 31, 20 - -

	ACCOUNT TITLE	INCOME STATEMENT DEBIT	INCOME STATEMENT CREDIT	BALANCE SHEET DEBIT	BALANCE SHEET CREDIT	
1	Cash			2 4 1 2 00		1
2	Accounts Receivable			8 9 6 00		2
3	Supplies			4 8 2 00		3
4	Prepaid Insurance			9 0 0 00		4
5	Office Equipment			3 0 0 0 00		5
6	Accum. Depr.—Office Equipment				2 0 0 0 00	6
7	Accounts Payable				2 1 9 0 00	7
8	Wages Payable				1 2 0 0 00	8
9	Notes Payable				3 0 0 0 00	9
10	Sam Ardery, Capital				2 2 0 0 00	10
11	Sam Ardery, Drawing			8 0 0 00		11
12	Advising Fees		3 8 0 2 00			12
13	Wages Expense	1 8 0 0 00				13
14	Advertising Expense	4 0 0 00				14
15	Rent Expense	1 5 0 0 00				15
16	Supplies Expense	1 2 0 00				16
17	Telephone Expense	3 0 0 00				17
18	Electricity Expense	4 4 00				18
19	Insurance Expense	2 0 0 00				19
20	Gas and Oil Expense	3 8 00				20
21	Depr. Expense—Office Equipment	1 0 0 0 00				21
22	Miscellaneous Expense	5 0 0 00				22
23		5 9 0 2 00	3 8 0 2 00	8 4 9 0 00	10 5 9 0 00	23
24	Net Loss		2 1 0 0 00	2 1 0 0 00		24
25		5 9 0 2 00	5 9 0 2 00	10 5 9 0 00	10 5 9 0 00	25

REQUIRED

During January, Ardery made an additional investment of $1,200. Prepare an income statement, statement of owner's equity, and balance sheet for Ardery Advising.

Chapter 6 Appendix
Statement of Cash Flows

Careful study of this appendix should enable you to:

LO1 **Classify business transactions as operating, investing, or financing.**

LO2 **Prepare a statement of cash flows by analyzing and categorizing a series of business transactions.**

Thus far, we have discussed three financial statements: the income statement, the statement of owner's equity, and the balance sheet. A fourth statement, the statement of cash flows, is also very important. It explains what the business did to generate cash and how the cash was used. This is done by categorizing all cash transactions into three types of activities: operating, investing, and financing.

TYPES OF BUSINESS ACTIVITIES

LO1 **Classify business transactions as operating, investing, or financing.**

Cash flows from **operating activities** are related to the revenues and expenses reported on the income statement. Examples include cash received for services performed and the payment of cash for expenses.

Investing activities are those transactions involving the purchase and sale of long-term assets, lending money, and collecting the principal on the related loans.

Financing activities are those transactions dealing with the exchange of cash between the business and its owners and creditors. Examples include cash received from the owner to finance the operations and cash paid to the owner as withdrawals. Financing activities also include borrowing cash and repaying the loan principal.

Figure 6A-1 provides a review of the transactions for Jessie Jane's Campus Delivery for the month of June. The transactions are classified as operating, investing, or financing, and an explanation for the classification is provided.

> **LEARNING KEY**
>
> There are three types of business activities: operating, investing, and financing.

> **LEARNING KEY**
>
> Lending money to another entity is an outflow of cash from investing activities. The collection of the principal when the loan is due is an inflow of cash from investing activities. Borrowing cash is an inflow from financing activities. Repayment of the loan principal is an outflow from financing activities.

FIGURE 6A-1 Summary of Transactions for Jessie Jane's Campus Delivery

SUMMARY OF TRANSACTIONS FOR JESSIE JANE'S CAMPUS DELIVERY	TYPE OF TRANSACTION	EXPLANATION
(a) Jessica Jane invested cash in her business, $2,000.	Financing	Cash received from the owner is an inflow from financing activities. Don't be fooled by the word "invested." From the company's point of view, this is a way to *finance* the business.
(b) Purchased delivery equipment for cash, $1,200.	Investing	Purchases of long-term assets are investments.
(c) Purchased delivery equipment on account from Big Red Scooters, $900. (Note: Big Red has loaned Jane $900.)	No cash involved	This transaction will not affect the main sections of the statement of cash flows. (This is a noncash investing and financing activity.)
(d) Paid first installment to Big Red Scooters, $300. [See transaction (c).]	Financing	Repayments of loans are financing activities.
(e) Received cash for delivery services rendered, $500.	Operating	Cash received as a result of providing services is classified as an operating activity.
(f) Paid cash for June office rent, $200.	Operating	Cash payments for expenses are classified as operating activities.
(g) Paid telephone bill, $50.	Operating	Cash payments for expenses are classified as operating activities.
(h) Made deliveries on account for a total of $600: $400 for the Accounting Department and $200 for the School of Music.	No cash involved	This transaction will not affect the statement of cash flows.
(i) Purchased supplies for cash, $80.	Operating	Cash payments for expenses are classified as operating activities. Most of these supplies were used up. Those that remain will be used in the near future. These are not long-term assets and, thus, do not qualify as investments.
(j) Paid cash for an eight-month liability insurance policy, $200. Coverage began on June 1.	Operating	Cash payments for expenses are classified as operating activities. Prepaid Insurance is not considered a long-term asset and, thus, does not qualify as an investment.
(k) Received $570 in cash for services performed in transaction (h): $400 from the Accounting Department and $170 from the School of Music.	Operating	Cash received as a result of providing services is classified as an operating activity.
(l) Purchased a third scooter from Big Red Scooters, $1,500. A down payment of $300 was made with the remaining payments expected over the next four months.	Investing	Purchases of long-term assets are investments. Only the $300 cash paid will be reported on the statement of cash flows.
(m) Paid wages of part-time employees, $650.	Operating	Cash payments for expenses are classified as operating activities.
(n) Earned delivery fees for the remainder of the month amounting to $1,050: $430 in cash and $620 on account. Deliveries on account: $250 for the Accounting Department and $370 for the Athletic Ticket Office.	Operating	Cash received ($430) as a result of providing services is classified as an operating activity.
(o) Jane withdrew cash for personal use, $150.	Financing	Cash payments to owners are classified as a financing activity.

PREPARING THE STATEMENT OF CASH FLOWS

LO2 Prepare a statement of cash flows by analyzing and categorizing a series of business transactions.

The classifications of the cash transactions for Jessie Jane's Campus Delivery are summarized in the expanded Cash T account shown in Figure 6A-2. Using this information, we can prepare a statement of cash flows. As shown in Figure 6A-3, the heading is similar to that used for the income statement. Since the statement of cash flows reports on the flow of cash for a period of time, the statement is dated for the month ended June 30, 20--.

FIGURE 6A-2   Cash T Account for Jessie Jane's Campus Delivery with Classifications of Cash Transactions

CASH

Event	Classification	Amount	Amount	Classification	Event	
(a) Investment by Jessie.	Financing	2,000	1,200	Investing	Purchased delivery equipment.	(b)
(e) Cash received for services.	Operating	500	300	Financing	Made payment on loan.	(d)
(k) Cash received for services.	Operating	570	200	Operating	Paid office rent.	(f)`
(n) Cash received for services.	Operating	430	50	Operating	Paid telephone bill.	(g)
		3,500	80	Operating	Purchased supplies.	(i)
			200	Operating	Paid for insurance.	(j)
			300	Investing	Purchased delivery equipment.	(l)
			650	Operating	Paid wages.	(m)
			150	Financing	Withdrawal by owner.	(o)
			3,130			
	Bal.	370				

FIGURE 6A-3   Statement of Cash Flows for Jessie Jane's Campus Delivery

Jessie Jane's Campus Delivery Statement of Cash Flows For Month Ended June 30, 20 - -										
Cash flows from operating activities:										
Cash received from customers for delivery services						$1	5	0	0	00
Cash paid for wages	$	(6	5	0	00)					
Cash paid for rent		(2	0	0	00)					
Cash paid for supplies			(8	0	00)					
Cash paid for telephone			(5	0	00)					
Cash paid for insurance		(2	0	0	00)					
Total cash paid for operations						(1	1	8	0	00)
Net cash provided by operating activities						$	3	2	0	00
Cash flows from investing activities:										
Cash paid for delivery equipment	$(1	5	0	0	00)					
Net cash used for investing activities						(1	5	0	0	00)
Cash flows from financing activities:										
Cash investment by owner	$2	0	0	0	00					
Cash withdrawal by owner		(1	5	0	00)					
Payment made on loan		(3	0	0	00)					
Net cash provided by financing activities						1	5	5	0	00
Net increase in cash						$	3	7	0	00

The main body of the statement is arranged in three sections: operating, investing, and financing activities. First, cash received from customers is listed under operating activities. Then, cash payments for operating activities are listed and totaled. The net amount is reported as net cash provided by operating activities. Since this is the main purpose of the business, it is important to be able to generate positive cash flows from operating activities.

The next two sections list the inflows and outflows from investing and financing activities. Debits to the cash account are inflows and credits are outflows. Note that there was an outflow, or net use of cash, from investing activities resulting from the purchase of the motor scooters. In addition, cash was provided from financing activities because Jessie's initial investment more than covered her withdrawal and the payment on the loan. These investing and financing activities are typical for a new business.

The sum of the inflows and outflows from operating, investing, and financing activities equals the net increase (or decrease) in the cash account during the period. Since this is a new business, the cash account had a beginning balance of zero. The ending balance is $370. This agrees with the net increase in cash of $370 reported on the statement of cash flows.

This appendix introduces you to the purpose and format of the statement of cash flows. Here, we classified entries made to the cash account as operating, investing, or financing. These classifications were then used to prepare the statement. Businesses have thousands of entries to the cash account. Thus, this approach to preparing the statement is not really practical. Other approaches to preparing the statement will be discussed in Chapter 23. However, the purpose and format of the statements are the same.

Learning Objectives	Key Points to Remember
LO1 Classify business transactions as operating, investing, or financing.	The purpose of the statement of cash flows is to report what the firm did to generate cash and how the cash was used. Business transactions are classified as operating, investing, and financing activities.
	Operating activities are those transactions related to the revenues and expenses reported on the income statement.
	Investing activities are those transactions involving the purchase and sale of long-term assets, lending money, and collecting the principal on the related loans.
	Financing activities are those transactions dealing with the exchange of cash between the business and its owners and creditors.
LO2 Prepare a statement of cash flows by analyzing and categorizing a series of business transactions.	The main body of the statement of cash flows consists of three sections: operating, investing, and financing activities.

<table>
<tr><td colspan="11" align="center">Name of Business
Statement of Cash Flows
For Period Ended Date</td></tr>
<tr><td>Cash flows from operating activities:</td><td></td><td></td><td></td><td></td><td></td><td></td><td></td><td></td><td></td><td></td></tr>
<tr><td>Cash received from customers</td><td></td><td></td><td></td><td></td><td></td><td>$ x</td><td>x</td><td>x</td><td>x</td><td>xx</td></tr>
<tr><td>List cash paid for various expenses</td><td>$</td><td>(x</td><td>x</td><td>x</td><td>xx)</td><td></td><td></td><td></td><td></td><td></td></tr>
<tr><td>Total cash paid for operations</td><td></td><td></td><td></td><td></td><td></td><td>(x</td><td>x</td><td>x</td><td>x</td><td>xx)</td></tr>
<tr><td>Net cash provided by (used for) operating activities</td><td></td><td></td><td></td><td></td><td></td><td>$</td><td>x</td><td>x</td><td>x</td><td>xx</td></tr>
<tr><td>Cash flows from investing activities:</td><td></td><td></td><td></td><td></td><td></td><td></td><td></td><td></td><td></td><td></td></tr>
<tr><td>List cash received from the sale of long-term assets and other</td><td></td><td></td><td></td><td></td><td></td><td></td><td></td><td></td><td></td><td></td></tr>
<tr><td> investing activities</td><td>$ x</td><td>x</td><td>x</td><td>x</td><td>xx</td><td></td><td></td><td></td><td></td><td></td></tr>
<tr><td>List cash paid for the purchase of long-term assets and other</td><td></td><td></td><td></td><td></td><td></td><td></td><td></td><td></td><td></td><td></td></tr>
<tr><td> investing activities</td><td>(x</td><td>x</td><td>x</td><td>x</td><td>xx)</td><td></td><td></td><td></td><td></td><td></td></tr>
<tr><td>Net cash provided by (used for) investing activities</td><td></td><td></td><td></td><td></td><td></td><td>x</td><td>x</td><td>x</td><td>x</td><td>xx</td></tr>
<tr><td>Cash flows from financing activities:</td><td></td><td></td><td></td><td></td><td></td><td></td><td></td><td></td><td></td><td></td></tr>
<tr><td>List cash received from owners and creditors</td><td>$ x</td><td>x</td><td>x</td><td>x</td><td>xx</td><td></td><td></td><td></td><td></td><td></td></tr>
<tr><td>List cash paid to owners and creditors</td><td></td><td>(x</td><td>x</td><td>x</td><td>xx)</td><td></td><td></td><td></td><td></td><td></td></tr>
<tr><td>Net cash provided by (used for) financing activities</td><td></td><td></td><td></td><td></td><td></td><td>x</td><td>x</td><td>x</td><td>x</td><td>xx</td></tr>
<tr><td>Net increase (decrease) in cash</td><td></td><td></td><td></td><td></td><td></td><td>$</td><td>x</td><td>x</td><td>x</td><td>xx</td></tr>
</table>

KEY TERMS

financing activities (219) Those transactions dealing with the exchange of cash between the business and its owners and creditors.

investing activities (219) Those transactions involving the purchase and sale of long-term assets, lending money, and collecting the principal on the related loans.

operating activities (219) Those transactions related to the revenues and expenses reported on the income statement.

REVIEW QUESTIONS

LO1   1. Explain the purpose of the statement of cash flows.

LO1   2. Define and provide examples of the three types of business activities.

SERIES A EXERCISE

E 6Apx-1A (LO1)

CLASSIFYING BUSINESS TRANSACTIONS Dolores Lopez opened a new consulting business. The following transactions occurred during January of the current year. Classify each transaction as an operating, investing, or financing activity.

(a) Invested cash in the business, $10,000.
(b) Paid office rent, $500.
(c) Purchased office equipment. Paid $1,500 cash and agreed to pay the balance of $2,000 in four monthly installments.
(d) Received cash for services rendered, $900.
(e) Paid telephone bill, $65.
(f) Made payment on loan in transaction (c), $500.
(g) Paid wages to part-time employee, $500.
(h) Received cash for services rendered, $800.
(i) Paid electricity bill, $85
(j) Withdrew cash for personal use, $100.
(k) Paid wages to part-time employee, $500.

SERIES A PROBLEM

P 6Apx-2A (LO2)

✓ Operating activities: $50;
Investing activities: ($1,500);
Financing activities: $9,400

PREPARING A STATEMENT OF CASH FLOWS Prepare a statement of cash flows based on the transactions reported in Exercise 6Apx-1A.

SERIES B EXERCISE

E 6Apx-1B (LO1)

CLASSIFYING BUSINESS TRANSACTIONS Bob Jacobs opened an advertising agency. The following transactions occurred during January of the current year. Classify each transaction as an operating, investing, or financing activity.

(a)   Invested cash in the business, $5,000.
(b)   Purchased office equipment. Paid $2,500 cash and agreed to pay the balance of $2,000 in four monthly installments.
(c)   Paid office rent, $400.
(d)   Received cash for services rendered, $700.
(e)   Paid telephone bill, $95.
(f)   Received cash for services rendered, $600.
(g)   Made payment on loan in transaction (b), $500.
(h)   Paid wages to part-time employee, $800.
(i)   Paid electricity bill, $100.
(j)   Withdrew cash for personal use, $500.
(k)   Paid wages to part-time employee, $600.

SERIES B PROBLEM

P 6Apx-2B (LO2)
✓ Operating activities: ($695);
Investing activities: ($2,500);
Financing activities: $4,000

PREPARING A STATEMENT OF CASH FLOWS Prepare a statement of cash flows based on the transactions reported in Exercise 6Apx-1B.

COMPREHENSIVE PROBLEM 1: THE ACCOUNTING CYCLE

Bob Night opened "The General's Favorite Fishing Hole." The fishing camp is open from April through September and attracts many famous college basketball coaches during the off-season. Guests typically register for one week, arriving on Sunday afternoon and returning home the following Saturday afternoon. The registration fee includes room and board, the use of fishing boats, and professional instruction in fishing techniques. The chart of accounts for the camping operations is provided below.

This comprehensive problem is intended to serve as a mini-practice set without the source documents. As such, students should plan on about three to four hours to complete this problem.

The General's Favorite Fishing Hole
Chart of Accounts

Assets		Revenues	
101	Cash	401	Registration Fees
142	Office Supplies		
144	Food Supplies		Expenses
145	Prepaid Insurance	511	Wages Expense
181	Fishing Boats	521	Rent Expense
181.1	Accum. Depr.—Fishing Boats	523	Office Supplies Expense
		524	Food Supplies Expense
Liabilities		525	Telephone Expense
202	Accounts Payable	533	Utilities Expense
219	Wages Payable	535	Insurance Expense
		536	Postage Expense
Owner's Equity		542	Depr. Exp.—Fishing Boats
311	Bob Night, Capital		
312	Bob Night, Drawing		
313	Income Summary		

THE FOLLOWING TRANSACTIONS TOOK PLACE DURING APRIL 20--.

Apr. 1	Night invested cash in business, $90,000.
1	Paid insurance premium for six-month camping season, $9,000.
2	Paid rent for lodge and campgrounds for the month of April, $40,000.
2	Deposited registration fees, $35,000.
2	Purchased 10 fishing boats on account for $60,000. The boats have estimated useful lives of five years, at which time they will be donated to a local day camp. Arrangements were made to pay for the boats in July.
3	Purchased food supplies from Acme Super Market on account, $7,000.
5	Purchased office supplies from Gordon Office Supplies on account, $500.
7	Deposited registration fees, $38,600.
10	Purchased food supplies from Acme Super Market on account, $8,200.
10	Paid wages to fishing guides, $10,000.
14	Deposited registration fees, $30,500.
16	Purchased food supplies from Acme Super Market on account, $9,000.
17	Paid wages to fishing guides, $10,000.

(continued)

Apr. 18   Paid postage, $150.

21   Deposited registration fees, $35,600.

24   Purchased food supplies from Acme Super Market on account, $8,500.

24   Paid wages to fishing guides, $10,000.

28   Deposited registration fees, $32,000.

29   Paid wages to fishing guides, $10,000.

30   Purchased food supplies from Acme Super Market on account, $6,000.

30   Paid Acme Super Market on account, $32,700.

30   Paid utilities bill, $2,000.

30   Paid telephone bill, $1,200.

30   Bob Night withdrew cash for personal use, $6,000.

Adjustment information for the end of April is provided below.

(a) Office supplies remaining on hand, $100.
(b) Food supplies remaining on hand, $8,000.
(c) Insurance expired during the month of April, $1,500.
(d) Depreciation on the fishing boats for the month of April, $1,000.
(e) Wages earned, but not yet paid, at the end of April, $500.

REQUIRED

1. Enter the transactions in a general journal. Enter transactions from April 1–5 on page 1, April 7–18 on page 2, April 21–29 and the first two entries for April 30 on page 3, and the remaining entries for April 30 on page 4.

2. Post the entries to the general ledger. (If you are not using the working papers that accompany this text, you will need to enter the account titles and account numbers in the general ledger accounts.)

3. Prepare a trial balance on a work sheet.

4. Complete the work sheet.

5. Journalize the adjusting entries (page 5).

6. Post the adjusting entries to the general ledger.

7. Prepare the income statement.

8. Prepare the statement of owner's equity.

9. Prepare the balance sheet.

10. Journalize the closing entries (pages 5 and 6).

11. Post the closing entries to the general ledger.

12. Prepare a post-closing trial balance.

COMPREHENSIVE PROBLEM 1, PERIOD 2: THE ACCOUNTING CYCLE

During the month of May 20--, The General's Favorite Fishing Hole engaged in the following transactions. These transactions required an expansion of the chart of accounts as shown below.

Assets
101	Cash
122	Accounts Receivable
142	Office Supplies
144	Food Supplies
145	Prepaid Insurance
146	Prepaid Subscriptions
161	Land
171	Buildings
171.1	Accum. Depr.—Buildings
181	Fishing Boats
181.1	Accum. Depr.—Fishing Boats
182	Surround Sound System
182.1	Accum. Depr.—Surround Sound Sys.
183	Big Screen TV
183.1	Accum. Depr.—Big Screen TV

Liabilities
202	Accounts Payable
219	Wages Payable

Owner's Equity
311	Bob Night, Capital
312	Bob Night, Drawing
313	Income Summary

Revenues
401	Registration Fees
404	Vending Revenue

Expenses
511	Wages Expense
512	Advertising Expense
521	Rent Expense
523	Office Supplies Expense
524	Food Supplies Expense
525	Telephone Expense
533	Utilities Expense
535	Insurance Expense
536	Postage Expense
537	Repair Expense
540	Depr. Exp.—Buildings
541	Depr. Exp.—Surround Sound Sys.
542	Depr. Exp.—Fishing Boats
543	Depr. Exp.—Big Screen TV
546	Satellite Programming Exp.
548	Subscriptions Expense

> This comprehensive problem is intended to serve as a mini-practice set without the source documents. As such, students should plan on about three to four hours to complete this problem.

May 1 In order to provide snacks for guests on a 24-hour basis, Night signed a contract with Snack Attack. Snack Attack will install vending machines with food and drinks and pay a 10% commission on all sales. Estimated payments are made at the beginning of each month. Night received a check for $200, the estimated commission on sales for May.

2 Night purchased a surround sound system and big screen TV with a Digital Satellite System for the guest lounge. The surround sound system cost $3,600 and has an estimated useful life of five years and no salvage value. The TV cost $8,000, has an estimated useful life of eight years, and has a salvage value of $800. Night paid cash for both items.

2 Paid for May's programming on the new Digital Satellite System, $125.

3 Night's office manager returned $100 worth of office supplies to Gordon Office Supply. Night received a $100 reduction on the account.

3 Deposited registration fees, $52,700.

3 Paid rent for lodge and campgrounds for the month of May, $40,000.

3 In preparation for the purchase of a nearby campground, Night invested an additional $600,000.

(continued)

May 4   Paid Gordon Office Supply on account, $400.

4   Purchased the assets of a competing business and paid cash for the following: land, $100,000; lodge, $530,000; and fishing boats, $9,000. The lodge has a remaining useful life of 50 years and a $50,000 salvage value. The boats have remaining lives of five years and no salvage value.

5   Paid May's insurance premium for the new camp, $1,000. (See above transaction.)

5   Purchased food supplies from Acme Super Market on account, $22,950.

5   Purchased office supplies from Gordon Office Supplies on account, $1,200.

7   Night paid $40 each for one-year subscriptions to *Fishing Illustrated*, *Fishing Unlimited*, and *Fish Master*. The magazines are published monthly.

10   Deposited registration fees, $62,750.

13   Paid wages to fishing guides, $30,000. (Don't forget wages payable.)

14   A guest became ill and was unable to stay for the entire week. A refund was issued in the amount of $1,000.

17   Deposited registration fees, $63,000.

19   Purchased food supplies from Acme Super Market on account, $18,400.

21   Deposited registration fees, $63,400.

23   Paid $2,500 for advertising spots on National Sports Talk Radio.

25   Paid repair fee for damaged boat, $850.

27   Paid wages to fishing guides, $30,000.

28   Paid $1,800 for advertising spots on billboards.

29   Purchased food supplies from Acme Super Market on account, $14,325.

30   Paid utilities bill, $3,300.

30   Paid telephone bill, $1,800.

30   Paid Acme Super Market on account, $47,350.

31   Bob Night withdrew cash for personal use, $7,500.

Adjustment information at the end of May is provided below.

(a)   Total vending machine sales were $2,300 for the month of May.

(b)   Straight-line depreciation is used for the 10 boats purchased on April 2 for $60,000. The useful life for these assets is five years and there is no salvage value. A full month's depreciation was taken in April on these boats. Straight-line depreciation is also used for the two boats purchased in May. Make one adjusting entry for all depreciation on the boats.

(c)   Straight-line depreciation is used to depreciate the surround sound system.

(d)   Straight-line depreciation is used to depreciate the big screen TV.

(e)   Straight-line depreciation is used for the building purchased in May.

(f)   On April 2, Night paid $9,000 for insurance during the six-month camping season. May's portion of this premium was used up during this month.

(g)   Night received his May issues of *Fishing Illustrated*, *Fishing Unlimited*, and *Fish Master*.
(h)   Office supplies remaining on hand, $150.
(i)   Food supplies remaining on hand, $5,925.
(j)   Wages earned, but not yet paid, at the end of May, $6,000.

REQUIRED

1.   Enter the transactions in a general journal. Enter transactions from May 1–4 on page 5, May 5–28 on page 6, and the remaining entries on page 7. To save time and space, don't enter descriptions for the journal entries.

2.   Post the entries to the general ledger. (If you are not using the working papers that accompany this text, you will need to enter the account titles, account numbers, and balances from April 30 in the general ledger accounts.)

3.   Prepare a trial balance on a work sheet.

4.   Complete the work sheet.

5.   Journalize the adjusting entries on page 8 of the general journal.

6.   Post the adjusting entries to the general ledger.

7.   Prepare the income statement.

8.   Prepare the statement of owner's equity.

9.   Prepare the balance sheet.

10.   Journalize the closing entries on page 9 of the general journal.

11.   Post the closing entries to the general ledger.

12.   Prepare a post-closing trial balance.

PART

2

Accounting for Cash and Payroll

7 Accounting for Cash

8 Payroll Accounting: Employee Earnings and Deductions

9 Payroll Accounting: Employer Taxes and Reports

Objectives

Careful study of this chapter should enable you to:

LO1
Describe how to open and use a checking account.

LO2
Prepare a bank reconciliation and related journal entries.

LO3
Establish and use a petty cash fund.

LO4
Establish a change fund and use the cash short and over account.

Accounting for Cash

Evan Taylor recently opened his own retail business called Parkway Pet Supplies. To protect and properly manage cash, Evan uses a checking account. All cash and checks received from customers are deposited promptly. All bills are paid by check. In this way, Evan can use the deposit slips and monthly bank statement to verify his records of cash received. Similarly, canceled checks and the monthly bank statement can be used to verify Evan's records of cash payments. Complete and accurate records of cash receipts and cash payments help Evan control this important asset and plan for future cash needs.

At the end of the month, the balance in the cash account in the store's books differs from the cash balance shown on the bank statement. In trying to reconcile the two amounts, how should Evan treat the checks he wrote during the month that have not yet been presented to the bank for payment?

Cash is an asset that is quite familiar and important to all of us. We generally think of **cash** as the currency and coins in our pockets and the money we have in our checking accounts. To a business, cash also includes checks received from customers, money orders, and bank cashier's checks.

Because it plays such a central role in operating a business, cash must be carefully managed and controlled. A business should have a system of **internal control**—a set of policies and procedures designed to ensure proper accounting for transactions. For good internal control of cash transactions, all cash received should be deposited daily in a bank. All disbursements, except for payments from petty cash, should be made by check.

CHECKING ACCOUNT

LO1   **Describe how to open and use a checking account.**

The key documents and forms required in opening and using a checking account are the signature card, deposit tickets, checks, and bank statements.

Opening a Checking Account

To open a checking account, each person authorized to sign checks must complete and sign a **signature card** (Figure 7-1). The bank uses this card to verify the depositor's signature on any banking transactions. The taxpayer identification number (TIN) is the depositor's social security number or employer identification number (EIN). This number is shown on the card to identify the depositor for income tax purposes. An EIN can be obtained from the Internal Revenue Service.

Making Deposits

A **deposit ticket** (Figure 7-2) is a form showing a detailed listing of items being deposited. Currency, coins, and checks are listed separately. Each check should be identified by its **ABA (American Bankers Association) Number**. This number is the small fraction printed in the upper right-hand corner of each check (Figure 7-5). Part of this number also appears in **magnetic ink character recognition (MICR) code** on the lower left side of the front of each check. The code is used to sort and route checks throughout the U.S. banking system. Normally, only the numerator of the fraction is used in identifying checks on the deposit ticket.

The depositor delivers or mails the deposit ticket and all items being deposited to the bank. The bank then gives or mails a receipt to the depositor. The deposit also can be made after business hours by using the night depository provided by most banks. The deposit is put in a locked bag, which is placed in a secure drawer or chute at the bank, for processing the following morning.

Endorsements

Each check being deposited must be endorsed by the depositor. The **endorsement** consists of stamping or writing the depositor's name and sometimes other information on the back of the check, in the space provided near the left end. There are two basic types of endorsements:

1. **Blank endorsement**—the depositor simply signs the back of the check. This makes the check payable to any bearer.

2. **Restrictive endorsement**—the depositor adds words such as "For deposit," "Pay to any bank," or "Pay to Daryl Beck only" to restrict the payment of the check.

FIGURE 7-1 Signature Card

ACCOUNT OWNER NAME & ADDRESS

ACCOUNT NUMBER

Number of signatures required for withdrawal _____ ☐ This is a temporary account agreement.

SIGNATURE(S) - THE UNDERSIGNED AGREE(S) TO THE TERMS STATED ON PAGES 1 AND 2 OF THIS FORM, AND ACKNOWLEDGE(S) RECEIPT OF A COMPLETED COPY ON TODAY'S DATE. THE UNDERSIGNED ALSO ACKNOWLEDGE(S) RECEIPT OF A COPY OF AND AGREE(S) TO THE TERMS OF THE FOLLOWING DISCLOSURE(S):

☐ Funds Availability Disclosure   ☐ Truth-In-Savings Disclosure

☐ Electronic Funds Transfer Disclosure   ☐ _____

Signature(s)	**Identifying Info.**
(1)	
(2)	
(3)	
(4)	

☐ **AUTHORIZED SIGNER (name)** _____
Individual Accounts Only

X _____

ADDITIONAL INFORMATION:

BACKUP WITHHOLDING CERTIFICATIONS

TIN: _____

☐ **TAXPAYER I.D. NUMBER -** The Taxpayer Identification Number shown above (TIN) is my correct taxpayer identification number.

☐ **BACKUP WITHHOLDING -** I am not subject to backup withholding either because I have not been notified that I am subject to backup withholding as a result of a failure to report all interest or dividends, or the Internal Revenue Service has notified me that I am no longer subject to backup withholding.

☐ **EXEMPT RECIPIENTS -** I am an exempt recipient under the Internal Revenue Service Regulations.

SIGNATURE - I certify under penalties of perjury the statements checked in this section.

X _____
(Date)

© 1983, 1988, 1990, 1991 Bankers Systems, Inc., St. Cloud, MN Form MPSC-KS 3/15/99

(page 1 of 2)

FIGURE 7-2 Deposit Ticket

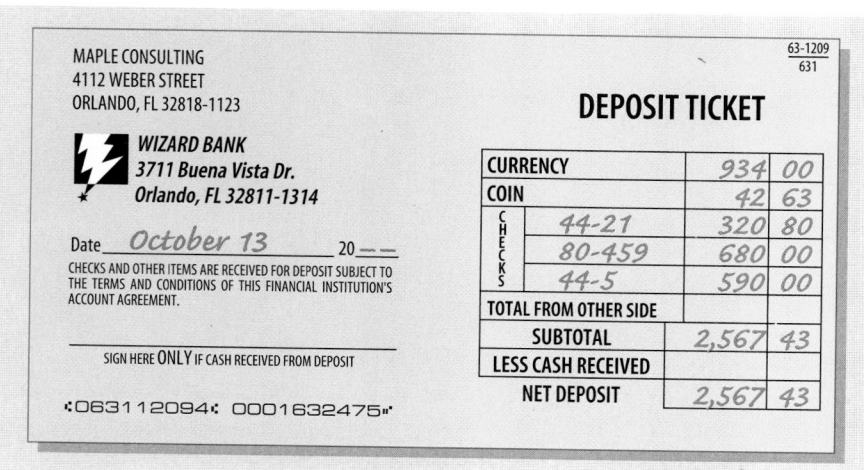

MAPLE CONSULTING
4112 WEBER STREET
ORLANDO, FL 32818-1123

63-1209 / 631

WIZARD BANK
3711 Buena Vista Dr.
Orlando, FL 32811-1314

DEPOSIT TICKET

Date _October 13_ 20 __

CHECKS AND OTHER ITEMS ARE RECEIVED FOR DEPOSIT SUBJECT TO THE TERMS AND CONDITIONS OF THIS FINANCIAL INSTITUTION'S ACCOUNT AGREEMENT.

SIGN HERE ONLY IF CASH RECEIVED FROM DEPOSIT

⑆063112094⑆ 0001632475⑈

CURRENCY		934	00
COIN		42	63
CHECKS	44-21	320	80
	80-459	680	00
	44-5	590	00
TOTAL FROM OTHER SIDE			
SUBTOTAL		2,567	43
LESS CASH RECEIVED			
NET DEPOSIT		2,567	43

Businesses commonly use a rubber stamp to endorse checks for deposit. The check shown in Figure 7-3 has been stamped with a restrictive endorsement.

FIGURE 7-3   Restrictive Endorsement

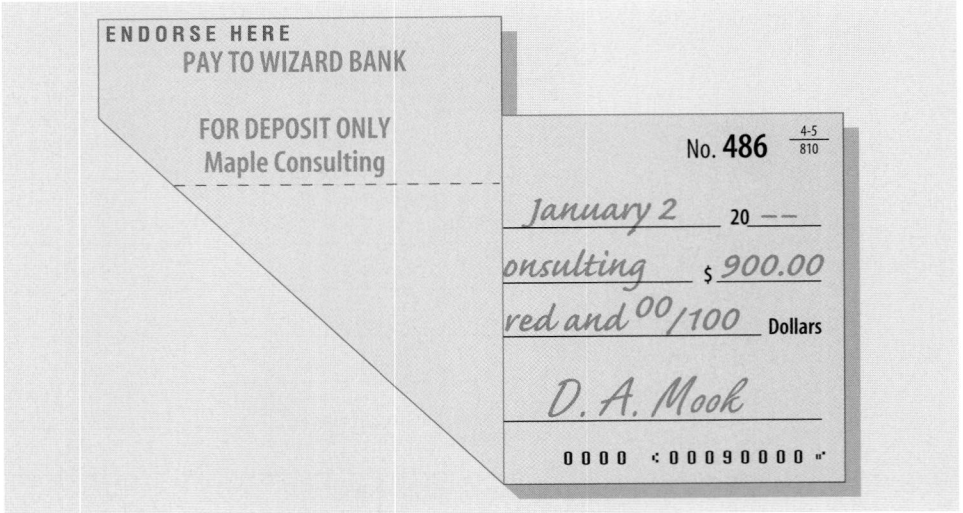

Automated Teller Machines

Most banks now make **automated teller machines (ATMs)** available at all times to depositors for making deposits or withdrawals. Each depositor has a plastic card (Figure 7-4) and a personal identification number (PIN). The depositor inserts the card, keys in the PIN, indicates whether the transaction is a withdrawal or a deposit, and enters the amount. The machine has a drawer or door for the withdrawal or deposit.

FIGURE 7-4   Automated Teller Machine Card

Most ATMs are now on a system such as Cirrus that allows noncustomers to use other ATMs in both the United States and foreign countries. There are also "cash machines" that supply only cash and do not take deposits. These are often found at airports and convenience stores.

It is important for the depositor to keep an accounting record of ATM withdrawals and deposits. This is done on the check stub or register described in the following section, and with an appropriate journal entry.

Writing Checks

A **check** is a document ordering a bank to pay cash from a depositor's account. There are three parties to every check:

1. **Drawer**—the depositor who orders the bank to pay the cash.

2. **Drawee**—the bank on which the check is drawn.

3. **Payee**—the person being paid the cash.

Checks used by businesses are usually bound in the form of a book. In some checkbooks, each check is attached to a **check stub** (Figure 7-5) that contains space to record all relevant information about the check. Other checkbooks are accompanied by a small register book in which the relevant information is noted. If a financial computer software package is used, both the check and the register can be prepared electronically.

Note that the check stubs in Figure 7-5 contain space to record amounts deposited. It generally is a good idea also to indicate the date of the deposit, as shown on check stub No. 108.

Use the following three steps in preparing a check.

STEP 1 Complete the check stub or register.

STEP 2 Enter the date, payee name, and amount on the check.

STEP 3 Sign the check.

The check stub is completed first so that the drawer retains a record of each check issued. This information is needed to determine the proper journal entry for the transaction.

The payee name is entered on the first long line on the check, followed by the amount in figures. The amount in words is then entered on the second long line. If the amount in figures does not agree with the amount in words, the bank usually contacts the drawer for the correct amount or returns the check unpaid.

The most critical point in preparing a check is signing it, and this should be done last. The signature authorizes the bank to pay cash from the drawer's account. The check signer should make sure that all other aspects of the check are correct before signing it.

The payee and amount written in words should be followed by something, such as a line, to make it difficult to alter the payee or the amount.

It is sometimes necessary to void a check. Proper procedures for doing so are to tear off or deface the signature box and to file the voided check numerically with the canceled checks.

LEARNING KEY

The check should not be signed until the check signer has verified that all aspects of the check are correct.

PROFILES IN ACCOUNTING

Lisa Davis, Legal Coordinator

Lisa Davis began working as a part-time legal secretary with Zegarelli Associates. Lisa continued her career with this company after earning an Associate Degree in Legal Office Management.

After graduation, Lisa was hired as a legal assistant and later promoted to legal coordinator. Her duties include budgeting, accounts receivable, supervising two employees, coordinating schedules, researching, and dealing with clients on a daily basis.

According to Lisa, dependability, initiative, and loyalty lead to success. Lisa chose the legal field because she always had an interest in law and wanted to work in a fast-paced environment.

FIGURE 7-5 Checks and Check Stubs

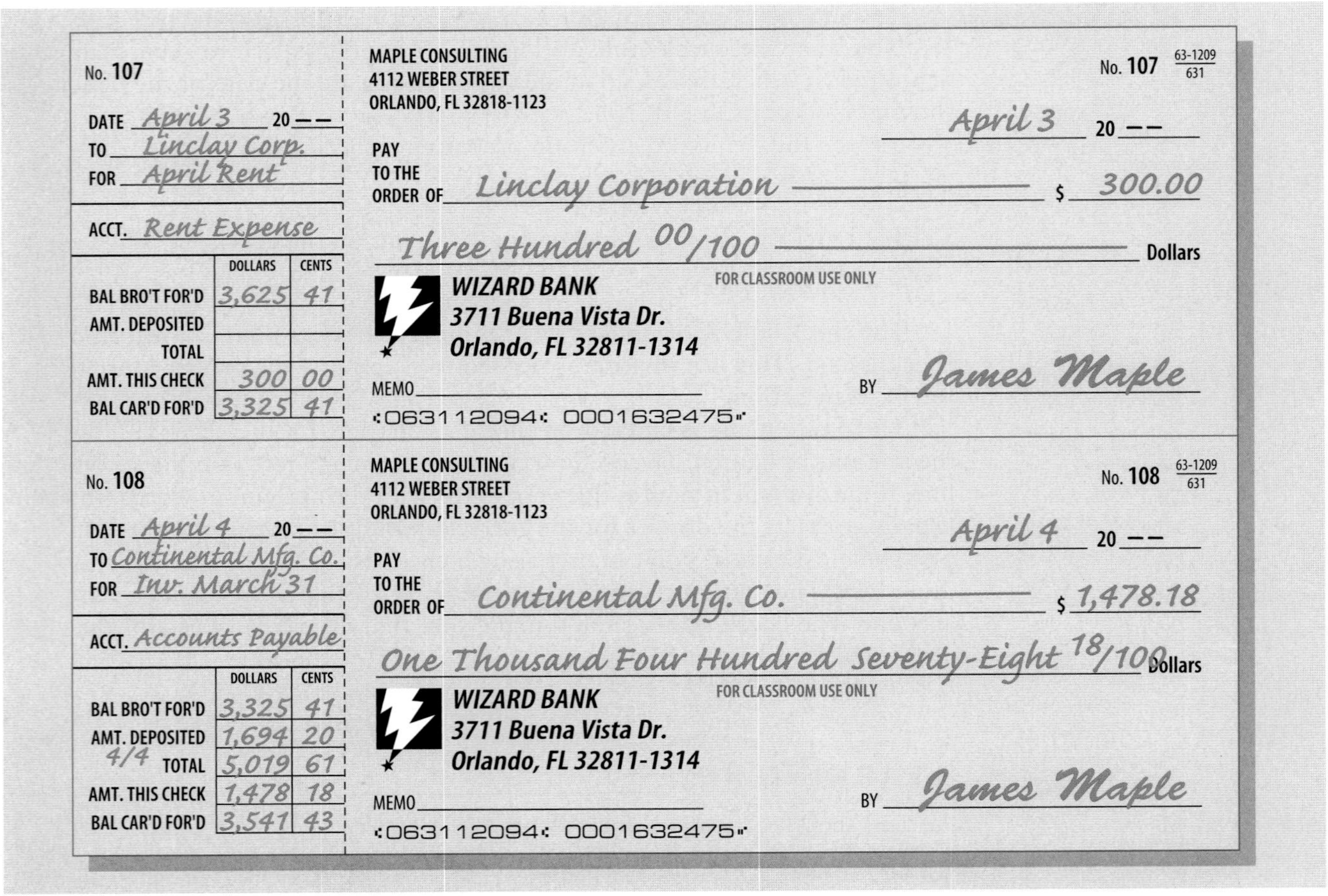

No. 107
DATE April 3 20--
TO Linclay Corp.
FOR April Rent
ACCT. Rent Expense

	DOLLARS	CENTS
BAL BRO'T FOR'D	3,625	41
AMT. DEPOSITED		
TOTAL		
AMT. THIS CHECK	300	00
BAL CAR'D FOR'D	3,325	41

MAPLE CONSULTING
4112 WEBER STREET
ORLANDO, FL 32818-1123
No. 107 63-1209/631
April 3 20--
PAY TO THE ORDER OF Linclay Corporation $ 300.00
Three Hundred 00/100 Dollars
WIZARD BANK
3711 Buena Vista Dr.
Orlando, FL 32811-1314
FOR CLASSROOM USE ONLY
MEMO
BY James Maple
:063112094: 0001632475"

No. 108
DATE April 4 20--
TO Continental Mfg. Co.
FOR Inv. March 31
ACCT. Accounts Payable

	DOLLARS	CENTS
BAL BRO'T FOR'D	3,325	41
AMT. DEPOSITED	1,694	20
4/4 TOTAL	5,019	61
AMT. THIS CHECK	1,478	18
BAL CAR'D FOR'D	3,541	43

MAPLE CONSULTING
4112 WEBER STREET
ORLANDO, FL 32818-1123
No. 108 63-1209/631
April 4 20--
PAY TO THE ORDER OF Continental Mfg. Co. $ 1,478.18
One Thousand Four Hundred Seventy-Eight 18/100 Dollars
WIZARD BANK
3711 Buena Vista Dr.
Orlando, FL 32811-1314
FOR CLASSROOM USE ONLY
MEMO
BY James Maple
:063112094: 0001632475"

Bank Statement

A statement of account issued by a bank to each depositor once a month is called a **bank statement**. Figure 7-6 is a bank statement for a checking account. The statement shows:

1.   The balance at the beginning of the period.

2.   Deposits and other amounts added during the period.

3.   Checks and other amounts subtracted during the period.

4.   The balance at the end of the period.

With the bank statement, the bank normally sends to the depositor:

1.   **Canceled checks**—the depositor's checks paid by the bank during the period. The bank may send the checks themselves, "imaged" sheets showing only the faces of the checks, or simply a listing of the checks on the bank statement.

2.   Any other forms representing items added to or subtracted from the account.

FIGURE 7-6   Bank Statement

STATEMENT   **WIZARD BANK**

MAPLE CONSULTING
4112 WEBER STREET
ORLANDO, FL 32818-1123

Account Number	16 3247 5	Page Number	1
Statement Date	Nov. 21, 20—		
Statement Instructions			

Beginning Balance	No. of Deposits and Credits	We Have Added these Deposits and Credits Totaling	No. of Withdrawals and Charges	We Have Subtracted these Withdrawals and Charges Totaling	Resulting in a Statement Balance of
$2,721.51	2	$2,599.31	17	$3,572.73	$1,748.09
Document Count	Average Daily Balance this Statement Period		Minimum Balance this Statement Period	Date	Amount

If Your Account does not Balance, Please See Reverse Side and Report any Discrepancies to our Customer Service Department.

DATE	DESCRIPTION	AMOUNT	BALANCE
10/20	Beginning Balance		2,721.51
10/27	Check No. 207	−242.00	2,479.51
10/28	Check No. 212	−68.93	2,410.58
10/28	Check No. 213	−58.00	2,352.58
10/29	Deposit	867.00	3,219.58
11/3	Deposit	1,732.31	4,951.89
11/3	Check No. 214	−18.98	4,932.91
11/3	Check No. 215	−229.01	4,703.90
11/3	Check No. 216	−452.13	4,251.77
11/3	Check No. 217	−94.60	4,157.17
11/10	Check No. 218	−1,800.00	2,357.17
11/10	DM: NSF	−200.00	2,157.17
11/10	Check No. 220	−32.42	2,124.75
11/10	Check No. 221	−64.08	2,060.67
11/10	Check No. 222	−110.87	1,949.80
11/13	ATM Withdrawal	−100.00	1,849.80
11/18	Check No. 223	−18.00	1,831.80
11/18	Check No. 225	−23.31	1,808.49
11/18	Check No. 226	−58.60	1,749.89
11/19	DM: Service Charge	−1.80	1,748.09

EC – Error Correction
CM – Credit Memo
DM – Debit Memo

NSF – Not Sufficient Funds
ATM – Automated Teller Machine

TR – Wire Transfer

RECONCILING THE BANK STATEMENT

LO2 Prepare a bank reconciliation and related journal entries.

On any given day, the balance in the cash account on the depositor's books (the book balance) is unlikely to be the same as that on the bank's books (the bank balance). This difference can be due to errors, but it usually is caused by timing. Transactions generally are recorded by the business at a time that is different from when the bank records them.

Deposits

Suppose there are cash receipts of $600 on April 30. These cash receipts would be recorded on the depositor's books on April 30 and a deposit of $600 would be sent to the bank. The deposit would not reach the bank, however, until at least the following day, May 1. This timing difference in recording the $600 of cash receipts is illustrated in Figure 7-7. Notice that on April 30, the balances in the depositor's books and in the bank's books would be different.

FIGURE 7-7 Depositor and Bank Records—Deposits

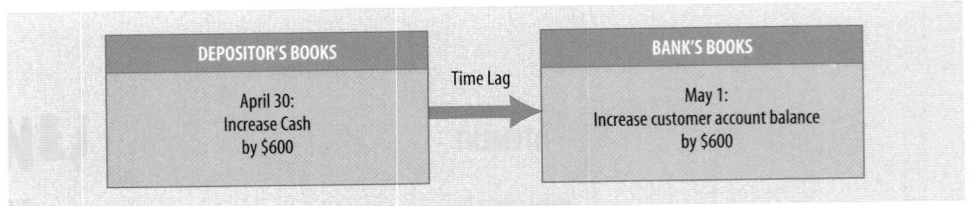

Cash Payments

Similar timing differences occur with cash payments. Suppose a check for $350 is written on April 30. This cash payment would be recorded on the depositor's books on April 30 and the check mailed to the payee. The check probably would not be received by the payee until May 3. If the payee deposited the check promptly, it still would not clear the bank until May 4. This timing difference in recording the $350 cash payment is illustrated in Figure 7-8. Notice once again that on April 30, the balances in the depositor's books and in the bank's books would be different.

FIGURE 7-8 Depositor and Bank Records—Cash Payments

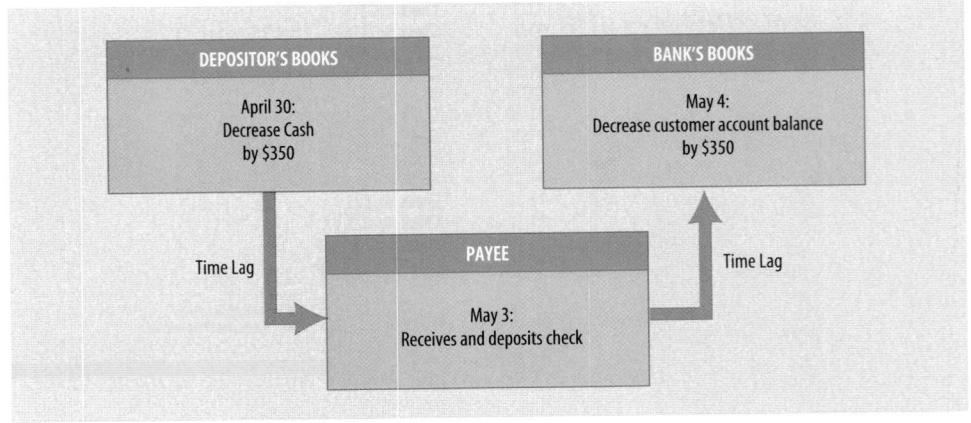

Reasons for Differences Between Bank and Book Balances

When the bank statement is received, the depositor examines the records to identify the items that explain the difference between the book and bank balances. This process of bringing the book and bank balances into agreement is called preparing a **bank reconciliation**.

The most common reasons for differences between the book and bank balances are the following:

1. **Deposits in transit.** Deposits that have not reached or been recorded by the bank before the statement is prepared.

2. **Outstanding checks.** Checks issued that have not been presented to the bank for payment before the statement is prepared.

3. **Service charges.** Bank charges for services such as check printing and processing.

4. **Collections.** Collections of promissory notes or charge accounts made by the bank on behalf of the depositor.

5. **Not sufficient funds (NSF) checks.** Checks deposited by the depositor that are not paid because the drawer did not have sufficient funds.

6. **Errors.** Errors made by the bank or the depositor in recording cash transactions.

Steps in Preparing the Bank Reconciliation

Use the following three steps in preparing the bank reconciliation.

STEP 1 Identify deposits in transit and any related errors.

STEP 2 Identify outstanding checks and any related errors.

STEP 3 Identify additional reconciling items.

Deposits in Transit and Related Errors
Follow these steps:

STEP 1 Compare deposits listed on the bank statement with deposits in transit on last month's bank reconciliation. All of last month's deposits in transit should appear on the current month's bank statement.

STEP 2 Compare the remaining deposits on the bank statement with deposits listed in the accounting records. Any deposits listed in the accounting records but not on the bank statement are deposits in transit on the current bank reconciliation.

STEP 3 Compare the individual deposit amounts on the bank statement and in the accounting records. If they differ, the error needs to be corrected.

Outstanding Checks and Related Errors
Follow these steps:

STEP 1 Compare canceled checks with the bank statement and the accounting records. If the amounts differ, the error needs to be corrected.

STEP 2 As each canceled check is compared with the accounting records, place a check mark on the check stub or other accounting record to indicate that the check has cleared.

STEP 3 Any checks written that have not been checked off represent outstanding checks on the bank reconciliation. This includes outstanding checks from last month's bank reconciliation that have not yet cleared.

Additional Reconciling Items

Compare any additions and deductions on the bank statement that are not deposits or checks with the accounting records. Items that the bank adds to the account are called **credit memos**. Items that the bank deducts from the account are called **debit memos**. Remember that a depositor's account is a liability to the bank. Thus, a credit memo increases this liability; a debit memo reduces the liability. Any of these items not appearing in the accounting records represent additional items on the bank reconciliation.

Illustration of a Bank Reconciliation

A general format for the bank reconciliation is shown in Figure 7-9. Not every item shown in this illustration would be in every bank reconciliation, but this format is helpful in determining where to put items. A bank reconciliation form also can be found on the back of most bank statements.

FIGURE 7-9   Bank Reconciliation Format

BANK RECONCILIATION		
Bank statement balance		$xxxx
Add: Deposits in transit	$xxxx	
Bank errors (that understate balance)	xxxx	xxxx
		$xxxx
Deduct: Outstanding checks	$xxxx	
Bank errors (that overstate balance)	xxxx	xxxx
Adjusted bank balance		$xxxx
Book balance		$xxxx
Add: Bank credit memos	$xxxx	
Book errors (that understate balance)	xxxx	xxxx
		$xxxx
Deduct: Bank debit memos	$xxxx	
Book errors (that overstate balance)	xxxx	xxxx
Adjusted book balance		$xxxx

To illustrate the preparation of a bank reconciliation, we will use the Maple Consulting bank statement shown in Figure 7-6. That statement shows a balance of $1,748.09 as of November 21. The balance in Maple's check stubs and general ledger cash account is $2,393.23. The three steps described on page 241 were used to identify the following items, and the reconciliation in Figure 7-10 was prepared.

1. A deposit of $637.02 recorded on November 21 had not been received by the bank. Maple has received the funds but the amount has not yet been counted by the bank. This deposit in transit is added to the bank statement balance.

2. Check numbers 219, 224, and 227 are outstanding. The funds have been disbursed by Maple but have not yet been paid out by the bank. The amount of these outstanding checks is subtracted from the bank statement balance.

3. Check number 214 was written for $18.98 but was entered on the check stub and on the books as $19.88. This $0.90 error is added to the book balance because $0.90 too much had been deducted from the book balance.

4. Maple made an ATM withdrawal of $100.00 on November 13 for personal use but did not record the withdrawal on the books. The bank has reduced Maple's balance by this amount. Thus, this amount is deducted from the book balance.

5. The bank returned an NSF check of $200.00. This was a check received by Maple from a customer. The bank has reduced Maple's balance by $200.00 but Maple has not yet recorded it. This amount is deducted from the book balance.

6. The bank service charge was $1.80. The bank has reduced Maple's balance by this amount but Maple has not yet recorded it. This amount is deducted from the book balance.

FIGURE 7-10   Bank Reconciliation

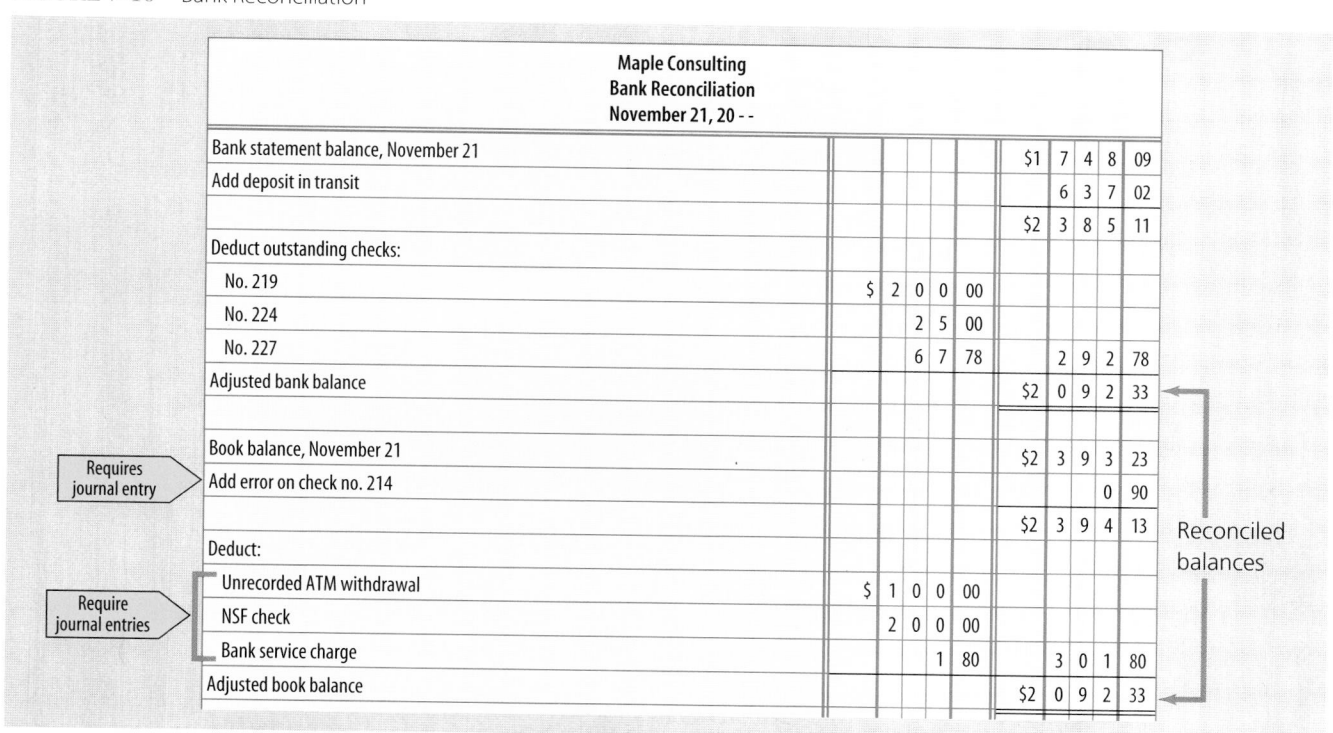

LEARNING KEY

Journal entries are needed to correct errors in the books and to record bank additions and deductions that are not in the books.

Journal Entries

Only two kinds of items appearing on a bank reconciliation require journal entries:

1. Errors in the depositor's books.

2. Bank additions and deductions that do not already appear in the books.

A B R O A D E R   V I E W

© GETTY IMAGES/PHOTODISC

Fraud—A Real Threat to Small Business

The bookkeeper for Kramer Iron, Inc., in Hamden, Connecticut, embezzled $213,539 from the company over a four-year period. She used two schemes. One was to alter the number of the dollar amount printed on checks payable to her. The other technique involved putting her own name on the "pay to" line on checks intended for other parties.

This fraud shows the importance of two procedures described in this chapter: (1) Make sure that all aspects of a check are correct before signing it. (2) In preparing the bank reconciliation, compare canceled checks with the accounting records.

Figure 7-11 contains a detailed list of items that require journal entries.

FIGURE 7-11   Bank Reconciliation Items that Require Journal Entries

ADDITIONS TO CASH BALANCE	DEDUCTIONS FROM CASH BALANCE
* Unrecorded deposits (including ATM)	* Unrecorded ATM withdrawals
* Note collected by bank	* NSF checks
* Interest earned	* Bank service charges
* Errors:	* Deposits recorded twice
1. Added too little as a deposit	* Unrecorded checks
2. Deducted too much as a check	* Loan payments
	* Interest payments
	* Errors:
	1. Added too much as a deposit
	2. Deducted too little as a check

Note the four items in the lower portion of the bank reconciliation in Figure 7-10. A journal entry always is required for each item in this book balance portion of the bank reconciliation.

The $0.90 item is an error in the accounting records that occurred when the check amount was incorrectly entered. Assume the $18.98 was in payment of an account payable which had been incorrectly debited for $19.88. The entry to correct this error is as follows:

4	Cash			0	90				4
5	Accounts Payable						0	90	5
6	Error in recording check								6

The $100.00 ATM withdrawal has been deducted from Maple's account by the bank. Maple has not yet recorded the withdrawal. Maple withdrew the funds for personal use, so the following journal entry is required:

8		James Maple, Drawing			1 0 0 00			8
9		Cash				1 0 0 00		9
10		Unrecorded ATM withdrawal						10

The $200.00 NSF check is a deduction by the bank for a check deposited by Maple that proved to be worthless. This amount must be deducted from the book balance. Assuming the $200.00 was received from a customer on account, the following journal entry is required:

12		Accounts Receivable			2 0 0 00			12
13		Cash				2 0 0 00		13
14		Unrecorded NSF check						14

The $1.80 bank service charge is a fee for bank services received by Maple. The bank has deducted this amount from Maple's account. Bank service charges are usually small and are charged to Miscellaneous Expense.

16		Miscellaneous Expense			1 80			16
17		Cash				1 80		17
18		Bank service charge						18

Electronic Funds Transfer

Electronic funds transfer (EFT) uses a computer rather than paper checks to complete transactions with the bank. This technique is being used increasingly today. Applications of EFT include payrolls, social security payments, retail purchases, mortgage payments, and the ATM transactions described earlier in the chapter.

Heavy use of EFT can present a challenge in preparing bank reconciliations. Many of the documents handled in a purely manual environment disappear when EFT is used. Bank accounts are just one of many areas where computers require accountants to think in new ways. Regardless of what system is used, the key point to remember is that the accounting records must be correctly updated.

THE PETTY CASH FUND

L03 Establish and use a petty cash fund.

For good control over cash, payments generally should be made by check. Unfortunately, payments of very small amounts by check can be both inconvenient and inefficient. For example, the time and cost required to write a check for $0.70 to mail a letter might be greater than the cost of the postage. Therefore, businesses customarily establish a **petty cash fund** to pay for small items with cash. "Petty" means small, and both the amount of the fund and the maximum amount of any bill that can be paid from the fund are small.

Establishing a Petty Cash Fund

To establish a petty cash fund, a check is written to the petty cash custodian for the amount to be set aside in the fund. The amount may be $50.00, $100.00, $200.00, or any amount considered necessary. The journal entry to establish a petty cash fund of $100.00 would be as follows:

4			Petty Cash		1 0 0 00		4
5			Cash			1 0 0 00	5
6			Establish petty cash fund				6

Petty Cash is an asset that is listed immediately below Cash on the balance sheet.

The custodian cashes the check and places the money in a petty cash box. For good control, the custodian should be the only person authorized to make payments from the fund. The custodian should be able to account for the full amount of the fund at any time.

Making Payments from a Petty Cash Fund

A receipt called a **petty cash voucher** (Figure 7-12) should be prepared for every payment from the fund. The voucher shows the name of the payee, the purpose of the payment, and the account to be charged for the payment. Each voucher should be signed by the custodian and by the person receiving the cash. The vouchers should be numbered consecutively so that all vouchers can be accounted for.

FIGURE 7-12 Petty Cash Voucher

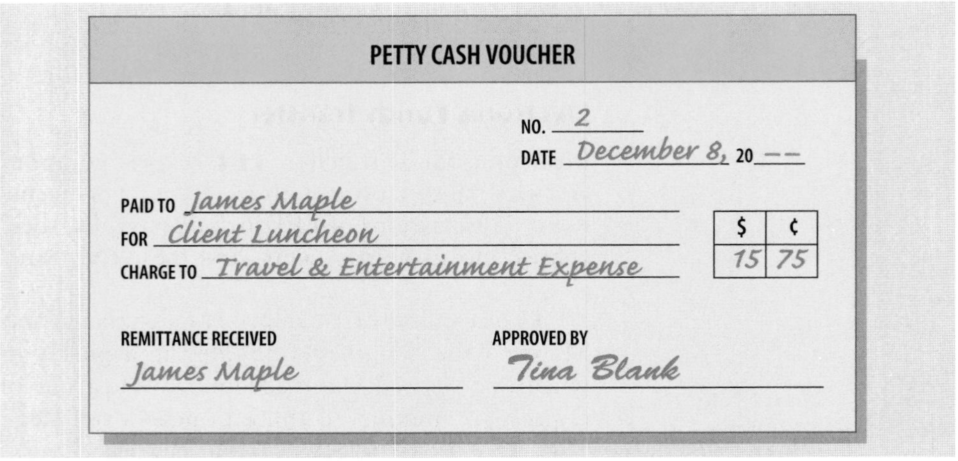
PETTY CASH VOUCHER

NO. 2
DATE December 8, 20--

PAID TO James Maple
FOR Client Luncheon
CHARGE TO Travel & Entertainment Expense

$	¢
15	75

REMITTANCE RECEIVED James Maple
APPROVED BY Tina Blank

Petty Cash Payments Record

When a petty cash fund is maintained, a formal record is often kept of all payments from the fund. The **petty cash payments record** (Figure 7-13) is a special multi-column record that supplements the regular accounting records. It is not a journal. The headings of the Distribution of Payments columns may vary, depending upon the types of expenditures.

The petty cash payments record of Maple Consulting is shown in Figure 7-13. A narrative of the petty cash transactions shown in Figure 7-13 is as follows:

Dec. 1 Maple issued a check for $200.00 payable to Tina Blank, Petty Cash Custodian. Blank cashed the check and placed the money in a secure cash box.

FIGURE 7-13 Maple Consulting's Petty Cash Payments Record

PETTY CASH PAYMENTS FOR THE MONTH OF December 20-- PAGE 1

	DAY	DESCRIPTION		VOU. NO.	TOTAL AMOUNT	DISTRIBUTION OF PAYMENTS						
						AUTO EXP.	POST. EXP.	TRAVEL/ ENTERT. EXP.	MISC. EXP.	ACCOUNT	AMOUNT	
1	1	Received in fund	200.00									1
2	5	Automobile repairs		1	32.80	32.80						2
3	8	Client luncheon		2	15.75			15.75				3
4	9	James Maple, personal use		3	30.00					James Maple, Drawing	30.00	4
5	15	Printer repairs		4	38.25				38.25			5
6	17	Traveling expenses		5	14.50			14.50				6
7	19	Washing automobile		6	8.00	8.00						7
8	22	Postage expense		7	9.50		9.50					8
9	29	Postage stamps		8	30.00		30.00					9
10					178.80	40.80	39.50	30.25	38.25		30.00	10
11	31	Balance	21.20									11
12	31	Replenished fund	178.80									12
13		Total	200.00									13
14												14
15												15
16												16
17												17
18												18
19												19
20												20
21												21
22												22
23												23
24												24
25												25
26												26
27												27
28												28

Credit to replenish petty cash fund

Debits to replenish petty cash fund

A notation of the amount received is made in the Description column of the petty cash payments record. In addition, this transaction is entered in the journal as follows:

8	Dec. 1	Petty Cash			2	0	0	00						8
9		Cash								2	0	0	00	9
10		Establish petty cash fund												10

During the month of December, the following payments were made from the petty cash fund:

Dec. 5   Paid $32.80 to Jerry's Auto for servicing the company automobile. Voucher No. 1.

8   Reimbursed Maple $15.75 for the amount spent for lunch with a client. Voucher No. 2.

9   Gave Maple $30.00 for personal use. Voucher No. 3.

There is no special Distribution column for entering amounts withdrawn by the owner for personal use. Therefore, this payment is entered by writing the account name in the Account column and $30.00 in the Amount column at the extreme right of the petty cash payments record.

15   Paid $38.25 for printer repairs. Voucher No. 4.

17   Reimbursed Maple $14.50 for travel expenses. Voucher No. 5.

19   Paid $8.00 to Big Red Car Care for washing the company automobile. Voucher No. 6.

22   Paid $9.50 for mailing a package. Voucher No. 7.

29   Paid $30.00 for postage stamps. Voucher No. 8.

Replenishing the Petty Cash Fund

The petty cash fund should be replenished whenever the fund runs low and at the end of each accounting period, so that the accounts are brought up to date. The amount columns of the petty cash payments record are totaled to verify that the total of the Total Amount column equals the total of the Distribution columns. The amount columns are then ruled as shown in Figure 7-13.

The information in the petty cash payments record is then used to replenish the petty cash fund. On December 31, a check for $178.80 is issued to the petty cash custodian. The journal entry to record the replenishment of the fund is as follows:

18	Dec.	31	Automobile Expense			4	0	80						18
19			Postage Expense			3	9	50						19
20			Travel and Entertainment Expense			3	0	25						20
21			Miscellaneous Expense			3	8	25						21
22			James Maple, Drawing			3	0	00						22
23			Cash							1	7	8	80	23
24			Replenishment of petty cash fund											24

Note two important aspects of the functioning of a petty cash fund:

LEARNING KEY

Once the petty cash fund is established, an entry is made to Petty Cash only if the amount of the fund is being changed.

1. Once the fund is established by debiting Petty Cash and crediting Cash, no further entries are made to Petty Cash. Notice in the journal entry to replenish the fund that the debits are to appropriate expense accounts and the credit is to Cash. Only if the amount of the fund itself is being changed would there be a debit or credit to Petty Cash.

2. The petty cash payments record is strictly a supplement to the regular accounting records. Because it is not a journal, no posting is done from this record. A separate entry must be made in the journal to replenish the fund and update the expense accounts.

THE CHANGE FUND AND CASH SHORT AND OVER

LO4 Establish a change fund and use the cash short and over account.

Businesses generally must be able to make change when customers use cash to pay for goods or services received. To do so, generally it is a good idea to establish a **change fund**. A change fund is a supply of currency and coins kept in a cash register or cash drawer for use in handling cash sales.

Establishing and Operating the Change Fund

The journal entries for establishing and maintaining a change fund are very similar to the ones just used for petty cash. To establish a change fund of $200.00 on June 1, the following entry would be made:

8	June 1	Change Fund		2	0	0	00						8
9		Cash							2	0	0	00	9
10		Establish change fund											10

At the end of the day, cash received during the day is deposited, but the change fund is held back for use the following business day. For example, if cash of $1,250.00 was received on June 3 for services provided, the cash drawer would contain $1,450.00, as follows:

Change fund	$ 200.00
Cash sales	1,250.00
Total cash on hand	$1,450.00

The $1,250 would be deposited in the bank, and the following journal entry would be made:

12	June 3	Cash		1	2	5	0	00						12
13		Service Fees							1	2	5	0	00	13
14		Cash received for services												14

LEARNING KEY

Once the change fund is established, an entry is made to Change Fund only if the amount of the fund is being changed.

Notice the additional similarity between the change fund and the petty cash fund. Once the change fund is established by a debit to Change Fund and a credit to Cash, no further entries are made to the change fund. Only if the amount of the change fund itself is being changed would there be a debit or credit to Change Fund.

Cash Short and Over

An unavoidable part of the change-making process is that errors can occur. It is important to know whether such errors have occurred and how to account for them.

Businesses commonly use cash registers with tapes that accumulate a record of the day's receipts. The amount of cash according to the tapes plus the amount of the change fund can be compared with the amount of cash in the register to determine any error. For example, assume a cash shortage is identified for June 19.

Change fund	$ 200.00
Receipts per register tapes	963.00
Total	$1,163.00
Cash count	1,161.00
Cash shortage	$ 2.00

Similarly, assume a cash overage is identified for June 20.

Change fund	$ 200.00
Receipts per register tapes	814.00
Total	$1,014.00
Cash count	1,015.00
Cash overage	$ 1.00

We account for such errors by using an account called Cash Short and Over. In T account form, Cash Short and Over appears as follows:

Cash Short and Over

Shortage (Expense)	Overage (Revenue)

The register tapes on June 19 showed receipts of $963.00 and the change fund was $200.00, but only $1,161.00 in cash was counted. The journal entry on June 19 to record the revenues and cash shortage (remember that we hold back the change fund) would be:

18	June	19	Cash			9	6	1	00						18
19			Cash Short and Over					2	00						19
20			Service Fees							9	6	3	00		20
21			Record service fees and cash shortage												21

The entry on June 20 to record the revenues and cash overage (holding back the change fund) would be:

23	June	20	Cash			8	1	5	00						23
24			Service Fees							8	1	4	00		24
25			Cash Short and Over									1	00		25
26			Record service fees and cash overage												26

The cash short and over account is used to accumulate cash shortages and overages throughout the accounting period. At the end of the period, a debit balance in the account (a net shortage) is treated as an expense. A credit balance in the account (a net overage) is treated as revenue.

S E L F   S T U D Y

Learning Objectives	Key Points to Remember
LO1 Describe how to open and use a checking account.	Three steps to follow in preparing a check are: 1. Complete the check stub or register. 2. Enter the date, payee name, and amount on the check. 3. Sign the check.
LO2 Prepare a bank reconciliation and related journal entries.	The most common reasons for differences between the book and bank cash balances are: 1. Deposits in transit 2. Outstanding checks 3. Bank service charges 4. Bank collections for the depositor 5. NSF checks 6. Errors by the bank or the depositor Three steps to follow in preparing a bank reconciliation are: 1. Identify deposits in transit and any related errors. 2. Identify outstanding checks and any related errors. 3. Identify additional reconciling items. Only two kinds of items on a bank reconciliation require journal entries: 1. Errors in the depositor's books. 2. Bank additions and deductions that do not already appear in the books.
LO3 Establish and use a petty cash fund.	Two important aspects of the functioning of a petty cash fund are: 1. Once the fund is established, subsequent entries do not affect the petty cash account balance, unless the size of the fund itself is being changed. 2. The petty cash payments record is supplemental to the regular accounting records. No posting is done from this record.
LO4 Establish a change fund and use the cash short and over account.	A change fund is established by debiting Change Fund and crediting Cash. Cash shortages and overages are accounted for using the cash short and over account. A debit balance in this account represents expense; a credit balance represents revenue.

DEMONSTRATION PROBLEM

Jason Kuhn's check stubs indicated a balance of $4,673.12 for Kuhn's Wilderness Outfitters on March 31. This included a record of a deposit of $926.10 mailed to the bank on March 30, but not credited to Kuhn's account until April 1. In addition, the following checks were outstanding on March 31:

No. 462	$524.26
No. 465	$213.41
No. 473	$543.58
No. 476	$351.38
No. 477	$197.45

The bank statement showed a balance of $5,419.00 as of March 31. The bank statement included a service charge of $4.10 with the date of March 29. In matching the canceled checks and record of deposits with the stubs, it was discovered that check no. 456, to Office Suppliers, Inc., for $93.00 was erroneously recorded on the stub as $39.00. This caused the bank balance on that stub and those following to be $54.00 too large. It was also discovered that an ATM withdrawal of $100.00 for personal use was not recorded on the books.

Kuhn maintains a $200.00 petty cash fund. His petty cash payments record showed the following totals at the end of March of the current year:

Automobile expense	$ 32.40
Postage expense	27.50
Charitable contributions expense	35.00
Telephone expense	6.20
Travel and entertainment expense	38.60
Miscellaneous expense	17.75
Jason Kuhn, Drawing	40.00
Total	$197.45

This left a balance of $2.55 in the petty cash fund, and the fund was replenished.

REQUIRED

1. Prepare a bank reconciliation for Jason Kuhn as of March 31, 20--.

2. Journalize the entries that should be made by Kuhn on his books as of March 31, 20--, (a) as a result of the bank reconciliation and (b) to replenish the petty cash fund.

3. Show proof that, after these entries, the total of the cash and petty cash account balances equals $4,715.02.

Solution

1.

Kuhn's Wilderness Outfitters										
Bank Reconciliation										
March 31, 20 - -										
Bank statement balance, March 31							$5	4	1	9	00
Add deposit in transit								9	2	6	10
							$6	3	4	5	10
Deduct outstanding checks:											
No. 462	$	5	2	4	26						
No. 465		2	1	3	41						
No. 473		5	4	3	58						
No. 476		3	5	1	38						
No. 477		1	9	7	45		1	8	3	0	08
Adjusted bank balance							$4	5	1	5	02
Book balance, March 31							$4	6	7	3	12
Deduct: Bank service charge	$			4	10						
Error on check no. 456				5	4	00					
Unrecorded ATM withdrawal		1	0	0	00			1	5	8	10
Adjusted book balance							$4	5	1	5	02

2a.

3										3
4	Mar.	31	Miscellaneous Expense		4	10				4
5			Cash					4	10	5
6			Bank service charge							6
7										7
8			Accounts Payable—Office Suppliers, Inc.		5	4	00			8
9			Cash					5	4	00	9
10			Error on check no. 456							10
11										11
12			Jason Kuhn, Drawing	1	0	0	00			12
13			Cash				1	0	0	00	13
14			Unrecorded ATM withdrawal							14
15										15

b.

16		31	Automobile Expense	3	2	40				16
17			Postage Expense	2	7	50				17
18			Charitable Contributions Expense	3	5	00				18
19			Telephone Expense		6	20				19
20			Travel and Entertainment Expense	3	8	60				20
21			Miscellaneous Expense	1	7	75				21
22			Jason Kuhn, Drawing	4	0	00				22
23			Cash				1	9	7	45	23
24			Replenishment of petty cash fund							24
25										25

(continued)

3. Cash in bank:

Check stub balance, March 31	$4,673.12	
Less bank charges	158.10	$4,515.02
Adjusted cash in bank		
Cash on hand:		
Petty cash fund	$ 2.55	
Add replenishment	197.45	200.00
Adjusted cash on hand		$4,715.02
Total cash in bank and petty cash on hand		

KEY TERMS

ABA (American Bankers Association) Number (234) The small fraction printed in the upper right-hand corner of each check.

automated teller machine (ATM) (236) A machine used by depositors to make withdrawals or deposits at any time.

bank reconciliation (241) A report used to bring the book and bank balances into agreement.

bank statement (239) A statement of account issued by a bank to each depositor once a month.

blank endorsement (234) An endorsement where the depositor simply signs the back of the check, making the check payable to any bearer.

canceled check (239) A depositor's check paid by the bank during the bank statement period.

cash (234) To a business, cash includes currency, coins, checks received from customers, money orders, and bank cashier's checks.

change fund (249) A supply of currency and coins kept in a cash register or cash drawer for use in handling cash sales.

check (237) A document ordering a bank to pay cash from a depositor's account.

check stub (237) In some checkbooks, a document attached to a check that contains space for relevant information about the check.

credit memo (242) An item that the bank adds to the account.

debit memo (242) An item that the bank deducts from the account.

deposit ticket (234) A form showing a detailed listing of items being deposited.

deposits in transit (241) Deposits that have not reached or been recorded by the bank before the bank statement is prepared.

drawee (237) The bank on which the check is drawn.

drawer (237) The depositor who orders the bank to pay the cash.

electronic funds transfer (EFT) (245) A process using a computer rather than paper checks to complete transactions with the bank.

endorsement (234) Stamping or writing the depositor's name and sometimes other information on the back of the check.

internal control (234) A set of procedures designed to ensure proper accounting for transactions.

magnetic ink character recognition (MICR) code (234) The character code used to print identifying information on the lower left front side of each check.

not sufficient funds (NSF) check (241) A check deposited by the depositor that is not paid because the drawer did not have sufficient funds.

outstanding check (241) A check issued that has not been presented to the bank for payment before the statement is prepared.

payee (237) The person being paid the cash.

petty cash fund (245) A fund established to pay for small items with cash.

petty cash payments record (246) A special multi-column record that supplements the regular accounting records.

petty cash voucher (246) A receipt that is prepared for every payment from the petty cash fund.

restrictive endorsement (234) An endorsement where the depositor adds words such as "For deposit" to restrict the payment of the check.

service charge (241) A bank charge for services such as check printing and processing.

signature card (234) A card that is completed and signed by each person authorized to sign checks.

Self-Study Test Questions

True/False

1. The primary purpose of a bank reconciliation is to detect and correct errors made by the bank in its records.

2. NSF checks are subtracted from the bank's ending balance on the bank reconciliation.

3. The bank service charge requires a journal entry to record its effects on the cash account.

4. Unrecorded ATM withdrawals are added to the checkbook balance on the bank reconciliation.

5. The petty cash record is a journal of original entry (entries are posted from it to the general ledger accounts).

Multiple Choice

1. To establish a petty cash fund, which account is debited?

   (a) Cash
   (b) Petty Cash
   (c) Miscellaneous Expense
   (d) Revenue

2. When the cash short and over account has a debit balance at the end of the month, it is considered

   (a) an expense.
   (b) an asset.
   (c) revenue.
   (d) a liability.

3. Which of these could be *added* to the ending checkbook balance?

   (a) service charges
   (b) NSF check
   (c) checkbook errors
   (d) outstanding checks

4. Which of these is *subtracted* from the ending checkbook balance?

   (a) deposits in transit
   (b) service charges
   (c) note collection
   (d) bank errors

5. Which of these is *added* to the ending bank statement balance?

   (a) outstanding checks
   (b) service charges
   (c) checkbook errors
   (d) deposits in transit

The answers to the Self-Study Test Questions are at the end of the text.

REVIEW QUESTIONS

LO1   1. Why must a signature card be filled out and signed to open a checking account?

LO1   2. Explain the difference between a blank endorsement and a restrictive endorsement.

LO1   3. Who are the three parties to every check?

LO1   4. What are the three steps to follow in preparing a check?

LO2   5. What are the most common reasons for differences between the book and bank cash balances?

LO2   6. What are the three steps to follow in preparing a bank reconciliation?

LO2   7. What two kinds of items on a bank reconciliation require journal entries?

LO2   8. Name five applications of electronic funds transfer in current use.

LO3   9. What is the purpose of a petty cash fund?

LO3   10. What should be prepared every time a petty cash payment is made?

LO3   11. At what two times should the petty cash fund be replenished?

LO3   12. From what source is the information obtained for issuing a check to replenish the petty cash fund?

LO4   13. At what two times would an entry be made affecting the change fund?

LO4   14. What does a debit balance in the cash short and over account represent? What does a credit balance in this account represent?

REVISITING THE OPENER

In the chapter opener on p. 233, Evan wondered how to reconcile the book and bank cash balances. In particular, he wanted to know how to handle some checks he had written.

(1) How should Evan treat the checks he wrote during the month that have not yet been presented to the bank for payment?

(2) Give an example of how such checks would appear on a bank reconciliation.

(3) Would journal entries be needed for these bank reconciliation items?

© DIGITAL IMAGING GROUP

SERIES A EXERCISES

E 7-1A (LO1)

CHECKING ACCOUNT TERMS Match the following words with their definitions.

1. An endorsement where the depositor simply signs on the back of the check
2. An endorsement that contains words like "For Deposit Only" together with the signature
3. A card filled out and signed by each person authorized to sign checks on an account
4. The depositor who orders the bank to pay cash from the depositor's account
5. The bank on which the check is drawn
6. The person being paid the cash
7. A check that has been paid by the bank and is being returned to the depositor

a. signature card
b. canceled check
c. blank endorsement
d. drawer
e. restrictive endorsement
f. drawee
g. payee

E 7-2A (LO1)

✓ Total deposit: $817.00

PREPARE DEPOSIT TICKET Based on the following information, prepare a deposit ticket.

Date:		January 15, 20--
Currency:		$334.00
Coin:		26.00
Checks:	No. 4-11	311.00
	No. 80-322	108.00
	No. 3-9	38.00

E 7-3A (LO1)

PREPARE CHECK AND STUB Based on the following information, prepare a check and stub.

Date:	January 15, 20--
Balance brought forward:	$2,841.50
Deposit:	(from Exercise 7-2A)
Check to:	J.M. Suppliers
Amount:	$150.00
For:	Office Supplies
Signature:	Sign your name

E 7-4A (LO2)

BANK RECONCILIATION PROCEDURES In a format similar to the following, indicate whether the action at the left will result in an addition to (+) or subtraction from (−) the ending bank balance or the ending checkbook balance.

(continued)

		Ending Bank Balance	Ending Checkbook Balance
1.	Deposits in transit to the bank	_____	_____
2.	Error in checkbook: check recorded as $32.00 but was actually for $23.00	_____	_____
3.	Service fee charged by bank	_____	_____
4.	Outstanding checks	_____	_____
5.	NSF check deposited earlier	_____	_____
6.	Error in checkbook: check recorded as $22.00 but was actually for $220.00	_____	_____
7.	Bank credit memo advising they collected a note for us	_____	_____

E 7-5A (LO2)

✓ NSF check: Dr. Accounts Receivable, $390.00

PREPARE JOURNAL ENTRIES FOR BANK RECONCILIATION Based on the following bank reconciliation, prepare the journal entries.

Lisa Choy Associates Bank Reconciliation July 31, 20 - -										
Bank statement balance, July 31						$2	7	6	4	40
Add deposits in transit	$	2	5	0	00					
			9	8	00		3	4	8	00
						$3	1	1	2	40
Deduct outstanding checks:										
No. 387	$	3	5	3	50					
No. 393			1	7	80					
No. 398			3	3	20		4	0	4	50
Adjusted bank balance						$2	7	0	7	90
Book balance, July 31						$3	1	3	0	90
Deduct: Error on check no. 394*	$		2	3	00					
NSF check		3	9	0	00					
Bank service charge			1	0	00		4	2	3	00
Adjusted book balance						$2	7	0	7	90
*Accounts Payable was debited in original entry.										

E 7-6A (LO3)

✓ Replenishment: Cr. Cash, $197.00

PETTY CASH JOURNAL ENTRIES Based on the following petty cash information, prepare (a) the journal entry to establish a petty cash fund, and (b) the journal entry to replenish the petty cash fund.

On January 1, 20--, a check was written in the amount of $200.00 to establish a petty cash fund. During January, the following vouchers were written for cash removed from the petty cash drawer.

Voucher No.	Account Debited	Amount
1	Telephone Expense	$17.50
2	Automobile Expense	33.00
3	Joseph Levine, Drawing	70.00
4	Postage Expense	12.50
5	Charitable Contributions Expense	15.00
6	Miscellaneous Expense	49.00

E 7-7A (LO4)

✓ Apr. 16: Cr. Cash Short and Over, $1.75

CASH SHORT AND OVER ENTRIES Based on the following information, prepare the weekly entries for cash receipts from service fees and cash short and over. A change fund of $100.00 is maintained.

Date	Change Fund	Cash Register Receipt Amount	Actual Cash Counted
Apr. 2	$100.00	$268.50	$366.50
9	100.00	237.75	333.50
16	100.00	309.25	411.00
23	100.00	226.50	324.00
30	100.00	318.00	422.00

SERIES A PROBLEMS

P 7-8A (LO2)

✓ Adjusted book balance: $4,182.00

BANK RECONCILIATION AND RELATED JOURNAL ENTRIES The balance in the checking account of Violette Enterprises as of October 31 is $4,765.00. The bank statement shows an ending balance of $4,235.00. The following information is discovered by (1) comparing last month's deposits in transit and outstanding checks with this month's bank statement, (2) comparing deposits and checks written per books and per bank in the current month, and (3) noting service charges and other debit and credit memos shown on the bank statement.

Deposits in transit:	10/29	$175.00
	10/30	334.00
Outstanding checks:	No. 1764	47.00
	No. 1767	146.00
	No. 1781	369.00
Unrecorded ATM withdrawal*:		180.00
Bank service charge:		43.00
NSF check:		370.00

Error on check no. 1754   Checkbook shows it was for $72.00, but it was actually written for $62.00. Accounts Payable was debited.

*Funds were withdrawn by Guy Violette for personal use.

REQUIRED

1. Prepare a bank reconciliation as of October 31, 20--.

2. Prepare the required journal entries.

P 7-9A (LO2)

✓ Adjusted bank balance: $3,069.95

KLOOSTER & ALLEN

BANK RECONCILIATION AND RELATED JOURNAL ENTRIES The balance in the checking account of Lyle's Salon as of November 30 is $3,282.95. The bank statement shows an ending balance of $2,127.00. By examining last month's bank reconciliation, comparing the deposits and checks written per books and per bank in November, and noting the service charges and other debit and credit memos shown on the bank statement, the following were found:

(a) An ATM withdrawal of $150.00 on November 18 by Lyle for personal use was not recorded on the books.

(b) A bank debit memo issued for an NSF check from a customer of $19.50.

(c) A bank credit memo issued for interest of $19.00 earned during the month.

(d) On November 30, a deposit of $1,177.00 was made, which is not shown on the bank statement.

(e) A bank debit memo issued for $17.50 for bank service charges.

(f) Checks No. 549, 561, and 562 for the amounts of $185.00, $21.00, and $9.40, respectively, were written during November but have not yet been received by the bank.

(g) The reconciliation from the previous month showed outstanding checks of $271.95. One of those checks, No. 471 for $18.65, has not yet been received by the bank.

(h) Check No. 523 written to a creditor in the amount of $372.90 was recorded in the books as $327.90.

REQUIRED

1. Prepare a bank reconciliation as of November 30.

2. Prepare the required journal entries.

P 7-10A (LO3)

✓ Replenishment: Cr. Cash, $138.00

PETTY CASH RECORD AND JOURNAL ENTRIES On May 1, a petty cash fund was established for $150.00. The following vouchers were issued during May:

Date	Voucher No.	Purpose	Amount
May 1	1	postage due	$ 3.50
3	2	office supplies	11.00
5	3	auto repair (miscellaneous)	22.00
7	4	drawing (Joy Adams)	25.00
11	5	donation (Red Cross)	10.00
15	6	travel expenses	28.00
22	7	postage stamps	3.50
26	8	telephone call	5.00
30	9	donation (Boy Scouts)	30.00

REQUIRED

1. Prepare the journal entry to establish the petty cash fund.

2. Record the vouchers in the petty cash record. Total and rule the petty cash record.

3. Prepare the journal entry to replenish the petty cash fund. Make the appropriate entry in the petty cash record.

P 7-11A (LO4)

✓ July 23: Dr. Cash Short and Over, $2.50

CASH SHORT AND OVER ENTRIES Listed below are the weekly cash register tape amounts for service fees and the related cash counts during the month of July. A change fund of $100.00 is maintained.

Date	Change Fund	Cash Register Receipt Amount	Actual Cash Counted
July 2	$100.00	$289.50	$387.00
9	100.00	311.50	411.50
16	100.00	306.00	408.50
23	100.00	317.50	415.00
30	100.00	296.00	399.50

REQUIRED

1. Prepare the journal entries to record the cash service fees and cash short and over for each of the five weeks.

2. Post to the cash short and over account (use account no. 516).

3. Determine the ending balance of the cash short and over account. Does it represent an expense or revenue?

SERIES B EXERCISES

E 7-1B (LO1)

CHECKING ACCOUNT TERMS Match the following words with their definitions.

1. Banking number used to identify checks for deposit tickets
2. A card filled out to open a checking account
3. A machine from which withdrawals can be taken or deposits made to accounts
4. A place where relevant information is recorded about a check
5. A set of procedures designed to ensure proper accounting for transactions
6. A statement of account issued to each depositor once a month
7. A detailed listing of items being deposited to an account

a. bank statement
b. deposit ticket
c. signature card
d. internal control
e. check stub
f. ATM
g. ABA number

E 7-2B (LO1)

✓ Total deposit: $645.00

PREPARE DEPOSIT TICKET Based on the following information, prepare a deposit ticket.

Date:		November 15, 20--
Currency:		$283.00
Coin:		19.00
Checks:	No. 3-22	201.00
	No. 19-366	114.00
	No. 3-2	28.00

E 7-3B (LO1)

PREPARE CHECK AND STUB Based on the following information, prepare a check and stub.

Date:	November 15, 20--
Balance brought forward:	$3,181.00
Deposit:	(from Exercise 7-2B)
Check to:	R.J. Smith Co.
Amount:	$120.00
For:	Payment on account
Signature:	Sign your name

E 7-4B (LO2)

BANK RECONCILIATION PROCEDURES In a format similar to the following, indicate whether the action at the left will result in an addition to (+) or subtraction from (−) the ending bank balance or the ending checkbook balance.

		Ending Bank Balance	Ending Checkbook Balance
1.	Service fee of $12 charged by bank	_____	_____
2.	Outstanding checks	_____	_____
3.	Error in checkbook: check recorded as $36.00 was actually for $28.00	_____	_____
4.	NSF check deposited earlier	_____	_____
5.	Bank credit memo advising they collected a note for us	_____	_____
6.	Deposits in transit to the bank	_____	_____
7.	Error in checkbook: check recorded as $182.00 was actually for $218.00	_____	_____

E 7-5B (LO2)

✓ NSF check: Dr. Accounts Receivable, $66.00

PREPARE JOURNAL ENTRIES FOR BANK RECONCILIATION Based on the following bank reconciliation, prepare the journal entries.

Regina D'Alfonso Associates Bank Reconciliation July 31, 20 - -										
Bank statement balance, July 31							$1	7	8 4	00
Add deposits in transit	$	4	1 8	50						
		1	0 0	50				5	1 9	00
							$2	3	0 3	00
Deduct outstanding checks:										
No. 185	$	2	0 6	50						
No. 203		3	1 7	40						
No. 210			5 6	10				5	8 0	00
Adjusted bank balance							$1	7	2 3	00
Book balance, July 31							$1	7	9 4	00
Add error on check no. 191*									1 0	00
							$1	8	0 4	00
Deduct: NSF check	$		6 6	00						
Bank service charge			1 5	00					8 1	00
Adjusted book balance							$1	7	2 3	00
*Accounts Payable was debited in original entry.										

E 7-6B (LO3)

✓ Replenishment: Cr. Cash, $190.00

PETTY CASH JOURNAL ENTRIES Based on the following petty cash information, prepare (a) the journal entry to establish a petty cash fund, and (b) the journal entry to replenish the petty cash fund.

On October 1, 20--, a check was written in the amount of $200.00 to establish a petty cash fund. During October, the following vouchers were written for cash taken from the petty cash drawer:

Voucher No.	Account Debited	Amount
1	Postage Expense	$13.00
2	Miscellaneous Expense	17.00
3	John Flanagan, Drawing	45.00
4	Telephone Expense	36.00
5	Charitable Contributions Expense	50.00
6	Automobile Expense	29.00

E 7-7B (LO4)

✓ June 15: Dr. Cash Short and Over, $2.00

CASH SHORT AND OVER ENTRIES Based on the following information, prepare the weekly entries for cash receipts from service fees and cash short and over. A change fund of $100.00 is maintained.

Date	Change Fund	Cash Register Receipt Amount	Actual Cash Counted
June 1	$100.00	$330.00	$433.00
8	100.00	297.00	400.00
15	100.00	233.00	331.00
22	100.00	302.00	396.50
29	100.00	316.00	412.00

SERIES B PROBLEMS

P 7-8B (LO2)

✓ Adjusted book balance: $2,674.00

BANK RECONCILIATION AND RELATED JOURNAL ENTRIES The balance in the checking account of Kyros Enterprises as of November 30 is $3,004.00. The bank statement shows an ending balance of $2,525.00. The following information is discovered by (1) comparing last month's deposits in transit and outstanding checks with this month's bank statement, (2) comparing deposits and checks written per books and per bank in the current month, and (3) noting service charges and other debit and credit memos shown on the bank statement.

Deposits in transit:	11/29	$125.00
	11/30	200.00
Outstanding checks:	No. 322	17.00
	No. 324	105.00
	No. 327	54.00
Unrecorded ATM withdrawal*:		100.00
Bank service charge:		25.00
NSF check:		185.00
Error on check no. 321	Checkbook shows it was for $44.00, but it was actually written for $64.00. Accounts Payable was debited.	

*Funds were withdrawn by Steve Kyros for personal use.

1. Prepare a bank reconciliation as of November 30, 20--.

2. Prepare the required journal entries.

P 7-9B (LO2)

✓ Adjusted bank balance: $4,518.70

BANK RECONCILIATION AND RELATED JOURNAL ENTRIES The balance in the checking account of Tori's Health Center as of April 30 is $4,690.30. The bank statement shows an ending balance of $3,275.60. By examining last month's bank reconciliation, comparing the deposits and checks written per books and per bank in April, and noting the service charges and other debit and credit memos shown on the bank statement, the following were found:

(a) An ATM withdrawal of $200.00 on April 20 by Tori for personal use was not recorded on the books.
(b) A bank debit memo issued for an NSF check from a customer of $29.10.
(c) A bank credit memo issued for interest of $28.00 earned during the month.
(d) On April 30, a deposit of $1,592.00 was made, which is not shown on the bank statement.
(e) A bank debit memo issued for $24.50 for bank service charges.
(f) Checks No. 481, 493, and 494 for the amounts of $215.00, $71.00, and $24.30, respectively, were written during April but have not yet been received by the bank.
(g) The reconciliation from the previous month showed outstanding checks of $418.25. One of these checks, No. 397 for $38.60, has not yet been received by the bank.
(h) Check No. 422 written to a creditor in the amount of $217.90 was recorded in the books as $271.90.

REQUIRED

1. Prepare a bank reconciliation as of April 30.

2. Prepare the required journal entries.

P 7-10B (LO3)

✓ Replenishment: Cr. Cash, $87.00

PETTY CASH RECORD AND JOURNAL ENTRIES On July 1, a petty cash fund was established for $100.00. The following vouchers were issued during July:

Date	Voucher No.	Purpose	Amount
July 1	1	office supplies	$ 3.00
3	2	donation (Goodwill)	15.00
5	3	travel expenses	5.00
7	4	postage due	2.00
8	5	office supplies	4.00
11	6	postage due	3.50
15	7	telephone call	5.00
21	8	travel expenses	11.00
25	9	withdrawal by owner (L. Ortiz)	20.00
26	10	copier repair (miscellaneous)	18.50

REQUIRED

1. Prepare the journal entry to establish the petty cash fund.

2. Record the vouchers in the petty cash record. Total and rule the petty cash record.

3.   Prepare the journal entry to replenish the petty cash fund. Make the appropriate entry in the petty cash record.

P 7-11B (LO4)

✓ Aug. 8: Dr. Cash Short and Over, $3.50

CASH SHORT AND OVER ENTRIES Listed below are the weekly cash register tape amounts for service fees and the related cash counts during the month of July. A change fund of $200.00 is maintained.

Date	Change Fund	Cash Register Receipt Amount	Actual Cash Counted
Aug. 1	$200.00	$292.50	$495.00
8	200.00	305.00	501.50
15	200.00	286.00	486.00
22	200.00	330.25	532.75
29	200.00	298.50	495.00

REQUIRED

1.   Prepare the journal entries to record the cash service fees and cash short and over for each of the five weeks.

2.   Post to the cash short and over account (use account no. 516).

3.   Determine the ending balance of the cash short and over account. Does it represent an expense or revenue?

MANAGING YOUR WRITING

The current month's bank statement for your account arrives in the mail. In reviewing the statement, you notice a deposit listed for $400.00 that you did not make. It has been credited in error to your account.

Discuss whether you have an ethical or legal obligation to inform the bank of the error. What action should you take?

ETHICS CASE

Ben Thomas works as a teller for First National Bank. When he arrived at work on Friday, the branch manager, Frank Mills, asked him to get his cash drawer out early because the head teller, Naomi Ray, was conducting a surprise cash count for all the tellers. Surprise cash counts are usually done four or five times a year by the branch manager or the head teller and once or twice a year by internal auditors. Ben's drawer was $100.00 short and his reconciliation tape showed that he was in balance on Thursday night. Naomi asked Ben for an explanation, and Ben immediately took $100.00 out of his pocket and handed it to her. He went on to explain he needed the cash to buy prescriptions for his son and pay for groceries and intended to put the $100.00 back in his cash drawer on Monday, which was pay day. He also told Naomi that this was the first time he had ever "borrowed" money from his cash drawer and that he would never do it again.

1.   What are the ethical considerations in this case from both Ben's and Naomi's perspectives?

2.   What options does Naomi have to address this problem?

(continued)

3. Assume Naomi chooses to inform the branch manager. Write a short incident report describing the findings.

4. In small groups, come up with as many ideas as possible on how to safeguard cash on hand in a bank (petty cash, teller drawer cash, and vault cash) from employee theft and mismanagement.

MASTERY PROBLEM

✓ Adjusted bank balance: $4,324.05

Turner Excavation maintains a checking account and has decided to open a petty cash fund. The following petty cash fund transactions occurred during July.

July 2   Established a petty cash fund by issuing Check No. 301 for $100.00.

5   Paid $25.00 from the petty cash fund for postage. Voucher No. 1.

7   Paid $30.00 from the petty cash fund for delivery of flowers (Miscellaneous Expense). Voucher No. 2.

8   Paid $20.00 from the petty cash fund to repair a tire on the company truck. Voucher No. 3.

12   Paid $22.00 from the petty cash fund for a newspaper advertisement. Voucher No. 4.

13   Issued Check No. 303 to replenish the petty cash fund. (Total and rule the petty cash payments record. Record the balance and the amount needed to replenish the fund in the Description column of the petty cash payments record.)

20   Paid $26.00 from the petty cash fund to reimburse an employee for expenses incurred to repair the company truck. Voucher No. 5.

24   Paid $12.50 from the petty cash fund for telephone calls made from a phone booth. Voucher No. 6.

28   Paid $25.00 from the petty cash fund as a contribution to the YMCA. Voucher No. 7.

31   Issued Check No. 308 to replenish the petty cash fund. (Total and rule the petty cash payments record. Record the balance and the amount needed to replenish the fund in the Description column of the petty cash payments record.)

The following additional transactions occurred during July.

July 5   Issued Check No. 302 to pay office rent, $650.00.

15   Issued Check No. 304 for office equipment, $525.00.

17   Issued Check No. 305 for the purchase of supplies, $133.00.

18   Issued Check No. 306 to pay attorney fees, $1,000.00.

30   Issued Check No. 307 to pay newspaper for an advertisement, $200.20.

REQUIRED

1. Record the petty cash transactions in a petty cash payments record.

2. Make all required general journal entries for the cash transactions. (Note: The petty cash fund was established and replenished twice during July.)

3. The following bank statement was received in the mail. Deposits were made on July 6 for $3,500.00 and on July 29 for $2,350.00. The checkbook balance on July 31 is $4,331.55. Notice the discrepancy in Check No. 302 that cleared the bank for $655.00. This check was written on July 5 for rent expense, but was incorrectly entered on the check stub and in the journal as $650.00. Prepare a bank reconciliation and make any necessary journal entries as of July 31.

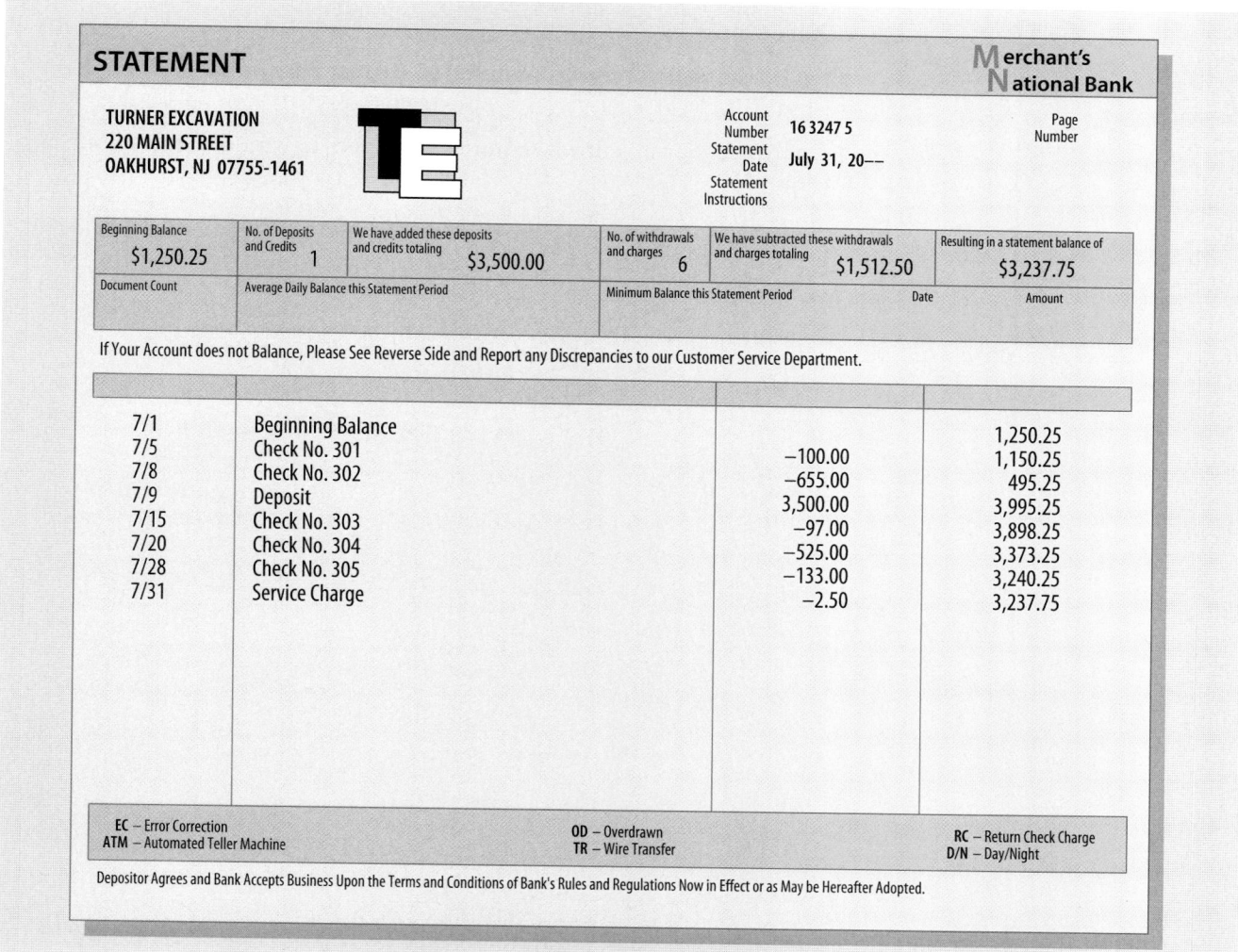

CHALLENGE PROBLEM

This problem challenges you to apply your cumulative accounting knowledge to move a step beyond the material in the chapter.

✓ 2. Item 4: Dr. Depositor Accounts, $350.00

Susan Panera is preparing the June 30 bank reconciliation for Panera Bakery. She discovers the following items that explain the difference between the cash balance on her books and the balance as reported by Lawrence Bank.

1. An ATM withdrawal of $200.00 for personal use was not recorded by Susan.

2. A deposit of $850.00 was recorded by Susan but has not been received by Lawrence Bank as of June 30.

(continued)

3. A check written in payment on account to Jayhawk Supply for $340.00 was recorded by Susan as $430.00 and by Lawrence Bank as $530.00.

4. An ATM deposit of $350.00 was recorded twice by Lawrence Bank.

5. An electronic funds transfer of $260.00 to Sunflower Mills as a payment on account was not recorded by Susan.

6. Check No. 103 for $235.00 and No. 110 for $127.00 had not cleared Lawrence Bank as of June 30.

REQUIRED

1. Prepare the journal entries required to correct Panera Bakery's books as of June 30.

2. Prepare the journal entries required to correct Lawrence Bank's books as of June 30.

Chapter 7 Appendix
Internal Controls

Objectives

Careful study of this appendix should enable you to:

LO1 Explain the importance of internal control.

LO2 Define internal control and describe its key components.

LO3 Describe selected internal controls over cash receipts.

LO4 Describe selected internal controls over cash payments and the use of a voucher system.

In Chapter 7, we introduced the concept of internal control and provided some examples of good internal control over cash transactions. Here, we examine internal control in greater depth. We (1) explain why it has achieved greater importance today, (2) identify its key components, (3) give examples of internal control in various business activities, and (4) describe internal control of cash payments using a voucher system.

IMPORTANCE OF INTERNAL CONTROL

LO1 Explain the importance of internal control.

To be successful, management must have adequate control of the operations of the business. For example, the records of business activities must be reliable and timely, so that management has the information it needs to take necessary actions. The assets of the business must be known and protected. Employees must follow the rules and procedures defined by management. Accurate information must be available to report to owners, lenders, and regulatory bodies, such as the IRS. Without good internal control, it simply would not be possible to effectively and efficiently run a business.

The importance of strong internal control for managing a business has been known for years. But a recent event has raised the importance of internal control to a whole new level. In July 2002, Congress passed the Sarbanes-Oxley Act (SOX). SOX applies to all **publicly held companies**—companies whose stock is traded on the major stock exchanges. Section 404 of SOX requires these companies to report annually on the effectiveness of internal control over financial reporting. For decades, these corporations have been required to provide audited financial statements. Now, they must also report on the quality of their internal control system. Figure 7A-1 provides an example of management's Section 404 report for Jacuzzi Brands, Inc.

One of the interesting effects of SOX is how widely its rules are being felt. Officially, SOX applies to all publicly held companies and their external auditors. But SOX is causing many other companies and managements to look closely at the quality of their internal controls. The logic is simple: if internal controls are so important for publicly held companies, they probably deserve attention in other companies as well. Clearly, internal controls are a hot topic today.

FIGURE 7A-1   Section 404 Internal Control Report

MANAGEMENT'S REPORT ON INTERNAL CONTROL OVER FINANCIAL REPORTING

Management of Jacuzzi Brands, Inc. is responsible for establishing and maintaining adequate internal control over financial reporting as defined in Rule I3a-15(f) under the Securities Exchange Act of 1934. We recognize that internal control over financial reporting cannot provide absolute assurance of achieving financial reporting objectives because of its inherent limitations. Internal control over financial reporting is a process that involves human diligence and is subject to the possibility of human error or the circumvention or the overriding of internal control. Therefore, there is a risk that material misstatements may not be prevented or detected on a timely basis by internal control over financial reporting. However, we believe we have designed into the process safeguards to reduce, though not eliminate, this risk. Projections of any evaluation of effectiveness to future periods are subject to the risk that controls may become inadequate because of changes in conditions, or that the degree of compliance with the policies or procedures may deteriorate.

In order to ensure that the Company's internal control over financial reporting was effective as of September 30, 2005, we conducted an assessment of its effectiveness under the supervision and with the participation of our management group including our Chief Executive Officer and Chief Financial Officer. This assessment was based on criteria established in Internal Control—Integrated Framework issued by the Committee of Sponsoring Organizations of the Treadway Commission (COSO). In accordance with the SEC's published guidance, we have excluded from our evaluation the 2005 acquisition of Spear and Jackson, which is included in the 2005 consolidated financial statements of Jacuzzi Brands, Inc. and which in the aggregate represent 5.2% of consolidated total assets, 0.2% of consolidated stockholders' equity as of September 30, 2005, 0.0% of consolidated net revenues and 2.5% of loss from discontinued operations for the year ended September 30, 2005.

Based on our assessment of internal control over financial reporting under the criteria established in Internal Control—Integrated Framework, we have concluded that, as of September 30, 2005, the Company's internal control over financial reporting is effective. Our assessment of the effectiveness of the Company's internal control over financial reporting as of September 30, 2005 has been audited by Ernst & Young LLP, an independent registered public accounting firm, as stated in their attestation report which is included herein.

December 8, 2005

KEY COMPONENTS OF INTERNAL CONTROL

LO2 Define internal control and describe its key components.

Internal control is really important. So what exactly do we mean by internal control? Both the concept and attempts to define it have existed for many years. For our purposes, the following is a good definition:

> Internal control is a system developed by a company to provide reasonable assurance of achieving (1) effective and efficient operations, (2) reliable financial reporting, and (3) compliance with laws and regulations.

Several internal control frameworks have been developed that are consistent with this definition. The most widely accepted framework in the United States contains the following five components:

- Control environment
- Risk assessment
- Control activities
- Information and communication system
- Monitoring processes

Control Environment

The control environment is the policies, procedures, and attitudes of the top management and owners of the business. It is often referred to as the "tone at the top." It includes the organization structure, management's philosophy and operating style, integrity and ethical values, and commitment to competent, trustworthy employees. The control environment provides the foundation for all other components of internal control.

Risk Assessment

Risk assessment is management's process for identifying, analyzing, and responding to its business risks. All businesses face various and changing risks from both external and internal sources. These risks include error and fraud. As part of the risk assessment component of internal control, management must deal with these risks. For example, if a business sells products like computers that are affected by rapid technology changes, its marketing and inventory plans should carefully guard against obsolete inventory. If a business has high employee turnover, its employee screening and training programs should be very thorough and up to date. If a business is growing rapidly, it should regularly review its internal controls to see that they fit the size and activities of the business.

Control Activities

Control activities are the policies and procedures established to help management meet its control objectives. Control activities can be classified in various ways. Four types of control activities are particularly important for our purposes.

1. Segregation of duties

2. Authorization procedures and related responsibilities

3. Adequate documents and records

4. Protection of assets and records

Segregation of duties means that:

1. Different employees should be responsible for different parts of a transaction; and

2. Employees who account for transactions should not also have custody of the assets.

For example, one employee should be responsible for ordering goods and another employee should be responsible for issuing the check to pay for them. One employee should be responsible for recording the purchase of goods and another employee should be responsible for receiving and placing the goods in inventory. This segregation of duties provides a built-in check by one employee on another. One employee cannot obtain goods for personal use without being caught by another employee.

    Authorization procedures and related responsibilities means that every business activity should be properly authorized. In addition, it should be possible to identify who is responsible for every activity that has occurred. For example, to acquire new equipment, a signed document should authorize the purchase. After the purchase is made, this signed document shows who is responsible for the action.

Adequate documents and records means that accounting documents and records should be used so that all business transactions are recorded. For example, every purchase that occurs should be supported by a document. These documents should be prenumbered, used in sequence, and subsequently accounted for. In this way, the business can be sure that it has made a record of each transaction.

Protection of assets and records means that assets and records should be physically and logically protected. For assets, this generally means physical protection. Some examples are vaults for cash, securities and precious gems, or secure storage rooms for inventory. For records, this can mean storing journals, ledgers, and key documents in physically secure locations. In computerized systems, both physical and logical protection are needed. Passwords are a common form of logical protection of data files and processing programs.

Information and Communication System

The information and communication system is the set of procedures, processes, and records established to initiate, process, record, and report the business's transactions. In addition, the system accounts for the related assets and liabilities. Typically, the system has several subcomponents for different business processes, such as sales, cash receipts, purchases, cash payments, etc. The journals and ledgers we learned to use in the previous chapters would be part of an information and communication system.

Monitoring Processes

Monitoring processes are the methods used by management to determine that controls are operating properly, and that the controls are modified in response to changes in assessed risks. Monitoring can be part of the ongoing activities of the business or a separate process. One ongoing activity could be comparisons of financial reports with expectations. If financial reports differ from expectations, it could indicate internal control failures. Follow-up on customer complaints regarding account balances might also uncover internal control weaknesses. The most common form of separate process is the work of the internal audit department. Internal auditors evaluate the design of the internal control system in light of the business risks. They also perform specific tests to determine whether internal controls are operating properly. If a business is not large enough to have an internal audit department, these responsibilities must be assumed by top management.

INTERNAL CONTROLS OVER CASH RECEIPTS

LO3 Describe selected internal controls over cash receipts.

The main purposes of internal controls over cash receipts are to make sure that (1) all cash received by the business is recorded in the accounts, and (2) the cash is promptly deposited in the business bank account. The exact form of some of these controls will vary depending on whether the cash is received directly from customers for sales, or is received by mail as a collection on account. Some of the key internal controls are described in the following paragraphs.

If cash is received directly from customers, the use of a cash register or terminal with a printed receipt is essential. Only authorized employees should be allowed to operate the register. The register should generate an internal record of all transactions entered, including a total of cash receipts. This amount should be reconciled with the actual cash (and checks) in the register drawer.

Any differences greater than a small amount to allow for errors in making change should be investigated. All cash receipts should be deposited daily in the business bank account. The total deposited and the total cash receipts according to the register should be reconciled and any differences investigated.

If cash is received as collections on account, the mail room should be supervised and employees who handle the cash (checks) should have no access to the accounting records. When the mail is opened, a remittance list should be prepared showing all amounts received and from whom they are received. Checks should be immediately endorsed "For deposit" to the business bank account.

The remittance list is sent to the accounting department for use in recording the collections in the journal and ledgers. The cash is sent to the cash receipts department to deposit in the business bank account. The total of the remittance list and the amount of the bank deposit should be independently verified and any differences investigated.

An additional internal control common to both systems described above is the independent monthly preparation of a bank reconciliation. Procedures for preparing the bank reconciliation are described in Chapter 7. The cash receipts, cash payments, and beginning and ending balances per bank and per books must be reconciled. The reconciliation should be prepared by employees who have no access to cash. Any differences should be investigated.

One of the reasons internal controls over cash are so important is that they help businesses manage their cash resources. Naturally, it is important to plan to have sufficient cash to meet current obligations. But it is also important not to allow too much cash to lie idle. Management should carefully monitor and plan for its cash needs. Strong internal controls help with this process.

INTERNAL CONTROLS OVER CASH PAYMENTS

LO4 Describe selected internal controls over cash payments and the use of a voucher system.

The main purpose of internal controls over cash payments is to make sure cash is paid only for goods and services received by the business, consistent with its best interests. To achieve this objective, controls are needed from the beginning of the process of acquiring goods and services, through the payment of cash for those goods and services. An effective way to do so is with a voucher system.

Voucher System

The three control activities described above can be combined to control cash payments by using a voucher system. A **voucher system** is a control technique that requires every acquisition and subsequent payment to be supported by an approved voucher. A **voucher** is a document which shows that an acquisition is proper and that payment is authorized.

The Purchasing Process

Figure 7A-2 is a simplified illustration of how the purchasing portion of a voucher system operates. An authorized person or department prepares a purchase requisition to indicate the need for goods. The purchasing department reviews and approves the purchase requisition and prepares a purchase order to send to the supplier. When the goods are received, a receiving report is prepared. A copy of each of these documents is sent to the vouchers payable section in the accounting department.

FIGURE 7A-2 Voucher System—Purchasing Process

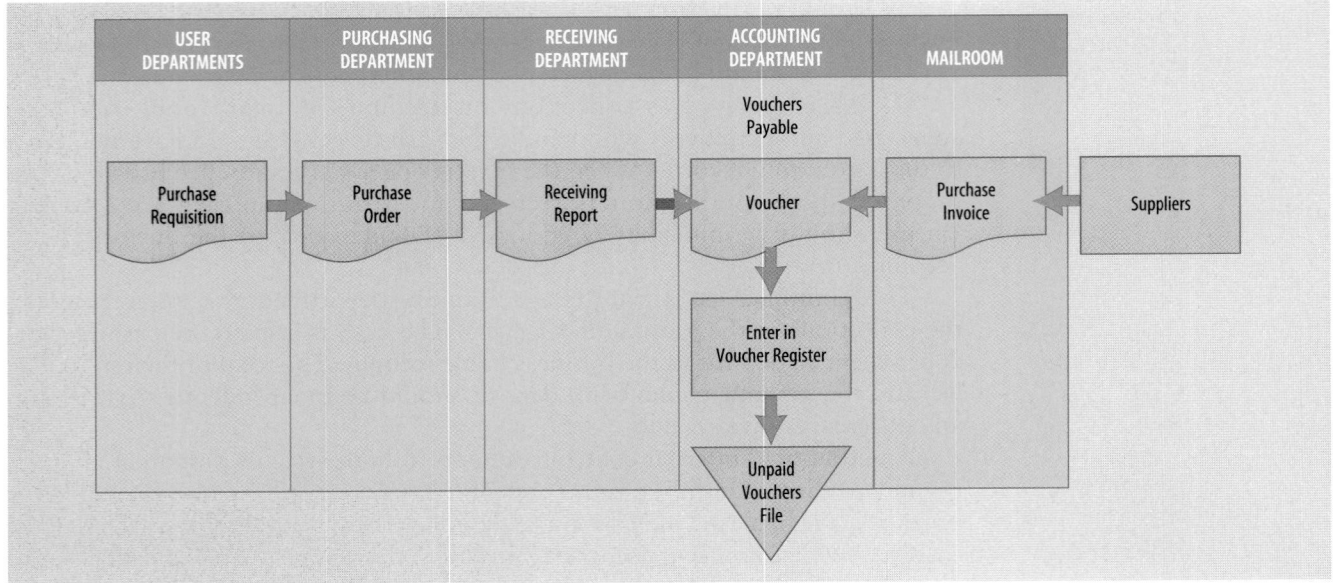

When the purchase invoice arrives, it is compared with the purchase requisition, purchase order, and receiving report. If the purchase invoice is

- for the goods ordered (purchase requisition and purchase order),
- at the correct price (purchase order),
- and for the correct quantity (receiving report),

then a voucher like the one in Figure 7A-3 is prepared. This is the first key control provided by the voucher system. If any aspect of the purchase is improper, it will be caught when the voucher is prepared.

The front of the voucher usually shows the voucher number, date, supplier, and what was purchased. The back indicates the accounts to be debited and the payment date, check number, and amount.

After the voucher is prepared and approved, it is entered in a special journal called a **voucher register**. A voucher register is used to record purchases of all types of assets and services.

After the voucher is entered in the voucher register, the voucher and supporting documents (purchase requisition, purchase order, receiving report, and purchase invoice) are stapled together. This "voucher packet" is then filed in an **unpaid vouchers file**, normally by due date. Alternatively, vouchers can be filed by supplier name. Filing by due date is preferred because this helps management plan for cash needs. It also helps ensure that vouchers are paid on the due date and cash discounts are taken.

The completed voucher provides the basis for paying the supplier's invoice on the due date. This is the second key control provided by the voucher system. No payment may be made without an approved voucher.

FIGURE 7A-3   Voucher

Notice how three of the four control activities that are part of an internal control system can be seen in this system. (1) *Duties are segregated* because different employees order, receive, and record the purchases. (2) *Authorization* is required to order the goods and to prepare the voucher. (3) The *documents and records* include purchase requisitions, purchase orders, receiving reports, and vouchers that are prenumbered and accounted for. This means that every recorded purchase is supported by the following five documents:

1. Voucher

2. Purchase invoice

3. Receiving report

4. Purchase order

5. Purchase requisition

This provides management with strong assurance that purchasing activities are properly controlled.

LEARNING KEY

The voucher system contains elements of internal control such as segregation of duties, authorization to order the goods and prepare the voucher, and accounting procedures that require prenumbering and accounting for the supporting documents.

The Payment Process

Figure 7A-4 is a simplified illustration of the payment process when a voucher system is used. On the due date, the voucher is pulled from the unpaid vouchers file. The voucher is given to the person responsible for preparing and signing checks (the cashier in this illustration). The cashier reviews each voucher and supporting documents to see that the expenditure is proper. The cashier then prepares and signs the check and sends it to the supplier. It is important for internal control that no check be prepared without a supporting voucher and that the check be mailed as soon as it is signed.

FIGURE 7A-4 Voucher System—Payment Process

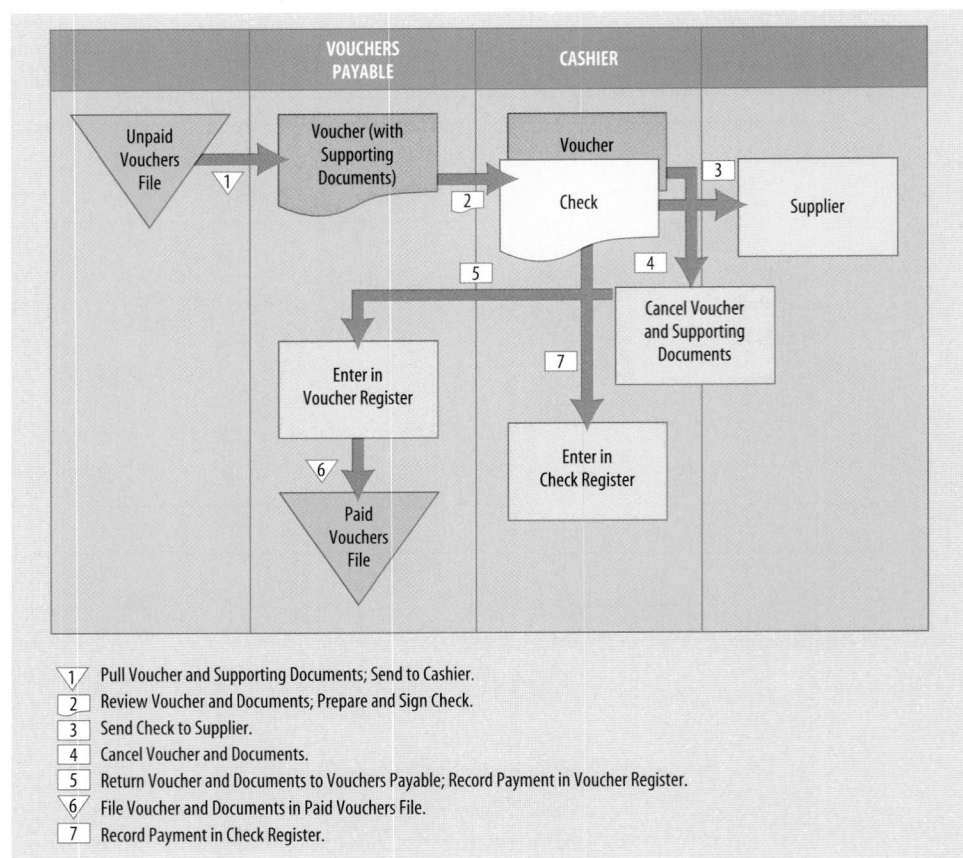

1. Pull Voucher and Supporting Documents; Send to Cashier.
2. Review Voucher and Documents; Prepare and Sign Check.
3. Send Check to Supplier.
4. Cancel Voucher and Documents.
5. Return Voucher and Documents to Vouchers Payable; Record Payment in Voucher Register.
6. File Voucher and Documents in Paid Vouchers File.
7. Record Payment in Check Register.

Ordinary checks may be used to make payments, but under the voucher system, voucher checks often are used. A **voucher check** is a check with space for entering data about the voucher being paid. Figure 7A-5 shows a voucher check used to pay Voucher No. 111 (Figure 7A-3).

The voucher check has two parts:

1. The check itself, which is similar to an ordinary check, and

2. An attached statement, which indicates the invoice being paid and any deductions.

In addition, the voucher check stub identifies the voucher number being paid.

FIGURE 7A-5   Voucher Check

After the voucher has been paid, the cashier completes the "Payment" approval on the back of the voucher. The voucher and supporting documents are then canceled to indicate payment. The canceling can be done with a rubber stamp, by perforating, or by simply writing "paid" on all relevant documents. This prevents a voucher from being processed again to create a duplicate payment. The canceled voucher and supporting documents are then returned to the vouchers payable section. The canceled voucher is used to record the payment of the voucher in the voucher register. The voucher and supporting documents are then filed either numerically or by supplier in a **paid vouchers file**. In either case, the numerical sequence should be accounted for to identify possible missing or duplicate vouchers.

A copy of the check is used to enter the payment in a check register. A **check register** is a special journal used to record all checks written in a voucher system. This completes the payment process using the voucher system.

This appendix provides an introduction to internal control concepts and procedures. We have focused on cash here, but internal controls are important in every area of the business. Internal controls can be a very complicated subject, particularly in dealing with computerized operations. More thorough analysis of internal controls is a subject for a more advanced text.

Learning Objectives	Key Points to Remember
LO1 Explain the importance of internal control.	Internal controls help assure management that it has reliable records to run the business and prepare needed reports. In addition, SOX requires publicly held companies to report annually on the quality of their internal control system.
LO2 Define internal control and describe its key components.	Internal control is a system developed by a company to provide reasonable assurance of achieving (1) effective and efficient operations, (2) reliable financial reporting, and (3) compliance with laws and regulations. The key components are: • Control environment • Risk assessment • Control activities • Information and communication system • Monitoring processes
LO3 Describe selected internal controls over cash receipts.	If cash is received directly from customers, a cash register should be used. The record of cash receipts per the register should be reconciled with the actual cash in the drawer. If cash is received by mail, a remittance list should be prepared and sent to accounting. The checks should be endorsed immediately "For deposit" and sent to the cash receipts department for deposit in the bank. The remittance list and bank deposit should be independently reconciled.
LO4 Describe selected internal controls over cash payments and the use of a voucher system.	Every acquisition and subsequent payment should be supported by an approved voucher. The voucher should be supported by a purchase requisition, purchase order, receiving report, and purchase invoice. On the due date, checks are written only for approved vouchers, and vouchers and supporting documents are canceled to prevent reuse.

KEY TERMS

check register (277) A special journal used to record all checks written in a voucher system.

paid vouchers file (277) A file in which paid vouchers and supporting documents are placed, organized either numerically or by supplier.

publicly held companies (269) Companies whose stock is traded on the major stock exchanges.

unpaid vouchers file (274) A file in which unpaid voucher packets are placed, normally organized by due date.

voucher (273) A document that shows that an acquisition is proper and that payment is authorized.

voucher check (276) A check with space for entering data about the voucher being paid.

voucher register (274) A special journal used to record purchases of all types of assets and services.

voucher system (273) A control technique that requires that every acquisition and subsequent payment be supported by an approved voucher.

REVIEW QUESTIONS

LO1   1. What does Section 404 of the Sarbanes-Oxley Act require?

LO2   2. What is the meaning of internal control?

LO2   3. What are the five components of internal control?

LO2   4. What are the four types of control activities?

LO3   5. What are the main purposes of internal controls over cash receipts?

LO4   6. What is the main purpose of internal controls over cash payments?

LO4   7. What is a voucher system?

LO4   8. In a voucher system, each recorded purchase is supported by what five documents?

LO4   9. What is the purpose of canceling the voucher and supporting documents when a payment is made?

SERIES A EXERCISES

E 7Apx-1A (LO2)

INTERNAL CONTROL COMPONENTS The most widely accepted internal control framework in the United States contains the following five components. Describe each of them.

1. Control environment
2. Risk assessment
3. Control activities
4. Information and communication system
5. Monitoring processes

E 7Apx-2A (LO2)

INTERNAL CONTROL PROCEDURES AND PROCESSES In the left column below, five different internal control procedures and processes are described. In the right column, the five components of internal control are listed. Match the procedures and processes with the components by placing the letter of the appropriate component on the blank provided.

1. ____ A company publishes and uses a code of ethical conduct.
2. ____ The accounting system automatically generates monthly sales reports for each product line.
3. ____ A company has established an internal audit department.
4. ____ All purchases above $5,000 must be approved in writing by the head of the purchasing department.
5. ____ A company invests heavily in employee training programs because of the technical nature of its products.

a. Control environment
b. Risk assessment
c. Control activities
d. Information and communication system
e. Monitoring processes

E 7Apx-3A (L04)   **PURCHASING PROCESS USING A VOUCHER SYSTEM** In the following flowchart, identify the documents, records, and procedures that illustrate the purchasing process in a voucher system.

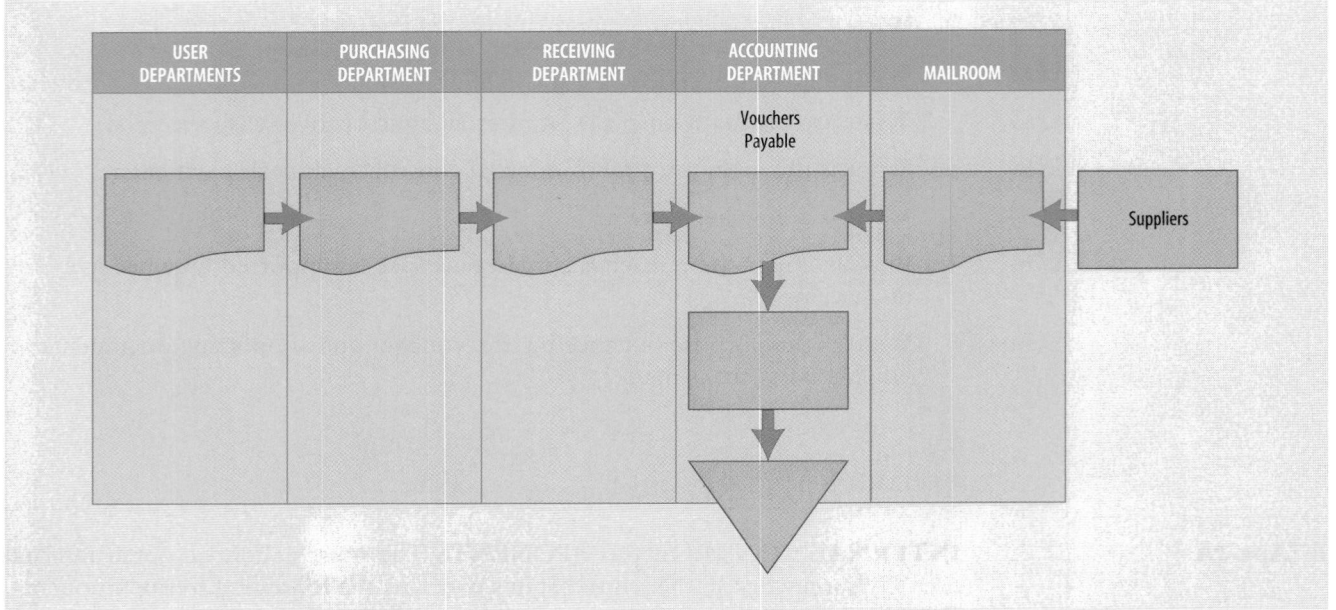

SERIES A PROBLEM

P 7Apx-4A (L02/3/4)   **USING INTERNAL CONTROLS TO PREVENT ERRORS** The following misstatements occurred in the records of ICW Company. For each misstatement, suggest a control to prevent it from happening.

1. A bill from a supplier was paid even though the shipment was not received.
2. A supplier's bill was paid twice for the same purchase.
3. A plant employee increased his pay rate by entering the computer system using a plant terminal and altering the payroll records.
4. The cash receipts clerk kept a portion of the regular bank deposits for personal use and concealed the theft by manipulating the monthly bank reconciliation she prepared.

SERIES B EXERCISES

E 7Apx-1B (L02)   **INTERNAL CONTROL COMPONENTS** Four types of internal control activities are listed below. Describe each of them.

1. Segregation of duties
2. Authorization procedures and related responsibilities
3. Adequate documents and records
4. Protection of assets and records

E 7Apx-2B (L02)

INTERNAL CONTROL PROCEDURES AND PROCESSES In the left column below, four different internal control procedures are described. In the right column, the four basic types of internal control activities are listed. Match the procedures with the activities by placing the letter of the appropriate activity on the blank provided.

1. ____ All passwords for access to sales and inventory databases must be changed monthly.
2. ____ All new hires must be approved by the department of human resources.
3. ____ All sales invoices are prenumbered and accounted for.
4. ____ Bank reconciliations are prepared by an employee with no other cash responsibilities.

a. Segregation of duties
b. Authorization procedures and related responsibilities
c. Adequate documents and records
d. Protection of assets and records

E 7Apx-3B (L04)

PAYMENT PROCESS USING A VOUCHER SYSTEM In the following flowchart, identify the documents, records, and procedures that illustrate the payment process using a voucher system.

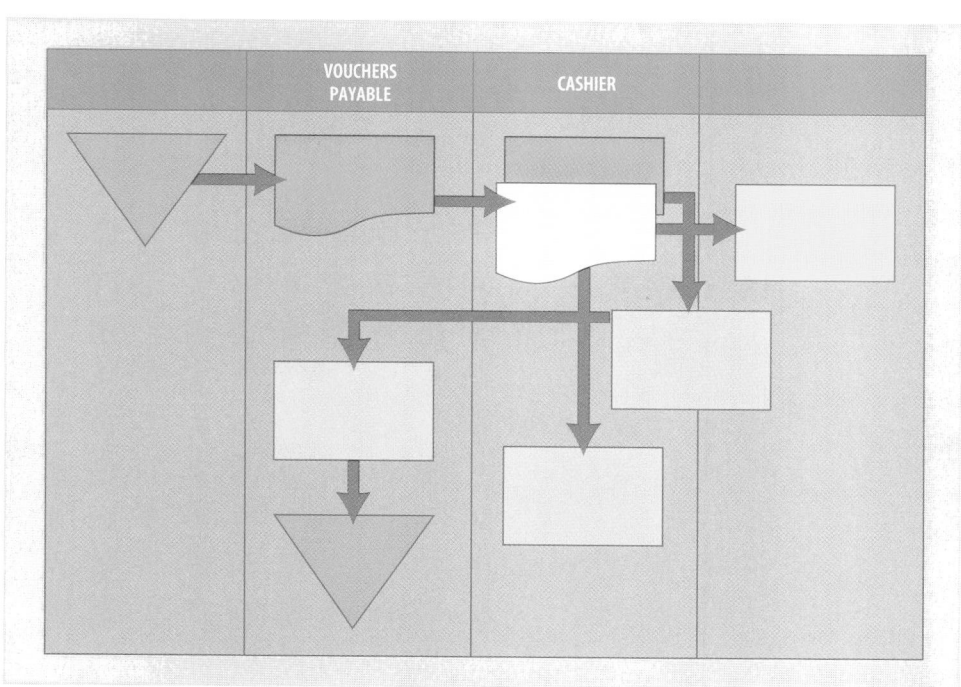

SERIES B PROBLEM

P 7Apx-4B (LO2/3/4)

USING INTERNAL CONTROLS TO PREVENT ERRORS The following misstatements occurred in the records of MW Company. For each misstatement, suggest a control to prevent it from happening.

1. A bill from a supplier was paid for goods that had not been ordered.
2. A supplier's bill for 50 boxes of materials was paid even though only 40 boxes were received.
3. Expensive product components were stolen by an employee from a loading dock area after hours.
4. No bill was sent to a customer for a shipment because the shipping document was lost after the shipment was made.

Objectives

Careful study of this chapter should enable you to:

LO1
Distinguish between employees and independent contractors.

LO2
Calculate employee earnings and deductions.

LO3
Describe and prepare payroll records.

LO4
Account for employee earnings and deductions.

LO5
Describe various payroll record-keeping methods.

Payroll Accounting: Employee Earnings and Deductions

Six months after opening his Parkway Pet Supplies store described at the beginning of Chapter 7, Evan Taylor is pleased to find that the business is doing very well. Evan has hired a student, who is studying accounting at the local college, as a part-time bookkeeper. He also has added an employee to help in the store during peak periods and to keep the inventory organized. Evan knows he needs to keep a record of each employee's work hours so he can compute the employees' earnings. His new bookkeeper says Evan also needs to withhold certain taxes from the wages. What taxes must Evan withhold from his employees' wages? How does he determine the correct amounts to withhold?

The only contact most of us have with payroll is receiving a paycheck. Few of us have seen the large amount of record keeping needed to produce that paycheck.

Employers maintain complete payroll accounting records for two reasons. First, payroll costs are major expenditures for most companies. Payroll accounting records provide data useful in analyzing and controlling these expenditures. Second, federal, state, and local laws require employers to keep payroll records. Companies must accumulate payroll data both for the business as a whole and for each employee.

There are two major types of payroll taxes: those paid by the employee and those paid by the employer. In this chapter, we discuss employee taxes. In Chapter 9, we address payroll taxes paid by the employer.

EMPLOYEES AND INDEPENDENT CONTRACTORS

LO1 Distinguish between employees and independent contractors.

Not every person who performs services for a business is considered an employee. An **employee** works under the control and direction of an employer. Examples include secretaries, maintenance workers, salesclerks, and plant supervisors. In contrast, an **independent contractor** performs a service for a fee and does not work under the control and direction of the company paying for the service. Examples of independent contractors include public accountants, real estate agents, and lawyers.

The distinction between an employee and an independent contractor is important for payroll purposes. Government laws and regulations regarding payroll are much more complex for employees than for independent contractors. Employers must deduct certain taxes, maintain payroll records, and file numerous reports for all employees. Only one form (Form 1099) must be filed for independent contractors. The payroll accounting procedures described in this chapter apply only to employer/employee relationships.

EMPLOYEE EARNINGS AND DEDUCTIONS

LO2 Calculate employee earnings and deductions.

Three steps are required to determine how much to pay an employee for a pay period:

1. Calculate total earnings.

2. Determine the amounts of deductions.

3. Subtract deductions from total earnings to compute net pay.

Salaries and Wages

Compensation for managerial or administrative services usually is called **salary**. A salary normally is expressed in biweekly (every two weeks), monthly, or annual terms. Compensation for skilled or unskilled labor usually is referred to as **wages**. Wages ordinarily are expressed in terms of hours, weeks, or units produced. The terms "salaries" and "wages" often are used interchangeably in practice.

The **Fair Labor Standards Act (FLSA)** requires employers to pay overtime at 1½ times the regular rate to any hourly employee who works over 40 hours in a week. Some companies pay a higher rate for hours worked on Saturday or Sunday, but this is not required by the FLSA. Some salaried employees are exempt from the FLSA rules and are not paid overtime.

Computing Total Earnings

Compensation usually is based on the time worked during the payroll period. Sometimes earnings are based on sales or units of output during the period. When compensation is based on time, a record must be kept of the time worked by each employee. Time cards (Figure 8-1) are helpful for this purpose. In large businesses with computer-based timekeeping systems, plastic cards or badges with special magnetic strips or barcodes (Figure 8-2) can be used. Employees use the cards to clock in and out at terminals with card readers. For increased security, these terminals also are available with fingerprint readers.

FIGURE 8-1   Time Card

Westly, Inc.
Time Card — Hourly Payroll

Emp. Name **Kuzmik, Helen**   Base Dept.: **Sales**

Emp. ID: **359-47-1138**   Pay Per. End: **12/19/20--**

					HOURS			
Date	Time In	Time Out	Time In	Time Out	Reg	OT	DT	Total
12/13	8:00	12:30	13:00	17:30	8	1		9
12/14	8:00	12:30	13:00	17:30	8	1		9
12/15	8:00	12:30	13:00	17:30	8	1		9
12/16	8:00	12:30	13:00	17:30	8	1		9
12/17	8:00	12:30	13:00	17:30	8	1		9
12/18	10:00	16:00				6		6
12/19	13:00	17:00					4	4
TOTAL					40	11	4	55

Remarks _____

_____

Approval _____ TM _____
         Dept. Head

FIGURE 8-2   Time Cards and Clock Terminal

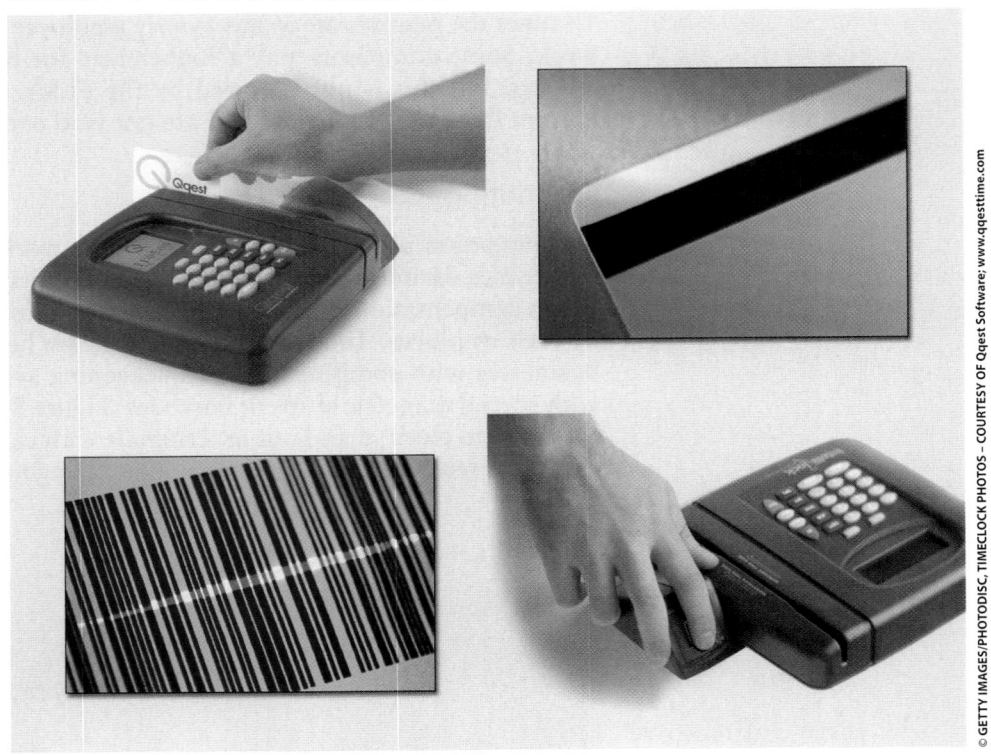

To illustrate the computation of total earnings, look at the time card of Helen Kuzmik in Figure 8-1. The card shows that Kuzmik worked 55 hours for the week.

Regular hours	40 hours
Overtime	11
Double time	4
Total hours worked	55 hours

Kuzmik's regular rate of pay is $12 per hour. She is paid 1½ times the regular rate for hours in excess of 8 on Monday through Friday and any hours worked on Saturday, and twice the regular rate for hours on Sunday. Kuzmik's total earnings for the week ended December 19 are computed as follows:

40 hours × $12	$480
11 hours × $18 (1½ × $12 = $18)	198
4 hours (on Sunday) × $24 (2 × $12 = $24)	96
Total earnings for the week	$774

An employee who is paid a salary may also be entitled to premium pay for overtime. If this is the case, it is necessary to compute the regular hourly rate of pay before computing the overtime rate. To illustrate, assume that Linda Swaney has a salary of $2,288 a month plus 1½ times the regular hourly rate for hours in excess of 40 per week. Swaney's overtime rate of pay is computed as follows:

$2,288 × 12 months	$27,456 annual pay
$27,456 ÷ 52 weeks	$528.00 pay per week
$528.00 ÷ 40 hours	$13.20 pay per regular hour
$13.20 × 1½	$19.80 overtime pay per hour

There are 52 weeks in each year but not 4 weeks in each month. That is why monthly salaries must be annualized in order to determine the hourly rate.

If Swaney worked 50 hours during the week ended December 19, her total earnings for the week would be computed as follows:

40 hours × $13.20	$528.00
10 hours × $19.80	198.00
Total earnings for the week	$726.00

Deductions from Total Earnings

An employee's total earnings are called **gross pay**. Various deductions are made from gross pay to yield take-home or **net pay**. Deductions from gross pay fall into three major categories:

1. Federal (and possibly state and city) income tax withholding

2. Employee FICA tax withholding

3. Voluntary deductions

Income Tax Withholding

Federal law requires employers to withhold certain amounts from the total earnings of each employee. These withholdings are applied toward the payment of the employee's federal income tax. Four factors determine the amount to be withheld from an employee's gross pay each pay period:

1. Total earnings

2. Marital status

3. Number of withholding allowances claimed

4. Length of the pay period

Withholding Allowances. Each employee is required to furnish the employer an Employee's Withholding Allowance Certificate, Form W-4 (Figure 8-3). The marital status of the employee and the number of allowances claimed on Form W-4 determine the dollar amount of earnings subject to withholding. A **withholding allowance** exempts a specific dollar amount of an employee's gross pay from federal income tax withholding. In general, each employee is permitted one personal withholding allowance, one for a spouse who does not also claim an allowance, and one for each dependent.

A withholding certificate completed by Ken Istone is shown in Figure 8-3. Istone is married, has a spouse who does not claim an allowance, and has four dependent children. On line 5 of the W-4 form, Istone claims six allowances, calculated as follows:

Personal allowance	1
Spouse allowance	1
Allowances for dependents	4
Total withholding allowances	6

FIGURE 8-3 Employee's Withholding Allowance Certificate (Form W-4)

Form **W-4**	**Employee's Withholding Allowance Certificate**	OMB No. 1545-0010
Department of the Treasury Internal Revenue Service	► **For Privacy Act and Paperwork Reduction Act Notice, see page 2.**	20--

1 Type or print your first name and middle initial	Last name	2 Your social security number
Ken M.	Istone	393 58 8194

Home address (number and street or rural route)
1546 Swallow Drive

3 ☐ Single ☒ Married ☐ Married, but withhold at higher Single rate.
Note: If married, but legally separated, or spouse is a nonresident alien, check the "Single" box.

City or town, state, and ZIP code
St. Louis, MO 63144-4752

4 If your last name differs from that shown on your social security card, check here. You must call 1-800-772-1213 for a new card. ► ☐

5 Total number of allowances you are claiming (from line **H** above **or** from the applicable worksheet on page 2) **5** 6

6 Additional amount, if any, you want withheld from each paycheck . . . . **6** $

7 I claim exemption from withholding for 20--, and I certify that I meet **both** of the following conditions for exemption:
- Last year I had a right to a refund of **all** Federal income tax withheld because I had **no** tax liability **and**
- This year I expect a refund of **all** Federal income tax withheld because I expect to have **no** tax liability.
If you meet both conditions, write "Exempt" here . . . . ► **7**

Under penalties of perjury, I certify that I am entitled to the number of withholding allowances claimed on this certificate, or I am entitled to claim exempt status.
Employee's signature
(Form is not valid unless you sign it.) ► Ken M. Istone   **Date** January 3, 20--

8 Employer's name and address (Employer: Complete lines 8 and 10 only if sending to the IRS.)	9 Office code (optional)	10 Employer identification number

Cat. No. 10220Q

A large number of IRS publications and forms can be found at the IRS Web site: http://www.irs.gov

LEARNING KEY

1. Find the row for wages.
2. Find the column for withholding allowances.
3. Find the amount where they cross.

Wage-Bracket Method. Employers generally use the **wage-bracket method** to determine the amount of tax to be withheld from an employee's pay. The employee's gross pay for a specific time period is traced into the appropriate wage-bracket table provided by the Internal Revenue Service (IRS). These tables cover various time periods, and there are separate tables for single and married taxpayers. Copies are provided in *Circular E—Employer's Tax Guide*, which may be obtained from any local IRS office or at the IRS Internet site.

Portions of weekly income tax wage-bracket withholding tables for single and married persons are illustrated in Figure 8-4. Assume that Ken Istone (who claims 6 allowances) had gross earnings of $545 for the week ending December 19, 20--. The table for married persons is used as follows:

1. Find the row for wages of "at least $540, but less than $550."

2. Find the column headed "6 withholding allowances."

3. Where the row and column cross, $1.00 is given as the amount to be withheld.

For state or city income taxes, withholding generally is handled in one of two ways: (1) forms and tables similar to those provided by the IRS are used or (2) an amount equal to a percentage of the federal withholding amount is withheld.

FIGURE 8-4   Federal Withholding Tax Table: Single Persons

SINGLE Persons—WEEKLY Payroll Period

(For Wages Paid in 2006)

If the wages are—		And the number of withholding allowances claimed is—										
At least	But less than	0	1	2	3	4	5	6	7	8	9	10
		The amount of income tax to be withheld is—										
200	210	16	9	3	0	0	0	0	0	0	0	0
210	220	18	10	4	0	0	0	0	0	0	0	0
220	230	19	11	5	0	0	0	0	0	0	0	0
230	240	21	12	6	0	0	0	0	0	0	0	0
240	250	22	13	7	0	0	0	0	0	0	0	0
250	260	24	14	8	1	0	0	0	0	0	0	0
260	270	25	16	9	2	0	0	0	0	0	0	0
270	280	27	17	10	3	0	0	0	0	0	0	0
280	290	28	19	11	4	0	0	0	0	0	0	0
290	300	30	20	12	5	0	0	0	0	0	0	0
300	310	31	22	13	6	0	0	0	0	0	0	0
310	320	33	23	14	7	1	0	0	0	0	0	0
320	330	34	25	15	8	2	0	0	0	0	0	0
330	340	36	26	17	9	3	0	0	0	0	0	0
340	350	37	28	18	10	4	0	0	0	0	0	0
350	360	39	29	20	11	5	0	0	0	0	0	0
360	370	40	31	21	12	6	0	0	0	0	0	0
370	380	42	32	23	13	7	1	0	0	0	0	0
380	390	43	34	24	14	8	2	0	0	0	0	0
390	400	45	35	26	16	9	3	0	0	0	0	0
400	410	46	37	27	17	10	4	0	0	0	0	0
410	420	48	38	29	19	11	5	0	0	0	0	0
420	430	49	40	30	20	12	6	0	0	0	0	0
430	440	51	41	32	22	13	7	0	0	0	0	0
440	450	52	43	33	23	14	8	1	0	0	0	0
450	460	54	44	35	25	15	9	2	0	0	0	0
460	470	55	46	36	26	17	10	3	0	0	0	0
470	480	57	47	38	28	18	11	4	0	0	0	0
480	490	58	49	39	29	20	12	5	0	0	0	0
490	500	60	50	41	31	21	13	6	0	0	0	0
500	510	61	52	42	32	23	14	7	1	0	0	0
510	520	63	53	44	34	24	15	8	2	0	0	0
520	530	64	55	45	35	26	16	9	3	0	0	0
530	540	66	56	47	37	27	18	10	4	0	0	0
540	550	67	58	48	38	29	19	11	5	0	0	0
550	560	69	59	50	40	30	21	12	6	0	0	0
560	570	70	61	51	41	32	22	13	7	1	0	0
570	580	72	62	53	43	33	24	14	8	2	0	0
580	590	73	64	54	44	35	25	16	9	3	0	0
590	600	75	65	56	46	36	27	17	10	4	0	0
600	610	76	67	57	47	38	28	19	11	5	0	0
610	620	78	68	59	49	39	30	20	12	6	0	0
620	630	80	70	60	50	41	31	22	13	7	0	0
630	640	82	71	62	52	42	33	23	14	8	1	0
640	650	85	73	63	53	44	34	25	15	9	2	0
650	660	87	74	65	55	45	36	26	17	10	3	0
660	670	90	76	66	56	47	37	28	18	11	4	0
670	680	92	77	68	58	48	39	29	20	12	5	0
680	690	95	79	69	59	50	40	31	21	13	6	0
690	700	97	81	71	61	51	42	32	23	14	7	1
700	710	100	84	72	62	53	43	34	24	15	8	2
710	720	102	86	74	64	54	45	35	26	16	9	3
720	730	105	89	75	65	56	46	37	27	18	10	4
730	740	107	91	77	67	57	48	38	29	19	11	5
740	750	110	94	78	68	59	49	40	30	21	12	6
750	760	112	96	80	70	60	51	41	32	22	13	7
760	770	115	99	83	71	62	52	43	33	24	14	8
770	780	117	101	85	73	63	54	44	35	25	16	9
780	790	120	104	88	74	65	55	46	36	27	17	10
790	800	122	106	90	76	66	57	47	38	28	19	11

FIGURE 8-4   Federal Withholding Tax Table: (*continued*) Married Persons

MARRIED Persons—WEEKLY Payroll Period

(For Wages Paid in 2006)

If the wages are—		And the number of withholding allowances claimed is—										
At least	But less than	0	1	2	3	4	5	6	7	8	9	10
		The amount of income tax to be withheld is—										
200	210	5	0	0	0	0	0	0	0	0	0	0
210	220	6	0	0	0	0	0	0	0	0	0	0
220	230	7	1	0	0	0	0	0	0	0	0	0
230	240	8	2	0	0	0	0	0	0	0	0	0
240	250	9	3	0	0	0	0	0	0	0	0	0
250	260	10	4	0	0	0	0	0	0	0	0	0
260	270	11	5	0	0	0	0	0	0	0	0	0
270	280	12	6	0	0	0	0	0	0	0	0	0
280	290	13	7	0	0	0	0	0	0	0	0	0
290	300	14	8	1	0	0	0	0	0	0	0	0
300	310	15	9	2	0	0	0	0	0	0	0	0
310	320	16	10	3	0	0	0	0	0	0	0	0
320	330	17	11	4	0	0	0	0	0	0	0	0
330	340	18	12	5	0	0	0	0	0	0	0	0
340	350	19	13	6	0	0	0	0	0	0	0	0
350	360	20	14	7	1	0	0	0	0	0	0	0
360	370	21	15	8	2	0	0	0	0	0	0	0
370	380	22	16	9	3	0	0	0	0	0	0	0
380	390	23	17	10	4	0	0	0	0	0	0	0
390	400	24	18	11	5	0	0	0	0	0	0	0
400	410	25	19	12	6	0	0	0	0	0	0	0
410	420	26	20	13	7	1	0	0	0	0	0	0
420	430	27	21	14	8	2	0	0	0	0	0	0
430	440	28	22	15	9	3	0	0	0	0	0	0
440	450	29	23	16	10	4	0	0	0	0	0	0
450	460	31	24	17	11	5	0	0	0	0	0	0
460	470	32	25	18	12	6	0	0	0	0	0	0
470	480	34	26	19	13	7	0	0	0	0	0	0
480	490	35	27	20	14	8	1	0	0	0	0	0
490	500	37	28	21	15	9	2	0	0	0	0	0
500	510	38	29	22	16	10	3	0	0	0	0	0
510	520	40	30	23	17	11	4	0	0	0	0	0
520	530	41	32	24	18	12	5	0	0	0	0	0
530	540	43	33	25	19	13	6	0	0	0	0	0
540	550	44	35	26	20	14	7	1	0	0	0	0
550	560	46	36	27	21	15	8	2	0	0	0	0
560	570	47	38	28	22	16	9	3	0	0	0	0
570	580	49	39	30	23	17	10	4	0	0	0	0
580	590	50	41	31	24	18	11	5	0	0	0	0
590	600	52	42	33	25	19	12	6	0	0	0	0
600	610	53	44	34	26	20	13	7	1	0	0	0
610	620	55	45	36	27	21	14	8	2	0	0	0
620	630	56	47	37	28	22	15	9	3	0	0	0
630	640	58	48	39	29	23	16	10	4	0	0	0
640	650	59	50	40	31	24	17	11	5	0	0	0
650	660	61	51	42	32	25	18	12	6	0	0	0
660	670	62	53	43	34	26	19	13	7	0	0	0
670	680	64	54	45	35	27	20	14	8	1	0	0
680	690	65	56	46	37	28	21	15	9	2	0	0
690	700	67	57	48	38	29	22	16	10	3	0	0
1,300	1,310	158	149	139	130	120	111	101	92	82	73	63
1,310	1,320	161	150	141	131	122	112	103	93	84	74	65
1,320	1,330	163	152	142	133	123	114	104	95	85	76	66
1,330	1,340	166	153	144	134	125	115	106	96	87	77	68
1,340	1,350	168	155	145	136	126	117	107	98	88	79	69
1,350	1,360	171	156	147	137	128	118	109	99	90	80	71
1,360	1,370	173	158	148	139	129	120	110	101	91	82	72
1,370	1,380	176	160	150	140	131	121	112	102	93	83	74
1,380	1,390	178	162	151	142	132	123	113	104	94	85	75
1,390	1,400	181	165	153	143	134	124	115	105	96	86	77

Employee FICA Tax Withholding

The Federal Insurance Contributions Act requires employers to withhold **FICA taxes** from employees' earnings. FICA taxes include amounts for both Social Security and Medicare programs. Social Security provides pensions and disability benefits. Medicare provides health insurance.

Congress has frequently changed the tax rates and the maximum amounts of earnings subject to FICA taxes. For this text, we assume the Social Security rate is 6.2% on maximum earnings of $94,200. The Medicare rate is 1.45% on all earnings; there is no maximum.

To illustrate the calculation of FICA taxes, assume the following earnings for Sarah Cadrain:

		Earnings
Pay Period	Week	Year-to-Date
Dec. 6–12	$1,600	$93,540
Dec. 13–19	$1,660	$95,200

For the week of December 6–12, FICA taxes on Cadrain's earnings would be:

Gross Pay	×	Tax Rate		=	Tax
$1,600		Social Security	6.2%		$ 99.20
		Medicare	1.45%		23.20
					$122.40

During the week of December 13–19, Cadrain's earnings for the calendar year went over the $94,200 Social Security maximum by $1,000 ($95,200 – $94,200). Therefore, $1,000 of her $1,660 earnings for the week would not be subject to the Social Security tax.

Year-to-date earnings	$95,200
Social Security maximum	94,200
Amount not subject to Social Security tax	$ 1,000

The Social Security tax on Cadrain's December 13–19 earnings would be:

Gross pay	$1,660.00
Amount not subject to Social Security tax	1,000.00
Amount subject to Social Security tax	$ 660.00
Tax rate	6.2%
Social Security tax	$ 40.92

Since there is no Medicare maximum, all of Cadrain's December 13–19 earnings would be subject to the Medicare tax.

Gross pay	$1,660.00
Tax rate	1.45%
Medicare tax	$ 24.07

The total FICA tax would be:

Social Security tax	$40.92
Medicare tax	24.07
Total FICA tax	$64.99

For the rest of the calendar year through December 31, Cadrain's earnings would be subject only to Medicare taxes.

Voluntary Deductions

In addition to the mandatory deductions from employee earnings for income and FICA taxes, many other deductions are possible. These deductions are usually voluntary and depend on specific agreements between the employee and employer. Examples of voluntary deductions are:

1. U.S. savings bond purchases

2. Health insurance premiums

3. Credit union deposits

4. Pension plan payments

5. Charitable contributions

Computing Net Pay

To compute an employee's net pay for the period, subtract all tax withholdings and voluntary deductions from the gross pay. Ken Istone's net pay for the week ended December 19 would be calculated as follows:

Gross pay		$545.00
Deductions:		
Federal income tax withholding	$ 1.00	
Social Security tax withholding	33.79	
Medicare tax withholding	7.90	
Health insurance premiums	10.00	
Total deductions		52.69
Net pay		$492.31

FIGURE 8-5   Payroll Register (left side)

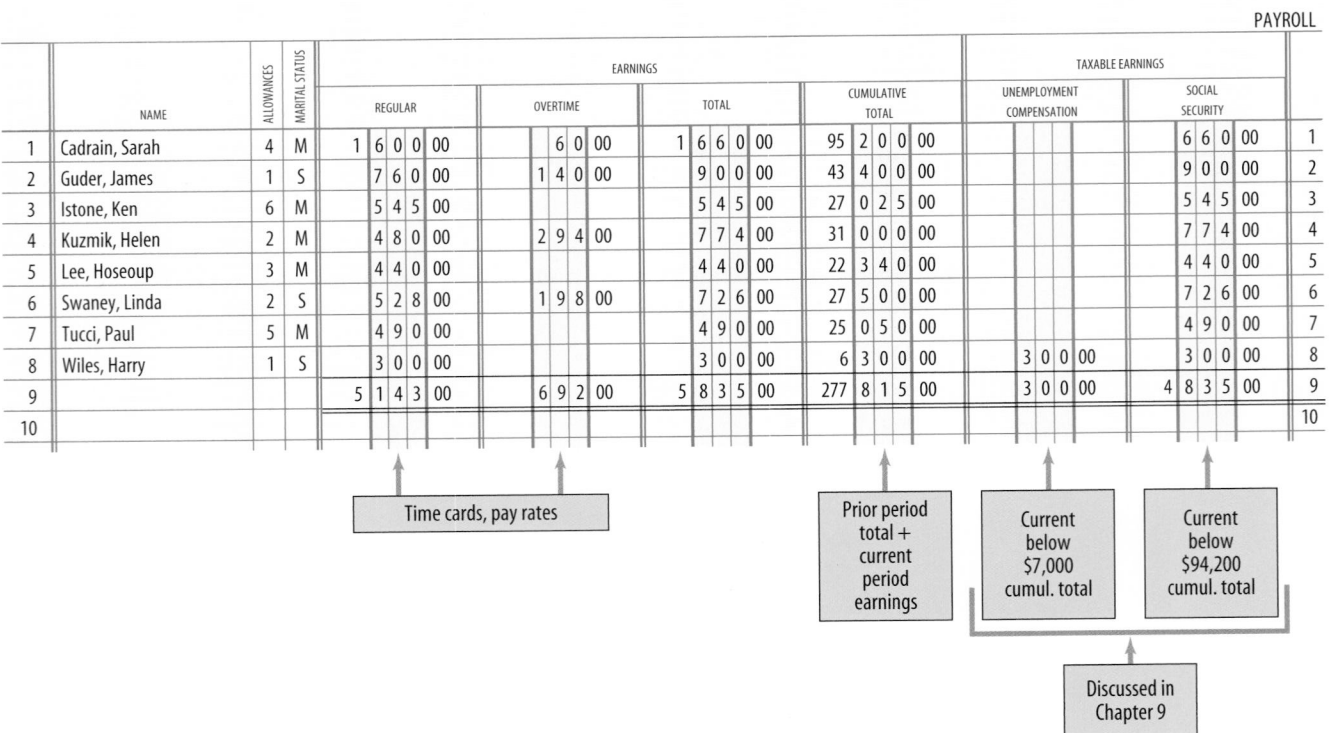

PAYROLL

	NAME	ALLOWANCES	MARITAL STATUS	EARNINGS				TAXABLE EARNINGS		
				REGULAR	OVERTIME	TOTAL	CUMULATIVE TOTAL	UNEMPLOYMENT COMPENSATION	SOCIAL SECURITY	
1	Cadrain, Sarah	4	M	1 6 0 0 00	6 0 00	1 6 6 0 00	95 2 0 0 00		6 6 0 00	1
2	Guder, James	1	S	7 6 0 00	1 4 0 00	9 0 0 00	43 4 0 0 00		9 0 0 00	2
3	Istone, Ken	6	M	5 4 5 00		5 4 5 00	27 0 2 5 00		5 4 5 00	3
4	Kuzmik, Helen	2	M	4 8 0 00	2 9 4 00	7 7 4 00	31 0 0 0 00		7 7 4 00	4
5	Lee, Hoseoup	3	M	4 4 0 00		4 4 0 00	22 3 4 0 00		4 4 0 00	5
6	Swaney, Linda	2	S	5 2 8 00	1 9 8 00	7 2 6 00	27 5 0 0 00		7 2 6 00	6
7	Tucci, Paul	5	M	4 9 0 00		4 9 0 00	25 0 5 0 00		4 9 0 00	7
8	Wiles, Harry	1	S	3 0 0 00		3 0 0 00	6 3 0 0 00	3 0 0 00	3 0 0 00	8
9				5 1 4 3 00	6 9 2 00	5 8 3 5 00	277 8 1 5 00	3 0 0 00	4 8 3 5 00	9
10										10

Time cards, pay rates

Prior period total + current period earnings

Current below $7,000 cumul. total

Current below $94,200 cumul. total

Discussed in Chapter 9

PAYROLL RECORDS

LO3 Describe and prepare payroll records.

Payroll records should provide the following information for each employee:

1. Name, address, occupation, social security number, marital status, and number of withholding allowances

2. Gross amount of earnings, date of payment, and period covered by each payroll

3. Gross amount of earnings accumulated for the year

4. Amounts of taxes and other items withheld

Three types of payroll records are used to accumulate this information:

1. The payroll register

2. The payroll check with earnings statement attached

3. The employee earnings record

These records can be prepared by either manual or automated methods. The illustrations in this chapter are based on a manual system. The forms and procedures illustrated are equally applicable to both manual and automated systems.

Payroll Register

A **payroll register** is a form used to assemble the data required at the end of each payroll period. Figure 8-5 illustrates Westly, Inc.'s payroll register for the payroll period ended December 19, 20--. Detailed information on earnings, taxable earnings, deductions, and net pay is provided for each employee. Column headings for deductions may vary, depending on which deductions are commonly used by a particular business. The sources of key information in the register are indicated in Figure 8-5.

FIGURE 8-5   Payroll Register (right side)

REGISTER—WEEK ENDED 12/19/--

	FEDERAL INCOME TAX	SOCIAL SECURITY TAX	MEDICARE TAX	HEALTH INSURANCE	UNITED WAY	OTHER	TOTAL	NET PAY	CHECK NO.	
1	1 8 4 00	4 0 92	2 4 07				2 4 8 99	1 4 1 1 01	409	1
2	1 3 4 00	5 5 80	1 3 05		2 0 00		2 2 2 85	6 7 7 15	410	2
3	1 00	3 3 79	7 90	1 0 00			5 2 69	4 9 2 31	411	3
4	6 0 00	4 7 99	1 1 22	1 3 00	2 0 00		1 5 2 21	6 2 1 79	412	4
5	1 0 00	2 7 28	6 38	1 3 00			5 6 66	3 8 3 34	413	5
6	7 5 00	4 5 01	1 0 53				1 3 0 54	5 9 5 46	414	6
7	2 00	3 0 38	7 11	1 0 00			4 9 49	4 4 0 51	415	7
8	2 2 00	1 8 60	4 35				4 4 95	2 5 5 05	416	8
9	4 8 8 00	2 9 9 77	8 4 61	4 6 00	4 0 00		9 5 8 38	4 8 7 6 62		9
10										10

Withholding Tax Table	6.2% × Social Security taxable earnings	1.45% × total earnings	Specific employer–employee agreements	Total earnings – total deductions

Westly, Inc., has eight employees. The first $94,200 of earnings of each employee is subject to Social Security tax. The Cumulative Total column, under the Earnings category, shows that Sarah Cadrain has exceeded this limit during the period. Thus, only $660 of her earnings for this pay period is subject to Social Security tax, as shown in the Taxable Earnings columns. Note that there are two Taxable Earnings columns: Unemployment Compensation and Social Security. Only one of these columns (Social Security) is needed to determine employee taxes. Both columns are shown here because they are a standard part of a payroll register. The Unemployment Compensation column is needed to determine this payroll tax on employers. The Social Security column is needed to determine both employee and employer Social Security taxes. The two employer taxes (Unemployment Compensation and Social Security) are discussed in Chapter 9.

Regular deductions are made from employee earnings for federal income tax and Social Security and Medicare taxes. In addition, voluntary deductions are made for health insurance and United Way contributions, based on agreements with individual employees.

After the data for each employee have been entered, the amount columns in the payroll register should be totaled and the totals verified as follows:

Regular earnings		$5,143.00
Overtime earnings		692.00
Gross earnings		$5,835.00
Deductions:		
Federal income tax	$488.00	
Social Security tax	299.77	
Medicare tax	84.61	
Health insurance premiums	46.00	
United Way	40.00	958.38
Net amount of payroll		$4,876.62

In a computerized accounting system, the payroll software performs this proof. An error in the payroll register could cause the payment of an incorrect amount to an employee. It also could result in sending an incorrect amount to the government or other agencies for whom funds are withheld.

Payroll Check

Employees may be paid in cash or by check. Data needed to prepare a paycheck for each employee are contained in the payroll register. In a computer-based system, the paychecks and payroll register normally are prepared at the same time. The employer furnishes an earnings statement to each employee along with each paycheck. Paychecks with detachable earnings statements, like the one for Ken Istone illustrated in Figure 8-6, are widely used for this purpose. Before the check is deposited or cashed, the employee should detach the stub and keep it.

In many cases, the employee does not even handle the paycheck. Rather, payment is made by **direct deposit** or electronic funds transfer (EFT) by the employer to the employee's bank. The employee receives only the earnings statement from the check indicating the deposit has been made. Payment by check or direct deposit provides better internal accounting control than payment by cash.

FIGURE 8-6　　Paycheck and Earnings Statement

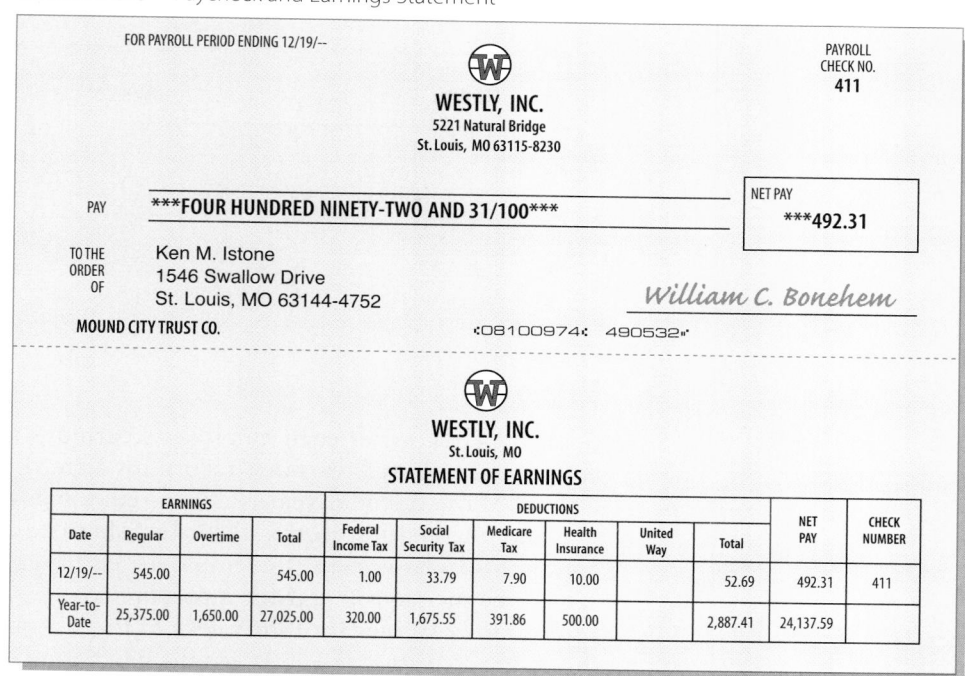

FOR PAYROLL PERIOD ENDING 12/19/--

PAYROLL CHECK NO. **411**

WESTLY, INC.
5221 Natural Bridge
St. Louis, MO 63115-8230

PAY　***FOUR HUNDRED NINETY-TWO AND 31/100***

NET PAY ***492.31

TO THE ORDER OF
Ken M. Istone
1546 Swallow Drive
St. Louis, MO 63144-4752

William C. Bonehem

MOUND CITY TRUST CO.　　⑈08100974⑈ 490532⑈

WESTLY, INC.
St. Louis, MO
STATEMENT OF EARNINGS

	EARNINGS			DEDUCTIONS						NET PAY	CHECK NUMBER
Date	Regular	Overtime	Total	Federal Income Tax	Social Security Tax	Medicare Tax	Health Insurance	United Way	Total		
12/19/--	545.00		545.00	1.00	33.79	7.90	10.00		52.69	492.31	411
Year-to-Date	25,375.00	1,650.00	27,025.00	320.00	1,675.55	391.86	500.00		2,887.41	24,137.59	

A BROADER VIEW

© GETTY IMAGES/PHOTODISC

Payroll Fraud—Paying for Ghosts

A supervisor at Haas Transfer Warehouse embezzled $12,000 from the company by collecting paychecks for former employees. When an employee left the company, the supervisor continued to submit a department time report for the employee. This caused a paycheck to be generated for the "ghost" employee. The supervisor then simply kept this paycheck when others were distributed to actual employees.

This fraud shows the importance of two procedures that appear in this chapter: (1) a time card, plastic card, or badge should be used for each employee to keep an accurate record of time worked and (2) payment by direct deposit or electronic funds transfer to the employee's bank is a good internal control.

FIGURE 8-7   Employee Earnings Record (left side)

EMPLOYEE EARNINGS RECORD

| PERIOD ENDED | EARNINGS | | | | TAXABLE EARNINGS | |
	REGULAR	OVERTIME	TOTAL	CUMULATIVE TOTAL	UNEMPLOYMENT COMPENSATION	SOCIAL SECURITY
11/28	5 4 5 00	7 5 00	6 2 0 00	25 2 4 0 00		6 2 0 00
12/5	5 4 5 00	7 5 00	6 2 0 00	25 8 6 0 00		6 2 0 00
12/12	5 4 5 00	7 5 00	6 2 0 00	26 4 8 0 00		6 2 0 00
12/19	5 4 5 00		5 4 5 00	27 0 2 5 00		5 4 5 00

GENDER	DEPARTMENT	OCCUPATION	SOCIAL SECURITY NUMBER	MARITAL STATUS	ALLOWANCES
M ✔ F	Maintenance	Service	393-58-8194	M	6

Employee Earnings Record

A separate record of each employee's earnings is called an **employee earnings record**. An employee earnings record for Ken M. Istone for a portion of the last quarter of the calendar year is illustrated in Figure 8-7.

The information in this record is obtained from the payroll register. In a computer-based system, the employee earnings record can be updated at the same time the payroll register is prepared.

Istone's earnings for four weeks of the last quarter of the year are shown on this form. Note that the entry for the pay period ended December 19 is the same as that in the payroll register illustrated in Figure 8-5. This linkage between the payroll register and the employee earnings record always exists. The payroll register provides a summary of the earnings of all employees for each pay period. The earnings record provides a summary of the annual earnings of an individual employee.

The earnings record illustrated in Figure 8-7 is designed to accumulate both quarterly and annual totals. The employer needs this information to prepare several reports. These reports will be discussed in Chapter 9.

ACCOUNTING FOR EMPLOYEE EARNINGS AND DEDUCTIONS

The payroll register described in the previous section provides complete payroll data for each pay period. But the payroll register is not a journal. We still need to make a journal entry for payroll.

Journalizing Payroll Transactions

The totals at the bottom of the columns of the payroll register in Figure 8-5 show the following information.

Regular earnings		$5,143.00
Overtime earnings		692.00
Gross earnings		$5,835.00
Deductions:		
Federal income tax	$488.00	
Social Security tax	299.77	
Medicare tax	84.61	
Health insurance premiums	46.00	
United Way contributions	40.00	958.38
Net amount of payroll		$4,876.62

LEARNING KEY

The payroll register and employee earnings record are linked. The payroll register shows the earnings of all employees for a single pay period. The employee earnings record summarizes the earnings of an individual employee for all pay periods.

LO4   Account for employee earnings and deductions.

FIGURE 8-7   Employee Earnings Record (right side)

FOR PERIOD ENDED   20--

FEDERAL INCOME TAX	SOCIAL SECURITY TAX	MEDICARE TAX	HEALTH INSURANCE	UNITED WAY	OTHER	TOTAL	CHECK NO.	AMOUNT
9 00	3 8 44	8 99	1 0 00			6 6 43	387	5 5 3 57
9 00	3 8 44	8 99	1 0 00			6 6 43	395	5 5 3 57
9 00	3 8 44	8 99	1 0 00			6 6 43	403	5 5 3 57
1 00	3 3 79	7 90	1 0 00			5 2 69	411	4 9 2 31

PAY RATE	DATE OF BIRTH	DATE HIRED	NAME/ADDRESS	EMPLOYEE NUMBER
$545/wk	8/17/64	1/3/87	Ken M. Istone 1546 Swallow Drive St. Louis, MO 63144-4752	3

The payroll register column totals thus provide the basis for recording the payroll. If the employee paychecks are written from the regular bank account, the following journal entry is made:

	DATE		DESCRIPTION	POST REF.	DEBIT	CREDIT	
5	Dec.	19	Wages and Salaries Expense		5 8 3 5 00		5
6			Employee Income Tax Payable			4 8 8 00	6
7			Social Security Tax Payable			2 9 9 77	7
8			Medicare Tax Payable			8 4 61	8
9			Health Insurance Premiums Payable			4 6 00	9
10			United Way Contributions Payable			4 0 00	10
11			Cash			4 8 7 6 62	11
12			Payroll for week ended Dec. 19				12

Employee paychecks also can be written from a special payroll bank account. Large businesses with many employees commonly use a payroll bank account. If Westly used a payroll bank account, it first would have made the following entry on December 19 to transfer funds from the regular bank account to the payroll bank account:

	DATE		DESCRIPTION	POST REF.	DEBIT	CREDIT	
5	Dec.	19	Payroll Cash		4 8 7 6 62		5
6			Cash			4 8 7 6 62	6
7			Cash for Dec. 19 payroll				7

LEARNING KEY

Wages and Salaries Expense is debited for the gross pay. A separate account is kept for each earnings deduction. Cash is credited for the net pay.

Then, the payroll entry shown above would be made, except that the credit of $4,876.62 would be to Payroll Cash rather than Cash.

If a payroll bank account is used, individual checks totaling $4,876.62 are written to the employees from that account. Otherwise, individual checks totaling that amount are written to the employees from the regular bank account.

Notice two important facts about the payroll entry. First, Wages and Salaries Expense is debited for the gross pay of the employees. The expense to the employer is the gross pay, not the employees' net pay after deductions. Second, a separate account is kept for each deduction.

The accounts needed in entering deductions depend upon the deductions involved. To understand the accounting for these deductions, consider what the employer is doing. By deducting amounts from employees' earnings, the employer is simply serving as an agent for the government and other groups. Amounts that are deducted from an employee's gross earnings must be paid by the employer to these groups. Therefore, a separate account should be kept for the liability for each type of deduction.

To help us understand the journal entry for payroll, let's use the accounting equation to examine the accounts involved. The seven accounts affected by the payroll entry on page 297 are shown in the accounting equation in Figure 8-8.

FIGURE 8-8   Accounting for Payroll

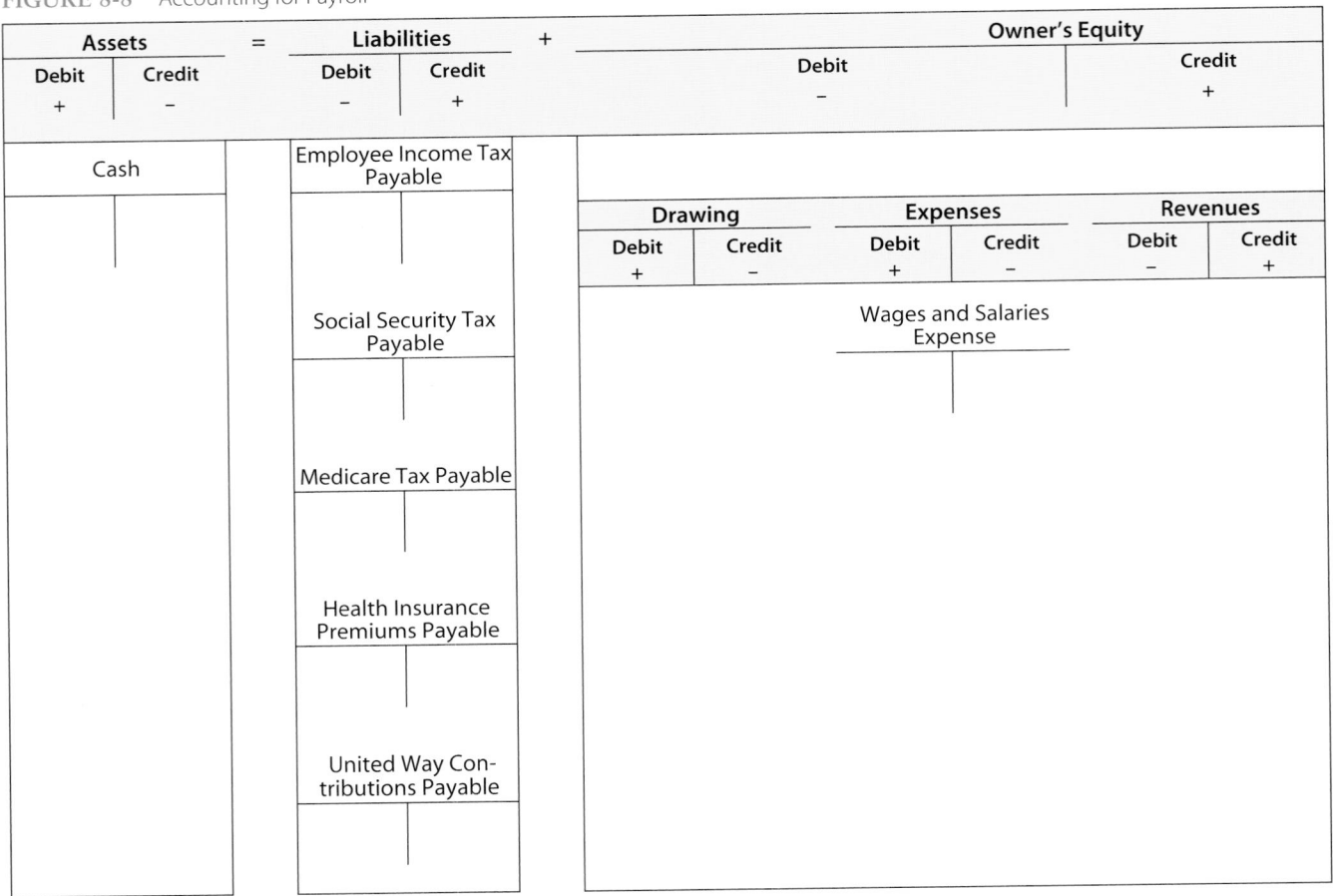

Wages and Salaries Expense

This account is debited for the gross pay of all employees for each pay period. Sometimes separate expense accounts are kept for the employees of different departments. Thus, separate accounts may be kept for Office Salaries Expense, Sales Salaries Expense, and Factory Wages Expense.

Wages and Salaries Expense

Debit	Credit
gross pay of employees for each pay period	

Employee Income Tax Payable

This account is credited for the total federal income tax withheld from employees' earnings. The account is debited for amounts paid to the IRS. When all of the income taxes withheld have been paid, the account will have a zero balance. A state or city income tax payable account is used in a similar manner.

Employee Income Tax Payable

Debit	Credit
payment of income tax previously withheld	federal income tax withheld from employees' earnings

Social Security and Medicare Taxes Payable

These accounts are credited for (1) the Social Security and Medicare taxes withheld from employees' earnings and (2) the Social Security and Medicare taxes imposed on the employer. Social Security and Medicare taxes imposed on the employer are discussed in Chapter 9. The accounts are debited for amounts paid to the IRS. When all of the Social Security and Medicare taxes have been paid, the accounts will have zero balances.

Social Security Tax Payable

Debit	Credit
payment of Social Security tax previously withheld or imposed	Social Security taxes (1) withheld from employees' earnings and (2) imposed on the employer

Medicare Tax Payable

Debit	Credit
payment of Medicare tax previously withheld or imposed	Medicare taxes (1) withheld from employees' earnings and (2) imposed on the employer

Other Deductions

Health Insurance Premiums Payable is credited for health insurance contributions deducted from an employee's pay. The account is debited for the subsequent payment of these amounts to the health insurer. United Way Contributions Payable is handled in a similar manner.

PAYROLL RECORD-KEEPING METHODS

LO5 **Describe various payroll record-keeping methods.**

Payroll typically is one of the first functions to be computerized by businesses.

You probably noticed that the same information appears in several places in the payroll records—in the payroll register, paycheck and stub, and employee earnings records. If all records are prepared by hand (a **manual system**), the same information would be recorded several times. Unless an employer has only a few employees, this can be very inefficient. Various approaches are available to make payroll accounting more efficient and accurate.

Both medium- and large-size businesses commonly use two approaches for payroll record keeping: payroll processing centers and electronic systems. A **payroll processing center** is a business that sells payroll record-keeping services. The employer provides the center with all basic employee data and each period's report of hours worked. The processing center maintains all payroll records and prepares each period's payroll checks. Payroll processing center fees tend to be much less than the cost to an employer of handling payroll internally.

An **electronic system** is a computer system based on a software package that performs all payroll record keeping and prepares payroll checks. In this system, only the employee number and hours worked need to be entered into a computer each pay period, as shown in Figure 8-9. All other payroll data needed to prepare the payroll records can be stored in the computer. The computer uses the employee number and hours worked to determine the gross pay, deductions, and net pay. The payroll register, checks, and employee earnings records are provided as outputs.

FIGURE 8-9   Electronic Payroll System

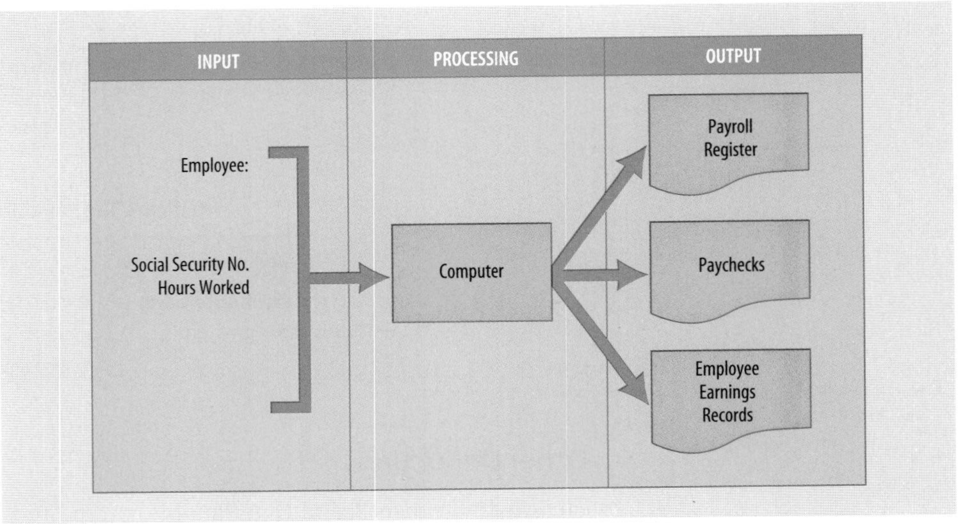

The same inputs and outputs are required in all payroll systems. Even with a computer, the data required for payroll processing have to be entered into the system at some point. The outputs—the payroll register, paychecks, and employee earnings records—are basically the same under each system.

Learning Objectives	Key Points to Remember
LO1 Distinguish between employees and independent contractors.	Employees work under the control and direction of an employer. Independent contractors perform a service for a fee and do not work under the control and direction of the company paying for the service. Payroll accounting procedures apply only to employees, not to independent contractors.
LO2 Calculate employee earnings and deductions.	Three steps are required to determine how much to pay an employee for a pay period: 1. Calculate total earnings. 2. Determine the amounts of deductions. 3. Subtract deductions from total earnings to compute net pay. Deductions from gross pay fall into three categories: 1. Income tax withholding 2. Employee Social Security and Medicare taxes withholding 3. Voluntary deductions Four factors determine the amount to be withheld from an employee's gross pay each pay period: 1. Total earnings 2. Marital status 3. Number of withholding allowances claimed 4. Length of the pay period
LO3 Describe and prepare payroll records.	The payroll register and the employee earnings record are linked. The payroll register provides a summary of earnings of all employees for each pay period. The earnings record provides a summary of the annual earnings of an individual employee.
LO4 Account for employee earnings and deductions.	The totals at the bottom of the columns of the payroll register provide the basis for the journal entry for payroll. Amounts withheld or deducted by the employer from employee earnings are credited to liability accounts. The employer must pay these amounts to the proper government groups and other appropriate groups.
LO5 Describe various payroll record-keeping methods.	In a manual payroll system, the same information needs to be recorded several times. An electronic payroll system is much more efficient.

DEMONSTRATION PROBLEM

Carole Vohsen operates a pet grooming salon called Canine Coiffures. She has five employees, all of whom are paid on a weekly basis. Canine Coiffures uses a payroll register, individual employee earnings records, a journal, and a general ledger.

The payroll data for each employee for the week ended January 21, 20--, are given below. Employees are paid 1½ times the regular rate for work over 40 hours a week and double time for work on Sunday.

Name	Employee No.	No. of Allowances	Marital Status	Total Hours Worked Jan. 15–21	Rate	Total Earnings Jan. 1–14
DeNourie, Katie	1	2	S	44	$11.50	$1,058.00
Garriott, Pete	2	1	M	40	12.00	1,032.00
Martinez, Sheila	3	3	M	39	12.50	987.50
Parker, Nancy	4	4	M	42	11.00	957.00
Shapiro, John	5	2	S	40	11.50	931.50

Sheila Martinez is the manager of the Shampooing Department. Her social security number is 500-88-4189, and she was born April 12, 1969. She lives at 46 Darling Crossing, Norwich, CT 06360. Martinez was hired September 1 of last year.

Canine Coiffures uses a federal income tax withholding table. A portion of this weekly table is provided in Figure 8-4 on pages 289 and 290. Social Security tax is withheld at the rate of 6.2% of the first $94,200 earned. Medicare tax is withheld at the rate of 1.45%, and city earnings tax at the rate of 1%, both applied to gross pay. Garriott and Parker each have $14.00 and DeNourie and Martinez each have $4.00 withheld for health insurance. DeNourie, Martinez, and Shapiro each have $15.00 withheld to be invested in the groomers' credit union. Garriott and Shapiro each have $18.75 withheld under a savings bond purchase plan.

Canine Coiffures' payroll is met by drawing checks on its regular bank account. This week, the checks were issued in sequence, beginning with no. 811.

REQUIRED

1. Prepare a payroll register for Canine Coiffures for the week ended January 21, 20--. (In the Taxable Earnings/Unemployment Compensation column, enter the same amounts as in the Social Security column.) Total the amount columns, verify the totals, and rule with single and double lines.

2. Prepare an employee earnings record for Sheila Martinez for the week ended January 21, 20--.

3. Assuming that the wages for the week ended January 21 were paid on January 23, prepare the journal entry for the payment of this payroll.

4. Post the entry in requirement (3) to the affected accounts in the ledger of Canine Coiffures. Do not enter any amounts in the Balance columns. Use account numbers as follows: Cash—101; Employee Income Tax Payable—211; Social Security Tax Payable—212; Medicare Tax Payable—213; City Earnings Tax Payable—215; Health Insurance Premiums Payable—216; Credit Union Payable—217; Savings Bond Deductions Payable—218; Wages and Salaries Expense—511.

graph paper

PAYROLL

		EARNINGS						TAXABLE EARNINGS		
	OVERTIME		TOTAL		CUMULATIVE TOTAL		UNEMPLOYMENT COMPENSATION		SOCIAL SECURITY	
00	6 9 00		5 2 9 00		1 5 8 7 00		5 2 9 00		5 2 9 00	1
00			4 8 0 00		1 5 1 2 00		4 8 0 00		4 8 0 00	2
50			4 8 7 50		1 4 7 5 00		4 8 7 50		4 8 7 50	3
00	3 3 00		4 7 3 00		1 4 3 0 00		4 7 3 00		4 7 3 00	4
Shapiro, John 5 2 3 4 6 0 00			4 6 0 00		1 3 9 1 50		4 6 0 00		4 6 0 00	5
2 3 2 7 50	1 0 2 00		2 4 2 9 50		7 3 9 5 50		2 4 2 9 50		2 4 2 9 50	6
										7

REGISTER—WEEK ENDED January 21, 20--

	FEDERAL INCOME TAX	SOCIAL SECURITY TAX	MEDICARE TAX	CITY TAX	HEALTH INSURANCE	CREDIT UNION	OTHER		TOTAL	NET PAY	CHECK NO.	
1	4 5 00	3 2 80	7 67	5 29	4 00	1 5 00			1 0 9 76	4 1 9 24	811	1
2	2 7 00	2 9 76	6 96	4 80	1 4 00		U.S. Savings Bond	1 8 75	1 0 1 27	3 7 8 73	812	2
3	1 4 00	3 0 23	7 07	4 88	4 00	1 5 00			7 5 18	4 1 2 32	813	3
4	7 00	2 9 33	6 86	4 73	1 4 00				6 1 92	4 1 1 08	814	4
5	3 6 00	2 8 52	6 67	4 60		1 5 00	U.S. Savings Bond	1 8 75	1 0 9 54	3 5 0 46	815	5
6	1 2 9 00	1 5 0 64	3 5 23	2 4 30	3 6 00	4 5 00		3 7 50	4 5 7 67	1 9 7 1 83		6
7												7

2.

EMPLOYEE EARNINGS RECORD

20-- PERIOD ENDED	EARNINGS								TAXABLE EARNINGS		
	REGULAR		OVERTIME		TOTAL		CUMULATIVE TOTAL		UNEMPLOYMENT COMPENSATION	SOCIAL SECURITY
1/7										
1/14										
1/21	4 8 7 50				4 8 7 50		1 4 7 5 00		4 8 7 50	4 8 7 50
1/28										

GENDER		DEPARTMENT	OCCUPATION	SOCIAL SECURITY NUMBER	MARITAL STATUS	ALLOWANCES
M	F ✔	Shampooing	Manager	500-88-4189	M	3

FOR PERIOD ENDED   20--

DEDUCTIONS										
FEDERAL INCOME TAX	SOCIAL SECURITY TAX	MEDICARE TAX	CITY TAX	HEALTH INSURANCE	CREDIT UNION	OTHER		TOTAL	CHECK NO.	AMOUNT
1 4 00	3 0 23	7 07	4 88	4 00	1 5 00			7 5 18	813	4 1 2 32

PAY RATE	DATE OF BIRTH	DATE HIRED	NAME/ADDRESS	EMPLOYEE NUMBER
$12.50	4/12/69	9/1/--	Sheila Martinez 46 Darling Crossing Norwich, CT 06360	3

(continued)

3.

	DATE		DESCRIPTION	POST. REF.	DEBIT					CREDIT					
	\multicolumn{15}{c}{GENERAL JOURNAL PAGE 1}
1	20-- Jan.	23	Wages and Salaries Expense	511	2	4	2	9	50						1
2			Employee Income Tax Payable	211						1	2	9	00		2
3			Social Security Tax Payable	212						1	5	0	64		3
4			Medicare Tax Payable	213							3	5	23		4
5			City Earnings Tax Payable	215							2	4	30		5
6			Health Insurance Premiums Payable	216							3	6	00		6
7			Credit Union Payable	217							4	5	00		7
8			Savings Bond Deductions Payable	218							3	7	50		8
9			Cash	101						1	9	7	1	83	9
10			Payroll for week ended Jan. 21												10

4.

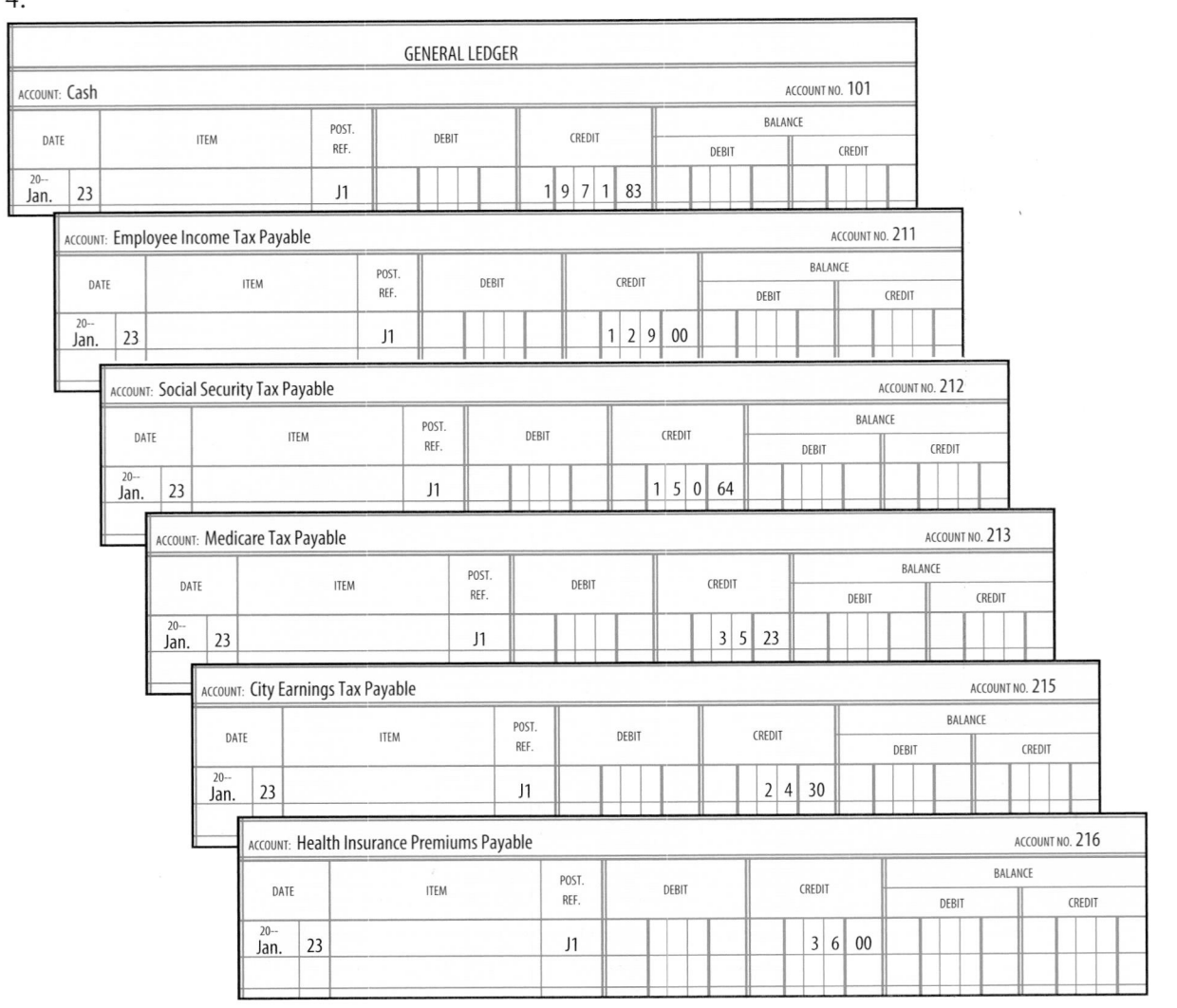

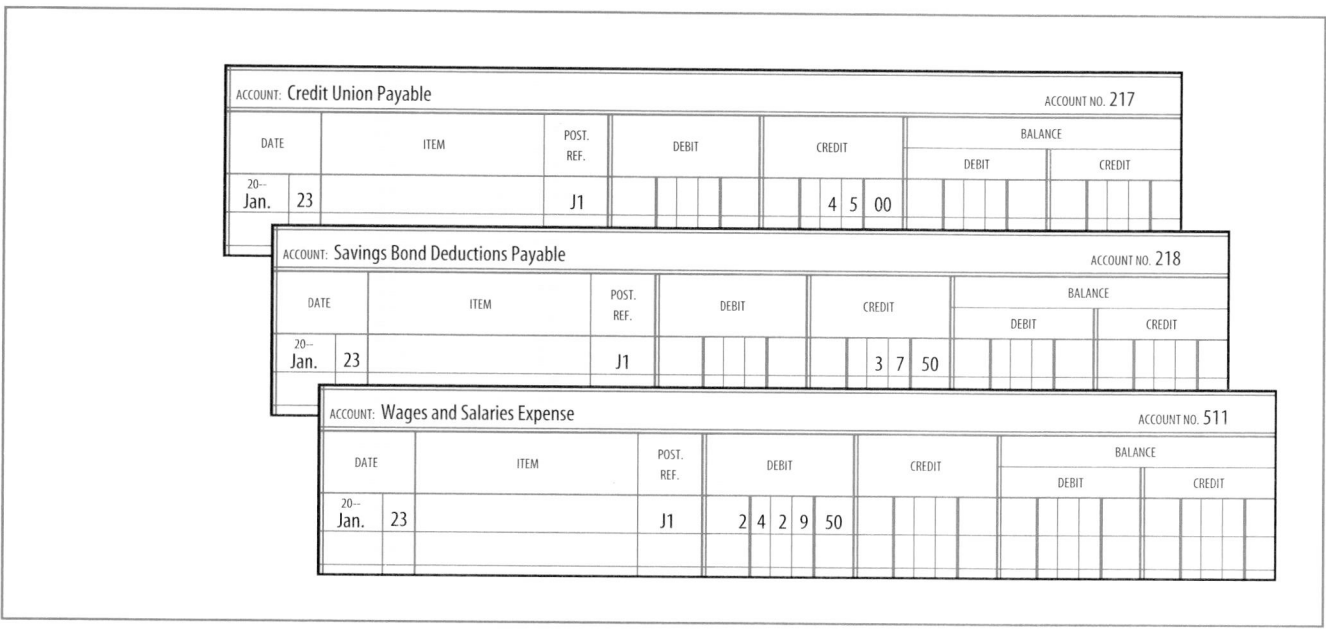

KEY TERMS

direct deposit (294)   A payroll method in which the employee does not handle the paycheck; payment is made by the employer directly to the employee's bank.

electronic system (300)   A computer system based on a software package that performs all payroll record keeping and prepares payroll checks.

employee (284)   Someone who works under the control and direction of an employer.

employee earnings record (296)   A separate record of each employee's earnings.

Fair Labor Standards Act (FLSA) (285)   A law that requires employers to pay overtime at 1½ times the regular rate to any hourly employee who works over 40 hours in a week.

FICA taxes (291)   Payroll taxes withheld to provide Social Security and Medicare benefits.

gross pay (287)   An employee's total earnings.

independent contractor (284)   Someone who performs a service for a fee and does not work under the control and direction of the company paying for the service.

manual system (300)   Payroll system in which all records are prepared by hand.

net pay (287)   Gross pay less mandatory and voluntary deductions.

payroll processing center (300)   A business that sells payroll record-keeping services.

payroll register (293)   A form used to assemble the data required at the end of each payroll period.

salary (284)   Compensation for managerial or administrative services.

wage-bracket method (288)   A method of determining the amount to withhold from an employee's gross pay for a specific time period. Wage-bracket tables are provided by the Internal Revenue Service.

wages (284)   Compensation for skilled or unskilled labor.

withholding allowance (287)   A specific dollar amount of an employee's gross pay that is exempt from federal income tax withholding.

Self-Study Test Questions

True/False

1. An independent contractor is one who works under the control and direction of an employer.

2. Government laws and regulations regarding payroll are more complex for employees than for independent contractors.

3. Compensation for skilled or unskilled labor expressed in terms of hours, weeks, or units is called salary.

4. An employee's total earnings is called gross pay.

5. A payroll register is a multi-column form used to assemble the data required at the end of each payroll period.

Multiple Choice

1. Jack Smith is married, has a spouse who is not employed, has five dependent children, and does not anticipate large itemized deductions. How many withholding allowances is Smith entitled to?

   (a) 5   (c) 7
   (b) 6   (d) 8

2. A separate record of each employee's earnings is called a(n)

   (a) payroll register.   (c) W-4.
   (b) employee earnings record. (d) earnings statement.

3. Nancy Summers worked 44 hours during the past week. She is entitled to 1½ times her regular pay for all hours worked in excess of 40 during the week. Her regular rate of pay is $12.00. Social Security tax is withheld at the rate of 6.2% and Medicare tax is withheld at the rate of 1.45%; federal income tax withheld is $68; and $5 of union dues are withheld. Her net pay for the week is

   (a) $440.89.   (c) $552.00.
   (b) $472.00.   (d) $436.78.

4. Social Security Tax Payable and Medicare Tax Payable are classified as

   (a) liabilities.   (c) owner's equity.
   (b) assets.   (d) expenses.

5. Which of the following is *not* a factor that determines the amount of federal income tax to be withheld from an employee's gross pay?

   (a) marital status   (c) total earnings
   (b) number of withholding allowances claimed   (d) age of employee

The answers to the Self-Study Test Questions are at the end of the text.

REVIEW QUESTIONS

LO1   1. Why is it important for payroll accounting purposes to distinguish between an employee and an independent contractor?

LO2   2. Name three major categories of deductions from an employee's gross pay.

LO2   3. Identify the four factors that determine the amount of federal income tax that is withheld from an employee's pay each pay period.

LO2   4. In general, an employee is entitled to withholding allowances for what purposes?

LO3   5. Identify the three payroll records usually needed by an employer.

LO3   6. Describe the information contained in the payroll register.

LO3   7. Why is it important to total and verify the totals of the payroll register after the data for each employee have been entered?

LO3   8. Distinguish between the payroll register and the employee earnings record.

LO4   9. Explain what an employer does with the amounts withheld from an employee's pay.

LO5   10. Explain why payroll processing centers and electronic systems are commonly used in payroll accounting.

© DIGITAL IMAGING GROUP

REVISITING THE OPENER

In the chapter opener on page 283, you are asked to consider the taxes Evan must withhold from his employees' wages.

(1) What taxes must Evan withhold from his employees' wages?

(2) How does Evan determine the correct amounts to withhold?

(3) Compute the amounts to withhold for federal income tax, Social Security tax, and Medicare tax for an employee with gross earnings of $200 for the week of February 7. The employee is single with one withholding allowance.

SERIES A EXERCISES

E 8-1A (LO2)

✓ Net pay: $443.51

COMPUTING NET PAY Mary Sue Guild works for a company that pays its employees 1½ times the regular rate for all hours worked in excess of 40 per week. Guild's pay rate is $10.00 per hour. Her wages are subject to deductions for federal income tax, Social Security tax, and Medicare tax. She is married and claims four withholding allowances. Guild has a ½-hour lunch break during an 8½-hour day. Her time card is shown on the next page.

Name	Mary Sue Guild						
Week Ending	March 30, 20--						
						Hours Worked	
Day	In	Out	In	Out		Regular	Overtime
M	7:57	12:05	12:35	4:33		8	
T	7:52	12:09	12:39	5:05		8	½
W	7:59	12:15	12:45	5:30		8	1
T	8:00	12:01	12:30	6:31		8	2
F	7:56	12:05	12:34	4:30		8	
S	8:00	10:31					2½

Complete the following:

(a) _____ regular hours × $10.00 per hour $_____

(b) _____ overtime hours × $15.00 per hour $_____

(c) Total gross wages $_____

(d) Federal income tax withholding (from tax tables in Figure 8-4, pages 289 and 290) $_____

(e) Social Security withholding at 6.2% $_____

(f) Medicare withholding at 1.45% $_____

(g) Total withholding $_____

(h) Net pay $_____

E 8-2A (LO2)

✓ Gross pay: $795.00

COMPUTING WEEKLY GROSS PAY Ryan Lawrence's regular hourly rate is $15.00. He receives 1½ times the regular rate for any hours worked over 40 a week and double the rate for work on Sunday. During the past week, Lawrence worked 8 hours each day Monday through Thursday, 10 hours on Friday, and 5 hours on Sunday. Compute Lawrence's gross pay for the past week.

E 8-3A (LO2)

✓ b: $712.50

COMPUTING OVERTIME RATE OF PAY AND GROSS WEEKLY PAY Rebecca Huang receives a regular salary of $2,600 a month and is paid 1½ times the regular hourly rate for hours worked in excess of 40 per week.

(a) Calculate Huang's overtime rate of pay.
(b) Calculate Huang's total gross weekly pay if she works 45 hours during the week.

E 8-4A (LO2)

✓ e: $7.00

COMPUTING FEDERAL INCOME TAX Using the table in Figure 8-4 on pages 289 and 290, determine the amount of federal income tax an employer should withhold weekly for employees with the following marital status, earnings, and withholding allowances:

	Marital Status	Total Weekly Earnings	Number of Allowances	Amount of Withholding
(a)	S	$327.90	2	_____
(b)	S	410.00	1	_____
(c)	M	438.16	5	_____
(d)	S	518.25	0	_____
(e)	M	603.98	6	_____

E 8-5A (LO2)

✓ 3d row, Soc. Sec. tax: $161.20

CALCULATING SOCIAL SECURITY AND MEDICARE TAXES Assume a Social Security tax rate of 6.2% is applied to maximum earnings of $94,200 and a Medicare tax rate of 1.45% is applied to all earnings. Calculate the Social Security and Medicare taxes for the following situations:

Cumul. Pay Before Current Weekly Payroll	Current Gross Pay	Year-to-Date Earnings	Soc. Sec. Maximum	Amount Over Max. Soc. Sec.	Amount Subject to Soc. Sec.	Soc. Sec. Tax Withheld	Medicare Tax Withheld
$22,000	$1,200	_____	$94,200	_____	_____	_____	_____
54,000	4,200	_____	94,200	_____	_____	_____	_____
91,600	3,925	_____	94,200	_____	_____	_____	_____
93,600	4,600	_____	94,200	_____	_____	_____	_____

E 8-6A (LO4)

✓ Med. tax: $126.15

JOURNALIZING PAYROLL TRANSACTIONS On December 31, the payroll register of Hamstreet Associates indicated the following information:

Wages and Salaries Expense	$8,700.00
Employee Income Tax Payable	920.00
United Way Contributions Payable	200.00
Earnings subject to Social Security tax	8,000.00

Determine the amount of Social Security and Medicare taxes to be withheld and record the journal entry for the payroll, crediting Cash for the net pay.

E 8-7A (LO4)

✓ Cr. Cash: $4,756.49

PAYROLL JOURNAL ENTRY Journalize the following data taken from the payroll register of University Printing as of April 15, 20--:

Regular earnings	$5,418.00
Overtime earnings	824.00
Deductions:	
Federal income tax	593.00
Social Security tax	387.00
Medicare tax	90.51
Pension plan	90.00
Health insurance premiums	225.00
United Way contributions	100.00

SERIES A PROBLEMS

P 8-8A (LO2/4)

✓ Net pay: $184.19

GROSS PAY, DEDUCTIONS, AND NET PAY Donald Chin works for Northwest Supplies. His rate of pay is $8.50 per hour, and he is paid 1½ times the regular rate for all hours worked in excess of 40 per week. During the last week of January of the current year, he worked 48 hours. Chin is married and claims four withholding allowances on his W-4 form. His weekly wages are subject to the following deductions:

(a) Employee income tax (use Figure 8-4 on pages 289 and 290)
(b) Social Security tax at 6.2%
(c) Medicare tax at 1.45%
(d) Health insurance premium, $85.00
(e) Credit union, $125.00
(f) United Way contribution, $10.00

(continued)

REQUIRED

1.   Compute Chin's regular pay, overtime pay, gross pay, and net pay.

2.   Journalize the payment of his wages for the week ended January 31, crediting Cash for the net amount.

P 8-9A (LO2/3/4)

✓ Cr. Cash: $1,817.01

KLOOSTER & ALLEN

PAYROLL REGISTER AND PAYROLL JOURNAL ENTRY Don McCullum operates a travel agency called Don's Luxury Travel. He has five employees, all of whom are paid on a weekly basis. The travel agency uses a payroll register, individual employee earnings records, and a general journal.

Don's Luxury Travel uses a weekly federal income tax withholding table. The payroll data for each employee for the week ended March 22, 20--, are given below. Employees are paid 1½ times the regular rate for working over 40 hours a week.

Name	No. of Allowances	Marital Status	Total Hours Worked Mar. 16–22	Rate	Total Earnings Jan. 1–Mar. 15
Ali, Loren	4	M	45	$11.00	$5,280.00
Carson, Judy	1	S	40	12.00	5,760.00
Hernandez, Maria	3	M	43	9.50	4,560.00
Knox, Wayne	1	S	39	11.00	5,125.50
Paglione, Jim	2	M	40	10.50	4,720.50

Social Security tax is withheld from the first $94,200 of earnings at the rate of 6.2%. Medicare tax is withheld at the rate of 1.45%, and city earnings tax at the rate of 1%, both applied to gross pay. Ali and Knox have $15.00 withheld and Carson and Hernandez have $5.00 withheld for health insurance. Ali and Knox have $20.00 withheld to be invested in the travel agency's credit union. Carson has $38.75 withheld and Hernandez has $18.75 withheld under a savings bond purchase plan.

Don's Luxury Travel's payroll is met by drawing checks on its regular bank account. The checks were issued in sequence, beginning with check no. 423.

REQUIRED

1.   Prepare a payroll register for Don's Luxury Travel for the week ended March 22, 20--. (In the Taxable Earnings/Unemployment Compensation column, enter the same amounts as in the Social Security column.) Total the amount columns, verify the totals, and rule with single and double lines.

2.   Assuming that the wages for the week ended March 22 were paid on March 24, prepare the journal entry for the payment of the payroll.

P 8-10A (LO3)

✓ Soc. Sec. tax: $29.76

EMPLOYEE EARNINGS RECORD Don's Luxury Travel in Problem 8-9A keeps employee earnings records. Judy Carson, employee number 62, is employed as a manager in the ticket sales department. She was born on May 8, 1959, and was hired on June 1 of last year. Her social security number is 544-67-1283. She lives at 28 Quarry Drive, Vernon, CT 06066.

REQUIRED

For the week ended March 22, complete an employee earnings record for Judy Carson. (Insert earnings data only for the week of March 22.)

SERIES B EXERCISES

E 8-1B (LO2)

✓ Net pay: $524.70

COMPUTING NET PAY Tom Hallinan works for a company that pays its employees 1½ times the regular rate for all hours worked in excess of 40 per week. Hallinan's pay rate is $12.00 per hour. His wages are subject to deductions for federal income tax, Social Security tax, and Medicare tax. He is married and claims five withholding allowances. Hallinan has a ½-hour lunch break during an 8½-hour day. His time card is shown below.

Name	Tom Hallinan					
Week Ending	March 30, 20--					
Day	In	Out	In	Out	Regular	Overtime
M	7:55	12:02	12:32	5:33	8	1
T	7:59	12:04	12:34	6:05	8	1½
W	7:59	12:05	12:35	4:30	8	
T	8:00	12:01	12:30	5:01	8	½
F	7:58	12:02	12:31	5:33	8	1
S	7:59	9:33				1½

Complete the following:

(a) _____ regular hours × $12.00 per hour $_____
(b) _____ overtime hours × $18.00 per hour $_____
(c) Total gross wages $_____
(d) Federal income tax withholding (from tax tables in Figure 8-4, pages 289 and 290) $_____
(e) Social Security withholding at 6.2% $_____
(f) Medicare withholding at 1.45% $_____
(g) Total withholding $_____
(h) Net pay $_____

E 8-2B (LO2)

✓ Gross pay: $678.00

COMPUTING WEEKLY GROSS PAY Manuel Soto's regular hourly rate is $12.00. He receives 1½ times the regular rate for hours worked in excess of 40 a week and double the rate for work on Sunday. During the past week, Soto worked 8 hours each day Monday through Thursday, 11 hours on Friday, and 6 hours on Sunday. Compute Soto's gross pay for the past week.

E 8-3B (LO2)

✓ b: $918.75

COMPUTING OVERTIME RATE OF PAY AND GROSS WEEKLY PAY Mike Fritz receives a regular salary of $3,250 a month and is paid 1½ times the regular hourly rate for hours worked in excess of 40 per week.

(a) Calculate Fritz's overtime rate of pay. (Compute to the nearest half cent.)
(b) Calculate Fritz's total gross weekly pay if he works 46 hours during the week.

E 8-4B (LO2)

✓ e: $78.00

COMPUTING FEDERAL INCOME TAX Using the table in Figure 8-4 on pages 289 and 290, determine the amount of federal income tax an employer should withhold weekly for employees with the following marital status, earnings, and withholding allowances:

	Marital Status	Total Weekly Earnings	Number of Allowances	Amount of Withholding
(a)	M	$546.00	4	_____
(b)	M	390.00	3	_____
(c)	S	461.39	2	_____
(d)	M	522.88	6	_____
(e)	S	612.00	0	_____

E 8-5B (LO2)

✓ 3rd row, Soc. Sec. tax: $179.80

CALCULATING SOCIAL SECURITY AND MEDICARE TAXES Assume a Social Security tax rate of 6.2% is applied to maximum earnings of $94,200 and a Medicare tax rate of 1.45% is applied to all earnings. Calculate the Social Security and Medicare taxes for the following situations:

Cumul. Pay Before Current Weekly Payroll	Current Gross Pay	Year-to-Date Earnings	Soc. Sec. Maximum	Amount Over Max. Soc. Sec.	Amount Subject to Soc. Sec.	Soc. Sec. Tax Withheld	Medicare Tax Withheld
$31,000	$1,500	_____	$94,200	_____	_____	_____	_____
53,000	2,860	_____	94,200	_____	_____	_____	_____
91,300	3,140	_____	94,200	_____	_____	_____	_____
93,600	2,920	_____	94,200	_____	_____	_____	_____

E 8-6B (LO4)

✓ Med. tax: $136.30

JOURNALIZING PAYROLL TRANSACTIONS On November 30, the payroll register of Webster & Smith indicated the following information:

Wages and Salaries Expense	$9,400.00
Employee Income Tax Payable	985.00
United Way Contributions Payable	200.00
Earnings subject to Social Security tax	9,400.00

Determine the amount of Social Security and Medicare taxes to be withheld and record the journal entry for the payroll, crediting Cash for the net pay.

E 8-7B (LO4)

✓ Cr. Cash: $5,696.54

PAYROLL JOURNAL ENTRY Journalize the following data taken from the payroll register of Himes Bakery as of June 12, 20--:

Regular earnings	$6,520.00
Overtime earnings	950.00
Deductions:	
Federal income tax	782.00
Social Security tax	463.14
Medicare tax	108.32
Pension plan	80.00
Health insurance premiums	190.00
United Way contributions	150.00

SERIES B PROBLEMS

P 8-8B (LO2/4)

✓ Net pay: $196.27

GROSS PAY, DEDUCTIONS, AND NET PAY Elyse Lin works for Columbia Industries. Her rate of pay is $9.00 per hour, and she is paid 1½ times the regular rate for all hours worked in excess of 40 per week. During the last week of January of the current year, she worked 46 hours. Lin is married and claims four withholding allowances on her W-4 form. Her weekly wages are subject to the following deductions:

(a) Employee income tax (use Figure 8-4 on pages 289 and 290)
(b) Social Security tax at 6.2%
(c) Medicare tax at 1.45%
(d) Health insurance premium, $92.00
(e) Credit union, $110.00
(f) United Way contribution, $5.00

REQUIRED

1. Compute Lin's regular pay, overtime pay, gross pay, and net pay.

2. Journalize the payment of her wages for the week ended January 31, crediting Cash for the net amount.

P 8-9B (LO2/3/4)

✓ Cr. Cash: $1,765.40

KA
KLOOSTER
& ALLEN

PAYROLL REGISTER AND PAYROLL JOURNAL ENTRY Karen Jolly operates a bakery called Karen's Cupcakes. She has five employees, all of whom are paid on a weekly basis. Karen's Cupcakes uses a payroll register, individual employee earnings records, and a general journal.

Karen's Cupcakes uses a weekly federal income tax withholding table. The payroll data for each employee for the week ended February 15, 20--, are given below. Employees are paid 1½ times the regular rate for working over 40 hours a week.

Name	No. of Allowances	Marital Status	Total Hours Worked Feb. 9–15	Rate	Total Earnings Jan. 1–Feb. 8
Barone, William	1	S	40	$10.00	$2,400.00
Hastings, Gene	4	M	45	12.00	3,360.00
Nitobe, Isako	3	M	46	8.75	2,935.00
Smith, Judy	4	M	42	11.00	2,745.00
Tarshis, Dolores	1	S	39	10.50	2,650.75

Social Security tax is withheld from the first $94,200 of earnings at the rate of 6.2%. Medicare tax is withheld at the rate of 1.45%, and city earnings tax at the rate of 1%, both applied to gross pay. Hastings and Smith have $35.00 withheld and Nitobe and Tarshis have $15.00 withheld for health insurance. Nitobe and Tarshis have $25.00 withheld to be invested in the bakers' credit union. Hastings has $18.75 withheld and Smith has $43.75 withheld under a savings bond purchase plan.

Karen's Cupcakes' payroll is met by drawing checks on its regular bank account. The checks were issued in sequence, beginning with no. 365.

REQUIRED

1. Prepare a payroll register for Karen's Cupcakes for the week ended February 15, 20--. (In the Taxable Earnings/Unemployment

Compensation column, enter the same amounts as in the Social Security column.) Total the amount columns, verify the totals, and rule with single and double lines.

2.   Assuming that the wages for the week ended February 15 were paid on February 17, prepare the journal entry for the payment of this payroll.

P 8-10B (LO3)
✓ Soc. Sec. tax: $24.80

EMPLOYEE EARNINGS RECORD Karen's Cupcakes in Problem 8-9B keeps employee earnings records. William Barone, employee number 19, is employed as a baker in the desserts department. He was born on August 26, 1959, and was hired on October 1 of last year. His social security number is 342-73-4681. He lives at 30 Timber Lane, Willington, CT 06279.

REQUIRED

For the week ended February 15, complete an employee earnings record for William Barone. (Insert earnings data only for the week of February 15.)

MANAGING YOUR WRITING

The minimum wage originally was only 25 cents an hour. Today it is $5.15 an hour. Assume that Congress is considering raising the minimum wage again and your U.S. representative is asking for public opinion on this issue. Write a letter to your representative with arguments for and against a higher minimum wage.

ETHICS CASE

Maura Lowe is a payroll accountant for N & L Company. She prepares and processes the company's payroll on a weekly basis and has been at N & L for only three months. All employees are paid on Friday. On Wednesday afternoon, Simon Lentz, one of the company's top sales associates, asks Maura to not take out any payroll deductions from his pay this week. He explains that he is short of cash and needs the full amount of his gross salary just to put food on the table and make his past-due car payment. He promises Maura that she can catch up on the deductions over the next month. The deductions include employee income tax, Social Security tax, Medicare tax, and health insurance premiums.

1.   Is Simon's request of Maura ethical? Why or why not?

2.   If this were the first pay period of the year and Maura agreed not to take out deductions from Simon's pay, what effect would this have on the liabilities section of the balance sheet?

3.   Write a short paragraph from Maura to Simon explaining how omitting deductions from a pay period will cause errors in the company's financial statements.

4.   In small groups, discuss what action Maura should take regarding Simon's request.

MASTERY PROBLEM

Abigail Trenkamp owns and operates the Trenkamp Collection Agency. Listed below are the name, number of allowances claimed, marital status, information from time cards on hours worked each day, and the hourly rate of each employee. All hours worked in excess of 40 hours for Monday through Friday are paid at 1½ times the regular rate. All weekend hours are paid at double the regular rate.

Trenkamp uses a weekly federal income tax withholding table (see Figure 8-4 on pages 289 and 290). Social Security tax is withheld at the rate of 6.2% for the first $94,200 earned. Medicare tax is withheld at 1.45% and state income tax at 3.5%. Each employee has $5.00 withheld for health insurance. All employees use payroll deduction to the credit union for varying amounts as listed below.

Trenkamp Collection Agency
Payroll Information for the Week Ended November 18, 20--

Name	Employee No.	No. of Allow.	Marital Status	Regular Hours Worked							Hourly Rate	Credit Union Deposit	Total Earnings 1/1–11/11
				S	S	M	T	W	T	F			
Berling, James	1	3	M	2	2	9	8	8	9	10	$12.00	$149.60	$24,525.00
Merz, Linda	2	4	M	4	3	8	8	8	8	11	10.00	117.00	20,480.00
Goetz, Ken	3	5	M	0	0	6	7	8	9	10	11.00	91.30	21,500.00
Menick, Judd	4	2	S	8	8	0	0	8	8	9	11.00	126.50	22,625.00
Morales, Eva	5	3	M	0	0	8	8	8	6	8	13.00	117.05	24,730.00
Heimbrock, Jacob	6	2	M	0	0	8	8	8	8	8	34.00	154.25	93,240.00
Townsley, Sarah	7	2	M	4	0	6	6	6	6	4	9.00	83.05	21,425.00
Salzman, Ben	8	4	M	6	2	8	8	6	6	6	11.00	130.00	6,635.00
Layton, Esther	9	4	M	0	0	8	8	8	8	8	11.00	88.00	5,635.00
Thompson, David	10	5	M	0	2	10	9	7	7	10	11.00	128.90	21,635.00
Vadillo, Carmen	11	2	S	8	0	4	8	8	8	9	13.00	139.11	24,115.00

The Trenkamp Collection Agency follows the practice of drawing a single check for the net amount of the payroll and depositing the check in a special payroll account at the bank. Individual checks issued were numbered consecutively, beginning with no. 331.

REQUIRED

1. Prepare a payroll register for Trenkamp Collection Agency for the week ended November 18, 20--. (In the Taxable Earnings/Unemployment Compensation column, enter $365 for Salzman and $440 for Layton. Leave this column blank for all other employees.) Total the amount columns, verify the totals, and rule with single and double lines.

2. Assuming that the wages for the week ended November 18 were paid on November 21, prepare the journal entry for the payment of this payroll.

3. The current employee earnings record for Ben Salzman is provided in the working papers. Update Salzman's earnings record to reflect the November 18 payroll. Although this information should have been entered earlier, complete the required information on the earnings record. The necessary information is as follows:

Name   Ben F. Salzman
Address   12 Windmill Lane
                              Trumbull, CT 06611
Employee No.   8
Gender   Male
Department   Administration
Occupation   Office Manager
Social Security No.   446-46-6321
Marital Status   Married
Allowances   4
Pay Rate $11.00 per hour
Date of Birth   4/5/64
Date Hired   7/22/--

CHALLENGE PROBLEM

This problem challenges you to apply your cumulative accounting knowledge to move a step beyond the material in the chapter.

✓ **Dr. Wages and Salaries Expense: $1,596**

Irina Company pays its employees weekly. The last pay period for 20-1 was on December 28. From December 28 through December 31, the employees earned $1,754.00, so the following adjusting entry was made:

	20-1													
5	Dec.	31	Wages and Salaries Expense		1 7 5 4 00				5
6			Wages and Salaries Payable				1 7 5 4 00	6
7			To record accrued wages and salaries					7

The first pay period in 20-2 was on January 4. The totals line from Irina Company's payroll register for the week ended January 4, 20-2, was as follows:

PAYROLL

			EARNINGS				TAXABLE EARNINGS	
			REGULAR	OVERTIME	TOTAL	CUMULATIVE TOTAL	UNEMPLOYMENT COMPENSATION	SOCIAL SECURITY
1	Totals		3 3 5 0 00		3 3 5 0 00	3 3 5 0 00	3 3 5 0 00	3 3 5 0 00	1

REGISTER—WEEK ENDED January 4, 20-2

	DEDUCTIONS						NET PAY
	FEDERAL INCOME TAX	SOCIAL SECURITY TAX	MEDICARE TAX	HEALTH INSURANCE	UNITED WAY	OTHER	TOTAL	
1	3 4 2 00	2 0 7 70	4 8 58	5 0 00	8 0 00		7 2 8 28	2 6 2 1 72	1

REQUIRED

1. Prepare the journal entry for the payment of the payroll on January 4, 20-2.

2. Prepare T accounts for Wages and Salaries Expense and Wages and Salaries Payable showing the beginning balance, January 4, 20-2, entry, and ending balance as of January 4, 20-2.

Objectives

Careful study of this chapter should enable you to:

LO1
Describe and calculate employer payroll taxes.

LO2
Account for employer payroll taxes expense.

LO3
Describe employer reporting and payment responsibilities.

LO4
Describe and account for workers' compensation insurance.

Payroll Accounting: Employer Taxes and Reports

Evan Taylor's new shop assistant has worked out extremely well. Parkway Pet Supplies is better organized, and customers receive more direct attention. Having worked in a store in another state, the new hire also was able to help Evan obtain accounts with two new vendors. The only negative feature of having the new employee has been the cost. Based on 25 hours per week at $8 an hour, Evan had budgeted a cost of $200 per week for help. In fact, as Evan's bookkeeper had warned him, the cost is substantially higher. In simple terms, Evan has discovered that he must pay numerous payroll taxes, in addition to the basic wages of the employee. What payroll taxes must Evan pay as an employer? Assuming the employee works a full year and is paid $10,400 (52 weeks × $200), what is the total payroll cost to Evan of having this employee?

The taxes we discussed in Chapter 8 had one thing in common—they all were levied on the employee. The employer withheld them from employees' earnings and paid them to the government. They did not add anything to the employer's payroll expenses.

In this chapter, we will examine several taxes that are imposed directly on the employer. All of these taxes represent additional payroll expenses.

EMPLOYER PAYROLL TAXES

LO1 Describe and calculate employer payroll taxes.

Most employers must pay FICA, FUTA (Federal Unemployment Tax Act), and SUTA (state unemployment tax) taxes.

Employer FICA Taxes

Employer FICA taxes are levied on employers at the same rates and on the same earnings bases as the employee FICA taxes. As explained in Chapter 8, we are assuming the Social Security component is 6.2% on maximum earnings of $94,200 for each employee. Since there is no maximum on the Medicare component, this tax is 1.45% on all earnings.

The payroll register we saw in Chapter 8 is a key source of information for computing employer payroll taxes. That payroll register is reproduced in Figure 9-1. The Taxable Earnings Social Security column shows that $4,835 of employee earnings were subject to Social Security tax for the pay period. The employer's Social Security tax on these earnings is computed as follows:

FIGURE 9-1 Payroll Register (left side)

PAYROLL

	NAME	ALLOWANCES	MARITAL STATUS	EARNINGS REGULAR	EARNINGS OVERTIME	EARNINGS TOTAL	CUMULATIVE TOTAL	TAXABLE EARNINGS UNEMPLOYMENT COMPENSATION	TAXABLE EARNINGS SOCIAL SECURITY	
1	Cadrain, Sarah	4	M	1 6 0 0 00	6 0 00	1 6 6 0 00	95 2 0 0 00		6 6 0 00	1
2	Guder, James	1	S	7 6 0 00	1 4 0 00	9 0 0 00	43 4 0 0 00		9 0 0 00	2
3	Istone, Ken	6	M	5 4 5 00		5 4 5 00	27 0 2 5 00		5 4 5 00	3
4	Kuzmik, Helen	2	M	4 8 0 00	2 9 4 00	7 7 4 00	31 0 0 0 00		7 7 4 00	4
5	Lee, Hoseoup	3	M	4 4 0 00		4 4 0 00	22 3 4 0 00		4 4 0 00	5
6	Swaney, Linda	2	S	5 2 8 00	1 9 8 00	7 2 6 00	27 5 0 0 00		7 2 6 00	6
7	Tucci, Paul	5	M	4 9 0 00		4 9 0 00	25 0 5 0 00		4 9 0 00	7
8	Wiles, Harry	1	S	3 0 0 00		3 0 0 00	6 3 0 0 00	3 0 0 00	3 0 0 00	8
9	Totals			5 1 4 3 00	6 9 2 00	5 8 3 5 00	277 8 1 5 00	3 0 0 00	4 8 3 5 00	9

Time cards, pay rates

Prior period total + current period earnings

Current below $7,000 cumul. total

Current below $94,200 cumul. total

LEARNING KEY

Use the information in the payroll register to compute employer payroll taxes.

Social Security Taxable Earnings	×	Tax Rate	=	Tax
$4,835		0.062		$299.77

The Medicare tax applies to the total earnings of $5,835. The employer's Medicare tax on these earnings is computed as follows:

Total Earnings	×	Tax Rate	=	Tax
$5,835		0.0145		$84.61

These amounts plus the employees' Social Security and Medicare taxes withheld must be paid by the employer to the Internal Revenue Service (IRS).

Self-Employment Tax

The self-employment tax rate is double the employee and employer Social Security and Medicare rates because the self-employed person is considered both the employer and employee.

Individuals who own and run their own business are considered self-employed. These individuals can be viewed as both employer and employee. They do not receive salary or wages from the business, but they do have earnings in the form of the business net income. **Self-employment income** is the net income of a trade or business run by an individual. Currently, persons earning net self-employment income of $400 or more must pay a **self-employment tax**. Self-employment tax is a contribution to the FICA program. The tax rates are double the Social Security and Medicare rates. They are applied to the same income bases as those used for the Social Security and Medicare taxes.

FIGURE 9-1   Payroll Register (right side)

REGISTER—WEEK ENDED 12/19/--

	FEDERAL INCOME TAX	SOCIAL SECURITY TAX	MEDICARE TAX	HEALTH INSURANCE	UNITED WAY	OTHER	TOTAL	NET PAY	CHECK NO.	
1	1 8 4 00	4 0 92	2 4 07				2 4 8 99	1 4 1 1 01	409	1
2	1 3 4 00	5 5 80	1 3 05		2 0 00		2 2 2 85	6 7 7 15	410	2
3	1 00	3 3 79	7 90	1 0 00			5 2 69	4 9 2 31	411	3
4	6 0 00	4 7 99	1 1 22	1 3 00	2 0 00		1 5 2 21	6 2 1 79	412	4
5	1 0 00	2 7 28	6 38	1 3 00			5 6 66	3 8 3 34	413	5
6	7 5 00	4 5 01	1 0 53				1 3 0 54	5 9 5 46	414	6
7	2 00	3 0 38	7 11	1 0 00			4 9 49	4 4 0 51	415	7
8	2 2 00	1 8 60	4 35				4 4 95	2 5 5 05	416	8
9	4 8 8 00	2 9 9 77	8 4 61	4 6 00	4 0 00		9 5 8 38	4 8 7 6 62		9

Withholding Tax Table

6.2% × Social Security taxable earnings

1.45% × total earnings

Specific employer–employee agreements

Total earnings – total deductions

Employer FUTA Tax

The **FUTA (Federal Unemployment Tax Act) tax** is levied only on employers. It is not deducted from employees' earnings. The purpose of this tax is to raise funds to administer the combined federal/state unemployment compensation program. The maximum amount of earnings subject to the FUTA tax and the tax rate can be changed by Congress. The current rate is 6.2% applied to maximum earnings of $7,000 for each employee, but employers are allowed a credit of up to 5.4% for participation in state unemployment programs. Thus, the effective federal rate is commonly 0.8%.

Gross FUTA rate	6.2%
Credit for state unemployment taxes	5.4%
Net FUTA rate	0.8%

To illustrate the computation of the FUTA tax, refer to Figure 9-1. The Taxable Earnings Unemployment Compensation column shows that only $300 of employee earnings were subject to the FUTA tax. This amount is low because the payroll period is late in the calendar year (December 19, 20--). It is common for most employees to exceed the $7,000 earnings limit by this time. The FUTA tax is computed as shown in Figure 9-2.

FIGURE 9-2   Computation of FUTA Tax

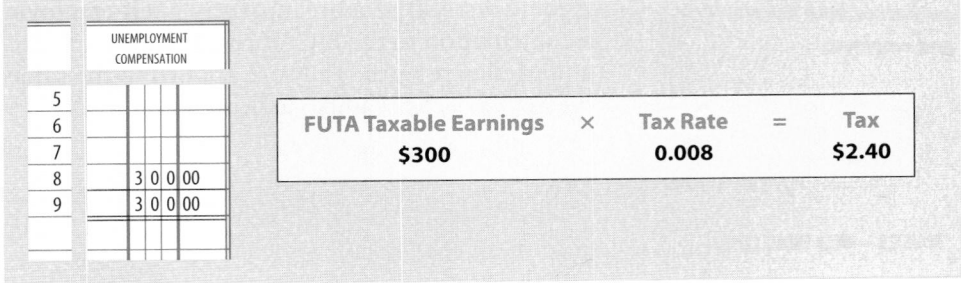

Employer SUTA Tax

The **SUTA (state unemployment tax) tax** is also levied only on employers in most states. The purpose of this tax is to raise funds to pay unemployment benefits. Tax rates and unemployment benefits vary among the states. A common rate is 5.4% applied to maximum earnings of $7,000 for each employee. Most states have a **merit-rating system** to encourage employers to provide regular employment to workers. If an employer has very few former employees receiving unemployment compensation, the employer qualifies for a lower state unemployment tax rate. If an employer qualifies for a lower state rate, the full credit of 5.4% would still be allowed in computing the federal unemployment tax due.

Refer to the payroll register in Figure 9-1. As we saw with the FUTA tax, only $300 of employee earnings for this pay period are subject to the state unemployment tax. The tax is computed as shown in Figure 9-3.

State unemployment tax rates and maximum earnings amounts vary greatly. Current rates range from 4.5% to 10%. Maximum earnings amounts are $7,000 to $29,300.

FIGURE 9-3   Computation of SUTA Tax

	UNEMPLOYMENT COMPENSATION	
5		
6		
7		
8	3 0 0 00	
9	3 0 0 00	

State Unemployment Taxable Earnings × Tax Rate = Tax
$300   0.054 $16.20

ACCOUNTING FOR EMPLOYER PAYROLL TAXES

LO2 Account for employer payroll taxes expense.

Now that we have computed the employer payroll taxes, we need to journalize them. It is common to debit all employer payroll taxes to a single account—Payroll Taxes Expense. However, we usually credit separate liability accounts for Social Security, Medicare, FUTA, and SUTA taxes payable.

Journalizing Employer Payroll Taxes

The employer payroll taxes computed in the previous section can be summarized as follows:

Employer's Social Security tax	$299.77
Employer's Medicare tax	84.61
FUTA tax	2.40
SUTA tax	16.20
Total employer payroll taxes	$402.98

These amounts provide the basis for the following journal entry:

5	Dec.	19	Payroll Taxes Expense		4 0 2 98			5
6			Social Security Tax Payable			2 9 9 77		6
7			Medicare Tax Payable			8 4 61		7
8			FUTA Tax Payable			2 40		8
9			SUTA Tax Payable			1 6 20		9
10			Employer payroll taxes for week ended Dec. 19					10

The steps needed to prepare this journal entry for employer payroll taxes are:

STEP 1 Obtain the total earnings and taxable earnings amounts from the Earnings—Total and Taxable Earnings columns of the payroll register. In this case, total earnings were $5,835; Social Security taxable earnings were $4,835; and Unemployment Compensation taxable earnings were $300.

STEP 2 Compute the amount of employer Social Security tax by multiplying the Social Security taxable earnings by 6.2%.

STEP 3 Compute the amount of employer Medicare tax by multiplying total earnings by 1.45%.

STEP 4 Compute the amount of FUTA tax by multiplying the Unemployment Taxable earnings by 0.8%.

STEP 5 Compute the amount of SUTA tax by multiplying the Unemployment Taxable earnings by 5.4%.

STEP 6 Prepare the appropriate journal entry using the amounts computed in steps 2–5.

To understand the journal entry for employer payroll taxes, let's use the accounting equation to examine the accounts involved. The five accounts affected by the payroll taxes entry above are shown in the accounting equation in Figure 9-4.

FIGURE 9-4   Accounting for Payroll Taxes

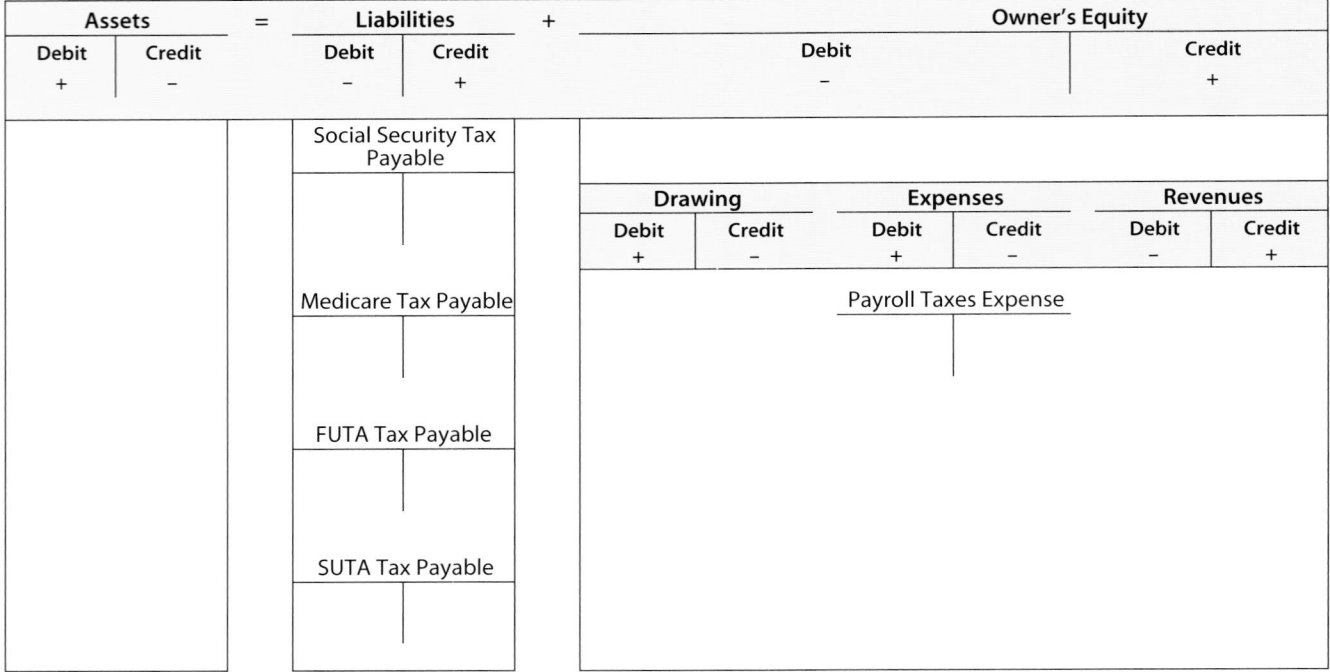

Payroll Taxes Expense

The Social Security, Medicare, FUTA, and SUTA taxes imposed on the employer are expenses of doing business. Each of the employer taxes is debited to Payroll Taxes Expense.

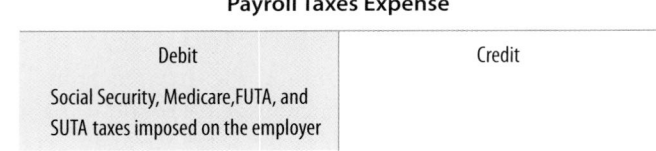

Social Security and Medicare Taxes Payable

These are the same liability accounts used in Chapter 8 to record the Social Security and Medicare taxes withheld from employees' earnings. The accounts are credited to enter the Social Security and Medicare taxes imposed on the employer. They are debited when the taxes are paid to the IRS. When all of the Social Security and Medicare taxes have been paid, the accounts will have zero balances.

Social Security Tax Payable

Debit	Credit
Payment of Social Security tax	Social Security taxes (1) withheld from employees' earnings and (2) imposed on the employer

Medicare Tax Payable

Debit	Credit
Payment of Medicare tax	Medicare taxes (1) with-held from employees' earnings and (2) imposed on the employer

FUTA Tax Payable

A separate liability account entitled FUTA Tax Payable is kept for the employer's FUTA tax. This account is credited for the tax imposed on employers under the Federal Unemployment Tax Act. The account is debited when this tax is paid. When all of the FUTA taxes have been paid, the account will have a zero balance.

FUTA Tax Payable

Debit	Credit
Payment of FUTA tax	FUTA tax imposed on the employer

SUTA Tax Payable

A separate liability account entitled SUTA Tax Payable is kept for the state unemployment tax. This account is credited for the tax imposed on employers under the state unemployment compensation laws. The account is debited when this tax is paid. When all of the state unemployment taxes have been paid, the account will have a zero balance.

SUTA Tax Payable

Debit	Credit
Payment of SUTA tax	SUTA tax imposed on the employer

Total Payroll Cost of an Employee

It is interesting to note what it really costs to employ a person. The employer must, of course, pay the gross wages of an employee. In addition, the employer must pay payroll taxes on employee earnings up to certain dollar limits.

To illustrate, assume that an employee earns $26,000 a year. The total cost of this employee to the employer is calculated as follows:

Gross wages	$26,000
Employer Social Security tax, 6.2% of $26,000	1,612
Employer Medicare tax, 1.45% of $26,000	377
State unemployment tax, 5.4% of $7,000	378
FUTA tax, 0.8% of $7,000	56
	$28,423

Thus, the total payroll cost of employing a person whose stated compensation is $26,000 is $28,423. Employer payroll taxes clearly are a significant cost of doing business. Employer-paid medical insurance and pension plans can further increase total payroll costs.

REPORTING AND PAYMENT RESPONSIBILITIES

LO3 Describe employer reporting and payment responsibilities.

Employer payroll reporting and payment responsibilities fall into five areas:

1. Federal income tax withholding and Social Security and Medicare taxes
2. FUTA taxes
3. SUTA taxes
4. Employee Wage and Tax Statement (Form W-2)
5. Summary of employee wages and taxes

Federal Income Tax Withholding and Social Security and Medicare Taxes

Three important aspects of employer reporting and payment responsibilities for federal income tax withholding and Social Security and Medicare taxes are:

1. Determining when payments are due
2. Use of Form 8109, Federal Tax Deposit Coupon
3. Use of Form 941, Employer's Quarterly Federal Tax Return

When Payments Are Due

The date by which federal income tax withholding and Social Security and Medicare taxes must be paid depends on the amount of these taxes. Figure 9-5 summarizes the deposit rules stated in *Circular E—Employer's Tax Guide*. In general, the larger the amount that needs to be deposited, the more frequently payments must be made. For simplicity, we will assume that deposits must be made 15 days after the end of each month.

FIGURE 9-5   Summary of Deposit Rules

ACCUMULATED TAX LIABILITY	DEPOSIT DUE
1. Less than $2,500 at the end of the current quarter	1. Pay with Form 941 at end of the month following end of the quarter
2. $2,500 or more at the end of the current quarter and $50,000 or less in total during the lookback period*	2. Deposit 15 days after end of the month
3. $2,500 or more at the end of the current quarter and more than $50,000 in total during the lookback period*	3. Deposit every other Wednesday or Friday, depending on day of the week payroll payments are made
4. $100,000 or more on any day during the current quarter	4. Deposit by the end of the next banking day

*Lookback period is the four quarters beginning July 1, two years ago, and ending June 30, one year ago.

Form 8109

Taxpayers who are not required to make electronic deposits may voluntarily participate in EFTPS.

Deposits may be made using either the **Electronic Federal Tax Payment System (EFTPS)** or Form 8109. The EFTPS is an electronic funds transfer system for making federal tax deposits. Any taxpayer whose deposits in the prior year exceeded $200,000 is required to use this system. Deposits other than EFTPS are made at an authorized commercial bank using Form 8109, Federal Tax Deposit Coupon (Figure 9-6). The **Employer Identification Number (EIN)** shown on this form is obtained by the employer from the IRS. This number identifies the employer and must be shown on all payroll forms and reports filed with the IRS.

FIGURE 9-6   Federal Tax Deposit Coupon (Form 8109)

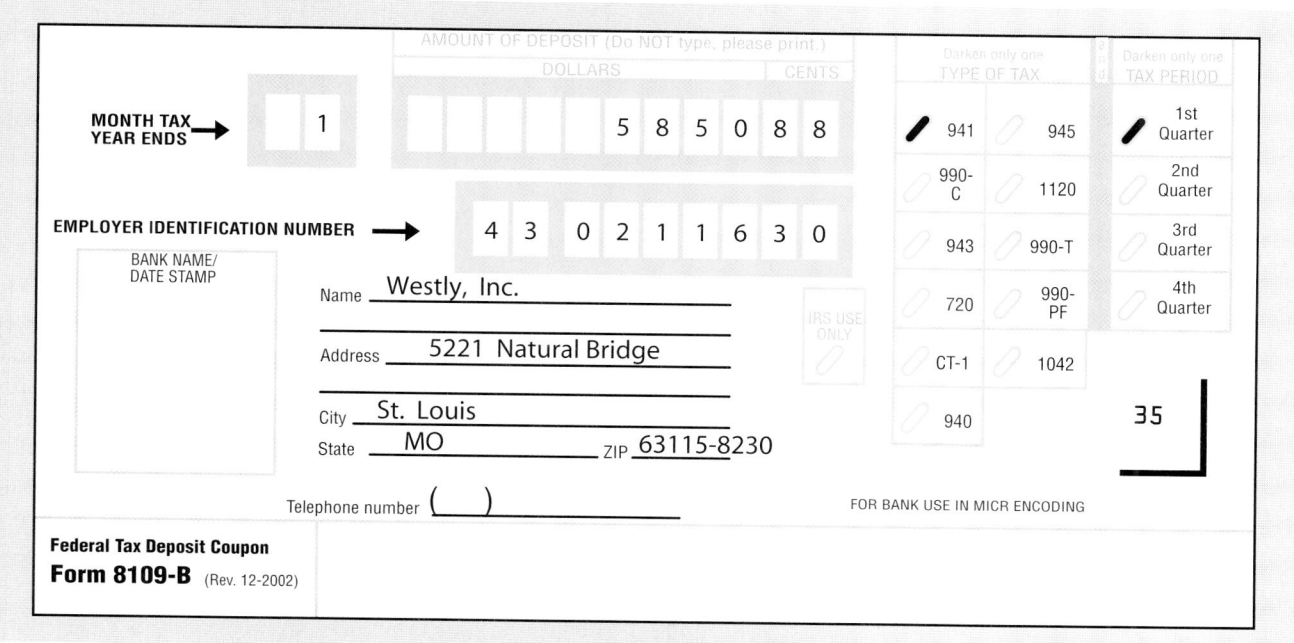

The $5,850.88 deposit shown in Figure 9-6 for Westly, Inc., was for the following taxes:

Employees' income tax withheld from wages		$2,526.80
Social Security tax:		
Withheld from employees' wages	$1,346.24	
Imposed on employer	1,346.24	2,692.48
Medicare tax:		
Withheld from employees' wages	$ 315.80	
Imposed on employer	315.80	631.60
Amount of check		$5,850.88

The journal entry for this deposit would be as follows:

5	Feb.	15	Employee Income Tax Payable	2 5 2 6 80		5
6			Social Security Tax Payable	2 6 9 2 48		6
7			Medicare Tax Payable	6 3 1 60		7
8			Cash		5 8 5 0 88	8
9			Deposit of employee federal income tax and			9
10			Social Security and Medicare taxes			10

Form 941

Form 941, Employer's Quarterly Federal Tax Return, must be filed with the IRS at the end of the month following each calendar quarter. This form reports the following taxes for the quarter:

1. Employee federal income tax withheld
2. Employee Social Security and Medicare taxes withheld
3. Employer Social Security and Medicare taxes

A completed form for Westly, Inc., for the first quarter of the calendar year is shown in Figure 9-7. Instructions for completing the form are provided with the form and in *Circular E.*

FUTA Taxes

Federal unemployment taxes must be calculated on a quarterly basis. If the accumulated liability exceeds $500, the total must be paid to an authorized commercial bank. The total is due by the end of the month following the close of the quarter. If the liability is $500 or less, no deposit is necessary. The amount is simply added to the amount to be deposited for the next quarter. FUTA taxes are deposited using either EFTPS or Form 8109 (Figure 9-6).

Assume that an employer's accumulated FUTA tax liability for the first quarter of the calendar year is $508. The employer would use Form 8109 to deposit this amount on April 30. The journal entry for this transaction would be as follows:

15	Apr.	30	FUTA Tax Payable	5 0 8 00		15
16			Cash		5 0 8 00	16
17			Paid federal unemployment tax			17

FIGURE 9-7   Employer's Quarterly Federal Tax Return (Form 941)

Form **941 for 2006:** **Employer's QUARTERLY Federal Tax Return**   950106
(Rev. January 2006)   Department of the Treasury — Internal Revenue Service
OMB No. 1545-0029

(EIN)
Employer identification number   4 3 – 0 2 1 1 6 3 0

Report for this Quarter ...
(Check one.)

Name (not your trade name)

Trade name (if any)   Westly, Inc.

[X] **1:** January, February, March

[ ] **2:** April, May, June

Address   5221 Natural Bridge
Number   Street   Suite or room number

[ ] **3:** July, August, September

St. Louis   MO   63115-8230
City   State   ZIP code

[ ] **4:** October, November, December

Read the separate instructions before you fill out this form. Please type or print within the boxes.

Part 1: Answer these questions for this quarter.

1 Number of employees who received wages, tips, or other compensation for the pay period
including: *Mar. 12* (Quarter 1), *June 12* (Quarter 2), *Sept. 12* (Quarter 3), *Dec. 12* (Quarter 4)   **1**   8

2 Wages, tips, and other compensation **2**   65,160.00

3 Total income tax withheld from wages, tips, and other compensation **3**   7,595.80

4 If no wages, tips, and other compensation are subject to social security or Medicare tax   .   [ ] Check and go to line 6.

5 Taxable social security and Medicare wages and tips:

		Column 1		Column 2
5a	Taxable social security wages	65,160.00	× .124 =	8,079.84
5b	Taxable social security tips	.	× .124 =	.
5c	Taxable Medicare wages & tips	65,160.00	× .029 =	1,889.64

5d Total social security and Medicare taxes (*Column 2*, lines 5a + 5b + 5c = line 5d)   .   **5d**   9,969.48

6 Total taxes before adjustments (lines 3 + 5d = line 6) **6**   17,565.28

7 **TAX ADJUSTMENTS** (Read the instructions for line 7 before completing lines 7a through 7h.):

7a Current quarter's fractions of cents   .   .   .   .

7b Current quarter's sick pay   .   .   .   .

7c Current quarter's adjustments for tips and group-term life insurance   .

7d Current year's income tax withholding (attach Form 941c)   .   .

7e Prior quarters' social security and Medicare taxes (attach Form 941c)

7f Special additions to federal income tax (attach Form 941c)   .   .   .

7g Special additions to social security and Medicare (attach Form 941c)

7h **TOTAL ADJUSTMENTS** (Combine all amounts: lines 7a through 7g.)   .   .   .   .   **7h**   . 0

8 Total taxes after adjustments (Combine lines 6 and 7h.) **8**   17,565.28

9 Advance earned income credit (EIC) payments made to employees   .   .   .   .   **9**   . 0

10 Total taxes after adjustment for advance EIC (line 8 – line 9 = line 10) **10**   17,565.28

11 Total deposits for this quarter, including overpayment applied from a prior quarter   .   .   **11**   17,565.28

12 **Balance due** (If line 10 is more than line 11, write the difference here.)   .   .   .   .   **12**   . 0
Make checks payable to *United States Treasury.*

13 **Overpayment** (If line 11 is more than line 10, write the difference here.)   .   [ ] Check one [ ] Apply to next return.
[ ] Send a refund.

▶ You **MUST** fill out both pages of this form and **SIGN** it.   Next ➡

For Privacy Act and Paperwork Reduction Act Notice, see the back of the Payment Voucher.   Cat. No. 17001Z   Form **941** (Rev. 1-2006)

FIGURE 9-7   Employer's Quarterly Federal Tax Return (Form 941) *(continued)*

990206

Name *(not your trade name)*   **Employer identification number (EIN)**

Part 2: Tell us about your deposit schedule and tax liability for this quarter.

If you are unsure about whether you are a monthly schedule depositor or a semiweekly schedule depositor, see *Pub. 15 (Circular E),* section 11.

14 | M | O | Write the state abbreviation for the state where you made your deposits OR write "MU" if you made your deposits in *multiple* states.

15   Check one: ☐   Line 10 is less than $2,500. Go to Part 3.

☒   You were a monthly schedule depositor for the entire quarter. Fill out your tax liability for each month. Then go to Part 3.

Tax liability:	Month 1	5,850.88
	Month 2	5,690.77
	Month 3	6,023.63
Total liability for quarter		17,565.28	Total must equal line 10.

☐   You were a semiweekly schedule depositor for any part of this quarter. Fill out *Schedule B (Form 941): Report of Tax Liability for Semiweekly Schedule Depositors,* and attach it to this form.

Part 3: Tell us about your business. If a question does NOT apply to your business, leave it blank.

16   If your business has closed or you stopped paying wages   . . . .   ☐ Check here, and

enter the final date you paid wages | / / | .

17   If you are a seasonal employer and you do not have to file a return for every quarter of the year   .   ☐ Check here.

Part 4: May we speak with your third-party designee?

Do you want to allow an employee, a paid tax preparer, or another person to discuss this return with the IRS? See the instructions for details.

☐ Yes. Designee's name

Phone   ( )   –   Personal Identification Number (PIN)   ☐ ☐ ☐ ☐ ☐

☒ No.

Part 5: Sign here. You MUST fill out both sides of this form and SIGN it.

Under penalties of perjury, I declare that I have examined this return, including accompanying schedules and statements, and to the best of my knowledge and belief, it is true, correct, and complete.

✗ Sign your name here   *William P. Jones*

Print name and title   *William P. Jones   Treasurer*

Date   *4 / 30 /--*   Phone   ( )   –

Part 6: For PAID preparers only *(optional)*

Paid Preparer's Signature	
Firm's name	
Address		EIN
		ZIP code
Date	/ / Phone ( ) –	SSN/PTIN

☐ Check if you are self-employed.

Page **2**   Form **941** (Rev. 1-2006)

Form 940

In addition to making quarterly deposits, employers are required to file an annual report of federal unemployment tax using Form 940 or 940-EZ, a simplified version of Form 940. Form 940-EZ (Figure 9-8) may be used by employers who pay

FIGURE 9-8 Employer's Annual Federal Unemployment (FUTA) Tax Return (Form 940-EZ)

Form **940-EZ**
Department of the Treasury
Internal Revenue Service

Employer's Annual Federal Unemployment (FUTA) Tax Return

▶ **See the separate Instructions for Form 940-EZ for information on completing this form.**

OMB No. 1545-1110
2005

You must complete this section.

Name (as distinguished from trade name)
Trade name, if any
Westly, Inc.
Address (number and street)
5221 Natural Bridge, St. Louis, MO 63115-8230

Calendar year
Employer identification number (EIN)
43-0211630
City, state, and ZIP code

T	
FF	
FD	
FP	
I	
T	

*Answer the questions under **Who May Use Form 940-EZ** on page 2. If you cannot use Form 940-EZ, you must use Form 940.*

A Enter the amount of contributions paid to your state unemployment fund (see the separate instructions) ▶ $ 3,007.80

B (1) Enter the name of the state where you have to pay contributions ▶ MO

(2) Enter your state reporting number as shown on your state unemployment tax return. ▶ 36112

If you will not have to file returns in the future, check here (see **Who Must File** in separate instructions) **and complete and sign the return.** ▶ ☐

If this is an Amended Return, check here (see **Amended Returns** in the separate instructions) ▶ ☐

Part I Taxable Wages and FUTA Tax

1	Total payments (including payments shown on lines 2 and 3) during the calendar year for services of employees			1	258,954 00
2	Exempt payments. (Explain all exempt payments, attaching additional sheets if necessary.) ▶	2			
3	Payments of more than $7,000 for services. Enter only amounts over the first $7,000 paid to each employee **(see the separate instructions)**	3	203,254 00		
4	Add lines 2 and 3			4	203,254 00
5	**Total taxable wages** (subtract line 4 from line 1) ▶			5	55,700 00
6	**FUTA tax.** Multiply the wages on line 5 by .008 and enter here. **(If the result is over $500, also complete Part II.)**			6	445 60
7	Total FUTA tax deposited for the year, including any overpayment applied from a prior year			7	427 60
8	**Balance due** (subtract line 7 from line 6). Pay to the "United States Treasury." ▶ If you owe more than $500, see **Depositing FUTA tax** in the separate instructions.			8	18 00
9	**Overpayment** (subtract line 6 from line 7). Check if it is to be: ☐ **Applied to next return** or ☐ **Refunded** ▶			9	

Part II Record of Quarterly Federal Unemployment Tax Liability (Do not include state liability.) **Complete only if line 6 is over $500.**

Quarter	First (Jan. 1 – Mar. 31)	Second (Apr. 1 – June 30)	Third (July 1 – Sept. 30)	Fourth (Oct. 1 – Dec. 31)	Total for year
Liability for quarter					

Third-Party Designee

Do you want to allow another person to discuss this return with the IRS (see the separate instructions)? ☐ **Yes.** Complete the following. ☐ **No**

Designee's name ▶ Phone no. ▶ ( ) Personal identification number (PIN) ▶

Under penalties of perjury, I declare that I have examined this return, including accompanying schedules and statements, and, to the best of my knowledge and belief, it is true, correct, and complete, and that no part of any payment made to a state unemployment fund claimed as a credit was, or is to be, deducted from the payments to employees.

Signature ▶ *William P. Jones* **Title (Owner, etc.)** ▶ *Treasurer* **Date** ▶ *1/31/--*

For Privacy Act and Paperwork Reduction Act Notice, see the separate instructions. ▼ **DETACH HERE** ▼ Cat. No. 10983G Form **940-EZ** (2005)

Form **940-V(EZ)**
Department of the Treasury
Internal Revenue Service

Payment Voucher

Use this voucher only when making a payment with your return.

OMB No. 1545-1110
2005

Complete boxes 1, 2, and 3. Do not send cash, and do not staple your payment to this voucher. Make your check or money order payable to the "United States Treasury." Be sure to enter your employer identification number (EIN), "Form 940-EZ," and "2005" on your payment.

1 Enter your employer identification number (EIN).

2 **Enter the amount of your payment.** ▶ Dollars Cents

3 Enter your business name (individual name for sole proprietors).

Enter your address.

Enter your city, state, and ZIP code.

unemployment contributions in only one state and have made all the payments by January 31. This form must be filed with the IRS by January 31 following the end of the calendar year. Figure 9-8 shows a completed Form 940-EZ for Westly, Inc. Instructions for completing the form are provided with the form and in *Circular E.*

SUTA Taxes

Deposit rules and forms for state unemployment taxes vary among the states. Deposits usually are required on a quarterly basis. Assume that Westly's accumulated state unemployment liability for the first quarter of the calendar year is $2,754. The journal entry for the deposit of this amount with the state on April 30 would be as follows:

19	Apr.	30	SUTA Tax Payable		2 7 5 4 00		19
20			Cash			2 7 5 4 00	20
21			Paid state unemployment tax				21

Employee Wage and Tax Statement

By January 31 of each year, employers must furnish each employee with a Wage and Tax Statement, Form W-2 (Figure 9-9). This form shows the total amount of wages paid to the employee and the amounts of taxes withheld during the preceding taxable year. The employee earnings record contains the information needed to complete this form.

FIGURE 9-9 Wage and Tax Statement (Form W-2)

a Control number 33333 Void ☐ For Official Use Only ▶ OMB No. 1545-0008

b Employer identification number 43 0211630

c Employer's name, address, and ZIP code
Westly, Inc.
5221 Natural Bridge
St. Louis, MO 63115-8230

d Employee's social security number 393-58-8194

e Employee's first name and initial Ken M. Last name Istone

1546 Swallow Dr.
St. Louis, MO 63144-4752

f Employee's address and ZIP code

Box	Amount	Box	Amount
1 Wages, tips, other compensation	$ 27,645.00	2 Federal income tax withheld	$ 528.00
3 Social security wages	$ 27,645.00	4 Social security tax withheld	$ 1,713.99
5 Medicare wages and tips	$ 27,645.00	6 Medicare tax withheld	$ 400.85
7 Social security tips	$	8 Allocated tips	$
9 Advance EIC payment	$	10 Dependent care benefits	$
11 Nonqualified plans	$	12a See instructions for box 12	$
13 Statutory employee ☐ Retirement plan ☐ Third-party sick pay ☐		12b	$
14 Other		12c	$
		12d	$

15 State	Employeris state ID number	16 State wages, tips, etc.	17 State income tax	18 Local wages, tips, etc.	19 Local income tax	20 Locality name
		$	$	$	$	
		$	$	$	$	

Form **W-2** Wage and Tax Statement (99) 20-- Department of the Treasury—Internal Revenue Service

Copy A For Social Security Administrationó Send this entire page with Form W-3 to the Social Security Administration; photocopies are **not** acceptable.

(Rev. February 2002) Cat. No. 10134D

For Privacy Act and Paperwork Reduction Act Notice, see separate instructions.

Do Not Cut, Fold, or Staple Forms on This Page—Do Not Cut, Fold, or Staple Forms on This Page

Multiple copies of Form W-2 are needed for the following purposes:

- Copy A—Employer sends to Social Security Administration
- Copy B—Employee attaches to federal income tax return
- Copy C—Employee retains for his or her own records

- Copy D—Employer retains for business records
- Copy 1—Employer sends to state or local tax department
- Copy 2—Employee attaches to state, city, or local income tax return

Summary of Employee Wages and Taxes

Employers send Form W-3, Transmittal of Wage and Tax Statements (Figure 9-10), with Copy A of Forms W-2 to the Social Security Administration. Form W-3 must be filed by February 28 following the end of each taxable year. This form summarizes the employee earnings and tax information presented on Forms W-2 for the year. Information needed to complete Form W-3 is contained in the employee earnings records.

FIGURE 9-10 Transmittal of Wage and Tax Statements (Form W-3)

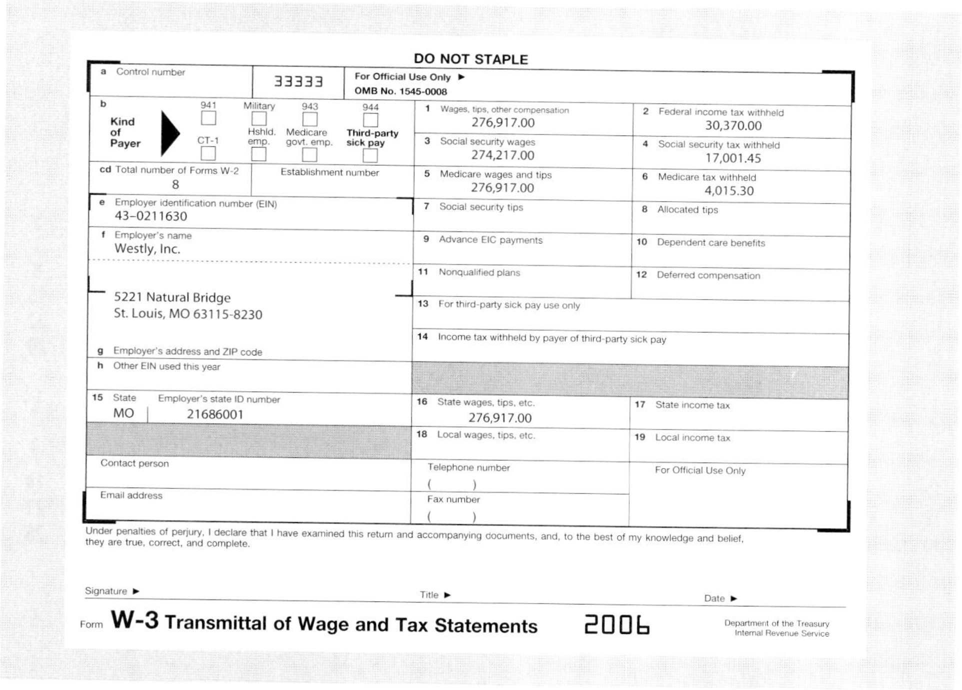

DO NOT STAPLE

a Control number 33333 For Official Use Only ► OMB No. 1545-0008

b Kind of Payer: 941 ☐ Military ☐ 943 ☐ 944 ☐ CT-1 ☐ Hshld. emp. ☐ Medicare govt. emp. ☐ Third-party sick pay ☐

1 Wages, tips, other compensation 276,917.00
2 Federal income tax withheld 30,370.00
3 Social security wages 274,217.00
4 Social security tax withheld 17,001.45
5 Medicare wages and tips 276,917.00
6 Medicare tax withheld 4,015.30
7 Social security tips
8 Allocated tips
9 Advance EIC payments
10 Dependent care benefits
11 Nonqualified plans
12 Deferred compensation
13 For third-party sick pay use only
14 Income tax withheld by payer of third-party sick pay

cd Total number of Forms W-2 8
Establishment number
e Employer identification number (EIN) 43-0211630
f Employer's name Westly, Inc.
5221 Natural Bridge
St. Louis, MO 63115-8230
g Employer's address and ZIP code
h Other EIN used this year

15 State MO Employer's state ID number 21686001
16 State wages, tips, etc. 276,917.00
17 State income tax
18 Local wages, tips, etc.
19 Local income tax

Contact person
Telephone number ( )
For Official Use Only
Email address
Fax number ( )

Under penalties of perjury, I declare that I have examined this return and accompanying documents, and, to the best of my knowledge and belief, they are true, correct, and complete.

Signature ► Title ► Date ►

Form **W-3 Transmittal of Wage and Tax Statements** 2006 Department of the Treasury Internal Revenue Service

Summary of Taxes, Reports, and Payments

Keeping track of the many payroll taxes can be a challenge for an employer. Figure 9-11 summarizes the various employee and employer taxes we have discussed in Chapters 8 and 9. Figure 9-12 shows a calendar that highlights the due dates for the various reports and deposits. The calendar assumes the following for an employer:

1. Undeposited FIT (federal income tax) and Social Security and Medicare taxes of $2,500 at the end of each quarter and less than $50,000 during the lookback period.
2. Undeposited FUTA taxes of more than $500 at the end of each quarter.
3. SUTA taxes deposited quarterly.

FIGURE 9-11   Summary of Employee and Employer Taxes

TAX	TAX APPLIES TO	
	EMPLOYEE	EMPLOYER
Federal income tax	X	
State income tax	X	
Social Security	X	X
Medicare	X	X
FUTA		X
SUTA		X*

*Also applies to employees in some states.

FIGURE 9-12   Payroll Calendar

Color Key

File Forms 940, 941, state unemployment tax report, and send W-2 to employees.	File form W-3 with Copy A of W-2s.	File Form 941 and make FUTA and SUTA tax deposits.	Deposit FIT and Social Security and Medicare taxes from previous month.

January

S	M	T	W	T	F	S
			1	2	3	4
5	6	7	8	9	10	11
12	13	14	15	16	17	18
19	20	21	22	23	24	25
26	27	28	29	30	31	

February

S	M	T	W	T	F	S
						1
2	3	4	5	6	7	8
9	10	11	12	13	14	15
16	17	18	19	20	21	22
23	24	25	26	27	28	29

March

S	M	T	W	T	F	S
1	2	3	4	5	6	7
8	9	10	11	12	13	14
15	16	17	18	19	20	21
22	23	24	25	26	27	28
29	30	31				

April

S	M	T	W	T	F	S
			1	2	3	4
5	6	7	8	9	10	11
12	13	14	15	16	17	18
19	20	21	22	23	24	25
26	27	28	29	30		

May

S	M	T	W	T	F	S
					1	2
3	4	5	6	7	8	9
10	11	12	13	14	15	16
17	18	19	20	21	22	23
24	25	26	27	28	29	30
31						

June

S	M	T	W	T	F	S
	1	2	3	4	5	6
7	8	9	10	11	12	13
14	15	16	17	18	19	20
21	22	23	24	25	26	27
28	29	30				

July

S	M	T	W	T	F	S
			1	2	3	4
5	6	7	8	9	10	11
12	13	14	15	16	17	18
19	20	21	22	23	24	25
26	27	28	29	30	31	

August

S	M	T	W	T	F	S
						1
2	3	4	5	6	7	8
9	10	11	12	13	14	15
16	17	18	19	20	21	22
23	24	25	26	27	28	29
30	31					

September

S	M	T	W	T	F	S
		1	2	3	4	5
6	7	8	9	10	11	12
13	14	15	16	17	18	19
20	21	22	23	24	25	26
27	28	29	30			

October

S	M	T	W	T	F	S
				1	2	3
4	5	6	7	8	9	10
11	12	13	14	15	16	17
18	19	20	21	22	23	24
25	26	27	28	29	30	31

November

S	M	T	W	T	F	S
1	2	3	4	5	6	7
8	9	10	11	12	13	14
15	16	17	18	19	20	21
22	23	24	25	26	27	28
29	30					

December

S	M	T	W	T	F	S
		1	2	3	4	5
6	7	8	9	10	11	12
13	14	15	16	17	18	19
20	21	22	23	24	25	26
27	28	29	30	31		

A BROADER VIEW

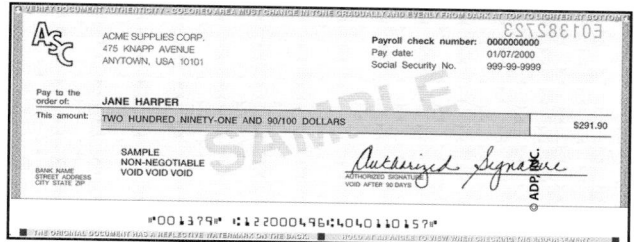

© ADP, INC.

Dealing with Payroll Complexity—Let Someone Else Do It

A common way for both small and large businesses to deal with the complexity of payroll reports, deposit rules, and due dates is to hire an outside company to handle the payroll. Payroll processing companies have combined payroll expertise with the power of computers to create a major business enterprise based on the efficient and effective provision of payroll services.

To give you some idea of the extent to which businesses have turned to outside companies to handle payroll, consider Automatic Data Processing, Inc. (ADP), the world's largest provider of payroll services. ADP currently processes payrolls for more than 590,000 clients, with over 32 million employees in 26 countries. ADP prepares employee paychecks, journals, and summary reports; collects and remits funds for federal, state, and local payroll taxes; and files all required forms with government taxing authorities.

The combination of payroll taxes, reports, deposit rules, and due dates can make payroll accounting rather complex. In fact, this is a major reason why small businesses often hire an accountant or an outside company to handle payroll.

WORKERS' COMPENSATION INSURANCE

LO4 Describe and account for workers' compensation insurance.

Most states require employers to carry workers' compensation insurance. **Workers' compensation insurance** provides insurance for employees who suffer a job-related illness or injury.

The employer usually pays the entire cost of workers' compensation insurance. The cost of the insurance depends on the number of employees, riskiness of the job, and the company's accident history. For example, the insurance premium for workers in a chemical plant could be higher than for office workers. Employers generally obtain the insurance either from the state in which they operate or from a private insurance company.

The employer usually pays the premium at the beginning of the year, based on the estimated payroll for the year. At the end of the year, after the actual amount of payroll is known, an adjustment is made. If the employer has overpaid, a credit is received from the state or insurance company. If the employer has underpaid, an additional premium is paid.

To illustrate the accounting for workers' compensation insurance, assume that Lockwood Co. expects its payroll for the year to be $210,000. If Lockwood's insurance premium rate is 0.2%, its payment for workers' compensation insurance at the beginning of the year would be $420.

Estimated Payroll	×	Rate	=	Estimated Insurance Premium
$210,000		0.002		$420.00

The journal entry for the payment of this $420 premium would be as follows:

7	Jan.	2	Workers' Compensation Insurance Expense		4 2 0 00		7
8			Cash			4 2 0 00	8
9			Paid insurance premium				9

If Lockwood's actual payroll for the year is $220,000, Lockwood would owe an additional premium of $20 at year-end.

Actual Payroll	×	Rate	=	Insurance Premium
$220,000		0.002		$440.00
Less premium paid				420.00
Additional premium due				$ 20.00

The adjusting entry at year-end for this additional expense would be as follows:

11	Dec.	31	Workers' Compensation Insurance Expense		2 0 00		11
12			Workers' Compensation Insurance Payable			2 0 00	12
13			Adjustment for insurance premium				13

In T account form, the total Workers' Compensation Insurance Expense of $440.00 would look like this.

Workers' Compensation Insurance Expense

Debit	Credit
420.00	
20.00	
440.00	

If Lockwood's actual payroll for the year is only $205,000, Lockwood would be due a refund of $10:

Payroll	×	Rate	=	Insurance Premium
$205,000		0.002		$410.00
Less premium paid				420.00
Refund due				$ (10.00)

The adjusting entry at year-end for this refund due would be as follows:

16	Dec.	31	Insurance Refund Receivable				1	0	00					16
17			Workers' Compensation Insurance Expense								1	0	00	17
18			Adjustment for insurance premium											18

In T account form, the total Workers' Compensation Insurance Expense of $410 would look like this.

Workers' Compensation Insurance Expense

Debit	Credit
420.00	10.00
410.00	

Computers and Accounting

Computerized Payroll Systems—Gary P. Schneider, University of San Diego, and Toni Hartley, Laurel Business Institute

Payroll, as you have learned in this and the previous chapter, is one of the most detailed and computation-laden parts of accounting. For this reason, payroll was one of the first accounting activities that companies computerized. All payroll systems divide the work into four main parts: (1) maintaining basic records about employees and tax rates, (2) recording employee activities such as time worked or commissions earned, (3) calculating net pay and payroll taxes, and (4) reporting the results of those calculations in a variety of formats. You can see parts (1), (2), and (4) illustrated in the accompanying figure [in a computerized payroll system, the part (3) calculations are done by the computer behind the scenes]. The figure shows the main payroll module screen for Peachtree®, a popular accounting software package for small- and medium-sized businesses.

As you can see in the figure, Peachtree is graphically oriented and you begin by setting up the employees by clicking on the Employees icon. Once employees are established in Peachtree, you proceed by entering their working time through the Time and Expense Ticket icon. The flow chart illustration in this module guides you through the rest of the process which would be to Pay Employees by either Direct Deposit or Payroll Checks.

The Payroll feature in Peachtree enables you to download current tax tables or allows you to create your own manually through the Payroll Tax Tables icon. Through the Forms icon, you can print applicable state reports and federal reports such as Forms 940 and 941. Peachtree also provides the option of preparing 1099s and voiding checks easily with the appropriate icons.

(continued)

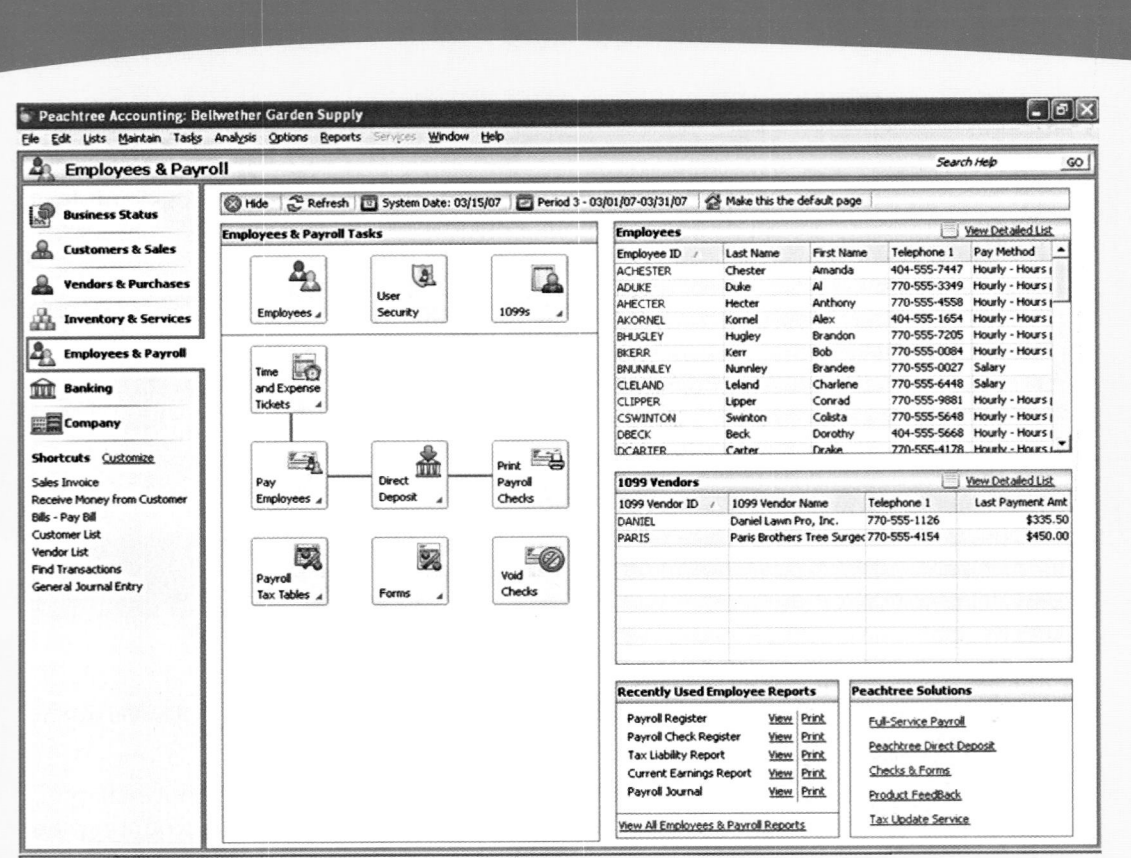

In smaller companies, the payroll module can provide all of the information that managers need to track the people they hire, promote, and fire. It also can do a good job of recording raises. However, as the business grows, hires more employees, and introduces more complex benefit plans, the company's information needs can exceed the capabilities of accounting software payroll modules.

When they grow to this point, many companies buy or create separate human resource management (HRM) information systems to keep track of hirings, firings, promotions, and benefit plan participation. Most of these HRM systems can share information with the payroll module of the accounting software. Virtually all of the information stored in the employee records section of a payroll module (for example, employee names, addresses, social security numbers, pay rates) is the same information a company will want to have in its HRM. It is more efficient to keep that information stored in one format and in one place. The employee information can then be shared effectively by the payroll and human resources departments.

Learning Objectives	Key Points to Remember

LO1 Describe and calculate employer payroll taxes.

LO2 Account for employer payroll taxes expense.

Employer payroll taxes include FICA, FUTA, and SUTA taxes. These taxes represent additional payroll expenses of the employer. The journal entry for payroll taxes is as follows:

8		Payroll Taxes Expense		x x x xx		8
9		Social Security Tax Payable			x x x xx	9
10		Medicare Tax Payable			x x x xx	10
11		FUTA Tax Payable			x x x xx	11
12		SUTA Tax Payable			x x x xx	12

The steps to be followed in preparing this journal entry are as follows:
1. Obtain the total earnings and taxable earnings amounts from the Earnings—Total and Taxable Earnings columns of the payroll register.
2. Compute the amount of employer Social Security tax by multiplying the Social Security taxable earnings by 6.2%.
3. Compute the amount of employer Medicare tax by multiplying total earnings by 1.45%.
4. Compute the amount of FUTA tax by multiplying the Unemployment Taxable earnings by 0.8%.
5. Compute the amount of SUTA tax by multiplying the Unemployment Taxable earnings by 5.4%.
6. Prepare the appropriate journal entry using the amounts computed in steps 2–5.

LO3 Describe employer reporting and payment responsibilities.

Employer payroll reporting and payment responsibilities fall into five areas.
1. Federal income tax withholding and Social Security and Medicare taxes
2. FUTA taxes
3. SUTA taxes
4. Employee Wage and Tax Statement (Form W-2)
5. Summary of employee wages and taxes

Key forms needed in reporting and paying employer payroll taxes are as follows:
1. Form 8109, Federal Tax Deposit Coupon
2. Form 941, Employer's Quarterly Federal Tax Return
3. Form 940, Employer's Annual Federal Unemployment Tax Return

By January 31 of each year, employers must provide each employee with a Wage and Tax Statement, Form W-2.

By February 28 of each year, employers must file Form W-3 and Copy A of Form W-2 with the Social Security Administration.

LO4 Describe and account for workers' compensation insurance.

Workers' compensation insurance provides insurance for employees who suffer a job-related illness or injury. Employers generally are required to carry and pay the entire cost of this insurance.

DEMONSTRATION PROBLEM

The totals line from Hart Company's payroll register for the week ended December 31, 20--, is as follows:

(left side)

PAYROLL

	NAME	EMPLOYEE NUMBER	ALLOWANCES	MARITAL STATUS	EARNINGS			CUMULATIVE TOTAL	TAXABLE EARNINGS		
					REGULAR	OVERTIME	TOTAL		UNEMPLOYMENT COMPENSATION	SOCIAL SECURITY	
21	Totals				3 5 0 0 00	3 0 0 00	3 8 0 0 00	197 6 0 0 00	4 0 0 00	3 8 0 0 00	21

(right side)

REGISTER—PERIOD ENDED December 31, 20--

	DEDUCTIONS							NET PAY	CHECK NO.	
	FEDERAL INCOME TAX	SOCIAL SECURITY TAX	MEDICARE TAX	HEALTH INSURANCE	UNITED WAY	OTHER	TOTAL			
21	3 8 0 00	2 3 5 60	5 5 10	5 0 00	1 0 0 00		8 2 0 70	2 9 7 9 30		21

Payroll taxes are imposed as follows: Social Security, 6.2%; Medicare, 1.45%; FUTA, 0.8%; and SUTA, 5.4%.

REQUIRED

1. a. Prepare the journal entry for payment of this payroll on December 31, 20--.

    b. Prepare the journal entry for the employer's payroll taxes for the period ended December 31, 20--.

2. Hart Company had the following balances in its general ledger *after* the entries for requirement (1) were made:

Employee Income Tax Payable	$1,620.00
Social Security Tax Payable	1,847.00
Medicare Tax Payable	433.00
FUTA Tax Payable	27.20
SUTA Tax Payable	183.60

    a. Prepare the journal entry for payment of the liabilities for employee federal income taxes and Social Security and Medicare taxes on January 15, 20--.

    b. Prepare the journal entry for payment of the liability for FUTA tax on January 31, 20--.

    c. Prepare the journal entry for payment of the liability for SUTA tax on January 31, 20--.

3. Hart Company paid a premium of $280 for workers' compensation insurance based on estimated payroll as of the beginning of the year. Based on actual payroll as of the end of the year, the premium is $298. Prepare the adjusting entry to reflect the underpayment of the insurance premium.

Solution 1.

	DATE		DESCRIPTION	POST. REF.	DEBIT					CREDIT					
1	20-- Dec.	31	Wages and Salaries Expense		3	8	0	0	00						1
2			Employee Income Tax Payable								3	8	0	00	2
3			Social Security Tax Payable								2	3	5	60	3
4			Medicare Tax Payable									5	5	10	4
5			Health Insurance Premiums Payable									5	0	00	5
6			United Way Contributions Payable								1	0	0	00	6
7			Cash							2	9	7	9	30	7
8			To record Dec. 31 payroll												8
9															9
10	Dec.	31	Payroll Taxes Expense			3	1	5	50						10
11			Social Security Tax Payable								2	3	5	60	11
12			Medicare Tax Payable									5	5	10	12
13			FUTA Tax Payable										3	20	13
14			SUTA Tax Payable									2	1	60	14
15			Employer payroll taxes for week ended Dec. 31												15

2. and 3.

	DATE		DESCRIPTION	POST. REF.	DEBIT					CREDIT					
18	Jan.	15	Employee Income Tax Payable		1	6	2	0	00						18
19			Social Security Tax Payable		1	8	4	7	00						19
20			Medicare Tax Payable			4	3	3	00						20
21			Cash							3	9	0	0	00	21
22			Deposit of employee federal income tax and												22
23			Social Security and Medicare taxes												23
24															24
25	Jan.	31	FUTA Tax Payable				2	7	20						25
26			Cash									2	7	20	26
27			Paid FUTA tax												27
28															28
29	Jan.	31	SUTA Tax Payable			1	8	3	60						29
30			Cash								1	8	3	60	30
31			Paid SUTA tax												31
32															32
33	Dec.	31	Workers' Compensation Insurance Expense				1	8	00						33
34			Workers' Compensation Insurance Payable									1	8	00	34
35			Adjustment for insurance premium												35

adjusted
less - Recoverable

KEY TERMS

Electronic Federal Tax Payment System (EFTPS) (325)   An electronic funds transfer system for making federal tax deposits.

employer FICA taxes (318)   Taxes levied on employers at the same rates and on the same earnings bases as the employee FICA taxes.

Employer Identification Number (EIN) (325)   A number that identifies the employer on all payroll forms and reports filed with the IRS.

FUTA (Federal Unemployment Tax Act) tax (320)   A tax levied on employers to raise funds to administer the federal/state unemployment compensation program.

merit-rating system (320)   A system to encourage employers to provide regular employment to workers.

self-employment income (319)   The net income of a trade or business run by an individual.

self-employment tax (319)   A contribution to the FICA program.

SUTA (state unemployment tax) tax (320)   A tax levied on employers to raise funds to pay unemployment benefits.

workers' compensation insurance (333)   Provides insurance for employees who suffer a job-related illness or injury.

Self-Study Test Questions

True/False

1. Employer payroll taxes are deducted from the employee's pay.

2. The payroll register is a key source of information for computing employer payroll taxes.

3. Self-employment income is the net income of a trade or business owned and run by an individual.

4. The FUTA tax is levied only on the employees.

5. The W-4, which shows total annual earnings and deductions for federal and state income taxes, must be completed by the employer and given to the employee by January 31.

Multiple Choice

1. The general ledger accounts commonly used to record the employer's Social Security, Medicare, FUTA, and SUTA taxes are classified as

   (a) assets.   (c) expenses.
   (b) liabilities.   (d) owner's equity.

2. Joyce Lee earns $30,000 a year. Her employer pays a matching Social Security tax of 6.2% on the first $94,200 in earnings, a Medicare tax of 1.45% on gross earnings, and a FUTA tax of 0.8% and a SUTA tax of 5.4%, both on the first $7,000 in earnings. What is the total cost of Joyce Lee to her employer?

   (a) $32,250   (c) $30,434
   (b) $30,000   (d) $32,729

3. The Form 941 tax deposit includes which of the following types of taxes withheld from the employee and paid by the employer?

(a) Federal income tax and FUTA tax
(b) Federal income tax and Social Security and Medicare taxes
(c) Social Security and Medicare taxes and SUTA tax
(d) FUTA tax and SUTA tax

4. Workers' compensation provides insurance for employees who

(a) are unemployed due to a layoff.
(b) are unemployed due to a plant closing.
(c) are underemployed and need additional compensation.
(d) suffer a job-related illness or injury.

5. The journal entry at the end of the year that recognizes an additional premium owed under workers' compensation insurance will include a

(a) debit to Workers' Compensation Insurance Expense.
(b) debit to Cash.
(c) debit to Workers' Compensation Insurance Payable.
(d) credit to Workers' Compensation Insurance Expense.

The answers to the Self-Study Test Questions are at the end of the text.

REVIEW QUESTIONS

LO1   1. Why do employer payroll taxes represent an additional expense to the employer, whereas the various employee payroll taxes do not?

LO1   2. At what rate and on what earnings base is the employer's Social Security tax levied?

LO1   3. What is the purpose of the FUTA tax, and who must pay it?

LO1   4. What is the purpose of the state unemployment tax, and who must pay it?

LO2   5. What accounts are affected when employer payroll tax expenses are properly recorded?

LO2   6. Identify all items that are debited or credited to Social Security Tax Payable and to Medicare Tax Payable.

LO2   7. Explain why an employee whose gross salary is $20,000 costs an employer more than $20,000 to employ. *Because of taxes paid*

LO3   8. What is the purpose of Form 8109, Federal Tax Deposit Coupon?

LO3   9. What is the purpose of Form 941, Employer's Quarterly Federal Tax Return?

LO3   10. What is the purpose of Form 940, Employer's Annual Federal Unemployment Tax Return?

LO3   11. What information appears on Form W-2, the employee's Wage and Tax Statement?

LO4   12. What is the purpose of workers' compensation insurance, and who must pay for it?

REVISITING THE OPENER

In the chapter opener on page 317, you were asked to consider what payroll taxes Evan must pay and what the total payroll cost of an employee is.

(1) What payroll taxes must Evan pay as an employer?

(2) Assuming the employee works a full year and is paid $10,400, what is the total payroll cost to Evan of having this employee?

SERIES A EXERCISES

E 9-1A (LO1/2)

✓ Payroll taxes expense: $1,584.30

CALCULATION AND JOURNAL ENTRY FOR EMPLOYER PAYROLL TAXES Portions of the payroll register for Barney's Bagels for the week ended July 15 are shown below. The SUTA tax rate is 5.4%, and the FUTA tax rate is 0.8%, both of which are levied on the first $7,000 of earnings. The Social Security tax rate is 6.2% on the first $94,200 of earnings. The Medicare rate is 1.45% on gross earnings.

Barney's Bagels
Payroll Register

| | Total Taxable Earnings of All Employees | |
Total Earnings	Unemployment Compensation	Social Security
$12,200	$10,500	$12,200

Calculate the employer's payroll taxes expense and prepare the journal entry to record the employer's payroll taxes expense for the week ended July 15 of the current year.

E 9-2A (LO1/2)

✓ Payroll taxes expense: $350.02

CALCULATION AND JOURNAL ENTRY FOR EMPLOYER PAYROLL TAXES Earnings for several employees for the week ended March 12, 20--, are as follows:

| | | Taxable Earnings | |
Employee Name	Total Earnings	Unemployment Compensation	Social Security
Aus, Glenn E.	$ 700	$200	$ 700
Diaz, Charles K.	350	350	350
Knapp, Carol S.	1,200	—	1,200
Mueller, Deborah F.	830	125	830
Yeager, Jackie R.	920	35	920

Calculate the employer's payroll taxes expense and prepare the journal entry as of March 12, 20--, assuming that FUTA tax is 0.8%, SUTA tax is 5.4%, Social Security tax is 6.2%, and Medicare tax is 1.45%.

E 9-3A (LO1/2)

✓ Payroll taxes expense: $886.86

CALCULATION OF TAXABLE EARNINGS AND EMPLOYER PAYROLL TAXES AND PREPARATION OF JOURNAL ENTRY Selected information from the payroll register of Raynette's Boutique for the week ended September

14, 20--, is as follows. Social Security tax is 6.2% on the first $94,200 of earnings for each employee. Medicare tax is 1.45% of gross earnings. FUTA tax is 0.8% and SUTA tax is 5.4% on the first $7,000 of earnings.

Employee Name	Cumulative Pay Before Current Earnings	Current Gross Pay	Taxable Earnings	
			Unemployment Compensation	Social Security
Burgos, Juan	$ 6,800	$1,250		
Ellis, Judy A.	6,300	1,100		
Lewis, Arlene S.	54,200	2,320		
Mason, Jason W.	53,900	2,270		
Yates, Ruby L.	27,650	1,900		
Zielke, Ronald M.	92,330	2,680		

Calculate the amount of taxable earnings for unemployment, Social Security, and Medicare taxes, and prepare the journal entry to record the employer's payroll taxes as of September 14, 20--.

E 9-4A (LO1/2)

✓ Total cost: $34,882.00

TOTAL COST OF EMPLOYEE J. B. Kenton employs Sharla Knox at a salary of $32,000 a year. Kenton is subject to employer Social Security taxes at a rate of 6.2% and Medicare taxes at a rate of 1.45% on Knox's salary. In addition, Kenton must pay SUTA tax at a rate of 5.4% and FUTA tax at a rate of 0.8% on the first $7,000 of Knox's salary.

Compute the total cost to Kenton of employing Knox for the year.

E 9-5A (LO3)

✓ 941 deposit: $20,700

JOURNAL ENTRIES FOR PAYMENT OF EMPLOYER PAYROLL TAXES
Angel Ruiz owns a business called Ruiz Construction Co. He does his banking at Citizens National Bank in Portland, Oregon. The amounts in his general ledger for payroll taxes and the employees' withholding of Social Security, Medicare, and federal income tax payable as of April 15 of the current year are as follows:

Social Security tax payable (includes both employer and employee)	$11,250
Medicare tax payable (includes both employer and employee)	2,625
FUTA tax payable	600
SUTA tax payable	4,050
Employee income tax payable	6,825

Journalize the payment of the employee federal income taxes and Social Security and Medicare taxes on April 15, 20--, and the payments of the FUTA and SUTA taxes on April 30, 20--.

E 9-6A (LO4)

✓ 2. Additional premium due: $14.00

WORKERS' COMPENSATION INSURANCE AND ADJUSTMENT General Manufacturing estimated that its total payroll for the coming year would be $425,000. The workers' compensation insurance premium rate is 0.2%.

REQUIRED

1. Calculate the estimated workers' compensation insurance premium and prepare the journal entry for the payment as of January 2, 20--.

2. Assume that General Manufacturing's actual payroll for the year is $432,000. Calculate the total insurance premium owed and prepare a journal entry as of December 31, 20--, to record the adjustment for the underpayment. The actual payment of the additional premium will take place in January of the next year.

SERIES A PROBLEMS

P 9-7A (LO1/2)

✓ Payroll taxes expense: $662.06

CALCULATING PAYROLL TAXES EXPENSE AND PREPARING JOURNAL ENTRY Selected information from the payroll register of Anderson's Dairy for the week ended July 7, 20--, is shown below. The SUTA tax rate is 5.4%, and the FUTA tax rate is 0.8%, both on the first $7,000 of earnings. Social Security tax on the employer is 6.2% on the first $94,200 of earnings, and Medicare tax is 1.45% on gross earnings.

			Taxable Earnings	
	Cumulative Pay	Current		
	Before Current	Weekly	Unemployment	Social
Employee Name	Earnings	Earnings	Compensation	Security
Barnum, Alex	$ 6,750	$ 820		
Duel, Richard	6,340	725		
Hunt, J. B.	23,460	1,235		
Larson, Susan	6,950	910		
Mercado, Denise	92,850	3,520		
Swan, Judy	25,470	1,125		
Yates, Keith	28,675	1,300		

REQUIRED

1. Calculate the total employer payroll taxes for these employees.

2. Prepare the journal entry to record the employer payroll taxes as of July 7, 20--.

P 9-8A (LO2/3)

✓ Payroll taxes expense: $3,864.00

JOURNALIZING AND POSTING PAYROLL ENTRIES Cascade Company has four employees. All are paid on a monthly basis. The fiscal year of the business is May 1 to April 30. Payroll taxes are imposed as follows:

1. Social Security tax of 6.2% withheld from employees' wages on the first $94,200 of earnings and Medicare tax withheld at 1.45% of gross earnings.
2. Social Security tax of 6.2% imposed on the employer on the first $94,200 of earnings and Medicare tax of 1.45% on gross earnings.
3. SUTA tax of 5.4% imposed on the employer on the first $7,000 of earnings.
4. FUTA tax of 0.8% imposed on the employer on the first $7,000 of earnings.

The accounts kept by Cascade include the following:

Account Number	Title	Balance on June 1
101	Cash	$70,200
211	Employee Income Tax Payable	3,553
212	Social Security Tax Payable	5,103
213	Medicare Tax Payable	1,197
218	Savings Bond Deductions Payable	1,225
221	FUTA Tax Payable	574
222	SUTA Tax Payable	2,835
511	Wages and Salaries Expense	0
530	Payroll Taxes Expense	0

The following transactions relating to payrolls and payroll taxes occurred during June and July:

June 15   Paid $9,853 covering the following May taxes:

Social Security tax	$ 5,103
Medicare tax	1,197
Employee income tax withheld	3,553
Total	$ 9,853

30   June payroll:

Total wages and salaries expense		$42,000
Less amounts withheld:		
Social Security tax	$2,604	
Medicare tax	609	
Employee income tax	3,570	
Savings bond deductions	1,225	8,008
Net amount paid		$33,992

30   Purchased savings bonds for employees, $2,450

30   Data for completing employer's payroll taxes expense for June:

Social Security taxable wages	$42,000
Unemployment taxable wages	10,500

July 15   Paid $9,996 covering the following June taxes:

Social Security tax	$ 5,208
Medicare tax	1,218
Employee income tax withheld	3,570
Total	$ 9,996

31   Paid SUTA tax for the quarter, $3,402

31   Paid FUTA tax, $658

REQUIRED

1. Journalize the preceding transactions using a general journal.

2. Open T accounts for the payroll expenses and liabilities. Enter the beginning balances and post the transactions recorded in the journal.

P 9-9A (LO4)

✓ 3. Refund due: $48.00

WORKERS' COMPENSATION INSURANCE AND ADJUSTMENT Willamette Manufacturing estimated that its total payroll for the coming year would be $650,000. The workers' compensation insurance premium rate is 0.3%.

REQUIRED

1. Calculate the estimated workers' compensation insurance premium and prepare the journal entry for the payment as of January 2, 20--.

2. Assume that Willamette Manufacturing's actual payroll for the year was $672,000. Calculate the total insurance premium owed and prepare a journal entry as of December 31, 20--, to record the adjustment for the underpayment. The actual payment of the additional premium will take place in January of the next year.

(continued)

3. Assume instead that Willamette Manufacturing's actual payroll for the year was $634,000. Prepare a journal entry as of December 31, 20--, for the total amount that should be refunded. The refund will not be received until the next year.

SERIES B EXERCISES

E 9-1B (LO1/2)

✓ Payroll taxes expense: $1,962.74

CALCULATION AND JOURNAL ENTRY FOR EMPLOYER PAYROLL TAXES Portions of the payroll register for Kathy's Cupcakes for the week ended June 21 are shown below. The SUTA tax rate is 5.4%, and the FUTA tax rate is 0.8%, both on the first $7,000 of earnings. The Social Security tax rate is 6.2% on the first $94,200 of earnings. The Medicare rate is 1.45% on gross earnings.

Kathy's Cupcakes
Payroll Register

| | Total Taxable Earnings of All Employees | |
Total Earnings	Unemployment Compensation	Social Security
$15,680	$12,310	$15,680

Calculate the employer's payroll taxes expense and prepare the journal entry to record the employer's payroll taxes expense for the week ended June 21 of the current year.

E 9-2B (LO1/2)

✓ Payroll taxes expense: $503.63

CALCULATION AND JOURNAL ENTRY FOR EMPLOYER PAYROLL TAXES Earnings for several employees for the week ended April 7, 20--, are as follows:

| | | Taxable Earnings | |
Employee Name	Total Earnings	Unemployment Compensation	Social Security
Boyd, Glenda L.	$ 850	$300	$ 850
Evans, Sheryl N.	970	225	970
Fox, Howard J.	830	830	830
Jacobs, Phyllis J.	1,825	—	1,825
Roh, William R.	990	25	990

Calculate the employer's payroll taxes expense and prepare the journal entry as of April 7, 20--, assuming that FUTA tax is 0.8%, SUTA tax is 5.4%, Social Security tax is 6.2%, and Medicare tax is 1.45%.

E 9-3B (LO1/2)

✓ Payroll taxes expense: $788.04

CALCULATION OF TAXABLE EARNINGS AND EMPLOYER PAYROLL TAXES, AND PREPARATION OF JOURNAL ENTRY Selected information from the payroll register of Howard's Cutlery for the week ended October 7, 20--, is presented on the next page. Social Security tax is 6.2% on the first $94,200 of earnings for each employee. Medicare tax is 1.45% on gross earnings. FUTA tax is 0.8% and SUTA tax is 5.4% on the first $7,000 of earnings.

Employee Name	Cumulative Pay Before Current Earnings	Current Gross Pay	Taxable Earnings	
			Unemployment Compensation	Social Security
Carlson, David J.	$ 6,635	$ 950		
Delgado, Luisa	6,150	1,215		
Lewis, Arlene S.	54,375	2,415		
Nixon, Robert R.	53,870	1,750		
Shippe, Lance W.	24,830	1,450		
Watts, Brandon Q.	92,800	2,120		

Calculate the amount of taxable earnings for unemployment, Social Security, and Medicare taxes, and prepare the journal entry to record the employer's payroll taxes as of October 7, 20--.

E 9-4B (LO1/2)

✓ Total cost: $49,953.00

TOTAL COST OF EMPLOYEE B. F. Goodson employs Eduardo Gonzales at a salary of $46,000 a year. Goodson is subject to employer Social Security taxes at a rate of 6.2% and Medicare taxes at a rate of 1.45% on Gonzales's salary. In addition, Goodson must pay SUTA tax at a rate of 5.4% and FUTA tax at a rate of 0.8% on the first $7,000 of Gonzales's salary.

Compute the total cost to Goodson of employing Gonzales for the year.

E 9-5B (LO3)

✓ 941 deposit: $19,058.00

JOURNAL ENTRIES FOR PAYMENT OF EMPLOYER PAYROLL TAXES Francis Baker owns a business called Baker Construction Co. She does her banking at the American National Bank in Seattle, Washington. The amounts in her general ledger for payroll taxes and employees' withholding of Social Security, Medicare, and federal income tax payable as of July 15 of the current year are as follows:

Social Security tax payable (includes both employer and employee)	$9,563
Medicare tax payable (includes both employer and employee)	2,250
FUTA tax payable	504
SUTA tax payable	3,402
Employee federal income tax payable	7,245

Journalize the payment of the employee federal income taxes and Social Security and Medicare taxes on July 15, 20--, and the payments of the FUTA and state unemployment taxes on July 31, 20--.

E 9-6B (LO4)

✓ 2. Additional premium due: $22.00

WORKERS' COMPENSATION INSURANCE AND ADJUSTMENT Columbia Industries estimated that its total payroll for the coming year would be $385,000. The workers' compensation insurance premium rate is 0.2%.

REQUIRED

1. Calculate the estimated workers' compensation insurance premium and prepare the journal entry for the payment as of January 2, 20--.

2. Assume that Columbia Industries' actual payroll for the year is $396,000. Calculate the total insurance premium owed and prepare a journal entry as of December 31, 20--, to record the adjustment for the underpayment. The actual payment of the additional premium will take place in January of the next year.

SERIES B PROBLEMS

P 9-7B (LO1/2)

✓ Payroll taxes expense: $738.34

CALCULATING PAYROLL TAXES EXPENSE AND PREPARING JOURNAL ENTRY Selected information from the payroll register of Wray's Drug Store for the week ended July 14, 20--, is shown below. The SUTA tax rate is 5.4%, and the FUTA tax rate is 0.8%, both on the first $7,000 of earnings. Social Security tax on the employer is 6.2% on the first $94,200 of earnings, and Medicare tax is 1.45% on gross earnings.

Employee Name	Cumulative Pay Before Current Earnings	Current Weekly Earnings	Taxable Earnings	
			Unemployment Compensation	Social Security
Ackers, Alice	$ 6,460	$ 645		
Conley, Dorothy	27,560	1,025		
Davis, James	6,850	565		
Lawrence, Kevin	52,850	2,875		
Rawlings, Judy	16,350	985		
Tanaka, Sumio	22,320	835		
Vadillo, Raynette	92,360	3,540		

REQUIRED

1. Calculate the total employer payroll taxes for these employees.

2. Prepare the journal entry to record the employer payroll taxes as of July 14, 20--.

P 9-8B (LO2/3)

✓ Payroll taxes expense: $2,105.85

JOURNALIZING AND POSTING PAYROLL ENTRIES Oxford Company has five employees. All are paid on a monthly basis. The fiscal year of the business is June 1 to May 31. Payroll taxes are imposed as follows:

1. Social Security tax of 6.2% to be withheld from employees' wages on the first $94,200 of earnings and Medicare tax of 1.45% on gross earnings.
2. Social Security tax of 6.2% imposed on the employer on the first $94,200 of earnings and Medicare tax of 1.45% on gross earnings.
3. SUTA tax of 5.4% imposed on the employer on the first $7,000 of earnings.
4. FUTA tax of 0.8% imposed on the employer on the first $7,000 of earnings.

The accounts kept by Oxford Company include the following:

Account Number	Title	Balance on June 1
101	Cash	$69,500.00
211	Employee Income Tax Payable	2,018.00
212	Social Security Tax Payable	2,735.00
213	Medicare Tax Payable	641.00
218	Savings Bond Deductions Payable	787.50
221	FUTA Tax Payable	540.00
222	SUTA Tax Payable	1,380.00
511	Wages and Salaries Expense	0.00
530	Payroll Taxes Expense	0.00

The following transactions relating to payrolls and payroll taxes occurred during June and July:

June 15   Paid $5,394.00 covering the following May taxes:

Social Security tax	$2,735.00
Medicare tax	641.00
Employee income tax withheld	2,018.00
Total	$5,394.00

30   June payroll:

Total wages and salaries expense		$22,050.00
Less amounts withheld:		
Social Security tax	$1,367.10	
Medicare tax	319.73	
Employee income tax	1,920.00	
Savings bond deductions	787.50	4,394.33
Net amount paid		$17,655.67

30   Purchased savings bonds for employees, $1,575.00

30   Data for completing employer's payroll taxes expense for June:

Social Security taxable wages	$22,050.00
Unemployment taxable wages	6,750.00

July 15   Paid $5,293.70 covering the following June taxes:

Social Security tax	$ 2,734.20
Medicare tax	639.50
Employee income tax withheld	1,920.00
Total	$ 5,293.70

31   Paid SUTA tax for the quarter, $1,745.00

31   Paid FUTA tax, $594.00

REQUIRED

1.   Journalize the preceding transactions using a general journal.

2.   Open T accounts for the payroll expenses and liabilities. Enter the beginning balances and post the transactions recorded in the journal.

P 9-9B (LO4)

✓ 3. Refund due: $16.00

WORKERS' COMPENSATION INSURANCE AND ADJUSTMENT
Multnomah Manufacturing estimated that its total payroll for the coming year would be $540,000. The workers' compensation insurance premium rate is 0.2%.

REQUIRED

1.   Calculate the estimated workers' compensation insurance premium and prepare the journal entry for the payment as of January 2, 20--.

2.   Assume that Multnomah Manufacturing's actual payroll for the year was $562,000. Calculate the total insurance premium owed and prepare a journal entry as of December 31, 20--, to record the adjustment for the underpayment. The actual payment of the additional premium will take place in January of the next year.

(continued)

3. Assume instead that Multnomah Manufacturing's actual payroll for the year was $532,000. Prepare a journal entry as of December 31, 20--, for the total amount that should be refunded. The refund will not be received until the next year.

MANAGING YOUR WRITING

The director of the art department, Wilson Watson, wants to hire new office staff. His boss tells him that to do so he must find in his budget not only the base salary for this position but an additional 30% for "fringe benefits." Wilson explodes: "How in the world can there be 30% in fringe benefits?" Write a memo to Wilson Watson explaining the costs that probably make up these fringe benefits.

ETHICS CASE

Bob Estes works at Cliffrock Company in the central receiving department. He unpacks incoming shipments and verifies quantities of goods received. Over the weekend, Bob pulled a muscle in his back while playing basketball. When he came to work on Monday and started unpacking shipments, his back started to hurt again. Bob called the human resources department and told them he hurt his back lifting a package at work. He was told to fill out an accident report and sent to an orthopedic clinic with a workers' compensation form. The doctor at the clinic told Bob not to lift anything heavy for two weeks and to stay home from work for at least one week.

1. Is Bob entitled to workers' compensation? Why or why not?

2. What effect will Bob's claim have on Cliffrock Company's workers' compensation insurance premium?

3. Write a short memo from the human resources department to Cliffrock Company's employees explaining the purpose of workers' compensation.

4. In small groups, discuss the job-related illness or injury risks of a computer input operator and measures an employer might take to minimize these risks.

MASTERY PROBLEM

✓ Payroll taxes expense: $730.75

The totals line from Nix Company's payroll register for the week ended March 31, 20--, is as follows:

(left side)   PAYROLL

	NAME	EMPLOYEE NUMBER	ALLOWANCES	MARITAL STATUS	EARNINGS				TAXABLE EARNINGS	
					REGULAR	OVERTIME	TOTAL	CUMULATIVE TOTAL	UNEMPLOYMENT COMPENSATION	SOCIAL SECURITY
21	Totals				5 4 0 0 00	1 0 0 00	5 5 0 0 00	71 5 0 0 00	5 0 0 0 00	5 5 0 0 00	21

(right side)

REGISTER—PERIOD ENDED March 31, 20--

	DEDUCTIONS							NET PAY	CHECK NO.	
	FEDERAL INCOME TAX	SOCIAL SECURITY TAX	MEDICARE TAX	HEALTH INSURANCE	LIFE INSURANCE	OTHER	TOTAL			
21	5 0 0 00	3 4 1 00	7 9 75	1 6 5 00	2 0 0 00		1 2 8 5 75	4 2 1 4 25		21

Payroll taxes are imposed as follows: Social Security tax, 6.2%; Medicare tax, 1.45%; FUTA tax, 0.8%; and SUTA tax, 5.4%.

REQUIRED

1. a. Prepare the journal entry for payment of this payroll on March 31, 20--.

   b. Prepare the journal entry for the employer's payroll taxes for the period ended March 31, 20--.

2. Nix Company had the following balances in its general ledger before the entries for requirement (1) were made:

Employee income tax payable	$2,500
Social Security tax payable	2,008
Medicare tax payable	470
FUTA tax payable	520
SUTA tax payable	3,510

   a. Prepare the journal entry for payment of the liabilities for federal income taxes and Social Security and Medicare taxes on April 15, 20--.

   b. Prepare the journal entry for payment of the liability for FUTA tax on April 30, 20--.

   c. Prepare the journal entry for payment of the liability for SUTA tax on April 30, 20--.

3. Nix Company paid a premium of $420 for workers' compensation insurance based on the estimated payroll as of the beginning of the year. Based on actual payroll as of the end of the year, the premium is only $400. Prepare the adjusting entry to reflect the overpayment of the insurance premium at the end of the year (December 31, 20--).

CHALLENGE PROBLEM

This problem challenges you to apply your cumulative accounting knowledge to move a step beyond the material in the chapter.

✓ **Payroll taxes expense: $1,306.25**

Payrex Co. has six employees. All are paid on a weekly basis. For the payroll period ending January 7, total employee earnings were $12,500, all of which were subject to SUTA, FUTA, Social Security, and Medicare taxes. The SUTA tax rate in Payrex's state is 5.4%, but Payrex qualifies for a rate of 2.0% because of its good record of providing regular employment to its employees. Other employer payroll taxes are at the rates described in the chapter.

REQUIRED

1. Calculate Payrex's FUTA, SUTA, Social Security, and Medicare taxes for the week ended January 7.

2. Prepare the journal entry for Payrex's payroll taxes for the week ended January 7.

3. What amount of payroll taxes did Payrex save because of its good employment record?

© CHARLES GULLUNG/GETTY IMAGES

PART 3

Accounting for a Merchandising Business

10 Accounting for Sales and Cash Receipts

11 Accounting for Purchases and Cash Payments

12 Special Journals

13 Accounting for Merchandise Inventory

14 Adjustments and the Work Sheet for a Merchandising Business

15 Financial Statements and Year-End Accounting for a Merchandising Business

Objectives

Careful study of this chapter should enable you to:

LO1
Describe merchandise sales transactions.

LO2
Describe and use merchandise sales accounts.

LO3
Describe and use the accounts receivable ledger.

LO4
Prepare a schedule of accounts receivable.

Accounting for Sales and Cash Receipts

When Evan Taylor opened Parkway Pet Supplies, he accepted only cash and personal checks from customers. Soon he had several customers asking to make large purchases of merchandise on account. Evan refused because he thought his business was too small to carry such receivables, and he was unsure about the credit risk of some customers. Evan had a similar attitude toward bank credit cards, such as MasterCard and Visa. A friend with a similar store in Lawrence, Kansas, encouraged Evan to reconsider. He said bank credit card sales are "just like cash" and can provide a major boost in sales. How are bank credit card sales "just like cash"? How should Evan's bookkeeper account for such sales?

Over the last nine chapters, we have learned how to account for a service business. We are now ready to consider accounting for a different kind of business—merchandising. A **merchandising business** purchases merchandise such as clothing, furniture, or computers, and sells that merchandise to customers. For example, Evan Taylor buys pet toys from vendors and manufacturers and sells them to his customers at Parkway Pet Supplies.

This chapter examines how to account for the sale of merchandise using the accrual basis of accounting. We will learn how to use four new accounts and a subsidiary ledger.

MERCHANDISE SALES TRANSACTIONS

LO1 Describe merchandise sales transactions.

A **sale** is a transfer of merchandise from one business or individual to another in exchange for cash or a promise to pay cash. Sales procedures and documents vary greatly, depending on the nature and size of the business.

Retailer

Retail businesses generally sell to customers who enter the store, select the merchandise they want, and bring it to a salesclerk. The salesclerk enters the sale in some type of electronic cash register that generates a receipt for the customer. A copy of the receipt is retained in the register. Most registers can print a summary of the day's sales activity, like the one in Figure 10-1. This summary can be used to journalize sales in the accounting records.

FIGURE 10-1   Cash Register Tape Summary

```
              (1)
    CASH SALES       327.79 *
              (3)
    MCARD/VISA       550.62 *
              (6)
    LAYAWAY           79.50 *
    TOTAL CASH       957.91 *
              (2)
    CHARGE SALES     543.84 *
              (5)
    APPROVAL         126.58 *
    TOTAL CHARGE     670.42 *

    TOTAL SALES    1,628.33 G*
    SALES TAX         81.42 *
                      81.42 *

    REC'D ON ACCT.   324.51 *
                     324.51 *

    PAID OUT          76.51 *
                      76.51 *

    NO SALE            0.00 *
                       0.00 *

    *     SUB-TOTAL
    G*    GRAND TOTAL
```

An additional document often created as evidence of a sale in a retail business is a **sales ticket** (Figure 10-2). One copy of the sales ticket is given to the customer and the other copy is sent to accounting.

FIGURE 10-2   Sales Ticket

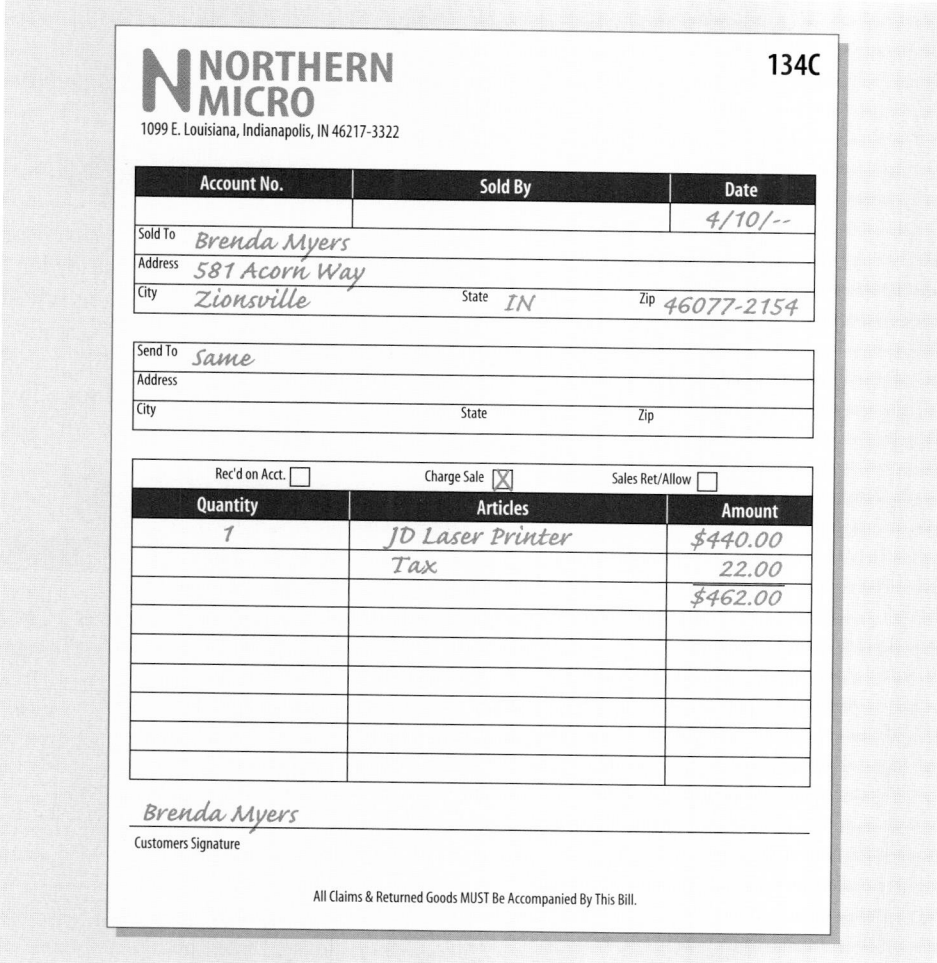

Wholesaler

Figure 10-3 shows how the wholesaler plays a different role than the retailer in the marketing chain. Retailers usually sell to final consumers, whereas wholesalers tend to sell to retailers. This causes the wholesale sales transaction process to differ, as shown in Figure 10-4.

FIGURE 10-3   Marketing Chain

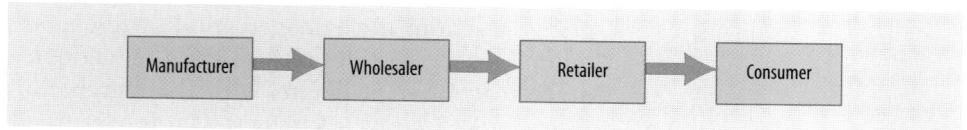

FIGURE 10-4   Wholesale Sales Transaction Process

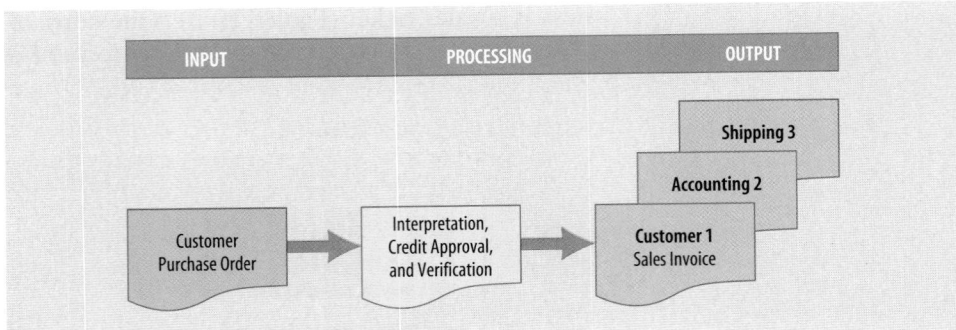

Customers commonly mail or fax written orders to buy merchandise from wholesalers. When the customer purchase order arrives, the customer name and items being ordered are determined. Since wholesalers typically make sales on account, credit approval is needed. Three copies of a **sales invoice** are then generated. One is sent to the customer as a bill for the merchandise, one is sent to accounting to record the sale, and one is shipped with the merchandise. Figure 10-5 shows the customer copy of a sales invoice for Aladdin Electric Supply.

FIGURE 10-5   Sales Invoice

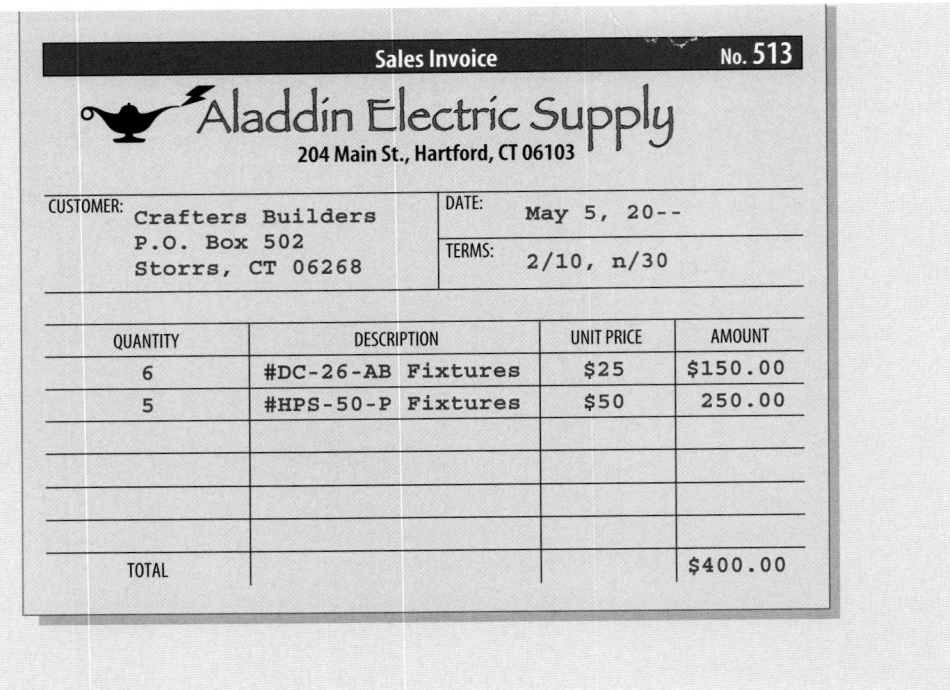

Credit Memorandum

Both retailers and wholesalers sometimes have customers return goods or seek price reductions for damaged goods. Merchandise returned by a customer for a refund is called a **sales return**. Price reductions granted by the seller because of defects or other problems with the merchandise are called **sales allowances**. When credit is given for merchandise returned or for an allowance, a **credit memo** is issued for the amount involved. This document is called a credit memo because the customer's account receivable is *credited* to reduce the amount the customer owes. One copy of the credit memo is given to the customer and one copy is sent to accounting. Figure 10-6 shows a credit memo issued by Northern Micro for merchandise returned by a customer.

FIGURE 10-6 Credit Memo

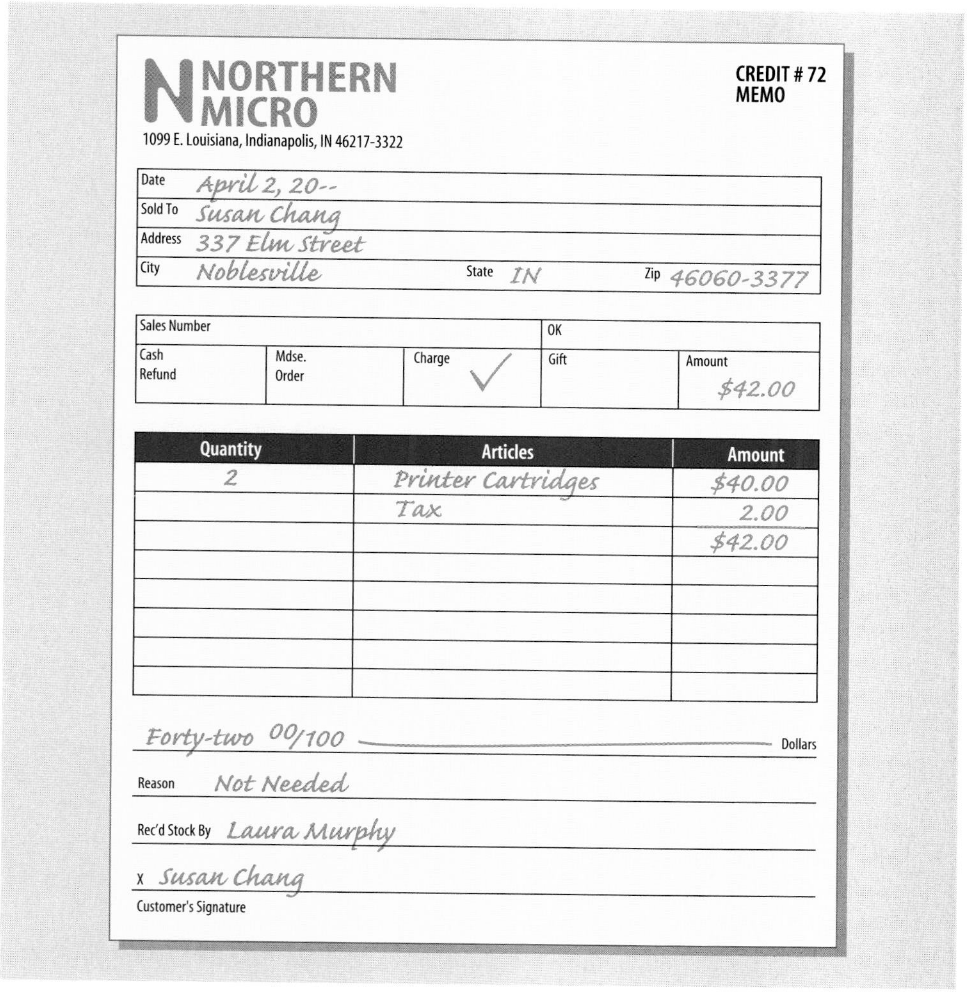

NORTHERN MICRO
1099 E. Louisiana, Indianapolis, IN 46217-3322

CREDIT # 72
MEMO

Date April 2, 20--
Sold To Susan Chang
Address 337 Elm Street
City Noblesville State IN Zip 46060-3377

Sales Number			OK	
Cash Refund	Mdse. Order	Charge ✓	Gift	Amount $42.00

Quantity	Articles	Amount
2	Printer Cartridges	$40.00
	Tax	2.00
		$42.00

Forty-two 00/100 Dollars
Reason Not Needed
Rec'd Stock By Laura Murphy
X Susan Chang
Customer's Signature

MERCHANDISE SALES ACCOUNTS

LO2 Describe and use merchandise sales accounts.

To account for merchandise sales transactions, we will use four new accounts:

1. Sales
2. Sales Tax Payable
3. Sales Returns and Allowances
4. Sales Discounts

The position of these accounts in the accounting equation and their normal balances are shown in Figure 10-7.

FIGURE 10-7 Accounting for Merchandise Sales Transactions

Assets		=	Liabilities		+	Owner's Equity	
Debit	**Credit**		**Debit**	**Credit**		**Debit**	**Credit**
+	−		−	+		−	+

Sales Tax Payable
XXX

Drawing		Expenses		Revenues	
Debit	**Credit**	**Debit**	**Credit**	**Debit**	**Credit**
+	−	+	−	−	+

Sales
XXX

Sales Returns and Allowances
XXX

Sales Discounts
XXX

Sales Account

The sales account is a revenue account used to record sales of merchandise. The account is credited for the selling price of merchandise sold during the period.

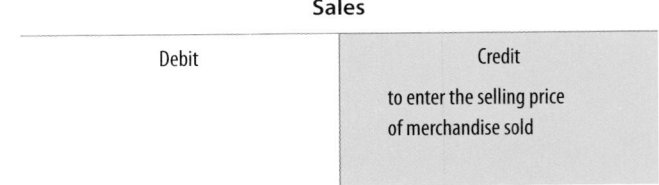

Sales

Debit	Credit
	to enter the selling price of merchandise sold

If a $100 sale is made for cash, the following entry is made:

5		Cash		1 0 0 00			5
6		Sales			1 0 0 00		6
7		Made cash sale					7

If the same sale is made on account, the entry is as follows:

5		Accounts Receivable/Customer		1 0 0 00			5
6		Sales			1 0 0 00		6
7		Made credit sale					7

Accounts Receivable is followed by a slash (/) and the name of the specific customer who owes the money.

Sales Tax Payable Account

Most states require retailers to collect sales tax on sales to final consumers. When sales tax is imposed on merchandise sold, a separate account for Sales Tax Payable is kept. This is a liability account that is credited for the taxes imposed on sales. The account is debited for sales taxes paid to the proper taxing authority or for sales taxes on merchandise returned by customers. A credit balance in the account indicates the amount owed to the taxing authority for taxes collected.

Sales Tax Payable

Debit	Credit
to enter payment of tax to taxing authority or adjustment of tax on merchandise returned by customers	to enter tax imposed on sales

If a cash sale for $100 plus 5% sales tax (5% × $100 = $5) occurs, the following entry is made:

10		Cash			1	0	5	00						10
11		Sales								1	0	0	00	11
12		Sales Tax Payable										5	00	12
13		Made cash sale												13

If the same sale is made on account, the entry is as follows:

10		Accounts Receivable/Customer			1	0	5	00						10
11		Sales								1	0	0	00	11
12		Sales Tax Payable										5	00	12
13		Made credit sale												13

The debit to Accounts Receivable indicates that the amount owed by customers to the business has increased. Since the buyer has accepted the merchandise and promised to pay for it, revenue is recognized by crediting Sales. Sales Tax Payable is credited because the amount of sales tax owed to the taxing authority has increased.

Sales Returns and Allowances Account

Sales Returns and Allowances is a contra-revenue account to which sales returns and sales allowances are debited. As shown in Figure 10-8, this account is reported as a deduction from Sales on the income statement. Returns and allowances are debited to a separate account rather than directly to Sales so that the business can more readily keep track of this activity.

Sales Returns and Allowances

Debit	Credit
to enter returns and allowances	

FIGURE 10-8 Sales Returns and Allowances on the Income Statement

Sales	$38,500.00
Less sales returns and allowances	200.00
Net sales	$38,300.00

Look at the credit memo in Figure 10-6 on page 359. The entry for the return of these printer cartridges by Susan Chang would be as follows:

19		Sales Returns and Allowances			4 0 00					19
20		Sales Tax Payable			2 00					20
21		Accounts Receivable/Susan Chang					4 2 00			21
22		Returned merchandise — Credit Memo #72								22

Note carefully the parts of this entry. Sales Returns and Allowances is debited for the amount of the sale, *excluding* the sales tax. Sales Tax Payable is debited separately for the sales tax on the original sale amount. Accounts Receivable is credited for the total amount originally billed to Chang.

Sales Discounts Account

Some businesses offer **cash discounts** to encourage prompt payment by customers who buy merchandise on account. Some possible credit terms are shown in Figure 10-9.

FIGURE 10-9 Credit Terms

TERMS	MEANING
2/10, n/30*	2% discount off sales price if paid within 10 days Total amount due within 30 days
1/10, n/30	Same as 2/10, n/30, except 1% discount instead of 2%
2/eom, n/60	2% discount if paid before end of month Total amount due within 60 days
3/10 eom, n/60	3% discount if paid within 10 days after end of month Total amount due within 60 days

*See Figure 10-5. A discount of $8 (2% × $400) is allowed if this invoice is paid by May 15 (invoice date of May 5 + 10 days).

To the seller, cash discounts are considered **sales discounts**. Sales Discounts is a contra-revenue account to which cash discounts allowed are debited. Like Sales Returns and Allowances, this account is reported as a deduction from Sales on the income statement, as shown in Figure 10-10.

Sales Discounts

Debit	Credit
to enter cash discounts	

FIGURE 10-10   Sales Discounts on the Income Statement

Sales		$38,500.00
Less: Sales returns and allowances	$200.00	
Sales discounts	140.00	340.00
Net sales		$38,160.00

If merchandise is sold for $100 with credit terms of 2/10, n/30, and cash is received within the discount period, two entries are made.

At time of sale:

26		Accounts Receivable/Customer		1 0 0 00		26
27		Sales			1 0 0 00	27
28		Made sale on account				28

At time of collection:

30		Cash		9 8 00		30
31		Sales Discounts		2 00		31
32		Accounts Receivable/Customer			1 0 0 00	32
33		Received cash on account				33

If any merchandise has been returned, the sales discount is calculated on the sale amount after deducting the return. If there is a sales tax, the discount is calculated on the sale amount excluding the sales tax.

JOURNALIZING AND POSTING SALES AND CASH RECEIPTS TRANSACTIONS

LO3 Describe and use the accounts receivable ledger.

To illustrate the journalizing and posting of sales and cash receipts transactions, we use Northern Micro, a retail computer business.

Sales

Assume the following sales transactions occurred during April 20--:

Apr. 4   Made sale no. 133C on account to Enrico Lorenzo, $1,520 plus $76 sales tax.

10   Made sale no. 134C on account to Brenda Myers, $440 plus $22 sales tax.

18   Made sale no. 105D on account to Edith Walton, $980 plus $49 sales tax.

21   Made sale no. 202B on account to Susan Chang, $620 plus $31 sales tax.

24   Made sale no. 162A on account to Heidi Schwitzer, $1,600 plus $80 sales tax.

These transactions are entered in a general journal, as shown in Figure 10-11.

FIGURE 10-11   Sales Entered in General Journal

4	Apr.	4	Accounts Receivable/E. Lorenzo		1	5	9	6	00											4
5			Sales								1	5	2	0	00		5
6			Sales Tax Payable										7	6	00		6
7			Sale No. 133C														7
8																	8
9		10	Accounts Receivable/B. Myers			4	6	2	00								9
10			Sales									4	4	0	00		10
11			Sales Tax Payable										2	2	00		11
12			Sale No. 134C														12
13																	13
14		18	Accounts Receivable/E. Walton		1	0	2	9	00								14
15			Sales									9	8	0	00		15
16			Sales Tax Payable										4	9	00		16
17			Sale No. 105D														17
18																	18
19		21	Accounts Receivable/S. Chang			6	5	1	00								19
20			Sales									6	2	0	00		20
21			Sales Tax Payable										3	1	00		21
22			Sale No. 202B														22
23																	23
24		24	Accounts Receivable/H. Schwitzer		1	6	8	0	00								24
25			Sales								1	6	0	0	00		25
26			Sales Tax Payable										8	0	00		26
27			Sale No. 162A														27

Posting Sales to the General Ledger

Sales transactions are posted from the general journal to the general ledger in the same manner as was illustrated in Chapter 4. Several steps are used, as indicated in Figure 10-12, for Northern Micro's April 4 and 10 sales transactions.

In the general ledger account:

STEP 1 Enter the date of the transaction in the Date column.

STEP 2 Enter the amount of the debit or credit in the Debit or Credit column.

STEP 3 Enter the new balance in the Balance columns under Debit or Credit.

STEP 4 Enter the journal page number from which each transaction is posted in the Posting Reference column.

In the journal:

STEP 5 Enter the ledger account number in the Posting Reference column of the journal for each transaction that is posted.

Other sales transactions would be posted in the same manner.

FIGURE 10-12   Posting Sales to the General Ledger

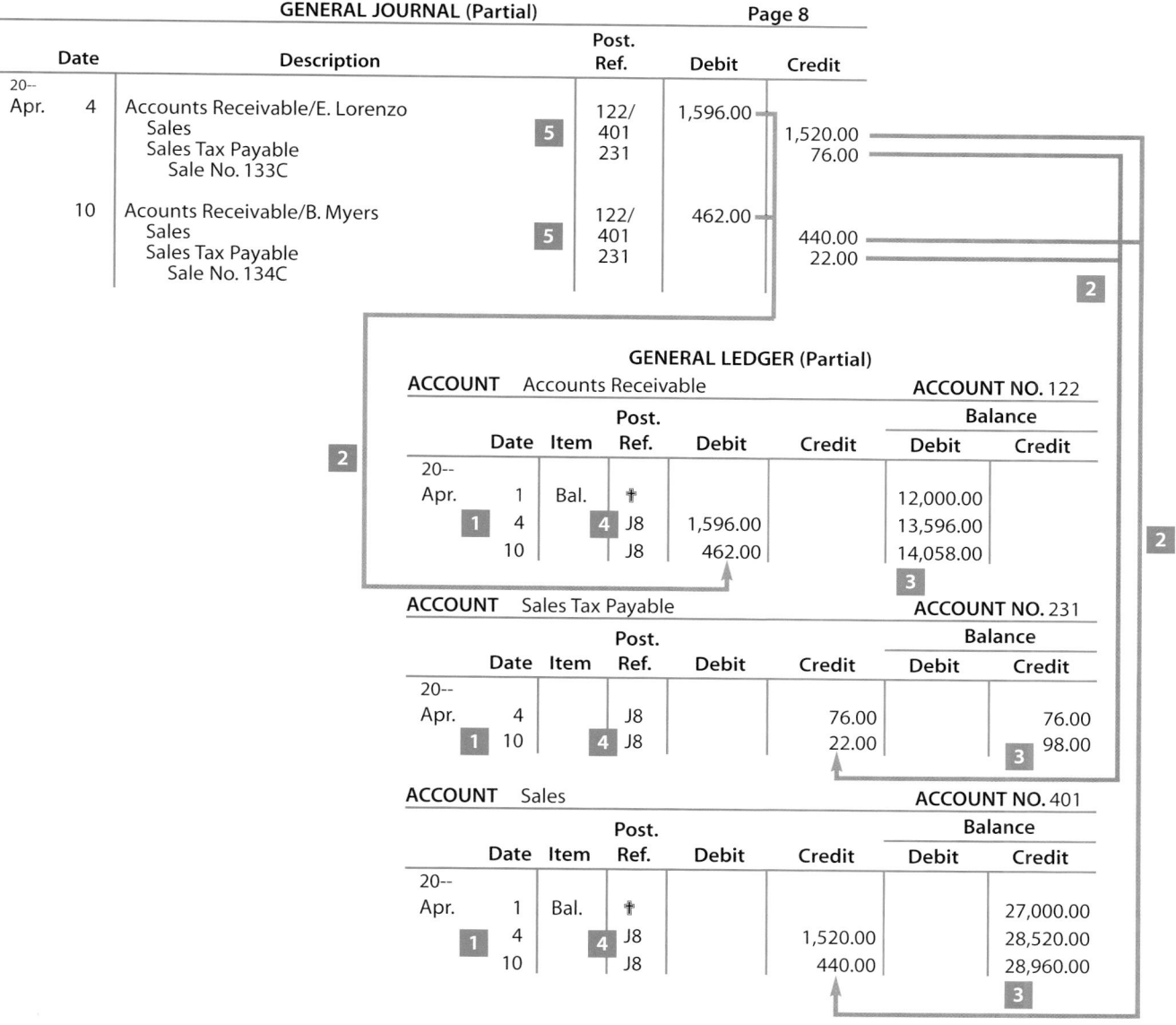

Posting Sales to the Accounts Receivable Ledger

After all posting to the general ledger is completed, the accounts receivable, sales tax payable, and sales accounts in the general ledger are up to date. But at this point, Northern Micro has no complete record of the account receivable from *individual customers*. To run the business properly, Northern Micro needs this information.

A common approach to keeping a record of each customer's account receivable is to use a subsidiary **accounts receivable ledger**. This is a separate ledger containing an individual account receivable for each customer. If there are many customer accounts, it is good practice to assign each customer an account number. The subsidiary ledger accounts are kept in either alphabetical or numerical order, depending on whether customer accounts are identified by number. A summary accounts receivable account called a **controlling account** is still maintained in the general ledger. The accounts receivable ledger is "subsidiary" to this account.

A three-column account form is commonly used for customer accounts. Only one balance column is needed because the normal balance is a debit. If a credit balance occurs, the amount may be bracketed.

Figure 10-13 illustrates the use of the accounts receivable ledger for Northern Micro's April 4 and 10 sales transactions. The accounts receivable ledger is posted from the journal *daily* so that current information is available for each customer at all times. Several steps are used to post from the general journal to the accounts receivable ledger, as shown in Figure 10-13.

In the accounts receivable ledger account:

STEP 1 Enter the date of the transaction in the Date column.

STEP 2 Enter the amount of the debit or credit in the Debit or Credit column.

STEP 3 Enter the new balance in the Balance column.

STEP 4 Enter the journal page number from which each transaction is posted in the Posting Reference column.

In the journal:

STEP 5 Enter a slash (/) followed by a check mark (✓) in the Posting Reference column of the journal for each transaction that is posted.

FIGURE 10-13 Posting Sales to the Accounts Receivable Ledger

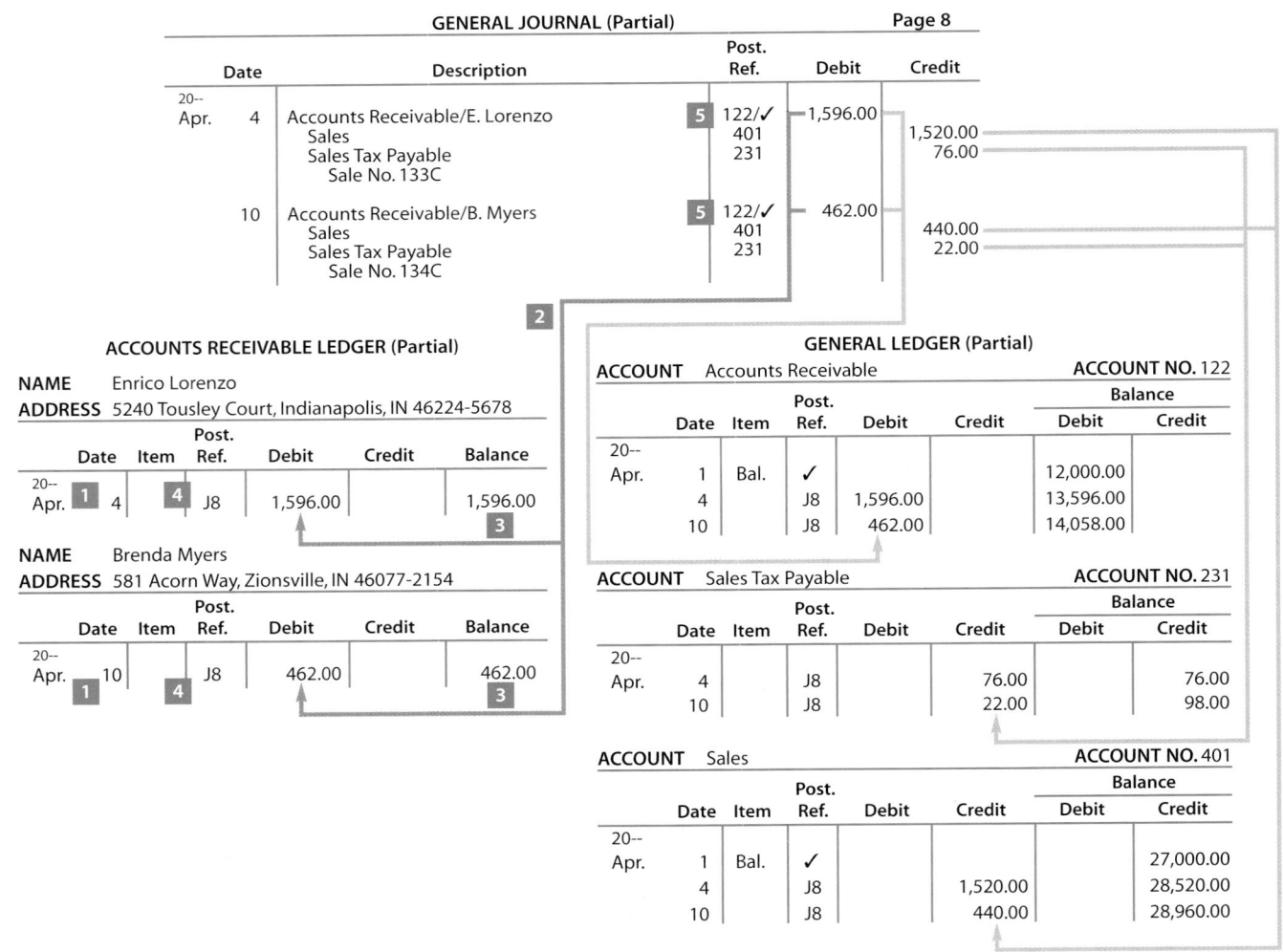

The accounts receivable ledger also can be posted from the source document used to make the general journal entry. For example, sales ticket no. 134C (see Figure 10-2) could be used to post that sale to Brenda Myers' account in the accounts receivable ledger. In this case, 134C would be inserted in the Posting Reference column of her account.

Note the relationship between the general journal, accounts receivable ledger, and general ledger. Entries in the general journal are posted to the general ledger and accounts receivable ledger. After the posting of the accounts receivable ledger and the general ledger is completed, the total of the accounts receivable ledger balances should equal the Accounts Receivable balance in the general ledger. Remember, the accounts receivable ledger is simply a detailed listing of the same information that is summarized in Accounts Receivable in the general ledger.

Sales Returns and Allowances

If a customer returns merchandise or is given an allowance for damaged merchandise, a general journal entry is required. On May 5, Susan Chang returned two printer cartridges costing $40 plus $2 sales tax (Figure 10-6, page 359). Figure 10-14 shows the general journal entry, general ledger posting, and accounts receivable ledger posting for this transaction.

The general journal entry is made in the usual manner. The general ledger is posted using the same five steps as were illustrated for sales transactions in Figure 10-12. The accounts receivable ledger is posted using the five steps below, as illustrated in Figure 10-14.

In the accounts receivable ledger account:

STEP 1 Enter the date of the transaction in the Date column.

STEP 2 Enter the amount of the debit or credit in the Debit or Credit column.

STEP 3 Enter the new balance in the Balance column.

STEP 4 Enter the journal page number from which each transaction is posted in the Posting Reference column.

In the journal:

STEP 5 Enter a slash (/) followed by a check mark (✔) in the Posting Reference column of the journal for each transaction that is posted.

Cash Receipts

Like sales transactions, cash receipt transactions occur frequently in most businesses. Sales on account lead to cash receipts, which are entered in the general journal. For example, assume that Northern Micro receives cash from Enrico Lorenzo for sale no. 133C on April 14. The transaction is recorded in the general journal as follows:

25	Apr.	14	Cash		1 5 9 6 00				25
26			Accounts Receivable/E. Lorenzo			1 5 9 6 00			26
27			Received cash on account						27

FIGURE 10-14   Accounting for Sales Returns and Allowances

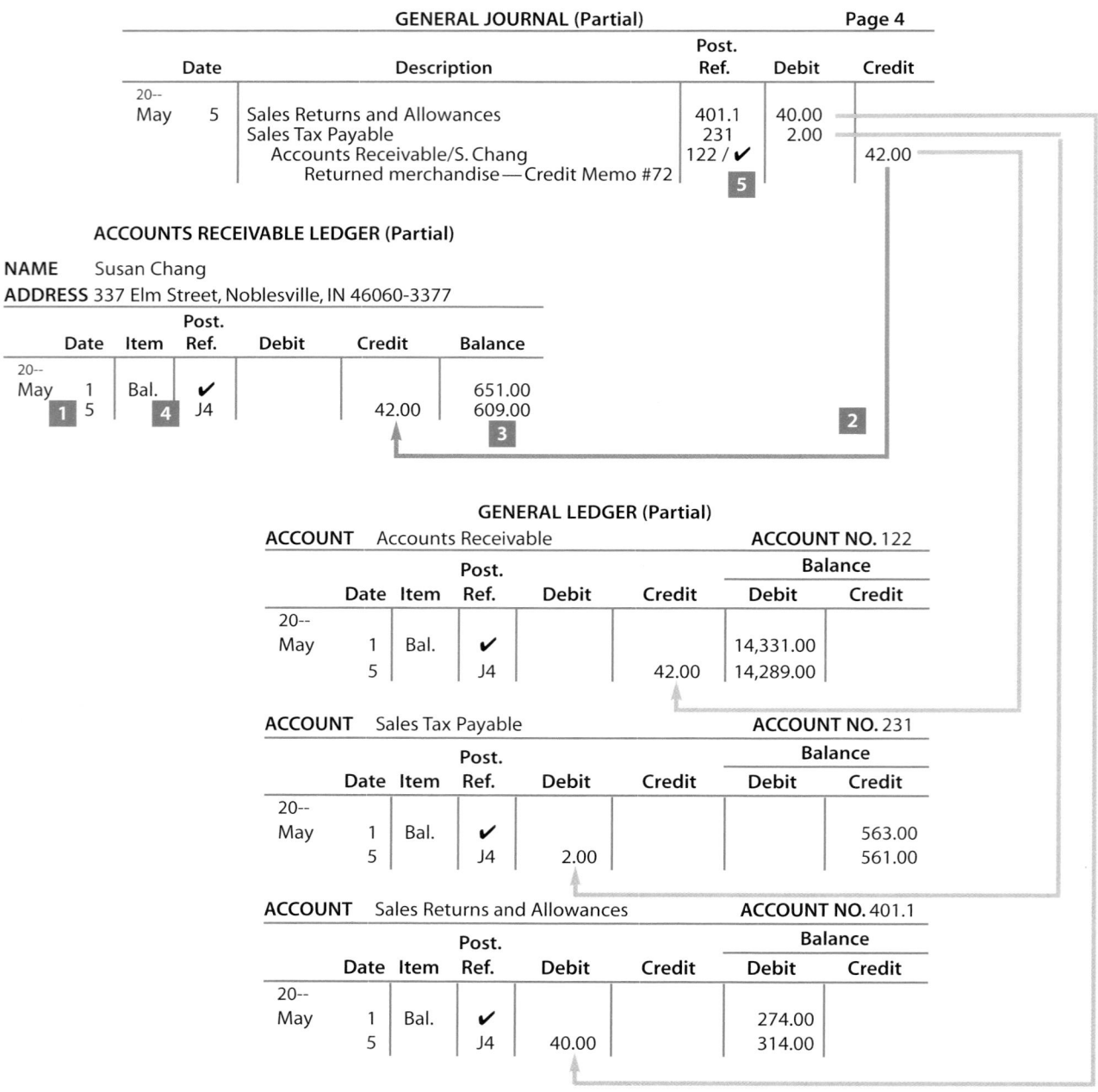

Most businesses also regularly make cash sales. The following entry shows cash sales of $500 recorded in the general journal on May 5:

	Date		Description		Debit				Credit				
3	May	5	Cash		5	0	0	00					3
4			Sales						5	0	0	00	4
5			Made cash sales										5

In addition, an increasing amount of sales today are made using bank credit cards. Bank credit card sales are similar to cash sales because the cash is available to the business as soon as an electronic deposit is made at the end of the day. The credit card company makes the electronic deposit to the merchandiser's bank account for the gross amount of credit card sales less a processing fee. The fee is based on the gross amount of the sale, including the sales tax. Thus, on a sale of $100 plus sales tax of $5, the credit card fee at 4% would be $4.20 (4% × $105). The following entry shows this credit card sale recorded on May 6:

8	May	6	Cash					1	0	0	80							8
9			Bank Credit Card Expense							4	20							9
10			Sales										1	0	0	00		10
11			Sales Tax Payable												5	00		11
12			Made credit card sale															12

To illustrate the journalizing and posting of cash receipts transactions, we continue to use Northern Micro. Assume the following cash receipts transactions related to sales occurred during April 20--. (To simplify the illustration, cash sales and bank credit card sales for the month are summarized as a single transaction at the end of the month.)

Apr. 14   Received cash on account from Enrico Lorenzo for sale no. 133C, $1,596.

20   Received cash on account from Brenda Myers for sale no. 134C, $462.

28   Received cash on account from Edith Walton for sale no. 105D, $1,029.

30   Cash sales for the month are $3,600 plus tax of $180.

30   Bank credit card sales for the month are $2,500 plus tax of $125. Bank credit card expenses on these sales are $100.

These transactions are entered in a general journal as shown in Figure 10-15.

FIGURE 10-15   Cash Receipts Entered in General Journal

4	Apr.	14	Cash			1	5	9	6	00								4
5			Accounts Receivable/E. Lorenzo									1	5	9	6	00		5
6			Received cash on account															6
7																		7
8		20	Cash				4	6	2	00								8
9			Accounts Receivable/B. Myers										4	6	2	00		9
10			Received cash on account															10
11																		11
12		28	Cash			1	0	2	9	00								12
13			Accounts Receivable/E. Walton									1	0	2	9	00		13
14			Received cash on account															14
15																		15
16		30	Cash			3	7	8	0	00								16
17			Sales									3	6	0	0	00		17
18			Sales Tax Payable										1	8	0	00		18
19			Made cash sales															19
20																		20
21		30	Cash			2	5	2	5	00								21
22			Bank Credit Card Expense				1	0	0	00								22
23			Sales									2	5	0	0	00		23
24			Sales Tax Payable										1	2	5	00		24
25			Made credit card sales															25

A B R O A D E R V I E W

Is This Sale for Real?

U.S. businesses lose billions of dollars annually because of credit card fraud and bad checks. To reduce credit card fraud, cashiers should do two things: (1) Watch the customer sign the credit card slip and match it to the signature on the card. (2) Obtain an approval code on all credit card transactions. To reduce bad check losses, cashiers should accept only a driver's license as identification. They should compare the picture with the customer, watch the check being signed, and match the check signature with that on the driver's license.

Posting Cash Receipts to the General Ledger and Accounts Receivable Ledger

Cash receipts transactions are posted to the general ledger in the same manner as was illustrated for sales transactions in Figure 10-12. To post cash receipts to the accounts receivable ledger, the steps below are used, as illustrated in Figure 10-16 for Northern Micro's April 14 and 20 cash receipts transactions.

In the accounts receivable ledger account:

STEP 1 Enter the date of the transaction in the Date column.

STEP 2 Enter the amount of the debit or credit in the Debit or Credit column.

STEP 3 Enter the new balance in the Balance column.

STEP 4 Enter the journal page number from which each transaction is posted in the Posting Reference column.

In the journal:

STEP 5 Enter a slash (/) followed by a check mark (✔) in the Posting Reference column of the journal for each transaction that is posted.

FIGURE 10-16 Posting Cash Receipts to the General Ledger and Accounts Receivable Ledger

SCHEDULE OF ACCOUNTS RECEIVABLE

L04 Prepare a schedule of accounts receivable.

At the end of the month, all postings to Accounts Receivable in the general ledger and to the accounts receivable ledger should be complete, as shown in Figure 10-17. At this point, the Accounts Receivable balance in the general ledger should equal the sum of the customer balances in the accounts receivable ledger.

To verify that the sum of the accounts receivable ledger balances equals the Accounts Receivable balance, a **schedule of accounts receivable** is prepared. This is an alphabetical or numerical listing of customer accounts and balances, usually prepared at the end of the month. Note that customers whose account balance is zero are not included. The schedule of accounts receivable for Northern Micro as of April 30 is illustrated in Figure 10-18.

FIGURE 10-17   General Ledger and Accounts Receivable Ledger after Posting

ACCOUNTS RECEIVABLE LEDGER

NAME   Helen Avery
ADDRESS   1739 Woodsage Trace, Indianapolis, IN 46237-1199

Date	Item	Post. Ref.	Debit	Credit	Balance
20-- Apr. 1	Bal.	✝			2,302.00

NAME   Susan Chang
ADDRESS   337 Elm Street, Noblesville, IN 46060-3377

Date	Item	Post. Ref.	Debit	Credit	Balance
20-- Apr. 21		J9	651.00		651.00

NAME   Enrico Lorenzo
ADDRESS   5240 Tousley Court, Indianapolis, IN 46224-5678

Date	Item	Post. Ref.	Debit	Credit	Balance
20-- Apr. 4		J8	1,596.00		1,596.00
14		J8		1,596.00	0

NAME   Brenda Myers
ADDRESS   581 Acorn Way, Zionsville, IN 46077-2154

Date	Item	Post. Ref.	Debit	Credit	Balance
20-- Apr. 10		J8	462.00		462.00
20		J8		462.00	0

NAME   Heidi Schwitzer
ADDRESS   5858 Wildflower Cir., Bloomington, IN 47401-6209

Date	Item	Post. Ref.	Debit	Credit	Balance
20-- Apr. 1	Bal.	✔			1,883.00
24		J9	1,680.00		3,563.00

ACCOUNTS RECEIVABLE LEDGER (Continued)

NAME   Ken Ulmet
ADDRESS   5260 Eagle Creek, Indianapolis, IN 46254-8275

Date	Item	Post. Ref.	Debit	Credit	Balance
20-- Apr. 1	Bal.	✔			3,315.00

NAME   Edith Walton
ADDRESS   1113 Stones Crossing, Zionsville, IN 46077-6601

Date	Item	Post. Ref.	Debit	Credit	Balance
20-- Apr. 18		J8	1,029.00		1,029.00
28		J9		1,029.00	0

NAME   Vivian Winston
ADDRESS   124 Main St., Zionsville, IN 46077-1358

Date	Item	Post. Ref.	Debit	Credit	Balance
20-- Apr. 1	Bal.	✝			4,500.00

GENERAL LEDGER (Partial)

ACCOUNT   Accounts Receivable   **ACCOUNT NO.** 122

Date	Item	Post. Ref.	Debit	Credit	Balance Debit	Balance Credit
20-- Apr. 1	Bal.	✝			12,000.00	
4		J8	1,596.00		13,596.00	
10		J8	462.00		14,058.00	
14		J8		1,596.00	12,462.00	
18		J8	1,029.00		13,491.00	
20		J8		462.00	13,029.00	
21		J9	651.00		13,680.00	
24		J9	1,680.00		15,360.00	
28		J9		1,029.00	14,331.00	

FIGURE 10-18   Schedule of Accounts Receivable

Northern Micro
Schedule of Accounts Receivable
April 30, 20--

Helen Avery	$ 2	3	0	2	00
Susan Chang		6	5	1	00
Heidi Schwitzer	3	5	6	3	00
Ken Ulmet	3	3	1	5	00
Vivian Winston	4	5	0	0	00
Total	$14	3	3	1	00

This schedule is prepared from the list of customer accounts in the accounts receivable ledger. The total calculated in the schedule is compared with the balance in Accounts Receivable in the general ledger. Note that the $14,331 total listed in the schedule equals the Accounts Receivable balance shown in Figure 10-17. If the schedule total and the Accounts Receivable balance do not agree, the error must be located and corrected. To find the error, use the following procedures:

STEP 1 Verify the total of the schedule.

STEP 2 Verify the postings to the accounts receivable ledger.

STEP 3 Verify the postings to Accounts Receivable in the general ledger.

Learning Objectives	Key Points to Remember
LO1 Describe merchandise sales transactions.	A merchandising business buys and sells merchandise. Retailers generally make sales in the store. Important accounting documents are cash register tapes and sales tickets. Wholesalers generally ship merchandise to retailers. A key accounting document is the sales invoice. When customers return merchandise or obtain price adjustments, a credit memo is issued.
LO2 Describe and use merchandise sales accounts.	Four accounts are used in accounting for merchandise sales transactions. 1. Sales 2. Sales Tax Payable 3. Sales Returns and Allowances 4. Sales Discounts
LO3 Describe and use the accounts receivable ledger.	To post sales transactions to the general ledger, use these five steps. **In the general ledger account:** STEP 1 Enter the date of the transaction in the Date column. STEP 2 Enter the amount of the debit or credit in the Debit or Credit column. STEP 3 Enter the new balance in the Balance columns under Debit or Credit. STEP 4 Enter the journal page number from which each transaction is posted in the Posting Reference column. **In the journal:** STEP 5 Enter the ledger account number in the Posting Reference column of the journal for each transaction that is posted. An accounts receivable ledger is a separate ledger containing an individual account receivable for each customer. To post sales transactions to the accounts receivable ledger, use these five steps.

(continued)

Learning Objectives	Key Points to Remember
LO3 (concluded)	**In the accounts receivable ledger account:**

STEP 1 Enter the date of the transaction in the Date column.

STEP 2 Enter the amount of the debit or credit in the Debit or Credit column.

STEP 3 Enter the new balance in the Balance column.

STEP 4 Enter the journal page number from which each transaction is posted in the Posting Reference column.

In the journal:

STEP 5 Enter a slash (/) followed by a check mark (✔) in the Posting Reference column of the journal for each transaction that is posted.

To post cash receipts transactions to the general ledger, use these five steps.

In the general ledger account:

STEP 1 Enter the date of the transaction in the Date column.

STEP 2 Enter the amount of the debit or credit in the Debit or Credit column.

STEP 3 Enter the new balance in the Balance columns under Debit or Credit.

STEP 4 Enter the journal page number from which each transaction is posted in the Posting Reference column.

In the journal:

STEP 5 Enter the ledger account number in the Posting Reference column of the journal for each transaction that is posted.

To post cash receipts transactions to the accounts receivable ledger, use these five steps.

In the accounts receivable ledger account:

STEP 1 Enter the date of the transaction in the Date column.

STEP 2 Enter the amount of the debit or credit in the Debit or Credit column.

STEP 3 Enter the new balance in the Balance column.

STEP 4 Enter the journal page number from which each transaction is posted in the Posting Reference column.

In the journal:

STEP 5 Enter a slash (/) followed by a check mark (✔) in the Posting Reference column of the journal for each transaction that is posted.

| **LO4** **Prepare a schedule of accounts receivable.** | The schedule of accounts receivable is used to verify that the sum of the accounts receivable ledger balances equals the Accounts Receivable balance. |

DEMONSTRATION PROBLEM

Karen Hunt operates Hunt's Audio-Video Store. The books include a general journal, general ledger, and accounts receivable ledger. The following transactions related to sales on account and cash receipts occurred during April 20--:

Apr. 3   Sold merchandise on account to Susan Haberman, $159.50 plus tax of $11.17. Sale no. 41.

4   Sold merchandise on account to Goro Kimura, $299.95 plus tax of $21.00. Sale no. 42.

6   Received payment from Tera Scherrer on account, $69.50.

7   Issued credit memo no. 48 to Kenneth Watt for merchandise returned that had been sold on account, $42.75 including tax of $2.80.

10   Received payment from Kellie Cokley on account, $99.95.

11   Sold merchandise on account to Victor Cardona, $499.95 plus tax of $35.00. Sale no. 43.

14   Received payment from Kenneth Watt in full settlement of account, $157.00.

17   Sold merchandise on account to Susan Haberman, $379.95 plus tax of $26.60. Sale no. 44.

19   Sold merchandise on account to Tera Scherrer, $59.95 plus tax of $4.20. Sale no. 45.

21   Issued credit memo no. 49 to Goro Kimura for merchandise returned that had been sold on account, $53.45 including tax of $3.50.

24   Received payment from Victor Cardona on account, $299.95.

25   Sold merchandise on account to Kellie Cokley, $179.50 plus tax of $12.57. Sale no. 46.

26   Received payment from Susan Haberman on account, $250.65.

28   Sold merchandise on account to Kenneth Watt, $49.95 plus tax of $3.50. Sale no. 47.

30   Bank credit card sales for the month were $1,220.00 plus tax of $85.40. Bank credit card expense on these sales was $65.27.

30   Cash sales for the month were $2,000.00 plus tax of $140.00.

(continued)

Hunt had the following general ledger account balances as of April 1:

Account Title	Account No.	General Ledger Balance on April 1
Cash	101	$5,000.00
Accounts Receivable	122	1,208.63
Sales Tax Payable	231	72.52
Sales	401	8,421.49
Sales Returns and Allowances	401.1	168.43
Bank Credit Card Expense	513	215.00

Hunt also had the following accounts receivable ledger account balances as of April 1:

Customer	Accounts Receivable Balance
Victor Cardona 6300 Washington Blvd. St. Louis, MO 63130-9523	$299.95
Kellie Cokley 4220 Kingsbury Blvd. St. Louis, MO 63130-1645	$99.95
Susan Haberman 9421 Garden Ct. Kirkwood, MO 63122-1878	$79.98
Goro Kimura 6612 Arundel Pl. Clayton, MO 63150-9266	$379.50
Tera Scherrer 315 W. Linden St. Webster Groves, MO 63119-9881	$149.50
Kenneth Watt 11742 Fawnridge Dr. St. Louis, MO 63131-1726	$199.75

REQUIRED

1. Open general ledger accounts and three-column accounts receivable ledger accounts for Hunt's Audio-Video Store as of April 1, 20--. Enter the April 1 balance in each of the accounts.

2. Enter each transaction in a general journal (page 7).

3. Post directly from the journal to the proper customers' accounts in the accounts receivable ledger. Each subsidiary ledger account should show the initial "J," followed by the appropriate journal page number as a posting reference for each transaction.

4. Post from the journal to the proper general ledger accounts. Each general ledger account should show the initial "J," followed by the appropriate journal page number as a posting reference for each transaction.

5. Prove the balance of the summary accounts receivable account by preparing a schedule of accounts receivable as of April 30, based on the accounts receivable ledger.

Solution 1. and 3.

ACCOUNTS RECEIVABLE LEDGER

NAME: Victor Cardona

DATE		ITEM	POST. REF.	DEBIT	CREDIT	BALANCE
20-- Apr.	1	Balance	✔			2 9 9 95
	11		J7	5 3 4 95		8 3 4 90
	24		J8		2 9 9 95	5 3 4 95

NAME: Kellie Cokley

DATE		ITEM	POST. REF.	DEBIT	CREDIT	BALANCE
20-- Apr.	1	Balance	✔			9 9 95
	10		J7		9 9 95	
	25		J8	1 9 2 07		1 9 2 07

NAME: Susan Haberman

DATE		ITEM	POST. REF.	DEBIT	CREDIT	BALANCE
20-- Apr.	1	Balance	✔			7 9 98
	3		J7	1 7 0 67		2 5 0 65
	17		J7	4 0 6 55		6 5 7 20
	26		J8		2 5 0 65	4 0 6 55

NAME: Goro Kimura

DATE		ITEM	POST REF.	DEBIT	CREDIT	BALANCE
20-- Apr.	1	Balance	✔			3 7 9 50
	4		J7	3 2 0 95		7 0 0 45
	21		J8		5 3 45	6 4 7 00

NAME: Tera Scherrer

DATE		ITEM	POST. REF.	DEBIT	CREDIT	BALANCE
20-- Apr.	1	Balance	✔			1 4 9 50
	6		J7		6 9 50	8 0 00
	19		J8	6 4 15		1 4 4 15

(continued)

NAME: Kenneth Watt																		
DATE		ITEM	POST REF.	DEBIT					CREDIT					BALANCE				
20-- Apr.	1	Balance	✔												1	9	9	75
	7		J7							4	2	75			1	5	7	00
	14		J7						1	5	7	00						
	28		J8		5	3	45									5	3	45

2., 3., and 4.

	DATE		DESCRIPTION	POST. REF.	DEBIT				CREDIT				
1	20-- Apr.	3	Accounts Receivable/Susan Haberman	122/✔	1	7	0	67					1
2			Sales	401					1	5	9	50	2
3			Sales Tax Payable	231						1	1	17	3
4			Sale No. 41										4
5													5
6		4	Accounts Receivable/Goro Kimura	122/✔	3	2	0	95					6
7			Sales	401					2	9	9	95	7
8			Sales Tax Payable	231						2	1	00	8
9			Sale No. 42										9
10													10
11		6	Cash	101		6	9	50					11
12			Accounts Receivable/Tera Scherrer	122/✔						6	9	50	12
13			Received cash on account										13
14													14
15		7	Sales Returns and Allowances	401.1		3	9	95					15
16			Sales Tax Payable	231			2	80					16
17			Accounts Receivable/Kenneth Watt	122/✔						4	2	75	17
18			Returned merchandise										18
19													19
20		10	Cash	101		9	9	95					20
21			Accounts Receivable/Kellie Cokley	122/✔						9	9	95	21
22			Received cash on account										22
23													23
24		11	Accounts Receivable/Victor Cardona	122/✔	5	3	4	95					24
25			Sales	401					4	9	9	95	25
26			Sales Tax Payable	231						3	5	00	26
27			Sale No. 43										27
28													28
29		14	Cash	101	1	5	7	00					29
30			Accounts Receivable/Kenneth Watt	122/✔					1	5	7	00	30
31			Received cash on account										31
32													32
33		17	Accounts Receivable/Susan Haberman	122/✔	4	0	6	55					33
34			Sales	401					3	7	9	95	34
35			Sales Tax Payable	231						2	6	60	35
36			Sale No. 44										36

GENERAL JOURNAL   PAGE 7

2., 3., and 4.

GENERAL JOURNAL
PAGE 8

	DATE		DESCRIPTION	POST. REF.	DEBIT	CREDIT	
1	20-- Apr.	19	Accounts Receivable/Tera Scherrer	122/✔	6 4 15		1
2			Sales	401		5 9 95	2
3			Sales Tax Payable	231		4 20	3
4			Sale No. 45				4
5							5
6		21	Sales Returns and Allowances	401.1	4 9 95		6
7			Sales Tax Payable	231	3 50		7
8			Accounts Receivable/Goro Kimura	122/✔		5 3 45	8
9			Returned merchandise—Credit Memo #49				9
10							10
11		24	Cash	101	2 9 9 95		11
12			Accounts Receivable/Victor Cardona	122/✔		2 9 9 95	12
13			Received cash on account				13
14							14
15		25	Accounts Receivable/Kellie Cokley	122/✔	1 9 2 07		15
16			Sales	401		1 7 9 50	16
17			Sales Tax Payable	231		1 2 57	17
18			Sale No. 46				18
19							19
20		26	Cash	101	2 5 0 65		20
21			Accounts Receivable/Susan Haberman	122/✔		2 5 0 65	21
22			Received cash on account				22
23							23
24		28	Accounts Receivable/Kenneth Watt	122/✔	5 3 45		24
25			Sales	401		4 9 95	25
26			Sales Tax Payable	231		3 50	26
27			Sale No. 47				27
28							28
29		30	Cash	101	1 2 4 0 13		29
30			Bank Credit Card Expense	513	6 5 27		30
31			Sales	401		1 2 2 0 00	31
32			Sales Tax Payable	231		8 5 40	32
33			Credit card sales				33
34							34
35		30	Cash	101	2 1 4 0 00		35
36			Sales	401		2 0 0 0 00	36
37			Sales Tax Payable	231		1 4 0 00	37
38			Made cash sales				38

1. and 4.

GENERAL LEDGER (PARTIAL)

ACCOUNT: Cash   ACCOUNT NO. 101

DATE		ITEM	POST. REF.	DEBIT	CREDIT	BALANCE DEBIT	BALANCE CREDIT
20-- Apr.	1	Balance	✔			5 0 0 0 00	
	6		J7	6 9 50		5 0 6 9 50	
	10		J7	9 9 95		5 1 6 9 45	
	14		J7	1 5 7 00		5 3 2 6 45	
	24		J8	2 9 9 95		5 6 2 6 40	
	26		J8	2 5 0 65		5 8 7 7 05	
	30		J8	1 2 4 0 13		7 1 1 7 18	
	30		J8	2 1 4 0 00		9 2 5 7 18	

(continued)

1. and 4.

ACCOUNT: Accounts Receivable   ACCOUNT NO. 122

DATE	ITEM	POST. REF.	DEBIT	CREDIT	BALANCE DEBIT	BALANCE CREDIT
20-- Apr. 1	Balance	✔			1 2 0 8 63	
3		J7	1 7 0 67		1 3 7 9 30	
4		J7	3 2 0 95		1 7 0 0 25	
6		J7		6 9 50	1 6 3 0 75	
7		J7		4 2 75	1 5 8 8 00	
10		J7		9 9 95	1 4 8 8 05	
11		J7	5 3 4 95		2 0 2 3 00	
14		J7		1 5 7 00	1 8 6 6 00	
17		J7	4 0 6 55		2 2 7 2 55	
19		J8	6 4 15		2 3 3 6 70	
21		J8		5 3 45	2 2 8 3 25	
24		J8		2 9 9 95	1 9 8 3 30	
25		J8	1 9 2 07		2 1 7 5 37	
26		J8		2 5 0 65	1 9 2 4 72	
28		J8	5 3 45		1 9 7 8 17	

ACCOUNT: Sales Tax Payable   ACCOUNT NO. 231

DATE	ITEM	POST. REF.	DEBIT	CREDIT	BALANCE DEBIT	BALANCE CREDIT
20-- Apr. 1	Balance	✔				7 2 52
3		J7		1 1 17		8 3 69
4		J7		2 1 00		1 0 4 69
7		J7	2 80			1 0 1 89
11		J7		3 5 00		1 3 6 89
17		J7		2 6 60		1 6 3 49
19		J8		4 20		1 6 7 69
21		J8	3 50			1 6 4 19
25		J8		1 2 57		1 7 6 76
28		J8		3 50		1 8 0 26
30		J8		8 5 40		2 6 5 66
30		J8		1 4 0 00		4 0 5 66

ACCOUNT: Sales   ACCOUNT NO. 401

DATE	ITEM	POST. REF.	DEBIT	CREDIT	BALANCE DEBIT	BALANCE CREDIT
20-- Apr. 1	Balance	✔				8 4 2 1 49
3		J7		1 5 9 50		8 5 8 0 99
4		J7		2 9 9 95		8 8 8 0 94
11		J7		4 9 9 95		9 3 8 0 89
17		J7		3 7 9 95		9 7 6 0 84
19		J8		5 9 95		9 8 2 0 79
25		J8		1 7 9 50		10 0 0 0 29
28		J8		4 9 95		10 0 5 0 24
30		J8		1 2 2 0 00		11 2 7 0 24
30		J8		2 0 0 0 00		13 2 7 0 24

1. and 4.

ACCOUNT: Sales Returns and Allowances											ACCOUNT NO. 401.1				

DATE		ITEM	POST. REF.	DEBIT			CREDIT			BALANCE					
										DEBIT			CREDIT		
20-- Apr.	1	Balance	✔							1 6 8	43				
	7		J7	3 9	95					2 0 8	38				
	21		J8	4 9	95					2 5 8	33				

ACCOUNT: Bank Credit Card Expense											ACCOUNT NO. 513				

DATE		ITEM	POST. REF.	DEBIT			CREDIT			BALANCE					
										DEBIT			CREDIT		
20-- Apr.	1	Balance	✔							2 1 5	00				
	30		J8	6 5	27					2 8 0	27				

5.

Hunt's Audio-Video Store Schedule of Accounts Receivable April 30, 20--		
Victor Cardona	5 3 4	95
Kellie Cokley	1 9 2	07
Susan Haberman	4 0 6	55
Goro Kimura	6 4 7	00
Tera Scherrer	1 4 4	15
Kenneth Watt	5 3	45
Total	1 9 7 8	17

KEY TERMS

accounts receivable ledger (365)   A separate ledger containing an individual account receivable for each customer, kept in either alphabetical or numerical order.

cash discounts (362)   Discounts to encourage prompt payment by customers who buy merchandise on account.

controlling account (365)   A summary account maintained in the general ledger with a subsidiary ledger (for example, the accounts receivable ledger).

credit memo (358)   A document issued when credit is given for merchandise returned or for an allowance.

merchandising business (356)   A business that purchases merchandise such as clothing, furniture, or computers, and sells that merchandise to its customers.

sale (356)   A transfer of merchandise from one business or individual to another in exchange for cash or a promise to pay cash.

sales allowances (358)   Reductions in the price of merchandise granted by the seller because of defects or other problems with the merchandise.

sales discounts (362)   To the seller, cash discounts are considered sales discounts.

sales invoice (358)   A document that is generated to bill the customer to whom the sale was made.

sales return (358)   Merchandise returned by a customer for a refund.
sales ticket (357)   A document created as evidence of a sale in a retail business.
schedule of accounts receivable (371)   An alphabetical or numerical listing of customer accounts and balances, usually prepared at the end of the month.

Self-Study Test Questions

True/False

1. All sales, for cash or on credit, can be recorded in the general journal.

2. Reductions in the price of merchandise granted by the seller because of defects or other problems with the merchandise are called sales allowances.

3. Sales Tax Payable is a liability account that is credited for the amount of tax imposed on sales.

4. Sales Returns and Allowances is debited for the amount of the sale, including the sales tax on that amount.

5. Cash discounts are offered to encourage prompt payment by customers who buy on account.

Multiple Choice

1. A credit sale of $250 plus a 6% sales tax would require a debit to Accounts Receivable of

   (a) $15.   (c) $30.
   (b) $280.   (d) $265.

2. When $25 of merchandise is returned for a credit on account, what is the amount of the credit to Accounts Receivable, assuming a 6% sales tax rate?

   (a) $1.50   (c) $26.50
   (b) $25.00   (d) $31.00

3. When $300, plus sales tax of 6%, is received for an amount previously owed, Cash is debited for what amount?

   (a) $18   (c) $300
   (b) $318   (d) $282

4. When credit sales are $325 plus sales tax of 5%, and there is a bank credit card fee of 3%, what is the debit to Bank Credit Card Expense?

   (a) $16.25   (c) $341.25
   (b) $10.24   (d) $331.01

5. Cash receipts should

   (a) be posted to customer accounts daily.
   (b) be posted to customer accounts weekly.
   (c) be posted to customer accounts at the end of the month.
   (d) not be posted.

The answers to the Self-Study Test Questions are at the end of the text.

REVIEW QUESTIONS

LO1   1. Identify the sales documents commonly used in retail and wholesale businesses.

LO1   2. What is the purpose of a credit memo?

LO2   3. Describe how each of the following accounts is used: (1) Sales, (2) Sales Tax Payable, (3) Sales Returns and Allowances, and (4) Sales Discounts.

LO3   4. What steps are followed in posting sales from the general journal to the general ledger?

LO3   5. What steps are followed in posting sales from the general journal to the accounts receivable ledger?

LO3   6. What steps are followed in posting sales returns and allowances from the general journal to the general ledger and accounts receivable ledger?

LO3   7. What steps are followed in posting cash receipts from the general journal to the general ledger?

LO3   8. What steps are followed in posting cash receipts from the general journal to the accounts receivable ledger?

LO4   9. If the total of the schedule of accounts receivable does not agree with the Accounts Receivable balance, what procedures should be used to search for the error?

REVISITING THE OPENER

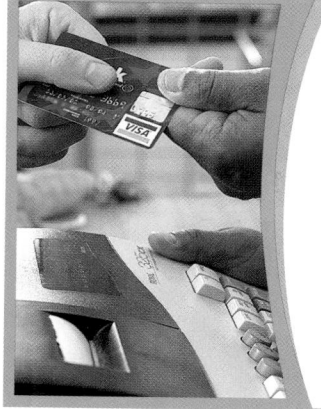

In the chapter opener on page 355, you are asked to consider whether Evan should make bank credit card sales at his store.

(1) Explain to Evan how bank credit card sales are "just like cash."

(2) Assume a bank credit card sale is made for $400 plus sales tax of 5%, with a bank credit card fee of 3%. What journal entry should Evan's bookkeeper prepare for this sale?

© DIGITAL IMAGING GROUP

SERIES A EXERCISES

E 10-1A (LO1)   **SALES DOCUMENTS** For each document or procedure listed below, indicate whether it would be used for a retail business or a wholesale business, as described in the chapter.

1. sales ticket   4. cash register tape summary
2. sales invoice   5. credit memo
3. credit approval   6. customer purchase order

E 10-2A (LO2)

✓ 3(d):

Sales Ret. & Allow.   35

  Accts. Rec.   35

SALES TRANSACTIONS AND T ACCOUNTS Using T accounts for Cash, Accounts Receivable, Sales Tax Payable, Sales, Sales Returns and Allowances, and Sales Discounts, enter the following sales transactions. Use a new set of accounts for each part, 1–5.

1. No sales tax.

   (a) Merchandise is sold for $300 cash.
   (b) Merchandise is sold on account for $285.
   (c) Payment is received for merchandise sold on account.

2. 5% sales tax.

   (a) Merchandise is sold for $300 cash plus sales tax.
   (b) Merchandise is sold on account for $285 plus sales tax.
   (c) Payment is received for merchandise sold on account.

3. Cash and credit sales, with returned merchandise.

   (a) Merchandise is sold for $325 cash.
   (b) $25 of merchandise sold for $325 is returned for refund.
   (c) Merchandise is sold on account for $350.
   (d) $35 of merchandise sold for $350 is returned for a credit.
   (e) Payment is received for balance owed on merchandise sold on account.

4. 5% sales tax, with returned merchandise.

   (a) Merchandise is sold on account for $400 plus sales tax.
   (b) Merchandise sold on account for $40 plus sales tax is returned for a credit.
   (c) Balance on account is paid in cash.
   (d) Merchandise is sold for $280 cash plus sales tax.
   (e) $20 of merchandise sold for $280 cash plus sales tax is returned for a refund.

5. Sales on account, with 2/10, n/30 cash discount terms.

   (a) Merchandise is sold on account for $350.
   (b) The balance is paid within the discount period.
   (c) Merchandise is sold on account for $290.
   (d) The balance is paid after the discount period.

E 10-3A (LO2)

✓ Net sales: $3,079

COMPUTING NET SALES Based on the following information, compute net sales.

Gross sales	$3,580
Sales returns and allowances	428
Sales discounts	73

E 10-4A (LO3)

✓ May 1:

A/R–J. Adams   2,120

  Sales   2,000

  Sales Tax Payable   120

JOURNALIZING SALES TRANSACTIONS Enter the following transactions in a general journal. Use a 6% sales tax rate.

May 1   Sold merchandise on account to J. Adams, $2,000 plus sales tax. Sale no. 488.

4   Sold merchandise on account to B. Clark, $1,800 plus sales tax. Sale no. 489.

8   Sold merchandise on account to A. Duck, $1,500 plus sales tax. Sale no. 490.

11   Sold merchandise on account to E. Hill, $1,950 plus sales tax. Sale no. 491.

E 10-5A (LO3)
✓ Ending Accts. Rec.
balance: $4,059

JOURNALIZING SALES RETURNS AND ALLOWANCES Enter the following transactions in a general journal and post them to the appropriate general ledger and accounts receivable ledger accounts. Use account numbers as shown in the chapter. Beginning balance in Accounts Receivable is $4,200. Beginning balances in customer accounts are Abramowitz, $850; Gruder, $428; and Perez, $1,018.

June 1   John B. Abramowitz returned merchandise previously purchased on account (sale no. 329), $73.

6   Marie L. Perez returned merchandise previously purchased on account (sale no. 321), $44.

8   L. B. Gruder returned merchandise previously purchased on account (sale no. 299), $24.

E 10-6A (LO3)
✓ July 6:
Cash   643
  A/R–J. Adler   643

JOURNALIZING CASH RECEIPTS Enter the following transactions in a general journal:

July 6   James Adler made payment on account, $643.

10   Cash sales for the week were $2,320.

14   Betty Havel made payment on account, $430.

15   J. L. Borg made payment on account, $117.

17   Cash sales for the week were $2,237.

E 10-7A (LO4)
✓ Accts. Rec. balance: $4,586

SCHEDULE OF ACCOUNTS RECEIVABLE From the accounts receivable ledger shown, prepare a schedule of accounts receivable for Pheng Co. as of August 31, 20--.

ACCOUNTS RECEIVABLE LEDGER

NAME B & G Distributors
ADDRESS 2628 Burlington Avenue, Chicago, IL 60604-1329

DATE		ITEM	POST. REF.	DEBIT	CREDIT	BALANCE
20-- Aug.	3		J1	1 3 8 0 00		1 3 8 0 00
	8		J1		1 4 0 00	1 2 4 0 00

NAME M. Chang
ADDRESS 1422 SW Pacific, Chicago, IL 60603-8596

DATE		ITEM	POST. REF.	DEBIT	CREDIT	BALANCE
20-- Aug.	5		J1	2 1 3 6 00		2 1 3 6 00
	11		J2		2 1 3 6 00	

NAME B. J. Hinschliff & Co.
ADDRESS 133 College Blvd., Des Plaines, IL 60611-4431

DATE		ITEM	POST. REF.	DEBIT	CREDIT	BALANCE
20-- Aug.	15		J2	1 1 0 6 00		1 1 0 6 00
	21		J3	3 8 4 00		1 4 9 0 00

(continued)

NAME	Sally M. Pitts					

ADDRESS   213 East 29th Place, Chicago, IL 60601-6287

DATE	ITEM	POST. REF.	DEBIT	CREDIT	BALANCE
20-- Aug. 21		J3	8 3 8 00		8 3 8 00

NAME	Trendsetters, Inc.

ADDRESS   29 Industrial Way, Chicago, IL 60600-5918

DATE	ITEM	POST. REF.	DEBIT	CREDIT	BALANCE
20-- Aug. 28		J4	1 0 1 8 00		1 0 1 8 00

SERIES A PROBLEMS

P 10-8A (LO3)

✓ Accts. Rec. balance: $16,345.20

SALES TRANSACTIONS J. K. Bijan owns a retail business and made the following sales on account during the month of August 20--. There is a 6% sales tax on all sales.

Aug. 1 Sale no. 213 to Jung Manufacturing Co., $1,200 plus sales tax.

3 Sale no. 214 to Hassad Co., $3,600 plus sales tax.

7 Sale no. 215 to Helsinki, Inc., $1,400 plus sales tax. (Open a new account for this customer. Address is 125 Fishers Dr., Noblesville, IN 47870-8867.)

11 Sale no. 216 to Ardis Myler, $1,280 plus sales tax.

18 Sale no. 217 to Hassad Co., $4,330 plus sales tax.

22 Sale no. 218 to Jung Manufacturing Co., $2,000 plus sales tax.

30 Sale no. 219 to Ardis Myler, $1,610 plus sales tax.

REQUIRED

1. Record the transactions in a general journal.

2. Post from the journal to the general ledger and accounts receivable ledger accounts. Use account numbers as shown in the chapter.

P 10-9A (LO3)

✓ Accts. Rec. balance: $3,533.08

CASH RECEIPTS TRANSACTIONS Zebra Imaginarium, a retail business, had the following cash receipts during December 20--. The sales tax is 6%.

Dec. 1 Received payment on account from Michael Anderson, $1,360.

2 Received payment on account from Ansel Manufacturing, $382.

7 Cash sales for the week were $3,160 plus tax. Bank credit card sales for the week were $1,000 plus tax. Bank credit card fee is 3%.

8 Received payment on account from J. Gorbea, $880.

11 Michael Anderson returned merchandise for a credit, $60 plus tax.

14 Cash sales for the week were $2,800 plus tax. Bank credit card sales for the week were $800 plus tax. Bank credit card fee is 3%.

Dec. 20   Received payment on account from Tom Wilson, $1,110.

21   Ansel Manufacturing returned merchandise for a credit, $22 plus tax.

21   Cash sales for the week were $3,200 plus tax.

24   Received payment on account from Rachel Carson, $2,000.

Beginning general ledger account balances were:

Cash	$9,862
Accounts Receivable	9,352

Beginning customer account balances were:

M. Anderson	$2,480
Ansel Manufacturing	982
J. Gorbea	880
R. Carson	3,200
T. Wilson	1,810

REQUIRED

1.   Record the transactions in a general journal.

2.   Post from the journal to the general ledger and accounts receivable ledger accounts. Use account numbers as shown in the chapter.

P 10-10A (LO3)

✓ Accts. Rec. balance: $8,133.33

KLOOSTER
& ALLEN

SALES AND CASH RECEIPTS TRANSACTIONS Owens Distributors is a retail business. The following sales, returns, and cash receipts occurred during March 20--. There is an 8% sales tax. Beginning general ledger account balances were Cash, $9,741.00; and Accounts Receivable, $1,058.25. Beginning customer account balances included Thompson Group, $1,058.25.

Mar. 1   Sale no. 33C to Able & Co., $1,800 plus sales tax.

3   Sale no. 33D to R. J. Kalas, Inc., $2,240 plus sales tax.

5   Able & Co. returned merchandise from sale no. 33C for a credit (credit memo no. 66), $30 plus sales tax.

7   Cash sales for the week were $3,160 plus sales tax.

10   Received payment from Able & Co. for sale no. 33C less credit memo no. 66.

11   Sale no. 33E to Blevins Bakery, $1,210 plus sales tax.

13   Received payment from R. J. Kalas for sale no. 33D.

14   Cash sales for the week were $4,200 plus sales tax.

16   Blevins Bakery returned merchandise from sale no. 33E for a credit (credit memo no. 67), $44 plus sales tax.

18   Sale no. 33F to R. J. Kalas, Inc., $2,620 plus sales tax.

20   Received payment from Blevins Bakery for sale no. 33E less credit memo no. 67.

21   Cash sales for the week were $2,400 plus sales tax.

25   Sale no. 33G to Blevins Bakery, $1,915 plus sales tax.

(continued)

Mar. 27   Sale no. 33H to Thompson Group, $2,016 plus sales tax.

28   Cash sales for the week were $3,500 plus sales tax.

REQUIRED

1.   Record the transactions in a general journal.

2.   Post from the journal to the general ledger and accounts receivable ledger accounts. Use account numbers as shown in the chapter.

P 10-11A (LO4)

✓ Accts. Rec. balance,
Thompson Group: $3,235.53

SCHEDULE OF ACCOUNTS RECEIVABLE Based on the information provided in Problem 10-10A, prepare a schedule of accounts receivable for Owens Distributors as of March 31, 20--. Verify that the accounts receivable account balance in the general ledger agrees with the schedule of accounts receivable total.

SERIES B EXERCISES

E 10-1B (LO1)

SALES DOCUMENTS Indicate whether each of the following documents or procedures is for a retail business or for a wholesale business, as described in the chapter.

1.   A cash register receipt is given to the customer.

2.   Credit approval is required since sales are almost always "on account."

3.   Three copies of the sales invoice are prepared: one for shipping, one for the customer (as a bill), and one for accounting.

4.   A sales ticket is given to a customer and another copy is sent to accounting.

5.   The sales process begins with a customer purchase order.

6.   The sales invoice itemizes what is sold, its cost, and the total amount owed.

E 10-2B (LO2)

✓ 3(d):
Sales Ret. & Allow.   24
   Accts. Rec.   24

SALES TRANSACTIONS AND T ACCOUNTS Using T accounts for Cash, Accounts Receivable, Sales Tax Payable, Sales, Sales Returns and Allowances, and Sales Discounts, enter the following sales transactions. Use a new set of accounts for each part, 1–5.

1.   No sales tax.

(a) Merchandise is sold for $250 cash.
(b) Merchandise is sold on account for $225.
(c) Payment is received for merchandise sold on account.

2.   6% sales tax.

(a) Merchandise is sold for $250 cash plus sales tax.
(b) Merchandise is sold on account for $225 plus sales tax.
(c) Payment is received for merchandise sold on account.

3.   Cash and credit sales, with returned merchandise.

   (a) Merchandise is sold for $481 cash.
   (b) $18 of merchandise sold for $481 is returned for a refund.
   (c) Merchandise is sold on account for $388.
   (d) $24 of merchandise sold for $388 is returned for a credit.
   (e) Payment is received for balance owed on merchandise sold on
        account.

4.   6% sales tax, with returned merchandise.

   (a) Merchandise is sold on account for $480 plus sales tax.
   (b) Merchandise sold on account for $30 plus sales tax is returned.
   (c) The balance on the account is paid in cash.
   (d) Merchandise is sold for $300 cash plus sales tax.
   (e) $30 of merchandise sold for $300 cash plus sales tax is returned for a
        refund.

5.   Sales on account, with 2/10, n/30 cash discount terms.

   (a) Merchandise is sold on account for $280.
   (b) The balance is paid within the discount period.
   (c) Merchandise is sold on account for $203.
   (d) The balance is paid after the discount period.

E 10-3B (LO2)
✓ Net sales: $2,502

COMPUTING NET SALES Based on the following information, compute net sales:

Gross sales	$2,880
Sales returns and allowances	322
Sales discounts	56

E 10-4B (LO3)

JOURNALIZING SALES TRANSACTIONS Enter the following transactions in a general journal. Use a 5% sales tax rate.

✓ Sept. 1:
A/R–K. Smith 1,890
  Sales   1,800
  Sales Tax Payable 90

Sept. 1 Sold merchandise on account to K. Smith, $1,800 plus sales tax. Sale no. 228.

3 Sold merchandise on account to J. Arnes, $3,100 plus sales tax. Sale no. 229.

5 Sold merchandise on account to M. Denison, $2,800 plus sales tax. Sale no. 230.

7 Sold merchandise on account to B. Marshall, $1,900 plus sales tax. Sale no. 231.

E 10-5B (LO3)
✓ Ending Accts. Rec. balance: $3,777

JOURNALIZING SALES RETURNS AND ALLOWANCES Enter the following transactions in a general journal and post them to the appropriate general ledger and accounts receivable ledger accounts. Use account numbers as shown in the chapter. Beginning balance in Accounts Receivable is $3,900. Beginning balances in customer accounts are Adams, $850; Greene, $428; and Phillips, $1,018.

June 1 Marie L. Phillips returned merchandise previously purchased on account (sale no. 33), $43.

11 John B. Adams returned merchandise previously purchased on account (sale no. 34), $59.

15 L. B. Greene returned merchandise previously purchased on account (sale no. 35), $21.

E 10-6B (LO3)

JOURNALIZING CASH RECEIPTS Enter the following transactions in a general journal:

✓ Nov. 1:
Cash   750
  A/R–J. Haghighat   750

Nov. 1 Jean Haghighat made payment on account, $750.

12 Marc Antonoff made payment on account, $464.

15 Cash sales were $3,763.

18 Will Mossein made payment on account, $241.

25 Cash sales were $2,648.

E 10-7B (LO4)

✓ Accts. Rec. balance: $6,402

SCHEDULE OF ACCOUNTS RECEIVABLE From the accounts receivable ledger shown, prepare a schedule of accounts receivable for Gelph Co. as of November 30, 20--.

ACCOUNTS RECEIVABLE LEDGER

NAME James L. Adams Co.

ADDRESS 24481 McAdams Road, Dallas, TX 77001-3465

DATE	ITEM	POST. REF.	DEBIT	CREDIT	BALANCE
20-- Nov. 1		J1	3 1 8 0 00		3 1 8 0 00
5		J1		1 8 0 00	3 0 0 0 00
7		J2	2 0 0 00		3 2 0 0 00

NAME Trish Berens

ADDRESS 34 West 55th Avenue, Fort Worth, TX 76310-8182

DATE	ITEM	POST. REF.	DEBIT	CREDIT	BALANCE
20-- Nov. 3		J1	1 3 6 0 00		1 3 6 0 00

NAME M and T Jenkins, Inc.

ADDRESS 100 NW Richfield, Austin, TX 78481-3791

DATE	ITEM	POST. REF.	DEBIT	CREDIT	BALANCE
20-- Nov. 5		J1	2 6 2 8 00		2 6 2 8 00
12		J2		2 6 2 8 00	—

NAME R & J Travis

ADDRESS 288 Beacon Street, Dallas, TX 79301-6642

DATE	ITEM	POST. REF.	DEBIT	CREDIT	BALANCE
20-- Nov. 22		J3	1 8 4 2 00		1 8 4 2 00

SERIES B PROBLEMS

P 10-8B (LO3)

✓ Accts. Rec. balance: $13,072.50

SALES TRANSACTIONS T. M. Maxwell owns a retail business and made the following sales on account during the month of July 20--. There is a 5% sales tax on all sales.

July 1   Sale no. 101 to Saga, Inc., $1,200 plus sales tax.

8   Sale no. 102 to Vinnie Ward, $2,100 plus sales tax.

15   Sale no. 103 to Dvorak Manufacturing, $4,300 plus sales tax.

21   Sale no. 104 to Vinnie Ward, $1,800 plus sales tax.

24   Sale no. 105 to Zapata Co., $1,600 plus sales tax. (Open a new account for this customer. Address is 789 N. Stafford Dr., Bloomington, IN 47401-6201.)

29   Sale no. 106 to Saga, Inc., $1,450 plus sales tax.

REQUIRED

1.   Record the transactions in a general journal.

2.   Post from the journal to the general ledger and accounts receivable ledger accounts. Use account numbers as shown in the chapter.

P 10-9B (LO3)

✓ Accts. Rec. balance: $2,744.45

CASH RECEIPTS TRANSACTIONS Color Florists, a retail business, had the following cash receipts during January 20--. The sales tax is 5%.

Jan. 1   Received payment on account from Ray Boyd, $880.

3   Received payment on account from Clint Hassell, $271.

5   Cash sales for the week were $2,800 plus tax. Bank credit card sales for the week were $1,200 plus tax. Bank credit card fee is 3%.

8   Received payment on account from Jan Sowada, $912.

11   Ray Boyd returned merchandise for a credit, $40 plus tax.

12   Cash sales for the week were $3,100 plus tax. Bank credit card sales for the week were $1,900 plus tax. Bank credit card fee is 3%.

15   Received payment on account from Robert Zehnle, $1,100.

18   Robert Zehnle returned merchandise for a credit, $31 plus tax.

19   Cash sales for the week were $2,230 plus tax.

25   Received payment on account from Dazai Manufacturing, $318.

Beginning general ledger account balances were:

Cash	$2,890.75
Accounts Receivable	6,300.00

Beginning customer account balances were:

R. Boyd	$1,400
Dazai Manufacturing	318
C. Hassell	815
J. Sowada	1,481
R. Zehnle	2,286

REQUIRED

1.   Record the transactions in a general journal.

2.   Post from the journal to the general ledger and accounts receivable ledger accounts. Use account numbers as shown in the chapter.

P 10-10B (LO3)

✓ Accts. Rec. balance: $6,104.25

KLOOSTER
& ALLEN

SALES AND CASH RECEIPTS TRANSACTIONS Paul Jackson owns a retail business. The following sales, returns, and cash receipts are for April 20--. There is a 7% sales tax.

Apr.	1	Sale no. 111 to O. L. Meyers, $2,100 plus sales tax.
	3	Sale no. 112 to Andrew Plaa, $1,000 plus sales tax.
	6	O. L. Meyers returned merchandise from sale no. 111 for a credit (credit memo no. 42), $50 plus sales tax.
	7	Cash sales for the week were $3,240 plus sales tax.
	9	Received payment from O. L. Meyers for sale no. 111 less credit memo no. 42.
	12	Sale no. 113 to Melissa Richfield, $980 plus sales tax.
	14	Cash sales for the week were $2,180 plus sales tax.
	17	Melissa Richfield returned merchandise from sale no. 113 for a credit (credit memo no. 43), $40 plus sales tax.
	19	Sale no. 114 to Kelsay Munkres, $1,020 plus sales tax.
	21	Cash sales for the week were $2,600 plus sales tax.
	24	Sale no. 115 to O. L. Meyers, $920 plus sales tax.
	27	Sale no. 116 to Andrew Plaa, $1,320 plus sales tax.
	28	Cash sales for the week were $2,800 plus sales tax.
	29	Received payment from Melissa Richfield for $2,186.

Beginning general ledger account balances were:

Cash	$2,864.54
Accounts Receivable	2,726.25

Beginning customer account balances were:

K. Munkres	$ 482.00
M. Richfield	2,244.25

REQUIRED

1. Record the transactions in a general journal.

2. Post from the journal to the general ledger and accounts receivable ledger accounts. Use account numbers as shown in the chapter.

P 10-11B (LO4)

✓ Accts. Rec. balance, Melissa Richfield: $1,064.05

SCHEDULE OF ACCOUNTS RECEIVABLE Based on the information provided in Problem 10-10B, prepare a schedule of accounts receivable for Paul Jackson as of April 30, 20--. Verify that the accounts receivable account balance in the general ledger agrees with the schedule of accounts receivable total.

MANAGING YOUR WRITING

You and your spouse have separate charge accounts at a local department store. When you tried to use your card last week, you were told that you were over your credit limit. This puzzled you because you had paid the entire account balance several weeks ago. When the monthly statements arrived yesterday, the error was clear. The store had credited your payment to your spouse's account.

Your account was treated as over the limit, and the store charged you interest on the unpaid balance. You suspect that part of the problem is that you and your spouse use the same last name (Morales) and have similar first names (Carmen and Carmelo).

Write a letter to the store requesting correction of your accounts and suggesting a way to identify your accounts so that this error does not happen again.

ETHICS CASE

Wholesale Health Supply sells a variety of medical equipment and supplies to retailers. When a new retailer is approved for credit, one of the criteria is that the retailer must have been in business for at least six months. Good Earth Foods placed a large order with Wholesale Health Supply and requested credit terms. Wholesale Health Supply faxed a credit request form to Good Earth Foods, and the buyer at Good Earth Foods faxed the completed form back to Wholesale Health Supply. Robin Sylvester, the sales manager at Wholesale Health Supply, saw the credit application and noticed Good Earth Foods had only been in business for two months. Thinking she might lose the order if Good Earth Foods wasn't extended credit, Robin authorized the shipment. She figured by the time the credit department rejected the application, Good Earth Foods would have received the order and the vice president would override the rejection to keep a new customer. Robin was sure that everything would turn out alright.

1. Do you think Robin's decision to ship the order was unethical? Why or why not?

2. What would you have done if you were in Robin's position?

3. Write a memo from the credit department manager to Robin Sylvester explaining the reasoning behind requiring a new credit customer to be in business for at least six months.

4. In small groups, discuss ways to prevent a situation like this from happening.

MASTERY PROBLEM

✓ Accts. Rec. balance: $1,900.54

Geoff and Sandy Harland own and operate Wayward Kennel and Pet Supply. Their motto is, "If your pet is not becoming to you, he should be coming to us." The Harlands maintain a sales tax payable account throughout the month to account for the 6% sales tax. They use a general journal, general ledger, and accounts receivable ledger. The following sales and cash collections took place during the month of September:

Sept. 2   Sold a fish aquarium on account to Ken Shank, $125.00 plus tax of $7.50, terms n/30. Sale no. 101.

3   Sold dog food on account to Nancy Truelove, $68.25 plus tax of $4.10, terms n/30. Sale no. 102.

(continued)

Sept. 5   Sold a bird cage on account to Jean Warkentin, $43.95 plus tax of $2.64, terms n/30. Sale no. 103.

8   Cash sales for the week were $2,332.45 plus tax of $139.95.

10   Received cash for boarding and grooming services, $625.00 plus tax of $37.50.

11   Jean Warkentin stopped by the store to point out a minor defect in the bird cage purchased in sale no. 103. The Harlands offered a sales allowance of $10.00 plus tax on the price of the cage which satisfied Warkentin.

12   Sold a cockatoo on account to Tully Shaw, $1,200.00 plus tax of $72.00, terms n/30. Sale no. 104.

14   Received cash on account from Rosa Alanso, $256.00

15   Rosa Alanso returned merchandise, $93.28 including tax of $5.28.

15   Cash sales for the week were $2,656.85 plus tax of $159.41.

16   Received cash on account from Nancy Truelove, $58.25.

18   Received cash for boarding and grooming services, $535.00 plus tax of $32.10.

19   Received cash on account from Ed Cochran, $63.25.

20   Sold pet supplies on account to Susan Hays, $83.33 plus tax of $5.00, terms n/30. Sale no. 105.

21   Sold three Labrador Retriever puppies to All American Day Camp, $375.00 plus tax of $22.50, terms n/30. Sale no. 106.

22   Cash sales for the week were $3,122.45 plus tax of $187.35.

23   Received cash for boarding and grooming services, $515.00 plus tax of $30.90.

25   Received cash on account from Ken Shank, $132.50.

26   Received cash on account from Nancy Truelove, $72.35.

27   Received cash on account from Joe Gloy, $273.25.

28   Borrowed cash to purchase a pet limousine, $11,000.00.

29   Cash sales for the week were $2,835.45 plus tax of $170.13.

30   Received cash for boarding and grooming services, $488.00 plus tax of $29.28.

Wayward had the following general ledger account balances as of September 1:

Account Title	Account No.	General Ledger Balance on Sept. 1
Cash	101	$23,500.25
Accounts Receivable	122	850.75
Notes Payable	201	2,500.00
Sales Tax Payable	231	909.90
Sales	401	13,050.48
Sales Returns and Allowances	401.1	86.00
Boarding and Grooming Revenue	402	2,115.00

Wayward also had the following accounts receivable ledger balances as of September 1:

Customer	Accounts Receivable Balance
Rosa Alanso 2541 East 2nd Street Bloomington, IN 47401-5356	$456.00
Ed Cochran 2669 Windcrest Drive Bloomington, IN 47401-5446	$63.25
Joe Gloy 1458 Parnell Avenue Muncie, IN 47304-2682	$273.25
Nancy Truelove 2300 E. National Road Cumberland, IN 46229-4824	$58.25

New customers opening accounts during September were as follows:

All American Day Camp
3025 Old Mill Run
Bloomington, IN 47408-1080

Susan Hays
1424 Jackson Creek Road
Nashville, IN 47448-2245

Ken Shank
6422 E. Bender Road
Bloomington, IN 47401-7756

Tully Shaw
3315 Longview Avenue
Bloomington, IN 47401-7223

Jean Warkentin
1813 Deep Well Court
Bloomington, IN 47401-5124

REQUIRED

1. Enter the transactions for the month of September in a general journal. (Begin with page 7.)

2. Post the entries to the general and subsidiary ledgers. Open new accounts for any customers who did not have a balance as of September 1.

3. Prepare a schedule of accounts receivable.

4. Compute the net sales for the month of September.

CHALLENGE PROBLEM

This problem challenges you to apply your cumulative accounting knowledge to move a step beyond the material in the chapter.

✓ **June 14: Dr. Sales Discounts, $12**

Enter the following transactions in a general journal:

June 4	Sold merchandise on account to T. Allen, $1,500.00 plus 6% sales tax, with 1/10, n/30 cash discount terms.
7	Sold merchandise on account to K. Bryant, $1,800.00 plus 6% sales tax, with 1/10, n/30 cash discount terms.
11	T. Allen returned merchandise totaling $300.00 from the June 4 sale, for credit.
14	T. Allen paid the balance due from the June 4 sale, less discount.
17	K. Bryant paid the balance due from the June 7 sale, less discount.

Objectives

Careful study of this chapter should enable you to:

LO1
Define merchandise purchases transactions.

LO2
Describe and use merchandise purchases accounts and compute gross profit.

LO3
Describe and use the accounts payable ledger.

LO4
Prepare a schedule of accounts payable.

Accounting for Purchases and Cash Payments

In the early months of operating Parkway Pet Supplies, Evan Taylor paid for his purchases by issuing a check to the vendors who delivered the items to his store. His store was new, so manufacturers and vendors would not sell to him on account. Accounting for such purchases was simple. As the business succeeded, Evan was able to buy on account and have merchandise shipped to his store. He had to pay the freight charges on such shipments. He also found that he was eligible for various discounts on his purchases and could return items for credit on his account. Accounting for purchases has become much more complicated. How should Evan's bookkeeper account for items like freight charges, discounts, and credits for purchases that he returns to the manufacturer or vendor?

Chapter 10 demonstrated how to account for sales in a merchandising business. This chapter continues the study of the merchandising business by examining how to account for merchandise purchases. We will learn how to use four new accounts and another subsidiary ledger.

MERCHANDISE PURCHASES TRANSACTIONS

LO1 Define merchandise purchases transactions.

In everyday language, purchases can refer to almost anything we have bought. For a merchandising business, however, **purchases** refers to merchandise acquired for resale. These are the goods a business buys for the sole purpose of selling them to its customers.

Purchasing procedures and documents vary, depending on the nature and size of a business. For example, in a small business, the owner or an employee might do the buying on a part-time basis. In a large business, there might be a separate purchasing department with a full-time manager and staff. In addition, the procedures and documents used can be affected by whether purchases are made on account or for cash.

The flowchart in Figure 11-1 shows some of the major documents used in the purchasing process of a merchandising business. In discussing the purchasing process, we will assume that the business makes purchases on account and has a purchasing department.

FIGURE 11-1   Purchasing Process Documents

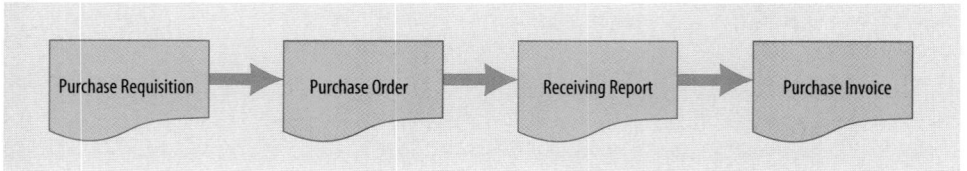

Purchase Requisition

A **purchase requisition** is a form used to request the purchase of merchandise or other property. Any authorized person or department can prepare this form and submit it to the purchasing department. Figure 11-2 shows a purchase requisition used by Northern Micro. One copy of this form is sent to the purchasing department, one to the accounting department, and one is kept by the department that prepared the requisition.

FIGURE 11-2   Purchase Requisition

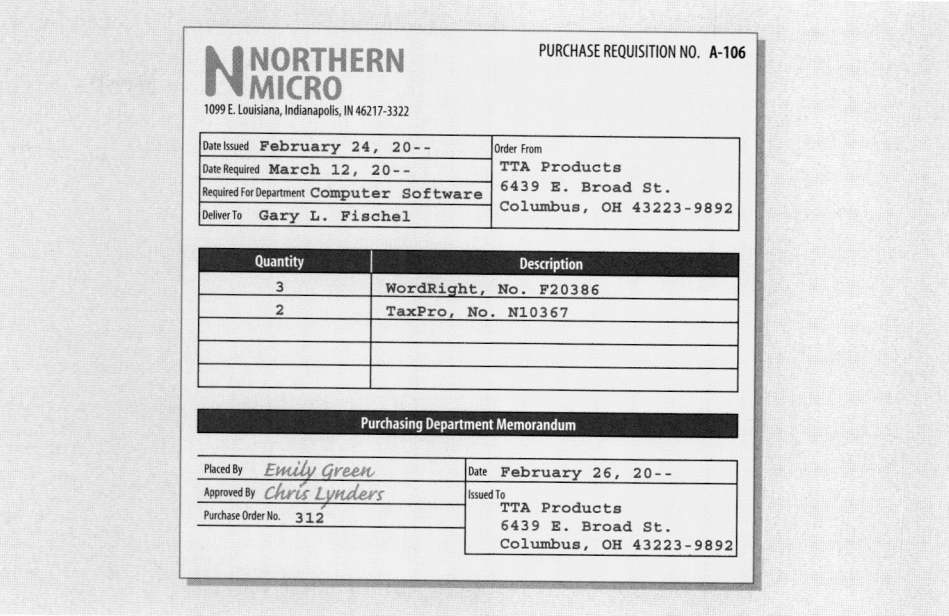

Purchase Order

In a computerized system, purchase orders can be submitted electronically. Signals are sent to the vendor and the accounting and purchasing departments at the same time.

The purchasing department reviews and approves the purchase requisition and prepares a purchase order. A **purchase order** is a written order to buy goods from a specific vendor (supplier). Figure 11-3 shows a purchase order prepared by Northern Micro based on the purchase requisition in Figure 11-2. One copy of the purchase order is sent to the vendor to order the goods, one to the accounting department, and one copy is kept in the purchasing department. Other copies may be sent to the department that prepared the purchase requisition and to the receiving area.

FIGURE 11-3   Purchase Order

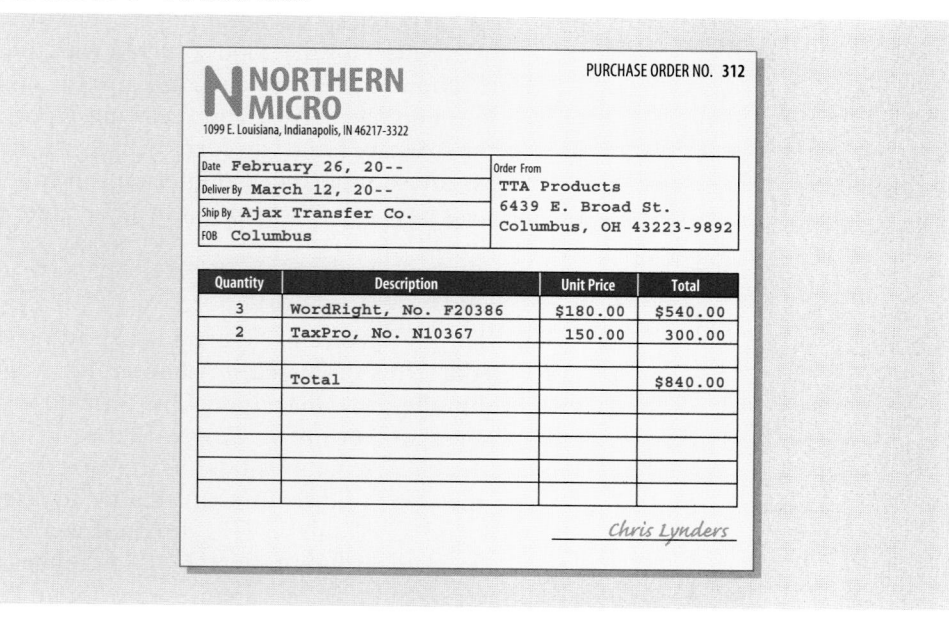

Receiving Report and Purchase Invoice

When the merchandise is received, a **receiving report** indicating what has been received is prepared. The receiving report can be a separate form, or one can be created from the vendor's purchase invoice. Figure 11-4 shows a vendor invoice on which a rubber stamp has been used to imprint a type of receiving report. The receiving clerk has indicated on the form the date and condition of the goods received.

FIGURE 11-4 Purchase Invoice

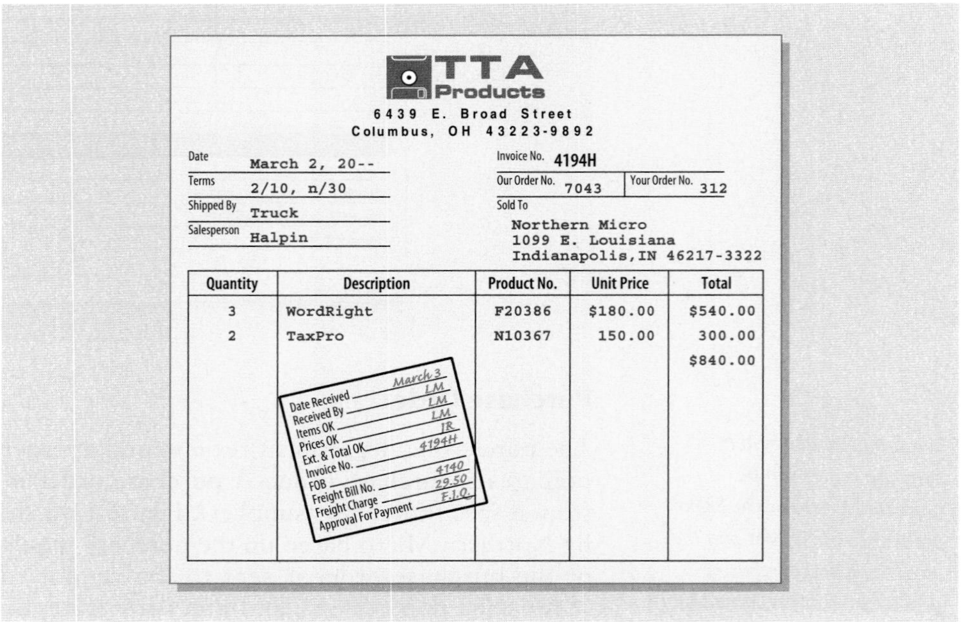

TTA Products
6439 E. Broad Street
Columbus, OH 43223-9892

Date: March 2, 20--
Terms: 2/10, n/30
Shipped By: Truck
Salesperson: Halpin

Invoice No. 4194H
Our Order No. 7043 Your Order No. 312
Sold To
Northern Micro
1099 E. Louisiana
Indianapolis, IN 46217-3322

Quantity	Description	Product No.	Unit Price	Total
3	WordRight	F20386	$180.00	$540.00
2	TaxPro	N10367	150.00	300.00
				$840.00

An **invoice** is a document prepared by the seller as a bill for the merchandise shipped. To the seller, this is a sales invoice, as explained in Chapter 10. To the buyer, this is a **purchase invoice.** Figure 11-4 shows an invoice sent by TTA Products to Northern Micro for the goods ordered with the purchase order in Figure 11-3.

The accounting department compares the purchase invoice with the purchase requisition, purchase order, and receiving report. If the invoice is for the goods ordered and received and the correct price, the invoice is paid by the due date.

This is an example of good internal control. The procedure helps ensure that the business pays only for goods it ordered and received, and at the correct price.

Cash and Trade Discounts

Notice that the invoice in Figure 11-4 shows terms of 2/10, n/30. These are the same credit terms discussed in Chapter 10. A discount is available if the bill is paid within the discount period. The only difference is that we are now looking from the buyer's point of view rather than the seller's. We will see how to account for these discounts later in the chapter.

Another type of discount, called a **trade discount,** is often offered by manufacturers and wholesalers. This discount is a reduction from the list or catalog price offered to different classes of customers. By simply adjusting the trade discount percentages, companies can avoid the cost of reprinting catalogs every time there is a change in prices. Trade discounts are usually shown as a deduction from the total amount of the invoice. For example, the invoice in Figure 11-5 includes a trade discount of 10%. The amount to be entered in the accounting records for this invoice is $756, the net amount after deducting the trade discount of $84. Trade discounts represent a reduction in the price of the merchandise and should not be entered in the accounts of either the seller or the buyer.

FIGURE 11-5   Purchase Invoice with Trade Discount

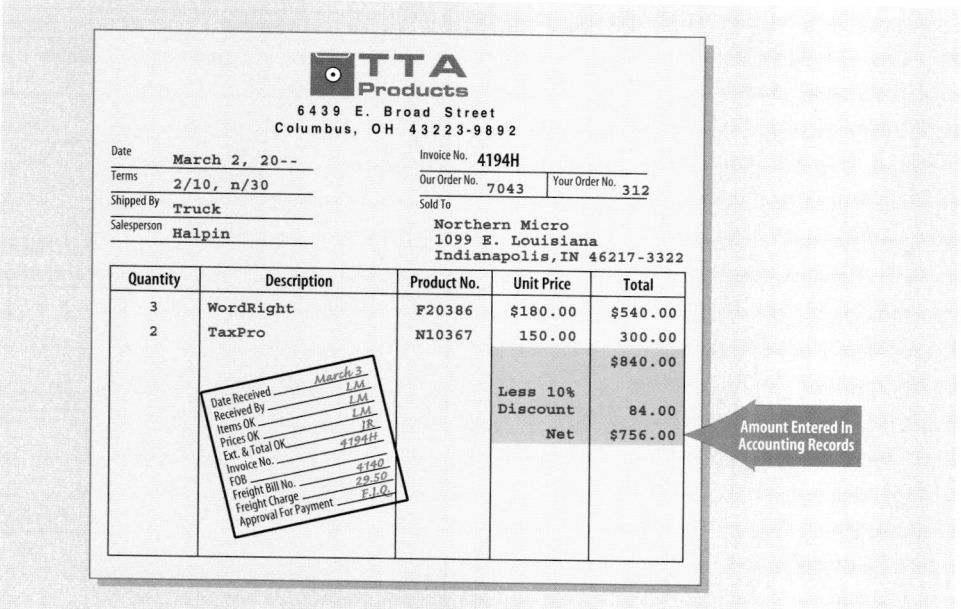

We need to be careful in computing the cash discount when an invoice has both cash and trade discounts. The cash discount applies to the *net amount* after deducting the trade discount. For example, the cash discount and amount to be paid on the invoice in Figure 11-5 would be calculated as follows:

Gross amount	$840.00
Less 10% trade discount	84.00
Net amount	$756.00
Less 2% cash discount	15.12
Amount to be paid	$740.88

MERCHANDISE PURCHASES ACCOUNTS

LO2 Describe and use merchandise purchases accounts and compute gross profit.

To account for merchandise purchases transactions, we will use four new accounts.

1. Purchases

2. Purchases Returns and Allowances

3. Purchases Discounts

4. Freight-In

The position of these accounts in the accounting equation and their normal balances are shown in Figure 11-6.

FIGURE 11-6   Accounting for Merchandise Purchases Transactions

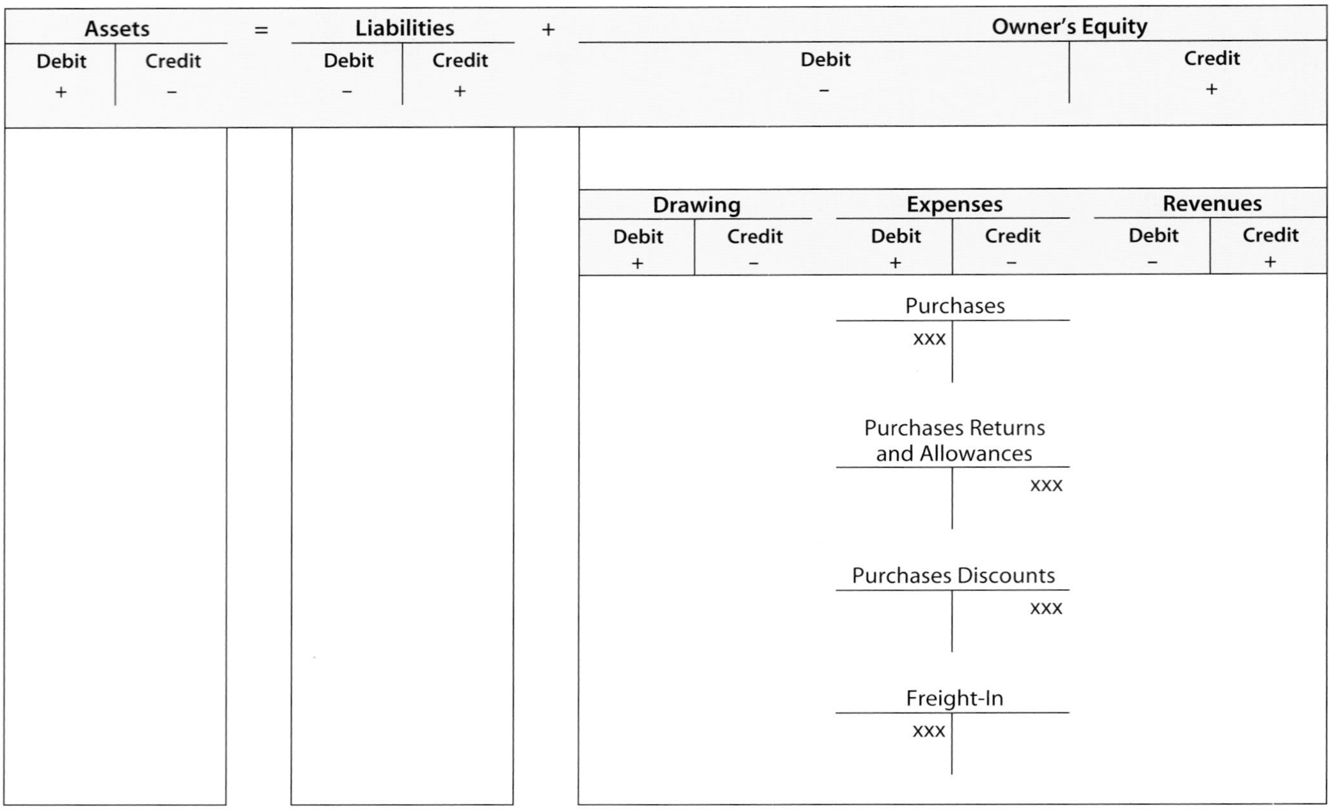

Assets		=	Liabilities		+	Owner's Equity		
Debit	Credit		Debit	Credit		Debit		Credit
+	–		–	+		–		+

Drawing		Expenses		Revenues	
Debit	Credit	Debit	Credit	Debit	Credit
+	–	+	–	–	+

Purchases
xxx |

Purchases Returns
and Allowances
| xxx

Purchases Discounts
| xxx

Freight-In
xxx |

Purchases Account

The purchases account is used to record the cost of merchandise purchased.

Purchases

Debit	Credit
to enter the cost of merchandise purchased	

If a $100 purchase is made for cash, the following entry is made:

5		Purchases			1 0 0 00			5
6		Cash				1 0 0 00		6
7		Made cash purchase						7

If the same purchase is made on account, the entry is as follows:

5		Purchases			1 0 0 00			5
6		Accounts Payable/Vendor				1 0 0 00		6
7		Made purchase on account						7

Accounts Payable is followed by a slash (/) and the name of the specific vendor to whom the purchaser owes money.

Purchases Returns and Allowances Account

Purchases Returns and Allowances is a contra-purchases account used to record purchases returns and purchases allowances. It is reported as a deduction from Purchases on the income statement (see Figure 11-7).

Purchases returns and allowances are similar to the sales returns and allowances we discussed in Chapter 10. We are simply looking at returns and allowances from the buyer's point of view. If merchandise is returned to a supplier, or the supplier grants a price reduction because of defects or other problems with merchandise purchased, Purchases Returns and Allowances is credited.

Purchases Returns and Allowances

Debit	Credit
	to enter returns and allowances

If merchandise that was purchased on account for $200 is defective and is returned to the supplier, the following entry is made:

9		Accounts Payable/Vendor		2 0 0 00		9
10		Purchases Returns and Allowances			2 0 0 00	10
11		Returned merchandise				11

If the same merchandise is retained but the supplier grants a price reduction of $45 because of the defects, the entry is as follows:

9		Accounts Payable/Vendor		4 5 00		9
10		Purchases Returns and Allowances			4 5 00	10
11		Allowance for defective merchandise				11

Purchases Discounts Account

Purchases Discounts is a contra-purchases account used to record cash discounts allowed on purchases. Like Purchases Returns and Allowances, it is reported as a deduction from Purchases on the income statement (see Figure 11-7).

Purchases Discounts

Debit	Credit
	to enter cash discounts taken

If merchandise is purchased for $100 on account, with credit terms of 2/10, n/30, the following entry is made:

14		Purchases		1 0 0 00		14
15		Accounts Payable/Vendor			1 0 0 00	15
16		Made purchase on account				16

If payment for the merchandise is then made within the discount period, the entry is as follows:

18		Accounts Payable/Vendor			1	0	0	00								18
19		Cash									9	8	00			19
20		Purchases Discounts										2	00			20
21		Made payment on account														21

This approach to accounting for purchases discounts is known as the "gross-price method." The "net-price method" is described in the appendix.

Note the parts of this entry. Accounts Payable is debited for $100, the full amount of the invoice, because the entire debt has been satisfied. Cash is credited for only $98 because that is all that was required to pay the debt. The difference of $2 ($100 – $98) is credited to Purchases Discounts, which represents a reduction in the purchase price of the merchandise. That is why Purchases Discounts is deducted from Purchases on the income statement.

Freight-In Account

Freight-In is an adjunct-purchases account used to record transportation charges on merchandise purchases. It is added to Purchases on the income statement (see Figure 11-7).

Freight-In

Debit	Credit
to enter transportation charges on merchandise purchases	

Transportation charges are expressed in FOB (free on board) terms that indicate who is responsible for paying the freight costs. **FOB shipping point** means that transportation charges are paid by the buyer. **FOB destination** means that transportation charges are paid by the seller.

When the terms are FOB shipping point, either the freight charges will be listed separately on the purchase invoice or a separate freight bill will be sent. Assume Northern Micro receives an invoice for $400 plus freight charges of $38. The entry for this purchase is as follows:

25		Purchases			4	0	0	00								25
26		Freight-In				3	8	00								26
27		Accounts Payable/Vendor									4	3	8	00		27
28		Made purchase on account														28

Assume instead that Northern Micro receives an invoice for $400 for the same merchandise, shipped FOB shipping point. Northern Micro then receives a separate bill from the transportation company for $38. These two transactions are entered as follows:

30		Purchases			4	0	0	00								30
31		Accounts Payable/Vendor									4	0	0	00		31
32		Made purchase on account														32
33																33
34		Freight-In				3	8	00								34
35		Accounts Payable/Vendor										3	8	00		35
36		Freight charges on merchandise purchase														36

When the terms are FOB destination, generally no freight charges appear on the purchase invoice. The buyer simply records the purchase at the amount of the invoice. The freight-in account is not used in recording this purchase.

Computation of Gross Profit

An important step in determining net income for a merchandising business is the calculation of its gross profit. **Gross profit** (also called **gross margin**) is the difference between net sales and cost of goods sold. **Cost of goods sold** (also called **cost of merchandise sold**) is the difference between the goods available for sale and the ending inventory. It indicates the cost of the goods sold during the period. Gross profit provides very important information. It tells management the amount of sales dollars available to cover expenses, after covering the cost of the goods sold.

To compute gross profit, we use two of the four new accounts described in Chapter 10, the four new accounts described above, and the merchandise inventory balances. Assume that Northern Micro has the following sales, purchases, and merchandise inventory balances for the year ended December 31, 20--:

From Chapter 10	Sales	$200,500
	Sales Returns and Allowances	1,200
From Chapter 11	Purchases	105,000
	Purchases Returns and Allowances	800
	Purchases Discounts	1,000
	Freight-In	300
	Merchandise Inventory, January 1, 20--	26,000
	Merchandise Inventory, December 31, 20--	18,000

A BROADER VIEW

© GETTY IMAGES/PHOTODISC

Cash Management—Those Discounts Matter

If a business makes a $2,000 purchase on account, with terms of 2/10, n/30, the available discount is only $40 ($2,000 × 0.02). On the surface, this seems unimportant, like "small change." But take a closer look. If the business does not pay $1,960 ($2,000 − $40) within 10 days, it must pay $2,000 within 30 days. This means that the business would pay $40 for the use of $1,960 for 20 more days. If we assume a 360-day year, the approximate annual interest rate for using the $1,960 for 20 days is 36%.

The innocent looking 2% cash discount represents a very high rate of interest. If a business regularly misses cash discount opportunities, the annual dollar cost can be substantial. For sound cash management, take advantage of discounts.

In Chapter 17, we discuss how to compute interest. There you will learn to compute the exact interest rate.

Figure 11-7 uses these balances to compute net sales, net purchases, cost of goods sold, and gross profit. The following four steps in computing gross profit are labeled in the figure:

STEP 1 Compute net sales.

(Sales — Sales Returns and Allowances)

STEP 2 Compute goods available for sale.

(Beginning Inventory + Cost of Goods Purchased)

STEP 3 Compute cost of goods sold.

(Goods Available for Sale — Ending Inventory)

STEP 4 Compute gross profit.

(Net Sales — Cost of Goods Sold)

LEARNING KEY

Cost of Goods Sold = Beginning Inventory + Net Purchases + Freight-In — Ending Inventory

Net Sales — Cost of Goods Sold = Gross Profit

FIGURE 11-7 Computation of Gross Profit

Sales				$200 5 0 0 00	
Less sales returns and allowances				1 2 0 0 00	
Step 1 — **Net sales**					$199 3 0 0 00
Cost of goods sold:					
Merchandise inventory, Jan. 1				$ 26 0 0 0 00	
Purchases			$105 0 0 0 00		
Less: Purchases returns and allowances	$ 8 0 0 00				
Purchases discounts	1 0 0 0 00		1 8 0 0 00		
Net purchases			$103 2 0 0 00		
Add freight-in			3 0 0 00		
Cost of goods purchased				103 5 0 0 00	
Step 2 — **Goods available for sale**				$129 5 0 0 00	
Less merchandise inventory, Dec. 31				18 0 0 0 00	
Step 3 — **Cost of goods sold**					111 5 0 0 00
Step 4 — **Gross profit**					$ 87 8 0 0 00

JOURNALIZING AND POSTING PURCHASES AND CASH PAYMENTS TRANSACTIONS

LO3 Describe and use the accounts payable ledger.

To illustrate the journalizing and posting of purchases transactions, we will continue with the transactions of Northern Micro.

Purchases

Assume the following purchases on account occurred during the month of April:

Apr. 4   Purchased merchandise from Compucraft, Inc., $3,300. Invoice no. 631, dated April 2, terms, n/30.

8   Purchased merchandise from Datasoft, $2,500. Invoice no. 927D, dated April 6, terms, n/30.

11   Purchased merchandise from EZX Corp., $8,700. Invoice no. 804, dated April 9, terms, 1/15, n/30.

17   Purchased merchandise from Printpro Corp., $800. Invoice no. 611, dated April 16, terms, n/30.

23   Purchased merchandise from Televax, Inc., $5,300. Invoice no. 1465, dated April 22, terms, 1/10, n/30.

These transactions are entered in a general journal as shown in Figure 11-8.

FIGURE 11-8   Purchases Entered in General Journal

GENERAL JOURNAL   PAGE 6

	DATE		DESCRIPTION	POST. REF.	DEBIT	CREDIT	
1	20-- Apr.	4	Purchases		3 3 0 0 00		1
2			Accounts Payable/Compucraft, Inc.			3 3 0 0 00	2
3			Invoice No. 631				3
4							4
5		8	Purchases		2 5 0 0 00		5
6			Accounts Payable/Datasoft			2 5 0 0 00	6
7			Invoice No. 927D				7
8							8
9		11	Purchases		8 7 0 0 00		9
10			Accounts Payable/EZX Corp.			8 7 0 0 00	10
11			Invoice No. 804				11
12							12
13		17	Purchases		8 0 0 00		13
14			Accounts Payable/Printpro Corp.			8 0 0 00	14
15			Invoice No. 611				15
16							16
17		23	Purchases		5 3 0 0 00		17
18			Accounts Payable/Televax, Inc.			5 3 0 0 00	18
19			Invoice No. 1465				19

Posting Purchases to the General Ledger

Purchases transactions are posted from the general journal to the general ledger in the same manner as was illustrated for sales in Chapter 10. The following steps are used, as indicated in Figure 11-9 for Northern Micro's April 4 and 8 purchases transactions:

In the general ledger account:

STEP 1 Enter the date of the transaction in the Date column.

STEP 2 Enter the amount of the debit or credit in the Debit or Credit column.

STEP 3 Enter the new balance in the Balance columns under Debit or Credit.

STEP 4 Enter the journal page number from which each transaction is posted in the Posting Reference column.

In the journal:

STEP 5 Enter the ledger account number in the Posting Reference column of the journal for each transaction that is posted.

Other purchases transactions would be posted in the same manner.

FIGURE 11-9   Posting Purchases to the General Ledger

GENERAL JOURNAL (Partial)   **Page 6**

Date	Description	Post. Ref.	Debit	Credit
20--				
Apr. 4	Purchases	501	3,300.00	
	Accounts Payable/Compucraft, Inc.	202		3,300.00
	Invoice No. 631			
8	Purchases	501	2,500.00	
	Accounts Payable/Datasoft	202		2,500.00
	Invoice No. 927D			

GENERAL LEDGER (Partial)

ACCOUNT   Accounts Payable   ACCOUNT NO. 202

Date	Item	Post. Ref.	Debit	Credit	Balance Debit	Balance Credit
20--						
Apr. 1	Bal.	✓				4,800.00
4		J6		3,300.00		8,100.00
8		J6		2,500.00		10,600.00

ACCOUNT   Purchases   ACCOUNT NO. 501

Date	Item	Post. Ref.	Debit	Credit	Balance Debit	Balance Credit
20--						
Apr. 1	Bal.	✓			17,400.00	
4		J6	3,300.00		20,700.00	
8		J6	2,500.00		23,200.00	

A three-column account form is commonly used for supplier accounts. Only one balance column is needed because the normal balance is a credit. If a debit balance occurs, the amount may be bracketed.

LEARNING KEY

When an accounts payable ledger is used, the Posting Reference column in the general journal serves two purposes. (1) The account number is inserted to indicate the general ledger account has been posted. (2) A slash (/) and a check mark (✓) are inserted to indicate the accounts payable ledger account has been posted.

Posting Purchases to the Accounts Payable Ledger

The Purchases and Accounts Payable resulting from merchandise purchases on account are now up to date in the general ledger. A record can be kept of the amount owed to each supplier by using a subsidiary **accounts payable ledger**. This is a separate ledger containing an individual account payable for each supplier. If there are many supplier accounts, it is a good practice to assign each supplier an account number. The subsidiary ledger accounts are kept in either alphabetical or numerical order, depending on whether the supplier accounts are identified by number. A summary accounts payable account called a controlling account is maintained in the general ledger. The accounts payable ledger is "subsidiary" to this account.

Figure 11-10 illustrates the use of the accounts payable ledger for Northern Micro's April 4 and 8 purchases transactions. The following steps are used to post from the general journal to the accounts payable ledger, as shown in Figure 11-10:

In the accounts payable ledger account:

STEP 1 Enter the date of the transaction in the Date column.

STEP 2 Enter the amount of the debit or credit in the Debit or Credit column.

STEP 3 Enter the new balance in the Balance column.

STEP 4 Enter the journal page number from which each transaction is posted in the Posting Reference column.

In the journal:

STEP 5 Enter a slash (/) followed by a check mark (✓) in the Posting Reference column of the journal for each transaction that is posted.

FIGURE 11-10   Posting Purchases to the Accounts Payable Ledger

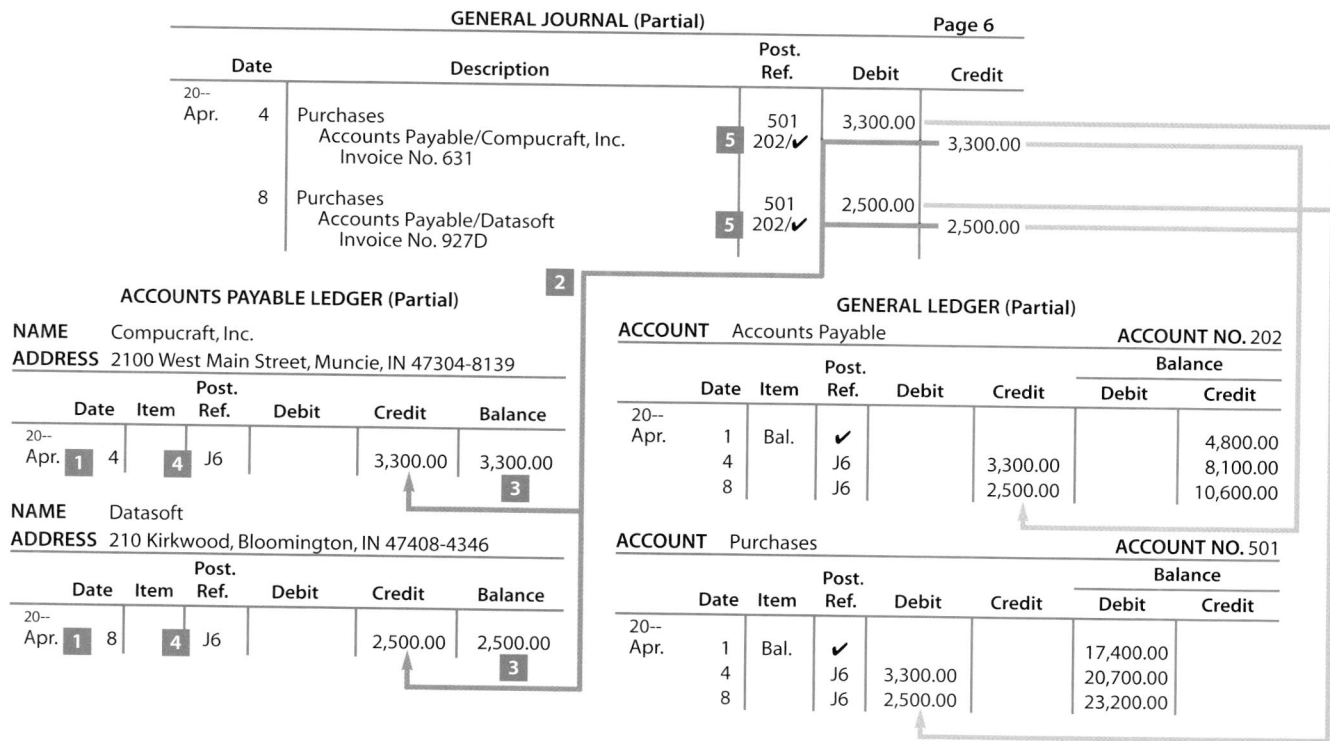

LEARNING KEY

The total of the accounts payable ledger balances must equal the Accounts Payable balance in the general ledger.

Note the relationship between the general journal, accounts payable ledger, and general ledger. All general journal entries are posted to both the general ledger and the accounts payable ledger. After the posting of the accounts payable ledger and general ledger is completed, the total of the accounts payable ledger balances should equal the Accounts Payable balance in the general ledger.

Purchases Returns and Allowances

If a buyer returns merchandise or is given an allowance for damaged merchandise, a general journal entry is required. Assume that on May 4, Northern Micro returns $200 of merchandise to Televax, Inc. These goods were part of a purchase made on April 23. Figure 11-11 shows the general journal entry, general ledger posting, and accounts payable ledger posting for this transaction.

The general journal entry is made in the usual manner. The general ledger is posted using the same five steps as were illustrated for purchases transactions in Figure 11-9. The accounts payable ledger is posted using the following five steps, as illustrated in Figure 11-11:

In the accounts payable ledger account:

STEP 1 Enter the date of the transaction in the Date column.

STEP 2 Enter the amount of the debit or credit in the Debit or Credit column.

STEP 3 Enter the new balance in the Balance column.

STEP 4 Enter the journal page number from which each transaction is posted in the Posting Reference column.

In the journal:

STEP 5 Enter a slash (/) followed by a check mark (✔) in the Posting Reference column of the journal for each transaction that is posted.

FIGURE 11-11   Accounting for Purchases Returns and Allowances

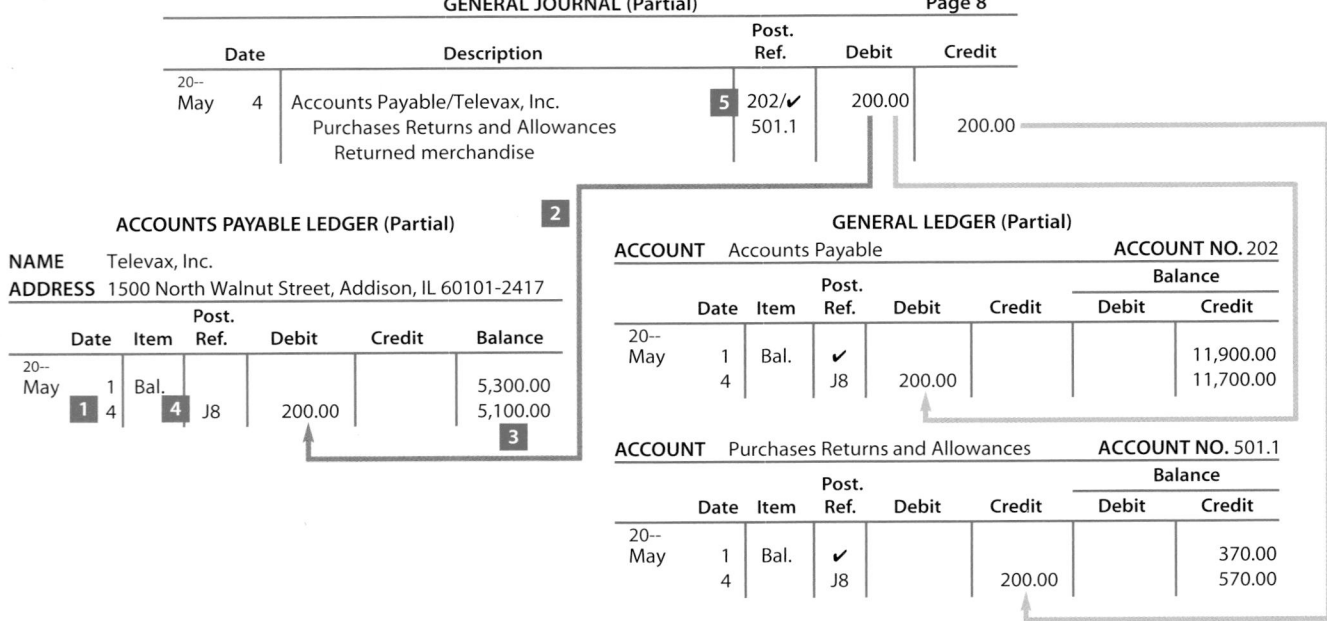

Cash Payments

To illustrate the journalizing and posting of cash payments, we will use Northern Micro's cash payment transactions. Assume Northern Micro made the following two payments on account during the month of April:

Apr. 10   Paid B. B. Small $4,800 for purchases made on account.

24   Paid EZX Corp. $8,700 less discount of 1% for purchases made on account.

These transactions are entered in a general journal as shown in Figure 11-12.

FIGURE 11-12   Cash Payments Entered in a General Journal

30	Apr.	10	Accounts Payable/B. B. Small		4	8	0	0	00						30
31			Cash							4	8	0	0	00	31
32			Made payment on account												32
33															33
34		24	Accounts Payable/EZX Corp.		8	7	0	0	00						34
35			Cash							8	6	1	3	00	35
36			Purchases Discounts									8	7	00	36
37			Made payment less discount on account												37

Posting Cash Payments to the General Ledger and Accounts Payable Ledger

Cash payment transactions are posted to the general ledger in the same manner as was illustrated for purchases transactions in Figure 11-9. To post cash payments to the accounts payable ledger, the following steps are used, as indicated in Figure 11-13 for Northern Micro's April 10 and 24 cash payment transactions:

In the accounts payable ledger account:

STEP 1 Enter the date of the transaction in the Date column.

STEP 2 Enter the amount of the debit or credit in the Debit or Credit column.

STEP 3 Enter the new balance in the Balance column.

STEP 4 Enter the journal page number from which each transaction is posted in the Posting Reference column.

In the journal:

STEP 5 Enter a slash (/) followed by a check mark (✔) in the Posting Reference column of the journal for each transaction that is posted.

FIGURE 11-13 Posting Cash Payments to the General Ledger and Accounts Payable Ledger

GENERAL JOURNAL (Partial) Page 6

	Date	Description	Post. Ref.	Debit	Credit
20--					
Apr.	10	Accounts Payable/B. B. Small	202/✔	4,800.00	
		Cash	101		4,800.00
		Made payment on account			
	24	Accounts Payable/EZX Corp.	202/✔	8,700.00	
		Cash	101		8,613.00
		Purchases Discounts	501.2		87.00
		Made payment less discount on account			

ACCOUNTS PAYABLE LEDGER (Partial)

NAME B. B. Small
ADDRESS 2323 High Street, Gurnee, IL 60031-5524

Date	Item	Post. Ref.	Debit	Credit	Balance
20--					
Apr. 1	Bal.	✔			4,800.00
10		J6	4,800.00		0

NAME EZX Corp.
ADDRESS 2928 Rhodes Ave., Chicago, IL 60658-5036

Date	Item	Post. Ref.	Debit	Credit	Balance
20--					
Apr. 11		J6		8,700.00	8,700.00
24		J6	8,700.00		0

GENERAL LEDGER (Partial)

ACCOUNT Cash ACCOUNT NO. 101

		Post.			Balance	
Date	Item	Ref.	Debit	Credit	Debit	Credit
20--						
Apr. 1	Bal.	✔			20,000.00	
10		J6		4,800.00	15,200.00	
24		J6		8,613.00	6,587.00	

ACCOUNT Accounts Payable ACCOUNT NO. 202

		Post.			Balance	
Date	Item	Ref.	Debit	Credit	Debit	Credit
20--						
Apr. 1	Bal.	✔				4,800.00
4		J6		3,300.00		8,100.00
8		J6		2,500.00		10,600.00
10		J6	4,800.00			5,800.00
11		J6		8,700.00		14,500.00
17		J6		800.00		15,300.00
23		J6		5,300.00		20,600.00
24		J6	8,700.00			11,900.00

ACCOUNT Purchases Discounts ACCOUNT NO. 501.2

		Post.			Balance	
Date	Item	Ref.	Debit	Credit	Debit	Credit
20--						
Apr. 1	Bal.	✔				330.00
24		J6		87.00		417.00

SCHEDULE OF ACCOUNTS PAYABLE

LO4 Prepare a schedule of accounts payable.

At the end of the month, all postings to Accounts Payable in the general ledger and to the accounts payable ledger should be complete, as shown in Figure 11-14. At this point, the Accounts Payable balance in the general ledger should equal the sum of the supplier balances in the accounts payable ledger.

FIGURE 11-14   General Ledger and Accounts Payable Ledger after Posting

ACCOUNTS PAYABLE LEDGER

NAME   B. B. Small
ADDRESS   2323 High Street, Gurnee, IL 60031-5524

Date		Item	Post. Ref.	Debit	Credit	Balance
20--						
Apr.	1	Bal.	✓			4,800.00
	10		J6	4,800.00		0

NAME   Compucraft, Inc.
ADDRESS   2100 West Main Street, Muncie, IN 47304-8139

Date		Item	Post. Ref.	Debit	Credit	Balance
20--						
Apr.	4		J6		3,300.00	3,300.00

NAME   Datasoft
ADDRESS   210 Kirkwood, Bloomington, IN 47408-4346

Date		Item	Post. Ref.	Debit	Credit	Balance
20--						
Apr.	8		J6		2,500.00	2,500.00

NAME   EZX Corp.
ADDRESS   2928 Rhodes Ave., Chicago, IL 60658-5036

Date		Item	Post. Ref.	Debit	Credit	Balance
20--						
Apr.	11		J6		8,700.00	8,700.00
	24		J6	8,700.00		0

NAME   Printpro Corp.
ADDRESS   1200 Chambers Pike, Lincolnwood, IL 60648-2417

Date		Item	Post. Ref.	Debit	Credit	Balance
20--						
Apr.	17		J6		800.00	800.00

NAME   Televax, Inc.
ADDRESS   1500 North Walnut Street, Addison, IL 60101-2417

Date		Item	Post. Ref.	Debit	Credit	Balance
20--						
Apr.	23		J6		5,300.00	5,300.00

GENERAL LEDGER (Partial)

ACCOUNT   Accounts Payable   **ACCOUNT NO. 202**

Date		Item	Post. Ref.	Debit	Credit	Balance Debit	Balance Credit
20--							
Apr.	1	Bal.	✓				4,800.00
	4		J6		3,300.00		8,100.00
	8		J6		2,500.00		10,600.00
	10		J6	4,800.00			5,800.00
	11		J6		8,700.00		14,500.00
	17		J6		800.00		15,300.00
	23		J6		5,300.00		20,600.00
	24		J6	8,700.00			11,900.00

To verify that the sum of the accounts payable ledger balances equals the Accounts Payable balance, a **schedule of accounts payable** is prepared. This is an alphabetical or numerical listing of supplier accounts and balances, usually prepared at the end of the month. Figure 11-15 shows the schedule of accounts payable for Northern Micro as of April 30. Note that suppliers whose account balance is zero are not included.

PROFILES IN ACCOUNTING

Christy Rankin, Accounts Payable Representative

Christy Rankin credits good training and a willingness to continue to learn for her success as an accounts payable representative for a home builder. After 18 months at Davis Homes LLC, Christy finds her job challenging and rewarding. She uses what she learned in her college accounting classes, including computer accounting, every day at work.

This is Christy's first job since graduating with an Associate Degree in Business Management. She firmly believes her degree, along with the skills she learned in college, has helped her earn a better salary and will continue to pay off in the future.

Christy believes her college education provided her with a foundation and she feels that she is building her skills each day. Asked if she had any advice for today's students, Christy said "stick with it."

FIGURE 11-15 Schedule of Accounts Payable

Northern Micro
Schedule of Accounts Payable
April 30, 20--

Compucraft, Inc.	$ 3,300.00
Datasoft	2,500.00
Printpro Corp.	800.00
Televax, Inc.	5,300.00
	$11,900.00

This schedule is prepared from the list of supplier accounts in the accounts payable ledger. The total calculated in the schedule is compared with the balance in Accounts Payable in the general ledger. Note that the $11,900 total listed in the schedule equals the Accounts Payable balance shown in Figure 11-14. If the schedule total and the Accounts Payable balance do not agree, the error must be located and corrected. To find the error, use the following procedures:

STEP 1 Verify the total of the schedule.

STEP 2 Verify the postings to the accounts payable ledger.

STEP 3 Verify the postings to Accounts Payable in the general ledger.

Learning Objectives	Key Points to Remember
LO1 Define merchandise purchases transactions.	For a merchandising business, purchases refers to merchandise acquired for resale. Major documents used in the purchasing process are the purchase requisition, purchase order, receiving report, and purchase invoice.
LO2 Describe and use merchandise purchases accounts and compute gross profit.	Four accounts are used in accounting for merchandise purchases transactions. 1. Purchases 2. Purchases Returns and Allowances 3. Purchases Discounts 4. Freight-In Cost of Goods Sold = Beginning Inventory + Net Purchases + Freight-In − Ending Inventory. Gross Profit = Net Sales − Cost of Goods Sold.
LO3 Describe and use the accounts payable ledger.	To post purchases transactions to the general ledger: **In the general ledger account:** STEP 1 Enter the date of the transaction in the Date column. STEP 2 Enter the amount of the debit or credit in the Debit or Credit column. STEP 3 Enter the new balance in the Balance columns under Debit or Credit. STEP 4 Enter the journal page number from which each transaction is posted in the Posting Reference column. **In the journal:** STEP 5 Enter the ledger account number in the Posting Reference column of the journal for each transaction that is posted. An accounts payable ledger is a separate ledger containing an individual account payable for each supplier. To post from the general journal to the accounts payable ledger: **In the accounts payable ledger account:** STEP 1 Enter the date of the transaction in the Date column. STEP 2 Enter the amount of the debit or credit in the Debit or Credit column. STEP 3 Enter the new balance in the Balance column. STEP 4 Enter the journal page number from which each transaction is posted in the Posting Reference column. **In the journal:** STEP 5 Enter a slash (/) followed by a check mark (✔) in the Posting Reference column of the journal for each transaction that is posted. To post cash payments transactions to the general ledger: **In the general ledger account:** STEP 1 Enter the date of the transaction in the Date column. STEP 2 Enter the amount of the debit or credit in the Debit or Credit column. STEP 3 Enter the new balance in the Balance columns under Debit or Credit. STEP 4 Enter the journal page number from which each transaction is posted in the Posting Reference column.

Learning Objectives	Key Points to Remember
LO3 (concluded)	**In the journal:**
	STEP 5 Enter the ledger account number in the Posting Reference column of the journal for each transaction that is posted.
	To post cash payments transactions to the accounts payable ledger:
	In the accounts payable ledger account:
	STEP 1 Enter the date of the transaction in the Date column.
	STEP 2 Enter the amount of the debit or credit in the Debit or Credit column.
	STEP 3 Enter the new balance in the Balance column.
	STEP 4 Enter the journal page number from which each transaction is posted in the Posting Reference column.
	In the journal:
	STEP 5 Enter a slash (/) followed by a check mark (✓) in the Posting Reference column of the journal for each transaction that is posted.
LO4 Prepare a schedule of accounts payable.	The schedule of accounts payable is used to verify that the sum of the accounts payable ledger balances equals the Accounts Payable balance.

DEMONSTRATION PROBLEM

Jodi Rutman operates a retail pharmacy called Rutman Pharmacy. The books include a general journal, a general ledger, and an accounts payable ledger. The following transactions are related to purchases and cash payments for the month of June 20--:

June 1   Purchased merchandise from Sullivan Co. on account, $234.20. Invoice no. 71 dated June 1, terms 2/10, n/30.

2   Issued check no. 536 for payment of June rent (Rent Expense), $1,000.00.

5   Purchased merchandise from Amfac Drug Supply on account, $562.40. Invoice no. 196 dated June 2, terms 1/15, n/30.

7   Purchased merchandise from University Drug Co. on account, $367.35. Invoice no. 914A dated June 5, terms 3/10 eom, n/30.

9   Issued check no. 537 to Sullivan Co. in payment of invoice no. 71 less 2% discount.

12   Received a credit memo from Amfac Drug Supply for merchandise returned that was purchased on June 5, $46.20.

14   Purchased merchandise from Mutual Drug Co. on account, $479.40. Invoice no. 745 dated June 14, terms 2/10, n/30.

15   Received a credit memo from University Drug Co. for merchandise returned that was purchased on June 7, $53.70.

16   Issued check no. 538 to Amfac Drug Supply in payment of invoice no. 196 less the credit memo of June 12 and less 1% discount.

June 23   Issued check no. 539 to Mutual Drug Co. in payment of invoice no. 745 less 2% discount.

27   Purchased merchandise from Flites Pharmaceuticals on account, $638.47. Invoice no. 675 dated June 27, terms 2/10 eom, n/30.

29   Issued check no. 540 to Dolgin Candy Co. for a cash purchase of merchandise, $270.20.

30   Issued check no. 541 to Vashon Medical Supply in payment of invoice no. 416, $1,217.69. No discount allowed.

REQUIRED

1. Enter the transactions in a general journal (start with page 7).

2. Post from the journal to the general ledger accounts and the accounts payable ledger. Account numbers and June 1 balances are as indicated in the accounts presented below. Then, update the account balances.

3. Prepare a schedule of accounts payable from the accounts payable ledger in the problem. Verify that the total of accounts payable in the schedule equals the June 30 balance of Accounts Payable in the general ledger.

Solution 1.

GENERAL JOURNAL   PAGE 7

	DATE		DESCRIPTION	POST. REF.	DEBIT	CREDIT	
1	20-- June	1	Purchases	501	2 3 4 20		1
2			Accounts Payable/Sullivan Co.	202/✔		2 3 4 20	2
3			Invoice No. 71				3
4							4
5		2	Rent Expense	521	1 0 0 0 00		5
6			Cash	101		1 0 0 0 00	6
7			Check No. 536				7
8							8
9		5	Purchases	501	5 6 2 40		9
10			Accounts Payable/Amfac Drug Supply	202/✔		5 6 2 40	10
11			Invoice No. 196				11
12							12
13		7	Purchases	501	3 6 7 35		13
14			Accounts Payable/University Drug Co.	202/✔		3 6 7 35	14
15			Invoice No. 914A				15
16							16
17		9	Accounts Payable/Sullivan Co.	202/✔	2 3 4 20		17
18			Cash	101		2 2 9 52	18
19			Purchases Discounts	501.2		4 68	19
20			Check No. 537				20
21							21
22		12	Accounts Payable/Amfac Drug Supply	202/✔	4 6 20		22
23			Purchases Returns and Allowances	501.1		4 6 20	23
24			Returned merchandise				24
25							25
26		14	Purchases	501	4 7 9 40		26
27			Accounts Payable/Mutual Drug Co.	202/✔		4 7 9 40	27
28			Invoice No. 745				28

(continued)

			GENERAL JOURNAL												PAGE 8	
	DATE		DESCRIPTION	POST. REF.	DEBIT					CREDIT						
1	20-- June	15	Accounts Payable/University Drug Co.	202/✔			5	3	70							1
2			Purchases Returns and Allowances	501.1								5	3	70		2
3			Returned merchandise													3
4																4
5		16	Accounts Payable/Amfac Drug Supply	202/✔		5	1	6	20							5
6			Cash	101								5	1	1	04	6
7			Purchases Discounts	501.2									5	16		7
8			Check No. 538													8
9																9
10		23	Accounts Payable/Mutual Drug Co.	202/✔		4	7	9	40							10
11			Cash	101								4	6	9	81	11
12			Purchases Discounts	501.2									9	59		12
13			Check No. 539													13
14																14
15		27	Purchases	501		6	3	8	47							15
16			Accounts Payable/Flites Pharmaceuticals	202/✔								6	3	8	47	16
17			Invoice No. 675													17
18																18
19		29	Purchases	501		2	7	0	20							19
20			Cash	101								2	7	0	20	20
21			Check No. 540													21
22																22
23		30	Accounts Payable/Vashon Medical Supply	202/✔	1	2	1	7	69							23
24			Cash	101							1	2	1	7	69	24
25			Check No. 541													25

2.

ACCOUNT: Cash															ACCOUNT NO. 101					
DATE		ITEM	POST. REF.	DEBIT				CREDIT					BALANCE							
													DEBIT					CREDIT		
20-- June	1	Balance	✔										9	1	8	0	00			
	2		J7					1	0	0	0	00	8	1	8	0	00			
	9		J7						2	2	9	52	7	9	5	0	48			
	16		J8						5	1	1	04	7	4	3	9	44			
	23		J8						4	6	9	81	6	9	6	9	63			
	29		J8						2	7	0	20	6	6	9	9	43			
	30		J8					1	2	1	7	69	5	4	8	1	74			

ACCOUNT: Accounts Payable ACCOUNT NO. 202

DATE		ITEM	POST. REF.	DEBIT	CREDIT	BALANCE DEBIT	BALANCE CREDIT
20-- June	1	Balance	✓				1 2 1 7 69
	1		J7		2 3 4 20		1 4 5 1 89
	5		J7		5 6 2 40		2 0 1 4 29
	7		J7		3 6 7 35		2 3 8 1 64
	9		J7	2 3 4 20			2 1 4 7 44
	12		J7	4 6 20			2 1 0 1 24
	14		J7		4 7 9 40		2 5 8 0 64
	15		J8	5 3 70			2 5 2 6 94
	16		J8	5 1 6 20			2 0 1 0 74
	23		J8	4 7 9 40			1 5 3 1 34
	27		J8		6 3 8 47		2 1 6 9 81
	30		J8	1 2 1 7 69			9 5 2 12

ACCOUNT: Purchases ACCOUNT NO. 501

DATE		ITEM	POST. REF.	DEBIT	CREDIT	BALANCE DEBIT	BALANCE CREDIT
20-- June	1	Balance	✓			13 8 2 6 25	
	1		J7	2 3 4 20		14 0 6 0 45	
	5		J7	5 6 2 40		14 6 2 2 85	
	7		J7	3 6 7 35		14 9 9 0 20	
	14		J7	4 7 9 40		15 4 6 9 60	
	27		J8	6 3 8 47		16 1 0 8 07	
	29		J8	2 7 0 20		16 3 7 8 27	

ACCOUNT: Purchases Returns and Allowances ACCOUNT NO. 501.1

DATE		ITEM	POST. REF.	DEBIT	CREDIT	BALANCE DEBIT	BALANCE CREDIT
20-- June	1	Balance	✓				3 1 2 63
	12		J7		4 6 20		3 5 8 83
	15		J8		5 3 70		4 1 2 53

ACCOUNT: Purchases Discounts ACCOUNT NO. 501.2

DATE		ITEM	POST. REF.	DEBIT	CREDIT	BALANCE DEBIT	BALANCE CREDIT
20-- June	1	Balance	✓				2 1 1 45
	9		J7		4 68		2 1 6 13
	16		J8		5 16		2 2 1 29
	23		J8		9 59		2 3 0 88

ACCOUNT: Rent Expense ACCOUNT NO. 521

DATE		ITEM	POST. REF.	DEBIT	CREDIT	BALANCE DEBIT	BALANCE CREDIT
20-- June	1	Balance	✓			5 0 0 0 00	
	2		J7	1 0 0 0 00		6 0 0 0 00	

(continued)

ACCOUNTS PAYABLE LEDGER

NAME: Amfac Drug Supply

DATE		ITEM	POST. REF.	DEBIT	CREDIT	BALANCE
20-- June	5		J7		5 6 2 40	5 6 2 40
	12		J7	4 6 20		5 1 6 20
	16		J8	5 1 6 20		

NAME: Flites Pharmaceuticals

DATE		ITEM	POST. REF.	DEBIT	CREDIT	BALANCE
20-- June	27		J8		6 3 8 47	6 3 8 47

NAME: Mutual Drug Co.

DATE		ITEM	POST. REF.	DEBIT	CREDIT	BALANCE
20-- June	14		J7		4 7 9 40	4 7 9 40
	23		J8	4 7 9 40		

NAME: Sullivan Co.

DATE		ITEM	POST. REF.	DEBIT	CREDIT	BALANCE
20-- June	1		J7		2 3 4 20	2 3 4 20
	9		J7	2 3 4 20		

NAME: University Drug Co.

DATE		ITEM	POST. REF.	DEBIT	CREDIT	BALANCE
20-- June	7		J7		3 6 7 35	3 6 7 35
	15		J8	5 3 70		3 1 3 65

NAME: Vashon Medical Supply

DATE		ITEM	POST. REF.	DEBIT	CREDIT	BALANCE
20-- June	1	Balance	✔			1 2 1 7 69
	30		J8	1 2 1 7 69		

3.

Rutman Pharmacy **Schedule of Accounts Payable** **June 30, 20--**	
Flites Pharmaceuticals	$ 6 3 8 47
University Drug Co.	3 1 3 65
	$ 9 5 2 12
Proof	
Balance of Accounts Payable, June 30	$ 9 5 2 12

KEY TERMS

accounts payable ledger (409)   A separate ledger containing an individual account payable for each supplier.

cost of goods sold (405)   The difference between the goods available for sale and the ending inventory.

cost of merchandise sold (405)   See cost of goods sold.

FOB destination (404)   Shipping terms indicating that transportation charges are paid by the seller.

FOB shipping point (404)   Shipping terms indicating that transportation charges are paid by the buyer.

gross margin (405)   See gross profit.

gross profit (405)   The difference between net sales and cost of goods sold.

invoice (400)   A document prepared by the seller as a bill for the merchandise shipped. To the seller, this is a sales invoice. To the buyer, this is a purchase invoice.

purchase invoice (400)   A document prepared by the seller as a bill for the merchandise shipped. To the buyer, this is a purchase invoice.

purchase order (399)   A written order to buy goods from a specific vendor (supplier).

purchase requisition (398)   A form used to request the purchase of merchandise or other property.

purchases (398)   Merchandise acquired for resale to customers.

receiving report (400)   A report indicating what has been received.

schedule of accounts payable (413)   An alphabetical or numerical listing of supplier accounts and balances, usually prepared at the end of the month.

trade discount (400)   A reduction from the list or catalog price offered to different classes of customers.

Self-Study Test Questions

True/False

1. In the purchasing process, the purchase invoice is the first document prepared.

2. A sales invoice prepared by the seller is called a purchase invoice by the buyer.

3. A trade discount is a reduction from the list or catalog price offered to different classes of customers.

4. Purchases Returns and Allowances is debited when merchandise is returned for credit.

5. FOB shipping point means that transportation charges are paid by the seller.

Multiple Choice

1. A purchase of merchandise for $300 with a trade discount of 10% would require a debit to Purchases of

    (a) $330.
    (b) $300.
    (c) $297.
    (d) $270.

2. In the income statement, Freight-In is

    (a) added to purchases.
    (b) subtracted from purchases.
    (c) added to sales.
    (d) subtracted from cost of goods sold.

3. The difference between net sales and cost of goods sold is called

(a) gross profit.
(b) net purchases.

(c) goods available for sale.
(d) the bottom line.

4. The difference between merchandise available for sale and the end-of-period merchandise inventory is called

(a) gross profit.
(b) net purchases.

(c) net sales.
(d) cost of goods sold.

5. A purchase invoice for $1,200 with credit terms 2/10, n/30, and a return of $300 received by the seller prior to payment, is paid within the discount period. A check should be sent for

(a) $1,200.
(b) $882.

(c) $900.
(d) $810.

The answers to the Self-Study Test Questions are at the end of the text.

REVIEW QUESTIONS

LO1   1. Identify the major documents commonly used in the purchasing process.

LO1   2. Distinguish between a cash discount and a trade discount.

LO2   3. Describe how each of the following accounts is used: (1) Purchases, (2) Purchases Returns and Allowances, (3) Purchases Discounts, and (4) Freight-In.

LO2   4. How are cost of goods sold and gross profit computed?

LO3   5. What steps are followed in posting purchases from the general journal to the general ledger?

LO3   6. What steps are followed in posting purchases from the general journal to the accounts payable ledger?

LO3   7. What steps are used to post purchases returns and allowances from the general journal to the general ledger and accounts payable ledger?

LO3   8. What steps are followed in posting cash payments from the general journal to the general ledger?

LO3   9. What steps are followed in posting cash payments from the general journal to the accounts payable ledger?

LO4   10. If the total of the schedule of accounts payable does not agree with the Accounts Payable balance, what procedures should be used to search for the error?

© DIGITAL IMAGING GROUP

REVISITING THE OPENER

In the chapter opener on page 397, you are asked to consider how Evan's bookkeeper should account for freight charges, discounts, and credits for purchases.

(1) How should Evan's bookkeeper account for (a) freight charges on purchases, (b) trade discounts, (c) cash discounts, and (d) credits for purchases returned to the manufacturer or vendor?

(2) Prepare the journal entry for each of the following transactions:

(a) Purchased merchandise on account for $1,500 less a trade discount of 10% plus freight charges of $80. (Terms: FOB shipping point.)

(b) Made payment within the discount period for merchandise purchased on account for $800, terms 2/10, n/30.

(c) Returned merchandise purchased for $760 less a trade discount of 10% to the supplier because it is defective.

SERIES A EXERCISES

E 11-1A (LO1)

PURCHASING DOCUMENTS AND FLOWCHART LABELING A partially completed flowchart showing some of the major documents commonly used in the purchasing function of a merchandise business is presented below. Identify documents 1, 3, and 4.

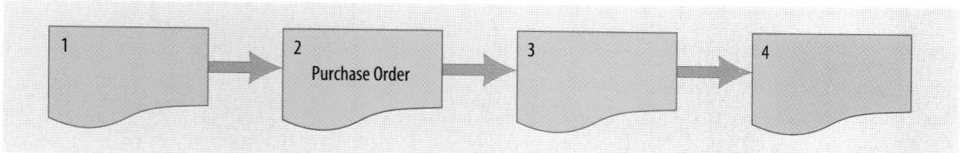

| 1 | | 2 Purchase Order | | 3 | | 4 |

E 11-2A (LO1/2)
✓ 2: $1,764

TRADE DISCOUNT AND CASH DISCOUNTS Merchandise was purchased on account from Jacob's Distributors on May 17. The purchase price was $2,000, subject to a 10% trade discount and credit terms of 2/10, n/30.

1. Calculate the net amount to record the invoice, subject to the 10% trade discount.
2. Calculate the amount to be paid on this invoice within the discount period.
3. Journalize the purchase of the merchandise on May 17 in a general journal. Journalize the payment on May 27 (within the discount period).

E 11-3A (LO2)
✓ 3(c): Purchases Discounts: $70

PURCHASE TRANSACTIONS AND T ACCOUNTS Using T accounts for Cash, Accounts Payable, Purchases, Purchases Returns and Allowances, Purchases Discounts, and Freight-In, enter the following purchase transactions. Identify each transaction with its corresponding letter. Use a new set of T accounts for each set of transactions, 1–4.

1. Purchase of merchandise with cash.

   (a) Merchandise is purchased for cash, $1,500.
   (b) Merchandise listed at $3,500, subject to a trade discount of 15%, is purchased for cash.

(continued)

2. Purchase of merchandise on account with credit terms.

   (a) Merchandise is purchased on account, credit terms 2/10, n/30, $2,000.
   (b) Merchandise is purchased on account, credit terms 3/10, n/30, $1,200.
   (c) Payment is made on invoice (a) within the discount period.
   (d) Payment is made on invoice (b) too late to receive the cash discount.

3. Purchase of merchandise on account with return of merchandise.

   (a) Merchandise is purchased on account, credit terms 2/10, n/30, $4,000.
   (b) Merchandise is returned for credit before payment is made, $500.
   (c) Payment is made within the discount period.

4. Purchase of merchandise with freight-in.

   (a) Merchandise is purchased on account, $2,500 plus freight charges of $100. Terms of the sale were FOB shipping point.
   (b) Payment is made for the cost of merchandise and the freight charge.

E 11-4A (LO2)
✓ Cost of goods sold: $74,500

COMPUTING GROSS PROFIT The following data were taken from the accounts of Delhi Hardware, a small retail business. Determine the gross profit.

Sales	$113,000
Sales returns and allowances	800
Merchandise inventory, January 1	34,000
Purchases during the period	76,000
Purchases returns and allowances during the period	4,000
Purchases discounts taken during the period	3,000
Freight-in on merchandise purchased during the period	1,500
Merchandise inventory, December 31	30,000

E 11-5A (LO3)
✓ May 9: Dr. Purchases, $2,300

JOURNALIZING PURCHASES TRANSACTIONS
Journalize the following transactions in a general journal:

May 3 Purchased merchandise from Cintron, $6,500. Invoice no. 321, dated May 1, terms n/30.

9 Purchased merchandise from Mitsui, $2,300. Invoice no. 614, dated May 8, terms 2/10, n/30.

18 Purchased merchandise from Aloha Distributors, $4,200. Invoice no. 180, dated May 15, terms 1/15, n/30.

23 Purchased merchandise from Soto, $6,300. Invoice no. 913, dated May 22, terms 1/10, n/30.

E 11-6A (LO3)
✓ Ending Accounts Payable balance: $8,600

JOURNALIZING PURCHASES RETURNS AND ALLOWANCES AND POSTING TO GENERAL LEDGER AND ACCOUNTS PAYABLE LEDGER
Using page 3 of a general journal and the following general ledger and accounts payable ledger accounts, journalize and post the following transactions:

July 7 Returned merchandise to Starcraft Industries, $700.

15 Returned merchandise to XYZ, Inc., $450.

27 Returned merchandise to Datamagic, $900.

General Ledger

Account No.	Account	Balance July 1, 20--
202	Accounts Payable	$10,650
501.1	Purchases Returns and Allowances	

Accounts Payable Ledger

Name	Balance July 1, 20--
Datamagic	$2,600
Starcraft Industries	4,300
XYZ, Inc.	3,750

E 11-7A (LO3)

✓ Sept. 12: Cr. Cash, $6,930

JOURNALIZING CASH PAYMENTS TRANSACTIONS Enter the following cash payments transactions in a general journal:

Sept. 5   Issued check no. 318 to Clinton Corp. for merchandise purchased August 28, $6,000, terms 2/10, n/30. Payment is made within the discount period.

12   Issued check no. 319 to Mitchell Company for merchandise purchased September 2, $7,500, terms 1/10, n/30. A credit memo had been received on September 8 from Mitchell Company for merchandise returned, $500. Payment is made within the discount period after deduction for the return dated September 8.

19   Issued check no. 320 to Expert Systems for merchandise purchased August 19, $4,100, terms n/30.

27   Issued check no. 321 to Graphic Data for merchandise purchased September 17, $9,000, terms 2/10, n/30. Payment is made within the discount period.

E 11-8A (LO4)

✓ Total Accounts Payable: $14,370

SCHEDULE OF ACCOUNTS PAYABLE Ryan's Express, a retail business, had the following beginning balances and purchases and payments activity in its accounts payable ledger during October. Prepare a schedule of accounts payable for Ryan's Express as of October 31, 20--.

Accounts Payable Ledger

Name	Balance Oct. 1, 20--	Purchases	Payments
Columbia Products	$4,350	$3,060	$2,060
Favorite Fashions	4,910	1,970	2,600
Rustic Legends	5,130	2,625	3,015

SERIES A PROBLEMS

P 11-9A (LO3)

✓ Purchases balance: $20,790

PURCHASES TRANSACTIONS J. B. Speck, owner of Speck's Galleria, made the following purchases of merchandise on account during the month of September:

Sept. 3   Purchase invoice no. 415, $2,650, from Smith Distributors.

8   Purchase invoice no. 132, $3,830, from Michaels Wholesaler.

11   Purchase invoice no. 614, $3,140, from J. B. Sanders & Co.

(continued)

Sept. 18   Purchase invoice no. 329, $2,250, from Bateman & Jones, Inc.

23   Purchase invoice no. 767, $4,160, from Smith Distributors.

27   Purchase invoice no. 744, $1,980, from Anderson Company.

30   Purchase invoice no. 652, $2,780, from Michaels Wholesaler.

REQUIRED

1.   Record the transactions in a general journal.

2.   Post from the general journal to the general ledger accounts and to the accounts payable ledger accounts. Use account numbers as shown in the chapter.

P 11-10A (LO3)

✓ Accounts Payable balance: $1,900

CASH PAYMENTS TRANSACTIONS Sam Santiago operates a retail variety store. The books include a general journal and an accounts payable ledger.

Selected account balances on May 1 are as follows:

General Ledger

Cash	$40,000
Accounts Payable	20,000

Accounts Payable Ledger

Fantastic Toys	$5,200
Goya Outlet	3,800
Mueller's Distributors	3,600
Van Kooning	7,400

The following are the transactions related to cash payments for the month of May:

May 1   Issued check no. 426 in payment of May rent (Rent Expense), $2,400.

3   Issued check no. 427 to Mueller's Distributors in payment of merchandise purchased on account, $3,600, less a 3% discount. Check was written for $3,492.

7   Issued check no. 428 to Van Kooning in partial payment of merchandise purchased on account, $5,500. A cash discount was not allowed.

12   Issued check no. 429 to Fantastic Toys for merchandise purchased on account, $5,200, less a 1% discount. Check was written for $5,148.

15   Issued check no. 430 to City Power and Light (Utilities Expense), $1,720.

18   Issued check no. 431 to A-1 Warehouse for a cash purchase of merchandise, $4,800.

26   Issued check no. 432 to Goya Outlet for merchandise purchased on account, $3,800, less a 2% discount. Check was written for $3,724.

30   Issued check no. 433 to Mercury Transit Company for freight charges on merchandise purchased (Freight-In), $1,200.

31   Issued check no. 434 to Town Merchants for a cash purchase of merchandise, $3,000.

REQUIRED

1. Enter the transactions in a general journal.

2. Post from the general journal to the general ledger and the accounts payable ledger. Use general ledger account numbers as shown in the chapter.

P 11-11A (L03)

✓ Cash balance: $8,830

KLOOSTER & ALLEN

PURCHASES AND CASH PAYMENTS TRANSACTIONS Freddy Flint owns a small retail business called Flint's Fantasy. The cash account has a balance of $20,000 on July 1. The following transactions occurred during July:

July	1	Issued check no. 414 in payment of July rent, $1,500.
	1	Purchased merchandise on account from Tang's Toys, invoice no. 311, $2,700, terms 2/10, n/30.
	3	Purchased merchandise on account from Sillas & Company, invoice no. 812, $3,100, terms 1/10, n/30.
	5	Returned merchandise purchased from Tang's Toys, receiving a credit memo on the amount owed, $500.
	8	Purchased merchandise on account from Daisy's Dolls, invoice no. 139, $1,900, terms 2/10, n/30.
	11	Issued check no. 415 to Tang's Toys for merchandise purchased on account, less return of July 5 and less 2% discount.
	13	Issued check no. 416 to Sillas & Company for merchandise purchased on account, less 1% discount.
	15	Returned merchandise purchased from Daisy's Dolls, receiving a credit memo on the amount owed, $400.
	18	Issued check no. 417 to Daisy's Dolls for merchandise purchased on account, less return of July 15 and less 2% discount.
	25	Purchased merchandise on account from Allied Business, invoice no. 489, $2,450, terms n/30.
	26	Purchased merchandise on account from Tang's Toys, invoice no. 375, $1,980, terms 2/10, n/30.
	29	Purchased merchandise on account from Sillas & Company, invoice no. 883, $3,460, terms 1/10, n/30.
	31	Freddy Flint withdrew cash for personal use, $2,000. Issued check no. 418.
	31	Issued check no. 419 to Glisan Distributors for a cash purchase of merchandise, $975.

REQUIRED

1. Enter the transactions in a general journal.

2. Post from the journal to the general ledger and accounts payable ledger accounts. Use general ledger account numbers as shown in the chapter.

P 11-12A (L04)

✓ Accounts Payable balance, Tang's Toys: $1,980

SCHEDULE OF ACCOUNTS PAYABLE Based on the information provided in Problem 11-11A, prepare a schedule of accounts payable for Flint's Fantasy as of July 31, 20--. Verify that the accounts payable account balance in the general ledger agrees with the schedule of accounts payable total.

SERIES B EXERCISES

E 11-1B (LO1)

PURCHASING DOCUMENTS AND FLOWCHART LABELING A flow-chart showing some of the major documents commonly used in the purchasing function of a merchandise business is presented below. Briefly describe each document.

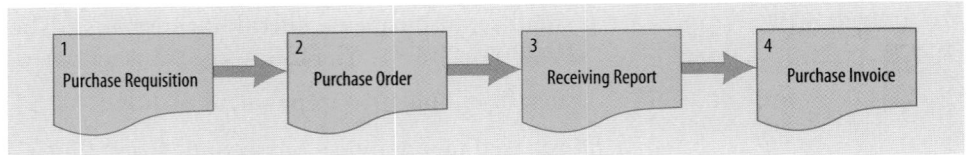

E 11-2B (LO1)

✓ 2: $4,365

TRADE DISCOUNT AND CASH DISCOUNTS Merchandise was purchased on account from Grant's Distributors on June 12. The purchase price was $5,000, subject to a 10% trade discount and credit terms of 3/10, n/30.

1. Calculate the net amount to record the invoice, subject to the 10% trade discount.
2. Calculate the amount to be paid on this invoice within the discount period.
3. Journalize the purchase of the merchandise on June 12 and the payment on June 22 (within the discount period) in a general journal.

E 11-3B (LO2)

✓ 3(c): Purchases Discounts, $100

PURCHASE TRANSACTIONS AND T ACCOUNTS Using T accounts for Cash, Accounts Payable, Purchases, Purchases Returns and Allowances, Purchases Discounts, and Freight-In, enter the following purchase transactions. Identify each transaction with its corresponding letter. Use a new set of T accounts for each set of transactions, 1–4.

1. Purchase of merchandise with cash.

    (a) Merchandise is purchased for cash, $2,300.
    (b) Merchandise listed at $4,000, subject to a trade discount of 10%, is purchased for cash.

2. Purchase of merchandise on account with credit terms.

    (a) Merchandise is purchased on account, credit terms 2/10, n/30, $4,000.
    (b) Merchandise is purchased on account, credit terms 3/10, n/30, $2,800.
    (c) Payment is made on invoice (a) within the discount period.
    (d) Payment is made on invoice (b) too late to receive the cash discount.

3. Purchase of merchandise on account with return of merchandise.

    (a) Merchandise is purchased on account, credit terms 2/10, n/30, $5,600.
    (b) Merchandise is returned for credit before payment is made, $600.
    (c) Payment is made within the discount period.

4. Purchase of merchandise with freight-in.

    (a) Merchandise is purchased on account, $3,800 plus freight charges of $200. Terms of the sale were FOB shipping point.
    (b) Payment is made for the cost of merchandise and the freight charge.

E 11-4B (LO2)

✓ Cost of goods sold: $76,700

COMPUTING GROSS PROFIT The following data were taken from the accounts of Burnside Bedknobs, a retail business. Determine the gross profit.

Sales	$116,500
Sales returns and allowances	1,100
Merchandise inventory, January 1	30,000
Purchases during the period	100,000
Purchases returns and allowances during the period	2,000
Purchases discounts taken during the period	2,800
Freight-in on merchandise purchased during the period	1,500
Merchandise inventory, December 31	50,000

E 11-5B (LO3)

✓ Jan. 12: Dr. Purchases, $9,000

JOURNALIZING PURCHASES TRANSACTIONS
Journalize the following transactions in a general journal:

Jan. 3   Purchased merchandise from Feng, $6,000. Invoice no. 416, dated January 1, terms 2/10, n/30.

12   Purchased merchandise from Miranda, $9,000. Invoice no. 624, dated January 10, terms n/30.

19   Purchased merchandise from J. B. Barba, $6,400. Invoice no. 190, dated January 18, terms 1/10, n/30.

26   Purchased merchandise from Ramirez, $3,700. Invoice no. 923, dated January 25, terms 1/15, n/30.

E 11-6B (LO3)

✓ Ending Accounts Payable balance: $6,950

JOURNALIZING PURCHASES RETURNS AND ALLOWANCES AND POSTING TO GENERAL LEDGER AND ACCOUNTS PAYABLE LEDGER
Using page 3 of a general journal and the following general ledger accounts and accounts payable ledger accounts, journalize and post the following transactions:

Mar. 5   Returned merchandise to Tower Industries, $500.

11   Returned merchandise to A & D Arms, $625.

23   Returned merchandise to Mighty Mansion, $275.

General Ledger

Account No.	Account	Balance Mar. 1, 20--
202	Accounts Payable	$8,350
501.1	Purchases Returns and Allowances	

Accounts Payable Ledger

Name	Balance Mar. 1, 20--
A & D Arms	$2,300
Mighty Mansion	1,450
Tower Industries	4,600

E 11-7B (LO3)

✓ Apr. 19: Cr. Cash, $4,950

JOURNALIZING CASH PAYMENTS TRANSACTIONS Enter the following cash payments transactions in a general journal:

Apr. 5   Issued check no. 429 to Standard Industries for merchandise purchased April 3, $8,000, terms 2/10, n/30. Payment is made within the discount period.

(continued)

Apr. 19   Issued check no. 430 to Finest Company for merchandise purchased April 10, $5,300, terms 1/10, n/30. A credit memo had been received on April 12 from Finest Company for merchandise returned, $300. Payment is made within the discount period after deduction for the return dated April 12.

21   Issued check no. 431 to Funny Follies for merchandise purchased March 21, $3,250, terms n/30.

29   Issued check no. 432 to Classic Data for merchandise purchased April 20, $7,000, terms 2/10, n/30. Payment is made within the discount period.

E 11-8B (LO4)
✓ Total accounts payable: $10,565

SCHEDULE OF ACCOUNTS PAYABLE Crystal's Candles, a retail business, had the following balances and purchases and payments activity in its accounts payable ledger during November. Prepare a schedule of accounts payable for Crystal's Candles as of November 30, 20--.

Accounts Payable Ledger			
Name	Balance Nov. 1, 20--	Purchases	Payments
Carl's Candle Wax	$4,135	$ 955	$1,610
Handy Supplies	3,490	1,320	1,850
Wishy Wicks	3,300	1,905	1,080

SERIES B PROBLEMS

P 11-9B (LO3)
✓ Purchases balance: $18,515

PURCHASES TRANSACTIONS Ann Benton, owner of Benton's Galleria, made the following purchases of merchandise on account during the month of October:

Oct. 2   Purchase invoice no. 321, $1,950, from Boggs Distributors.

7   Purchase invoice no. 152, $2,915, from Wolfs Wholesaler.

10   Purchase invoice no. 634, $3,565, from Komuro & Co.

16   Purchase invoice no. 349, $2,845, from Fritz & McCord, Inc.

24   Purchase invoice no. 587, $3,370, from Boggs Distributors.

26   Purchase invoice no. 764, $2,240, from Sanderson Company.

31   Purchase invoice no. 672, $1,630, from Wolfs Wholesaler.

REQUIRED

1.   Record the transactions in a general journal.

2.   Post from the general journal to the general ledger accounts and to the accounts payable ledger accounts. Use account numbers as shown in the chapter.

P 11-10B (LO3)
✓ Accounts Payable balance: $600

CASH PAYMENTS TRANSACTIONS Kay Zembrowski operates a retail variety store. The books include a general journal and an accounts payable ledger. Selected account balances on May 1 are as follows:

General Ledger

Cash	$40,000
Accounts Payable	20,000

Accounts Payable Ledger

Cortez Distributors	$4,200
Indra & Velga	6,800
Toy Corner	4,600
Troutman Outlet	4,400

The following transactions are related to cash payments for the month of May:

May 1   Issued check no. 326 in payment of May rent (Rent Expense), $2,600.

4   Issued check no. 327 to Cortez Distributors in payment of merchandise purchased on account, $4,200, less a 3% discount. Check was written for $4,074.

7   Issued check no. 328 to Indra & Velga in partial payment of merchandise purchased on account, $6,200. A cash discount was not allowed.

11   Issued check no. 329 to Toy Corner for merchandise purchased on account, $4,600, less a 1% discount. Check was written for $4,554.

15   Issued check no. 330 to County Power and Light (Utilities Expense), $1,500.

19   Issued check no. 331 to Builders Warehouse for a cash purchase of merchandise, $3,500.

25   Issued check no. 332 to Troutman Outlet for merchandise purchased on account, $4,400, less a 2% discount. Check was written for $4,312.

30   Issued check no. 333 to Rapid Transit Company for freight charges on merchandise purchased (Freight-In), $800.

31   Issued check no. 334 to City Merchants for a cash purchase of merchandise, $2,350.

REQUIRED

1. Enter the transactions in a general journal.

2. Post from the general journal to the general ledger and the accounts payable ledger. Use general ledger account numbers as shown in the chapter.

P 11-11B (LO3)

✓ Cash balance: $9,240

KLOOSTER & ALLEN

PURCHASES AND CASH PAYMENTS TRANSACTIONS Debbie Mueller owns a small retail business called Debbie's Doll House. The cash account has a balance of $20,000 on July 1. The following transactions occurred during July:

July 1   Issued check no. 314 for July rent, $1,400.

1   Purchased merchandise on account from Topper's Toys, invoice no. 211, $2,500, terms 2/10, n/30.

3   Purchased merchandise on account from Jones & Company, invoice no. 812, $2,800, terms 1/10, n/30.

5   Returned merchandise purchased from Topper's Toys receiving a credit memo on the amount owed, $400.

8   Purchased merchandise on account from Downtown Merchants, invoice no. 159, $1,600, terms 2/10, n/30.

11   Issued check no. 315 to Topper's Toys for merchandise purchased on account, less return of July 5 and less 2% discount.

(continued)

July 13   Issued check no. 316 to Jones & Company for merchandise purchased on account, less 1% discount.

15   Returned merchandise purchased from Downtown Merchants receiving a credit memo on the amount owed, $600.

18   Issued check no. 317 to Downtown Merchants for merchandise purchased on account, less return of July 15 and less 2% discount.

25   Purchased merchandise on account from Columbia Products, invoice no. 468, $3,200, terms n/30.

26   Purchased merchandise on account from Topper's Toys, invoice no. 395, $1,430, terms 2/10, n/30.

29   Purchased merchandise on account from Jones & Company, invoice no. 853, $2,970 terms 1/10, n/30.

31   Mueller withdrew cash for personal use, $2,500. Issued check no. 318.

31   Issued check no. 319 to Burnside Warehouse for a cash purchase of merchandise, $1,050.

REQUIRED

1.   Enter the transactions in a general journal.

2.   Post from the journal to the general ledger and accounts payable ledger accounts. Use general ledger account numbers as shown in the chapter.

P 11-12B (LO4)

✓ Accounts Payable balance,
Topper's Toys: $1,430

SCHEDULE OF ACCOUNTS PAYABLE Based on the information provided in Problem 11-11B, prepare a schedule of accounts payable for Debbie's Doll House as of July 31, 20--. Verify that the accounts payable account balance in the general ledger agrees with the schedule of accounts payable total.

MANAGING YOUR WRITING

You are working as a summer intern at a rapidly growing organic food distributor. Part of your responsibility is to assist in the accounts payable department. You notice that most bills from suppliers are not paid within the discount period. The manager of accounts payable says the bills are organized by vendor, like the accounts payable ledger, and she is too busy to keep track of the discount periods. Besides, the owner has told her that the 1% and 2% discounts available are not worth worrying about.

Write a memo to the owner explaining why it is expensive not to take advantage of cash discounts on credit purchases. In addition, suggest a way to file (organize) supplier invoices so that they are paid within the discount period.

ETHICS CASE

Bob's Discount Auto Parts receives a cash discount of 2% from Auto Warehouse if it pays an invoice within 10 days. Bob, the owner, consistently sends payments 15 to 20 days after receiving the invoice and still deducts the amount of the discount. Last week, Bob received a call from Auto Warehouse reminding him that in order to get the discount, an invoice must be paid within 10 days. When Bob received the next invoice, he dated the check exactly 10 days from the date of the invoice but didn't mail the check for another week. The receivables manager from Auto Warehouse called Bob and again reminded him that the check should be mailed by the 10th day in order to receive the 2% discount. When Bob received the next invoice, he mailed it on time but post-dated the check for the following week.

1. Are Bob's attempts to extend the discount period unethical?

2. What alternatives can Auto Warehouse take to prevent Bob's Discount Auto Parts from stretching the discount period?

3. Write a short note from Auto Warehouse to Bob's Discount Auto Parts explaining cash discounts and credit terms.

4. In small groups, make a list of the advantages and disadvantages of offering cash discounts.

MASTERY PROBLEM

✓ Accounts Payable balance: $10,000

KA
KLOOSTER
& ALLEN

Michelle French owns and operates Books and More, a retail book store. Selected account balances on June 1 are as follows:

General Ledger

Cash	$32,200.00
Accounts Payable	2,000.00
M. French, Drawing	18,000.00
Purchases	67,021.66
Purchases Returns and Allowances	2,315.23
Purchases Discounts	905.00
Freight-In	522.60
Rent Expense	3,125.00
Utilities Expense	1,522.87

Accounts Payable Ledger

Northeastern Publishing Co.	$2,000.00

The following purchases and cash payments transactions took place during the month of June:

June 1   Purchased books on account from Irving Publishing Company, $2,100. Invoice no. 101, terms 2/10, n/30, FOB destination.

2   Issued check no. 300 to Northeastern Publishing Co. for goods purchased on May 23, terms 2/10, n/30, $1,960 (the $2,000 invoice amount less the 2% discount).

3   Purchased books on account from Broadway Publishing, Inc., $2,880. Invoice no. 711, subject to 20% trade discount, and invoice terms of 3/10, n/30, FOB shipping point.

3   Issued check no. 301 to Mayday Shipping for delivery from Broadway Publishing, Inc., $250.

4   Issued check no. 302 for June rent, $625.

(continued)

June 8 Purchased books on account from Northeastern Publishing Co. $5,825. Invoice no. 268, terms 2/eom, n/60, FOB destination.

10 Received a credit memo from Irving Publishing Company, $550. Books had been returned because the covers were on upside down.

13 Issued check no. 304 to Broadway Publishing, Inc., for the purchase made on June 3. (Check no. 303 was voided because an error was made in preparing it.)

28 Made the following purchases:

Invoice No.	Company	Amount	Terms
579	Broadway Publishing, Inc.	$2,350	2/10, n/30 FOB destination
406	Northeastern Publishing Co.	4,200	2/eom, n/60 FOB destination
964	Riley Publishing Co.	3,450	3/10, n/30 FOB destination

30 Issued check no. 305 to Taylor County Utility Co. for June utilities, $325.

30 French withdrew cash for personal use, $4,500. Issued check no. 306.

30 Issued check no. 307 to Irving Publishing Company for purchase made on June 1 less returns made on June 10.

30 Issued check no. 308 to Northeastern Publishing Co. for purchase made on June 8.

30 Issued check no. 309 for books purchased at an auction, $1,328.

REQUIRED

1. Enter the transactions in a general journal (start with page 16).

2. Post from the journal to the general ledger accounts and the accounts payable ledger. Use account numbers as indicated in the chapter.

3. Prepare a schedule of accounts payable.

4. If merchandise inventory was $35,523 on January 1 and $42,100 as of June 30, prepare the cost of goods sold section of the income statement for the six months ended June 30, 20--.

CHALLENGE PROBLEM

This problem challenges you to apply your cumulative accounting knowledge to move a step beyond the material in the chapter.

Record the following transactions in a general journal:

✓ **May 14: Cr. Purchases Discounts, $9**

May 4 Merchandise listed at $2,900, subject to a trade discount of 10%, is purchased on account, credit terms of 1/10, n/30, shipping terms FOB destination.

8 Merchandise purchased on May 4, listed at $520, is returned for credit.

14 Partial payment is made for the merchandise purchased on May 4, listed at $1,000, less 1% discount.

June 3 Payment is made of the balance due on the May 4 purchase.

Chapter 11 Appendix
The Net-Price Method of Recording Purchases

Objectives

Careful study of this appendix should enable you to:

LO1 **Describe the net-price method of recording purchases.**

LO2 **Record purchases and cash payments using the net-price method.**

NET-PRICE METHOD

LO1 Describe the net-price method of recording purchases.

In this chapter, purchases were recorded using the **gross-price method**. Under this method, purchases are recorded at the gross amount, regardless of available cash discounts. An alternative approach to accounting for purchases is the **net-price method**. Under this method, purchases are recorded at the net amount, assuming that all available cash discounts will be taken.

RECORDING WITH THE NET-PRICE METHOD

LO1 Record purchases and cash payments using the net-price method.

To compare the gross-price and net-price methods, reconsider the purchase for $100 on account, with credit terms of 2/10, n/30, on page 403. At the time of the purchase, the following entries are made under the two methods:

Gross-Price			Net-Price		
Purchases	100.00		Purchases	98.00*	
Accounts Payable		100.00	Accounts Payable		98.00

*$100 − $2 (2% cash discount)

If the payment for the merchandise is made within the discount period, the entries are as follows:

Gross-Price			Net-Price		
Accounts Payable	100.00		Accounts Payable	98.00	
Cash		98.00	Cash		98.00
Purchases Discounts		2.00			

If payment for the merchandise is not made until after the discount period, the entries are as follows:

Gross-Price			Net-Price		
Accounts Payable	100.00		Accounts Payable	98.00	
Cash		100.00	Purchases Discounts Lost	2.00	
			Cash		100.00

Note that under the net-price method a new account, Purchases Discounts Lost, is used. Purchases Discounts Lost is a temporary owner's equity account used to record cash discounts lost on purchases. It is reported as an expense on the income statement.

Purchases Discounts Lost

Debit	Credit
to enter discounts lost because of late payment of invoices	

Purchases Discounts Lost represents a finance charge for postponing the payment for merchandise. If the balance in this account is large relative to the amount of gross purchases, management should review its cash payment procedures.

Learning Objectives	Key Points to Remember
LO1 Describe the net-price method of recording purchases.	Under the net-price method, purchases are recorded at the net amount, assuming all available cash discounts will be taken.
LO2 Record purchases and cash payments using the net-price method.	Assume a purchase is made for $100 on account, with credit terms of 2/10, n/30. Under the net-price method, the entry at the time of purchase is as follows: Purchases 98.00 Accounts Payable 98.00 If payment is made within the discount period, the entry is as follows: Accounts Payable 98.00 Cash 98.00 If payment is not made until after the discount period, the entry is as follows: Accounts Payable 98.00 Purchases Discounts Lost 2.00 Cash 100.00

KEY TERMS

gross-price method (435)   Under this method, purchases are recorded at the gross amount.

net-price method (435)   Under this method, purchases are recorded at the net amount, assuming all available cash discounts are taken.

REVIEW QUESTIONS

LO1   1.   At what amount are purchases recorded under the net-price method?

LO2   2.   Under the net-price method, if payment for merchandise is not made within the discount period, what accounts are debited when the payment is made?

LO2   3.   (a)   What kind of an account is Purchases Discounts Lost?
            (b)   How is this item reported on the income statement?

SERIES A EXERCISE

E 11Apx-1A (LO2)
✓ 1. Apr. 11: Dr. Purchases Discounts, $20

PURCHASES TRANSACTIONS—GROSS-PRICE AND NET-PRICE METHODS Romero's Heating and Cooling had the following transactions during April:

Apr. 2   Purchased merchandise on account from Alanon Valve for $1,000, terms 2/10, n/30.

      5   Purchased merchandise on account from Leon's Garage for $1,400, terms 1/10, n/30.

     11   Paid the amount due to Alanon Valve for the purchase on April 2.

     25   Paid the amount due to Leon's Garage for the purchase on April 5.

     1.   Prepare general journal entries for these transactions using the gross-price method.
     2.   Prepare general journal entries for these transactions using the net-price method.

SERIES B EXERCISE

E 11Apx-1B (LO2)
✓ 2. May 27: Dr. Purchases Discounts Lost, $12

PURCHASES TRANSACTIONS—GROSS-PRICE AND NET-PRICE METHODS Gloria's Repair Shop had the following transactions during May:

May 2   Purchased merchandise on account from Delgado's Supply for $900, terms 2/10, n/30.

      6   Purchased merchandise on account from Goro's Auto Care for $1,200, terms 1/10, n/30.

     11   Paid the amount due to Delgado's Supply for the purchase on May 2.

     27   Paid the amount due to Goro's Auto Care for the purchase on May 6.

     1.   Prepare general journal entries for these transactions using the gross-price method.
     2.   Prepare general journal entries for these transactions using the net-price method.

PHOTO: © DIGITAL IMAGING GROUP

Objectives

Careful study of this chapter should enable you to:

LO1
Describe, explain the purpose of, and identify transactions recorded in special journals.

LO2
Describe and use the sales journal.

LO3
Describe and use the cash receipts journal.

LO4
Describe and use the purchases journal.

LO5
Describe and use the cash payments journal.

Special Journals

As Evan Taylor's business has grown, the hours required for his part-time bookkeeper, Betty Jenkins, to maintain the books for Parkway Pet Supplies have grown substantially. Recently, she informed Evan that the increased hours were starting to affect her college studies, so they needed to adopt more efficient accounting methods. She seemed particularly annoyed about the sales, cash receipts, purchases, and cash payments transactions. Each week, she has to write the same account names in the general journal and then post to the same accounts in the general ledger hundreds of times for these transactions. Betty suggested that one way to improve the recording process would be to use the special journals she has studied in her accounting classes. What are special journals? How would they make the record keeping more efficient?

Chapters 10 and 11 demonstrated how to account for sales, cash receipts, purchases, and cash payments in a merchandising business. We also saw how to use accounts receivable and accounts payable ledgers to keep track of individual customer and supplier accounts. In this chapter, we continue to study how to account for sales, cash receipts, purchases, and cash payments, but our objective is to find a way to be more efficient. We will learn how to use four special journals that enable us to achieve this objective.

SPECIAL JOURNALS

LO1 Describe, explain the purpose of, and identify transactions recorded in special journals.

A **special journal** is a journal designed for recording only certain kinds of transactions. A special journal can be created for almost any kind of transaction. The types of special journals a business uses should depend on the types of transactions that occur most frequently for a business. The more transactions of a specific type that occur, the more likely a special journal of that type would be useful for the business.

The primary purpose of using special journals is to save time journalizing and posting transactions. In a general journal, we recorded transactions by writing the account names, debit and credit amounts, and an explanation for each transaction on several lines in the journal. In contrast, most transactions are entered in a special journal on a single line, with the debit and credit amounts indicated in special columns provided for each account. This enables substantial time saving. The posting process also is more efficient. Using the general journal, each transaction is posted separately to the appropriate general ledger accounts. With a special journal, summary postings of column totals are made to appropriate accounts on a periodic basis.

Of course, even if a business uses special journals, there still is a need for a general journal. For example, transactions that occur infrequently, and adjusting and closing entries, usually are recorded in the general journal.

Four special journals commonly used by businesses are as follows:

LEARNING KEY

The special journals and general journal are books of original entry. Each transaction is recorded in only <u>one</u> of these journals.

- Sales journal
- Cash receipts journal
- Purchases journal
- Cash payments journal

Figure 12-1 identifies the types of transactions recorded in each of the four special journals and the general journal. You might find it helpful to refer back to Figure 12-1 as the four special journals are introduced in this chapter.

FIGURE 12-1   Types of Journals and Transactions

TYPE OF JOURNAL	TYPE OF TRANSACTIONS RECORDED
Sales journal	All sales of merchandise on account
Cash receipts journal	All cash receipts
Purchases journal	All purchases of merchandise on account
Cash payments journal	All cash payments
General journal	All other transactions

In the following sections, we will examine the journalizing and posting process using each of the four special journals.

SALES JOURNAL

LO2 Describe and use the sales journal.

A **sales journal** is a special journal used to record only sales of merchandise on account. To illustrate the journalizing and posting of sales transactions in the sales journal, the sales transactions and general journal entries for Northern Micro from Chapter 10 are reproduced below and reported in Figure 12-2.

Apr. 4   Made sale no. 133C on account to Enrico Lorenzo, $1,520, plus $76 sales tax.

10   Made sale no. 134C on account to Brenda Myers, $440, plus $22 sales tax.

18   Made sale no. 105D on account to Edith Walton, $980, plus $49 sales tax.

21   Made sale no. 202B on account to Susan Chang, $620, plus $31 sales tax.

24   Made sale no. 162A on account to Heidi Schwitzer, $1,600, plus $80 sales tax.

FIGURE 12-2   Sales Entered in General Journal

4	Apr.	4	Accounts Receivable/E. Lorenzo	1 5 9 6 00		4
5			Sales		1 5 2 0 00	5
6			Sales Tax Payable		7 6 00	6
7			Sale No. 133C			7
8						8
9		10	Accounts Receivable/B. Myers	4 6 2 00		9
10			Sales		4 4 0 00	10
11			Sales Tax Payable		2 2 00	11
12			Sale No. 134C			12
13						13
14		18	Accounts Receivable/E. Walton	1 0 2 9 00		14
15			Sales		9 8 0 00	15
16			Sales Tax Payable		4 9 00	16
17			Sale No. 105D			17
18						18
19		21	Accounts Receivable/S. Chang	6 5 1 00		19
20			Sales		6 2 0 00	20
21			Sales Tax Payable		3 1 00	21
22			Sale No. 202B			22
23						23
24		24	Accounts Receivable/H. Schwitzer	1 6 8 0 00		24
25			Sales		1 6 0 0 00	25
26			Sales Tax Payable		8 0 00	26
27			Sale No. 162A			27

Notice that each of these five entries involved the same three accounts. The same account titles were recorded five times. Similarly, to post these entries to the general ledger, five separate postings would be made to each of the three accounts, a total of 15 postings.

These transactions can be recorded more efficiently by using a sales journal. To illustrate, reconsider the five sales made on account by Northern Micro. They are entered in the sales journal in Figure 12-3. The sales journal provides separate columns for Accounts Receivable Debit, Sales Credit, and Sales Tax Payable Credit, the three accounts used repeatedly in the general journal in Figure 12-2. A sale is recorded in the sales journal by entering the following information:

LEARNING KEY

Use a sales journal only for recording sales of merchandise on account.

Remember that sales returns and allowances are recorded in the general journal, as illustrated in Chapter 10, not in the sales journal.

1. Date

2. Sale number

3. Customer (to whom sold)

4. Dollar amounts

There is no need to enter any general ledger account titles, since they appear in the column headings.

FIGURE 12-3   Northern Micro Sales Journal

	DATE		SALE NO.	TO WHOM SOLD	POST. REF.	ACCOUNTS RECEIVABLE DEBIT					SALES CREDIT					SALES TAX PAYABLE CREDIT				
1	20-- Apr.	4	133C	Enrico Lorenzo		1	5	9	6	00	1	5	2	0	00		7	6	00	1
2		10	134C	Brenda Myers			4	6	2	00		4	4	0	00		2	2	00	2
3		18	105D	Edith Walton		1	0	2	9	00		9	8	0	00		4	9	00	3
4		21	202B	Susan Chang			6	5	1	00		6	2	0	00		3	1	00	4
5		24	162A	Heidi Schwitzer		1	6	8	0	00	1	6	0	0	00		8	0	00	5

SALES JOURNAL — PAGE 6

This chapter illustrates a manual accounting system. With a computerized system, journals/ledgers can be updated simultaneously when a transaction is entered (see pp. 458–461).

The sales journal in Figure 12-3 is designed for a company, like Northern Micro, that charges sales tax. For a wholesaler or any other company that does not charge sales tax, a sales journal like that in Figure 12-4 would be sufficient. In this case, there is only a single amount column headed Accounts Receivable Debit/Sales Credit. With no sales tax, the Accounts Receivable Debit and Sales Credit amounts are identical for each sale. Thus, only a single column is needed.

FIGURE 12-4   Sales Journal Without Sales Tax

SALES JOURNAL — PAGE 1

DATE	SALE NO.	TO WHOM SOLD	POST. REF.	ACCOUNTS RECEIVABLE DEBIT/ SALES CREDIT

Posting from the Sales Journal

Posting from the sales journal also is very efficient. Each general ledger account used in the sales journal requires only one posting each period. Figure 12-5 illustrates the general ledger posting process for Northern Micro's sales journal for the month of April.

The following steps are used to post from the sales journal to the general ledger at the end of each month, as indicated in Figure 12-5:

In the sales journal:

STEP 1 Total the amount columns, verify that the total of the debit column equals the total of the credit columns, and rule the columns.

In the ledger account:

STEP 2 Enter the date of the transaction in the Date column.

STEP 3 Enter the amount of the debit or credit in the Debit or Credit column.

Step 1 is the main difference in posting the sales journal to the general ledger. The remaining steps 2–6 are essentially the same as steps 1–5 used to post the general journal.

STEP 4 Enter the new balance in the Balance columns under Debit or Credit.

STEP 5 Enter the initial "S" and the journal page number in the Posting Reference column.

In the sales journal:

STEP 6 Enter the ledger account number immediately below the column totals for each account that is posted.

FIGURE 12-5   Posting the Sales Journal to the General Ledger

SALES JOURNAL   Page 6

Date	Sale No.	To Whom Sold	Post. Ref.	Accounts Receivable Debit	Sales Credit	Sales Tax Payable Credit	
20--							
Apr. 4	133C	Enrico Lorenzo		1,596.00	1,520.00	76.00	
10	134C	Brenda Myers		462.00	440.00	22.00	
18	105D	Edith Walton		1,029.00	980.00	49.00	
21	202B	Susan Chang		651.00	620.00	31.00	
24	162A	Heidi Schwitzer		1,680.00	1,600.00	80.00	
				5,418.00	5,160.00	258.00	**1**
				(122)	(401)	(231)	**6** **3**

GENERAL LEDGER (Partial)

1 Debit total: $5,418

Credit total: $5,160
                        258
                  $5,418

ACCOUNT   Accounts Receivable   **ACCOUNT NO.** 122

	Date	Item	Post. Ref.	Debit	Credit	Balance Debit	Balance Credit
	20--						
	Apr. 1	Bal.	✝			12,000.00	
2	30	**5** S6		5,418.00		17,418.00	
						4	

ACCOUNT   Sales Tax Payable   **ACCOUNT NO.** 231

	Date	Item	Post. Ref.	Debit	Credit	Balance Debit	Balance Credit
	20--						
2	Apr. 30	**5** S6			258.00		258.00
							4

ACCOUNT   Sales   **ACCOUNT NO.** 401

	Date	Item	Post. Ref.	Debit	Credit	Balance Debit	Balance Credit
	20--						
	Apr. 1	Bal.	✝				27,000.00
2	30	**5** S6			5,160.00		32,160.00
							4

As we saw in Chapter 10, Northern Micro also needs a record of the accounts receivable from *individual customers*. Figure 12-6 illustrates the use of the accounts receivable ledger. The accounts receivable ledger is posted *daily* so that current information is available for each customer at all times. The following steps are used to post the sales journal to the accounts receivable ledger, as shown in Figure 12-6:

In the accounts receivable ledger account:

STEP 1 Enter the date of the transaction in the Date column.

STEP 2 Enter the amount of the debit or credit in the Debit or Credit column.

STEP 3 Enter the new balance in the Balance column.

STEP 4 Enter the initial "S" and the journal page number in the Posting Reference column.

In the sales journal:

STEP 5 Enter a check mark (✓) in the Posting Reference column of the journal for each transaction that is posted.

The accounts receivable ledger also can be posted from the source document used to make the sales journal entry. For example, sales ticket #134C (see Figure 10-2) could be used to post that sale to Brenda Myers' account in the accounts receivable ledger. In this case, 134C would be inserted in the Posting Reference column of her account.

Note the relationship between the sales journal, accounts receivable ledger, and general ledger. All individual entries in the sales journal are posted to the accounts receivable ledger. The totals of all entries in the sales journal are posted to the general ledger accounts. After the posting of the accounts receivable ledger and the general ledger is completed, the total of the accounts receivable ledger balances should equal the Accounts Receivable balance in the general ledger.

If the accounts receivable ledger is posted daily and the general ledger is posted at the end of the month, the accounts receivable ledger total will equal the general ledger Accounts Receivable total only at the end of the month.

LEARNING KEY

The total of the accounts receivable ledger balances must equal the Accounts Receivable balance in the general ledger.

CASH RECEIPTS JOURNAL

LO3 **Describe and use the cash receipts journal.**

A **cash receipts journal** is a special journal used to record only cash receipts transactions. To illustrate its use, we continue with the transactions of Northern Micro. Northern Micro's cash receipts journal for the month of April is shown in Figure 12-7, with the following transactions:

Apr. 14 Received cash on account from Enrico Lorenzo for sale no. 133C, $1,596.

20 Received cash on account from Brenda Myers for sale no. 134C, $462.

28 Received cash on account from Edith Walton for sale no. 105D, $1,029.

30 Made cash sales for the month of $3,600 plus tax of $180.

30 Made bank credit card sales for the month of $2,500 plus tax of $125. Bank credit card expenses on these sales are $100.

30 Received cash for rent revenue, $600.

30 Borrowed cash from the bank by signing a note, $3,000.

FIGURE 12-6   Posting from the Sales Journal to the Accounts Receivable Ledger

SALES JOURNAL

Page 6

Date	Sale No.	To Whom Sold	Post. Ref.	Accounts Receivable Debit	Sales Credit	Sales Tax Payable Credit
20--						
Apr. 4	133C	Enrico Lorenzo	✝	1,596.00	1,520.00	76.00
10	134C	Brenda Myers	✝	462.00	440.00	22.00
18	105D	Edith Walton	✝	1,029.00	980.00	49.00
21	202B	Susan Chang	✝	651.00	620.00	31.00
24	162A	Heidi Schwitzer	✝	1,680.00	1,600.00	80.00
			5	5,418.00	5,160.00	258.00
				(122)	(401)	(231)

2

ACCOUNTS RECEIVABLE LEDGER

NAME   Helen Avery
ADDRESS 1739 Woodsage Trace, Indianapolis, IN 46237-1199

Date	Item	Post. Ref.	Debit	Credit	Balance
20--					
Apr. 1	Bal.	✝			2,302.00

NAME   Susan Chang
ADDRESS 337 Elm Street, Noblesville, IN 46060-3377

Date	Item	Post. Ref.	Debit	Credit	Balance
20--					
Apr. 21	**4**	S6	651.00		651.00 **3**

1

NAME   Enrico Lorenzo
ADDRESS 5240 Tousley Court, Indianapolis, IN 46224-5678

Date	Item	Post. Ref.	Debit	Credit	Balance
20--					
Apr. 4	**4**	S6	1,596.00		1,596.00 **3**

1

NAME   Brenda Myers
ADDRESS 581 Acorn Way, Zionsville, IN 46077-2154

Date	Item	Post. Ref.	Debit	Credit	Balance
20--					
Apr. 10	**4**	S6	462.00		462.00 **3**

1

NAME   Heidi Schwitzer
ADDRESS 5858 Wildflower Cir., Bloomington, IN 47401-6209

Date	Item	Post. Ref.	Debit	Credit	Balance
20--					
Apr. 1	Bal.	✝			1,883.00
24	**4**	S6	1,680.00		3,563.00 **3**

1

NAME   Ken Ulmet
ADDRESS 5260 Eagle Creek, Indianapolis, IN 46254-8275

Date	Item	Post. Ref.	Debit	Credit	Balance
20--					
Apr. 1	Bal.	✝			3,315.00

NAME   Edith Walton
ADDRESS 1113 Stones Crossing, Zionsville, IN 46077-6601

Date	Item	Post. Ref.	Debit	Credit	Balance
20--					
Apr. 18	**4**	S6	1,029.00		1,029.00 **3**

1

NAME   Vivian Winston
ADDRESS 124 Main St., Zionsville, IN 46077-1358

Date	Item	Post. Ref.	Debit	Credit	Balance
20--					
Apr. 1	Bal.	✝			4,500.00

GENERAL LEDGER (Partial)

ACCOUNT   Accounts Receivable   **ACCOUNT NO.** 122

Date	Item	Post. Ref.	Debit	Credit	Balance Debit	Balance Credit
20--						
Apr. 1	Bal.	✝			12,000.00	
30		S6	5,418.00		17,418.00	

ACCOUNT   Sales Tax Payable   **ACCOUNT NO.** 231

Date	Item	Post. Ref.	Debit	Credit	Balance Debit	Balance Credit
20--						
Apr. 30		S6		258.00		258.00

ACCOUNT   Sales   **ACCOUNT NO.** 401

Date	Item	Post. Ref.	Debit	Credit	Balance Debit	Balance Credit
20--						
Apr. 1	Bal.	✝				27,000.00
30		S6		5,160.00		32,160.00

FIGURE 12-7   Northern Micro Cash Receipts Journal (left side)

	DATE		ACCOUNT CREDITED	POST. REF.	GENERAL CREDIT				
1	20-- Apr.	14	Enrico Lorenzo						
2		20	Brenda Myers						
3		28	Edith Walton						
4		30							
5		30							
6		30	Rent Revenue			6	0	0	00
7		30	Notes Payable		3	0	0	0	00
8									

(Title: CASH RECEIPTS JOURNAL)

Northern Micro's cash receipts journal provides separate columns for Accounts Receivable Credit, Sales Credit, Sales Tax Payable Credit, Bank Credit Card Expense Debit, and Cash Debit. These are the accounts most frequently affected by Northern Micro's cash receipts transactions. In addition, a General Credit column is provided for credits to any other accounts affected by cash receipts transactions.

A cash receipt is recorded in the cash receipts journal by entering the following information:

A BROADER VIEW

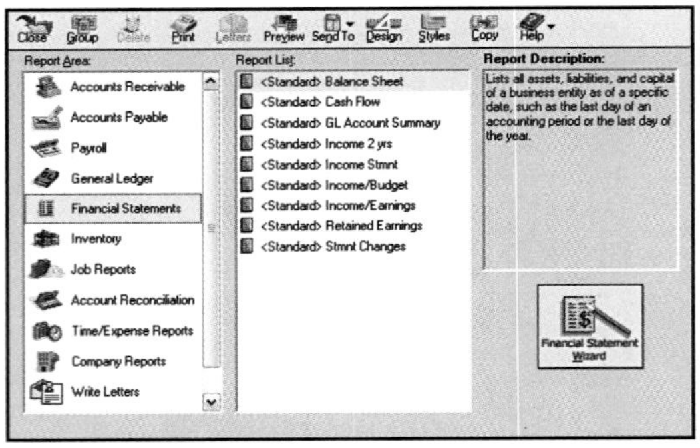

Improving Efficiency— The Power of Computerized Bookkeeping

In this chapter, we see many examples of the ways in which special journals can make the bookkeeping process more efficient. Yet, these efficiency gains pale by comparison with the power of computerized bookkeeping. By means of a single keyboard entry, journals, general and subsidiary ledgers, customer and supplier accounts, periodic financial reports, and more can be updated. You can even pay bills when due electronically as part of the system.

A good example of computerized bookkeeping software is Peachtree®. This software utilizes the one entry–many reports feature. The system makes entries using the keyboard, then tracks the effects on the financial status of the business. Software like Peachtree can produce income statements, balance sheets, reports of expenses by vendor or revenues by customer, and many other types of reports and graphs.

FIGURE 12-7   Northern Micro Cash Receipts Journal (right side)

PAGE 7

	ACCOUNTS RECEIVABLE CREDIT					SALES CREDIT					SALES TAX PAYABLE CREDIT				BANK CREDIT CARD EXPENSE DEBIT				CASH DEBIT					
	1	5	9	6	00														1	5	9	6	00	1
		4	6	2	00															4	6	2	00	2
	1	0	2	9	00														1	0	2	9	00	3
						3	6	0	0	00	1	8	0	00					3	7	8	0	00	4
						2	5	0	0	00	1	2	5	00	1	0	0	00	2	5	2	5	00	5
																				6	0	0	00	6
																			3	0	0	0	00	7
																								8

1. Date

2. Account credited (if applicable)

3. Dollar amounts

   The Account Credited column is used for two purposes.

1. To identify the customer name for any collection on account. This column is used whenever the Accounts Receivable Credit column is used.

2. To enter the appropriate account name whenever the General Credit column is used.

   The Account Credited column is left blank whenever the entry is for cash sales or bank credit card sales.

   The cash receipts journal in Figure 12-7 is designed for a company like Northern Micro, which charges sales tax, makes bank credit card sales, and offers no cash discounts. For a wholesaler who does not charge sales tax, makes no bank credit card sales, and offers cash discounts, a cash receipts journal like the one in Figure 12-8 would be used. Recall that a special journal should be designed with column headings for frequently used accounts. Thus, the cash receipts journal in Figure 12-8 has no Sales Tax Payable Credit or Bank Credit Card Expense Debit column. Instead, a Sales Discounts Debit column is provided. In this way, the common cash receipts transactions of the wholesaler can be easily and efficiently recorded.

FIGURE 12-8   Cash Receipts Journal Without Sales Tax

CASH RECEIPTS JOURNAL   PAGE 1

	DATE	ACCOUNT CREDITED	POST. REF.	GENERAL CREDIT	ACCOUNTS RECEIVABLE CREDIT	SALES CREDIT	SALES DISCOUNTS DEBIT	CASH DEBIT	
1									1

Posting from the Cash Receipts Journal

The cash receipts journal is posted to the general ledger in two stages, as illustrated in Figure 12-9. First, on a daily basis, the individual amounts in the General Credit column are posted. Second, at the end of the month, the totals of each of the other amount columns are posted.

To post the General Credit column, on a daily basis, use the following steps:

In the general ledger account:

STEP 1 Enter the date of the transaction in the Date column.

STEP 2 Enter the amount of the debit or credit in the Debit or Credit column.

STEP 3 Enter the new balance in the Balance columns under Debit or Credit.

STEP 4 Enter the initials "CR" and the journal page number in the Posting Reference column.

In the cash receipts journal:

STEP 5 Enter the ledger account number in the Posting Reference column for each account that is posted.

To post the other amount columns, at the end of the month, use the following steps:

In the cash receipts journal:

STEP 6 Total the amount columns, verify that the total of the debit columns equals the total of the credit columns, and rule the columns.

In the general ledger account:

STEP 7 Enter the date in the Date column.

STEP 8 Enter the amount of the debit or credit in the Debit or Credit column.

STEP 9 Enter the new balance in the Balance columns under Debit or Credit.

STEP 10 Enter the initials "CR" and the journal page number in the Posting Reference column.

In the cash receipts journal:

STEP 11 Enter the ledger account number immediately below the column totals for each account that is posted.

STEP 12 Enter a check mark (✓) in the Posting Reference column for the cash sales and bank credit card sales, and immediately below the General Credit column.

The general ledger accounts affected by the cash receipts transactions are now up to date. Postings to the accounts receivable ledger also must be made. These postings are made daily. Figure 12-10 illustrates the posting procedures, as follows:

In the accounts receivable ledger account:

STEP 1 Enter the date of the transaction in the Date column.

STEP 2 Enter the amount of the debit or credit in the Debit or Credit column.

STEP 3 Enter the new balance in the Balance column.

STEP 4 Enter the initials "CR" and the journal page number in the Posting Reference column.

In the cash receipts journal:

STEP 5 Enter a check mark (✓) in the Posting Reference column of the journal for each transaction that is posted.

FIGURE 12-9   Posting from the Cash Receipts Journal to the General Ledger

CASH RECEIPTS JOURNAL   Page 7

Date	Account Credited	Post. Ref.	General Credit	Accounts Receivable Credit	Sales Credit	Sales Tax Payable Credit	Bank Credit Card Expense Debit	Cash Debit
20--								
Apr. 14	Enrico Lorenzo			1,596.00				1,596.00
20	Brenda Myers			462.00				462.00
28	Edith Walton			1,029.00				1,029.00
30		✔			3,600.00	180.00		3,780.00
30		✔			2,500.00	125.00	100.00	2,525.00
30	Rent Revenue	412	600.00					600.00
30	Notes Payable	201	3,000.00					3,000.00
			3,600.00	3,087.00	6,100.00	305.00	100.00	12,992.00
			(✔)	(122)	(401)	(231)	(513)	(101)

6 Debit total: $ 100
                    12,992
                    $13,092

Credit total: $ 3,600
                    3,087
                    6,100
                    305
                    $13,092

GENERAL LEDGER (Partial)

ACCOUNT   Cash   **ACCOUNT NO.** 101

Date	Item	Post. Ref.	Debit	Credit	Balance Debit	Balance Credit
20--						
Apr. 1	Bal.	✝			20,000.00	
30		CR7	12,992.00		32,992.00	

ACCOUNT   Accounts Receivable   **ACCOUNT NO.** 122

Date	Item	Post. Ref.	Debit	Credit	Balance Debit	Balance Credit
20--						
Apr. 1	Bal.	✝			12,000.00	
30		S6	5,418.00		17,418.00	
30		CR7		3,087.00	14,331.00	

ACCOUNT   Notes Payable   **ACCOUNT NO.** 201

Date	Item	Post. Ref.	Debit	Credit	Balance Debit	Balance Credit
20--						
Apr. 1	Bal.	✝				6,000.00
30		CR7		3,000.00		9,000.00

ACCOUNT   Sales Tax Payable   **ACCOUNT NO.** 231

Date	Item	Post. Ref.	Debit	Credit	Balance Debit	Balance Credit
20--						
Apr. 30		S6		258.00		258.00
30		CR7		305.00		563.00

ACCOUNT   Sales   **ACCOUNT NO.** 401

Date	Item	Post. Ref.	Debit	Credit	Balance Debit	Balance Credit
20--						
Apr. 1	Bal.	✝				27,000.00
30		S6		5,160.00		32,160.00
30		CR7		6,100.00		38,260.00

ACCOUNT   Rent Revenue   **ACCOUNT NO.** 412

Date	Item	Post. Ref.	Debit	Credit	Balance Debit	Balance Credit
20--						
Apr. 1	Bal.	✝				1,800.00
30		CR7		600.00		2,400.00

ACCOUNT   Bank Credit Card Expense   **ACCOUNT NO.** 513

Date	Item	Post. Ref.	Debit	Credit	Balance Debit	Balance Credit
20--						
Apr. 1	Bal.	✝			430.00	
30		CR7	100.00		530.00	

FIGURE 12-10 Posting from the Cash Receipts Journal to the Accounts Receivable Ledger

CASH RECEIPTS JOURNAL   Page 7

Date	Account Credited	Post. Ref.	General Credit	Accounts Receivable Credit	Sales Credit	Sales Tax Payable Credit	Bank Credit Card Expense Debit	Cash Debit
20--								
Apr. 14	Enrico Lorenzo	✝		1,596.00				1,596.00
20	Brenda Myers	✝		462.00				462.00
28	Edith Walton	✝		1,029.00				1,029.00
30		✝			3,600.00	180.00		3,780.00
30		✝			2,500.00	125.00	100.00	2,525.00
30	Rent Revenue	412	600.00					600.00
30	Notes Payable	201	3,000.00					3,000.00
			3,600.00	3,087.00	6,100.00	305.00	100.00	12,992.00
			(✝)	(122)	(401)	(231)	(513)	(101)

ACCOUNTS RECEIVABLE LEDGER

NAME   Helen Avery
ADDRESS 1739 Woodsage Trace, Indianapolis, IN 46237-1199

Date	Item	Post. Ref.	Debit	Credit	Balance
20--					
Apr. 1	Bal.	✝			2,302.00

NAME   Susan Chang
ADDRESS 337 Elm Street, Noblesville, IN 46060-3377

Date	Item	Post. Ref.	Debit	Credit	Balance
20--					
Apr. 21		S6	651.00		651.00

NAME   Enrico Lorenzo
ADDRESS 5240 Tousley Court, Indianapolis, IN 46224-5678

Date	Item	Post. Ref.	Debit	Credit	Balance
20--					
Apr. 4		S6	1,596.00		1,596.00
14		CR7		1,596.00	—

NAME   Brenda Myers
ADDRESS 581 Acorn Way, Zionsville, IN 46077-2154

Date	Item	Post. Ref.	Debit	Credit	Balance
20--					
Apr. 10		S6	462.00		462.00
20		CR7		462.00	—

NAME   Heidi Schwitzer
ADDRESS 5858 Wildflower Cir., Bloomington, IN 47401-6209

Date	Item	Post. Ref.	Debit	Credit	Balance
20--					
Apr. 1	Bal.	✝			1,883.00
24		S6	1,680.00		3,563.00

NAME   Ken Ulmet
ADDRESS 5260 Eagle Creek, Indianapolis, IN 46254-8275

Date	Item	Post. Ref.	Debit	Credit	Balance
20--					
Apr. 1	Bal.	✝			3,315.00

NAME   Edith Walton
ADDRESS 1113 Stones Crossing, Zionsville, IN 46077-6601

Date	Item	Post. Ref.	Debit	Credit	Balance
20--					
Apr. 18		S6	1,029.00		1,029.00
28		CR7		1,029.00	—

NAME   Vivian Winston
ADDRESS 124 Main St., Zionsville, IN 46077-1358

Date	Item	Post. Ref.	Debit	Credit	Balance
20--					
Apr. 1	Bal.	✝			4,500.00

GENERAL LEDGER (Partial)

ACCOUNT   Cash   ACCOUNT NO. 101

Date	Item	Post. Ref.	Debit	Credit	Balance Debit	Balance Credit
20--						
Apr. 1	Bal.	✝			20,000.00	
30		CR7	12,992.00		32,992.00	

ACCOUNT   Accounts Receivable   ACCOUNT NO. 122

Date	Item	Post. Ref.	Debit	Credit	Balance Debit	Balance Credit
20--						
Apr. 1	Bal.	✝			12,000.00	
30		S6	5,418.00		17,418.00	
30		CR7		3,087.00	14,331.00	

ACCOUNT   Notes Payable   ACCOUNT NO. 201

Date	Item	Post. Ref.	Debit	Credit	Balance Debit	Balance Credit
20--						
Apr. 1	Bal.	✝				6,000.00
30		CR7		3,000.00		9,000.00

ACCOUNT   Sales Tax Payable   ACCOUNT NO. 231

Date	Item	Post. Ref.	Debit	Credit	Balance Debit	Balance Credit
20--						
Apr. 30		S6		258.00		258.00
30		CR7		305.00		563.00

ACCOUNT   Sales   ACCOUNT NO. 401

Date	Item	Post. Ref.	Debit	Credit	Balance Debit	Balance Credit
20--						
Apr. 1	Bal.	✝				27,000.00
30		S6		5,160.00		32,160.00
30		CR7		6,100.00		38,260.00

ACCOUNT   Rent Revenue   ACCOUNT NO. 412

Date	Item	Post. Ref.	Debit	Credit	Balance Debit	Balance Credit
20--						
Apr. 1	Bal.	✝				1,800.00
30		CR7		600.00		2,400.00

ACCOUNT   Bank Credit Card Expense   ACCOUNT NO. 513

Date	Item	Post. Ref.	Debit	Credit	Balance Debit	Balance Credit
20--						
Apr. 1	Bal.	✝			430.00	
30		CR7	100.00		530.00	

PURCHASES JOURNAL

A **purchases journal** is a special journal used to record only purchases of merchandise on account. To illustrate the journalizing and posting of purchases transactions in the purchases journal, we will continue with the transactions of Northern Micro. The following purchases on account are reproduced from Chapter 11:

Apr. 4   Purchased merchandise from Compucraft, Inc., $3,300. Invoice no. 631, dated April 2, terms n/30.

8   Purchased merchandise from Datasoft, $2,500. Invoice no. 927D, dated April 6, terms n/30.

11   Purchased merchandise from EZX Corp., $8,700. Invoice no. 804, dated April 9, terms 1/15, n/30.

17   Purchased merchandise from Printpro Corp., $800. Invoice no. 611, dated April 16, terms n/30.

23   Purchased merchandise from Televax, Inc., $5,300. Invoice no. 1465, dated April 22, terms 1/10, n/30.

As we saw with sales transactions, these purchases transactions can be recorded efficiently in a special journal, in this case a purchases journal. To illustrate, the five purchases on account of Northern Micro are entered in the purchases journal in Figure 12-11. Northern Micro's purchases journal has a single column for Purchases Debit/Accounts Payable Credit, the two accounts used repeatedly when these transactions are recorded in a general journal. A purchase is recorded in the purchases journal by entering the following information:

LEARNING KEY

Use a purchases journal only for recording purchases of merchandise on account.

1. Date

2. Invoice number

3. Supplier (from whom purchased)

Remember that purchases returns and allowances are recorded in the general journal, as illustrated in Chapter 11, not in the purchases journal.

4. Dollar amount

There is no need to enter any general ledger account titles, since they appear in the column heading.

FIGURE 12-11   Northern Micro Purchases Journal

	DATE		INVOICE NO.	FROM WHOM PURCHASED	POST. REF.	PURCHASES DEBIT/ACCOUNTS PAYABLE CREDIT					
	PURCHASES JOURNAL									PAGE 8	
1	20-- Apr.	4	631	Compucraft, Inc.		3	3	0	0	00	1
2		8	927D	Datasoft		2	5	0	0	00	2
3		11	804	EZX Corp.		8	7	0	0	00	3
4		17	611	Printpro Corp.			8	0	0	00	4
5		23	1465	Televax, Inc.		5	3	0	0	00	5
6						20	6	0	0	00	6

The purchases journal in Figure 12-11 is designed for a company like Northern Micro, whose suppliers generally pay freight charges. For a company that frequently pays freight charges as part of the purchase price of merchandise, a purchases journal like the one in Figure 12-12 would be used. In this case, there are three columns: (1) Purchases Debit, (2) Freight-In Debit, and (3) Accounts Payable Credit.

FIGURE 12-12   Purchases Journal with Freight-In Column

PURCHASES JOURNAL

DATE	INVOICE NO.	FROM WHOM PURCHASED	POST. REF.	PURCHASES DEBIT	FREIGHT-IN DEBIT	ACCOUNTS PAYABLE CREDIT

Posting from the Purchases Journal

Each general ledger account used in the purchases journal requires only one posting each period. Figure 12-13 illustrates the general ledger posting process for Northern Micro's purchases journal for the month of April.

FIGURE 12-13   Posting from the Purchases Journal to the General Ledger

PURCHASES JOURNAL   **Page 8**

Date	Invoice No.	From Whom Purchased	Post. Ref.	Purchases Debit/ Accounts Payable Credit
20--				
Apr. 4	631	Compucraft, Inc.		3,300.00
8	927D	Datasoft		2,500.00
11	804	EZX Corp.		8,700.00
17	611	Printpro Corp.		800.00
23	1465	Televax, Inc.		5,300.00
				20,600.00 [1]
				(501) (202) [6] [3]

GENERAL LEDGER (Partial)

ACCOUNT   Accounts Payable   ACCOUNT NO. 202

Date	Item	Post. Ref.	Debit	Credit	Balance Debit	Balance Credit
20--						
Apr. 1	Bal.	†				4,800.00
[2] 30 [5]		P8		20,600.00		25,400.00 [4]

ACCOUNT   Purchases   ACCOUNT NO. 501

Date	Item	Post. Ref.	Debit	Credit	Balance Debit	Balance Credit
20--						
Apr. 1	Bal.	†			17,400.00	
[2] 30 [5]		P8	20,600.00		38,000.00 [4]	

The following steps are used to post from the purchases journal to the general ledger at the end of each month, as indicated in Figure 12-13:

In the purchases journal:

STEP 1 Total and rule the amount column.

In the general ledger account:

STEP 2 Enter the date in the Date column.

STEP 3 Enter the amount of the debit or credit in the Debit or Credit column.

STEP 4 Enter the new balance in the Balance columns under Debit or Credit.

STEP 5 Enter the initial "P" and the journal page number in the Posting Reference column.

In the purchases journal:

STEP 6 Enter the Purchases and Accounts Payable account numbers immediately below the column total.

To maintain a record of the amount owed to each supplier, an accounts payable ledger is used. Figure 12-14 illustrates the use of the accounts payable ledger. The following steps are used to post from the purchases journal to the accounts payable ledger daily, as shown in Figure 12-14:

In the accounts payable ledger account:

STEP 1 Enter the date of the transaction in the Date column.

STEP 2 Enter the amount of the debit or credit in the Debit or Credit column.

STEP 3 Enter the new balance in the Balance column.

STEP 4 Enter the initial "P" and the journal page number in the Posting Reference column.

In the purchases journal:

STEP 5 Enter a check mark (✔) in the Posting Reference column of the journal for each transaction that is posted.

After the posting of the accounts payable ledger and general ledger is completed, the total of the accounts payable ledger balances should equal the Accounts Payable balance in the general ledger.

Step 1 is the main difference in posting the purchases journal to the general ledger. The remaining steps 2–6 are essentially the same as steps 1–5 used to post the general journal.

If the accounts payable ledger is posted daily and the general ledger is posted at the end of the month, the accounts payable ledger total will equal the general ledger

Accounts Payable total only at the end of the month.

FIGURE 12-14   Posting from the Purchases Journal to the Accounts Payable Ledger

PURCHASES JOURNAL   **Page 8**

Date	Invoice No.	From Whom Purchased	Post. Ref.	Purchases Debit/ Accounts Payable Credit
20--				
Apr. 4	631	Compucraft, Inc.	†	3,300.00
8	927D	Datasoft	†	2,500.00
11	804	EZX Corp.	†	8,700.00
17	611	Printpro Corp.	†	800.00
23	1465	Televax, Inc.	†	5,300.00
			5	20,600.00

(501) (202)

2

ACCOUNTS PAYABLE LEDGER (Partial)

NAME   B. B. Small
ADDRESS 2323 High Street, Gurnee, IL 60031-5524

Date	Item	Post. Ref.	Debit	Credit	Balance
20-- Apr. 1	Bal.	†			4,800.00

NAME   Compucraft, Inc.
ADDRESS 2100 West Main Street, Muncie, IN 47304-8139

Date	Item	Post. Ref.	Debit	Credit	Balance
20-- Apr. 4	**4**	P8		3,300.00	3,300.00 **3**

NAME   Datasoft
ADDRESS 210 Kirkwood, Bloomington, IN 47408-4346

Date	Item	Post. Ref.	Debit	Credit	Balance
20-- Apr. 8	**4**	P8		2,500.00	2,500.00 **3**

NAME   EZX Corp.
ADDRESS 2928 Rhodes Ave., Chicago, IL 60658-5036

Date	Item	Post. Ref.	Debit	Credit	Balance
20-- Apr. 11	**4**	P8		8,700.00	8,700.00 **3**

NAME   Printpro Corp.
ADDRESS 1200 Chambers Pike, Lincolnwood, IL 60648-2417

Date	Item	Post. Ref.	Debit	Credit	Balance
20-- Apr. 17	**4**	P8		800.00	800.00 **3**

NAME   Televax, Inc.
ADDRESS 1500 North Walnut Street, Addison, IL 60101-7328

Date	Item	Post. Ref.	Debit	Credit	Balance
20-- Apr. 23	**4**	P8		5,300.00	5,300.00 **3**

GENERAL LEDGER (Partial)

ACCOUNT   Accounts Payable   **ACCOUNT NO.** 202

Date	Item	Post. Ref.	Debit	Credit	Balance Debit	Balance Credit
20-- Apr. 1	Bal.	†				4,800.00
30		P8		20,600.00		25,400.00

ACCOUNT   Purchases   **ACCOUNT NO.** 501

Date	Item	Post. Ref.	Debit	Credit	Balance Debit	Balance Credit
20-- Apr. 1	Bal.	†			17,400.00	
30		P8	20,600.00		38,000.00	

CASH PAYMENTS JOURNAL

LO5 Describe and use the cash payments journal.

A **cash payments journal** is a special journal used to record only cash payments transactions. To illustrate its use, we will record the cash payments transactions of Northern Micro. Northern Micro's cash payments journal for the month of April is shown in Figure 12-15. Five types of cash payments transactions are shown as follows:

1. Payment of an expense (April 2)

2. Cash purchase (April 4)

3. Payment of an account payable (April 10 and 24)

4. Payment of a note payable (April 14)

5. Withdrawal by the owner (April 22)

FIGURE 12-15 Northern Micro Cash Payments Journal (left side)

CASH PAYMENTS JOURNAL

	DATE		CK. NO.	ACCOUNT DEBITED	POST. REF.	GENERAL DEBIT
1	Apr.	2	307	Rent Expense		2 4 0 0 00
2		4	308			
3		10	309	B. B. Small		
4		14	310	Notes Payable		2 0 0 0 00
5		22	311	Gary L. Fishel, Drawing		1 6 0 0 00
6		24	312	EZX Corp.		
7						6 0 0 0 00

FIGURE 12-15 Northern Micro Cash Payments Journal (right side)

ACCOUNTS PAYABLE DEBIT	PURCHASES DEBIT	PURCHASES DISCOUNTS CREDIT	CASH CREDIT	
			2 4 0 0 00	1
	1 4 0 0 00		1 4 0 0 00	2
4 8 0 0 00			4 8 0 0 00	3
			2 0 0 0 00	4
			1 6 0 0 00	5
8 7 0 0 00		8 7 00	8 6 1 3 00	6
13 5 0 0 00	1 4 0 0 00	8 7 00	20 8 1 3 00	7

LEARNING KEY

Use a cash payments journal to streamline journalizing and posting of cash payments.

Northern Micro's cash payments journal provides separate columns for Accounts Payable Debit, Purchases Debit, Purchases Discounts Credit, and Cash Credit. These are the accounts most frequently affected by Northern Micro's cash payments transactions. In addition, a General Debit column is provided for debits to any other accounts affected by cash payments transactions. For good internal control over cash payments, all payments (except out of petty cash) should be made by check. Therefore, the cash payments journal also includes a Check No. column.

A cash payment is recorded in the cash payments journal by entering the following information:

1. Date

2. Check number

3. Account debited (if applicable)

4. Dollar amounts

The Account Debited column is used for two purposes:

1. To identify the supplier name for any payment on account. This column is used whenever the Accounts Payable Debit column is used.

2. To enter the appropriate account name whenever the General Debit column is used.

Note that the column is left blank if the entry is for cash purchases.

Posting from the Cash Payments Journal

The cash payments journal is posted to the general ledger in two stages, as illustrated in Figure 12-16. First, on a daily basis, the individual amounts in the General Debit column are posted. Second, at the end of the month, the totals of each of the other amount columns are posted.

To post the General Debit column, on a daily basis, the following steps are used:

In the general ledger account:

STEP 1 Enter the date of the transaction in the Date column.

STEP 2 Enter the amount of the debit or credit in the Debit or Credit column.

STEP 3 Enter the new balance in the Balance columns under Debit or Credit.

STEP 4 Enter the initials "CP" and the journal page number in the Posting Reference column.

In the cash payments journal:

STEP 5 Enter the ledger account number in the Posting Reference column for each account that is posted.

To post the other amount columns, at the end of the month, the following steps are used:

In the cash payments journal:

STEP 6 Total the amount columns, verify that the total of the debit columns equals the total of the credit columns, and rule the columns.

In the general ledger account:

STEP 7 Enter the date in the Date column.

STEP 8 Enter the amount of the debit or credit in the Debit or Credit column.

STEP 9 Enter the new balance in the Balance columns under Debit or Credit.

STEP 10 Enter the initials "CP" and the journal page number in the Posting Reference column.

FIGURE 12-16   Posting from the Cash Payments Journal to the General Ledger

CASH PAYMENTS JOURNAL   Page 12

Date	Check No.	Account Debited	Post. Ref.	General Debit	Accounts Payable Debit	Purchases Debit	Purchases Discounts Credit	Cash Credit
20--								
Apr. 2	307	Rent Expense [5]	521	2,400.00				2,400.00
4	308		[12]	†		1,400.00		1,400.00
10	309	B. B. Small			4,800.00			4,800.00
14	310	Notes Payable [5]	201	2,000.00				2,000.00
22	311	Gary L. Fishel, Drawing [5]	312	1,600.00				1,600.00
24	312	EZX Corp.			8,700.00		87.00	8,613.00
				6,000.00	13,500.00	1,400.00	87.00	20,813.00 [6]
				(†)	(202)	(501)	(501.2)	(101) [11]
				[12]				

[6] Debit total: $ 6,000
                         13,500
                          1,400
                       $20,900

Credit total: $ 87
                       20,813
                      $20,900

GENERAL LEDGER (Partial)   [8]

ACCOUNT   Cash   ACCOUNT NO. 101

| | | | Post. | | | Balance | |
Date	Item	Ref.	Debit	Credit	Debit	Credit
20--						
Apr. 1	Bal.	†			20,000.00	
30		CR7	12,992.00		32,992.00	
[7] 30	[10]	CP12		20,813.00	12,179.00 [9]	

[2]   ACCOUNT   Notes Payable   ACCOUNT NO. 201

| | | | Post. | | | Balance | |
Date	Item	Ref.	Debit	Credit	Debit	Credit
20--						
Apr. 1	Bal.	†				6,000.00
[1] 14	[4]	CP12	2,000.00			4,000.00 [3]

ACCOUNT   Accounts Payable   ACCOUNT NO. 202

| | | | Post. | | | Balance | |
Date	Item	Ref.	Debit	Credit	Debit	Credit
20--						
Apr. 1	Bal.	†				4,800.00
30		P8		20,600.00		25,400.00
[7] 30	[10]	CP12	13,500.00			11,900.00 [9]

ACCOUNT   Gary L. Fishel, Drawing   ACCOUNT NO. 312

| | | | Post. | | | Balance | |
Date	Item	Ref.	Debit	Credit	Debit	Credit
20--						
Apr. 1	Bal.	†			4,500.00	
[1] 22	[4]	CP12	1,600.00		6,100.00 [3]	

ACCOUNT   Purchases   ACCOUNT NO. 501

| | | | Post. | | | Balance | |
Date	Item	Ref.	Debit	Credit	Debit	Credit
20--						
Apr. 1	Bal.	†			17,400.00	
30		P8	20,600.00		38,000.00	
[7] 30	[10]	CP12	1,400.00		39,400.00 [9]	

ACCOUNT   Purchases Discounts   ACCOUNT NO. 501.2

| | | | Post. | | | Balance | |
Date	Item	Ref.	Debit	Credit	Debit	Credit
20--						
Apr. 1	Bal.	†				330.00
[7] 30	[10]	CP12		87.00		417.00 [9]

ACCOUNT   Rent Expense   ACCOUNT NO. 521

| | | | Post. | | | Balance | |
Date	Item	Ref.	Debit	Credit	Debit	Credit
20--						
Apr. 1	Bal.	†			6,600.00	
[1] 2	[4]	CP12	2,400.00		9,000.00 [3]	

In the cash payments journal:

STEP 11 Enter the ledger account number immediately below the column totals for each account that is posted.

STEP 12 Enter a check mark (✓) in the Posting Reference column for the cash purchases, and immediately below the General Debit column.

Postings from the cash payments journal to the accounts payable ledger also must be made. These postings are made daily. Posting procedures are as follows, as shown in Figure 12-17:

In the accounts payable ledger account:

STEP 1 Enter the date of the transaction in the Date column.

STEP 2 Enter the amount of the debit or credit in the Debit or Credit column.

STEP 3 Enter the new balance in the Balance column.

STEP 4 Enter the initials "CP" and the journal page number in the Posting Reference column.

In the cash payments journal:

STEP 5 Enter a check mark (✓) in the Posting Reference column of the journal for each transaction that is posted.

Computers and Accounting

Special Journals in Computerized Accounting Systems—Gary P. Schneider, University of San Diego, and Toni Hartley, Laurel Business Institute

Special journals are an important part of manual accounting systems because they make it easy for accountants to record the types of transactions that occur most frequently in businesses. The common special journals are those used to record sales, cash receipts, purchases, and cash payments (also called cash disbursements). When working with an accounting system that uses special journals, accountants use the general journal to record the relatively few transactions that are not recorded in special journals.

Computerized accounting systems are organized somewhat differently than manual accounting systems. Instead of recording transactions directly in journals, they often use specialized entry screens designed to make recording transactions even easier than in a manual system with special journals. These entry screens are organized into modules. Each module is devoted to a specific transaction type, much as a manual system uses special journals to organize things. Figure A, on page 460, shows the modular organization of a typical computerized accounting system.

FIGURE 12-17   Posting from the Cash Payments Journal to the Accounts Payable Ledger

CASH PAYMENTS JOURNAL

Page 12

Date	Check No.	Account Debited	Post. Ref.	General Debit	Accounts Payable Debit	Purchases Debit	Purchases Discounts Credit	Cash Credit
20--								
Apr. 2	307	Rent Expense	521	2,400.00				2,400.00
4	308		✝ [5]			1,400.00		1,400.00
10	309	B. B. Small	✝		4,800.00			4,800.00
14	310	Notes Payable	201	2,000.00				2,000.00
22	311	Gary L. Fishel, Drawing	312	1,600.00				1,600.00
24	312	EZX Corp.	✝ [5]		8,700.00		87.00	8,613.00
				6,000.00	13,500.00	1,400.00	87.00	20,813.00
				(✝)	(202)	(501)	(501.2)	(101)

[2]

ACCOUNTS PAYABLE LEDGER (Partial)

NAME   B. B. Small
ADDRESS 2323 High Street, Gurnee, IL 60031-5524

Date	Item	Post. Ref.	Debit	Credit	Balance
20--					
Apr. 1 [1]	Bal.	✝			4,800.00
10		CP12 [4]	4,800.00		[3]

NAME   Compucraft, Inc.
ADDRESS 2100 West Main Street, Muncie, IN 47304-8139

Date	Item	Post. Ref.	Debit	Credit	Balance
20--					
Apr. 4		P8		3,300.00	3,300.00

NAME   Datasoft
ADDRESS 210 Kirkwood, Bloomington, IN 47408-4346

Date	Item	Post. Ref.	Debit	Credit	Balance
20--					
Apr. 8		P8		2,500.00	2,500.00

NAME   EZX Corp.
ADDRESS 2928 Rhodes Ave., Chicago, IL 60658-5036

Date	Item	Post. Ref.	Debit	Credit	Balance
20--					
Apr. 11 [1]		P8		8,700.00	8,700.00
24		CP12 [4]	8,700.00		[3]

NAME   Printpro Corp.
ADDRESS 1200 Chambers Pike, Lincolnwood, IL 60648-2417

Date	Item	Post. Ref.	Debit	Credit	Balance
20--					
Apr. 17		P8		800.00	800.00

NAME   Televax, Inc.
ADDRESS 1500 North Walnut Street, Addison, IL 60101-7328

Date	Item	Post. Ref.	Debit	Credit	Balance
20--					
Apr. 23		P8		5,300.00	5,300.00

GENERAL LEDGER (Partial)

ACCOUNT   Cash   ACCOUNT NO. 101

Date	Item	Post. Ref.	Debit	Credit	Balance Debit	Balance Credit
20--						
Apr. 1	Bal.	✝			20,000.00	
30		CR7	12,992.00		32,992.00	
30		CP12		20,813.00	12,179.00	

ACCOUNT   Notes Payable   ACCOUNT NO. 201

Date	Item	Post. Ref.	Debit	Credit	Balance Debit	Balance Credit
20--						
Apr. 1	Bal.	✝				6,000.00
14		CP12	2,000.00			4,000.00

ACCOUNT   Accounts Payable   ACCOUNT NO. 202

Date	Item	Post. Ref.	Debit	Credit	Balance Debit	Balance Credit
20--						
Apr. 1	Bal.	✝				4,800.00
30		P8		20,600.00		25,400.00
30		CP12	13,500.00			11,900.00

ACCOUNT   Gary L. Fishel, Drawing   ACCOUNT NO. 312

Date	Item	Post. Ref.	Debit	Credit	Balance Debit	Balance Credit
20--						
Apr. 1	Bal.	✝			4,500.00	
22		CP12	1,600.00		6,100.00	

ACCOUNT   Purchases   ACCOUNT NO. 501

Date	Item	Post. Ref.	Debit	Credit	Balance Debit	Balance Credit
20--						
Apr. 1	Bal.	✝			17,400.00	
30		P8	20,600.00		38,000.00	
30		CP12	1,400.00		39,400.00	

ACCOUNT   Purchases Discounts   ACCOUNT NO. 501.2

Date	Item	Post. Ref.	Debit	Credit	Balance Debit	Balance Credit
20--						
Apr. 1	Bal.	✝				330.00
30		CP12		87.00		417.00

ACCOUNT   Rent Expense   ACCOUNT NO. 521

Date	Item	Post. Ref.	Debit	Credit	Balance Debit	Balance Credit
20--						
Apr. 1	Bal.	✝			6,600.00	
2		CP12	2,400.00		9,000.00	

Figure A

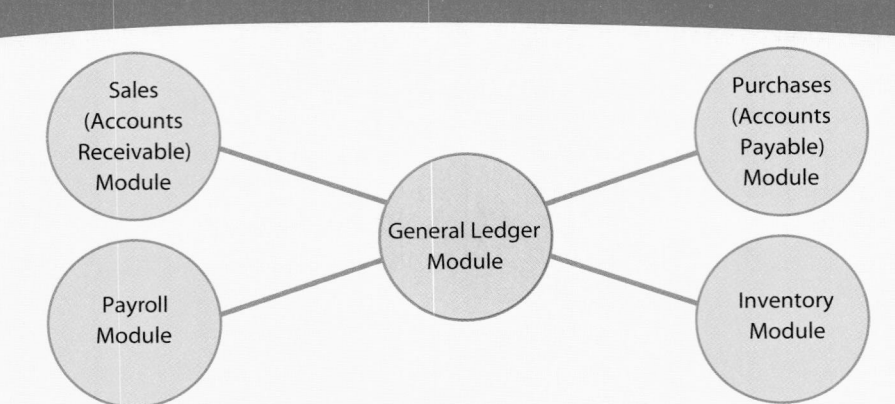

As you can see in the figure, this accounting system includes five modules: general ledger, sales (accounts receivable), purchases (accounts payable), payroll, and inventory. The general ledger module includes tools that accountants can use to record any type of transaction. In fact, some simple computerized accounting systems have only this module. Each of the other modules includes tools that accountants can use to record transactions of a specific type. For example, the sales module will have data entry screens for invoices and cash receipts. The details of the sales module for Peachtree®, a popular accounting software package, appear in Figure B.

To enter information into Peachtree's sales module, the accountant clicks on one of the icons to open the appropriate data entry screen. For example, you can click the Receive Money icon to record a payment from a customer on account. By accessing the Reports menu on the menu bar and selecting Accounts Receivable, you can print out the Sales Journal, Cash Receipts Journal, and Customer Ledger.

By storing the sales information in a database, instead of a pen-and-ink journal, a computerized accounting system records the information only once. Accountants can then extract information from the database to create journals, subsidiary ledgers, and even the entire general ledger at any time. The computerized accounting system, in effect, updates all of the accounting records simultaneously when transaction information is entered. This updating occurs immediately.

The purchases module of the computerized accounting system is similar. It helps accountants perform purchase-related functions such as issuing purchase orders and writing checks to pay vendors. Figure C shows details of the Peachtree Purchases module. This module includes icons for various purchases transactions such as purchase orders, paying vendors, and recording credits and returns.

Most accounting software packages include the ability to calculate payroll and print the necessary reports and government-required forms. You learned about these computerized payroll modules at the end of Chapter 9. Peachtree also includes an inventory module to help accountants track inventory that the company buys. More complex accounting software includes additional modules to record inventory movements from one warehouse to another and to record the manufacturing activities that some businesses undertake.

Figure B

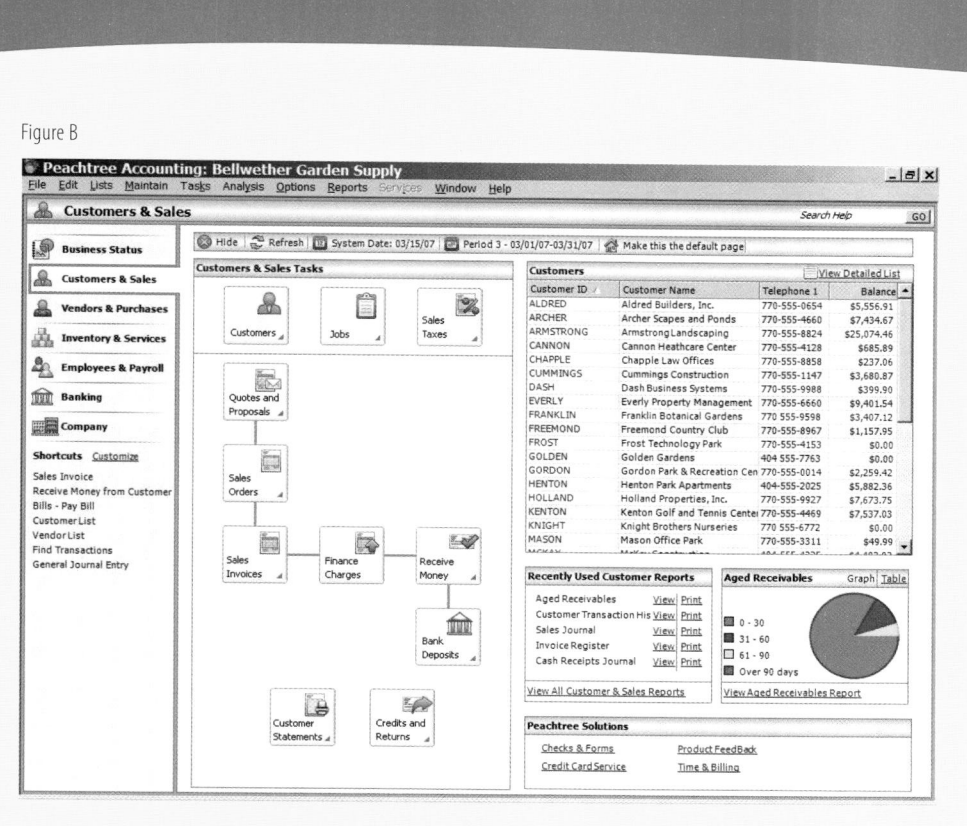

Figure C

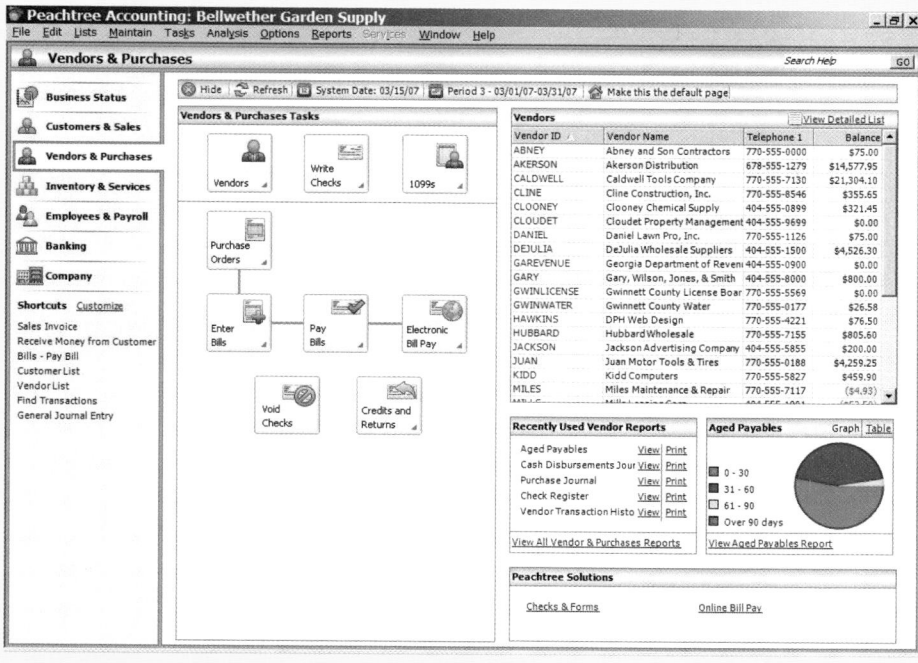

Learning Objectives	Key Points to Remember
LO1 Describe, explain the purpose of, and identify transactions recorded in special journals.	A special journal is a journal designed for recording only certain kinds of transactions. The primary purpose of using special journals is to save time journalizing and posting transactions.
LO2 Describe and use the sales journal.	A sales journal is a special journal for recording sales of merchandise on account. A sale is recorded by entering the following:

1. Date
2. Sale number
3. Customer (to whom sold)
4. Dollar amounts

To post from the sales journal to the general ledger, use the following steps:

In the sales journal:

STEP 1 Total the amount columns, verify that the total of the debit column equals the total of the credit columns, and rule the columns.

In the general ledger account:

STEP 2 Enter the date of the transaction in the Date column.

STEP 3 Enter the amount of the debit or credit in the Debit or Credit column.

STEP 4 Enter the new balance in the Balance columns under Debit or Credit.

STEP 5 Enter the initial "S" and the journal page number in the Posting Reference column.

In the sales journal:

STEP 6 Enter the ledger account number immediately below the column totals for each account that is posted.

To post from the sales journal to the accounts receivable ledger:

In the accounts receivable ledger account:

STEP 1 Enter the date of the transaction in the Date column.

STEP 2 Enter the amount of the debit or credit in the Debit or Credit column.

STEP 3 Enter the new balance in the Balance column.

STEP 4 Enter the initial "S" and the journal page number in the Posting Reference column.

In the sales journal:

STEP 5 Enter a check mark (✓) in the Posting Reference column of the journal for each transaction that is posted.

LO3 Describe and use the cash receipts journal.	A cash receipts journal is a special journal for recording cash receipts. A cash receipt is recorded by entering the following:

1. Date
2. Account credited (if applicable)
3. Dollar amounts

Learning Objectives	Key Points to Remember
LO3 **(continued)**	To post from the cash receipts journal to the general ledger:

To post the General Credit column, on a daily basis, use the following steps:

In the general ledger account:

STEP 1 Enter the date of the transaction in the Date column.

STEP 2 Enter the amount of the debit or credit in the Debit or Credit column.

STEP 3 Enter the new balance in the Balance columns under Debit or Credit.

STEP 4 Enter the initials "CR" and the journal page number in the Posting Reference column.

In the cash receipts journal:

STEP 5 Enter the ledger account number in the Posting Reference column for each account that is posted.

To post the other amount columns, at the end of the month, use the following steps:

In the cash receipts journal:

STEP 6 Total the amount columns, verify that the total of the debit columns equals the total of the credit columns, and rule the columns.

In the general ledger account:

STEP 7 Enter the date in the Date column.

STEP 8 Enter the amount of the debit or credit in the Debit or Credit column.

STEP 9 Enter the new balance in the Balance columns under Debit or Credit.

STEP 10 Enter the initials "CR" and the journal page number in the Posting Reference column.

In the cash receipts journal:

STEP 11 Enter the ledger account number immediately below the column totals for each account that is posted.

STEP 12 Enter a check mark (✓) in the Posting Reference column for the cash sales and bank credit card sales, and immediately below the General Credit column.

To post from the cash receipts journal to the accounts receivable ledger, use the following steps:

In the accounts receivable ledger account:

STEP 1 Enter the date of the transaction in the Date column.

STEP 2 Enter the amount of the debit or credit in the Debit or Credit column.

STEP 3 Enter the new balance in the Balance column.

STEP 4 Enter the initials "CR" and the journal page number in the Posting Reference column.

Learning Objectives	Key Points to Remember
LO3 (concluded)	**In the cash receipts journal:** STEP 5 Enter a check mark (✓) in the Posting Reference column of the journal for each transaction that is posted.
LO4 **Describe and use the purchases journal.**	A purchases journal is a special journal for recording purchases of merchandise on account. A purchase is recorded by entering the following: 1. Date 2. Invoice number 3. Supplier (from whom purchased) 4. Dollar amount To post from the purchases journal to the general ledger, use the following steps: **In the purchases journal:** STEP 1 Total and rule the amount column. **In the general ledger account:** STEP 2 Enter the date in the Date column. STEP 3 Enter the amount of the debit or credit in the Debit or Credit column. STEP 4 Enter the new balance in the Balance columns under Debit or Credit. STEP 5 Enter the initial "P" and the journal page number in the Posting Reference column. **In the purchases journal:** STEP 6 Enter the Purchases and Accounts Payable account numbers immediately below the column total. To post from the purchases journal to the accounts payable ledger, use the following steps: **In the accounts payable ledger account:** STEP 1 Enter the date of the transaction in the Date column. STEP 2 Enter the amount of the debit or credit in the Debit or Credit column. STEP 3 Enter the new balance in the Balance column. STEP 4 Enter the initial "P" and the journal page number in the Posting Reference column. **In the purchases journal:** STEP 5 Enter a check mark (✓) in the Posting Reference column of the journal for each transaction that is posted.
LO5 **Describe and use the cash payments journal.**	A cash payments journal is a special journal for recording cash payments. A cash payment is recorded by entering the following: 1. Date 2. Check number 3. Account debited (if applicable) 4. Dollar amounts

Learning Objectives	Key Points to Remember
LO5 (concluded)	

To post from the cash payments journal to the general ledger:

> To post the General Debit column, on a daily basis, use the following steps:

In the general ledger account:

STEP 1 Enter the date of the transaction in the Date column.

STEP 2 Enter the amount of the debit or credit in the Debit or Credit column.

STEP 3 Enter the new balance in the Balance columns under Debit or Credit.

STEP 4 Enter the initials "CP" and the journal page number in the Posting Reference column.

In the cash payments journal:

STEP 5 Enter the ledger account number in the Posting Reference column for each account that is posted.

> To post the other amount columns, at the end of the month, use the following steps:

In the cash payments journal:

STEP 6 Total the amount columns, verify that the total of the debit columns equals the total of the credit columns, and rule the columns.

In the general ledger account:

STEP 7 Enter the date in the Date column.

STEP 8 Enter the amount of the debit or credit in the Debit or Credit column.

STEP 9 Enter the new balance in the Balance columns under Debit or Credit.

STEP 10 Enter the initials "CP" and the journal page number in the Posting Reference column.

In the cash payments journal:

STEP 11 Enter the ledger account number immediately below the column totals for each account that is posted.

STEP 12 Enter a check mark (✓) in the Posting Reference column for the cash purchases, and immediately below the General Debit column.

> To post from the cash payments journal to the accounts payable ledger, use the following steps:

In the accounts payable ledger account:

STEP 1 Enter the date of the transaction in the Date column.

STEP 2 Enter the amount of the debit or credit in the Debit or Credit column.

STEP 3 Enter the new balance in the Balance column.

STEP 4 Enter the initials "CP" and the journal page number in the Posting Reference column.

In the cash payments journal:

STEP 5 Enter a check mark (✓) in the Posting Reference column of the journal for each transaction that is posted.

DEMONSTRATION PROBLEM

During the month of May 20--, David's Specialty Shop engaged in the following transactions:

May 1   Sold merchandise on account to Molly Mac, $2,000, plus tax of $100. Sale no. 533.

2   Issued check no. 750 to Kari Co. in partial payment of May 1 balance, $800, less 2% discount.

3   Purchased merchandise on account from Scanlan Wholesalers, $2,000. Invoice no. 621, dated May 3, terms 2/10, n/30.

4   Purchased merchandise on account from Simpson Enterprises, $1,500. Invoice no. 767, dated May 4, terms 2/15, n/30.

4   Issued check no. 751 in payment of telephone expense for the month of April, $200.

8   Sold merchandise for cash, $3,600, plus tax of $180.

9   Received payment from Cody Slaton in full settlement of account, $2,500.

10   Issued check no. 752 to Scanlan Wholesalers in payment of May 1 balance of $1,200.

12   Sold merchandise on account to Cody Slaton, $3,000, plus tax of $150. Sale no. 534.

12   Received payment from Kori Reynolds on account, $2,100.

13   Issued check no. 753 to Simpson Enterprises in payment of May 4 purchase. Invoice no. 767, less 2% discount.

13   Cody Slaton returned merchandise for a credit, $1,000, plus sales tax of $50.

17   Returned merchandise to Johnson Essentials for credit, $500.

22   Received payment from Natalie Gabbert on account, $1,555.

27   Sold merchandise on account to Natalie Gabbert, $2,000, plus tax of $100. Sale no. 535.

29   Issued check no. 754 in payment of wages (Wages Expense) for the four-week period ending May 30, $1,100.

Selected account balances as of May 1 were as follows:

Account	Account No.	Debit	Credit
Cash	101	$10,050.00	
Accounts Receivable	122	6,900.00	
Accounts Payable	202		$4,550.00

David also had the following subsidiary ledger balances as of May 1:

Accounts Receivable:

Customer	Accounts Receivable Balance
Natalie Gabbert 12 Jude Lane Hartford, CT 06117	$1,821.00
Molly Mac 52 Juniper Road Hartford, CT 06118	279.00
Kori Reynolds 700 Hobbes Dr. Avon, CT 06108	2,300.00
Cody Slaton 5200 Hamilton Ave. Hartford, CT 06111	2,500.00

Accounts Payable:

Vendor	Accounts Payable Balance
Johnson Essentials 34 Harry Ave. East Hartford, CT 05234	$2,350.00
Kari Co. 1009 Drake Rd. Farmington, CT 06082	1,000.00
Scanlan Wholesalers 43 Lucky Lane Bristol, CT 06007	1,200.00
Simpson Enterprises 888 Anders Street Newington, CT 06789	—

REQUIRED

1. Record the transactions in the sales journal, cash receipts journal, purchases journal, cash payments journal, and general journal. Total, verify, and rule the columns where appropriate at the end of the month.

2. Post from the journals to the general ledger, accounts receivable ledger, and accounts payable ledger accounts. Use account numbers as shown in the chapter.

(continued)

Solution 1.

SALES JOURNAL   PAGE 7

	DATE		SALE NO.	TO WHOM SOLD	POST. REF.	ACCOUNTS RECEIVABLE DEBIT	SALES CREDIT	SALES TAX PAYABLE CREDIT	
1	20-- May	1	533	Molly Mac	✝	2 1 0 0 00	2 0 0 0 00	1 0 0 00	1
2		12	534	Cody Slaton	✝	3 1 5 0 00	3 0 0 0 00	1 5 0 00	2
3		27	535	Natalie Gabbert	✝	2 1 0 0 00	2 0 0 0 00	1 0 0 00	3
4						7 3 5 0 00	7 0 0 0 00	3 5 0 00	4
5						(1 2 2)	(4 0 1)	(2 3 1)	5

PURCHASES JOURNAL   PAGE 6

	DATE		INVOICE NO.	FROM WHOM PURCHASED	POST. REF.	PURCHASES DEBIT/ACCOUNTS PAYABLE CREDIT	
1	20-- May	3	621	Scanlan Wholesalers	✝	2 0 0 0 00	1
2		4	767	Simpson Enterprises	✝	1 5 0 0 00	2
3						3 5 0 0 00	3
4						(50 1) (2 02)	4

GENERAL JOURNAL   PAGE 5

	DATE		DESCRIPTION	POST. REF.	DEBIT	CREDIT	
1	20-- May	13	Sales Returns and Allowances	401.1	1 0 0 0 00		1
2			Sales Tax Payable	231	5 0 00		2
3			Accounts Receivable/Cody Slaton	122/✝		1 0 5 0 00	3
4			Accepted returned merchandise				4
5							5
6		17	Accounts Payable/Johnson Essentials	202/✝	5 0 0 00		6
7			Purchases Returns and Allowances	501.1		5 0 0 00	7
8			Returned merchandise				8
9							9

CASH PAYMENTS JOURNAL   PAGE 11

	DATE		CK. NO.	ACCOUNT DEBITED	POST. REF.	GENERAL DEBIT	ACCOUNTS PAYABLE DEBIT	PURCHASES DEBIT	PURCHASES DISCOUNTS CREDIT	CASH CREDIT	
1	20-- May	2	750	Kari Co.	✓		8 0 0 00		1 6 00	7 8 4 00	1
2		4	751	Telephone Expense	525	2 0 0 00				2 0 0 00	2
3		10	752	Scanlan Wholesalers	✓		1 2 0 0 00			1 2 0 0 00	3
4		13	753	Simpson Enterprises	✓		1 5 0 0 00		3 0 00	1 4 7 0 00	4
5		29	754	Wages Expense	511	1 1 0 0 00				1 1 0 0 00	5
6						1 3 0 0 00	3 5 0 0 00		4 6 00	4 7 5 4 00	6
7						(✓)	(2 0 2)		(5 0 1 .2)	(1 0 1)	7

CASH RECEIPTS JOURNAL   PAGE 10

	DATE		ACCOUNT CREDITED	POST. REF.	GENERAL CREDIT	ACCOUNTS RECEIVABLE CREDIT	SALES CREDIT	SALES TAX PAYABLE CREDIT	CASH DEBIT	
1	20-- May	8					3 6 0 0 00	1 8 0 00	3 7 8 0 00	1
2		9	C. Slaton	✝		2 5 0 0 00			2 5 0 0 00	2
3		12	K. Reynolds	✝		2 1 0 0 00			2 1 0 0 00	3
4		22	N. Gabbert	✝		1 5 5 5 00			1 5 5 5 00	4
5						6 1 5 5 00	3 6 0 0 00	1 8 0 00	9 9 3 5 00	5
6						(1 2 2)	(4 0 1)	(2 3 1)	(1 0 1)	6

2.

GENERAL LEDGER

ACCOUNT: Cash   ACCOUNT NO. 101

DATE		ITEM	POST. REF.	DEBIT	CREDIT	BALANCE DEBIT	BALANCE CREDIT
20-- May	1	Balance	✓			10 0 5 0 00	
	31		CR10	9 9 3 5 00		19 9 8 5 00	
	31		CP11		4 7 5 4 00	15 2 3 1 00	

ACCOUNT: Accounts Receivable   ACCOUNT NO. 122

DATE		ITEM	POST. REF.	DEBIT	CREDIT	BALANCE DEBIT	BALANCE CREDIT
20-- May	1	Balance	✓			6 9 0 0 00	
	13		J5		1 0 5 0 00	5 8 5 0 00	
	31		S7	7 3 5 0 00		13 2 0 0 00	
	31		CR10		6 1 5 5 00	7 0 4 5 00	

ACCOUNT: Accounts Payable   ACCOUNT NO. 202

DATE		ITEM	POST. REF.	DEBIT	CREDIT	BALANCE DEBIT	BALANCE CREDIT
20-- May	1	Balance	✝				4 5 5 0 00
	17		J5	5 0 0 00			4 0 5 0 00
	31		P6		3 5 0 0 00		7 5 5 0 00
	31		CP11	3 5 0 0 00			4 0 5 0 00

ACCOUNT: Sales Tax Payable   ACCOUNT NO. 231

DATE		ITEM	POST. REF.	DEBIT	CREDIT	BALANCE DEBIT	BALANCE CREDIT
20-- May	13		J5	5 0 00		5 0 00	
	31		S7		3 5 0 00		3 0 0 00
	31		CR10		1 8 0 00		4 8 0 00

ACCOUNT: Sales   ACCOUNT NO. 401

DATE		ITEM	POST. REF.	DEBIT	CREDIT	BALANCE DEBIT	BALANCE CREDIT
20-- May	31		S7		7 0 0 0 00		7 0 0 0 00
	31		CR10		3 6 0 0 00		10 6 0 0 00

(continued)

ACCOUNT: Sales Returns and Allowances   **ACCOUNT NO.** 401.1

DATE		ITEM	POST. REF.	DEBIT	CREDIT	BALANCE DEBIT	BALANCE CREDIT
20-- May	13		J5	1 0 0 0 00		1 0 0 0 00	

ACCOUNT: Purchases   **ACCOUNT NO.** 501

DATE		ITEM	POST. REF.	DEBIT	CREDIT	BALANCE DEBIT	BALANCE CREDIT
20-- May	31		P6	3 5 0 0 00		3 5 0 0 00	

ACCOUNT: Purchases Returns and Allowances   **ACCOUNT NO.** 501.1

DATE		ITEM	POST. REF.	DEBIT	CREDIT	BALANCE DEBIT	BALANCE CREDIT
20-- May	17		J5		5 0 0 00		5 0 0 00

ACCOUNT: Purchases Discounts   **ACCOUNT NO.** 501.2

DATE		ITEM	POST. REF.	DEBIT	CREDIT	BALANCE DEBIT	BALANCE CREDIT
20-- May	31		CP11		4 6 00		4 6 00

ACCOUNT: Wages Expense   **ACCOUNT NO.** 511

DATE		ITEM	POST. REF.	DEBIT	CREDIT	BALANCE DEBIT	BALANCE CREDIT
20-- May	29		CP11	1 1 0 0 00		1 1 0 0 00	

ACCOUNT: Telephone Expense   **ACCOUNT NO.** 525

DATE		ITEM	POST. REF.	DEBIT	CREDIT	BALANCE DEBIT	BALANCE CREDIT
20-- May	4		CP11	2 0 0 00		2 0 0 00	

ACCOUNTS RECEIVABLE LEDGER

NAME: Natalie Gabbert
ADDRESS: 12 Jude Lane, Hartford, CT 06117

DATE		ITEM	POST. REF.	DEBIT	CREDIT	BALANCE
20-- May	1	Balance	✓			1 8 2 1 00
	22		CR10		1 5 5 5 00	2 6 6 00
	27		S7	2 1 0 0 00		2 3 6 6 00

NAME: Molly Mac
ADDRESS: 52 Juniper Road, Hartford, CT 06118

DATE		ITEM	POST. REF.	DEBIT	CREDIT	BALANCE
20-- May	1	Balance	✓			2 7 9 00
	1		S7	2 1 0 0 00		2 3 7 9 00

NAME: Kori Reynolds
ADDRESS: 700 Hobbes Dr., Avon, CT 06108

DATE		ITEM	POST. REF.	DEBIT	CREDIT	BALANCE
20-- May	1	Balance	✝			2 3 0 0 00
	12		CR10		2 1 0 0 00	2 0 0 00

NAME: Cody Slaton
ADDRESS: 5200 Hamilton Ave., Hartford, CT 06111

DATE		ITEM	POST. REF.	DEBIT	CREDIT	BALANCE
20-- May	1	Balance	✝			2 5 0 0 00
	9		CR10		2 5 0 0 00	
	12		S7	3 1 5 0 00		3 1 5 0 00
	13		J5		1 0 5 0 00	2 1 0 0 00

ACCOUNTS PAYABLE LEDGER

NAME: Johnson Essentials
ADDRESS: 34 Harry Ave., East Hartford, CT 05234

DATE		ITEM	POST. REF.	DEBIT	CREDIT	BALANCE
20-- May	1	Balance	✝			2 3 5 0 00
	17		J5	5 0 0 00		1 8 5 0 00

NAME: Kari Co.
ADDRESS: 1009 Drake Rd., Farmington, CT 06082

DATE		ITEM	POST. REF.	DEBIT	CREDIT	BALANCE
20-- May	1	Balance	✝			1 0 0 0 00
	2		CP11	8 0 0 00		2 0 0 00

NAME: Scanlan Wholesalers
ADDRESS: 43 Lucky Lane, Bristol, CT 06007

DATE		ITEM	POST. REF.	DEBIT	CREDIT	BALANCE
20-- May	1	Balance	✝			1 2 0 0 00
	3		P6		2 0 0 0 00	3 2 0 0 00
	10		CP11	1 2 0 0 00		2 0 0 0 00

NAME: Simpson Enterprises
ADDRESS: 888 Anders Street, Newington, CT 06789

DATE		ITEM	POST. REF.	DEBIT	CREDIT	BALANCE
20-- May	1	Balance	✝			
	4		P6		1 5 0 0 00	1 5 0 0 00
	13		CP11	1 5 0 0 00		

KEY TERMS

cash payments journal (455)   A special journal used to record only cash payments transactions.

cash receipts journal (444)   A special journal used to record only cash receipts transactions.

purchases journal (451)   A special journal used to record only purchases of merchandise on account.

sales journal (441)   A special journal used to record only sales of merchandise on account.

special journal (440)   A journal designed for recording only certain kinds of transactions.

Self-Study Test Questions

True/False

1. The types of special journals a business uses should depend on the types of transactions it has most frequently.

2. If a business uses special journals, it generally will not need a general journal.

3. All sales, for cash or on credit, are recorded in the sales journal.

4. A cash receipts journal is used to record all cash receipts transactions.

5. Purchases returns and allowances are recorded in the general journal.

Multiple Choice

1. In the cash receipts journal, each amount in the General Credit column is posted

   (a) daily.   (c) at the end of the month.
   (b) weekly.   (d) at the end of the year.

2. In the cash payments journal, each amount in the General Debit column is posted

   (a) daily.   (c) at the end of the month.
   (b) weekly.   (d) at the end of the year.

3. The journal that should be used to record the return of merchandise for credit is the

   (a) purchases journal.   (c) general journal.
   (b) cash payments journal.   (d) accounts payable journal.

4. A purchases journal is used to record all

   (a) purchases.   (c) purchases of merchandise on account.
   (b) cash purchases.   (d) purchases returns and allowances.

5. The first step in posting the sales journal to the general ledger is to

   (a) total and verify the equality of the amount columns.
   (b) enter the date in the Date column of the ledger account.
   (c) enter the new balance in the Balance columns of the ledger account.
   (d) enter the ledger account number below the column totals in the journal.

The answers to the Self-Study Test Questions are at the end of the text.

REVIEW QUESTIONS

LO1   1. What is the primary purpose of using special journals?

LO2   2. List four items of information about each sale entered in the sales journal.

LO2   3. What steps are followed in posting from the sales journal to the general ledger?

LO2   4. What steps are followed in posting from the sales journal to the accounts receivable ledger?

LO3   5. List three items of information about each cash receipt entered in the cash receipts journal.

LO3   6. What steps are followed in posting from the cash receipts journal to the general ledger?

LO3   7. What steps are followed in posting from the cash receipts journal to the accounts receivable ledger?

LO4   8. List four items of information about each purchase entered in the purchases journal.

LO4   9. What steps are followed in posting from the purchases journal to the general ledger?

LO4   10. What steps are followed in posting from the purchases journal to the accounts payable ledger?

LO5   11. List four items of information about each cash payment entered in the cash payments journal.

LO5   12. What steps are followed in posting from the cash payments journal to the general ledger?

LO5   13. What steps are followed in posting from the cash payments journal to the accounts payable ledger?

© DIGITAL IMAGING GROUP

REVISITING THE OPENER

In the chapter opener on page 439, you are asked whether Evan should use special journals in his business.

(1) What are special journals?

(2) How do special journals make record keeping more efficient?

(3) (a) If a company makes all sales on account and charges sales tax, what amount columns would be needed in the sales journal?

(b) If a company charges sales tax, makes bank credit card sales and other credit sales, and offers cash discounts, what amount columns would be needed in the cash receipts journal?

(c) If a company makes purchases on account and pays no separate freight charges, what amount columns would be needed in the purchases journal?

(d) If a company normally makes cash payments for amounts due on account within the discount period, and for cash purchases, what amount columns would be needed in the cash payments journal?

SERIES A EXERCISE

E 12-1A (LO1)

RECORDING TRANSACTIONS IN THE PROPER JOURNAL Identify the journal (sales, cash receipts, purchases, cash payments, or general) in which each of the following transactions should be recorded:

(a)   Sold merchandise on account.
(b)   Purchased delivery truck on account for use in the business.
(c)   Received payment from customer on account.
(d)   Purchased merchandise on account.
(e)   Issued check in payment of electric bill.
(f)   Recorded depreciation on factory building.

E 12-2A (LO2)
✓ May 1:Dr. Accounts Receivable/
J. Adams, $2,120

JOURNALIZING SALES TRANSACTIONS Enter the following transactions in a sales journal. Use a 6% sales tax rate.

May   1   Sold merchandise on account to J. Adams, $2,000, plus sales tax. Sale no 488.

4   Sold merchandise on account to B. Clark, $1,800, plus sales tax. Sale no. 489.

8   Sold merchandise on account to A. Duck, $1,500, plus sales tax. Sale no. 490.

11   Sold merchandise on account to E. Hill, $1,950, plus sales tax. Sale no. 491.

E 12-3A (LO3)
✓ July 6: Cr. Accounts Receivable/
J. Adler, $643

JOURNALIZING CASH RECEIPTS Enter the following transactions in a cash receipts journal:

July   6   James Adler made payment on account, $643.

10   Made cash sales for the week, $2,320.

14   Betty Havel made payment on account, $430.

15   J. L. Borg made payment on account, $117.

17   Made cash sales for the week, $2,237.

E 12-4A (LO4)
✓ May 9: Purchases Dr./Accounts
Payable Cr., $2,300

JOURNALIZING PURCHASES TRANSACTIONS Enter the following transactions in a purchases journal like the one below.

May   3   Purchased merchandise from Cintron, $6,500. Invoice no. 321, dated May 1, terms n/30.

9   Purchased merchandise from Mitsui, $2,300. Invoice no. 614, dated May 8, terms 2/10, n/30.

18   Purchased merchandise from Aloha Distributors, $4,200. Invoice no. 180, dated May 15, terms 1/15, n/30.

23   Purchased merchandise from Soto, $6,300. Invoice no. 913, dated May 22, terms 1/10, n/30.

		PURCHASES JOURNAL		PAGE
DATE	INVOICE NO.	FROM WHOM PURCHASED	POST. REF.	PURCHASES DEBIT/ACCOUNTS PAYABLE CREDIT

E 12-5A (LO5)
✓ Sept. 12: Cash Cr., $6,930

JOURNALIZING CASH PAYMENTS Landmark Industries uses a cash payments journal. Prepare a cash payments journal using the same format and account titles as illustrated in the chapter. Record the following payments for merchandise purchased:

Sept. 5   Issued check no. 318 to Clinton Corp. for merchandise purchased August 28, $6,000, terms 2/10, n/30. Payment is made within the discount period.

12   Issued check no. 319 to Mitchell Co. for merchandise purchased September 2, $7,500, terms 1/10, n/30. A credit memo had previously been received from Mitchell Company for merchandise returned, $500. Payment is made within the discount period after deduction for the return dated September 8.

19   Issued check no. 320 to Expert Systems for merchandise purchased August 19, $4,100, terms n/30.

27   Issued check no. 321 to Graphic Data for merchandise purchased September 17, $9,000, terms 2/10, n/30. Payment is made within the discount period.

SERIES A PROBLEMS

P 12-6A (LO2)

✓ Total Accounts Receivable Dr.: $16,345.20

SALES JOURNAL J. K. Bijan owns a retail business and made the following sales during the month of August 20--. There is a 6% sales tax on all sales.

Aug. 1   Sale no. 213 to Jung Manufacturing Co., $1,200, plus sales tax.

3   Sale no. 214 to Hassad Co., $3,600, plus sales tax.

7   Sale no. 215 to Helsinki, Inc., $1,400, plus sales tax. (Open a new account for this customer. Address is 125 Fishers Dr., Noblesville, IN 47870–8867.)

11   Sale no. 216 to Ardis Myler, $1,280, plus sales tax.

18   Sale no. 217 to Hassad Co., $4,330, plus sales tax.

22   Sale no. 218 to Jung Manufacturing Co., $2,000, plus sales tax.

30   Sale no. 219 to Ardis Myler, $1,610, plus sales tax.

REQUIRED

1.   Record the transactions in the sales journal. Total and verify the column totals and rule the columns.

2.   Post from the sales journal to the general ledger and accounts receivable ledger accounts. Use account numbers as shown in the chapter.

P 12-7A (LO3)

✓ Total Accounts Receivable Cr.: $5,732

CASH RECEIPTS JOURNAL Zebra Imaginarium, a retail business, had the following cash receipts during December 20--. The sales tax is 6%.

Dec. 1   Received payment on account from Michael Anderson, $1,360.

2   Received payment on account from Ansel Manufacturing, $382.

7   Made cash sales for the week, $3,160, plus tax. Bank credit card sales for the week, $1,000 plus tax. Bank credit card fee is 3%.

8   Received payment on account from J. Gorbea, $880.

11   Michael Anderson returned merchandise for a credit, $60 plus tax.

14   Made cash sales for the week, $2,800, plus tax. Bank credit card sales for the week, $800, plus tax. Bank credit card fee is 3%.

(continued)

Dec. 20   Received payment on account from Tom Wilson, $1,110.

21   Ansel Manufacturing returned merchandise for a credit, $22, plus tax.

21   Made cash sales for the week, $3,200, plus tax.

24   Received payment on account from Rachel Carson, $2,000.

Beginning general ledger account balances were as follows:

Cash	$9,862
Accounts Receivable	9,352

Beginning customer account balances were as follows:

M. Anderson	$2,480
Ansel Manufacturing	982
J. Gorbea	880
R. Carson	3,200
T. Wilson	1,810

REQUIRED

1.   Record the transactions in the cash receipts journal. Total and verify column totals and rule the columns. Use the general journal to record sales returns and allowances.

2.   Post from the journals to the general ledger and accounts receivable ledger accounts. Use account numbers as shown in the chapter.

P 12-8A (LO2/3)

✓ Total Accounts Receivable Dr.:
$12,745.08

SALES JOURNAL, CASH RECEIPTS JOURNAL, AND GENERAL JOURNAL
Owens Distributors is a retail business. The following sales, returns, and cash receipts occurred during March 20--. There is an 8% sales tax. Beginning general ledger account balances were Cash, $9,741.00; and Accounts Receivable, $1,058.25. Beginning customer account balances were Thompson Group, $1,058.25.

Mar. 1   Sold merchandise to Able & Co., $1,800, plus sales tax. Sale no. 33C.

3   Sold merchandise to R. J. Kalas, Inc., $2,240, plus sales tax. Sale no. 33D.

5   Able & Co. returned merchandise from sale no. 33C for a credit (credit memo no. 66), $30, plus sales tax.

7   Made cash sales for the week, $3,160, plus sales tax.

10   Received payment from Able & Co. for sale no. 33C less credit memo no. 66.

11   Sold merchandise to Blevins Bakery, $1,210, plus sales tax. Sale no. 33E.

13   Received payment from R. J. Kalas for sale no. 33D.

14   Made cash sales for the week, $4,200, plus sales tax.

16   Blevins Bakery returned merchandise from sale no. 33E for a credit (credit memo no. 67), $44, plus sales tax.

18   Sold merchandise to R. J. Kalas, Inc., $2,620, plus sales tax. Sale no. 33F.

20   Received payment from Blevins Bakery for sale no. 33E less credit memo no. 67.

21   Made cash sales for the week, $2,400, plus sales tax.

Mar. 25   Sold merchandise to Blevins Bakery, $1,915, plus sales tax. Sale no. 33G.

27   Sold merchandise to Thompson Group, $2,016, plus sales tax. Sale no. 33H.

28   Made cash sales for the week, $3,500, plus sales tax.

REQUIRED

1.   Record the transactions in the sales journal, cash receipts journal, and general journal. Total, verify, and rule the columns where appropriate at the end of the month.

2.   Post from the journals to the general ledger and accounts receivable ledger accounts. Use account numbers as shown in the chapter.

P 12-9A (LO4)

✓ Total Purchases Dr.: $20,790

PURCHASES JOURNAL J. B. Speck, owner of Speck's Galleria, made the following purchases of merchandise on account during the month of September:

Sept. 3   Purchase invoice no. 415, $2,650, from Smith Distributors.

8   Purchase invoice no. 132, $3,830, from Michaels Wholesaler.

11   Purchase invoice no. 614, $3,140, from J. B. Sanders & Co.

18   Purchase invoice no. 329, $2,250, from Bateman & Jones, Inc.

23   Purchase invoice no. 867, $4,160, from Smith Distributors.

27   Purchase invoice no. 744, $1,980, from Anderson Company.

30   Purchase invoice no. 652, $2,780, from Michaels Wholesaler.

REQUIRED

1.   Record the transactions in the purchases journal. Total and rule the journal.

2.   Post from the purchases journal to the general ledger and accounts payable ledger accounts. Use account numbers as shown in the chapter.

P 12-10A (LO4)

✓ Helmut's Hair Supply account balance: $4,240

PURCHASES JOURNAL, GENERAL LEDGER, AND ACCOUNTS PAYABLE LEDGER The purchases journal of Kevin's Kettle, a small retail business, is as follows:

PURCHASES JOURNAL   PAGE 1

	DATE		INVOICE NO.	FROM WHOM PURCHASED	POST. REF.	PURCHASES DEBIT/ACCOUNTS PAYABLE CREDIT					
1	20-- Jan.	2	101	Ruiz Imports		3	0	0	0	00	1
2		3	621	Helmut's Hair Supply		2	4	8	0	00	2
3		7	195	Viola's Boutique		4	3	6	0	00	3
4		12	267	Royal Flush		1	9	5	0	00	4
5		18	903	Maria's Melodies		4	7	0	0	00	5
6		25	680	Helmut's Hair Supply		1	7	6	0	00	6
7						18	2	5	0	00	7

(continued)

REQUIRED

1. Post the total of the purchases journal to the appropriate general ledger accounts. Use account numbers as shown in the chapter.

2. Post the individual purchase amounts to the accounts payable ledger.

P 12-11A (LO5)

✓ Total Cash Cr.: $30,984

CASH PAYMENTS JOURNAL Sam Santiago operates a retail variety store. The books include a cash payments journal and an accounts payable ledger. All cash payments (except petty cash) are entered in the cash payments journal.

Selected account balances on May 1 are as follows:

General Ledger

Cash	$40,000
Accounts Payable	20,000

Accounts Payable Ledger

Fantastic Toys	$5,200
Goya Outlet	3,800
Mueller's Distributors	3,600
Van Kooning	7,400

The following are the transactions related to cash payments for the month of May:

May	1	Issued check no. 426 in payment of May rent (Rent Expense), $2,400.
	3	Issued check no. 427 to Mueller's Distributors in payment of merchandise purchased on account, $3,600, less a 3% discount. Check was written for $3,492.
	7	Issued check no. 428 to Van Kooning in partial payment of merchandise purchased on account, $5,500. A cash discount was not allowed.
	12	Issued check no. 429 to Fantastic Toys for merchandise purchased on account, $5,200, less a 1% discount. Check was written for $5,148.
	15	Issued check no. 430 to City Power and Light (Utilities Expense), $1,720.
	18	Issued check no. 431 to A-1 Warehouse for a cash purchase of merchandise, $4,800.
	26	Issued check no. 432 to Goya Outlet for merchandise purchased on account, $3,800, less a 2% discount. Check was written for $3,724.
	30	Issued check no. 433 to Mercury Transit Company for freight charges on merchandise purchased (Freight-In), $1,200.
	31	Issued check no. 434 to Town Merchants for a cash purchase of merchandise, $3,000.

REQUIRED

1. Enter the transactions in a cash payments journal. Total, rule, and prove the cash payments journal.

2. Post from the cash payments journal to the general ledger and accounts payable ledger. Use general ledger account numbers as shown in the chapter.

P 12-12A (LO4/5)

✓Total Cash Cr.: $11,170

KLOOSTER & ALLEN

PURCHASES JOURNAL, CASH PAYMENTS JOURNAL, AND GENERAL JOURNAL Freddy Flint owns a small retail business called Flint's Fantasy. The cash account has a balance of $20,000 on July 1. The following transactions occurred during July:

July 1   Issued check no. 414 in payment of July rent, $1,500.

1   Purchased merchandise on account from Tang's Toys, invoice no. 311, $2,700, terms 2/10, n/30.

3   Purchased merchandise on account from Sillas & Company, invoice no. 812, $3,100, terms 1/10, n/30.

5   Returned merchandise purchased from Tang's Toys, receiving a credit memo on the amount owed, $500.

8   Purchased merchandise on account from Daisy's Dolls, invoice no. 139, $1,900, terms 2/10, n/30.

11   Issued check no. 415 to Tang's Toys for merchandise purchased on account, less return of July 5 and less 2% discount.

13   Issued check no. 416 to Sillas & Company for merchandise purchased on account, less 1% discount.

15   Returned merchandise purchased from Daisy's Dolls, receiving a credit memo on the amount owed, $400.

18   Issued check no. 417 to Daisy's Dolls for merchandise purchased on account, less return of July 15 and less 2% discount.

25   Purchased merchandise on account from Allied Business, invoice no. 489, $2,450, terms n/30.

26   Purchased merchandise on account from Tang's Toys, invoice no. 375, $1,980, terms 2/10, n/30.

29   Purchased merchandise on account from Sillas & Company, invoice no. 883, $3,460, terms 1/10, n/30.

31   Freddy Flint withdrew cash for personal use, $2,000. Issued check no. 418.

31   Issued check no. 419 to Glisan Distributors for a cash purchase of merchandise, $975.

REQUIRED

1.   Record the transactions in the purchases journal, cash payments journal, and general journal. Total and rule the purchases and cash payments journals. Prove the cash payments journal.

2.   Post from the journals to the general ledger and accounts payable ledger accounts. Use general ledger account numbers as shown in the chapter.

SERIES B EXERCISES

E 12-1B (LO1)

RECORDING TRANSACTIONS IN THE PROPER JOURNAL Identify the journal (sales, cash receipts, purchases, cash payments, or general) in which each of the following transactions should be recorded.

(continued)

   (a)   Issued credit memo to customer for merchandise returned.
   (b)   Sold merchandise for cash.
   (c)   Purchased merchandise on account.
   (d)   Issued checks to employees in payment of wages.
   (e)   Purchased factory supplies on account.
   (f)   Sold merchandise on account.

E 12-2B (LO2)

✓ Sept. 1: Dr. Accounts Receivable/
K. Smith, $1,890

JOURNALIZING SALES TRANSACTIONS Enter the following transactions in a sales journal. Use a 5% sales tax rate.

Sept. 1   Sold merchandise on account to K. Smith, $1,800, plus sales tax. Sale no. 228.

      3   Sold merchandise on account to J. Arnes, $3,100, plus sales tax. Sale no. 229.

      5   Sold merchandise on account to M. Denison, $2,800, plus sales tax. Sale no. 230.

      7   Sold merchandise on account to B. Marshall, $1,900, plus sales tax. Sale no. 231.

E 12-3B (LO3)

✓ Nov. 1: Cr. Accounts Receivable/
Jean Haghighat, $750

JOURNALIZING CASH RECEIPTS Enter the following transactions in a cash receipts journal:

Nov. 1   Jean Haghighat made payment on account, $750.

     12   Marc Antonoff made payment on account, $464.

     15   Made cash sales, $3,763.

     18   Will Mossein made payment on account, $241.

     25   Made cash sales, $2,648.

E 12-4B (LO4)

✓ Jan. 3: Purchases Dr./Accounts
Payable Cr., $6,000

JOURNALIZING PURCHASES TRANSACTIONS Enter the following transactions in a purchases journal like the one below.

Jan. 3   Purchased merchandise from Feng, $6,000. Invoice no. 416, dated January 1, terms 2/10, n/30.

     12   Purchased merchandise from Miranda, $9,000. Invoice no. 624, dated January 10, terms n/30.

     19   Purchased merchandise from J. B. Barba, $6,400. Invoice no. 190, dated January 18, terms 1/10, n/30.

     26   Purchased merchandise from Ramirez, $3,700. Invoice no. 923, dated January 25, terms 1/15, n/30.

		PURCHASES JOURNAL		PAGE
DATE	INVOICE NO.	FROM WHOM PURCHASED	POST. REF.	PURCHASES DEBIT/ACCOUNTS PAYABLE CREDIT

E 12-5B (LO5)

✓ Apr. 19: Cash Cr., $4,950

JOURNALIZING CASH PAYMENTS Sandcastles Northwest uses a cash payments journal. Prepare a cash payments journal using the same format and account titles as illustrated in the chapter. Record the following payments for merchandise purchased:

Apr. 5   Issued check no. 429 to Standard Industries for merchandise purchased April 3, $8,000, terms 2/10, n/30. Payment is made within the discount period.

Apr. 19	Issued check no. 430 to Finest Company for merchandise purchased April 10, $5,300, terms 1/10, n/30. A credit memo had previously been received from Finest Company for merchandise returned, $300. Payment is made within the discount period after deduction for the return dated April 12.
21	Issued check no. 431 to Funny Follies for merchandise purchased March 21, $3,250, terms n/30.
29	Issued check no. 432 to Classic Data for merchandise purchased April 20, $7,000, terms 2/10, n/30. Payment is made within the discount period.

SERIES B PROBLEMS

P 12-6B (LO2)

✓ Total Accounts Receivable Dr.: $13,072.50

SALES JOURNAL T. M. Maxwell owns a retail business and made the following sales during the month of July 20--. There is a 5% sales tax on all sales.

July 1	Sale no. 101 to Saga, Inc., $1,200, plus sales tax.
8	Sale no. 102 to Vinnie Ward, $2,100, plus sales tax.
15	Sale no. 103 to Dvorak Manufacturing, $4,300, plus sales tax.
21	Sale no. 104 to Vinnie Ward, $1,800, plus sales tax.
24	Sale no. 105 to Zapata Co., $1,600, plus sales tax. (Open a new account for this customer. Address is 789 N. Stafford Dr., Bloomington, IN 47401–6201.)
29	Sale no. 106 to Saga, Inc., $1,450, plus sales tax.

REQUIRED

1. Record the transactions in the sales journal. Total and verify the column totals and rule the columns.

2. Post the sales journal to the general ledger and accounts receivable ledger accounts. Use account numbers as shown in the chapter.

P 12-7B (LO3)

✓ Total Accounts Receivable Cr.: $3,481

CASH RECEIPTS JOURNAL Color Florists, a retail business, had the following cash receipts during January 20--. The sales tax is 5%.

Jan. 1	Received payment on account from Ray Boyd, $880.
3	Received payment on account from Clint Hassell, $271.
5	Made cash sales for the week, $2,800, plus tax. Bank credit card sales for the week, $1,200, plus tax. Bank credit card fee is 3%.
8	Received payment on account from Jan Sowada, $912.
11	Ray Boyd returned merchandise for a credit, $40, plus tax.
12	Made cash sales for the week, $3,100, plus tax. Bank credit card sales for the week, $1,900, plus tax. Bank credit card fee is 3%.
15	Received payment on account from Robert Zehnle, $1,100.
18	Robert Zehnle returned merchandise for a credit, $31, plus tax.
19	Made cash sales for the week, $2,230, plus tax.
25	Received payment on account from Dazai Manufacturing, $318.

(continued)

Beginning general ledger account balances were as follows:

Cash $2,890.75
Accounts Receivable 6,300.00

Beginning customer account balances were as follows:

R. Boyd $1,400
Dazai Manufacturing 318
C. Hassell 815
J. Sowada 1,481
R. Zehnle 2,286

REQUIRED

1. Record the transactions in the cash receipts journal. Total and verify the column totals and rule the columns. Use the general journal to record sales returns and allowances.

2. Post from the journals to the general ledger and accounts receivable ledger accounts. Use account numbers as shown in the chapter.

P 12-8B (LO2/3)

✓ Total Accounts Receivable Dr.:
$7,853.80

KLOOSTER
.& ALLEN.

SALES JOURNAL, CASH RECEIPTS JOURNAL, AND GENERAL JOURNAL
Paul Jackson owns a retail business. The following sales, returns, and cash receipts are for April 20--. There is a 7% sales tax.

Apr. 1　Sold merchandise to O. L. Meyers, $2,100, plus sales tax. Sale no. 111.

3　Sold merchandise to Andrew Plaa, $1,000, plus sales tax. Sale no. 112.

6　O. L. Meyers returned merchandise from sale no. 111 for a credit (credit memo no. 42), $50, plus sales tax.

7　Made cash sales for the week, $3,240, plus sales tax.

9　Received payment from O. L. Meyers for sale no. 111. less credit memo no. 42.

12　Sold merchandise to Melissa Richfield, $980, plus sales tax. Sale no. 113.

14　Made cash sales for the week, $2,180, plus sales tax.

17　Melissa Richfield returned merchandise from sale no. 113 for a credit (credit memo no. 43), $40, plus sales tax.

19　Sold merchandise to Kelsay Munkres, $1,020, plus sales tax. Sale no. 114.

21　Made cash sales for the week, $2,600, plus sales tax.

24　Sold merchandise to O. L. Meyers, $920, plus sales tax. Sale no. 115.

27　Sold merchandise to Andrew Plaa, $1,320, plus sales tax. Sale no. 116.

28　Made cash sales for the week, $2,800, plus sales tax.

Beginning general ledger account balances were as follows:

Cash $2,864.54
Accounts Receivable 2,726.25

Beginning customer account balances were as follows:

O. L. Meyers	$2,186.00
K. Munkres	482.00
M. Richfield	58.25

REQUIRED

1. Record the transactions in the sales journal, cash receipts journal, and general journal. Total, verify, and rule the columns where appropriate at the end of the month.

2. Post from the journals to the general ledger and accounts receivable ledger accounts. Use account numbers as shown in the chapter.

P 12-9B (LO4)

✓ Total Purchases Dr.: $18,515

PURCHASES JOURNAL Ann Benton, owner of Benton's Galleria, made the following purchases of merchandise on account during the month of October:

Oct. 2   Purchase invoice no. 321, $1,950, from Boggs Distributors.

7   Purchase invoice no. 152, $2,915, from Wolfs Wholesaler.

10   Purchase invoice no. 634, $3,565, from Komuro & Co.

16   Purchase invoice no. 349, $2,845, from Fritz & McCord, Inc.

24   Purchase invoice no. 587, $3,370, from Boggs Distributors.

26   Purchase invoice no. 764, $2,240, from Sanderson Company.

31   Purchase invoice no. 672, $1,630, from Wolfs Wholesaler.

REQUIRED

1. Record the transactions in the purchases journal. Total and rule the journal.

2. Post from the purchases journal to the general ledger and accounts payable ledger accounts. Use account numbers as shown in the chapter.

P 12-10B (LO4)

✓ Amelia & Vincente account balance: $7,810

PURCHASES JOURNAL, GENERAL LEDGER, AND ACCOUNTS PAYABLE LEDGER The purchases journal of Ryan's Rats Nest, a small retail business, is as follows:

	DATE	INVOICE NO.	FROM WHOM PURCHASED	POST. REF.	PURCHASES DEBIT/ACCOUNTS PAYABLE CREDIT	
1	20-- Jan. 3	121	Sandra's Sweets		4 4 9 0 00	1
2	5	641	Amelia & Vincente		5 9 2 0 00	2
3	9	215	Nobuko's Nature Store		2 6 8 0 00	3
4	15	227	Smith and Johnson Company		6 5 6 0 00	4
5	21	933	Hidemi, Inc.		1 3 0 0 00	5
6	30	650	Amelia & Vincente		1 8 9 0 00	6
7					22 8 4 0 00	7

PURCHASES JOURNAL   PAGE 1

REQUIRED

1. Post the total of the purchases journal to the appropriate general ledger accounts. Use account numbers as shown in the chapter.

2. Post the individual purchase amounts to the accounts payable ledger.

P 12-11B (LO5)

✓ Total Cash Cr.: $29,890

CASH PAYMENTS JOURNAL Kay Zembrowski operates a retail variety store. The books include a cash payments journal and an accounts payable ledger. All cash payments (except petty cash) are entered in the cash payments journal. Selected account balances on May 1 are as follows:

General Ledger	
Cash	$40,000
Accounts Payable	20,000

Accounts Payable Ledger	
Cortez Distributors	$4,200
Indra & Velga	6,800
Toy Corner	4,600
Troutman Outlet	4,400

The following transactions are related to cash payments for the month of May:

May 1   Issued check no. 326 in payment of May rent (Rent Expense), $2,600.

4   Issued check no. 327 to Cortez Distributors in payment of merchandise purchased on account, $4,200, less a 3% discount. Check was written for $4,074.

7   Issued check no. 328 to Indra & Velga in partial payment of merchandise purchased on account, $6,200. A cash discount was not allowed.

11   Issued check no. 329 to Toy Corner for merchandise purchased on account, $4,600, less a 1% discount. Check was written for $4,554.

15   Issued check no. 330 to County Power and Light (Utilities Expense), $1,500.

19   Issued check no. 331 to Builders Warehouse for a cash purchase of merchandise, $3,500.

25   Issued check no. 332 to Troutman Outlet for merchandise purchased on account, $4,400, less a 2% discount. Check was written for $4,312.

30   Issued check no. 333 to Rapid Transit Company for freight charges on merchandise purchased (Freight-In), $800.

31   Issued check no. 334 to City Merchants for a cash purchase of merchandise, $2,350.

REQUIRED

1. Enter the transactions in a cash payments journal. Total, rule, and prove the cash payments journal.

2. Post from the cash payments journal to the general ledger and accounts payable ledger. Use general ledger account numbers as shown in the chapter.

P 12-12B (LO4/5)

✓ Total Cash Cr.: $10,760

PURCHASES JOURNAL, CASH PAYMENTS JOURNAL, AND GENERAL JOURNAL Debbie Mueller owns a small retail business called Debbie's Doll House. The cash account has a balance of $20,000 on July 1. The following transactions occurred during July.

July	1	Issued check no. 314 for July rent, $1,400.
	1	Purchased merchandise on account from Topper's Toys, invoice no. 211, $2,500, terms 2/10, n/30.
	3	Purchased merchandise on account from Jones & Company, invoice no. 812, $2,800, terms 1/10, n/30.
	5	Returned merchandise purchased from Topper's Toys receiving a credit memo on the amount owed, $400.
	8	Purchased merchandise on account from Downtown Merchants, invoice no. 159, $1,600, terms 2/10, n/30.
	11	Issued check no. 315 to Topper's Toys for merchandise purchased on account, less return of July 5 and less 2% discount.
	13	Issued check no. 316 to Jones & Company for merchandise purchased on account, less 1% discount.
	15	Returned merchandise purchased from Downtown Merchants receiving a credit memo on the amount owed, $600.
	18	Issued check no. 317 to Downtown Merchants for merchandise purchased on account, less return of July 15 and less 2% discount.
	25	Purchased merchandise on account from Columbia Products, invoice no. 468, $3,200, terms n/30.
	26	Purchased merchandise on account from Topper's Toys, invoice no. 395, $1,430, terms 2/10, n/30.
	29	Purchased merchandise on account from Jones & Company, invoice no. 853, $2,970, terms 1/10, n/30.
	31	Mueller withdrew cash for personal use, $2,500. Issued check no. 318.
	31	Issued check no. 319 to Burnside Warehouse for a cash purchase of merchandise, $1,050.

REQUIRED

1. Record the transactions in the purchases journal, cash payments journal, and general journal. Total and rule the purchases and cash payments journals. Prove the cash payments journal.

2. Post from the journals to the general ledger and accounts payable ledger accounts. Use general ledger account numbers as shown in the chapter.

MANAGING YOUR WRITING

You have a part-time job as a bookkeeper at a local office supply store. The accounting records consist of a general journal and general ledger. The manager is concerned about efficiency and feels that too much time is spent recording transactions. In addition, there sometimes is difficulty determining the amount owed to specific suppliers. The manager knows you are an accounting student and asks for your suggestions to improve the accounting function.

Write a memo to the manager describing how to increase efficiency and accuracy by using different accounting records.

ETHICS CASE

Judy Baresford, the store manager of Comfort Futons, noticed that the amount of time the two bookkeepers were spending on accounts receivable, accounts payable, and cash receipts was increasing due to the store's increase in sales. A friend of Judy's who is also a store manager suggested that she might want to have some special journals designed that would reduce the amount of work involved in the day-to-day bookkeeping at her store. Judy approached Jon Fortner and Sue Stavio, the bookkeepers, and asked them to come up with a proposal for special journals. During lunch, Jon told Sue he thought designing special journals would be a lot of work and it was not in his job description. Sue told him not to worry because she would just copy pages of special journals from her accounting textbook and they could submit these journals as their own design. Jon liked the idea and they agreed to meet the next night, scan the journals into Word, and submit them to Judy the following morning.

1. Do you think Sue's suggestion is unethical? Why or why not?

2. In using the generic special journals from Sue's accounting textbook, what possible problems can you foresee?

3. If you were Judy, how would you respond to Sue and Jon's "plan"?

MASTERY PROBLEM

✓ Total Accounts Receivable Cr.: $7,235

KLOOSTER & ALLEN

During the month of October 20--, The Pink Petal flower shop engaged in the following transactions:

Oct.	1	Sold merchandise on account to Elizabeth Shoemaker, $1,000, plus tax of $50. Sale no. 222.
	2	Issued check no. 190 to Jill Hand in payment of October 1 balance of $500, less 2% discount.
	2	Purchased merchandise on account from Flower Wholesalers, $4,000. Invoice no. 500, dated October 2, terms 2/10, n/30.
	4	Purchased merchandise on account from Seidl Enterprises, $700. Invoice no. 527, dated October 4, terms 2/15, n/30.
	5	Issued check no. 191 in payment of telephone expense for the month of September, $150.
	7	Sold merchandise for cash, $3,500, plus tax of $175.
	9	Received payment from Leigh Summers in full settlement of account, $2,000.
	11	Issued check no. 192 to Flower Wholesalers in payment of October 1 balance of $1,500.
	12	Sold merchandise on account to Leigh Summers, $2,000, plus tax of $100. Sale no. 223.
	12	Received payment from Meg Johnson on account, $3,100.
	13	Issued check no. 193 to Seidl Enterprises in payment of October 4 purchase. Invoice no. 527, less 2% discount.
	14	Meg Johnson returned merchandise for a credit, $300, plus sales tax of $15.

Oct. 17   Returned merchandise to Vases Etc. for credit, $900.

   24   Received payment from David's Decorating on account, $2,135.

   27   Sold merchandise on account to David's Decorating, $3,000, plus tax of $150. Sale no. 224.

   29   Issued check no. 194 in payment of wages (Wages Expense) for the four-week period ending October 30, $900.

Selected account balances as of October 1 were as follows:

Account	Account No.	Debit	Credit
Cash	101	$18,225.00	
Accounts Receivable	122	9,619.00	
Accounts Payable	202		$5,120.00

The Pink Petal also had the following subsidiary ledger balances as of October 1:

Accounts Receivable:

Customer	Accounts Receivable Balance
David's Decorating 12 Jude Lane Hartford, CT 06117	$3,340.00
Elizabeth Shoemaker 52 Juniper Road Hartford, CT 06118	279.00
Meg Johnson 700 Hobbes Dr. Avon, CT 06108	4,000.00
Leigh Summers 5200 Hamilton Ave. Hartford, CT 06111	2,000.00

Accounts Payable:

Vendor	Accounts Payable Balance
Vases Etc. 34 Harry Ave. East Hartford, CT 05234	$3,120.00
Jill Hand 1009 Drake Rd. Farmington, CT 06082	500.00
Flower Wholesalers 43 Lucky Lane Bristol, CT 06007	1,500.00
Seidl Enterprises 888 Anders Street Newington, CT 06789	—

REQUIRED:

1.   Record the transactions in a sales journal (page 7), cash receipts journal (page 10), purchases journal (page 6), cash payments journal (page 11), and general journal (page 5). Total, verify, and rule the columns where appropriate at the end of the month.

2.   Post from the journals to the general ledger, accounts receivable ledger, and accounts payable ledger accounts. Use account numbers as shown in the chapter.

CHALLENGE PROBLEM

This problem challenges you to apply your cumulative accounting knowledge to move a step beyond the material in the chapter.

✓ June 3: Cr. City Sales Tax Payable, $4.22

Screpcap Co. had the following transactions during the first week of June:

June 1	Purchased merchandise on account from Acme Supply, $2,700, plus freight charges of $160.
1	Issued check no. 219 to Denver Wholesalers for merchandise purchased on account, $720, less 1% discount.
1	Sold merchandise on account to F. Colby, $246, plus 5% state sales tax plus 2% city sales tax.
2	Received cash on account from N. Dunlop, $315.
2	Made cash sale of $413 plus 5% state sales tax plus 2% city sales tax.
2	Purchased merchandise on account from Permon Co., $3,200, plus freight charges of $190.
3	Sold merchandise on account to F. Ayres, $211, plus 5% state sales tax plus 2% city sales tax.
3	Issued check no. 220 to Ellis Co. for merchandise purchased on account, $847, less 1% discount.
3	Received cash on account from F. Graves, $463.
4	Issued check no. 221 to Penguin Warehouse for merchandise purchased on account, $950, less 1% discount.
4	Sold merchandise on account to K. Stanga, $318, plus 5% state sales tax plus 2% city sales tax.
4	Purchased merchandise on account from Mason Milling, $1,630, plus freight charges of $90.
4	Received cash on account from O. Alston, $381.
5	Made cash sale of $319 plus 5% state sales tax plus 2% city sales tax.
5	Issued check no. 222 to Acme Supply for merchandise purchased on account, $980, less 1% discount.

REQUIRED

1. Record the transactions in a general journal.

2. Assuming these are the types of transactions Screpcap Co. experiences on a regular basis, design the following special journals for Screpcap:

   (a) Sales journal
   (b) Cash receipts journal
   (c) Purchases journal
   (d) Cash payments journal

Objectives
Careful study of this chapter should enable you to:

LO1
Explain the impact of merchandise inventory on the financial statements.

LO2
Describe the two principal systems of accounting for merchandise inventory—the periodic system and the perpetual system.

LO3
Compute the costs allocated to the ending inventory and cost of goods sold using different inventory methods.

LO4
Estimate the ending inventory and cost of goods sold by using the gross profit and retail inventory methods.

Accounting for Merchandise Inventory

As you walk through a grocery store, have you ever wondered what the store paid for each item? It would be nice to know which items really are "good buys" and which are "overpriced." What happens when management pays different amounts for identical products on the shelf? The selling price for each unit is the same. Otherwise, we could have customers arguing over identical items marked with different prices. Evan Taylor has a similar situation with his pet supplies inventory. Many of the product units are identical, but he paid different prices for them. If the units are identical, how does he know which unit was sold: the one with the higher or lower purchase price? Does it matter?

In Chapters 10 and 11, you learned how to account for the purchase and sale of merchandise. One of the major reasons for keeping accounting records is to determine the net income (or net loss) of a business. A major component of net income is the gross profit. In Chapter 11, you learned how to compute gross profit. An abbreviated form of this calculation is shown below.

Calculation of Gross Profit		
Net sales		$110
Cost of goods sold		
Merchandise inventory, Jan. 1	$ 20	
Purchases	80	
Cost of goods available for sale	$100	
Less merchandise inventory, Dec. 31	30	
Cost of goods sold		70
Gross profit		$ 40

> *The terms <u>goods</u> and <u>merchandise</u> mean the same thing and are used interchangeably.*

For a merchandising business, the cost of goods available for sale ($100) during the accounting period must be divided between cost of goods sold ($70) and ending merchandise inventory ($30). In Chapter 11, the costs assigned to these accounts were provided. In this chapter, you will learn how to determine the dollar amounts assigned to cost of goods sold and ending merchandise inventory. In Chapter 14, we will illustrate the end-of-period adjustments required to bring the cost of goods sold and merchandise inventory accounts up to date to reflect their proper balances.

THE IMPACT OF MERCHANDISE INVENTORY ON FINANCIAL STATEMENTS

LO1 Explain the impact of merchandise inventory on the financial statements.

A company's ending inventory must be reported accurately. An error in the reported inventory will cause errors on the income statement, statement of owner's equity, and balance sheet. In addition, since this year's ending inventory becomes next year's beginning inventory, financial statements for the following year will also contain errors.

Figure 13-1 illustrates the impact of an error in the *ending inventory*. The first pair of columns presents partial financial statements when the ending inventory is correct. For this illustration, sales, cost of goods sold, and operating expenses are assumed to be the same for 20-1 and 20-2. Thus, the same net income of $30 and beginning and ending merchandise inventories of $20 are reported for both years.

> *This year's ending inventory becomes next year's beginning inventory.*

The second pair of columns in Figure 13-1 illustrates the effects of understating the ending inventory. Understating the ending inventory for 20-1 by $5 causes the cost of goods sold to be overstated by $5 and net income to be understated by $5. Since net income is reported on the statement of owner's equity, Erv Bultman's capital on December 31 is understated by $5. The understated capital also appears in the owner's equity section of the balance sheet. The understated ending inventory is reported in the current assets section of the balance sheet.

Even if the ending inventory for 20-2 is accurately reported, we still have a problem with the income statement. Since the ending inventory for 20-1 was understated, the beginning inventory for 20-2 is understated also ($15 instead of $20). This error causes cost of goods sold to be understated by $5 and net income to be overstated by $5.

LEARNING KEY

If the ending inventory for 20-1 is understated, net income for 20-1 is understated and net income for 20-2 is overstated.

At this point, we can see that this inventory error "washes out" over the two-year period. The understated net income for 20-1 is offset by overstated net income in 20-2. Thus, Bultman's capital account as of December 31, 20-2, is reported accurately on the statement of owner's equity and balance sheet at $160. Assuming no future inventory errors, the financial statements for 20-3 and thereafter will be correct.

FIGURE 13-1　Effect of Inventory Errors on Net Income

	ENDING INVENTORY FOR 20-1 IS CORRECT		ENDING INVENTORY FOR 20-1 IS UNDERSTATED		ENDING INVENTORY FOR 20-1 IS OVERSTATED	
	20-1	**20-2**	**20-1**	**20-2**	**20-1**	**20-2**
Income Statement						
Sales	80	80	80	80	80	80
Cost of goods sold:						
Beginning merchandise inventory	20	20	20	15	20	25
Add purchases (net)	40	40	40	40	40	40
Cost of goods available for sale	60	60	60	55	60	65
Less ending merchandise inventory	(20)	(20)	(15)	(20)	(25)	(20)
Cost of goods sold		(40)		(40)	(45)	(35)	(35)	(45)
Gross profit	40	40	35	45	45	35
Operating expenses	(10)	(10)	(10)	(10)	(10)	(10)
Net income	30	30	25	35	35	25
Statement of Owner's Equity						
Erv Bultman, capital, January 1	100	130	100	125	100	135
Net income	30	30	25	35	35	25
Erv Bultman, capital, December 31		130	160		125	160		135	160
Balance Sheet (Partial)						
Current assets:						
Merchandise inventory	20	20	15	20	25	20
Owner's equity:						
Erv Bultman, capital	130	160	125	160	135	160

LEARNING KEY

If the ending inventory for 20-1 is overstated, net income for 20-1 is overstated and net income for 20-2 is understated.

The third pair of columns in Figure 13-1 illustrates the effects of overstating the ending inventory in 20-1. This causes net income to be overstated in 20-1 and understated in 20-2. As previously discussed, these errors "wash out" by the end of 20-2. Thus, Bultman's capital account is correct in the 20-2 financial statements.

It is very important to have an accurate count and valuation for the ending inventory. Since errors in the ending inventory have a direct effect on net income for the period, managers may be tempted to manipulate this amount to achieve a desired result: to either increase net income to make the company look good, or decrease net income to reduce taxes or smooth earnings. For this reason, observing and verifying the ending inventory is an important aspect of an external auditor's job.

TYPES OF INVENTORY SYSTEMS: PERIODIC AND PERPETUAL

The two principal systems of accounting for merchandise inventory are the periodic and the perpetual systems. Entries made for inventory transactions under these systems are illustrated in Figure 13-2. Though not identified as such, Chapter 11 illustrated the periodic inventory system. As shown in Figure 13-2 under the **periodic inventory system**, no entries are made to the merchandise inventory or cost of goods sold account during the year. Thus, the balance in the merchandise inventory account is based on the physical count of inventory taken at the end of the last accounting period. The merchandise inventory and the cost of goods sold for the current period are not determined until the end of the current accounting period, when a physical inventory is taken. At that time, the following formula is applied to calculate cost of goods sold.

Beginning Inventory (based on last year's ending physical count)

+ Net Purchases (account balance at end of this year)

= Cost of Goods Available for Sale

− Ending Inventory (based on this year's ending physical count)

= Cost of Goods Sold (for this year)

Adjusting entries are needed at the end of the fiscal year to update the merchandise inventory account and cost of goods sold. These entries are illustrated in Chapter 14.

As shown in Figure 13-2, under the **perpetual inventory system**, entries are made to the merchandise inventory and cost of goods sold accounts as transactions take place during the accounting period. The merchandise inventory account is debited for the cost of all goods purchased, including freight charges, and credited for the cost of all goods sold. In addition, this account is debited when customers return merchandise and is credited when suppliers grant returns, allowances, and discounts. Thus, the balance of the account represents the cost of goods on hand at all times. The cost of goods sold account is debited when merchandise is sold and credited when customers return merchandise. Thus, the balance of the account reflects the cost of goods sold at any point during the accounting period. No year-end adjusting entry is necessary as long as the physical inventory agrees with the amount reported in the merchandise inventory account. In Chapter 14, we will illustrate the proper adjustment if this is not true.

LEARNING KEY

Under the periodic inventory system, the ending inventory and cost of goods sold are determined at the end of the accounting period, when a physical inventory is taken.

LEARNING KEY

Under the perpetual inventory system, cost of goods sold and the amount of merchandise inventory on hand are continually updated as merchandise is bought and sold.

FIGURE 13-2   Entries for Periodic and Perpetual Inventory Systems

TRANSACTION	PERIODIC SYSTEM		PERPETUAL SYSTEM	
1. Purchased merchandise on account, $100.	Purchases 100		Merchandise Inventory 100	
	Accounts Payable	100	Accounts Payable	100
2. Paid freight charge, $30.	Freight-In 30		Merchandise Inventory 30	
	Cash	30	Cash	30
3. Sold merchandise on account, $80. The cost of the merchandise was $50.	Accounts Receivable 80		Accounts Receivable 80	
	Sales	80	Sales	80
			Cost of Goods Sold 50	
			Merchandise Inventory	50
4. Merchandise costing $10 was returned to the supplier.	Accounts Payable 10		Accounts Payable 10	
	Purchases Ret. & Allow.	10	Merchandise Inventory	10
5. Customers returned merchandise sold for $20. The cost of the merchandise was $15.	Sales Ret. and Allow. 20		Sales Ret. and Allow. 20	
	Accounts Receivable	20	Accounts Receivable	20
			Merchandise Inventory 15	
			Cost of Goods Sold	15
6. Paid for merchandise costing $100. The supplier granted a 2% discount for prompt payment.	Accounts Payable 100		Accounts Payable 100	
	Purchases Discounts	2	Merchandise Inventory	2
	Cash	98	Cash	98

ASSIGNING COST TO INVENTORY AND COST OF GOODS SOLD

LO3 Compute the costs allocated to the ending inventory and cost of goods sold using different inventory methods.

To determine the cost of goods sold and ending inventory, it is important to understand:

1. the purpose of a physical inventory,

2. the specific calculations used under the periodic and perpetual systems, and

3. the role of the lower-of-cost-or-market rule.

Taking a Physical Inventory

Even under the perpetual inventory system, there will be differences between the actual inventory on the floor and the amount on the books. These differences are the result of breakage,

spoilage, and theft. Thieves rarely yell "Debit Loss Due to Theft and credit Merchandise Inventory" as they attempt to leave the store with merchandise under their coats.

Under the periodic system, the goods on hand at the end of the period are counted to allocate merchandise costs between sold and unsold goods. This process is called taking a **physical inventory**. A physical inventory is also important under the perpetual system. It verifies that the amount of merchandise actually held agrees with what is reported in the accounting records.

Taking a physical inventory can be a sizable task. Frequently, it is done after regular business hours. Some companies even close for a few days to take inventory. The ideal time to count the goods is when the quantity on hand is at its lowest level. A fiscal year that starts and ends at the time the stock of goods is normally at its lowest level is known as a **natural business year**. Such a year is used by many businesses for accounting purposes.

Various procedures are followed in taking an inventory to be sure that no items are missed and that no items are included more than once. Frequently, persons taking inventory work in pairs: one counts the items and the other records the information. Usually, this information is entered on a special form called an **inventory sheet**, like the one illustrated in Figure 13-3. The inventory sheet has columns for recording the description of each item, the quantity on hand, the cost per unit, and the extension.

FIGURE 13-3 Inventory Sheet

INVENTORY Aug. 31 20-- **Page** 1					
Sheet No. 1				Costed by C.M.H.	
Called by L.M.M.		Department A		Extended by C.M.H.	
Entered by K.N.		Location Storeroom		Examined by C.J.C.	

Description	Quantity	Unit	Unit Cost	Extensions	
Table Lamp	20	ea.	62.80	1,256.00	
Wall Rack	18	ea.	19.70	354.60	
Bookcase	7	ea.	88.10	616.70	
End Table	13	ea.	53.20	691.60	
Desk	6	ea.	158.30	949.80	
Total					6,465.10

Only goods that are the property of the company should be included in a physical inventory. Two special situations that require care to determine ownership are (1) goods held for sale on **consignment** and (2) goods **in transit**. Sometimes

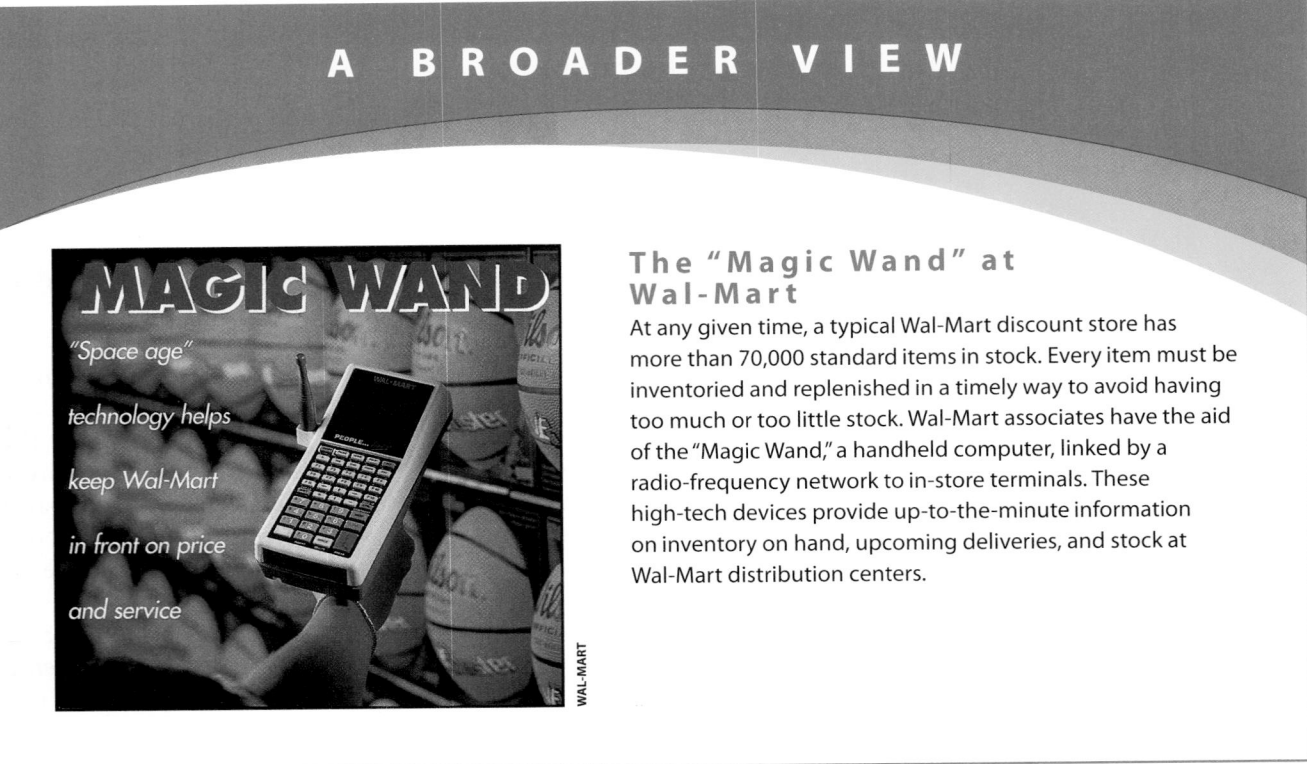

A BROADER VIEW

The "Magic Wand" at Wal-Mart

At any given time, a typical Wal-Mart discount store has more than 70,000 standard items in stock. Every item must be inventoried and replenished in a timely way to avoid having too much or too little stock. Wal-Mart associates have the aid of the "Magic Wand," a handheld computer, linked by a radio-frequency network to in-store terminals. These high-tech devices provide up-to-the-minute information on inventory on hand, upcoming deliveries, and stock at Wal-Mart distribution centers.

LEARNING KEY

Under FOB shipping point, the goods belong to the buyer as soon as they are shipped. Under FOB destination, the goods belong to the seller until they are received by the buyer.

one business will try to sell merchandise for another business or individual on a commission basis. This is called selling goods on consignment. Goods held on consignment remain the property of the shipper (**consignor**). They should not be included in the inventory of the company holding the goods (**consignee**).

To determine whether goods in transit at year-end should be included in inventory, we must know the FOB (free on board) terms. If goods are shipped FOB shipping point, the buyer pays for shipping and the goods belong to the buyer as soon as they are shipped. If goods are shipped FOB destination, the seller pays for shipping and the goods belong to the seller until they are received by the buyer.

After calculating the quantities of goods owned at the end of the period, the proper cost must be assigned to the inventory. In addition to the purchase price, we include delivery costs (freight-in), insurance, and, occasionally, storage fees. Therefore, cost means all necessary and reasonable costs incurred to get the goods to the buyer's place of business.

If all purchases of the same item were made at the same price per unit, computing the cost of the ending inventory would be simple. We would multiply the number of units by the cost per unit. In a world of changing prices, however, identical items are purchased at different times and at different costs per unit. Of the goods available for sale, how do we decide which units were sold and which units remain on the shelf? As shown in Figure 13-4, this decision affects the income statement and balance sheet. The following four inventory methods have become generally accepted for answering this question:

1. Specific identification

2. First-in, first-out (FIFO)

3. Weighted-average

4. Last-in, first-out (LIFO)

These methods may be applied under the periodic or perpetual inventory systems.

FIGURE 13-4   Allocation of Goods Available for Sale to Cost of Goods Sold and Ending Inventory

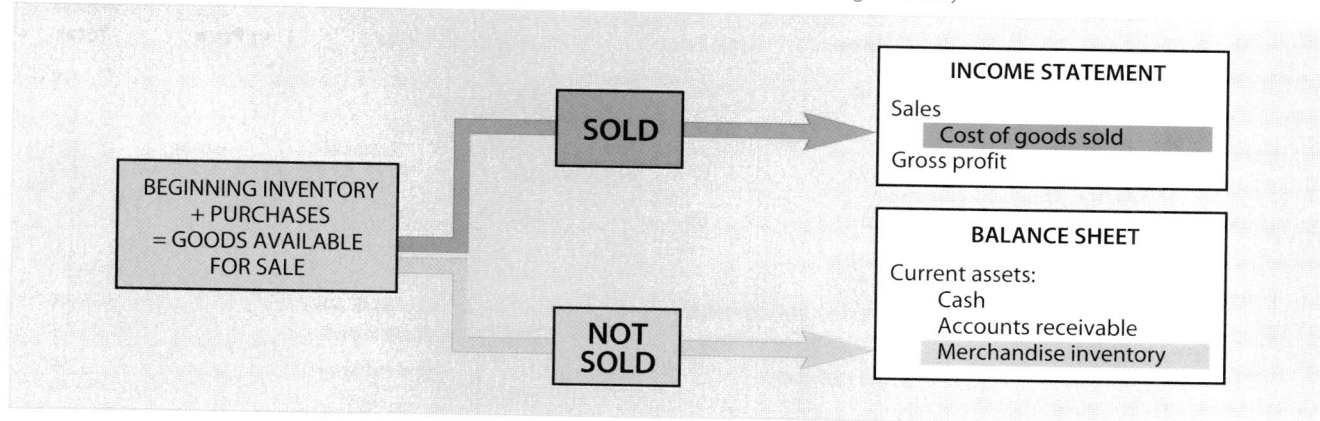

The Periodic Inventory System

Specific Identification Method

When each unit of inventory can be specifically identified, the **specific identification method** can be used. To use this method, inventory items must be physically different from each other, or they must have serial numbers. Examples include cars, motorcycles, furniture, appliances, and fine jewelry. When a unit is sold, its cost is determined from the supplier's invoice. Unless computerized, this method is practical only for businesses in which sales volume is relatively low and inventory unit value is relatively high. Otherwise, record keeping becomes expensive and time consuming.

To illustrate how specific identification costing works, assume the following data for an inventory of one specific model of children's bicycles:

Children's Bicycles (Model ZX007)

	Units	Unit Price	Total Cost
On hand at start of period	40	$62	$ 2,480
Purchased during period:			
1st purchase	60	65	3,900
2nd purchase	80	67	5,360
3rd purchase	70	68	4,760
Number of units available for sale	250		$16,500
On hand at end of period	50		
Number of units sold during period	200		

Of the 200 units sold during the period, the bicycle serial numbers show that 30 were from the beginning inventory, 50 were from the first purchase, 60 were from the second purchase, and 60 were from the last purchase. The cost of goods sold and the cost of inventory at the end of the period are determined as shown in Figure 13-5.

FIGURE 13-5 Specific Identification Inventory Method

	COST OF GOODS SOLD			COST OF ENDING INVENTORY		
	Units	Unit Price	Total	Units	Unit Price	Total
Beginning inventory	30	$62	$ 1,860	10	$62	$ 620
1st purchase	50	65	3,250	10	65	650
2nd purchase	60	67	4,020	20	67	1,340
3rd purchase	60	68	4,080	10	68	680
Total	200		$13,210	50		$ 3,290
Alternative calculation given goods available for sale and cost of goods sold or ending inventory.	Cost of goods available for sale		$16,500	Cost of goods available for sale		$ 16,500
	Less cost of ending inventory		(3,290)	Less cost of goods sold		(13,210)
	Cost of goods sold		$13,210	Cost of ending inventory		$ 3,290

First-In, First-Out (FIFO) Method

Another widely used method of allocating merchandise cost is called the **first-in, first-out,** or **FIFO, method.** This costing method assumes that the first goods purchased were the first goods sold. Therefore, the latest goods purchased remain in inventory.

Whenever possible, a business will attempt to sell the older goods first. This is particularly true of businesses that sell perishable items or merchandise that may become obsolete. Grocery stores, fresh fruit stands, and computer software businesses are good examples. These businesses must rotate their stock forward. They pull the oldest bread, milk, fruit, and vegetables to the front of the shelves and try to sell all copies of the current software before a new version arrives. FIFO costing is, therefore, widely used because it often follows the actual movement of goods. It assumes that the oldest units have been sold and the newest or freshest units are in the ending inventory.

Applying FIFO to the bicycle inventory data, the cost of goods sold and the cost of inventory at the end of the period are determined as shown in Figure 13-6.

FIGURE 13-6   FIFO Inventory Method

	COST OF GOODS SOLD			COST OF ENDING INVENTORY		
	Units	Unit Price	Total	Units	Unit Price	Total
Beginning inventory	40	$62	$ 2,480		$62	$ 0
1st purchase	60	65	3,900		65	0
2nd purchase	80	67	5,360		67	0
3rd purchase	20	68	1,360	50	68	3,400
Total	200		$13,100	50		$ 3,400
Alternative calculation given goods available for sale and cost of goods sold or ending inventory.	Cost of goods available for sale		$16,500	Cost of goods available for sale		$ 16,500
	Less cost of ending inventory		(3,400)	Less cost of goods sold		(13,100)
	Cost of goods sold		$13,100	Cost of ending inventory		$ 3,400

Note that the 50 items on hand at the end of the period are considered to be those most recently purchased.

FIFO costing is widely used because businesses have used this method for a long time. Accountants are reluctant to change a long-followed method of accounting when such a change would affect the comparability of their income calculations over a period of years. **Consistency** based on comparability is an important accounting principle.

Weighted-Average Method

Another method of allocating merchandise cost is called the **weighted-average method,** or **average cost method.** This costing method is based on the average cost of identical units.

Consider the bicycle inventory data again. The average cost of identical units is determined by dividing the total cost of units available for sale ($16,500) by the total number of units available for sale (250).

$$\frac{\$16,500 \text{ (cost of units available for sale)}}{250 \text{ (units available for sale)}} = \$66 \text{ weighted-average cost per unit}$$

The cost of goods sold and the cost of the end-of-period inventory are calculated as follows:

Cost of goods sold	200 units @ $66 =	$13,200
Cost of ending inventory	50 units @ $66 =	3,300
Total	250 units	$16,500

There is a logical appeal to the weighted-average method of allocating cost between goods sold and goods on hand. In this example, one-fifth (50) of the total units available (250) were unsold. The weighted-average method assigns one-fifth ($3,300) of the total cost ($16,500) to these goods.

Last-In, First-Out (LIFO) Method

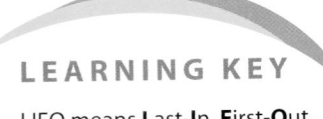

LEARNING KEY

LIFO means **L**ast-**I**n, **F**irst-**O**ut.

A fourth method of allocating merchandise cost is called the **last-in, first-out**, or **LIFO, method.** It assumes that the sales in the period were made from the most recently purchased goods. Therefore, the earliest goods purchased remain in inventory.

This physical flow is associated with businesses selling products that are not perishable or likely to become obsolete, and may be difficult to handle. Imagine a large barrel of nails at a lumberyard. Customers take nails from the top of the barrel. When the supply gets low, new nails are simply piled on top of the old ones. There is no need to rotate the nails from the bottom to the top of the barrel.

Applying LIFO to the bicycle inventory data, the cost of goods sold and the cost of inventory at the end of the period are determined as shown in Figure 13-7.

FIGURE 13-7   LIFO Inventory Method

	COST OF GOODS SOLD			COST OF ENDING INVENTORY		
	Units	**Unit Price**	**Total**	**Units**	**Unit Price**	**Total**
Beginning inventory	0	$62	$ 0	40	$62	$ 2,480
1st purchase	50	65	3,250	10	65	650
2nd purchase	80	67	5,360		67	0
3rd purchase	70	68	4,760		68	0
Total	200		$13,370	50		$ 3,130
Alternative calculation given goods available for sale and cost of goods sold or ending inventory.	Cost of goods available for sale		$16,500	Cost of goods available for sale		$ 16,500
	Less cost of ending inventory		(3,130)	Less cost of goods sold		(13,370)
	Cost of goods sold		$13,370	Cost of ending inventory		$ 3,130

Note that the 50 units on hand at the end of the period are considered to be the 40 units in the beginning inventory plus 10 of the units from the first purchase.

The LIFO method has been justified on the grounds that the physical movement of goods in some businesses is actually last-in, first-out. This is rarely the case, but the method has become popular for other reasons. One persuasive argument for the use of the LIFO method is that it matches the most current cost of items purchased against the current sales revenue. When the most current costs of purchases are subtracted from sales revenue, the impact of changing prices on the resulting gross profit figure is minimized. In the opinion of many accountants, this is proper and desirable.

Another reason for the popularity of the LIFO method is its effect on income taxes. When prices are rising, net income calculated under the LIFO method is less than net income calculated under either the FIFO or the weighted-average method. Since the net income amount under LIFO is less, the related income tax will be less. The reverse would be true if prices were falling. However, periods of falling prices over the past two centuries have been few and brief.

Opponents of the LIFO method contend that its use causes old, out-of-date inventory costs to be shown on the balance sheet. The theoretical and practical merits of FIFO versus LIFO are the subject of much professional debate.

Physical Flows and Cost Flows

Of the four inventory costing methods described, only the specific identification costing method will necessarily reflect cost flows that match physical flows of goods. Each of the other three methods—FIFO, weighted-average, and LIFO—is based on assumed cost flows. The assumed cost flows *are not required to reflect the actual physical movement of goods* within the company. Any one of the three assumed cost flow methods could be used under any set of physical flow conditions. For example, a fresh fruit stand with an actual FIFO flow of inventory may use LIFO for accounting purposes. Similarly, a supplier of building materials that sells nails, lumber, and sand off the top of the pile may use FIFO even though the physical flow of goods is LIFO.

LEARNING KEY

The inventory method used does not have to match the physical flow of goods.

Comparison of Methods

To compare the results of the four inventory methods, let's assume that the 200 bicycle units in our example were sold for $18,000. Figure 13-8 contrasts the ending inventory, cost of goods sold, and gross profit under each of the four methods.

FIGURE 13-8   Comparison of Inventory Methods

	SPECIFIC IDENTIFICATION		FIFO		WEIGHTED-AVERAGE		LIFO	
Sales		$18,000		$18,000		$18,000		$18,000
Cost of goods sold:								
Beginning inventory	$ 2,480		$ 2,480		$ 2,480		$ 2,480	
Purchases	14,020		14,020		14,020		14,020	
Goods available for sale	$16,500		$16,500		$16,500		$16,500	
Less ending inventory	3,290		3,400		3,300		3,130	
Cost of goods sold		13,210		13,100		13,200		13,370
Gross profit		$ 4,790		$ 4,900		$ 4,800		$ 4,630

During periods of rising prices, we can observe the following: LIFO generally produces the highest cost of goods sold, lowest gross profit, and lowest ending inventory. Since the most recent units purchased are assumed to have been sold, the most recent costs are matched against revenues and this provides the best measure of gross profit and net income. After all, the units sold must be replaced at current prices. However, under LIFO, the first units purchased are assumed to remain in inventory (FISH: First-In, Still Here). This means that units purchased many years ago may remain in the ending inventory. These dollar amounts are likely to have little meaning when measuring the firm's performance or financial health.

FIFO generally produces the lowest cost of goods sold, highest gross profit, and highest ending inventory. Since the last units purchased are assumed to be in ending inventory, these most recent costs provide the best inventory measure on the balance sheet (LISH: Last-In, Still Here). However, under FIFO, the first units purchased are assumed to have been sold. This means that somewhat older prices are used to compute cost of goods sold and gross profit than under LIFO. Thus, these measures are somewhat less useful than those computed under LIFO.

The weighted-average inventory method produces measures between LIFO and FIFO. The specific identification method will produce measures based on the actual units sold.

The Internal Revenue Service requires the use of the same inventory method for tax and financial reporting purposes. Since LIFO generally produces the highest cost of goods sold, lowest gross profit, and lowest tax liability, many firms use the LIFO inventory method to minimize federal income taxes. The tax dollars saved are then available for other purposes.

As discussed earlier, keep the following in mind when selecting the inventory method to be used by a business:

1. The physical flow of the inventory does not need to match the flow assumed by the inventory method.

2. The consistency principle requires that the same accounting methods be followed from period to period. Although it is acceptable to make changes, it is not appropriate to switch back and forth from FIFO to LIFO based on the desire to maximize or minimize earnings for a given year.

The Perpetual Inventory System

Under the perpetual inventory system, a continuous record is maintained for the quantities and costs of goods on hand at all times. The general ledger account for Merchandise Inventory under such a system is somewhat like the account for Cash. It provides a chronological record of each addition (purchase) and subtraction (sale). The balance of the account at any time shows the cost of goods that should be on hand.

When perpetual inventory records are kept, the merchandise inventory account in the general ledger is usually a controlling account. A subsidiary ledger is maintained with an account for each type of merchandise. These accounts are often recorded on cards or in computer files. As shown in Figure 13-9, the subsidiary accounts are designed to handle additions and subtractions and determine the new balance after each change. Goods sold usually are assigned cost on either a FIFO, moving-average, or LIFO basis. Procedures for applying the FIFO method in a perpetual inventory system are similar to those illustrated for a periodic system. The first merchandise purchased is treated as the first merchandise sold. The illustration in Figure 13-9 is based on the FIFO method. The specific techniques used to apply the moving-average and LIFO methods in a perpetual system are more complicated. They are illustrated in the chapter appendix.

FIGURE 13-9   Perpetual Inventory Record: FIFO Method

DATE	PURCHASES			COST OF GOODS SOLD				INVENTORY ON HAND				
	Units	Cost/Unit	Total	Units	Cost/Unit	CGS	Cumulative CGS	Layer	Units	Cost/Unit	Layer Cost	Total
Jan. 1 (BI)								(1)	40	$62	$2,480	$2,480
Feb. 15				30	$62	$1,860	$ 1,860	(1)	10	$62	$ 620	$ 620
Mar. 1	60	$65	$3,900					(1)	10	$62	$ 620	
								(2)	60	65	3,900	$4,520
Apr. 1				10	$62	$ 620		(2)	30	$65	$1,950	
				30	$65	1,950	$ 4,430					$1,950
May 15	80	$67	$5,360					(2)	30	$65	$1,950	
								(3)	80	67	5,360	$7,310
June 30				30	$65	$1,950		(3)	20	$67	$1,340	
				60	67	4,020	$10,400					$1,340
Aug. 28	70	$68	$4,760					(3)	20	$67	$1,340	
								(4)	70	68	4,760	$6,100
Oct. 30				20	$67	$1,340		(4)	50	$68	$3,400	
				20	68	1,360	$13,100					$3,400
Cost of Goods Sold during 20--							$13,100					

BI: Beginning Inventory

Lower-of-Cost-or-Market Method of Inventory Valuation

It is a well-established tradition in accounting that gains should not be recognized unless a sale has occurred. If the value of an asset increases while it is being held, no formal entry of the gain is made on the books. On the other hand, if an asset's value declines while it is being held, it is generally considered proper to recognize a loss. This is in keeping with the accounting practice of **conservatism**, which states that when in doubt, the lower asset value and net income measure should be used. Thus, we should never anticipate gains, but we should always anticipate and account for losses.

As applied to inventory, conservatism means that if the value of inventory declines while it is being held, the loss should be recognized in the period of the decline. The purpose of the **lower-of-cost-or-market method** is to recognize such losses on the income statement and to report the lower inventory valuation on the balance sheet.

In applying the lower-of-cost-or-market method, "**cost**" means the dollar amount calculated using one of the four inventory costing methods. "**Market**" means the cost to replace the inventory. It is the price in the market in which goods are purchased by the business—not the price in the market in which they are normally sold by the business. The lower-of-cost-or-market method assumes that a decline in the purchase (replacement) price of inventory is accompanied by a decline in the selling price. In this sense, a decline in the purchase (replacement) price signals a decline in the value of the inventory.

To illustrate the lower-of-cost-or-market method, assume the following end-of-period inventory data for three items:

Item	Recorded Purchase Cost	End-of-Period Market Value	Lower-of-Cost-or-Market
1	$ 8,000	$ 7,000	$ 7,000
2	9,000	10,000	9,000
3	7,000	6,500	6,500
	$24,000	$23,500	$22,500

The illustration shows two ways to calculate the lower-of-cost-or-market. First, the lower-of-cost-or-market method can be applied to the total inventory. This involves comparing the $24,000 total cost with the $23,500 *total end-of-period market value*. Under the second approach, the method is applied to each item in inventory. This involves comparing the $24,000 total cost with the $22,500 lower-of-cost-or-market value determined by comparing cost with market value for *each item*. Either approach is acceptable, but the one chosen should be applied consistently across periods.

The difference between the cost and market value is considered a loss due to holding inventory. Normally it is charged to an account such as **Loss on Write-Down of Inventory**. For example, based on application of the method to the total inventory in the previous illustration, a $500 loss ($24,000 − $23,500) is recognized as follows:

14		Loss on Write-Down of Inventory		5 0 0 00		14
15		Merchandise Inventory			5 0 0 00	15
16		To recognize loss in value of inventory held				16

The loss due to write-down of inventory should be reported on the income statement as an expense. Although not a preferred treatment, some businesses include it in cost of goods sold if the amounts are small.

ESTIMATING ENDING INVENTORY AND COST OF GOODS SOLD

LO4 Estimate the ending inventory and cost of goods sold by using the gross profit and retail inventory methods.

Many businesses prepare monthly or quarterly financial statements. To do this, the business must estimate the inventory at the end of the month or quarter and the cost of goods sold for the period. This is not a problem for businesses using the perpetual inventory method. Although these amounts need to be verified by a physical inventory at the end of the year, the unverified amounts are generally reliable estimates and can be used for these "interim" statements.

Businesses using the periodic inventory method must use other methods to estimate the ending inventory and cost of goods sold. Two generally accepted methods are the gross profit method and the retail inventory method.

Gross Profit Method of Estimating Inventory

Under the **gross profit method**, a business's normal gross profit (net sales − cost of goods sold) is used to estimate the cost of goods sold and ending inventory. To illustrate the gross profit method, assume the following data with respect to Groomer Company:

Inventory, start of period	$80,000
Net purchases, first month	$70,000
Net sales, first month	$110,000
Normal gross profit as a percentage of sales	40%

The estimated cost of goods sold for the month and the estimated merchandise inventory at the end of the month would be determined as shown in Figure 13-10.

FIGURE 13-10   Steps for the Gross Profit Method

STEP 1	Compute the cost of goods available for sale.	Cost of goods available for sale:		
		Inventory, start of period	$ 80,000	
		Net purchases, first month	70,000	
		Cost of goods available for sale		$150,000
STEP 2	Estimate cost of goods sold by deducting the normal gross profit from net sales.	Estimated cost of goods sold:		
		Net sales	$110,000	
		Normal gross profit ($110,000 × 40%)	44,000	
		Estimated cost of goods sold		66,000
STEP 3	Estimate the ending inventory by deducting cost of goods sold from the cost of goods available for sale.	Estimated end-of-month inventory		$ 84,000

This calculation is appropriate only if the firm's normal gross profit as a percentage of net sales has been relatively stable over time. This type of calculation also can be used to test the reasonableness of the amount of inventory that was computed on the basis of a physical count. A large difference between the two amounts might indicate a mistake in the count, a mistake in the costing of the items, or a marked change in the gross profit rate. The gross profit procedure also can be used to estimate the cost of an inventory that was destroyed by fire or other casualty.

Retail Method of Estimating Inventory

Many retail businesses, such as department and clothing stores, use a variation of the gross profit method to calculate cost of goods sold and ending inventory. The procedure used, called the **retail method** of inventory, requires keeping records of both the cost and selling (retail) prices of all goods purchased. This information can be used to estimate cost of goods sold and ending inventory, as shown in Figure 13-11.

FIGURE 13-11   Steps in the Retail Inventory Method

			COST	RETAIL
STEP 1	Compute the cost of goods available for sale at cost and retail.	Inventory, start of period	$ 60,000	$ 85,000
		Net purchases during period	126,000	163,000
		Goods available for sale	$186,000	$248,000
STEP 2	Compute the ending inventory at retail by subtracting sales at retail from goods available for sale at retail.	Less net sales for period		180,000
		Inventory, end of period, at retail		$ 68,000
STEP 3	Compute the cost-to-retail ratio by dividing the cost of goods available for sale by the retail value of the goods available for sale.	Ratio of cost-to-retail prices of goods available for sale ($186,000 ÷ $248,000)		75%
STEP 4	Estimate the cost of the ending inventory by multiplying the ending inventory at retail (step 2) by the cost-to-retail ratio.	Inventory, end of period, at estimated cost (75% of $68,000)	(51,000)	
STEP 5	Estimate cost of goods sold by: a. multiplying sales at retail by the cost-to-retail ratio, or b. subtracting the estimated ending inventory from the cost of goods available for sale.	Estimated cost of goods sold (or, sales of $180,000 × 75% = $135,000)	$135,000	

Learning Objectives	Key Points to Remember

LO1 Explain the impact of merchandise inventory on the financial statements.

The cost of goods available for sale during the accounting period must be divided between the cost of goods sold and the ending merchandise inventory. Cost of goods sold is reported on the income statement and used to determine the gross profit for the period. The ending merchandise inventory is reported as a current asset on the balance sheet. Figure 13-12 illustrates the allocation of cost of goods available for sale into cost of goods sold and ending inventory.

FIGURE 13-12   Allocation of Goods Available for Sale to Cost of Goods Sold and Ending Inventory

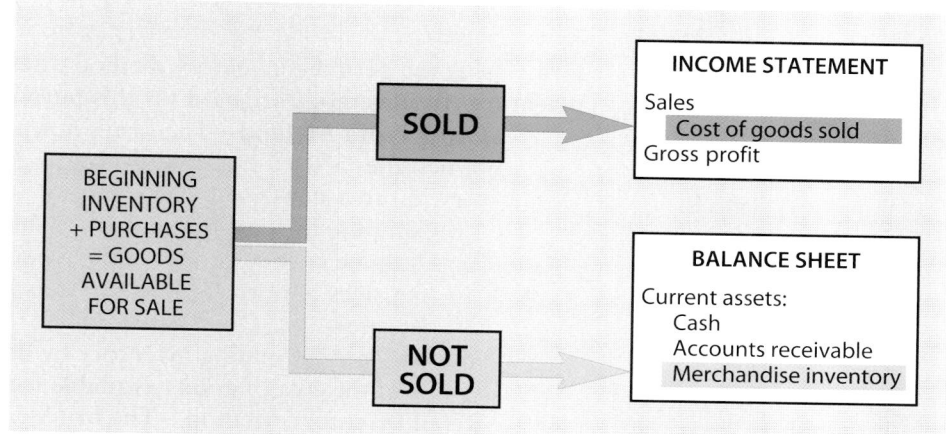

LO2 Describe the two principal systems of accounting for merchandise inventory—the periodic system and the perpetual system.

There are two systems of accounting for merchandise.

Periodic Inventory System
1. The purchases account is debited for the cost of all goods purchased.
2. The sales account is credited for the selling prices of all goods sold.
3. At the end of the accounting period, a physical inventory is taken, and the following formula is applied to calculate cost of goods sold:

Beginning Inventory (last year's ending physical count)
+ Net Purchases (account balance at end of this year)
= Cost of Goods Available for Sale
− Ending Inventory (this year's ending physical count)
= Cost of Goods Sold (for this year)

Perpetual Inventory System
1. The merchandise inventory account is debited for all purchases.
2. The cost of goods sold account is debited, and the merchandise inventory account is credited for all sales.
3. Thus, the merchandise inventory account provides a running balance of the goods on hand.

Learning Objectives	Key Points to Remember
LO3 **Compute the costs allocated to the ending inventory and cost of goods sold using different inventory methods.**	One of the following four inventory methods is generally used to determine the costs assigned to the goods sold and ending inventory: • Specific identification • FIFO: first-in, first-out • Weighted-average • LIFO: last-in, first-out The actual physical flow of inventory does not have to match the method used. During periods of rising prices, LIFO produces the lowest net income, and FIFO produces the highest net income.

LO4 **Estimate the ending inventory and cost of goods sold by using the gross profit and retail inventory methods.**	Firms using the periodic inventory method often need to estimate their inventory. Two methods are used for this purpose.
	• **Gross Profit Method**—The firm's normal gross profit as a percentage of net sales is used to estimate cost of goods sold and ending inventory in three steps.
	  1. Compute the cost of goods available for sale.
	  2. Estimate cost of goods sold by deducting the normal gross profit (net sales × normal gross profit as percentage of net sales) from net sales.
	  3. Estimate the ending inventory by deducting cost of goods sold from the cost of goods available for sale.
	• **Retail Inventory Method**—The firm's ratio of cost-to-retail prices of goods available for sale is used to estimate ending inventory and cost of goods sold in five basic steps:
	  1. Compute the cost of goods available for sale at cost and retail.
	  2. Compute the ending inventory at retail by subtracting sales at retail from goods available for sale at retail.
	  3. Compute the cost-to-retail ratio by dividing the cost of goods available for sale by the retail value of the goods available for sale.
	  4. Estimate the cost of ending inventory by multiplying the ending inventory at retail (step 2) by the cost-to-retail ratio.
	  5. Estimate cost of goods sold by:
	    a. multiplying sales at retail by the cost-to-retail ratio, or
	    b. subtracting the estimated ending inventory from the cost of goods available for sale.

DEMONSTRATION PROBLEM

Fialka Company's beginning inventory and purchases during the fiscal year ended October 31, 20-2, were as follows:

		Units	Unit Price	Total Cost
November 1, 20-1	Beginning inventory	500	$25.00	$ 12,500
November 12, 20-1	1st purchase	600	26.25	15,750
December 28, 20-1	2nd purchase	400	27.50	11,000
March 29, 20-2	3rd purchase	1,000	28.00	28,000
May 31, 20-2	4th purchase	750	28.50	21,375
July 29, 20-2	5th purchase	350	29.00	10,150
August 30, 20-2	6th purchase	675	30.00	20,250
October 21, 20-2	7th purchase	225	31.00	6,975
		4,500		$126,000

There are 1,600 units of inventory on hand on October 31, 20-2.

REQUIRED

1. Calculate the total amount to be assigned to cost of goods sold for the fiscal year and ending inventory on October 31, 20-2, under each of the following periodic inventory methods:

    (a) FIFO
    (b) LIFO
    (c) Weighted-average cost (round calculations to two decimal places)

2. Assume that the market price per unit (cost to replace) of Fialka's inventory on October 31, 20-2, was $29. Calculate the total amount to be assigned to the ending inventory on October 31, 20-2, under each of the following methods:

    (a) FIFO lower-of-cost-or-market
    (b) Weighted-average lower-of-cost-or-market

3. Assume that a fire destroyed Fialka's store and all inventory on October 31, just prior to taking a physical inventory. Thus, Fialka must estimate the ending inventory and cost of goods sold. During the fiscal year ended October 31, 20-2, net sales of $134,000 were made. The normal gross profit rate is 40%. Use the gross profit method to estimate the cost of goods sold for the fiscal year ended October 31, 20-2, and the inventory on October 31, 20-2.

(continued)

Solution 1a.

Date		FIFO INVENTORY METHOD Cost of Goods Sold			Cost of Ending Inventory		
20-1/-2		Units	Unit Price	Total	Units	Unit Price	Total
Nov. 1	Beginning inventory	500	$25.00	$ 12,500		$25.00	$ 0
Nov. 12	1st purchase	600	26.25	15,750		26.25	0
Dec. 28	2nd purchase	400	27.50	11,000		27.50	0
Mar. 29	3rd purchase	1,000	28.00	28,000		28.00	0
May 31	4th purchase	400	28.50	11,400	350	28.50	9,975
July 29	5th purchase		29.00	0	350	29.00	10,150
Aug. 30	6th purchase		30.00	0	675	30.00	20,250
Oct. 21	7th purchase		31.00	0	225	31.00	6,975
	Total	2,900		$ 78,650	1,600		$ 47,350

Alternative calculation given goods available for sale and cost of goods sold or ending inventory.	Cost of goods available for sale	$126,000	Cost of goods available for sale	$126,000
	Less cost of ending inventory	(47,350)	Less cost of goods sold	(78,650)
	Cost of goods sold	$ 78,650	Cost of ending inventory	$ 47,350

1b.

Date		LIFO INVENTORY METHOD Cost of Goods Sold			Cost of Ending Inventory		
20-1/-2		Units	Unit Price	Total	Units	Unit Price	Total
Nov. 1	Beginning inventory		$25.00	$ 0	500	$25.00	$ 12,500
Nov. 12	1st purchase		26.25	0	600	26.25	15,750
Dec. 28	2nd purchase		27.50	0	400	27.50	11,000
Mar. 29	3rd purchase	900	28.00	25,200	100	28.00	2,800
May 31	4th purchase	750	28.50	21,375		28.50	0
July 29	5th purchase	350	29.00	10,150		29.00	0
Aug. 30	6th purchase	675	30.00	20,250		30.00	0
Oct. 21	7th purchase	225	31.00	6,975		31.00	0
	Total	2,900		$ 83,950	1,600		$ 42,050

Alternative calculation given goods available for sale and cost of goods sold or ending inventory.	Cost of goods available for sale	$126,000	Cost of goods available for sale	$126,000
	Less cost of ending inventory	(42,050)	Less cost of goods sold	(83,950)
	Cost of goods sold	$ 83,950	Cost of ending inventory	$ 42,050

1c. Weighted-average method:
Average cost per unit: $126,000 ÷ 4,500 units = $28
Inventory, October 31, 20-2:
       1,600 units @ $28 = $44,800
Cost of goods sold for 20-1/-2:
       2,900 units @ $28 = $81,200

2a. FIFO lower-of-cost-or-market:
FIFO cost $47,350
Market 1,600 units @ $29   46,400
Choose market   46,400

2b. Weighted-average lower-of-cost-or-market:
Weighted-average cost $44,800
Market 1,600 units @ $29   46,400
Choose weighted-average cost   44,800

3.   Estimated inventory on October 31, 20-2:
Inventory, November 1, 20-1 $ 12,500
Net purchases, November 1, 20-1
   through October 31, 20-2   113,500
Cost of goods available for sale $126,000
Estimated cost of goods sold:
   Net sales $134,000
   Normal gross profit ($134,000 × 40%)   53,600
Estimated cost of goods sold   80,400
Estimated inventory on October 31, 20-2 $ 45,600

KEY TERMS

average cost method (499)   See weighted-average method.

conservatism (503)   The accounting practice of conservatism states that we should never anticipate gains, but always anticipate and account for losses. As applied to inventory, conservatism means that if the value of inventory declines while it is being held, the loss should be recognized in the period of the decline.

consignee (497)   The company holding the merchandise of another business to be sold.

consignment (496)   Goods that are held by one business for sale but that are owned by another business.

consignor (497)   The owner of the merchandise that is held by another business.

consistency (499)   The principle that states that a business should use the same accounting methods from period to period. This improves the comparability of the financial statements over time.

cost (503)   In applying the lower-of-cost-or-market method, cost means the dollar amount calculated using one of the four inventory costing methods.

first-in, first-out (FIFO) method (499)   A method of allocating merchandise cost which assumes that the first goods purchased were the first goods sold and, therefore, that the latest goods purchased remain in inventory.

gross profit method (505)   A method of estimating inventory in which a business's normal gross profit percentage is used to estimate the cost of goods sold and ending inventory.

in transit (496)   Goods that are in the process of being shipped between the seller and the buyer.

inventory sheet (495)   A form used for recording inventory items. It has columns for recording the description of each item, the quantity on hand, the cost per unit, and the extension.

last-in, first-out (LIFO) method (500)   A method of allocating merchandise cost which assumes that the sales in the period were made from the most recently purchased goods. Therefore, the earliest goods purchased remain in inventory.

Loss on Write-Down of Inventory (504)   This account is debited when the market value (replacement cost) of the inventory is below cost when applying the lower of cost or market method of inventory valuation. It is reported on the income statement as an expense.

lower-of-cost-or-market method (503)   An inventory valuation method under which inventory is valued at the lower of cost or market value (replacement cost).

market (503)   In applying the lower-of-cost-or-market method, market means the cost to replace the inventory. It is the prevailing price in the market in which goods are purchased—not the prevailing price in the market in which they are normally sold.

natural business year (495)   A fiscal year that starts and ends at the time the stock of goods is normally at its lowest level.

periodic inventory system (494)   Under this system, the ending inventory and cost of goods sold are determined at the end of the accounting period, when a physical inventory is taken.

perpetual inventory system (494)   Under this system, the merchandise inventory and cost of goods sold accounts are updated when merchandise is bought and sold.

physical inventory (495)   A physical count of the goods on hand.

retail method, (505)   A variation of the gross profit method that is used by many retail businesses, such as department and clothing stores, to estimate the cost of goods sold and ending inventory.

specific identification method, (498)   A method of allocating merchandise cost in which each unit of inventory is specifically identified.

weighted-average method, (499)   A method of allocating merchandise cost based on the average cost of identical units. The average cost of identical units is determined by dividing the total cost of units available for sale by the total number of units available for sale.

Self-Study Test Questions

True/False

1. An overstatement of ending inventory in the year 20-1 will cause net income to be overstated in the year 20-1.

2. An understatement of ending inventory in the year 20-1 will cause net income to be overstated in the year 20-2, assuming no other errors.

3. Under the perpetual system of accounting for inventory, the current merchandise inventory and the cost of goods sold are not determined until the end of the accounting period when a physical inventory is taken.

4. A fiscal year that starts and ends at the time the stock of goods is normally at its lowest level is known as a natural business year.

5. If goods are shipped FOB shipping point, the seller pays for the shipping costs.

Multiple Choice

1. Goods held on consignment remain the property of the

    (a) consignee.   (c) buyer.
    (b) consignor.   (d) seller.

2. In times of rising prices, the inventory cost method that will yield the lowest net income is

    (a) FIFO.   (c) LIFO.
    (b) weighted-average.   (d) none of the above.

3. In times of rising prices, the inventory cost method that will yield the highest cost of goods sold is

    (a) LIFO.   (c) FIFO.
    (b) weighted-average.   (d) none of the above.

4. In the application of "lower-of-cost-or-market," market is the

    (a) lowest sales price.   (c) replacement cost.
    (b) highest sales price. (d) average sales price.

5. An understatement of ending inventory in the year 20-1 will cause the owner's equity account at the end of the year 20-2, assuming no other errors, to be

    (a) understated.   (c) overstated.
    (b) correctly stated.   (d) none of the above.

The answers to the Self-Study Test Questions are at the end of the text.

REVIEW QUESTIONS

LO1   1. What financial statements are affected by an error in the ending inventory?

LO2   2. What is the main difference between the periodic system of accounting for inventory and the perpetual system of accounting for inventory?

LO3   3. Is a physical inventory necessary under the periodic system? Why or why not?

LO3   4. Is a physical inventory necessary under the perpetual system? Why or why not?

LO3   5. In a period of rising prices, which inventory method will result in:

     (a) the highest cost of goods sold?
     (b) the lowest cost of goods sold?
     (c) the highest ending inventory?
     (d) the lowest ending inventory?
     (e) the highest gross profit?
     (f) the lowest gross profit?

LO3   6. What two factors are taken into account by the weighted-average method of merchandise cost allocation?

LO3   7. Which inventory method always follows the actual physical flow of merchandise?

LO3   8. When lower-of-cost-or-market is assigned to the items that comprise the ending merchandise inventory, what does "cost" mean? What does "market" mean?

LO4   9. List the three steps followed under the gross profit method of estimating inventory.

LO4   10. List the five steps followed under the retail method of estimating inventory.

REVISITING THE OPENER

In the chapter opener on page 491, you are asked to consider an inventory problem. Most businesses buy identical units of inventory, but at different costs throughout the year. If all of the units look the same, how does the business know which units were sold and the cost of those units? Does it matter?

SERIES A EXERCISES

E 13-1A (LO1)

INVENTORY ERRORS Assume that in year 1, the ending merchandise inventory is overstated by $50,000. If this is the only error in years 1 and 2, indicate which items will be understated, overstated, or correctly stated for years 1 and 2.

	Year 1	Year 2
Ending merchandise inventory	_____	_____
Beginning merchandise inventory	_____	_____
Cost of goods sold	_____	_____
Gross profit	_____	_____
Net income	_____	_____
Ending owner's capital	_____	_____

E 13-2A (LO2)

JOURNAL ENTRIES—PERIODIC INVENTORY Bill Diamond owns a business called Diamond Distributors. The following transactions took place during January of the current year. Journalize the transactions in a general journal using the periodic inventory method.

Jan. 5 Purchased merchandise on account from Prestigious Jewelers, $3,700.

8 Paid freight charge on merchandise purchased, $200.

12 Sold merchandise on account to Diamonds Unlimited, $4,900.

15 Received a credit memo from Prestigious Jewelers for merchandise returned, $600.

22 Issued a credit memo to Diamonds Unlimited for merchandise returned, $800.

E 13-3A (LO2)

JOURNAL ENTRIES—PERPETUAL INVENTORY Sandy Johnson owns a small variety store. The following transactions took place during March of the current year. Journalize the transactions in a general journal using the perpetual inventory method.

Mar. 3 Purchased merchandise on account from City Galleria, $2,700.

7 Paid freight charge on merchandise purchased, $175.

13 Sold merchandise on account to Amber Specialties, $3,000. The cost of the merchandise was $1,800.

18 Received a credit memo from City Galleria for merchandise returned, $500.

22 Issued a credit memo to Amber Specialties for merchandise returned, $400. The cost of the merchandise was $240.

E 13-4A (LO3)
✓ End. inv.: $45,500

ENDING INVENTORY COSTS Sandy Chen owns a small specialty store, named Chen's Chattel, whose year-end is June 30. Determine the total amount that should be included in Chen's Chattel's year-end inventory. A physical inventory taken on June 30 reveals the following:

Cost of merchandise on the showroom floor and in the warehouse	$37,800
Goods held on consignment (consignor is National Manufacturer)	6,400
Goods that Chen's Chattel, as the consignor, has for sale at the location of the Grand Avenue Vista	4,600

(continued)

Sales invoices indicate that merchandise was shipped on June 29, terms FOB shipping point, delivered at buyer's receiving dock on July 3 $3,800

Sales invoices indicate that merchandise was shipped on June 25, terms FOB destination, delivered at buyer's receiving dock on July 5   3,100

E 13-5A (L03)

✓ 1. End. inv., FIFO: $300.00; Weighted-avg.: $242.50

LOWER-OF-COST-OR-MARKET Stalberg Company's beginning inventory and purchases during the fiscal year ended December 31, 20--, were as follows:

		Units	Unit Price	Total Cost
Jan. 1	Beginning inventory	10	$20	$200
Mar. 5	1st purchase	10	22	220
Sept. 9	2nd purchase	10	25	250
Dec. 8	3rd purchase	10	30	300
		40		$970

There are 10 units of inventory on hand on December 31.

1. Calculate the total amount to be assigned to the ending inventory under each of the following Periodic Inventory methods:

   (a) FIFO
   (b) Weighted-average (round calculations to two decimal places)

2. Assume that the market price per unit (cost to replace) of Stalberg's inventory on December 31, 20--, was $26. Calculate the total amount to be assigned to the ending inventory on December 31 under each of the following methods:

   (a) FIFO lower-of-cost-or-market
   (b) Weighted-average lower-of-cost-or-market
   (c) What journal entry would be made under lower-of-cost-or-market for parts (a) and (b) above?

SERIES A PROBLEMS

P 13-6A (L03)

✓ Cost of goods sold, FIFO: $77,100; LIFO: $81,150; Weighted-avg.: $79,050; Specific I.D.: $78,450

SPECIFIC IDENTIFICATION, FIFO, LIFO, AND WEIGHTED-AVERAGE Hamilton Company's beginning inventory and purchases during the fiscal year ended September 30, 20-2, were as follows:

		Units	Unit Price	Total Cost
October 1, 20-1	Beginning inventory	300	$20.00	$ 6,000
October 18	1st purchase	500	21.50	10,750
November 25	2nd purchase	400	22.00	8,800
January 12, 20-2	3rd purchase	800	23.00	18,400
March 17	4th purchase	900	23.50	21,150
June 2	5th purchase	600	24.00	14,400
August 21	6th purchase	500	25.00	12,500
September 27	7th purchase	400	25.75	10,300
		4,400		$102,300

There are 1,000 units of inventory on hand on September 30, 20-2. Of these 1,000 units:

100 are from the October 18, 20-1	1st purchase
300 are from the January 12, 20-2	3rd purchase
100 are from the March 17	4th purchase
200 are from the June 2	5th purchase
100 are from the August 21	6th purchase
200 are from the September 27	7th purchase

REQUIRED

Calculate the total amount to be assigned to cost of goods sold for the fiscal year ended September 30, 20-2, and ending inventory on September 30, 20-2, under each of the following periodic inventory methods:

1. FIFO

2. LIFO

3. Weighted-average (round calculations to two decimal places)

4. Specific identification

P 13-7A (LO3)

✓ 1. Ending inv., FIFO: $13,825; LIFO: $8,000; Weighted-avg.: $10,500

COST ALLOCATION AND LOWER-OF-COST-OR-MARKET Douglas Company's beginning inventory and purchases during the fiscal year ended December 31, 20--, were as follows:

		Units	Unit Price	Total Cost
January 1, 20--	Beginning inventory	1,100	$ 8.00	$ 8,800
March 5	1st purchase	900	9.00	8,100
April 16	2nd purchase	400	9.50	3,800
June 3	3rd purchase	700	10.25	7,175
August 18	4th purchase	600	11.00	6,600
September 13	5th purchase	800	12.00	9,600
November 14	6th purchase	400	14.00	5,600
December 3	7th purchase	500	14.05	7,025
		5,400		$56,700

There are 1,000 units of inventory on hand on December 31.

REQUIRED

1. Calculate the total amount to be assigned to the ending inventory and cost of goods sold on December 31 under each of the following methods:

    (a) FIFO
    (b) LIFO
    (c) Weighted-average (round calculations to two decimal places)

2. Assume that the market price per unit (cost to replace) of Douglas's inventory on December 31 was $13. Calculate the total amount to be assigned to the ending inventory on December 31 under each of the following methods:

    (a) FIFO lower-of-cost-or-market
    (b) Weighted-average lower-of-cost-or-market

P 13-8A (LO4)

✓ Est. ending inv.: $80,800

GROSS PROFIT METHOD A fire completely destroyed all the inventory of Glisan Lumber Yard on August 5, 20--. Fortunately, the books were not destroyed in the fire. The following information is taken from the books of Glisan Lumber Yard for the time period January 1 through August 5:

Beginning inventory, January 1, 20--	$100,000
Net purchases, January 1 through August 5	420,000
Net sales, January 1 through August 5	732,000
Normal gross profit as a percentage of sales	40%

REQUIRED

Estimate the amount of merchandise inventory destroyed in the fire on August 5 using the gross profit method.

P 13-9A (LO4)

✓ Est. ending inv.: $39,000

RETAIL INVENTORY METHOD The following information is taken from the books of Raynette's Pharmacy for the last quarter of its fiscal year ending on March 31, 20--:

	Cost	Retail
Inventory, start of period, January 1, 20--	$ 32,000	$ 52,000
Net purchases during the period	176,000	268,000
Net sales for the period		260,000

REQUIRED

1. Estimate the ending inventory as of March 31 using the retail inventory method.

2. Estimate the cost of goods sold for the time period January 1 through March 31 using the retail inventory method.

SERIES B EXERCISES

E 13-1B (LO1)

INVENTORY ERRORS Assume that in year 1, the ending merchandise inventory is understated by $40,000. If this is the only error in years 1 and 2, indicate which items will be understated, overstated, or correctly stated for years 1 and 2.

	Year 1	Year 2
Ending merchandise inventory	_____	_____
Beginning merchandise inventory	_____	_____
Cost of goods sold	_____	_____
Gross profit	_____	_____
Net income	_____	_____
Ending owner's capital	_____	_____

E 13-2B (LO2)

JOURNAL ENTRIES—PERIODIC INVENTORY Amy Douglas owns a business called Douglas Distributors. The following transactions took place during January of the current year. Journalize the transactions in a general journal using the periodic inventory method.

Jan. 5 Purchased merchandise on account from Elite Warehouse, $4,100.

8 Paid freight charge on merchandise purchased, $300.

Jan. 12   Sold merchandise on account to Memories Unlimited, $5,200.

15   Received a credit memo from Elite Warehouse for merchandise returned, $700.

22   Issued a credit memo to Memories Unlimited for merchandise returned, $400.

E 13-3B (LO2)

JOURNAL ENTRIES—PERPETUAL INVENTORY Doreen Woods owns a small variety store. The following transactions took place during March of the current year. Journalize the transactions in a general journal using the perpetual inventory method.

Mar. 3   Purchased merchandise on account from Corner Galleria, $3,500.

7   Paid freight charge on merchandise purchased, $200.

13   Sold merchandise on account to Sonya Specialties, $4,250. The cost of the merchandise was $2,550.

18   Received a credit memo from Corner Galleria for merchandise returned, $900.

22   Issued a credit memo to Sonya Specialties for merchandise returned, $500. The cost of the merchandise was $300.

E 13-4B (LO3)

✓ Ending inv.: $53,700

ENDING INVENTORY COSTS Danny Steele owns a small specialty store, named Steele's Storeroom, whose year-end is June 30. Determine the total amount that should be included in Steele's Storeroom's year-end inventory. A physical inventory taken on June 30 reveals the following:

Cost of merchandise on the showroom floor and in the warehouse	$42,600
Goods held on consignment (consignor is Quality Manufacturer)	7,600
Goods that Steele's Storeroom, as the consignor, has for sale at the location of Midtown Galleria	8,300
Sales invoices indicate that merchandise was shipped on June 28, terms FOB shipping point, delivered at buyer's receiving dock on July 6	4,350
Sales invoices indicate that merchandise was shipped on June 26, terms FOB destination, delivered at buyer's receiving dock on July 1	2,800

E 13-5B (LO3)

✓ 1. Ending inv., FIFO: $800;
Weighted-avg.: $697.20

LOWER-OF-COST-OR-MARKET Bouie Company's beginning inventory and purchases during the fiscal year ended December 31, 20--, were as follows:

		Units	Unit Price	Total Cost
Jan. 1	Beginning inventory	20	$30	$ 600
Mar. 5	1st purchase	22	34	748
Sept. 9	2nd purchase	24	35	840
Dec. 8	3rd purchase	22	40	880
		88		$3,068

There are 20 units of inventory on hand on December 31.

1.   Calculate the total amount to be assigned to the ending inventory under each of the following periodic inventory methods:

(a)   FIFO

(b)   Weighted-average (round calculations to two decimal places)

(continued)

2. Assume that the market price per unit (cost to replace) of Bouie's inventory on December 31, 20--, was $39. Calculate the total amount to be assigned to the ending inventory on December 31 under each of the following methods:

(a) FIFO lower-of-cost-or-market
(b) Weighted-average lower-of-cost-or-market
(c) What entry would be made under lower-of-cost-or-market for (a) and (b) above?

SERIES B PROBLEMS

P 13-6B (LO3)

✓ Ending inv., FIFO: $19,075; LIFO: $14,350; Weighted-avg.: $16,290; Specific I.D.: $17,000

SPECIFIC IDENTIFICATION, FIFO, LIFO, AND WEIGHTED-AVERAGE Boyce Company's beginning inventory and purchases during the fiscal year ended September 30, 20-2, were as follows:

		Units	Unit Price	Total Cost
October 1, 20-1	Beginning inventory	400	$15.00	$ 6,000
October 18	1st purchase	300	16.50	4,950
November 25	2nd purchase	600	17.00	10,200
January 12, 20-2	3rd purchase	700	17.25	12,075
March 17	4th purchase	800	18.00	14,400
June 2	5th purchase	400	19.00	7,600
August 21	6th purchase	300	21.00	6,300
September 27	7th purchase	500	21.75	10,875
		4,000		$72,400

There are 900 units of inventory on hand on September 30, 20-2. Of these 900 units:

50 are from the October 18, 20-1	1st purchase
300 are from the January 12, 20-2	3rd purchase
100 are from the March 17	4th purchase
200 are from the June 2	5th purchase
50 are from the August 21	6th purchase
200 are from the September 27	7th purchase

REQUIRED

Calculate the total amount to be assigned to the cost of goods sold for the fiscal year ended September 30, 20-2, and ending inventory on September 30, 20-2, under each of the following periodic inventory methods:

1. FIFO

2. LIFO

3. Weighted-average (round calculations to two decimal places)

4. Specific identification

P 13-7B (LO3)

COST ALLOCATION AND LOWER-OF-COST-OR-MARKET Hall Company's beginning inventory and purchases during the fiscal year ended December 31, 20--, were as follows:

		Units	Unit Price	Total Cost
January 1	Beginning inventory	800	$11.00	$ 8,800
March 5	1st purchase	600	12.00	7,200
April 16	2nd purchase	500	12.50	6,250
June 3	3rd purchase	700	14.00	9,800
August 18	4th purchase	800	15.00	12,000
September 13	5th purchase	900	17.00	15,300
November 14	6th purchase	400	18.00	7,200
December 3	7th purchase	500	20.30	10,150
		5,200		$76,700

There are 1,100 units of inventory on hand on December 31.

REQUIRED

1. Calculate the total amount to be assigned to the ending inventory and cost of goods sold on December 31 under each of the following methods:

    (a)   FIFO
    (b)   LIFO
    (c)   Weighted-average (round calculations to two decimal places)

2. Assume that the market price per unit (cost to replace) of Hall's inventory on December 31 was $16. Calculate the total amount to be assigned to the ending inventory on December 31 under each of the following methods:

    (a)   FIFO lower-of-cost-or-market
    (b)   Weighted-average lower-of-cost-or-market

P 13-8B (LO4)

GROSS PROFIT METHOD A flood completely destroyed all the inventory of Bayside Waterworks Company on July 1, 20--. Fortunately, the books were not destroyed in the flood. The following information is taken from the books of Bayside Waterworks for the time period January 1 through July 1, 20--.

Beginning inventory, January 1, 20--	$ 60,000
Net purchases, January 1 through July 1	380,000
Net sales, January 1 through July 1	650,000
Normal gross profit as a percentage of sales	45%

REQUIRED

Estimate the amount of merchandise inventory destroyed in the flood on July 1 using the gross profit method.

P 13-9B (LO4)

✓ Est. cost of goods sold: $193,750

RETAIL INVENTORY METHOD The following information is taken from the books of Beverly's Basket Corner for the last quarter of its fiscal year ending on March 31, 20--:

	Cost	Retail
Inventory, start of period, January 1, 20--	$ 50,000	$ 80,000
Net purchases during the period	220,000	352,000
Net sales for the period		310,000

REQUIRED

1. Estimate the ending inventory as of March 31 using the retail inventory method.

2. Estimate the cost of goods sold for the time period January 1 through March 31 using the retail inventory method.

MANAGING YOUR WRITING

Most major grocery chains have optical scanning devices at the checkout stands and they certainly reduce the time required to check out. What benefits do they provide to the business? Next time you go to the grocery store, take a few minutes to chat with the manager. Ask the manager to describe the benefits of the scanning devices over the old machines that required the clerk to key in each purchase. Pay particular attention to the linkage between the scanning devices and the inventory systems. Be sure to ask whether the grocery store is on a periodic or perpetual system.

After your visit, write a memo to your instructor describing the benefits of the scanning devices and how they are linked with the inventory system.

ETHICS CASE

Electronics, Inc., is a high-volume, wholesale merchandising company. Most of its inventory turns over four or five times a year. The company has had 50 units of a particular brand of computers on hand for over a year. These computers have not sold and probably will not sell unless they are discounted 60 to 70%. The accountant is carrying them on the books at cost and intends to recognize the loss when they are sold. This way, she can avoid a significant write-down in inventory on the current year's financial statements.

1. Is the accountant correct in her treatment of the inventory? Why or why not?

2. If the computers cost $1,000 each and their market value is 40% of their cost, journalize the entry necessary for the write-down.

3. In a short paragraph, explain what is meant by conservatism and how it ties in with the lower-of-cost-or-market method of accounting for inventory.

4. In groups of three or four, make a list of reasons why inventories of electronic equipment might have to be written down.

MASTERY PROBLEM

Tiller Company's beginning inventory and purchases during the fiscal year ended December 31, 20-2, were as follows:

		Units	Unit Price	Total Cost
January 1, 20-2	Beginning inventory	1,500	$10.00	$15,000
January 12	1st purchase	500	11.50	5,750
February 28	2nd purchase	600	14.50	8,700
June 29	3rd purchase	1,200	15.00	18,000
August 31	4th purchase	800	16.50	13,200
October 29	5th purchase	300	18.00	5,400
November 30	6th purchase	700	18.50	12,950
December 21	7th purchase	400	20.00	8,000
		6,000		$87,000

There are 1,200 units of inventory on hand on December 31, 20-2.

REQUIRED

1. Calculate the total amount to be assigned to the cost of goods sold for 20-2 and ending inventory on December 31 under each of the following periodic inventory methods:

    (a)   FIFO
    (b)   LIFO
    (c)   Weighted-average (round calculations to two decimal places)

2. Assume that the market price per unit (cost to replace) of Tiller's inventory on December 31 was $18. Calculate the total amount to be assigned to the ending inventory on December 31 under each of the following methods:

    (a)   FIFO lower-of-cost-or-market
    (b)   Weighted-average lower-of-cost-or-market

3. In addition to taking a physical inventory on December 31, Tiller decides to estimate the ending inventory and cost of goods sold. During the fiscal year ended December 31, 20-2, net sales of $100,000 were made at a normal gross profit rate of 35%. Use the gross profit method to estimate the cost of goods sold for the fiscal year ended December 31 and the inventory on December 31.

CHALLENGE PROBLEM

Bhushan Company has been using LIFO for inventory purposes because it would prefer to keep gross profits low for tax purposes. In its second year of operation (20-2), the controller pointed out that this strategy did not appear to work and suggested that FIFO cost of goods sold would have been higher than LIFO cost of goods sold for 20-2. Is this possible?

20-1	Units	Cost/Unit
Purchase 1	100	$1.00
Purchase 2	200	2.00
Purchase 3	300	3.00
Ending inventory	200	

20-2	Units	Cost/Unit
Beginning inventory	200	
Purchase 4	150	$4.00
Purchase 5	250	5.00
Purchase 6	350	6.00
Ending inventory	50	

REQUIRED

Using the information provided, compute the cost of goods sold for 20-1 and 20-2 comparing the LIFO and FIFO methods.

Chapter 13 Appendix
Perpetual Inventory Method: LIFO
and Moving-Average Methods

Objectives

Careful study of this appendix should enable you to:

LO1 Compute the costs allocated to the ending inventory and cost of goods sold using the perpetual LIFO inventory method.

LO2 Compute the costs allocated to the ending inventory and cost of goods sold using the perpetual moving-average inventory method.

In Chapter 13, you learned how to apply the LIFO and weighted-averge inventory methods under the periodic inventory system. Recall that all calculations under the periodic system are done at the end of the accounting period. Under the perpetual system, costs are computed every time merchandise is purchased and sold. These costs are used to maintain a running record of the cost of goods sold to date and the balance of inventory on hand.

PERPETUAL LIFO

LO1 Compute the costs allocated to the ending inventory and cost of goods sold using the perpetual LIFO inventory method.

When using the **perpetual LIFO inventory method**, every time inventory is purchased a new layer is formed. When inventory is sold, we assume that the most recently purchased layer is sold first. As those units are used up, units are taken from the next most recently purchased layer. To illustrate, let's assume that Phaler's Fishing Supplies has the following beginning inventory, purchases, and sales of one type of bobber during the month of June. Note that the beginning inventory also has layers based on the prices paid in earlier periods.

Date	Beginning Inventory and Purchases		Sales
	Units	Cost/Unit	Units
June 1 (BI)	20	$0.80	
	160	1.00	
	20	1.20	
June 4	300	1.50	
June 20			400
June 30	100	1.80	

BI: Beginning Inventory

As shown in Figure 13A-1, the beginning inventory of 200 units forms Phaler's first three layers of inventory. The purchase on June 4 forms a fourth layer (300 units @ $1.50 = $450). At this point, Phaler has a total of 500 units at a total cost of $650. On June 20, Phaler sells 400 units. Under perpetual LIFO, we assume that the 300 units purchased on June 4 are sold first, followed by 20 that cost $1.20 each and 80 units that cost $1.00 each from the beginning inventory.

The cost of goods sold on June 20 is $554. The cost of the inventory on hand is $96. At this point, Phaler has 100 units remaining from the beginning inventory.

On June 30, Phaler purchases 100 units at $1.80 each. This forms a new fifth layer (100 @ $1.80 = $180). This layer is added to the two layers remaining from the beginning inventory for a total of 200 units at a total cost of $276 of inventory on hand on June 30. Note that the third ($1.20 layer) and fourth ($1.50 layer) layers of inventory are gone. They will never reappear. If Phaler makes additional sales before buying more inventory, they will come from the fifth layer at $1.80 each, followed by units from the second ($1.00) and then the first ($0.80) layers.

FIGURE 13A-1   Perpetual LIFO Inventory System

DATE	PURCHASES			COST OF GOODS SOLD				INVENTORY ON HAND				
	Units	Cost/Unit	Total	Units	Cost/Unit	CGS	Cumulative CGS	Layer	Units	Cost/Unit	Layer Cost	Total
June 1 (BI)								(1)	20	$0.80	$ 16.00	
								(2)	160	1.00	160.00	
								(3)	20	1.20	24.00	$200.00
June 4								(1)	20	$0.80	$ 16.00	
								(2)	160	1.00	160.00	
								(3)	20	1.20	24.00	
	300	$1.50	$450.00					(4)	300	1.50	450.00	$650.00
June 20				300	$1.50	$450.00		(1)	20	$0.80	$ 16.00	
				20	1.20	24.00		(2)	80	1.00	80.00	$ 96.00
				80	1.00	80.00	$554.00					
June 30								(1)	20	$0.80	$ 16.00	
								(2)	80	1.00	80.00	
	100	$1.80	$180.00					(5)	100	1.80	180.00	$276.00
Cost of Goods Sold for June							$554.00					

BI: Beginning Inventory

PERPETUAL MOVING-AVERAGE

LO2 Compute the costs allocated to the ending inventory and cost of goods sold using the perpetual moving-average inventory method.

When using the **perpetual moving-average inventory method**, every time inventory is purchased a new average cost per unit is calculated. When inventory is sold, the most recent average cost is used to measure cost of goods sold and the remaining inventory on hand. To illustrate, let's look again at the purchases and sales of Phaler's Fishing Supplies for the month of June.

Date	Beginning Inventory and Purchases		Sales
	Units	Cost/Unit	Units
June 1 (BI)	20	$0.80	
	160	1.00	
	20	1.20	
June 4	300	1.50	
June 20			400
June 30	100	1.80	

BI: Beginning Inventory

When using the moving-average inventory method, it is best to do the calculations on a calculator or computer spreadsheet. Carry each calculation out to the number

of decimal places allowed by the technology used. This will reduce rounding errors.

As shown in Figure 13A-2, a new average cost is calculated each time a purchase is made. The average cost of the June 1 beginning inventory is shown as $1.00 ($200 cost/200 units). To compute the average cost after buying more inventory on June 4, we take the cost of the inventory on hand ($200 + $450 = $650) and divide by the number of units on hand (200 + 300 = 500). Thus, the average cost of the inventory on hand on June 4 is $1.30 per unit. To compute the cost of the 400 units sold on June 20, multiply the 400 units by $1.30 to get the cost of goods sold of $520. The remaining cost of the inventory on hand is $130 ($650 − $520). The number of units on hand is reduced to 100 (500 − 400).

On June 30, 100 additional units are purchased. This increases the units on hand to 200 (100 + 100) and the cost of the inventory on hand to $310 ($130 + $180). Dividing the cost of the inventory on hand by the number of units on hand provides a new moving-average cost of $1.55 ($310 ÷ 200). If Phaler makes another sale before buying additional units, this average cost will be used to compute the cost of goods sold and determine the cost of the inventory remaining on hand. Note that selling inventory does not change the moving-average cost. This is because the units are being removed at the most recent average cost.

FIGURE 13A-2   Perpetual Moving-Average Inventory System

DATE	PURCHASES			COST OF GOODS SOLD				INVENTORY ON HAND AND AVG. COST/UNIT			
	Units	Cost/ Unit	Total	Units	Cost/ Unit	CGS	Cumulative CGS	Cost of Purchase or (Sale)	Cost of Inventory on Hand	Units on Hand	Avg. Cost/Unit
June 1 (BI)									$200.00	200.00	$1.0000
June 4	300.00	$1.50	$450.00					$ 450.00	650.00	500.00	1.3000
June 20				400.00	$1.30	$520.00	$520.00	(520.00)	130.00	100.00	1.3000
June 30	100.00	$1.80	$180.00					180.00	310.00	200.00	1.5500
Cost of Goods Sold during January							$520.00				

BI: Beginning Inventory

Learning Objectives	Key Points to Remember
LO1 **Compute the costs allocated to the ending inventory and cost of goods sold using the perpetual LIFO inventory method.**	When using the perpetual LIFO inventory method, every time inventory is purchased, a new layer is formed. When inventory is sold, we assume the units were sold out of the most recent layer. As those units are used up, additional sales are taken from the next most recently purchased layer.
LO2 **Compute the costs allocated to the ending inventory and cost of goods sold using the perpetual moving-average inventory method.**	When using the perpetual moving-average inventory method, every time inventory is purchased, a new average cost per unit is calculated. When inventory is sold, the most recent average cost is used to measure cost of goods sold and the remaining inventory on hand.

KEY TERMS

perpetual LIFO inventory method (525)   A method of allocating merchandise cost which assumes that every time inventory is purchased, a new layer is formed. When inventory is sold, units were sold out of the most recent layer. As those units are used up, additional sales are taken from the next most recently purchased layer.

perpetual moving-average inventory method (526)   A method of allocating merchandise cost which assumes that every time inventory is purchased, a new average cost per unit is calculated. When inventory is sold, the most recent average cost is used to measure cost of goods sold and the remaining inventory on hand.

REVIEW QUESTION

LO1   1.   Explain the primary difference between the periodic and perpetual inventory systems when calculating cost of goods sold and merchandise inventory.

SERIES A EXERCISE

E 13Apx-1A (LO1/2)
✓ CGS under perpetual LIFO: $3,345; CGS under perpetual moving-average: $3,250

The beginning inventory, purchases, and sales for Myrl Sign Company for the month of April follow.

Date	Beginning Inventory and Purchases		Sales
	Units	Cost/Unit	Units
April 1 (BI)	100	$4.30	
	100	4.50	
	200	4.60	
April 20	400	5.50	
April 30			650

BI: Beginning Inventory

REQUIRED

Calculate the total amount to be assigned to cost of goods sold for April and the ending inventory on April 30, under each of the following methods:

1.   Perpetual LIFO inventory method

2.   Perpetual moving-average inventory method

SERIES A PROBLEM

P 13Apx-2A (LO1/2)

✓ CGS under perpetual LIFO: $1,900;
CGS under perpetual moving-average:
$1,856.64

PERPETUAL—LIFO AND MOVING-AVERAGE Kelley Company began business on January 1, 20-1. Purchases and sales during the month of January follow.

Date	Purchases		Sales
	Units	Cost/Unit	Units
Jan. 1	100	$1.00	
Jan. 4	400	1.10	
Jan. 5			300
Jan. 10	300	1.30	
Jan. 12			200
Jan. 15	200	1.35	
Jan. 18	500	1.60	
Jan. 22			800
Jan. 27			100
Jan. 31	300	1.80	

REQUIRED

Calculate the total amount to be assigned to cost of goods sold for January and the ending inventory on January 31, under each of the following methods:

1. Perpetual LIFO inventory method

2. Perpetual moving-average inventory method

SERIES B EXERCISE

E 13Apx-1B (LO1/2)

✓ CGS under perpetual LIFO: $5,435;
CGS under perpetual moving-average:
$5,395

The beginning inventory, purchases, and sales for Harrington Equipment Company for the month of August follow.

Date	Beginning Inventory and Purchases		Sales
	Units	Cost/Unit	Units
Aug. 1 (BI)	100	$8.00	
	150	8.10	
	250	8.30	
Aug. 15	300	8.50	
Aug. 31			650

BI: Beginning Inventory

REQUIRED

Calculate the total amount to be assigned to cost of goods sold for August and the ending inventory on August 31, under each of the following methods:

1. Perpetual LIFO inventory method

2. Perpetual moving-average inventory method

SERIES B PROBLEM

P 13Apx-2B (LO1/2)

✓ CGS under perpetual LIFO: $3,720;
CGS under perpetual moving-average:
$3,665.25

PERPETUAL—LIFO AND MOVING-AVERAGE Vozniak Company began business on January 1, 20-1. Purchases and sales during the month of January follow.

Date	Purchases		Sales
	Units	Cost/Unit	Units
Jan. 1	100	$2.00	
Jan. 5	500	2.30	
Jan. 7			300
Jan. 12	300	2.40	
Jan. 15			300
Jan. 17	200	2.50	
Jan. 19	500	2.70	
Jan. 24			800
Jan. 28			100
Jan. 31	200	2.90	

REQUIRED

Calculate the total amount to be assigned to cost of goods sold for January and the ending inventory on January 31, under each of the following methods:

1. Perpetual LIFO inventory method

2. Perpetual moving-average inventory method

PHOTO: © GETTY IMAGES/PHOTODISC

Adjustments and the Work Sheet for a Merchandising Business

Often, we are expected to pay in advance for goods and services. This is true for season tickets for sporting events, magazine subscriptions, or tickets for popular operas or rock concerts. In return, we expect to receive the goods or services. When customers place special orders, Evan Taylor requires them to pay a cash deposit of half of the total sales amount. How should these cash receipts be treated by his business?

Objectives
Careful study of this chapter should enable you to:

LO1
Prepare an adjustment for merchandise inventory using the periodic inventory system.

LO2
Prepare an adjustment for unearned revenue.

LO3
Prepare a work sheet for a merchandising business.

LO4
Journalize adjusting entries for a merchandising business.

LO5
Prepare adjusting journal entries under the perpetual inventory system.

In Chapters 10 through 13, we learned how to account for the day-to-day transactions of a merchandising business. In this chapter, we focus on end-of-period adjustments and the preparation of the work sheet. Finally, in Chapter 15, we will complete the accounting cycle by preparing financial statements and closing entries.

A work sheet for a merchandising business is similar to the work sheet prepared for a service business (Chapter 5). It is used to prepare adjustments for supplies, prepaid insurance, wages earned but not paid, depreciation, and other necessary year-end adjustments. A merchandising business must also make an adjustment to properly report the amount of merchandise inventory held at the end of the accounting period. While revisiting the work sheet, we will also introduce a new adjustment for unearned revenue.

ADJUSTMENT FOR MERCHANDISE INVENTORY: PERIODIC INVENTORY SYSTEM

LO1 Prepare an adjustment for merchandise inventory using the periodic inventory system.

As discussed in Chapter 13, when merchandise inventory is purchased, the purchases account is debited and Cash or Accounts Payable is credited. When inventory is sold, Cash or Accounts Receivable is debited and Sales is credited. This method of accounting for inventory transactions is called the periodic inventory system. Figure 14-1 provides a review of these entries.

FIGURE 14-1   Review of Entries for Purchase and Sale of Merchandise

TRANSACTION	ENTRY		
Purchase of merchandise	Purchases	xxx	
	Accounts Payable or Cash		xxx
Sale of merchandise	Accounts Receivable or Cash	xxx	
	Sales		xxx

Note that the merchandise inventory account is not debited or credited in either of these entries. Since sales and purchases have taken place during the year, the beginning balance of the merchandise inventory account no longer provides an accurate picture of the inventory held at the end of the year. Thus, an adjustment must be made to remove the beginning inventory and enter the ending inventory in the merchandise inventory account. The quantity of inventory on hand at the end of the accounting period is determined by taking a physical count of the goods on hand. The cost of these goods is determined by using one of the inventory methods described in Chapter 13 (FIFO, LIFO, etc.). Of course, this year's ending inventory becomes next year's beginning inventory.

To illustrate the adjustment for merchandise inventory, let's assume that Ponder's Bike Parts had a beginning merchandise inventory of $25,000. During the year, the entries shown in Figure 14-1 were made as merchandise was purchased and sold. At the end of the accounting period, a physical inventory of the merchandise determined that merchandise costing $30,000 was still on hand.

The adjustment process for merchandise inventory is a bit different from other adjustments you have learned. To appreciate the reason for this difference, recall how the beginning and ending inventories are used when computing cost of goods sold, as shown in the bottom portion of Figure 14-2. The beginning inventory is added to purchases to compute cost of goods available for sale. The ending inventory is subtracted from cost of goods available for sale to compute cost of goods sold.

FIGURE 14-2   Calculation of Cost of Goods Sold Using Information in the Income Statement Columns of the Work Sheet

Ponder's Bike Parts
Work Sheet (Partial)
For Year Ended December 31, 20- -

Work sheet account titles:
- Merchandise Inventory
- Income Summary
- Purchases
- Purchases Returns/Allowances
- Purchases Discounts
- Freight-In

Step 1: Remove beginning inventory

| Income Summary | 25,000 |
| Merchandise Inventory | 25,000 |

Step 2: Insert ending inventory

| Merchandise Inventory | 30,000 |
| Income Summary | 30,000 |

Income Statement columns — Debit: Beginning Inventory; Credit: Ending Inventory

Cost of goods sold:

Merchandise inventory, January 1			$ 25 0 0 0 00
Purchases		$80 0 0 0 00	
Less: Purchases returns and allowances	$ 1 0 0 0 00		
Purchases discounts	5 0 0 00	1 5 0 0 00	
Net purchases		$78 5 0 0 00	
Add freight-in		7 0 0 00	
Cost of goods purchased			79 2 0 0 00
Goods available for sale			$104 2 0 0 00
Less merchandise inventory, December 31			30 0 0 0 00
Cost of goods sold			$ 74 2 0 0 00

Many firms use the work sheet to prepare financial statements. Thus, all of the information needed to compute cost of goods sold should be readily available in the Income Statement columns of the work sheet. To provide this information, we need an adjustment technique that results in the beginning inventory being extended into the Income Statement *Debit* column so it can be *added* to purchases. Further, we need the ending inventory extended into the Income Statement *Credit* column so it will be *subtracted* when computing cost of goods sold. As shown in Figure 14-2, this can be accomplished in two steps by using the income summary account.

STEP 1 The beginning inventory ($25,000) is removed by crediting Merchandise Inventory. Income Summary is debited because this amount is used in the calculation of cost of goods sold and net income.

STEP 2 The ending inventory ($30,000) is entered by debiting Merchandise Inventory. Income Summary is credited because this amount is also used in the calculation of cost of goods sold and net income.

Note that the debit *and* credit adjustments made to Income Summary are extended into the Adjusted Trial Balance and Income Statement columns. *This is the only time individual figures, rather than the net amount, are extended on the work sheet.* It is done in this case because the individual amounts are needed for the calculation of cost of goods sold on the income statement (beginning

A BROADER VIEW

The Importance of Inventory

Note the important role of the ending inventory in the calculation of cost of goods sold in Figure 14-2. If the ending inventory is overstated for any reason, net income will also be overstated. Given this important relationship, auditors observe and verify the accuracy of the physical inventory. However, unethical managers, desperate to improve profits, have on occasion found ways to mislead auditors.

In one case, managers overstated inventory counts for items that the auditors had not physically verified. In another case, auditors found a barrel whose contents had been valued by management at thousands of dollars. It actually contained floor sweepings. Finally, there was a case where management called the auditor, the day after the inventory audit, to report that additional inventory had arrived and should be included in the inventory count. The auditor never verified that the inventory was real. It turned out to be a scam that helped the company double its reported profits for the year. These unfortunate events highlight the reason auditors must exercise great care when conducting an inventory audit.

© ED PRITCHARD/GETTY IMAGES

inventory + purchases − ending inventory = cost of goods sold). Note, also, that all of the information needed to compute cost of goods sold is readily available in the Income Statement columns of the work sheet.

ADJUSTMENT FOR UNEARNED REVENUE

LO2 Prepare an adjustment for unearned revenue.

LEARNING KEY

Remember, under the accrual basis of accounting, revenue is recorded when *earned* regardless of when cash is received.

Some businesses require payment before delivering a product or performing a service. Examples include insurance companies, magazine publishers, apartment complexes, college food services, and professional sports and theater companies that sell season tickets. The cash received in advance is called **unearned revenue**. Since the cash has been received in advance, the company owes the customers the product or service, or must refund their money. Thus, unearned revenue is reported as a *liability* on the balance sheet.

To illustrate, let's assume that Brown County Playhouse sells season tickets for five plays produced throughout the year. Tickets sell for $10 for each play ($50 for a season ticket) and a maximum of 1,000 seats can be sold for each play. For simplicity, let's assume that all shows sell out during the first week that season tickets are available for sale. As shown below and in Figure 14-3, the sale of the tickets would be recorded as follows:

8	(1) Cash		50 0 0 0 00		8
9	Unearned Ticket Revenue			50 0 0 0 00	9
10	Season ticket sales				10
11	($10 × 1,000 seats × 5 shows)				11

To prepare financial statements following production of the third show, an adjusting entry is needed to recognize that $30,000 ($10 × 1,000 seats × 3 shows) in ticket revenue has been earned. To do this, the following adjusting entry is made:

13	Adjusting Entries				13
14	Unearned Ticket Revenue		30 0 0 0 00		14
15	Ticket Revenue			30 0 0 0 00	15

The remaining balance of $20,000 in Unearned Ticket Revenue is reported as a current liability on the balance sheet.

FIGURE 14-3   Entries for Unearned Revenue

Expanded Chart of Accounts

Let's take a look at where the new accounts for a merchandising business fit into a chart of accounts. Recall that the chart of accounts follows the form of the accounting equation (assets = liabilities + owner's equity + revenues − expenses). A chart of accounts for Northern Micro is provided in Figure 14-4. Note the classification of the new accounts introduced in Chapters 10 and 11 for a merchandising firm.

Merchandise Inventory is listed as a current asset. Since Northern Micro sells subscriptions to a computer magazine that it produces, Unearned Subscriptions Revenue is listed as a current liability, and Subscriptions Revenue is listed as a revenue. Sales Returns and Allowances and Sales Discounts are **contra-revenue accounts**. Recall, however, that Northern Micro does not offer sales discounts.

Purchases, Purchases Returns and Allowances, Purchases Discounts, and Freight-In are used to compute cost of goods sold. Thus, they are listed under this heading. Purchases Returns and Allowances and Purchases Discounts are often called **contra-cost accounts** or contra-purchases accounts.

FIGURE 14-4 Chart of Accounts for Northern Micro

NORTHERN MICRO CHART OF ACCOUNTS			
Assets		**Revenue**	
Current Assets		401	Sales
101	Cash	401.1	Sales Returns and Allowances
122	Accounts Receivable		
131	Merchandise Inventory	**Other Revenue**	
141	Supplies	411	Interest Revenue
145	Prepaid Insurance	412	Rent Revenue
		413	Subscriptions Revenue
Property, Plant, and Equipment		**Expenses**	
161	Land	**Cost of Goods Sold**	
171	Building	501	Purchases
171.1	Accumulated Depreciation— Building	501.1	Purchases Returns and Allowances
181	Store Equipment	501.2	Purchases Discounts
181.1	Accumulated Depreciation— Store Equipment	502	Freight-In
		Operating Expenses	
Liabilities		511	Wages Expense
Current Liabilities		512	Advertising Expense
201	Notes Payable	513	Bank Credit Card Expense
202	Accounts Payable		
219	Wages Payable	521	Rent Expense
231	Sales Tax Payable	523	Supplies Expense
241	Unearned Subscriptions Revenue	525	Telephone Expense
		533	Utilities Expense
Long-Term Liabilities		535	Insurance Expense
251	Mortgage Payable	540	Depreciation Expense— Building
		541	Depreciation Expense— Store Equipment
Owner's Equity			
311	Gary L. Fishel, Capital	549	Miscellaneous Expense
312	Gary L. Fishel, Drawing		
313	Income Summary	**Other Expenses**	
		551	Interest Expense

Interest Expense is classified as "Other Expenses" instead of being listed under Operating Expenses. This is because it represents the expense of obtaining money to do business, rather than an expense directly associated with operating the business.

PREPARING A WORK SHEET FOR A MERCHANDISING BUSINESS

LO3 Prepare a work sheet for a merchandising business.

The work sheet for a merchandising business is similar to the one shown in Chapter 5 for a service business. Recall the five steps taken to prepare a work sheet.

STEP 1 Prepare the trial balance.

STEP 2 Prepare the adjustments.

STEP 3 Prepare the adjusted trial balance.

STEP 4 Extend the adjusted trial balance amounts to the Income Statement and Balance Sheet columns.

STEP 5 Total the Income Statement and Balance Sheet columns to compute the net income or net loss.

The work sheet format and the five steps taken when preparing the work sheet are illustrated in Figure 14-5. Note that the new accounts introduced for a merchandising firm and the unearned revenue account are highlighted so that you can see their proper placement and extensions. (The abbreviation BI stands for beginning inventory; EI stands for ending inventory.) Pay particular attention to the extension of Income Summary. Both the debit and credit amounts for this account must be extended.

Adjustments for Northern Micro

Before preparing a work sheet for Northern Micro, let's review the preparation of adjustments in T account form. Figure 14-6 provides year-end adjustment information for Northern Micro. Figure 14-7 shows adjusting entries based on this information. The unadjusted balances for these accounts were taken from Northern Micro's trial balance.

Preparing a Work Sheet for Northern Micro

Let's prepare a work sheet for Northern Micro following the five steps illustrated in Figure 14-5.

STEP 1 In Figure 14-8, the Trial Balance columns are completed by copying the balances of all accounts from the general ledger (not shown).

STEP 2 In Figure 14-9, the adjustments are entered. These entries are exactly the same as those made in T account form in Figure 14-7.

STEP 3 In Figure 14-10, extensions are made to the Adjusted Trial Balance columns. Note that both the debit and credit amounts for Income Summary are extended.

STEP 4 In Figure 14-11, the Adjusted Trial Balance amounts are extended to the Income Statement and Balance Sheet columns.

STEP 5 In Figure 14-11, the work sheet is completed by totaling the Income Statement and Balance Sheet columns. The difference between the debits and credits for each pair of columns represents the net income or net loss.

FIGURE 14-5 Overview of Work Sheet for a Merchandising Business

Name of Company
Work Sheet
For Year Ended December 31, 20 --

#	ACCOUNT TITLE	TRIAL BALANCE DEBIT	TRIAL BALANCE CREDIT	ADJUSTMENTS DEBIT	ADJUSTMENTS CREDIT	ADJUSTED TRIAL BALANCE DEBIT	ADJUSTED TRIAL BALANCE CREDIT	INCOME STATEMENT DEBIT	INCOME STATEMENT CREDIT	BALANCE SHEET DEBIT	BALANCE SHEET CREDIT
		Step 1: Prepare a Trial Balance		Step 2: Prepare the Adjustments		Step 3: Prepare the Adjusted Trial Balance		Step 4: Extend Adjusted Account Balances		Step 5: Complete the work sheet (1) Sum columns (2) Compute net income (loss)	
1	---------										
2	---------										
3	(Insert Ledger Account Titles)										
4		Assets				Assets				Assets	
5		Mdse. Inv. (BI)		EI	BI	Mdse. Inv. (EI)				Mdse. Inv. (EI)	
6			Liabilities				Liabilities				Liabilities
7			Unearned				Unearned				Unearned
8			Revenues				Revenues				Revenues
9											
10			Capital				Capital				Capital
11		Drawing				Drawing				Drawing	
12											
13	Income Summary			BI	EI	BI	EI	BI	EI		
14	---------										
15			Revenues				Revenues		Revenues		
16			Sales				Sales		Sales		
17		Sales R&A				Sales R&A		Sales R&A			
18		Sales Discounts				Sales Discounts		Sales Discounts			
19											
20		Expenses				Expenses		Expenses			
21		Purchases				Purchases		Purchases			
22			Purch. R&A				Purch. R&A		Purch. R&A		
23			Purch. Discounts				Purch. Discounts		Purch. Discounts		
24		Freight-In				Freight-In		Freight-In			
25											
26											
27											
28											
29											
30								Net	Net	Net	Net
31								Income	Loss	Loss	Income
32											

BI = Beginning Inventory
EI = Ending Inventory

FIGURE 14-6   Year-End Adjustment Data for Northern Micro

YEAR-END ADJUSTMENT DATA FOR NORTHERN MICRO	
(a, b)	A physical count showed that merchandise inventory costing $18,000 is on hand as of December 31.
(c)	Supplies remaining at the end of the year, $400.
(d)	Unexpired insurance on December 31, $600.
(e)	Depreciation expense on the building for the year, $4,000.
(f)	Depreciation expense on the store equipment for the year, $3,000.
(g)	Wages earned but not paid as of December 31, $450.
(h)	Northern Micro publishes a computer magazine. Subscribers pay in advance. Unearned subscriptions revenue as of December 31, $2,000.

FIGURE 14-7   Adjusting Entries for Northern Micro

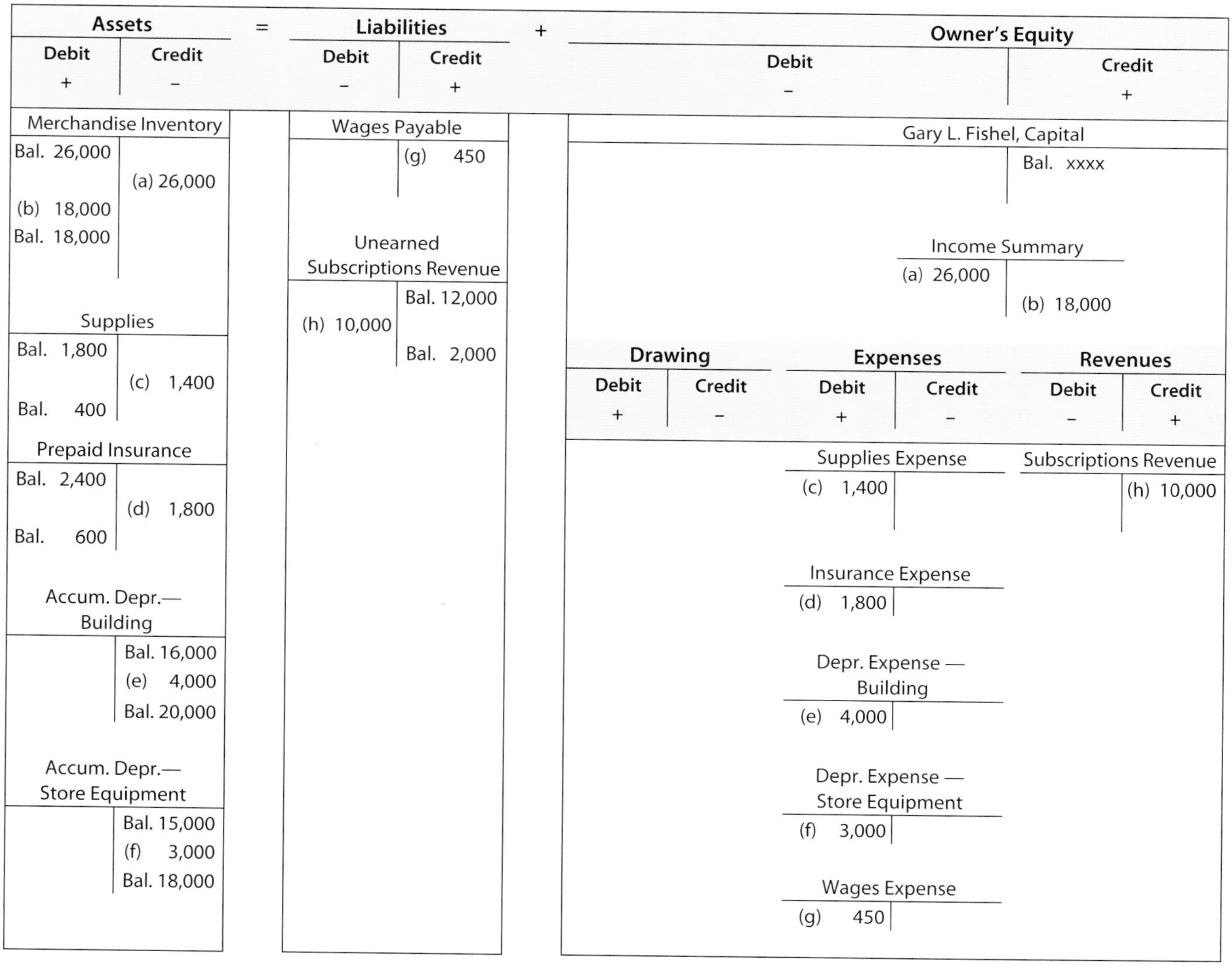

FIGURE 14-8   Step 1: Completion of the Trial Balance Columns

Northern Micro
Work Sheet
For Year Ended December 31, 20- -

#	Account Title	Trial Balance Debit	Trial Balance Credit	Adjustments Debit	Adjustments Credit	Adjusted Trial Balance Debit	Adjusted Trial Balance Credit	Income Statement Debit	Income Statement Credit	Balance Sheet Debit	Balance Sheet Credit
1	Cash	20 0 0 0 00									
2	Accounts Receivable	15 0 0 0 00									
3	Merchandise Inventory	26 0 0 0 00									
4	Supplies	1 8 0 0 00									
5	Prepaid Insurance	2 4 0 0 00									
6	Land	10 0 0 0 00									
7	Building	90 0 0 0 00									
8	Accum. Depr.—Building		16 0 0 0 00								
9	Store Equipment	50 0 0 0 00									
10	Accum. Depr.—Store Equipment		15 0 0 0 00								
11	Notes Payable		5 0 0 0 00								
12	Accounts Payable		10 0 0 0 00								
13	Wages Payable										
14	Sales Tax Payable		1 5 0 0 00								
15	Unearned Subscriptions Revenue		12 0 0 0 00								
16	Mortgage Payable		30 0 0 0 00								
17	Gary L. Fishel, Capital		114 4 0 0 00								
18	Gary L. Fishel, Drawing	20 0 0 0 00									
19	Income Summary										
20	Sales		214 0 0 0 00								
21	Sales Returns and Allowances	1 2 0 0 00									
22	Interest Revenue		9 0 0 00								
23	Rent Revenue		8 0 0 0 00								
24	Subscriptions Revenue										
25	Purchases	105 0 0 0 00									
26	Purchases Returns and Allowances		8 0 0 00								
27	Purchases Discounts		1 0 0 0 00								
28	Freight-In	3 0 0 0 00									
29	Wages Expense	42 0 0 0 00									
30	Advertising Expense	2 5 0 0 00									
31	Bank Credit Card Expense	1 5 0 0 00									
32	Rent Expense	20 0 0 0 00									
33	Supplies Expense										
34	Telephone Expense	3 5 0 0 00									
35	Utilities Expense	12 0 0 0 00									
36	Insurance Expense										
37	Depr. Expense—Building										
38	Depr. Expense—Store Equipment										
39	Miscellaneous Expense	2 5 0 0 00									
40	Interest Expense	3 1 5 0 00									
41		428 6 0 0 00	428 6 0 0 00								
42											

STEP 1

FIGURE 14-9   Step 2: Preparation of the Adjustments

Northern Micro
Work Sheet
For Year Ended December 31, 20 - -

ACCOUNT TITLE	TRIAL BALANCE DEBIT	TRIAL BALANCE CREDIT	ADJUSTMENTS DEBIT	ADJUSTMENTS CREDIT	ADJUSTED TRIAL BALANCE DEBIT	ADJUSTED TRIAL BALANCE CREDIT	INCOME STATEMENT DEBIT	INCOME STATEMENT CREDIT	BALANCE SHEET DEBIT	BALANCE SHEET CREDIT
1 Cash	20 0 0 0 00									
2 Accounts Receivable	15 0 0 0 00									
3 Merchandise Inventory	26 0 0 0 00		(b) 18 0 0 0 00	(a) 26 0 0 0 00						
4 Supplies	1 8 0 0 00			(c) 1 4 0 0 00						
5 Prepaid Insurance	2 4 0 0 00			(d) 1 8 0 0 00						
6 Land	10 0 0 0 00									
7 Building	90 0 0 0 00									
8 Accum. Depr.—Building		16 0 0 0 00		(e) 4 0 0 0 00						
9 Store Equipment	50 0 0 0 00									
10 Accum. Depr.—Store Equipment		15 0 0 0 00		(f) 3 0 0 0 00						
11 Notes Payable		5 0 0 0 00								
12 Accounts Payable		10 0 0 0 00								
13 Wages Payable				(g) 4 5 0 00						
14 Sales Tax Payable		1 5 0 0 00								
15 Unearned Subscriptions Revenue		12 0 0 0 00	(h) 10 0 0 0 00							
16 Mortgage Payable		30 0 0 0 00								
17 Gary L. Fishel, Capital		114 4 0 0 00								
18 Gary L. Fishel, Drawing	20 0 0 0 00									
19 Income Summary			(a) 26 0 0 0 00	(b) 18 0 0 0 00						
20 Sales		214 0 0 0 00								
21 Sales Returns and Allowances	1 2 0 0 00									
22 Interest Revenue		9 0 0 00								
23 Rent Revenue		8 0 0 0 00								
24 Subscriptions Revenue				(h) 10 0 0 0 00						
25 Purchases	105 0 0 0 00									
26 Purchases Returns and Allowances		8 0 0 00								
27 Purchases Discounts		1 0 0 0 00								
28 Freight-In	3 0 0 0 00									
29 Wages Expense	42 0 0 0 00		(g) 4 5 0 00							
30 Advertising Expense	2 5 0 0 00									
31 Bank Credit Card Expense	1 5 0 0 00									
32 Rent Expense	20 0 0 0 00									
33 Supplies Expense			(c) 1 4 0 0 00							
34 Telephone Expense	3 5 0 0 00									
35 Utilities Expense	12 0 0 0 00									
36 Insurance Expense			(d) 1 8 0 0 00							
37 Depr. Expense—Building			(e) 4 0 0 0 00							
38 Depr. Expense—Store Equipment			(f) 3 0 0 0 00							
39 Miscellaneous Expense	2 2 5 0 00									
40 Interest Expense	3 1 5 0 00									
41	428 6 0 0 00	428 6 0 0 00	64 6 5 0 00	64 6 5 0 00						
42										

BEGINNING INVENTORY

ENDING INVENTORY

ENDING INVENTORY

BEGINNING INVENTORY

STEP 1   STEP 2

FIGURE 14-10   Step 3: Extensions to the Adjusted Trial Balance Columns

Northern Micro
Work Sheet
For Year Ended December 31, 20 - -

#	Account Title	Trial Balance Debit	Trial Balance Credit	Adjustments Debit	Adjustments Credit	Adjusted Trial Balance Debit	Adjusted Trial Balance Credit	Income Statement Debit	Income Statement Credit	Balance Sheet Debit	Balance Sheet Credit
1	Cash	20 0 0 0 00				20 0 0 0 00					
2	Accounts Receivable	15 0 0 0 00				15 0 0 0 00					
3	Merchandise Inventory	26 0 0 0 00		(b) 18 0 0 0 00	(a) 26 0 0 0 00	18 0 0 0 00	18 0 0 0 00				
4	Supplies	1 8 0 0 00			(c) 1 4 0 0 00	4 0 0 00					
5	Prepaid Insurance	2 4 0 0 00			(d) 1 8 0 0 00	6 0 0 00					
6	Land	10 0 0 0 00				10 0 0 0 00					
7	Building	90 0 0 0 00				90 0 0 0 00					
8	Accum. Depr.—Building		16 0 0 0 00		(e) 4 0 0 0 00		20 0 0 0 00				
9	Store Equipment	50 0 0 0 00				50 0 0 0 00					
10	Accum. Depr.—Store Equipment		15 0 0 0 00		(f) 3 0 0 0 00		18 0 0 0 00				
11	Notes Payable		5 0 0 0 00				5 0 0 0 00				
12	Accounts Payable		10 0 0 0 00				10 0 0 0 00				
13	Wages Payable				(g) 4 5 0 00		4 5 0 00				
14	Sales Tax Payable		1 5 0 0 00				1 5 0 0 00				
15	Unearned Subscriptions Revenue		12 0 0 0 00	(h) 10 0 0 0 00			2 0 0 0 00				
16	Mortgage Payable		30 0 0 0 00				30 0 0 0 00				
17	Gary L. Fishel, Capital		114 4 0 0 00				114 4 0 0 00				
18	Gary L. Fishel, Drawing	20 0 0 0 00				20 0 0 0 00					
19	Income Summary			(a) 26 0 0 0 00	(b) 18 0 0 0 00	26 0 0 0 00	18 0 0 0 00				
20	Sales		214 0 0 0 00				214 0 0 0 00				
21	Sales Returns and Allowances	1 2 0 0 00				1 2 0 0 00					
22	Interest Revenue		9 0 0 00				9 0 0 00				
23	Rent Revenue		8 0 0 0 00				8 0 0 0 00				
24	Subscriptions Revenue				(h) 10 0 0 0 00		10 0 0 0 00				
25	Purchases	105 0 0 0 00				105 0 0 0 00					
26	Purchases Returns and Allowances		8 0 0 0 00				8 0 0 0 00				
27	Purchases Discounts		1 0 0 0 00				1 0 0 0 00				
28	Freight-In	3 0 0 0 00				3 0 0 0 00					
29	Wages Expense	42 0 0 0 00		(g) 4 5 0 00		42 4 5 0 00					
30	Advertising Expense	2 5 0 0 00				2 5 0 0 00					
31	Bank Credit Card Expense	1 5 0 0 00				1 5 0 0 00					
32	Rent Expense	20 0 0 0 00				20 0 0 0 00					
33	Supplies Expense			(c) 1 4 0 0 00		1 4 0 0 00					
34	Telephone Expense	3 5 0 0 00				3 5 0 0 00					
35	Utilities Expense	12 0 0 0 00				12 0 0 0 00					
36	Insurance Expense			(d) 1 8 0 0 00		1 8 0 0 00					
37	Depr. Expense—Building			(e) 4 0 0 0 00		4 0 0 0 00					
38	Depr. Expense—Store Equipment			(f) 3 0 0 0 00		3 0 0 0 00					
39	Miscellaneous Expense	2 2 5 0 00				2 2 5 0 00					
40	Interest Expense	3 1 5 0 00				3 1 5 0 00					
41		428 6 0 0 00	428 6 0 0 00	64 6 5 0 00	64 6 5 0 00	454 0 5 0 00	454 0 5 0 00				
42											

Ending Inventory

Beginning Inventory

Both the debit and credit are extended

Ending Inventory

STEP 1   STEP 2   STEP 3

FIGURE 14-11   Step 4: Extensions to the Income Statement and Balance Sheet Columns   Step 5: Completing the Work Sheet and Computing Net Income

Northern Micro
Work Sheet
For Year Ended December 31, 20- -

#	Account Title	Trial Balance Debit	Trial Balance Credit	Adjustments Debit	Adjustments Credit	Adjusted Trial Balance Debit	Adjusted Trial Balance Credit	Income Statement Debit	Income Statement Credit	Balance Sheet Debit	Balance Sheet Credit
1	Cash	20 0 0 0 00				20 0 0 0 00				20 0 0 0 00	
2	Accounts Receivable	15 0 0 0 00				15 0 0 0 00				15 0 0 0 00	
3	Merchandise Inventory	26 0 0 0 00		(b) 18 0 0 0 00	(a) 26 0 0 0 00	18 0 0 0 00				18 0 0 0 00	
4	Supplies	1 8 0 0 00			(c) 1 4 0 0 00	4 0 0 00				4 0 0 00	
5	Prepaid Insurance	2 4 0 0 00			(d) 1 8 0 0 00	6 0 0 00				6 0 0 00	
6	Land	10 0 0 0 00				10 0 0 0 00				10 0 0 0 00	
7	Building	90 0 0 0 00				90 0 0 0 00				90 0 0 0 00	
8	Accum. Depr.—Building		16 0 0 0 00		(e) 4 0 0 0 00		20 0 0 0 00				20 0 0 0 00
9	Store Equipment	50 0 0 0 00				50 0 0 0 00				50 0 0 0 00	
10	Accum. Depr.—Store Equipment		15 0 0 0 00		(f) 3 0 0 0 00		18 0 0 0 00				18 0 0 0 00
11	Notes Payable		5 0 0 0 00				5 0 0 0 00				5 0 0 0 00
12	Accounts Payable		10 0 0 0 00				10 0 0 0 00				10 0 0 0 00
13	Wages Payable				(g) 4 5 0 00		4 5 0 00				4 5 0 00
14	Sales Tax Payable		1 5 0 0 00				1 5 0 0 00				1 5 0 0 00
15	Unearned Subscriptions Revenue		12 0 0 0 00	(h) 10 0 0 0 00			2 0 0 0 00				2 0 0 0 00
16	Mortgage Payable		30 0 0 0 00				30 0 0 0 00				30 0 0 0 00
17	Gary L. Fishel, Capital		114 4 0 0 00				114 4 0 0 00				114 4 0 0 00
18	Gary L. Fishel, Drawing	20 0 0 0 00				20 0 0 0 00				20 0 0 0 00	
19	Income Summary			(a) 26 0 0 0 00	(b) 18 0 0 0 00	26 0 0 0 00	18 0 0 0 00	26 0 0 0 00	18 0 0 0 00		
20	Sales		214 0 0 0 00				214 0 0 0 00		214 0 0 0 00		
21	Sales Returns and Allowances	1 2 0 0 00				1 2 0 0 00		1 2 0 0 00			
22	Interest Revenue		9 0 0 00				9 0 0 00		9 0 0 00		
23	Rent Revenue		8 0 0 0 00				8 0 0 0 00		8 0 0 0 00		
24	Subscriptions Revenue				(h) 10 0 0 0 00		10 0 0 0 00		10 0 0 0 00		
25	Purchases	105 0 0 0 00				105 0 0 0 00		105 0 0 0 00			
26	Purchases Returns and Allowances		8 0 0 0 00				8 0 0 0 00		8 0 0 0 00		
27	Purchases Discounts		1 0 0 0 00				1 0 0 0 00		1 0 0 0 00		
28	Freight-In	3 0 0 0 00				3 0 0 0 00		3 0 0 0 00			
29	Wages Expense	42 0 0 0 00		(g) 4 5 0 00		42 4 5 0 00		42 4 5 0 00			
30	Advertising Expense	2 5 0 0 00				2 5 0 0 00		2 5 0 0 00			
31	Bank Credit Card Expense	1 5 0 0 00				1 5 0 0 00		1 5 0 0 00			
32	Rent Expense	20 0 0 0 00				20 0 0 0 00		20 0 0 0 00			
33	Supplies Expense			(c) 1 4 0 0 00		1 4 0 0 00		1 4 0 0 00			
34	Telephone Expense	3 5 0 0 00				3 5 0 0 00		3 5 0 0 00			
35	Utilities Expense	12 0 0 0 00				12 0 0 0 00		12 0 0 0 00			
36	Insurance Expense			(d) 1 8 0 0 00		1 8 0 0 00		1 8 0 0 00			
37	Depr. Expense—Building			(e) 4 0 0 0 00		4 0 0 0 00		4 0 0 0 00			
38	Depr. Expense—Store Equipment			(f) 3 0 0 0 00		3 0 0 0 00		3 0 0 0 00			
39	Miscellaneous Expense	2 2 5 0 00				2 2 5 0 00		2 2 5 0 00			
40	Interest Expense	3 1 5 0 00				3 1 5 0 00		3 1 5 0 00			
41		428 6 0 0 00	428 6 0 0 00	64 6 5 0 00	64 6 5 0 00	454 0 5 0 00	454 0 5 0 00	230 0 5 0 00	252 7 0 0 00	224 0 0 0 00	201 3 5 0 00
42	Net Income							22 6 5 0 00			22 6 5 0 00
43								252 7 0 0 00	252 7 0 0 00	224 0 0 0 00	224 0 0 0 00

STEP 1   STEP 2   STEP 3   STEPS 4 AND 5

ADJUSTING ENTRIES

LO4 Journalize adjusting entries for a merchandising business.

LO4 Journalize adjusting entries for a merchandising business.

Recall that making the adjustments on the work sheet has no effect on the actual accounts in the general ledger. Journal entries must be made to enter the adjustments into the accounting system. Figure 14-12 shows the adjusting entries for Northern Micro.

LEARNING KEY

Recall that the work sheet is just a planning tool. The adjusting entries must be entered in the general journal.

FIGURE 14-12   Adjusting Entries for Northern Micro

	DATE		DESCRIPTION	POST. REF.	DEBIT					CREDIT					
1			Adjusting Entries												1
2	20-- Dec.	31	Income Summary		26	0	0	0	00						2
3			Merchandise Inventory							26	0	0	0	00	3
4															4
5		31	Merchandise Inventory		18	0	0	0	00						5
6			Income Summary							18	0	0	0	00	6
7															7
8		31	Supplies Expense		1	4	0	0	00						8
9			Supplies							1	4	0	0	00	9
10															10
11		31	Insurance Expense		1	8	0	0	00						11
12			Prepaid Insurance							1	8	0	0	00	12
13															13
14		31	Depr. Expense—Building		4	0	0	0	00						14
15			Accumulated Depr.—Building							4	0	0	0	00	15
16															16
17		31	Depr. Expense—Store Equipment		3	0	0	0	00						17
18			Accumulated Depr.—Store Equipment							3	0	0	0	00	18
19															19
20		31	Wages Expense			4	5	0	00						20
21			Wages Payable								4	5	0	00	21
22															22
23		31	Unearned Subscriptions Revenue		10	0	0	0	00						23
24			Subscriptions Revenue							10	0	0	0	00	24
25															25

GENERAL JOURNAL — PAGE 3

PREPARING AND JOURNALIZING ADJUSTING ENTRIES UNDER THE PERPETUAL INVENTORY SYSTEM

LO5 Prepare adjusting journal entries under the perpetual inventory system.

Under the perpetual inventory method, two entries are required to record the sale of merchandise.

Under the perpetual inventory system, the merchandise inventory and cost of goods sold accounts are continually updated throughout the year to reflect purchases and sales of inventory. When inventory is purchased, the merchandise inventory account is debited and Cash or Accounts Payable is credited. When inventory is sold, two entries are made.

1. Cash or Accounts Receivable is debited and Sales is credited.

2. Cost of Goods Sold is debited and Merchandise Inventory is credited.

A comparison of the entries under the periodic and perpetual inventory systems is provided in Figure 14-13.

FIGURE 14-13   Entries for Periodic and Perpetual Inventory Systems

TRANSACTION	PERIODIC SYSTEM		PERPETUAL SYSTEM		

Purchased merchandise on account, $800.	Purchases
	    Accounts Payable
		800
		800
			Merchandise Inventory
			    Accounts Payable
				800
				800	

Sold merchandise on account, $400. The cost of the merchandise sold was $300.	Accounts Receivable
	    Sales
		400
		400
			Accounts Receivable
			    Sales
				400
				400	

			Cost of Goods Sold Merchandise Inventory	300 300	

As discussed in Chapter 13, the perpetual inventory system does not eliminate the need for taking physical inventories. The perpetual records must be compared with the physical inventory to discover and correct any errors or losses of merchandise from theft, breakage, or spoilage. If a difference is found between the physical count and the amount in the perpetual inventory records, the records must be corrected by an adjusting entry. Some firms use Cost of Goods Sold to make this adjustment. A preferable approach is to use an account called **Inventory Short and Over**. For example, if the book balance is $3,840 and the physical count shows $3,710 worth of merchandise, the $130 shortage would be entered as follows:

Adjusting Entry

4		Inventory Short and Over		1 3 0 00			4
5		Merchandise Inventory			1 3 0 00		5
6		To adjust inventory per physical count					6

Similarly, if the book balance is $3,840 and the physical count shows $3,900 worth of merchandise, this $60 overage would be entered as follows:

Adjusting Entry

4		Merchandise Inventory		6 0 00			4
5		Inventory Short and Over			6 0 00		5
6		To adjust inventory per physical count					6

If Inventory Short and Over has a debit balance, the account is listed with other expenses on the income statement. If it has a credit balance, the account is listed with other revenues on the income statement.

Using a separate account, Inventory Short and Over, makes it easier for management to track inventory problems associated with errors, theft, breakage, and spoilage. Further, it removes these items from the calculation of cost of goods sold and provides a better measure of the gross profit on sales.

A business that sells a wide selection of low-cost goods may not find it practical to keep a perpetual inventory. In contrast, a business that sells a few high-cost items (cars, fine jewelry, stereo equipment) can maintain such a record without incurring excessive processing costs. The increasing use of computers and optical scanning devices at the point of sale has enabled more businesses to switch from the periodic to the perpetual inventory method.

Learning Objectives	Key Points to Remember

LO1 Prepare an adjustment for merchandise inventory using the periodic inventory system.

Extra care is required for the end-of-period adjustment for merchandise inventory and the related extensions on the work sheet. The two-step adjustment process used on the work sheet is shown below. This technique is used so that all of the information required to compute cost of goods sold on the income statement is provided in the Income Statement columns of the work sheet.

ACCOUNT TITLE	TRIAL BALANCE DEBIT	TRIAL BALANCE CREDIT	ADJUSTMENTS DEBIT	ADJUSTMENTS CREDIT	ADJUSTED TRIAL BALANCE DEBIT	ADJUSTED TRIAL BALANCE CREDIT	INCOME STATEMENT DEBIT	INCOME STATEMENT CREDIT	BALANCE SHEET DEBIT	BALANCE SHEET CREDIT
							BI	EI		
Merchandise Inventory	20		STEP 2 30	20 STEP 1	30				30	
Income Summary			STEP 1 20	30 STEP 2	20	30	20	30		
Purchases	80						80			
							Purchases			

Step 1: Remove beginning inventory Income Summary 20
                                        Merchandise Inventory 20

Step 2: Insert ending inventory Merchandise Inventory 30
                                          Income Summary 30

BI: Beginning inventory ($20); EI: Ending inventory ($30)

Cost of goods sold:
  Merchandise inventory, January 1 $ 20
  Purchases   80
  Goods available for sale $100
  Less merchandise inventory, December 31   30
    Cost of goods sold $ 70

LO2 Prepare an adjustment for unearned revenue.

Some firms receive cash before providing a service or selling a product. The cash received in advance is considered a liability, unearned revenue, until earned. The adjusting entry to recognize that unearned revenue has become earned is as follows:

      Unearned Revenue   xxx
           Revenue   xxx

LO3 Prepare a work sheet for a merchandising business.

Steps to follow when preparing a work sheet are as follows:
1. Prepare the trial balance.
2. Prepare the adjustments.
3. Prepare the adjusted trial balance.
4. Extend the adjusted trial balance amounts to the Income Statement and Balance Sheet columns.
5. Total the Income Statement and Balance Sheet columns to compute the net income or net loss.

LO4 Journalize adjusting entries for a merchandising business.

The work sheet is a useful tool when preparing end-of-period adjustments and financial statements. Remember: The work sheet is NOT a formal part of the accounting system. Adjustments made on the work sheet must be entered in a journal and posted to the ledger.

Learning Objectives	Key Points to Remember
LO5 Prepare adjusting journal entries under the perpetual inventory system.	Under the perpetual inventory system, the cost of goods sold and merchandise inventory accounts are updated whenever merchandise is purchased or sold. Thus, the firm knows how much inventory should be on hand at any given point in time. However, the balance of the merchandise inventory account must be verified with an actual physical count of the inventory before issuing financial statements. If there is a difference, an adjusting entry is made. If the balance in the inventory account is greater than the physical count, the following entry is made:

Inventory Short and Over	xxx	
Merchandise Inventory		xxx

If the balance in the inventory account is less than the physical count, the following entry is made:

Merchandise Inventory	xxx	
Inventory Short and Over		xxx

DEMONSTRATION PROBLEM

Aaron Patton owns and operates Patton's Bait Shop and Boat Rental. A year-end trial balance is shown on the next page.

Year-end adjustment data for Patton's Bait Shop and Boat Rental are as follows:

(a and b)   A physical count shows that merchandise inventory costing $15,000 is on hand as of December 31, 20--.

(c)   Supplies remaining at the end of the year, $200.

(d)   Unexpired insurance on December 31, $300.

(e)   Depreciation expense on the building for 20--, $2,000.

(f)   Depreciation expense on the store equipment for 20--, $1,500.

(g)   Wages earned but not paid as of December 31, $225.

(h)   Unearned boat rental revenue as of December 31, $1,000.

REQUIRED

1.   Prepare a year-end work sheet.

2.   Journalize the adjusting entries.

(continued)

Patton's Bait Shop and Boat Rental
Trial Balance
December 31, 20 - -

ACCOUNT TITLE	DEBIT BALANCE					CREDIT BALANCE				
Cash	10	0	0	0	00					
Accounts Receivable	7	5	0	0	00					
Merchandise Inventory	19	0	0	0	00					
Supplies		9	0	0	00					
Prepaid Insurance	1	2	0	0	00					
Land	5	0	0	0	00					
Building	45	0	0	0	00					
Accumulated Depreciation—Building						8	0	0	0	00
Store Equipment	25	0	0	0	00					
Accumulated Depreciation—Store Equipment						7	5	0	0	00
Notes Payable						2	5	0	0	00
Accounts Payable						5	0	0	0	00
Wages Payable										
Unearned Boat Rental Revenue						11	0	0	0	00
Aaron Patton, Capital						77	9	0	0	00
Aaron Patton, Drawing	10	0	0	0	00					
Income Summary										
Sales						100	2	5	0	00
Sales Returns and Allowances		6	0	0	00					
Boat Rental Revenue										
Purchases	52	5	0	0	00					
Purchases Returns and Allowances							4	0	0	00
Purchases Discounts							5	0	0	00
Freight-In		1	5	0	00					
Wages Expense	21	0	0	0	00					
Advertising Expense	3	7	5	0	00					
Supplies Expense										
Telephone Expense	1	7	5	0	00					
Utilities Expense	6	0	0	0	00					
Insurance Expense										
Depreciation Expense—Building										
Depreciation Expense—Store Equipment										
Miscellaneous Expense	3	6	2	5	00					
Interest Expense			7	5	00					
	213	0	5	0	00	213	0	5	0	00

Solution 1.

Patton's Bait Shop and Boat Rental
Work Sheet
For Year Ended December 31, 20--

#	Account Title	Trial Balance Debit	Trial Balance Credit	Adjustments Debit	Adjustments Credit	Adjusted Trial Balance Debit	Adjusted Trial Balance Credit	Income Statement Debit	Income Statement Credit	Balance Sheet Debit	Balance Sheet Credit
1	Cash	10,000.00				10,000.00				10,000.00	
2	Accounts Receivable	7,500.00				7,500.00				7,500.00	
3	Merchandise Inventory	19,000.00		(b) 15,000.00	(a) 19,000.00	15,000.00				15,000.00	
4	Supplies	9,000.00			(c) 7,000.00	2,000.00				2,000.00	
5	Prepaid Insurance	12,000.00			(d) 9,000.00	3,000.00				3,000.00	
6	Land	5,000.00				5,000.00				5,000.00	
7	Building	45,000.00				45,000.00				45,000.00	
8	Accum. Depr.—Building		8,000.00		(e) 2,000.00		10,000.00				10,000.00
9	Store Equipment	25,000.00				25,000.00				25,000.00	
10	Accum. Depr.—Store Equipment		7,500.00		(f) 1,500.00		9,000.00				9,000.00
11	Notes Payable		2,500.00				2,500.00				2,500.00
12	Accounts Payable		5,000.00				5,000.00				5,000.00
13	Wages Payable				(g) 225.00		225.00				225.00
14	Unearned Boat Rental Revenue		11,000.00	(h) 10,000.00			1,000.00				1,000.00
15	Aaron Patton, Capital		77,900.00				77,900.00				77,900.00
16	Aaron Patton, Drawing	10,000.00				10,000.00				10,000.00	
17	Income Summary			(a) 19,000.00	(b) 15,000.00	19,000.00	15,000.00	19,000.00	15,000.00		
18	Sales		100,250.00				100,250.00		100,250.00		
19	Sales Returns and Allowances	6,000.00				6,000.00		6,000.00			
20	Boat Rental Revenue				(h) 10,000.00		10,000.00		10,000.00		
21	Purchases	52,500.00				52,500.00		52,500.00			
22	Purchases Returns and Allowances		4,000.00				4,000.00		4,000.00		
23	Purchases Discounts		5,000.00				5,000.00		5,000.00		
24	Freight-In	1,500.00				1,500.00		1,500.00			
25	Wages Expense	21,000.00		(g) 225.00		21,225.00		21,225.00			
26	Advertising Expense	3,750.00				3,750.00		3,750.00			
27	Supplies Expense			(c) 7,000.00		7,000.00		7,000.00			
28	Telephone Expense	1,750.00				1,750.00		1,750.00			
29	Utilities Expense	6,000.00				6,000.00		6,000.00			
30	Insurance Expense			(d) 9,000.00		9,000.00		9,000.00			
31	Depr. Expense—Building			(e) 2,000.00		2,000.00		2,000.00			
32	Depr. Expense—Store Equipment			(f) 1,500.00		1,500.00		1,500.00			
33	Miscellaneous Expense	3,625.00				3,625.00		3,625.00			
34	Interest Expense	750.00				750.00		750.00			
35		213,050.00	213,050.00	49,325.00	49,325.00	231,775.00	231,775.00	113,775.00	126,150.00	118,000.00	105,625.00
36	Net Income							12,375.00			12,375.00
37								126,150.00	126,150.00	118,000.00	118,000.00

(continued)

2.

		GENERAL JOURNAL													PAGE 3	
	DATE	DESCRIPTION	POST REF.	DEBIT					CREDIT						
1		Adjusting Entries													1
2	20-- Dec. 31	Income Summary		19	0	0	0	00							2
3		Merchandise Inventory							19	0	0	0	00		3
4															4
5	31	Merchandise Inventory		15	0	0	0	00							5
6		Income Summary							15	0	0	0	00		6
7															7
8	31	Supplies Expense			7	0	0	00							8
9		Supplies								7	0	0	00		9
10															10
11	31	Insurance Expense			9	0	0	00							11
12		Prepaid Insurance								9	0	0	00		12
13															13
14	31	Depreciation Expense—Building		2	0	0	0	00							14
15		Accumulated Depreciation—Building							2	0	0	0	00		15
16															16
17	31	Depreciation Expense—Store Equipment		1	5	0	0	00							17
18		Accumulated Depreciation—Store Equipment							1	5	0	0	00		18
19															19
20	31	Wages Expense			2	2	5	00							20
21		Wages Payable								2	2	5	00		21
22															22
23	31	Unearned Boat Rental Revenue		10	0	0	0	00							23
24		Boat Rental Revenue							10	0	0	0	00		24
25															25

KEY TERMS

contra-cost accounts (536)   Accounts that are deducted from the purchases account when computing cost of goods sold—Purchases Returns and Allowances, and Purchases Discounts.

contra-revenue accounts (536)   Accounts that are deducted from Sales on the income statement—Sales Returns and Allowances, and Sales Discounts.

Inventory Short and Over (545)   An account used to adjust the perpetual inventory records when a difference exists between the physical count and the amount in the perpetual inventory records.

unearned revenue (535)   Cash received in advance of delivering a product or performing a service.

Self-Study Test Questions

True/False

1. The beginning inventory is removed from the merchandise inventory account with a credit to Merchandise Inventory and a debit to Income Summary.

2. The ending inventory is entered by debiting Merchandise Inventory and crediting Income Summary.

3. The cash received in advance before delivering a product or performing a service is called unearned revenue.

4. Unearned revenue is adjusted into an expense account at the end of the accounting period.

5. Sales Returns and Allowances is classified as a contra-expense account on the income statement.

Multiple Choice

1. Purchases Returns and Allowances and Purchases Discounts are classified as _____ on the income statement.

   (a) expense accounts   (c) revenue accounts
   (b) contra-cost accounts   (d) contra-revenue accounts

2. The first step in preparing a work sheet is to

   (a) prepare the trial balance.
   (b) prepare the income statement.
   (c) prepare the adjustments.
   (d) prepare the balance sheet.

3. The last step in preparing a work sheet is to

   (a) prepare the adjusted trial balance.
   (b) total the Income Statement and Balance Sheet columns to compute net income or net loss.
   (c) prepare the adjustments.
   (d) extend the Adjusted Trial Balance columns.

4. Unearned Revenue is extended into the _____ on the work sheet.

   (a) Adjustments columns   (c) Income Statement columns
   (b) Balance Sheet columns   (d) Trial Balance columns

5. The most useful tool in preparing end-of-period adjustments and financial statements is the

   (a) general ledger.   (c) general journal.
   (b) work sheet.   (d) physical inventory.

The answers to the Self-Study Test Questions are at the end of the text.

REVIEW QUESTIONS

LO1   1.   A firm is preparing to make adjusting entries at the end of the accounting period. The balance of the merchandise inventory account is $200,000. If the firm is using the periodic inventory system, what does this balance represent?

LO1   2.   What work sheet amounts are used to compute cost of goods sold?

LO1   3.   Why are both the debit and credit amounts in the Adjustments columns on the Income Summary line of the work sheet extended to the Adjusted Trial Balance columns?

LO2   4.   What is an unearned revenue?

LO2   5.   Give three examples of unearned revenue.

LO3   6.   List the five steps taken to prepare a work sheet.

LO3   7.   What does the difference between the totals of the Income Statement columns represent? What does the difference between the Balance Sheet column totals represent?

LO5   8.   A firm is preparing to make adjusting entries at the end of the accounting period. The balance of the merchandise inventory account is $100,000. If the firm is using the perpetual inventory system, what does this balance represent?

REVISITING THE OPENER

In the chapter opener on page 531, you are asked to consider how Evan should account for cash deposits on special order sales. Please write a brief memo explaining the proper accounting treatment.

SERIES A EXERCISES

E 14-1A (LO1)

ADJUSTMENT FOR MERCHANDISE INVENTORY USING T ACCOUNTS: PERIODIC INVENTORY SYSTEM Sam Baker owns a business called Sam's Sporting Goods. His beginning inventory as of January 1, 20--, was $47,000 and his ending inventory as of December 31, 20--, was $53,000. Set up T accounts for Merchandise Inventory and Income Summary and perform the year-end adjustment for Merchandise Inventory.

E 14-2A (LO1)
✓ Cost of goods sold: $65,200

CALCULATION OF COST OF GOODS SOLD: PERIODIC INVENTORY SYSTEM Prepare the cost of goods sold section for Adams Gift Shop. The following amounts are known:

Beginning merchandise inventory	$26,000
Ending merchandise inventory	23,000
Purchases	71,000
Purchases returns and allowances	3,500
Purchases discounts	5,500
Freight-in	200

E 14-3A (LO2)

ADJUSTMENT FOR UNEARNED REVENUES USING T ACCOUNTS Set up T accounts for Cash, Unearned Ticket Revenue, and Ticket Revenue. Post the following two transactions to the appropriate accounts, indicating each transaction by letter:

(a) Sold 1,500 season tickets at $30 each, receiving cash of $45,000.
(b) An end-of-period adjustment is needed to recognize that $35,000 in ticket revenue has been earned.

E 14-4A (LO3)
✓ Cost of goods sold: $75,500

WORK SHEET EXTENSIONS FOR MERCHANDISE INVENTORY ADJUSTMENTS: PERIODIC INVENTORY SYSTEM The following partial work sheet is taken from Kevin's Gift Shop for the year ended December 31, 20--. The ending merchandise inventory is $50,000.

1. Complete the Adjustments columns for the merchandise inventory.
2. Extend the merchandise inventory to the Adjusted Trial Balance and Balance Sheet columns.
3. Extend the remaining accounts to the Adjusted Trial Balance and Income Statement columns.
4. Prepare a cost of goods sold section from the partial work sheet.

Kevin's Gift Shop
Work Sheet (Partial)
For Year Ended December 31, 20 - -

	ACCOUNT TITLE	TRIAL BALANCE		ADJUSTMENTS		
		DEBIT	CREDIT	DEBIT	CREDIT	
1	Merchandise Inventory	40 0 0 0 00				1
12	Income Summary					12
13	Purchases	90 0 0 0 00				13
14	Purchases Returns and Allowances		2 0 0 0 00			14
15	Purchases Discounts		3 0 0 0 00			15
16	Freight-In	5 0 0 00				16
17						17
18						18

E 14-5A (LO3)
✓ Beg. inv.: $55,000

DETERMINING THE BEGINNING AND ENDING INVENTORY FROM A PARTIAL WORK SHEET: PERIODIC INVENTORY SYSTEM From the following partial work sheet, indicate the dollar amount of beginning and ending merchandise inventory:

	ACCOUNT TITLE	ADJUSTMENTS		ADJUSTED TRIAL BALANCE		INCOME STATEMENT		BALANCE SHEET		
		DEBIT	CREDIT	DEBIT	CREDIT	DEBIT	CREDIT	DEBIT	CREDIT	
1	Merchandise Inventory	(b) 60 0 0 0 00	(a) 55 0 0 0 00	60 0 0 0 00				60 0 0 0 00		1
2	Income Summary	(a) 55 0 0 0 00	(b) 60 0 0 0 00	55 0 0 0 00	60 0 0 0 00	55 0 0 0 00	60 0 0 0 00			2

E 14-6A (LO4)

✓ (a)

Inc. Sum   45,000

    Mdse. Inv.   45,000

JOURNALIZE ADJUSTING ENTRIES FOR A MERCHANDISING BUSINESS

The following partial work sheet is taken from the books of Kelly's Kittens, a local pet kennel, for the year ended December 31, 20--. Journalize the adjustments in a general journal.

Kelly's Kittens
Work Sheet (Partial)
For Year Ended December 31, 20 - -

	ACCOUNT TITLE	TRIAL BALANCE DEBIT	TRIAL BALANCE CREDIT	ADJUSTMENTS DEBIT	ADJUSTMENTS CREDIT	
1	Merchandise Inventory	45 0 0 0 00		(b) 50 0 0 0 00	(a) 45 0 0 0 00	1
2	Supplies	10 0 0 0 00			(d) 7 0 0 0 00	2
3	Building	60 0 0 0 00				3
4	Accum. Depr.—Building		15 0 0 0 00		(e) 5 0 0 0 00	4
5	Wages Payable				(f) 1 2 0 0 00	5
6	Unearned Grooming Revenue		3 0 0 0 00	(c) 2 0 0 0 00		6
7	Income Summary			(a) 45 0 0 0 00	(b) 50 0 0 0 00	7
8	Grooming Revenue		20 0 0 0 00		(c) 2 0 0 0 00	8
9	Wages Expense	37 0 0 0 00		(f) 1 2 0 0 00		9
10	Supplies Expense			(d) 7 0 0 0 00		10
11	Depr. Expense—Building			(e) 5 0 0 0 00		11
12				110 2 0 0 00	110 2 0 0 00	12
13						13

E 14-7A (LO5)

JOURNAL ENTRIES UNDER THE PERPETUAL INVENTORY SYSTEM

Bhushan Building Supplies entered into the following transactions. Prepare journal entries under the perpetual inventory system.

June 1   Purchased merchandise on account from Brij Builder's Materials, $500,000.

     3   Purchased merchandise for cash, $400,000.

     5   Sold merchandise on account to Champa Construction for $20,000. The merchandise cost $15,000.

E 14-8A (LO5)

JOURNALIZE ADJUSTING ENTRY FOR A MERCHANDISING BUSINESS: PERPETUAL INVENTORY SYSTEM

On December 31, Anup Enterprises completed a physical count of its inventory. Although the merchandise inventory account shows a balance of $350,000, the physical count comes to $325,000. Prepare the appropriate adjusting entry under the perpetual inventory system.

SERIES A PROBLEMS

P 14-9A (LO1/2/3/4)

✓ Adj. col. total: $78,600;

Net income: $39,390

COMPLETION OF A WORK SHEET SHOWING A NET INCOME

The trial balance for the Seaside Kite Shop, a business owned by Joyce Kennington, is shown on page 555. Year-end adjustment information is as follows:

(a and b)   Merchandise inventory costing $30,000 is on hand as of December 31, 20--. (The periodic inventory system is used.)

(c)   Supplies remaining at the end of the year, $2,700.

(d)   Unexpired insurance on December 31, $2,900.

(e)   Depreciation expense on the building for 20--, $5,000.

(f)   Depreciation expense on the store equipment for 20--, $3,200.

(g) Unearned rent revenue as of December 31, $2,200.

(h) Wages earned but not paid as of December 31, $900.

REQUIRED

1. Complete the Adjustments columns, identifying each adjustment with its corresponding letter.

2. Complete the work sheet.

3. Enter the adjustments in a general journal.

Seaside Kite Shop
Trial Balance
December 31, 20 - -

ACCOUNT TITLE	DEBIT BALANCE					CREDIT BALANCE				
Cash	20	0	0	0	00					
Accounts Receivable	14	0	0	0	00					
Merchandise Inventory	25	0	0	0	00					
Supplies	8	0	0	0	00					
Prepaid Insurance	5	4	0	0	00					
Land	30	0	0	0	00					
Building	50	0	0	0	00					
Accumulated Depreciation—Building						20	0	0	0	00
Store Equipment	35	0	0	0	00					
Accumulated Depreciation—Store Equipment						14	0	0	0	00
Accounts Payable						9	6	0	0	00
Wages Payable										
Sales Tax Payable						5	9	0	0	00
Unearned Rent Revenue						8	9	0	0	00
Mortgage Payable						45	0	0	0	00
J. Kennington, Capital						65	4	1	0	00
J. Kennington, Drawing	26	0	0	0	00					
Income Summary										
Sales						118	0	0	0	00
Sales Returns and Allowances	1	7	0	0	00					
Rent Revenue										
Purchases	27	0	0	0	00					
Purchases Returns and Allowances						1	4	0	0	00
Purchases Discounts						1	8	0	0	00
Freight-In	2	1	0	0	00					
Wages Expense	32	0	0	0	00					
Advertising Expense	3	6	0	0	00					
Supplies Expense										
Telephone Expense	1	3	5	0	00					
Utilities Expense	8	0	0	0	00					
Insurance Expense										
Depreciation Expense—Building										
Depreciation Expense—Store Equipment										
Miscellaneous Expense		8	6	0	00					
	290	0	1	0	00	290	0	1	0	00

P 14-10A (LO1/2/3/4)

✓ **Adj. col. total: $72,650;**
Net loss: $45,760

COMPLETION OF A WORK SHEET SHOWING A NET LOSS The trial balance for Cascade Bicycle Shop, a business owned by David Lamond, is shown below. Year-end adjustment information is as follows:

(a and b)   Merchandise inventory costing $22,000 is on hand as of December 31, 20--. (The periodic inventory system is used.)
(c)   Supplies remaining at the end of the year, $2,400.
(d)   Unexpired insurance on December 31, $1,750.
(e)   Depreciation expense on the building for 20--, $4,000.
(f)   Depreciation expense on the store equipment for 20--, $3,600.
(g)   Unearned storage revenue as of December 31, $1,950.
(h)   Wages earned but not paid as of December 31, $750.

Cascade Bicycle Shop
Trial Balance
December 31, 20 - -

ACCOUNT TITLE	DEBIT BALANCE	CREDIT BALANCE
Cash	23 0 0 0 00	
Accounts Receivable	15 0 0 0 00	
Merchandise Inventory	31 0 0 0 00	
Supplies	7 2 0 0 00	
Prepaid Insurance	4 6 0 0 00	
Land	28 0 0 0 00	
Building	53 0 0 0 00	
Accumulated Depreciation—Building		17 0 0 0 00
Store Equipment	27 0 0 0 00	
Accumulated Depreciation—Store Equipment		9 0 0 0 00
Accounts Payable		3 8 0 0 00
Wages Payable		
Sales Tax Payable		3 0 5 0 00
Unearned Storage Revenue		5 6 0 0 00
Mortgage Payable		42 0 0 0 00
D. Lamond, Capital		165 7 6 0 00
D. Lamond, Drawing	33 0 0 0 00	
Income Summary		
Sales		51 0 0 0 00
Sales Returns and Allowances	2 4 0 0 00	
Storage Revenue		
Purchases	21 0 0 0 00	
Purchases Returns and Allowances		1 3 0 0 00
Purchases Discounts		1 9 0 0 00
Freight-In	1 8 0 0 00	
Wages Expense	35 0 0 0 00	
Advertising Expense	5 7 0 0 00	
Supplies Expense		
Telephone Expense	2 2 0 0 00	
Utilities Expense	9 6 0 0 00	
Insurance Expense		
Depreciation Expense—Building		
Depreciation Expense—Store Equipment		
Miscellaneous Expense	9 1 0 00	
	300 4 1 0 00	300 4 1 0 00

REQUIRED

1. Complete the Adjustments columns, identifying each adjustment with its corresponding letter.
2. Complete the work sheet.
3. Enter the adjustments in the general journal.

P 14-11A (LO1/2/4)
✓ Adj. col. total: $88,155

WORKING BACKWARD FROM ADJUSTED TRIAL BALANCE TO DETERMINE ADJUSTING ENTRIES The partial work sheet shown below is taken from the books of Stark Street Computers, a business owned by Logan Cowart, for the year ended December 31, 20--.

Stark Street Computers
Work Sheet (Partial)
For Year Ended December 31, 20 - -

#	ACCOUNT TITLE	TRIAL BALANCE DEBIT	TRIAL BALANCE CREDIT	ADJUSTMENTS DEBIT	ADJUSTMENTS CREDIT	ADJUSTED TRIAL BALANCE DEBIT	ADJUSTED TRIAL BALANCE CREDIT	#
1	Cash	18 000 00				18 000 00		1
2	Accounts Receivable	11 000 00				11 000 00		2
3	Merchandise Inventory	25 000 00				35 000 00		3
4	Supplies	8 000 00				2 820 00		4
5	Prepaid Insurance	5 400 00				1 225 00		5
6	Land	27 000 00				27 000 00		6
7	Building	48 000 00				48 000 00		7
8	Accum. Depr.—Building		20 000 00				27 000 00	8
9	Store Equipment	33 000 00				33 000 00		9
10	Accum. Depr.—Store Equipment		8 700 00				12 800 00	10
11	Accounts Payable		6 400 00				6 400 00	11
12	Wages Payable						1 300 00	12
13	Sales Tax Payable		5 700 00				5 700 00	13
14	Unearned Repair Revenue		8 200 00				1 800 00	14
15	Mortgage Payable		44 000 00				44 000 00	15
16	L. Cowart, Capital		80 025 00				80 025 00	16
17	L. Cowart, Drawing	35 000 00				35 000 00		17
18	Income Summary					25 000 00	35 000 00	18
19	Sales		122 000 00				122 000 00	19
20	Sales Returns and Allowances	2 250 00				2 250 00		20
21	Repair Revenue						6 400 00	21
22	Purchases	29 750 00				29 750 00		22
23	Purchases Returns and Allowances		1 850 00				1 850 00	23
24	Purchases Discounts		1 425 00				1 425 00	24
25	Freight-In	3 200 00				3 200 00		25
26	Wages Expense	37 000 00				38 300 00		26
27	Advertising Expense	4 125 00				4 125 00		27
28	Supplies Expense					5 180 00		28
29	Telephone Expense	1 650 00				1 650 00		29
30	Utilities Expense	9 150 00				9 150 00		30
31	Insurance Expense					4 175 00		31
32	Depr. Expense—Building					7 000 00		32
33	Depr. Expense—Store Equipment					4 100 00		33
34	Miscellaneous Expense	775 00				775 00		34
35		298 300 00	298 300 00			345 700 00	345 700 00	35

REQUIRED

1. Determine the adjusting entries by analyzing the difference between the adjusted trial balance and the trial balance.

2. Journalize the adjusting entries in a general journal.

P 14-12A (LO1/2/3/4)

✓ Adj. col. total: $92,335;
Cost of goods sold: $33,145

WORKING BACKWARD FROM THE INCOME STATEMENT AND BALANCE SHEET COLUMNS OF THE WORK SHEET TO DETERMINE ADJUSTED TRIAL BALANCE AND ADJUSTING ENTRIES The partially completed work sheet from the books of Lewis Music Store, a business owned by Hugo Lewis, for the year ended December 31, 20--, is shown on page 559.

REQUIRED

1. Analyze the work sheet and determine the adjusted trial balance and the adjusting entries by working backward from the Income Statement and Balance Sheet columns.

2. Journalize the adjusting entries in a general journal.

3. Prepare the cost of goods sold section of the income statement for Lewis Music Store.

SERIES B EXERCISES

E 14-1B (LO1)

ADJUSTMENT FOR MERCHANDISE INVENTORY USING T ACCOUNTS: PERIODIC INVENTORY SYSTEM Sandra Owens owns a business called Sandra's Sporting Goods. Her beginning inventory as of January 1, 20--, was $33,000 and her ending inventory as of December 31, 20--, was $36,000. Set up T accounts for Merchandise Inventory and Income Summary and perform the year-end adjustment for Merchandise Inventory.

E 14-2B (LO1)

✓ Cost of goods sold: $58,100

CALCULATION OF COST OF GOODS SOLD: PERIODIC INVENTORY SYSTEM Prepare the cost of goods sold section for Havens Gift Shop. The following amounts are known:

Beginning merchandise inventory	$29,000
Ending merchandise inventory	27,000
Purchases	62,000
Purchases returns and allowances	2,800
Purchases discounts	3,400
Freight-in	300

E 14-3B (LO2)

ADJUSTMENT FOR UNEARNED REVENUES USING T ACCOUNTS Set up T accounts for Cash, Unearned Ticket Revenue, and Ticket Revenue. Post the following two transactions to the appropriate accounts, indicating each transaction by letter:

(a) Sold 1,200 season tickets at $20 each, receiving cash of $24,000.
(b) An end-of-period adjustment is needed to recognize that $19,000 in ticket revenue has been earned.

Lewis Music Store
Work Sheet
For Year Ended December 31, 20 - -

P14-12A

#	Account Title	Trial Balance Debit	Trial Balance Credit	Adjustments Debit	Adjustments Credit	Adjusted Trial Balance Debit	Adjusted Trial Balance Credit	Income Statement Debit	Income Statement Credit	Balance Sheet Debit	Balance Sheet Credit
1	Cash	27 0 0 0 00								27 0 0 0 00	
2	Accounts Receivable	13 3 0 0 00								13 3 0 0 00	
3	Merchandise Inventory	34 0 0 0 00								38 0 0 0 00	
4	Supplies	5 3 0 0 00								1 5 0 0 00	
5	Prepaid Insurance	6 1 0 0 00								1 7 8 5 00	
6	Land	31 0 0 0 00								31 0 0 0 00	
7	Building	52 0 0 0 00								52 0 0 0 00	
8	Accum. Depr.—Building		17 0 0 0 00								21 1 4 5 00
9	Store Equipment	39 0 0 0 00								39 0 0 0 00	
10	Accum. Depr.—Store Equipment		11 9 0 0 00								14 8 7 5 00
11	Accounts Payable		6 2 5 0 00								6 2 5 0 00
12	Wages Payable										8 7 5 00
13	Sales Tax Payable		6 2 0 0 00								6 2 0 0 00
14	Unearned Rent Revenue		7 4 0 0 00								3 1 7 5 00
15	Mortgage Payable		46 0 0 0 00								46 0 0 0 00
16	H. Lewis, Capital		111 6 2 0 00								111 6 2 0 00
17	H. Lewis, Drawing	37 0 0 0 00								37 0 0 0 00	
18	Income Summary							34 0 0 0 00	38 0 0 0 00		
19	Sales		136 0 0 0 00						136 0 0 0 00		
20	Sales Returns and Allowances	3 5 0 0 00						3 5 0 0 00			
21	Rent Revenue								4 2 2 5 00		
22	Purchases	39 0 0 0 00						39 0 0 0 00			
23	Purchases Returns and Allowances		2 5 3 0 00						2 5 3 0 00		
24	Purchases Discounts		1 9 7 5 00						1 9 7 5 00		
25	Freight-In	2 6 5 0 00						2 6 5 0 00			
26	Wages Expense	42 0 0 0 00						42 8 7 5 00			
27	Advertising Expense	4 1 7 5 00						4 1 7 5 00			
28	Supplies Expense							3 8 0 0 00			
29	Telephone Expense	1 9 8 0 00						1 9 8 0 00			
30	Utilities Expense	7 9 4 5 00						7 9 4 5 00			
31	Insurance Expense							4 3 1 5 00			
32	Depr. Expense—Building							4 1 4 5 00			
33	Depr. Expense—Store Equipment							2 9 7 5 00			
34	Miscellaneous Expense	9 2 5 00						9 2 5 00			
35		346 8 7 5 00	346 8 7 5 00					152 2 8 5 00	182 7 3 0 00	240 5 8 5 00	210 1 4 0 00
36	Net Income							30 4 4 5 00			30 4 4 5 00
37								182 7 3 0 00	182 7 3 0 00	240 5 8 5 00	240 5 8 5 00

E 14-4B (LO3)

✓ Cost of goods sold: $73,400

WORK SHEET EXTENSIONS FOR MERCHANDISE INVENTORY ADJUSTMENTS: PERIODIC INVENTORY SYSTEM The following partial work sheet is taken from Nicole's Gift Shop for the year ended December 31, 20--. The ending merchandise inventory is $37,000.

1. Complete the Adjustments columns for the merchandise inventory.
2. Extend the merchandise inventory to the Adjusted Trial Balance and Balance Sheet columns.
3. Extend the remaining accounts to the Adjusted Trial Balance and Income Statement columns.
4. Prepare a cost of goods sold section from the partial work sheet.

Nicole's Gift Shop
Work Sheet (Partial)
For Year Ended December 31, 20 - -

	ACCOUNT TITLE	TRIAL BALANCE		ADJUSTMENTS		
		DEBIT	CREDIT	DEBIT	CREDIT	
1	Merchandise Inventory	30 0 0 0 00				1
12	Income Summary					12
13	Purchases	85 0 0 0 00				13
14	Purchases Returns and Allowances		2 2 0 0 00			14
15	Purchases Discounts		2 5 0 0 00			15
16	Freight-In	1 0 0 00				16
17						17
18						18

E 14-5B (LO3)

✓ Beg. inv.: $49,000

DETERMINING THE BEGINNING AND ENDING INVENTORY FROM A PARTIAL WORK SHEET: PERIODIC INVENTORY SYSTEM From the following partial work sheet, indicate the dollar amount of beginning and ending merchandise inventory.

	ACCOUNT TITLE	ADJUSTMENTS		ADJUSTED TRIAL BALANCE		INCOME STATEMENT		BALANCE SHEET		
		DEBIT	CREDIT	DEBIT	CREDIT	DEBIT	CREDIT	DEBIT	CREDIT	
1	Merchandise Inventory	(b) 45 0 0 0 00	(a) 49 0 0 0 00	45 0 0 0 00				45 0 0 0 00		1
2	Income Summary	(a) 49 0 0 0 00	(b) 45 0 0 0 00	49 0 0 0 00	45 0 0 0 00	49 0 0 0 00	45 0 0 0 00			2

E 14-6B (LO4)

(b)

✓ Mdse. Inv.   30,000

   Inc. Sum   30,000

JOURNALIZE ADJUSTING ENTRIES FOR A MERCHANDISING BUSINESS The following partial work sheet is taken from the books of Carmen's Collies, a local pet kennel, for the year ended December 31, 20--. Journalize the adjustments in a general journal.

Carmen's Collies
Work Sheet (Partial)
For Year Ended December 31, 20 - -

	ACCOUNT TITLE	TRIAL BALANCE DEBIT	TRIAL BALANCE CREDIT	ADJUSTMENTS DEBIT	ADJUSTMENTS CREDIT	
1	Merchandise Inventory	35 0 0 0 00		(b) 30 0 0 0 00	(a) 35 0 0 0 00	1
2	Supplies	4 5 0 0 00			(d) 3 1 0 0 00	2
3	Building	50 0 0 0 00				3
4	Accum. Depr.—Building		23 0 0 0 00		(e) 6 0 0 0 00	4
5	Wages Payable				(f) 1 3 0 0 00	5
6	Unearned Grooming Revenue		7 0 0 0 00	(c) 5 5 0 0 00		6
7	Income Summary			(a) 35 0 0 0 00	(b) 30 0 0 0 00	7
8	Grooming Revenue		24 0 0 0 00		(c) 5 5 0 0 00	8
9	Wages Expense	41 0 0 0 00		(f) 1 3 0 0 00		9
10	Supplies Expense			(d) 3 1 0 0 00		10
11	Depr. Expense—Building			(e) 6 0 0 0 00		11
12				80 9 0 0 00	80 9 0 0 00	12
13						13

E 14-7B (LO5)

JOURNAL ENTRIES UNDER THE PERPETUAL INVENTORY SYSTEM Sunita Computer Supplies entered into the following transactions. Prepare journal entries under the perpetual inventory system.

May 1   Purchased merchandise on account from Anju Enterprises, $200,000.

8   Purchased merchandise for cash, $100,000.

15   Sold merchandise on account to Salil's Pharmacy for $8,000. The merchandise cost $5,000.

E 14-8B (LO5)

JOURNALIZE ADJUSTING ENTRY FOR A MERCHANDISING BUSINESS: PERPETUAL INVENTORY SYSTEM On December 31, Anup Enterprises completed a physical count of its inventory. Although the merchandise inventory account shows a balance of $200,000, the physical count comes to $210,000. Prepare the appropriate adjusting entry under the perpetual inventory system.

SERIES B PROBLEMS

P 14-9B (LO1/2/3/4)

✓ Adj. col. total: $76,500;
Net income: $13,950

COMPLETION OF A WORK SHEET SHOWING A NET INCOME A trial balance for the Basket Corner, a business owned by Linda Palermo, is shown on page 562. Year-end adjustment information is provided below.

(a and b)   Merchandise inventory costing $24,000 is on hand as of December 31, 20--.
(c)   Supplies remaining at the end of the year, $2,100.
(d)   Unexpired insurance on December 31, $2,600.
(e)   Depreciation expense on the building for 20--, $5,300.
(f)   Depreciation expense on the store equipment for 20--, $3,800.
(g)   Unearned decorating revenue as of December 31, $1,650.
(h)   Wages earned but not paid as of December 31, $750.

(continued)

REQUIRED

1. Complete the Adjustments columns, identifying each adjustment with its corresponding letter.

2. Complete the work sheet.

3. Enter the adjustments in a general journal.

Basket Corner
Trial Balance
December 31, 20 - -

ACCOUNT TITLE	DEBIT BALANCE					CREDIT BALANCE				
Cash	25	0	0	0	00					
Accounts Receivable	8	1	0	0	00					
Merchandise Inventory	32	0	0	0	00					
Supplies	7	1	0	0	00					
Prepaid Insurance	3	6	0	0	00					
Land	40	0	0	0	00					
Building	45	0	0	0	00					
Accumulated Depreciation—Building						16	0	0	0	00
Store Equipment	27	0	0	0	00					
Accumulated Depreciation—Store Equipment						5	5	0	0	00
Accounts Payable						3	6	0	0	00
Wages Payable										
Sales Tax Payable						6	2	0	0	00
Unearned Decorating Revenue						6	3	0	0	00
Mortgage Payable						36	0	0	0	00
L. Palermo, Capital						112	0	5	0	00
L. Palermo, Drawing	31	0	0	0	00					
Income Summary										
Sales						125	0	0	0	00
Sales Returns and Allowances	2	6	0	0	00					
Decorating Revenue										
Purchases	38	0	0	0	00					
Purchases Returns and Allowances						2	2	0	0	00
Purchases Discounts						1	7	0	0	00
Freight-In	1	9	0	0	00					
Wages Expense	38	0	0	0	00					
Advertising Expense	4	2	0	0	00					
Supplies Expense										
Telephone Expense	1	8	7	0	00					
Utilities Expense	8	4	0	0	00					
Insurance Expense										
Depreciation Expense —Building										
Depreciation Expense —Store Equipment										
Miscellaneous Expense		7	8	0	00					
	314	5	5	0	00	314	5	5	0	00

P 14-10B (LO1/2/3/4)

✓ Adj. col. total: $86,730;
Net loss: $53,630

KLOOSTER
·& ALLEN·

COMPLETION OF A WORK SHEET SHOWING A NET LOSS The trial balance for Oregon Bike Company, a business owned by Craig Moody, is shown below. Year-end adjustment information is provided below.

(a and b)   Merchandise inventory costing $26,000 is on hand as of December 31, 20--.

(c)   Supplies remaining at the end of the year, $2,500.

(d)   Unexpired insurance on December 31, $1,820.

(e)   Depreciation expense on the building for 20--, $6,400.

(f)   Depreciation expense on the store equipment for 20--, $2,800.

(g)   Unearned rent revenue as of December 31, $2,350.

(h)   Wages earned but not paid as of December 31, $1,100.

Oregon Bike Company
Trial Balance
December 31, 20 - -

ACCOUNT TITLE	DEBIT BALANCE	CREDIT BALANCE
Cash	27 0 0 0 00	
Accounts Receivable	12 0 0 0 00	
Merchandise Inventory	39 0 0 0 00	
Supplies	6 2 0 0 00	
Prepaid Insurance	5 8 0 0 00	
Land	32 0 0 0 00	
Building	58 0 0 0 00	
Accumulated Depreciation—Building		27 0 0 0 00
Store Equipment	31 0 0 0 00	
Accumulated Depreciation—Store Equipment		14 0 0 0 00
Accounts Payable		4 9 0 0 00
Wages Payable		
Sales Tax Payable		2 9 0 0 00
Unearned Rent Revenue		6 1 0 0 00
Mortgage Payable		49 0 0 0 00
C. Moody, Capital		169 5 0 0 00
C. Moody, Drawing	36 0 0 0 00	
Income Summary		
Sales		58 0 0 0 00
Sales Returns and Allowances	3 3 0 0 00	
Rent Revenue		
Purchases	19 0 0 0 00	
Purchases Returns and Allowances		9 0 0 00
Purchases Discounts		1 4 5 0 00
Freight-In	8 0 0 00	
Wages Expense	47 0 0 0 00	
Advertising Expense	6 2 0 0 00	
Supplies Expense		
Telephone Expense	1 8 6 0 00	
Utilities Expense	8 1 0 0 00	
Insurance Expense		
Depreciation Expense—Building		
Depreciation Expense—Store Equipment		
Miscellaneous Expense	4 9 0 00	
	333 7 5 0 00	333 7 5 0 00

(continued)

REQUIRED

1. Complete the Adjustments columns, identifying each adjustment with its corresponding letter.

2. Complete the work sheet.

3. Enter the adjustments in a general journal.

P 14-11B (LO1/2/4)
✓ Adj. col. total: $88,805

WORKING BACKWARD FROM ADJUSTED TRIAL BALANCE TO DETERMINE ADJUSTING ENTRIES The partial work sheet shown below is taken from the books of Burnside Auto Parts, a business owned by Barbara Davis, for the year ended December 31, 20--.

Burnside Auto Parts
Work Sheet (Partial)
For Year Ended December 31, 20 - -

	ACCOUNT TITLE	TRIAL BALANCE DEBIT	TRIAL BALANCE CREDIT	ADJUSTMENTS DEBIT	ADJUSTMENTS CREDIT	ADJUSTED TRIAL BALANCE DEBIT	ADJUSTED TRIAL BALANCE CREDIT	
1	Cash	21 0 0 0 00				21 0 0 0 00		1
2	Accounts Receivable	8 3 0 0 00				8 3 0 0 00		2
3	Merchandise Inventory	32 0 0 0 00				36 0 0 0 00		3
4	Supplies	6 1 5 0 00				1 8 6 5 00		4
5	Prepaid Insurance	5 9 2 5 00				1 8 3 5 00		5
6	Land	41 7 5 0 00				41 7 5 0 00		6
7	Building	43 0 0 0 00				43 0 0 0 00		7
8	Accum. Depr.—Building		24 0 0 0 00				27 5 0 0 00	8
9	Store Equipment	25 4 0 0 00				25 4 0 0 00		9
10	Accum. Depr.—Store Equipment		12 4 0 0 00				14 7 5 0 00	10
11	Accounts Payable		8 1 0 0 00				8 1 0 0 00	11
12	Wages Payable						9 8 0 00	12
13	Sales Tax Payable		5 2 0 0 00				5 2 0 0 00	13
14	Unearned Rent-A-Junk Revenue		7 9 5 0 00				2 3 5 0 00	14
15	Mortgage Payable		26 0 0 0 00				26 0 0 0 00	15
16	B. Davis, Capital		109 1 3 0 00				109 1 3 0 00	16
17	B. Davis, Drawing	40 0 0 0 00				40 0 0 0 00		17
18	Income Summary					32 0 0 0 00	36 0 0 0 00	18
19	Sales		123 5 0 0 00				123 5 0 0 00	19
20	Sales Returns and Allowances	2 8 6 0 00				2 8 6 0 00		20
21	Rent-A-Junk Revenue						5 6 0 0 00	21
22	Purchases	32 5 2 5 00				32 5 2 5 00		22
23	Purchases Returns and Allowances		2 1 5 0 00				2 1 5 0 00	23
24	Purchases Discounts		2 4 0 0 00				2 4 0 0 00	24
25	Freight-In	3 1 7 5 00				3 1 7 5 00		25
26	Wages Expense	44 1 7 5 00				45 1 5 5 00		26
27	Advertising Expense	3 2 7 5 00				3 2 7 5 00		27
28	Supplies Expense					4 2 8 5 00		28
29	Telephone Expense	2 2 0 0 00				2 2 0 0 00		29
30	Utilities Expense	8 2 5 0 00				8 2 5 0 00		30
31	Insurance Expense					4 0 9 0 00		31
32	Depr. Expense—Building					3 5 0 0 00		32
33	Depr. Expense—Store Equipment					2 3 5 0 00		33
34	Miscellaneous Expense	8 4 5 00				8 4 5 00		34
35		320 8 3 0 00	320 8 3 0 00			363 6 6 0 00	363 6 6 0 00	35

REQUIRED

1. Determine the adjusting entries by analyzing the difference between the adjusted trial balance and the trial balance.

2. Journalize the adjusting entries in a general journal.

P 14-12B (LO1/2/3/4)
✓ Adj. col. total: $99,545;
Cost of goods sold: $31,975

WORKING BACKWARD FROM THE INCOME STATEMENT AND BALANCE SHEET COLUMNS OF THE WORK SHEET TO DETERMINE ADJUSTED TRIAL BALANCE AND ADJUSTING ENTRIES The partial work sheet shown on page 566 is taken from the books of Diamond Music Store, a business owned by Ned Diamond, for the year ended December 31, 20--.

REQUIRED

1. Analyze the work sheet and determine the adjusted trial balance and the adjusting entries by working backward from the Income Statement and Balance Sheet columns.

2. Journalize the adjusting entries in a general journal.

3. Prepare the cost of goods sold section of the income statement for Diamond Music Store.

MANAGING YOUR WRITING

A friend of yours recently opened Abracadabra, a sportswear shop specializing in monogrammed athletic gear. Most merchandise is special ordered for customers. However, a small inventory is on hand. Your friend does not understand why a physical inventory is necessary before preparing the financial statements. She knows how much she paid for all merchandise purchased. Why not simply use this amount for cost of goods sold? After all, it has been paid for. Write a brief memo explaining the purpose of the physical inventory and why she should not use the cost of purchases as cost of goods sold.

P14-12B

Diamond Music Store
Work Sheet
For Year Ended December 31, 20 - -

#	ACCOUNT TITLE	TRIAL BALANCE DEBIT	TRIAL BALANCE CREDIT	ADJUSTMENTS DEBIT	ADJUSTMENTS CREDIT	ADJUSTED TRIAL BALANCE DEBIT	ADJUSTED TRIAL BALANCE CREDIT	INCOME STATEMENT DEBIT	INCOME STATEMENT CREDIT	BALANCE SHEET DEBIT	BALANCE SHEET CREDIT
1	Cash	31 000 00								31 000 00	
2	Accounts Receivable	11 980 00								11 980 00	
3	Merchandise Inventory	33 600 00								39 100 00	
4	Supplies	7 140 00								1 965 00	
5	Prepaid Insurance	5 985 00								1 235 00	
6	Land	36 200 00								36 200 00	
7	Building	51 850 00								51 850 00	
8	Accum. Depr.—Building		13 590 00								18 875 00
9	Store Equipment	32 675 00								32 675 00	
10	Accum. Depr.—Store Equipment		10 290 00								14 755 00
11	Accounts Payable		5 895 00								5 895 00
12	Wages Payable										1 250 00
13	Sales Tax Payable		6 375 00								6 375 00
14	Unearned Rent Revenue		8 850 00								2 930 00
15	Mortgage Payable		42 400 00								42 400 00
16	N. Diamond, Capital		116 350 00								116 350 00
17	N. Diamond, Drawing	39 500 00								39 500 00	
18	Income Summary							33 600 00	39 100 00		
19	Sales		148 000 00						148 000 00		
20	Sales Returns and Allowances	2 800 00						2 800 00			
21	Rent Revenue								5 920 00		
22	Purchases	40 700 00						40 700 00			
23	Purchases Returns and Allowances		2 775 00						2 775 00		
24	Purchases Discounts		2 325 00						2 325 00		
25	Freight-In	1 875 00						1 875 00			
26	Wages Expense	47 000 00						48 250 00			
27	Advertising Expense	4 695 00						4 695 00			
28	Supplies Expense							5 175 00			
29	Telephone Expense	2 250 00						2 250 00			
30	Utilities Expense	6 825 00						6 825 00			
31	Insurance Expense							4 750 00			
32	Depr. Expense—Building							5 285 00			
33	Depr. Expense—Store Equipment							4 465 00			
34	Miscellaneous Expense	775 00						775 00			
35		356 850 00	356 850 00					161 445 00	198 120 00	245 505 00	208 830 00
36	Net Income							36 675 00			36 675 00
37								198 120 00	198 120 00	245 505 00	245 505 00

ETHICS CASE

Jason Tierro, an inventory clerk at Lexmar Company, is responsible for taking a physical count of the goods on hand at the end of the year. He has been performing this duty for several years. This year, Jason was very busy due to a shortage of personnel at the company, so he decided to just estimate the amount of ending inventory instead of doing an accurate count. He reasoned that he could come very close to the true amount because of his past experience working with inventory. Besides, he was sure that the sophisticated computer program that Lexmar had just invested in kept an accurate record of inventory on hand.

1.   What is your opinion of Jason's reasoning?

2.   If Jason underestimates the dollar amount of ending inventory, what effect will it have on net income for the current accounting period?

3.   Write a short paragraph explaining why a physical inventory should be taken at least once a year.

4.   In groups of three or four, make a list of possible reasons that the actual ending inventory might not agree with the ending inventory according to a computer system.

MASTERY PROBLEM

✓ Adj. T.B. col. total: $695,325; Net income: $37,125

John Neff owns and operates Waikiki Surf Shop. A year-end trial balance is provided on page 568. Year-end adjustment data for the Waikiki Surf Shop are shown below.

(a and b)   A physical count shows merchandise inventory costing $45,000 on hand as of December 31, 20--. Neff uses the periodic inventory system.
(c)   Supplies remaining at the end of the year, $600.
(d)   Unexpired insurance on December 31, $900.
(e)   Depreciation expense on the building for 20--, $6,000.
(f)   Depreciation expense on the store equipment for 20--, $4,500.
(g)   Wages earned but not paid as of December 31, $675.
(h)   Unearned boat rental revenue as of December 31, $3,000.

REQUIRED

1.   Prepare a year-end work sheet.

2.   Journalize the adjusting entries.

	Waikiki Surf Shop Trial Balance December 31, 20 - -										
ACCOUNT TITLE	DEBIT BALANCE					CREDIT BALANCE				
Cash	30	0	0	0	00					
Accounts Receivable	22	5	0	0	00					
Merchandise Inventory	57	0	0	0	00					
Supplies	2	7	0	0	00					
Prepaid Insurance	3	6	0	0	00					
Land	15	0	0	0	00					
Building	135	0	0	0	00					
Accumulated Depreciation—Building						24	0	0	0	00
Store Equipment	75	0	0	0	00					
Accumulated Depreciation—Store Equipment						22	5	0	0	00
Notes Payable						7	5	0	0	00
Accounts Payable						15	0	0	0	00
Wages Payable										
Unearned Boat Rental Revenue						33	0	0	0	00
J. Neff, Capital						233	7	0	0	00
J. Neff, Drawing	30	0	0	0	00					
Income Summary										
Sales						300	7	5	0	00
Sales Returns and Allowances	1	8	0	0	00					
Boat Rental Revenue										
Purchases	157	5	0	0	00					
Purchases Returns and Allowances						1	2	0	0	00
Purchases Discounts						1	5	0	0	00
Freight-In		4	5	0	00					
Wages Expense	63	0	0	0	00					
Advertising Expense	11	2	5	0	00					
Supplies Expense										
Telephone Expense	5	2	5	0	00					
Utilities Expense	18	0	0	0	00					
Insurance Expense										
Depreciation Expense —Building										
Depreciation Expense —Store Equipment										
Miscellaneous Expense	10	8	7	5	00					
Interest Expense		2	2	5	00					
	639	1	5	0	00	639	1	5	0	00

CHALLENGE PROBLEM

This problem challenges you to apply your cumulative accounting knowledge to move a step beyond the material in the chapter.

✓ Net purchases in 20-1: $410,000

Block Food's, a retail grocery store, has agreed to purchase all of its merchandise from Square Wholesalers. In return, Block receives a special discount on purchases. Over recent months, Square noticed that purchases by Block had been falling off. At first, Square simply thought that business might be down for Block and was hopeful that their purchases would pick up. When business with Block did not return to a normal level, Square requested financial statements from Block. Square's records indicate that Block purchased $300,000 worth of merchandise during 20-1, the most recent year.

Selected information taken from Block's financial statements is as follows:

Balance Sheet	12/31/-1	12/31/-0
Inventory	$30,000	$20,000

Income Statement	
Cost of goods sold	$400,000

REQUIRED

Compute net purchases made by Block during 20-1. Does it appear that Block violated the agreement?

Chapter 14 Appendix
Expense Method of Accounting for Prepaid Expenses

Objectives

Careful study of this appendix should enable you to:

LO1 Use the expense method of accounting for prepaid expenses.

LO2 Make the appropriate adjusting entries when the expense method is used for prepaid expenses.

THE EXPENSE METHOD

LO1 Use the expense method of accounting for prepaid expenses.

Under the **expense method** of accounting for prepaid expenses, supplies and other prepaid items are entered as expenses when purchased. Under this method, we must adjust the accounts at the end of each accounting period to record the unused portions as assets. To illustrate, let's assume that the following entry was made when office supplies were purchased:

4		Office Supplies Expense			4	2	5	00						4
5		Cash								4	2	5	00	5
6		Purchased office supplies												6

In the next section, we will illustrate the proper adjusting entry when using the expense method.

ADJUSTING ENTRIES UNDER THE EXPENSE METHOD

LO2 Make the appropriate adjusting entries when the expense method is used for prepaid expenses.

Office Supplies Expense was debited for a total of $425 during the period. An inventory taken at the end of the period shows that supplies on hand amounted to $150. The following adjusting entry is made for supplies on hand:

8		Office Supplies			1	5	0	00						8
9		Office Supplies Expense								1	5	0	00	9
10														10

As shown in the T accounts below, after this entry is posted, the office supplies expense account has a debit balance of $275. This amount is reported on the income statement as an operating expense. The office supplies account has a debit balance of $150. It is reported on the balance sheet as a current asset.

Office Supplies			Office Supplies Expense	
			425	
Adj. 150			Adj. 150	
			Bal. 275	

Let's consider another example of the use of the expense method. The following entry was made for the payment of $6,000 for a three-year insurance policy:

11		Insurance Expense			6 0 0 0 00			11
12		Cash				6 0 0 0 00		12
13		Paid insurance premium						13

At the end of the first year, one-third of the premium has expired and two-thirds remains. Thus, $2,000 for insurance expense should be reported on the income statement and $4,000 in prepaid insurance should be reported on the balance sheet. The following adjusting entry is made:

15		Prepaid Insurance			4 0 0 0 00			15
16		Insurance Expense				4 0 0 0 00		16
17								17

As shown in the T accounts below, after this entry is posted, the prepaid insurance account has a debit balance of $4,000. The insurance expense account has a debit balance of $2,000.

Prepaid Insurance		Insurance Expense	
		6,000	
Adj. 4,000			Adj. 4,000
		Bal. 2,000	

The asset and expense methods of accounting for prepaid expenses give the same final result. In the **asset method**, the prepaid item is first debited to an asset account. At the end of each period, the amount consumed is debited to an expense account. In the expense method, the original amount is debited to an expense account. At the end of each accounting period, the portion not consumed is debited to an asset account.

Learning Objectives	Key Points to Remember
LO1 **Use the expense method of accounting for prepaid expenses.**	Under the expense method, an expense account is debited when prepaid items are acquired.
LO2 **Make the appropriate adjusting entries when the expense method is used for prepaid expenses.**	At the end of the accounting period, an asset must be recognized for the amount of the prepaid item remaining. The expense account must be credited so that the ending balance represents the amount of the item consumed.

KEY TERMS

asset method (572)   Under this method, the acquisition of a prepaid item is debited to an asset account.

expense method (571)   Under this method, the acquisition of a prepaid item is debited to an expense account.

SERIES A EXERCISE

E 14APX-1A (LO1/2)

EXPENSE METHOD OF ACCOUNTING FOR PREPAID EXPENSES Davidson's Food Mart paid $1,200 in advance to the local newspaper for advertisements that will appear monthly. The following entry was made:

4		Advertising Expense		1 2 0 0 00		4
5		Cash			1 2 0 0 00	5
6		Paid prepaid advertising				6

At the end of the year, December 31, 20--, Davidson received notification that advertisements costing $800 had been run. Prepare the adjusting entry.

SERIES B EXERCISE

E 14APX-1B (LO1/2)

EXPENSE METHOD OF ACCOUNTING FOR PREPAID EXPENSES Ryan's Fish House purchased supplies costing $3,000 for cash. This amount was debited to the supplies expense account. At the end of the year, December 31, 20--, an inventory showed that supplies costing $500 remained. Prepare the adjusting entry.

Objectives

Careful study of this chapter should enable you to:

LO1
Prepare a single-step and multiple-step income statement for a merchandising business.

LO2
Prepare a statement of owner's equity.

LO3
Prepare a classified balance sheet.

LO4
Compute standard financial ratios.

LO5
Prepare closing entries for a merchandising business.

LO6
Prepare reversing entries.

Financial Statements and Year-End Accounting for a Merchandising Business

After closing Parkway Pet Supplies' books for the year, Betty Jenkins, the bookkeeper, went to Florida for a vacation. She plans to return during the second week of January. Before leaving, Betty gave Evan careful instructions on how to enter basic transactions while she is gone. Unfortunately, Evan is a bit confused about the proper entry for the first payroll of the new year. He knows that those first paychecks of the year cover wages earned at the end of last year, but not yet paid, as well as wages earned this year. Evan decides to check with Betty to get the proper allocation before he records the paychecks. Although he didn't want to interrupt Betty's vacation, he called her in Florida to get the information. Surprisingly, Betty said, "Don't worry about it. Just make the 'normal' entry by debiting Wages Expense and crediting Cash." Why is Betty not concerned about the proper allocation for the first payroll period?

The first six chapters of this text illustrated the accounting cycle for a service business. In this chapter, we complete the accounting cycle for a merchandising business.

In Chapter 14, we prepared the year-end work sheet and adjusting entries for Northern Micro. In this chapter, we will prepare financial statements, look briefly at financial statement analysis, and demonstrate closing and reversing entries.

THE INCOME STATEMENT

LO1 Prepare a single-step and multiple-step income statement for a merchandising business.

As you know, a primary purpose of the work sheet is to serve as an aid in preparing the financial statements. Figure 15-1 shows the completed work sheet for Northern Micro. We will use it to prepare financial statements.

The purpose of an income statement is to summarize the results of operations during an accounting period. The income statement shows the sources of revenue, types of expenses, and the amount of the net income or net loss for the period. Two forms of the income statement commonly used are the single step and the multiple step. The **single-step income statement** lists all revenue items and their total first, followed by all expense items and their total. The difference, which is either net income or net loss, is then calculated. A single-step income statement for Northern Micro is illustrated in Figure 15-2.

The use of the work sheet to prepare a **multiple-step income statement** is illustrated in Figure 15-3. This type of income statement is commonly used for merchandising businesses. The term "multiple-step" is used because the final net income is calculated on a step-by-step basis. Gross sales is shown first, less sales returns and allowances and sales discounts. This difference is called **net sales**. (Many published income statements begin with the amount of net sales.) Cost of goods sold is subtracted next to arrive at **gross profit** (sometimes called **gross margin**).

Operating expenses are then listed and subtracted from the gross profit to compute **income from operations** (sometimes called **operating income**). Operating expenses are directly associated with providing the primary goods and services of the business. Some companies divide operating expenses into the following subcategories.

Selling expenses. These expenses are directly associated with selling activities. Examples include:
- Sales Salaries Expense
- Sales Commissions Expense
- Advertising Expense
- Bank Credit Card Expense
- Delivery Expense
- Depreciation Expense—Store Equipment and Fixtures

FIGURE 15-1   Northern Micro Work Sheet

Northern Micro
Work Sheet
For Year Ended December 31, 20--

	Account Title	Trial Balance Debit	Trial Balance Credit	Adjustments Debit	Adjustments Credit	Adjusted Trial Balance Debit	Adjusted Trial Balance Credit	Income Statement Debit	Income Statement Credit	Balance Sheet Debit	Balance Sheet Credit	
1	Cash	20 0 0 0 00				20 0 0 0 00				20 0 0 0 00		1
2	Accounts Receivable	15 0 0 0 00				15 0 0 0 00				15 0 0 0 00		2
3	Merchandise Inventory	26 0 0 0 00		(b) 18 0 0 0 00	(a) 26 0 0 0 00	18 0 0 0 00				18 0 0 0 00		3
4	Supplies	1 8 0 0 00			(c) 1 4 0 0 00	4 0 0 00				4 0 0 00		4
5	Prepaid Insurance	2 4 0 0 00			(d) 1 8 0 0 00	6 0 0 00				6 0 0 00		5
6	Land	10 0 0 0 00				10 0 0 0 00				10 0 0 0 00		6
7	Building	90 0 0 0 00				90 0 0 0 00				90 0 0 0 00		7
8	Accum. Depr.—Building		16 0 0 0 00		(e) 4 0 0 0 00		20 0 0 0 00				20 0 0 0 00	8
9	Store Equipment	50 0 0 0 00				50 0 0 0 00				50 0 0 0 00		9
10	Accum. Depr.—Store Equipment		15 0 0 0 00		(f) 3 0 0 0 00		18 0 0 0 00				18 0 0 0 00	10
11	Notes Payable		5 0 0 0 00				5 0 0 0 00				5 0 0 0 00	11
12	Accounts Payable		10 0 0 0 00				10 0 0 0 00				10 0 0 0 00	12
13	Wages Payable				(g) 4 5 0 00		4 5 0 00				4 5 0 00	13
14	Sales Tax Payable		1 5 0 0 00				1 5 0 0 00				1 5 0 0 00	14
15	Unearned Subscriptions Revenue		12 0 0 0 00	(h) 10 0 0 0 00			2 0 0 0 00				2 0 0 0 00	15
16	Mortgage Payable		30 0 0 0 00				30 0 0 0 00				30 0 0 0 00	16
17	Gary L. Fishel, Capital		114 4 0 0 00				114 4 0 0 00				114 4 0 0 00	17
18	Gary L. Fishel, Drawing	20 0 0 0 00				20 0 0 0 00				20 0 0 0 00		18
19	Income Summary			(a) 26 0 0 0 00	(b) 18 0 0 0 00	26 0 0 0 00	18 0 0 0 00	26 0 0 0 00	18 0 0 0 00			19
20	Sales		214 0 0 0 00				214 0 0 0 00		214 0 0 0 00			20
21	Sales Returns and Allowances	1 2 0 0 00				1 2 0 0 00		1 2 0 0 00				21
22	Interest Revenue		9 0 0 00				9 0 0 00		9 0 0 00			22
23	Rent Revenue		8 0 0 0 00				8 0 0 0 00		8 0 0 0 00			23
24	Subscriptions Revenue				(h) 10 0 0 0 00		10 0 0 0 00		10 0 0 0 00			24
25	Purchases	105 0 0 0 00				105 0 0 0 00		105 0 0 0 00				25
26	Purchases Returns and Allowances		8 0 0 0 00				8 0 0 0 00		8 0 0 0 00			26
27	Purchases Discounts		1 0 0 0 00				1 0 0 0 00		1 0 0 0 00			27
28	Freight-In	3 0 0 0 00				3 0 0 0 00		3 0 0 0 00				28
29	Wages Expense	42 0 0 0 00		(g) 4 5 0 00		42 4 5 0 00		42 4 5 0 00				29
30	Advertising Expense	2 5 0 0 00				2 5 0 0 00		2 5 0 0 00				30
31	Bank Credit Card Expense	1 5 0 0 00				1 5 0 0 00		1 5 0 0 00				31
32	Rent Expense	20 0 0 0 00				20 0 0 0 00		20 0 0 0 00				32
33	Supplies Expense			(c) 1 4 0 0 00		1 4 0 0 00		1 4 0 0 00				33
34	Telephone Expense	3 5 0 0 00				3 5 0 0 00		3 5 0 0 00				34
35	Utilities Expense	12 0 0 0 00				12 0 0 0 00		12 0 0 0 00				35
36	Insurance Expense			(d) 1 8 0 0 00		1 8 0 0 00		1 8 0 0 00				36
37	Depr. Expense—Building			(e) 4 0 0 0 00		4 0 0 0 00		4 0 0 0 00				37
38	Depr. Expense—Store Equipment			(f) 3 0 0 0 00		3 0 0 0 00		3 0 0 0 00				38
39	Miscellaneous Expense	2 2 5 0 00				2 2 5 0 00		2 2 5 0 00				39
40	Interest Expense	3 1 5 0 00				3 1 5 0 00		3 1 5 0 00				40
41		428 6 0 0 00	428 6 0 0 00	64 6 5 0 00	64 6 5 0 00	454 0 5 0 00	454 0 5 0 00	230 0 5 0 00	252 7 0 0 00	224 0 0 0 00	201 3 5 0 00	41
42	Net Income							22 6 5 0 00			22 6 5 0 00	42
43								252 7 0 0 00	252 7 0 0 00	224 0 0 0 00	224 0 0 0 00	43

FIGURE 15-2 Single-Step Income Statement

Northern Micro Income Statement For Year Ended December 31, 20 - -										
Revenues:										
Net sales	$212	8	0	0	00					
Interest revenue		9	0	0	00					
Rent revenue	8	0	0	0	00					
Subscriptions revenue	10	0	0	0	00					
Total revenues						$231	7	0	0	00
Expenses:										
Cost of goods sold	$111	5	0	0	00					
Wages expense	42	4	5	0	00					
Advertising expense	2	5	0	0	00					
Bank credit card expense	1	5	0	0	00					
Rent expense	20	0	0	0	00					
Supplies expense	1	4	0	0	00					
Telephone expense	3	5	0	0	00					
Utilities expense	12	0	0	0	00					
Insurance expense	1	8	0	0	00					
Depreciation expense—building	4	0	0	0	00					
Depreciation expense—store equipment	3	0	0	0	00					
Miscellaneous expense	2	2	5	0	00					
Interest expense	3	1	5	0	00					
Total expenses						209	0	5	0	00
Net income						$ 22	6	5	0	00

General expenses. These expenses are associated with administrative, office, or general operating activities. Examples include:

- Rent Expense
- Office Salaries Expense
- Office Supplies Expense
- Telephone Expense
- Utilities Expense
- Insurance Expense
- Depreciation Expense—Office Equipment

Finally, other revenues are added and other expenses are subtracted to arrive at net income (or net loss). Note that the operating expenses are arranged according to the order given in the chart of accounts. They could also be listed by descending amount, with Miscellaneous Expense last.

By showing other revenues and other expenses separately, it is possible to show income from operations. This makes it easier for the reader to see how the business is doing in its main activity.

LEARNING KEY

Although the formats for the single-step and multiple-step income statements are different, the reported net income is the same.

FIGURE 15-3   Using a Work Sheet to Prepare a Multiple-Step Income Statement

Northern Micro
Work Sheet (Partial)
For Year Ended December 31, 20--

	ACCOUNT TITLE	INCOME STATEMENT DEBIT	INCOME STATEMENT CREDIT
1	Cash		
2	Accounts Receivable		
3	Merchandise Inventory		
4	Supplies		
5	Prepaid Insurance		
6	Land		
7	Building		
8	Accum. Depr.—Building		
9	Store Equipment		
10	Accum. Depr.—Store Equipment		
11	Notes Payable		
12	Accounts Payable		
13	Wages Payable		
14	Sales Tax Payable		
15	Unearned Subscriptions Revenue		
16	Mortgage Payable		
17	Gary L. Fishel, Capital		
18	Gary L. Fishel, Drawing		
19	Income Summary	26 0 0 0 00	18 0 0 0 00
20	Sales		214 0 0 0 00
21	Sales Returns and Allowances	1 2 0 0 00	
22	Interest Revenue		9 0 0 0 00
23	Rent Revenue		8 0 0 0 00
24	Subscriptions Revenue		10 0 0 00
25	Purchases	105 0 0 0 00	
26	Purchases Returns and Allowances		1 8 0 0 00
27	Purchases Discounts		1 2 0 0 00
28	Freight-In	3 0 0 00	
29	Wages Expense	42 4 5 0 00	
30	Advertising Expense	2 5 0 0 00	
31	Bank Credit Card Expense	1 5 0 0 00	
32	Rent Expense	20 0 0 0 00	
33	Supplies Expense	1 4 0 0 00	
34	Telephone Expense	3 5 0 0 00	
35	Utilities Expense	12 0 0 0 00	
36	Insurance Expense	1 8 0 0 00	
37	Depr. Expense—Building	4 0 0 0 00	
38	Depr. Expense—Store Equipment	3 0 0 0 00	
39	Miscellaneous Expense	2 2 5 0 00	
40	Interest Expense	3 1 5 0 00	
41		230 5 0 0 00	252 7 0 0 00
42	Net Income	22 6 5 0 00	
43		252 7 0 0 00	252 7 0 0 00

Northern Micro
Income Statement
For Year Ended December 31, 20--

Revenue from sales:			
Sales		$214 0 0 0 00	
Less sales returns and allowances		1 2 0 0 00	
Net sales			$212 8 0 0 00
Cost of goods sold:			
Merchandise inventory, January 1, 20--		$ 26 0 0 0 00	
Purchases	$105 0 0 0 00		
Less: Purchases returns and allowances	1 8 0 0 00		
Purchases discounts	1 2 0 0 00		
Net purchases	$103 0 0 0 00		
Add freight-in	3 0 0 00		
Cost of goods purchased		103 5 0 0 00	
Goods available for sale		$129 5 0 0 00	
Less merchandise inventory, December 31, 20--		18 0 0 0 00	
Cost of goods sold			111 5 0 0 00
Gross profit			$101 3 0 0 00
Operating expenses:			
Wages expense		$ 42 4 5 0 00	
Advertising expense		2 5 0 0 00	
Bank credit card expense		1 5 0 0 00	
Rent expense		20 0 0 0 00	
Supplies expense		1 4 0 0 00	
Telephone expense		3 5 0 0 00	
Utilities expense		12 0 0 0 00	
Insurance expense		1 8 0 0 00	
Depreciation expense—building		4 0 0 0 00	
Depreciation expense—store equipment		3 0 0 0 00	
Miscellaneous expense		2 2 5 0 00	
Total operating expenses			94 4 0 0 00
Income from operations			$ 6 9 0 0 00
Other revenues:			
Interest revenue		$ 9 0 0 0 00	
Rent revenue		8 0 0 0 00	
Subscriptions revenue		10 0 0 00	
Total other revenues			18 9 0 0 00
Other expenses:			
Interest expense			3 1 5 0 00
Net income			$22 6 5 0 00

THE STATEMENT OF OWNER'S EQUITY

LO2 Prepare a statement of owner's equity.

The statement of owner's equity summarizes all changes in the owner's equity during the period. It includes the net income or loss and any additional investments or withdrawals by the owner. These changes result in the end-of-period balance shown on this statement and the balance sheet.

To prepare the statement of owner's equity for Northern Micro, two sources of information are needed: (1) the work sheet, and (2) Gary Fishel's capital account (no. 311) in the general ledger. The work sheet (Figure 15-1) shows net income of $22,650 and withdrawals of $20,000 during the year. Fishel's capital account (Figure 15-4) shows a beginning balance of $104,400. An additional $10,000 was invested in the business in February of the current year. The statement of owner's equity for Northern Micro for the year ended December 31, 20--, is shown in Figure 15-5.

FIGURE 15-4 Capital Account for Gary L. Fishel

ACCOUNT: Gary L. Fishel, Capital — ACCOUNT NO. 311

DATE		ITEM	POST. REF.	DEBIT	CREDIT	BALANCE DEBIT	BALANCE CREDIT
20-- Jan.	1	Balance	✓				104 4 0 0 00
Feb.	12		CR7		10 0 0 0 00		114 4 0 0 00

FIGURE 15-5 Statement of Owner's Equity

The statement of owner's equity is the same for service and merchandising businesses.

Northern Micro
Statement of Owner's Equity
For Year Ended December 31, 20 - -

Gary L. Fishel, capital, January 1, 20 - -		$104 4 0 0 00
Add additional investments		10 0 0 0 00
Total investment		$114 4 0 0 00
Net income for the year	$22 6 5 0 00	
Less withdrawals for the year	20 0 0 0 00	
Increase in capital		2 6 5 0 00
Gary L. Fishel, capital, December 31, 20 - -		$117 0 5 0 00

BALANCE SHEET

LO3 Prepare a classified balance sheet.

The use of the work sheet to prepare a report form classified balance sheet is illustrated in Figure 15-6. The balance sheet classifications used by Northern Micro are explained on pages 582 and 583.

LEARNING KEY

Note the use of the ending balance for merchandise inventory. It is reported on the income statement as part of the calculation of cost of goods sold. It also is reported on the balance sheet as a current asset.

FIGURE 15-6   Using a Work Sheet to Prepare a Report Form Classified Balance Sheet

Northern Micro
Work Sheet (Partial)
For Year Ended December 31, 20--

	ACCOUNT TITLE	BALANCE SHEET DEBIT	BALANCE SHEET CREDIT
1	Cash	20 0 0 0 00	
2	Accounts Receivable	15 0 0 0 00	
3	Merchandise Inventory	18 0 0 0 00	
4	Supplies	4 0 0 00	
5	Prepaid Insurance	6 0 0 00	
6	Land	10 0 0 0 00	
7	Building	90 0 0 0 00	
8	Accum. Depr.—Building		20 0 0 0 00
9	Store Equipment	50 0 0 0 00	
10	Accum. Depr.—Store Equipment		18 0 0 0 00
11	Notes Payable		5 0 0 0 00
12	Accounts Payable		10 0 0 0 00
13	Wages Payable		4 5 0 00
14	Sales Tax Payable		1 5 0 0 00
15	Unearned Subscriptions Revenue		2 0 0 0 00
16	Mortgage Payable		30 0 0 0 00
17	Gary L. Fishel, Capital		114 4 0 0 00
18	Gary L. Fishel, Drawing	20 0 0 0 00	
19	Income Summary		
20	Sales		
21	Sales Returns and Allowances		
22	Interest Revenue		
23	Rent Revenue		
24	Subscriptions Revenue		
25	Purchases		
26	Purchases Returns and Allowances		
27	Purchases Discounts		
28	Freight-In		
29	Wages Expense		
30	Advertising Expense		
31	Bank Credit Card Expense		
32	Rent Expense		
33	Supplies Expense		
34	Telephone Expense		
35	Utilities Expense		
36	Insurance Expense		
37	Depr. Expense—Building		
38	Depr. Expense—Store Equipment		
39	Miscellaneous Expense		
40	Interest Expense		
41		224 0 0 0 00	201 3 5 0 00
42	Net Income		22 6 5 0 00
43		224 0 0 0 00	224 0 0 0 00

Northern Micro
Balance Sheet
December 31, 20--

Assets			
Current assets:			
Cash		$20 0 0 0 00	
Accounts receivable		15 0 0 0 00	
Merchandise inventory		18 0 0 0 00	
Supplies		4 0 0 00	
Prepaid insurance		6 0 0 00	
Total current assets			$ 54 0 0 0 00
Property, plant, and equipment:			
Land		$10 0 0 0 00	
Building	$90 0 0 0 00		
Less accum. depr.—bld.	20 0 0 0 00	70 0 0 0 00	
Store equipment	$50 0 0 0 00		
Less accum. depr.—store equip.	18 0 0 0 00	32 0 0 0 00	
Total property, plant, and equipment			112 0 0 0 00
Total assets			$166 0 0 0 00

Liabilities			
Current liabilities:			
Notes payable	$ 5 0 0 0 00		
Accounts payable	10 0 0 0 00		
Wages payable	4 5 0 00		
Sales tax payable	1 5 0 0 00		
Unearned subscriptions revenue	2 0 0 0 00		
Mortgage payable (current portion)	5 0 0 00		
Total current liabilities		$19 4 5 0 00	
Long-term liabilities:			
Mortgage payable	$30 0 0 0 00		
Less current portion	5 0 0 00	29 5 0 0 00	
Total liabilities			$ 48 9 5 0 00
Owner's Equity			
Gary L. Fishel, capital			117 0 5 0 00*
Total liabilities and owner's equity			$166 0 0 0 00

*From statement of owner's equity.

Current Assets

Current assets include cash and all other assets expected to be converted into cash or consumed within one year or the normal operating cycle of the business, whichever is longer. The **operating cycle** is the length of time generally required for a business to buy inventory, sell it, and collect the cash. This time period is generally less than a year. Thus, most firms use one year for classifying current assets. In a merchandising business, the current assets usually include cash, receivables (such as accounts receivable and notes receivable), and merchandise inventory. Since prepaid expenses, such as unused supplies and unexpired insurance, are likely to be consumed within a year, they also are reported as current assets.

Current assets are listed on the balance sheet from the most liquid to least liquid. **Liquidity** refers to the speed with which the company can convert the asset to cash. Cash is the most liquid asset and is always listed first. Notes Receivable, Accounts Receivable, and Merchandise Inventory often follow it on the balance sheet.

Property, Plant, and Equipment

Assets that are expected to be used for more than one year in the operation of a business are called **property, plant, and equipment.** Examples include land, buildings, office equipment, store equipment, and delivery equipment. Of these assets, only land is permanent; however, all of these assets have useful lives that are comparatively long. Typically, assets with longer useful lives are listed first.

The balance sheet of Northern Micro shows Land, Building, and Store Equipment. Land is not depreciated. Accumulated depreciation amounts are shown as deductions from the costs of the building and store equipment. The difference represents the **undepreciated cost**, or **book value**, of the assets. This amount less any salvage value will be written off as depreciation expense in future periods.

Current Liabilities

The current portion of long-term debt, the amount due within one year, is reported as a current liability. The remainder is reported under long-term liabilities.

Current liabilities include those obligations that are due within one year or the normal operating cycle of the business, whichever is longer, and will require the use of current assets. As of December 31, the current liabilities of Northern Micro consist of Notes Payable, Accounts Payable, Wages Payable, Sales Tax Payable, Unearned Subscriptions Revenue, and the portion of Mortgage Payable that is due within the next year.

Long-Term Liabilities

Long-term liabilities include those obligations that will extend beyond one year or the normal operating cycle, whichever is longer. A common long-term liability is a mortgage payable.

A **mortgage** is a written agreement specifying that if the borrower does not repay a debt, the lender has the right to take over specific property to satisfy the debt. When the debt is paid, the mortgage becomes void. **Mortgage Payable** is an account that is used to reflect an obligation that is secured by a mortgage on certain property.

Owner's Equity

The permanent owner's equity accounts reported on the balance sheet are determined by the type of organization. The accounts for a sole proprietorship, a partnership, and a corporation differ. Northern Micro is a sole proprietorship and reports one owner's equity account, Gary L. Fishel, Capital. The balance of this account is taken from the statement of owner's equity. Partnerships are illustrated in Chapter 19 and corporations are discussed in Chapters 20 and 21.

FINANCIAL STATEMENT ANALYSIS

LO4 Compute standard financial ratios.

Both management and creditors are interested in using the financial statements to evaluate the financial condition and profitability of the firm. This can be done by making a few simple calculations.

Balance Sheet Analysis

Recall the following:

1. Current assets include cash, items that will be converted to cash, and items that will be consumed within one year.

2. Current liabilities are obligations that will require the use of current assets.

Thus, the difference between current assets and current liabilities represents the amount of capital the business has available for current operations. This is called **working capital**.

Working Capital = Current Assets − Current Liabilities

The balance sheet in Figure 15-6 shows that Northern Micro has current assets of $54,000 and current liabilities of $19,450. Thus, the working capital at year end is $34,550 ($54,000 − $19,450). This amount should be more than adequate to satisfy current operating requirements.

Two measures of the firm's ability to pay its current liabilities are the **current ratio** and **quick ratio**. The formulas for calculating these ratios are as follows:

Northern Micro

$$\text{Current Ratio} = \frac{\text{Current Assets}}{\text{Current Liabilities}} = \frac{\$54,000}{\$19,450} = 2.8 \text{ to } 1$$

$$\text{Quick Ratio} = \frac{\text{Quick Assets}}{\text{Current Liabilities}} = \frac{\$35,000}{\$19,450} = 1.8 \text{ to } 1$$

LEARNING KEY

Ratio analysis is most informative when the ratios are compared with past performance and with those of similar businesses.

Information on industry averages is available in various publications from Dun & Bradstreet, Standard & Poor's, and Moody's.

Northern Micro's current ratio of 2.8 to 1 is quite high, which indicates a favorable financial position. The traditional "rule of thumb" has been that a current ratio should be about 2 to 1, but many businesses operate successfully on a current ratio of 1.5 to 1. Although a rule of thumb is helpful, it is better to compare an individual company to industry averages, which are available in most public libraries or on the Internet.

Quick assets include cash and all other current assets that can be converted into cash quickly, such as accounts receivable and temporary investments. Temporary investments are discussed in more advanced textbooks. The balance sheet in Figure 15-6 shows total quick assets of $35,000 ($20,000 in cash + $15,000 in accounts receivable). This produces a quick ratio of 1.8 to 1. Quick assets appear to be more than adequate to meet current obligations. The traditional rule of thumb has been that a quick ratio should be about 1 to 1, but many businesses operate successfully on a quick ratio of 0.6 to 1.

Interstatement Analysis

Interstatement analysis provides a comparison of the relationships between selected income statement and balance sheet amounts. A good example of interstatement analysis is the ratio of net income to owner's equity in the business. This ratio is known as **return on owner's equity**.

$$\text{Return on Owner's Equity} = \frac{\text{Net Income}}{\text{Average Owner's Equity}} = \frac{\text{Northern Micro}}{(\$104,400 + \$117,050) \div 2}$$

$$= \frac{\$22,650}{\$110,725}$$

$$= 20.5\%$$

The statement of owner's equity in Figure 15-5 shows that the owner's equity of Northern Micro was $104,400 on January 1 and $117,050 on December 31. The net income for the year of $22,650 is 20.5% of the average owner's equity. A comparison of this ratio with the return on owner's equity in prior years should be of interest to the owner. It may also be of interest to compare the return on owner's equity of Northern Micro with the same ratio for other businesses of comparable nature and size.

A second ratio involving both income statement and balance sheet accounts is a measure of the time required to collect cash from credit customers. This financial measure is often computed in two ways. The **accounts receivable turnover** is the number of times the accounts receivable "turned over," or were collected, during the accounting period. Of course, a higher number indicates that cash is collected more quickly. This ratio is calculated as follows:

> *Net credit sales is generally not reported in the financial statements. Use net sales, instead. As long as the proportion of cash and credit sales is reasonably stable over time, this ratio will provide a reasonable measure of the business's ability to collect receivables in a timely manner from year to year.*

$$\text{Accounts Receivable Turnover} = \frac{\text{Net Credit Sales for the Period}}{\text{Average Accounts Receivable}}$$

The accounts receivable turnover for Northern Micro for the year ended December 31 is computed as follows:

Net credit sales for the year (determined from the accounting records)	$110,000
Accounts receivable balance, January 1, 20-- (taken from last year's balance sheet)	10,000
Accounts receivable balance, December 31, 20--	15,000

$$\text{Average Accounts Receivable} = \frac{\text{Beginning Balance} + \text{Ending Balance}}{2} = \frac{\text{Northern Micro}}{2}$$
$$= \frac{\$10,000 + \$15,000}{2}$$
$$= \$12,500$$

$$\text{Accounts Receivable Turnover} = \frac{\text{Net Credit Sales for the Period}}{\text{Average Accounts Receivable}} = \frac{\$110,000}{\$12,500}$$
$$= 8.8$$

The **average collection period** is calculated by dividing the number of days in the year (365) by the rate of turnover to determine the number of days credit customers take to pay for their purchases. Northern Micro's customers are taking about 42 days.

365 days ÷ 8.8 = 41.5 days

Comparing the average collection period with a business's credit terms offers an indication of whether customers are paying within the terms. If Northern Micro allows credit terms of n/45, an average collection period of 41.5 days would suggest that customers are paying on a timely basis.

A third ratio involving both income statement and balance sheet accounts is the rate of **inventory turnover**. This is the number of times the merchandise inventory turned over, or was sold, during the accounting period. This ratio is calculated as follows:

$$\text{Inventory Turnover} = \frac{\text{Cost of Goods Sold for the Period}}{\text{Average Inventory}}$$

If inventory is taken only at the end of each accounting period, the average inventory for the period can be calculated by adding the beginning and ending inventories and dividing their sum by two. Northern Micro's turnover for the year ended December 31 is computed as follows:

Cost of goods sold for the period	$111,500
Beginning inventory	26,000
Ending inventory	18,000

$$\text{Average Inventory} = \frac{\text{Beginning Inventory} + \text{Ending Inventory}}{2} = \frac{\$26,000 + \$18,000}{2} = \$22,000$$

Northern Micro

A   BROADER   VIEW

© LESTER LEFKOWITZ/GETTY IMAGES

Who Cares About Tracking Financial Ratios?

Tracking a business's average collection period for receivables can help investors avoid making poor investments. Take the case of Kendall Square, a supercomputer maker. In an effort to increase sales and profits, Kendall Square recognized large amounts of revenues that had not actually been earned. Since no cash was received for these sales, accounts receivable increased dramatically (by 57%). Similarly, the average collection period increased to 157 days. Large increases in the average collection period should warn potential investors that something might be wrong. What happened at Kendall Square? Over $10 million of sales on account was never collected. This was equal to almost half of the revenues reported for the year. When eventually discovered, Kendall Square's stock price fell from $24.25 to $2.28 a share.

$$\text{Inventory Turnover} = \frac{\text{Cost of Goods Sold for the Period}}{\text{Average Inventory}} = \frac{\$111,500}{\$22,000} = 5.1$$

The **average days to sell inventory** can be computed by dividing the number of days in the year (365) by the inventory turnover. For Northern Micro, it takes about two months.

365 days ÷ 5.1 = 71.6 days

The higher the rate of inventory turnover, the smaller the profit required on each dollar of sales to produce a satisfactory gross profit. This is because the increase in the number of units sold offsets the smaller amount of gross profit earned per unit. For example, grocery stores have a very small gross profit on each item sold, but make up for this with a rapid inventory turnover. Other types of businesses, jewelers for example, need a high gross profit on each item because their inventory turnover is quite slow. Evaluations of Northern Micro's rate of inventory turnover would require comparison with prior years, other companies, or its industry.

CLOSING ENTRIES

LO5 Prepare closing entries for a merchandising business.

Closing entries for a service business were illustrated in Chapter 6. The process is essentially the same for a merchandising business. All revenues and expenses reported on the income statement must be closed to Income Summary. Then, the income summary and drawing accounts are closed to the owner's capital account. Keep in mind, however, that a few new accounts were needed for a merchandising business. These include Sales Returns and Allowances, Sales Discounts, Purchases Returns and Allowances, and Purchases Discounts. Since these are temporary accounts reported on the income statement, they also must be closed. The easiest way to complete the closing process is by using the work sheet to prepare the closing entries in four basic steps, as illustrated in Figures 15-7 and 15-8.

FIGURE 15-7   The Closing Process

THE CLOSING PROCESS FOR A MERCHANDISING BUSINESS

STEP 1   All income statement accounts with credit balances are debited, with an offsetting credit to Income Summary.

STEP 2   All income statement accounts with debit balances are credited, with an offsetting debit to Income Summary.

STEP 3   The resulting balance in Income Summary, which is the net income or loss for the period, is transferred to the owner's capital account.

ACCOUNT: Income Summary						ACCOUNT NO. 331			
DATE	ITEM	POST. REF.	DEBIT	CREDIT	BALANCE		Adjustments to:		
					DEBIT	CREDIT			
20-- Dec. 31	Adjusting	J5	26 0 0 0 00		26 0 0 0 00		← Remove Beg. Inventory		
31	Adjusting	J5		18 0 0 0 00	8 0 0 0 00		← Enter End. Inventory		
31	Closing	J6		234 7 0 0 00		226 7 0 0 00	← Closing step 1		
31	Closing	J6	204 0 5 0 00			22 6 5 0 00	← Closing step 2		
31	Closing	J6	22 6 5 0 00				← Closing step 3		

STEP 4   The balance in the owner's drawing account is transferred to the owner's capital account.

FIGURE 15-8   Closing Entries for a Merchandising Business

Northern Micro
Work Sheet (Partial)
For Year Ended December 31, 20--

	ACCOUNT TITLE	INCOME STATEMENT DEBIT	CREDIT	BALANCE SHEET DEBIT	CREDIT
17	Gary L. Fishel, Capital				114 4 0 0 00
18	Gary L. Fishel, Drawing			20 0 0 0 00	
19	Income Summary	26 0 0 0 00	18 0 0 0 00		
20	Sales		214 0 0 0 00		
21	Sales Returns and Allowances	1 2 0 0 00			
22	Interest Revenue		9 0 0 00		
23	Rent Revenue		8 0 0 0 00		
24	Subscriptions Revenue		10 0 0 0 00		
25	Purchases	105 0 0 0 00			
26	Purchases Returns and Allow.		8 0 0 0 00		
27	Purchases Discounts		1 0 0 0 00		
28	Freight-In	3 0 0 0 00			
29	Wages Expense	42 4 5 0 00			
30	Advertising Expense	2 5 0 0 00			
31	Bank Credit Card Expense	1 5 0 0 00			
32	Rent Expense	20 0 0 0 00			
33	Supplies Expense	1 4 0 0 00			
34	Telephone Expense	3 5 0 0 00			
35	Utilities Expense	12 0 0 0 00			
36	Insurance Expense	1 8 0 0 00			
37	Depr. Expense—Building	4 0 0 0 00			
38	Depr. Expense—Store Equip.	3 0 0 0 00			
39	Miscellaneous Expense	2 2 5 0 00			
40	Interest Expense	3 1 5 0 00			
41		230 0 5 0 00	252 7 0 0 00	224 0 0 0 00	201 3 5 0 00
42	Net Income	22 6 5 0 00			22 6 5 0 00
43		252 7 0 0 00	252 7 0 0 00	224 0 0 0 00	224 0 0 0 00
44					

GENERAL JOURNAL   PAGE 6

	DATE	DESCRIPTION	POST. REF.	DEBIT	CREDIT
1	20--	Closing Entries			
2	Dec. 31	Sales		214 0 0 0 00	
3		Interest Revenue		9 0 0 00	
4		Rent Revenue		8 0 0 0 00	
5		Subscriptions Revenue		10 0 0 0 00	
6		Purchases Returns and Allowances		8 0 0 0 00	
7		Purchases Discounts		1 0 0 0 00	
8		Income Summary			234 7 0 0 00
9					
10	31	Income Summary		204 0 5 0 00	
11		Sales Returns and Allowances			1 2 0 0 00
12		Purchases			105 0 0 0 00
13		Freight-In			3 0 0 0 00
14		Wages Expense			42 4 5 0 00
15		Advertising Expense			2 5 0 0 00
16		Bank Credit Card Expense			1 5 0 0 00
17		Rent Expense			20 0 0 0 00
18		Supplies Expense			1 4 0 0 00
19		Telephone Expense			3 5 0 0 00
20		Utilities Expense			12 0 0 0 00
21		Insurance Expense			1 8 0 0 00
22		Depreciation Exp.—Building			4 0 0 0 00
23		Depreciation Exp.—Store Equip.			3 0 0 0 00
24		Miscellaneous Expense			2 2 5 0 00
25		Interest Expense			3 1 5 0 00
26					
27	31	Income Summary		22 6 5 0 00	
28		Gary L. Fishel, Capital			22 6 5 0 00
29					
30	31	Gary L. Fishel, Capital		20 0 0 0 00	
31		Gary L. Fishel, Drawing			20 0 0 0 00
32					

Post-Closing Trial Balance

A trial balance of the general ledger accounts taken after the temporary owner's equity accounts have been closed is called a **post-closing trial balance**. The purpose of the post-closing trial balance is to prove that the general ledger is in balance at the beginning of a new accounting period, before any transactions for the new accounting period are entered. It should also confirm that all temporary accounts have zero balances. Figure 15-9 shows a post-closing trial balance for Northern Micro.

FIGURE 15-9   Post-Closing Trial Balance

The post-closing trial balance must be prepared by taking the balances from the general ledger accounts. It should not be prepared from the balances on the work sheet.

Using the general ledger accounts makes sure that all adjusting and closing entries were entered and posted correctly.

Northern Micro
Post-Closing Trial Balance
December 31, 20 - -

ACCOUNT TITLE	ACCOUNT NO.	DEBIT BALANCE	CREDIT BALANCE
Cash	101	20 0 0 0 00	
Accounts Receivable	122	15 0 0 0 00	
Merchandise Inventory	131	18 0 0 0 00	
Supplies	141	4 0 0 00	
Prepaid Insurance	145	6 0 0 00	
Land	161	10 0 0 0 00	
Building	171	90 0 0 0 00	
Accumulated Depreciation—Building	171.1		20 0 0 0 00
Store Equipment	181	50 0 0 0 00	
Accumulated Depreciation—Store Equipment	181.1		18 0 0 0 00
Notes Payable	201		5 0 0 0 00
Accounts Payable	202		10 0 0 0 00
Wages Payable	219		4 5 0 00
Sales Tax Payable	231		1 5 0 0 00
Unearned Subscriptions Revenue	241		2 0 0 0 00
Mortgage Payable	251		30 0 0 0 00
Gary L. Fishel, Capital	311		117 0 5 0 00
		204 0 0 0 00	204 0 0 0 00

REVERSING ENTRIES

LO6 Prepare reversing entries.

Numerous adjusting entries are needed at the end of the accounting period to bring the account balances up to date for presentation in the financial statements. Although not required, some of these adjusting entries should be reversed at the beginning of the next accounting period. This is done to simplify the recording of transactions in the new accounting period. As its name implies, a **reversing entry** is the reverse or opposite of the adjusting entry.

ADJUSTING ENTRY

| 4 | Dec. | 31 | Wages Expense | | | 4 5 0 00 | | | 4 |
| 5 | | | Wages Payable | | | | 4 5 0 00 | 5 |

REVERSING ENTRY
(OPPOSITE)

| 7 | Jan. | 1 | Wages Payable | | | 4 5 0 00 | | | 7 |
| 8 | | | Wages Expense | | | | 4 5 0 00 | 8 |

To see the advantage of using reversing entries, let's consider the effect of reversing Northern Micro's adjusting entry for wages earned, but not paid, at the end of the year. Figure 15-10 shows that accrued wages on December 31 were $450. These wages are for work performed by the employees on the last three days of the accounting period ($150 × 3 = $450). The employees will be paid on Friday, January 2, the normal payday.

FIGURE 15-10   Adjusting, Closing, and Reversing Entries for Wages

	20-1			20-2	
	12/29/-1 Monday	12/30/-1 Tuesday	12/31/-1 Wednesday	1/1/-2 Thursday	1/2/-2 Friday
Wages Earned	150	150	150	150	150
Wages Paid	0	0	0	0	750
Total Earned			450		300
Total Paid			0		750
Accrued Wages on 12/31/-1			450		

Date	Without Reversing Entry		With Reversing Entry	

12/31/-1 Adj. Entry	Wages Expense 450
	   Wages Payable
		450	Wages Expense 450
			   Wages Payable
				450

12/31/-1 Closing Entry	Income Summary 42,450
	   Wages Expense
		42,450	Income Summary 42,450
			   Wages Expense
				42,450

1/1/-2 Rev. Entry	No Entry		Wages Payable 450 Wages Expense	450

1/2/-2 Payment of Payroll	Wages Expense 300
	Wages Payable 450
	   Cash
		750	Wages Expense 750
			   Cash
				750

Description	Wages Expense	Description
Bal.	42,000	
12/31/-1 Adj.	450	
	42,450	12/31/-1 Close
1/2/-2 Payroll	300	

Description	Wages Expense	Description
Bal.	42,000	
12/31/-1 Adj.	450	
	42,450	12/31/-1 Close
	450	1/1/-2 Reversing
1/2/-2 Payroll	750	
Bal.	300	

Wages Payable		
	450	12/31/-1 Adj.
1/2/-2 Payroll 450		

Wages Payable		
	450	12/31/-1 Adj.
1/1/-2 Reverse 450		

Cash		
750	1/2/-2 Payroll	

Cash		
750	1/2/-2 Payroll	

Note that the adjusting and closing entries are the same, regardless of whether a reversing entry is made. However, the reversing entry on January 1 has an impact on the entry made when the employees are paid. **Without** a reversing entry, the payment on January 2, 20-2, must be split between reduction of the wages payable account for wages earned in 20-1 and Wages Expense for wages earned in 20-2. **With** a reversing entry, the bookkeeper simply debits Wages Expense and credits Cash, as is done on every other payday. Thus, the likelihood of error is reduced. Reversing entries are particularly important in large businesses where the individual recording the entry for wages may not even know what adjusting entries were made.

Not all adjusting entries should be reversed. To determine which adjusting entries to reverse, follow this rule: *Except for the first year of operations, reverse all adjusting entries that increase an asset or liability account from a zero balance.*

Except for the first year of operation, merchandise inventory, and contra-assets like accumulated depreciation, will have existing balances. Thus, they should never be reversed. The adjusting entries for Northern Micro are shown in Figure 15-11. Note that only the adjustment for accrued wages is reversed in Figure 15-12.

LEARNING KEY

Reverse all adjusting entries that increase an asset or liability account from a zero balance.

FIGURE 15-11   Which Adjusting Entries to Reverse?

	DATE	DESCRIPTION	POST. REF.	DEBIT	CREDIT	
1		Adjusting Entries				1
2	20-- Dec. 31	Income Summary		26 0 0 0 00		2
3		Merchandise Inventory			26 0 0 0 00	3
5	31	Merchandise Inventory		18 0 0 0 00		5
6		Income Summary			18 0 0 0 00	6
8	31	Supplies Expense		1 4 0 0 00		8
9		Supplies			1 4 0 0 00	9
11	31	Insurance Expense		1 8 0 0 00		11
12		Prepaid Insurance			1 8 0 0 00	12
14	31	Depr. Expense—Building		4 0 0 0 00		14
15		Accum. Depr.—Building			4 0 0 0 00	15
17	31	Depr. Expense—Store Equipment		3 0 0 0 00		17
18		Accum. Depr.—Store Equipment			3 0 0 0 00	18
20	31	Wages Expense		4 5 0 00		20
21		Wages Payable			4 5 0 00	21
23	31	Unearned Subscriptions Revenue		10 0 0 0 00		23
24		Subscriptions Revenue			10 0 0 0 00	24

GENERAL JOURNAL   PAGE 5

SHOULD THE ADJUSTMENT BE REVERSED?

Never reverse adjustments for merchandise inventory.

Never reverse adjustments for merchandise inventory.

No. No asset or liability with a zero balance has been increased.

No. No asset or liability with a zero balance has been increased.

Never reverse adjustments for depreciation.

Never reverse adjustments for depreciation.

Yes. A liability account with a zero balance has been increased.

No. No asset or liability with a zero balance has been increased.

FIGURE 15-12   Reversing Entry for Northern Micro

	DATE		DESCRIPTION	POST. REF.	DEBIT	CREDIT	
1			Reversing Entries				1
2	20-- Jan.	1	Wages Payable		4 5 0 00		2
3			Wages Expense			4 5 0 00	3
4							4
5							5

Learning Objectives	Key Points to Remember

LO1 Prepare a single-step and multiple-step income statement for a merchandising business.

The general format for a single-step and multiple-step income statement is shown below.

Single-Step
Income Statement
For Year Ended December 31, 20--

Revenues:		
List all revenues	$xxx	
Total revenues		$xxx
Expenses:		
Cost of goods sold	$xxx	
List all other expenses	xxx	
Total expenses		xxx
Net income		$xxx

Multiple-Step
Income Statement
For Year Ended December 31, 20--

Revenue from sales:		
Sales	$xxx	
Less sales returns and allowances	xxx	
Net sales		$xxx
Cost of goods sold		xxx
Gross profit		$xxx
Operating expenses:		
List all operating expenses	$xxx	
Total operating expenses		xxx
Income from operations		$xxx
Other revenue:		
List all other revenue	$xxx	
Total other revenue		xxx
Other expenses:		
List all other expenses	$xxx	
Total other expenses		xxx
Net income		$xxx

Learning Objectives	Key Points to Remember

LO2 Prepare a statement of owner's equity.

A statement of owner's equity has the following format:

Business Name
Statement of Owner's Equity
For Year Ended December 31, 20--

Capital, January 1, 20--		$xxx
Add additional investments		xxx
Total investment		$xxx
Net income for the year	$xxx	
Less withdrawals	xxx	
Increase in capital		xxx
Capital, December 31, 20--		$xxx

LO3 Prepare a classified balance sheet.

A classified balance sheet has the following major headings:

Business Name
Balance Sheet
December 31, 20--

Assets

Current assets:			
All are listed		$xxx	
Total current assets			$xxx
Property, plant, and equipment:			
All are listed	$xxx		
Less accumulated depreciation (if appropriate)	xxx	$xxx	
Total property, plant, and equipment			xxx
Total assets			$xxx

Liabilities

Current liabilities:			
All are listed		$xxx	
Total current liabilities			$xxx
Long-term liabilities:			
All are listed		$xxx	
Total long-term liabilities			xxx
Total liabilities			$xxx

Owner's Equity

Owner's capital	xxx
Total liabilities and owner's equity	$xxx

Learning Objectives	Key Points to Remember
LO4 Compute standard financial ratios.	The following measures of financial condition may be computed from financial statement information:

$$\text{Working Capital} = \text{Current Assets} - \text{Current Liabilities}$$

$$\text{Current Ratio} = \text{Current Assets} \div \text{Current Liabilities}$$

$$\text{Quick Ratio} = \text{Quick Assets} \div \text{Current Liabilities}$$

$$\text{Return on Owner's Equity} = \text{Net Income} \div \text{Average Owner's Equity}$$

$$\text{Accounts Receivable Turnover} = \frac{\text{Net Credit Sales for the Period}}{\text{Average Accounts Receivable}}$$

$$\text{Average Collection Period} = \frac{365}{\text{Accounts Receivable Turnover}}$$

$$\text{Inventory Turnover} = \frac{\text{Cost of Goods Sold for the Period}}{\text{Average Inventory}}$$

$$\text{Average Days to Sell Inventory} = \frac{365}{\text{Inventory Turnover}}$$

Learning Objectives	Key Points to Remember
LO5 Prepare closing entries for a merchandising business.	The four steps in the closing process for a merchandising business are as follows:

STEP 1 All income statement accounts with credit balances are debited, with an offsetting credit to Income Summary.

STEP 2 All income statement accounts with debit balances are credited, with an offsetting debit to Income Summary.

STEP 3 The resulting balance in Income Summary, which is the net income or loss for the period, is transferred to the owner's capital account.

STEP 4 The balance in the owner's drawing account is transferred to the owner's capital account.

Learning Objectives	Key Points to Remember
LO6 Prepare reversing entries.	Use the following rule to determine which adjusting entries to reverse:

Except for the first year of operations, reverse all adjusting entries that increase an asset or liability account from a zero balance.

DEMONSTRATION PROBLEM

Tom McKinney owns and operates McK's Home Electronics. He has a store where he sells and repairs televisions and stereo equipment. A completed work sheet for 20-1 is provided on page 595. McKinney made a $20,000 additional investment during 20-1. The current portion of Mortgage Payable is $1,000. Net credit sales for 20-1 were $200,000, and the balance of Accounts Receivable on January 1 was $26,000.

REQUIRED

1. Prepare a multiple-step income statement.

2. Prepare a statement of owner's equity.

3. Prepare a balance sheet.

4. Compute the following measures of performance and financial condition for 20-1:

    (a) current ratio
    (b) quick ratio
    (c) working capital
    (d) return on owner's equity
    (e) accounts receivable turnover and the average number of days required to collect receivables
    (f) inventory turnover and the average number of days required to sell inventory

5. Prepare adjusting entries and indicate which should be reversed and why.

6. Prepare closing entries.

7. Prepare reversing entries for the adjustments where appropriate.

McK's Home Electronics
Work Sheet
For Year Ended December 31, 20-1

#	Account Title	Trial Balance Debit	Trial Balance Credit	Adjustments Debit	Adjustments Credit	Adjusted Trial Balance Debit	Adjusted Trial Balance Credit	Income Statement Debit	Income Statement Credit	Balance Sheet Debit	Balance Sheet Credit
1	Cash	10,000.00				10,000.00				10,000.00	
2	Accounts Receivable	22,500.00				22,500.00				22,500.00	
3	Merchandise Inventory	39,000.00		(b) 45,000.00	(a) 39,000.00	45,000.00				45,000.00	
4	Supplies	2,700.00			(c) 2,100.00	600.00				600.00	
5	Prepaid Insurance	3,600.00			(d) 2,700.00	900.00				900.00	
6	Land	15,000.00				15,000.00				15,000.00	
7	Building	135,000.00				135,000.00				135,000.00	
8	Accum. Depr.—Building		24,000.00		(e) 6,000.00		30,000.00				30,000.00
9	Store Equipment	75,000.00				75,000.00				75,000.00	
10	Accum. Depr.—Store Equipment		22,500.00		(f) 4,500.00		27,000.00				27,000.00
11	Notes Payable		7,500.00				7,500.00				7,500.00
12	Accounts Payable		15,000.00				15,000.00				15,000.00
13	Wages Payable				(g) 675.00		675.00				675.00
14	Sales Tax Payable		2,250.00				2,250.00				2,250.00
15	Unearned Repair Fees		18,000.00	(h) 15,000.00			3,000.00				3,000.00
16	Mortgage Payable		45,000.00				45,000.00				45,000.00
17	Tom McKinney, Capital		151,600.00				151,600.00				151,600.00
18	Tom McKinney, Drawing	30,000.00				30,000.00				30,000.00	
19	Income Summary			(a) 39,000.00	(b) 45,000.00	39,000.00	45,000.00	39,000.00	45,000.00		
20	Sales		300,750.00				300,750.00		300,750.00		
21	Sales Returns and Allowances	1,800.00				1,800.00		1,800.00			
22	Repair Fees				(h) 15,000.00		15,000.00		15,000.00		
23	Interest Revenue		1,350.00				1,350.00		1,350.00		
24	Purchases	157,500.00				157,500.00		157,500.00			
25	Purchases Returns and Allowances		1,200.00				1,200.00		1,200.00		
26	Purchases Discounts		1,500.00				1,500.00		1,500.00		
27	Freight-In	450.00				450.00		450.00			
28	Wages Expense	63,000.00		(g) 675.00		63,675.00		63,675.00			
29	Advertising Expense	3,750.00				3,750.00		3,750.00			
30	Supplies Expense			(c) 2,100.00		2,100.00		2,100.00			
31	Telephone Expense	5,250.00				5,250.00		5,250.00			
32	Utilities Expense	18,000.00				18,000.00		18,000.00			
33	Insurance Expense			(d) 2,700.00		2,700.00		2,700.00			
34	Depr. Expense—Building			(e) 6,000.00		6,000.00		6,000.00			
35	Depr. Expense—Store Equipment			(f) 4,500.00		4,500.00		4,500.00			
36	Miscellaneous Expense	3,375.00				3,375.00		3,375.00			
37	Interest Expense	4,725.00				4,725.00		4,725.00			
38		590,650.00	590,650.00	114,975.00	114,975.00	646,825.00	646,825.00	312,825.00	364,800.00	334,000.00	282,025.00
39	Net Income							51,975.00			51,975.00
40								364,800.00	364,800.00	334,000.00	334,000.00

(continued)

Solution 1.

McK's Home Electronics Income Statement For Year Ended December 31, 20 -1					
Revenue from sales:					
Sales			$300 7 5 0 00		
Less sales returns and allowances			1 8 0 0 00		
Net sales				$298 9 5 0 00	
Cost of goods sold:					
Merchandise inventory, January 1, 20-1			$ 39 0 0 0 00		
Purchases		$157 5 0 0 00			
Less: Purchases returns and allowances	$1 2 0 0 00				
Purchases discounts	1 5 0 0 00	2 7 0 0 00			
Net purchases		$154 8 0 0 00			
Add freight-in		4 5 0 00			
Cost of goods purchased			155 2 5 0 00		
Goods available for sale			$194 2 5 0 00		
Less merchandise inventory, December 31, 20-1			45 0 0 0 00		
Cost of goods sold				149 2 5 0 00	
Gross profit				$149 7 0 0 00	
Operating expenses:					
Wages expense			$ 63 6 7 5 00		
Advertising expense			3 7 5 0 00		
Supplies expense			2 1 0 0 00		
Telephone expense			5 2 5 0 00		
Utilities expense			18 0 0 0 00		
Insurance expense			2 7 0 0 00		
Depreciation expense—building			6 0 0 0 00		
Depreciation expense—store equipment			4 5 0 0 00		
Miscellaneous expense			3 3 7 5 00		
Total operating expenses				109 3 5 0 00	
Income from operations				$ 40 3 5 0 00	
Other revenues:					
Repair fees			$ 15 0 0 0 00		
Interest revenue			1 3 5 0 00		
Total other revenues			$ 16 3 5 0 00		
Other expenses:					
Interest expense			4 7 2 5 00	11 6 2 5 00	
Net income				$ 51 9 7 5 00	

2.

McK's Home Electronics Statement of Owner's Equity For Year Ended December 31, 20-1		
Tom McKinney, capital, January 1, 20-1		$131 6 0 0 00
Add additional investments		20 0 0 0 00
Total investment		$151 6 0 0 00
Net income for the year	$51 9 7 5 00	
Less withdrawals	30 0 0 0 00	
Increase in capital		21 9 7 5 00
Tom McKinney, capital, December 31, 20-1		$173 5 7 5 00

3.

McK's Home Electronics Balance Sheet December 31, 20 -1																			
Assets																			
Current assets:																			
Cash								$ 10	0	0	0	00						
Accounts receivable								22	5	0	0	00						
Merchandise inventory								45	0	0	0	00						
Supplies									6	0	0	00						
Prepaid insurance									9	0	0	00						
Total current assets													$ 79	0	0	0	00
Property, plant, and equipment:																	
Land								$ 15	0	0	0	00						
Building	$135	0	0	0	00												
Less accumulated depreciation	30	0	0	0	00	105	0	0	0	00							
Store equipment	$ 75	0	0	0	00												
Less accumulated depreciation	27	0	0	0	00	48	0	0	0	00							
Total property, plant and equipment													168	0	0	0	00
Total assets													$247	0	0	0	00
Liabilities																	
Current liabilities:																	
Notes payable	$ 7	5	0	0	00												
Accounts payable	15	0	0	0	00												
Wages payable		6	7	5	00												
Sales tax payable	2	2	5	0	00												
Unearned repair fees	3	0	0	0	00												
Mortgage payable (current portion)	1	0	0	0	00												
Total current liabilities						$ 29	4	2	5	00							
Long-term liabilities:																	
Mortgage payable	$ 45	0	0	0	00												
Less current portion	1	0	0	0	00	44	0	0	0	00							
Total liabilities													$ 73	4	2	5	00
Owner's Equity																	
Tom McKinney, capital													173	5	7	5	00
Total liabilities and owner's equity													$247	0	0	0	00

4. (a) Current Ratio   = Current Assets ÷ Current Liabilities
                         = $79,000 ÷ $29,425 = 2.68 to 1

    (b) Quick Ratio   = Quick Assets ÷ Current Liabilities
                         = $32,500 ÷ $29,425 = 1.10 to 1

    (c) Working Capital = Current Assets − Current Liabilities
                         = $79,000 − $29,425 = $49,575

    (d) Return on Owner's Equity = Net Income ÷ Average Owner's Equity

$$= \frac{\$51,975}{(\$131,600 + \$173,575) \div 2}$$

                                   = $51,975 ÷ $152,587.50
                                   = 34%

(continued)

(e) Account Receivable Turnover $= \dfrac{\text{Net Credit Sales for the Period}}{\text{Average Accounts Receivable}}$

$= \dfrac{\$200,000}{(\$26,000 + \$22,500) \div 2}$

$= \$200,000 \div \$24,250$

$= 8.25$

Average number of days to collect an account receivable:
$365 \div 8.25 = 44.24$ days

(f) Inventory Turnover $= \dfrac{\text{Cost of Goods Sold for the Period}}{\text{Average Inventory}}$

$= \dfrac{\$149,250}{(\$39,000 + \$45,000) \div 2}$

$= \$149,250 \div \$42,000$

$= 3.6$

Average number of days to sell inventory:
$365 \div 3.6 = 101.39$ days

5.

	DATE		DESCRIPTION	POST. REF.	DEBIT		CREDIT		
			GENERAL JOURNAL				PAGE 3		
1			Adjusting Entries						1
2	20-1 Dec.	31	Income Summary		39 0 0 0 00				2
3			Merchandise Inventory				39 0 0 0 00		3
4									4
5		31	Merchandise Inventory		45 0 0 0 00				5
6			Income Summary				45 0 0 0 00		6
7									7
8		31	Supplies Expense		2 1 0 0 00				8
9			Supplies				2 1 0 0 00		9
10									10
11		31	Insurance Expense		2 7 0 0 00				11
12			Prepaid Insurance				2 7 0 0 00		12
13									13
14		31	Depr. Expense—Building		6 0 0 0 00				14
15			Accum. Depr.—Building				6 0 0 0 00		15
16									16
17		31	Depr. Expense—Store Equipment		4 5 0 0 00				17
18			Accum. Depr.—Store Equipment				4 5 0 0 00		18
19									19
20		31	Wages Expense		6 7 5 00				20
21			Wages Payable				6 7 5 00		21
22									22
23		31	Unearned Repair Fees		15 0 0 0 00				23
24			Repair Fees				15 0 0 0 00		24
25									25

SHOULD THE ADJUSTMENT BE REVERSED?

Never reverse adjustments for merchandise inventory.

Never reverse adjustments for merchandise inventory.

No. No asset or liability with a zero balance has been increased.

No. No asset or liability with a zero balance has been increased.

Never reverse adjustments for depreciation.

Never reverse adjustments for depreciation.

Yes. A liability account with a zero balance has been increased.

No. No asset or liability with a zero balance has been increased.

6.

	DATE		DESCRIPTION	POST. REF.	DEBIT					CREDIT					
			GENERAL JOURNAL										PAGE 4		
1			Closing Entries												1
2	20-1 Dec.	31	Repair Fees		15	0	0	0	00						2
3			Sales		300	7	5	0	00						3
4			Interest Revenue		1	3	5	0	00						4
5			Purchases Returns and Allowances		1	2	0	0	00						5
6			Purchases Discounts		1	5	0	0	00						6
7			Income Summary							319	8	0	0	00	7
8															8
9		31	Income Summary		273	8	2	5	00						9
10			Sales Returns and Allowances							1	8	0	0	00	10
11			Purchases							157	5	0	0	00	11
12			Freight-In								4	5	0	00	12
13			Wages Expense							63	6	7	5	00	13
14			Advertising Expense							3	7	5	0	00	14
15			Supplies Expense							2	1	0	0	00	15
16			Telephone Expense							5	2	5	0	00	16
17			Utilities Expense							18	0	0	0	00	17
18			Insurance Expense							2	7	0	0	00	18
19			Depr. Expense—Building							6	0	0	0	00	19
20			Depr. Expense—Store Equipment							4	5	0	0	00	20
21			Miscellaneous Expense							3	3	7	5	00	21
22			Interest Expense							4	7	2	5	00	22
23															23
24		31	Income Summary		51	9	7	5	00						24
25			Tom McKinney, Capital							51	9	7	5	00	25
26															26
27		31	Tom McKinney, Capital		30	0	0	0	00						27
28			Tom McKinney, Drawing							30	0	0	0	00	28
29															29

7.

	DATE		DESCRIPTION	POST. REF.	DEBIT					CREDIT					
			GENERAL JOURNAL										PAGE 5		
1			Reversing Entries												1
2	20-2 Jan.	1	Wages Payable			6	7	5	00						2
3			Wages Expense								6	7	5	00	3
4															4

KEY TERMS

accounts receivable turnover (584)   The number of times the accounts receivable turned over, or were collected, during the accounting period. When 365 is divided by the turnover, this measure can be expressed in terms of the average number of days required to collect receivables.

average collection period (584)   The number of days in the year (365) divided by the accounts receivable turnover. Provides an indication of the number of days credit customers take to pay for their purchases.

average days to sell inventory (586)   The number of days in the year (365) divided by the inventory turnover. Provides an indication of the average number of days required to sell inventory.

book value (582)   See undepreciated cost.

current assets (582)   Cash and all other assets expected to be converted into cash or consumed within one year or the normal operating cycle of the business, whichever is longer.

current liabilities (582)   Those obligations that are due within one year or the normal operating cycle of the business, whichever is longer, and will require the use of current assets.

current ratio (583)   Current assets divided by current liabilities.

general expenses (578)   Those expenses associated with administrative, office, or general operating activities.

gross margin (576)   See gross profit.

gross profit (576)   Net sales minus cost of goods sold.

income from operations (576)   Gross profit minus operating expenses on a multiple-step income statement.

interstatement analysis (584)   Compares the relationship between certain amounts in the income statement and balance sheet.

inventory turnover (585)   The number of times the merchandise inventory turned over, or was sold, during the accounting period. When 365 is divided by the turnover, this measure can be expressed in terms of the average number of days required to sell inventory.

liquidity (582)   Refers to the speed with which an asset can be converted to cash.

long-term liabilities (582)   Those obligations that will extend beyond one year or the normal operating cycle, whichever is longer.

mortgage (582)   A written agreement specifying that if the borrower does not repay a debt, the lender has the right to take over specific property to satisfy the debt.

Mortgage Payable (582)   An account that is used to reflect an obligation that is secured by a mortgage on certain property.

multiple-step income statement (576)   This statement shows a step-by-step calculation of net sales, cost of goods sold, gross profit, operating expenses, income from operations, other revenues and expenses, and net income.

net sales (576)   Gross sales less sales returns and allowances and less sales discounts.

operating cycle (582)   The length of time generally required for a business to buy inventory, sell it, and collect the cash.

operating income (576)   See income from operations.

post-closing trial balance (588)   A trial balance taken after the temporary owner's equity accounts have been closed.

property, plant, and equipment (582)   Assets that are expected to be used for more than one year in the operation of a business.

quick assets (583)   Cash and all other current assets that can be converted into cash quickly, such as accounts receivable and temporary investments.

quick ratio (583)   Quick assets divided by current liabilities.

return on owner's equity (584)   Net income divided by average owner's equity.

reversing entry (588)   The opposite of the adjusting entry. It is made on the first day of the next accounting period and simplifies recording transactions in the new period.

selling expenses (576)   Those expenses directly associated with selling activities.

single-step income statement (576)   This statement lists all revenue items and their total first, followed by all expense items and their total.

undepreciated cost (582)   Cost of plant and equipment less the accumulated depreciation amounts. Also called book value.

working capital (583)   The difference between current assets and current liabilities, which represents the amount of capital the business has available for current operations.

Self-Study Test Questions

True/False

1. A multiple-step form of income statement calculates gross profit, before subtracting operating expenses.

2. Current assets include cash, items expected to convert into cash, and items that will be consumed during a year or the normal operating cycle, whichever is shorter.

3. Current assets are listed on the balance sheet in order of liquidity.

4. Working capital is the difference between current assets and current liabilities.

5. Accounts receivable turnover is the number of times merchandise inventory turned over or was sold during the accounting period.

Multiple Choice

1. Which of these assets is *not* a current asset?

   (a) Cash
   (b) Accounts Receivable
   (c) Office Equipment
   (d) Merchandise Inventory

2. Which of these would be listed *first* on a balance sheet?

   (a) Accounts Receivable
   (b) Delivery Equipment
   (c) Accounts Payable
   (d) Prepaid Insurance

3. Which of these is considered a *quick asset*?

   (a) Merchandise Inventory
   (b) Accounts Receivable
   (c) Office Equipment
   (d) Prepaid Insurance

4. To calculate the accounts receivable turnover ratio, _____ is divided by average accounts receivable.

   (a) Net sales
   (b) Cost of goods sold
   (c) Total sales
   (d) Net credit sales

5. Inventory turnover is calculated by dividing cost of goods sold by

   (a) average accounts receivable.
   (b) average owner's equity.
   (c) average inventory.
   (d) accounts receivable turnover.

The answers to the Self-Study Test Questions are at the end of the text.

REVIEW QUESTIONS

LO1   1. Describe the nature of the two forms of an income statement.

LO4   2. Name and describe the calculation of two measures that provide an indication of a business's ability to pay current obligations.

LO4   3. Describe how to calculate the following ratios:

   (a) return on owner's equity
   (b) accounts receivable turnover
   (c) inventory turnover

LO5   4. Where is the information obtained that is needed in journalizing the closing entries?

LO5   5. Explain the function of each of the four closing entries made by Northern Micro.

LO5   6. What is the purpose of a post-closing trial balance?

LO6   7. What is the primary purpose of reversing entries?

LO6   8. What is the customary date for reversing entries?

LO6   9. What adjusting entries should be reversed?

R E V I S I T I N G   T H E   O P E N E R

In the chapter opener on page 575, you are asked to consider why Betty Jenkins was not concerned about the entries made to record the first payroll payment. Some of the payment was for work performed last year, and the remainder was for work done this year. This seems unusual given the importance of properly matching revenues and expenses. Why do you think Betty was not concerned?

SERIES A EXERCISES

E 15-1A (LO1)

✓ Net sales: $133,700

REVENUE SECTION, MULTIPLE-STEP INCOME STATEMENT Based on the information that follows, prepare the revenue section of a multiple-step income statement.

Sales	$140,000
Sales Returns and Allowances	3,500
Sales Discounts	2,800

E 15-2A (LO1)

✓ Cost of goods sold: $102,560

COST OF GOODS SOLD SECTION, MULTIPLE-STEP INCOME STATEMENT Based on the information that follows, prepare the cost of goods sold section of a multiple-step income statement.

Merchandise Inventory, January 1, 20--	$ 34,000
Purchases	102,000
Purchases Returns and Allowances	4,200
Purchases Discounts	2,040
Freight-In	800
Merchandise Inventory, December 31, 20--	28,000

E 15-3A (LO1)

✓ Cost of goods sold: $87,860;

Net income: $15,634

MULTIPLE-STEP INCOME STATEMENT Use the following information to prepare a multiple-step income statement, including the revenue section and the cost of goods sold section, for Rau Office Supplies for the year ended December 31, 20--.

Sales	$148,300
Sales Returns and Allowances	1,380
Sales Discounts	2,166
Interest Revenue	240
Merchandise Inventory, January 1, 20--	26,500
Purchases	98,000
Purchases Returns and Allowances	2,180
Purchases Discounts	1,960
Freight-In	750
Merchandise Inventory, December 31, 20--	33,250
Wages Expense	23,800
Supplies Expense	900
Telephone Expense	1,100
Utilities Expense	7,000
Insurance Expense	1,000
Depreciation Expense—Equipment	3,100
Miscellaneous Expense	720
Interest Expense	3,880

E 15-4A (LO5)

CLOSING ENTRIES From the work sheet on page 604, prepare closing entries for Gimbel's Gifts and Gadgets in a general journal.

E 15-5A (LO6)

REVERSING ENTRIES From the work sheet used in Exercise 15-4A, identify the adjusting entry(ies) that should be reversed and prepare the reversing entry(ies).

E 15-6A (LO5/6)

ADJUSTING, CLOSING, AND REVERSING ENTRIES Based on the information provided on page 605, prepare two sets of entries—one that will have a reversing entry and the other without a reversing entry. Enter existing balances and post all entries to two sets of T accounts for Wages Expense and Wages Payable.

(continued on page 605)

EXERCISE 15-4A

Gimbel's Gifts and Gadgets
Work Sheet
For Year Ended December 31, 20-1

No.	Account Title	Trial Balance Debit	Trial Balance Credit	Adjustments Debit	Adjustments Credit	Adjusted Trial Balance Debit	Adjusted Trial Balance Credit	Income Statement Debit	Income Statement Credit	Balance Sheet Debit	Balance Sheet Credit
1	Cash	8,214.00				8,214.00				8,214.00	
2	Accounts Receivable	6,720.00				6,720.00				6,720.00	
3	Merchandise Inventory	14,210.00		(b) 16,800.00	(a) 14,210.00	16,800.00				16,800.00	
4	Supplies	6,800.00			(c) 6,500.00	300.00				300.00	
5	Prepaid Insurance	800.00			(d) 200.00	600.00				600.00	
6	Building	80,000.00				80,000.00				80,000.00	
7	Accum. Depr.—Building		13,600.00		(e) 4,000.00		17,600.00				17,600.00
8	Accounts Payable		5,280.00				5,280.00				5,280.00
9	Wages Payable				(f) 280.00		280.00				280.00
10	Sales Tax Payable		326.00				326.00				326.00
11	J. M. Gimbel, Capital		87,883.00				87,883.00				87,883.00
12	J. M. Gimbel, Drawing	8,000.00				8,000.00				8,000.00	
13	Income Summary			(a) 14,210.00	(b) 16,800.00	14,210.00	16,800.00	14,210.00	16,800.00		
14	Sales		86,000.00				86,000.00		86,000.00		
15	Sales Returns and Allowances	1,840.00				1,840.00		1,840.00			
16	Purchases	36,272.00				36,272.00		36,272.00			
17	Purchases Returns and Allowances		2,813.00				2,813.00		2,813.00		
18	Purchases Discounts		1,084.00				1,084.00		1,084.00		
19	Freight-In	800.00				800.00		800.00			
20	Wages Expense	16,800.00		(f) 280.00		17,080.00		17,080.00			
21	Advertising Expense	7,840.00				7,840.00		7,840.00			
22	Supplies Expense			(c) 6,500.00		6,500.00		6,500.00			
23	Telephone Expense	2,100.00				2,100.00		2,100.00			
24	Utilities Expense	1,310.00				1,310.00		1,310.00			
25	Insurance Expense			(d) 200.00		200.00		200.00			
26	Depr. Expense—Building			(e) 4,000.00		4,000.00		4,000.00			
27	Miscellaneous Expense	3,860.00				3,860.00		3,860.00			
28	Interest Expense	1,420.00				1,420.00		1,420.00			
29		196,986.00	196,986.00	41,990.00	41,990.00	218,066.00	218,066.00	97,432.00	106,697.00	120,634.00	111,369.00
30	Net Income							9,265.00			9,265.00
31								106,697.00	106,697.00	120,634.00	120,634.00

(a)   Wages paid during 20-1 are $20,800.

(b)   Wages earned but not paid (accrued) as of December 31, 20-1, are $300.

(c)   On January 3, 20-2, payroll of $800 is paid, which includes the $300 of wages earned but not paid in December.

E 15-7A (LO4)

✓ Current ratio: 4.64 to 1;

Return on owner's equity: 28.9%;

Inventory turnover: 3.13

FINANCIAL RATIOS Based on the financial statements for Jackson Enterprises (income statement, statement of owner's equity, and balance sheet) shown below and on the next page, prepare the following financial ratios. All sales are credit sales. The Accounts Receivable balance on January 1, 20--, was $21,600.

1.   Working capital
2.   Current ratio
3.   Quick ratio
4.   Return on owner's equity
5.   Accounts receivable turnover and average number of days required to collect receivables
6.   Inventory turnover and average number of days required to sell inventory

Jackson Enterprises Income Statement For Year Ended December 31, 20 - -								
Revenue from sales:								
Sales				$184 2 0 0 00				
Less sales returns and allowances				2 1 0 0 00				
Net sales						$182 1 0 0 00		
Cost of goods sold:								
Merchandise inventory, January 1, 20- -				$ 31 3 0 0 00				
Purchases			$92 8 0 0 00					
Less: Purchases returns and allowances	$1 8 0 0 00							
Purchases discounts	1 8 5 6 00		3 6 5 6 00					
Net purchases			$89 1 4 4 00					
Add freight-in			9 3 3 00					
Cost of goods purchased				90 0 7 7 00				
Goods available for sale				$121 3 7 7 00				
Less merchandise inventory, December 31, 20- -				28 1 7 7 00				
Cost of goods sold						93 2 0 0 00		
Gross profit						$ 88 9 0 0 00		
Operating expenses:								
Wages expense				$ 38 0 0 0 00				
Advertising expense				1 1 8 0 00				
Supplies expense				3 8 0 00				
Telephone expense				2 2 1 0 00				
Utilities expense				11 0 0 0 00				
Insurance expense				9 0 0 00				
Depreciation expense—building				4 0 0 0 00				
Depreciation expense—equipment				3 8 0 0 00				
Miscellaneous expense				5 3 0 00				
Total operating expenses						62 0 0 0 00		
Income from operations						$ 26 9 0 0 00		
Other revenues:								
Interest revenue				$ 1 8 0 0 00				
Other expenses:								
Interest expense				9 0 0 00		9 0 0 00		
Net income						$ 27 8 0 0 00		

(*continued*)

Jackson Enterprises Statement of Owner's Equity For Year Ended December 31, 20 - -										
J. B. Gray, capital, January 1, 20- -							$ 88	0	0	0	00
Net income for the year	$27	8	0	0	00					
Less withdrawals for the year	11	6	0	0	00					
Increase in capital							16	2	0	0	00
J. B. Gray, capital, December 31, 20- -							$104	2	0	0	00

Jackson Enterprises
Balance Sheet
December 31, 20 - -

Assets																
Current assets:																
Cash						$20	8	0	0	00						
Accounts receivable						18	9	0	0	00						
Merchandise inventory						28	1	7	7	00						
Supplies						1	3	2	3	00						
Prepaid insurance							9	0	0	00						
Total current assets											$ 70	1	0	0	00
Property, plant, and equipment:																
Building	$90	0	0	0	00											
Less accumulated depreciation—building	28	0	0	0	00	$62	0	0	0	00						
Equipment	$33	0	0	0	00											
Less accumulated depreciation—equipment	7	5	0	0	00	25	5	0	0	00						
Total property, plant, and equipment											87	5	0	0	00
Total assets											$157	6	0	0	00
Liabilities																
Current liabilities:																
Accounts payable	$12	6	0	0	00											
Wages payable		5	0	0	00											
Sales tax payable	1	2	0	0	00											
Mortgage payable (current portion)		8	0	0	00											
Total current liabilities						$15	1	0	0	00						
Long-term liabilities:																
Mortgage payable	$39	1	0	0	00											
Less current portion		8	0	0	00	38	3	0	0	00						
Total liabilities											$ 53	4	0	0	00
Owner's Equity																
J. B. Gray, capital											104	2	0	0	00
Total liabilities and owner's equity											$157	6	0	0	00

SERIES A PROBLEMS

P 15-8A (LO5/6)

✓ Net income: $10,610; Post-closing trial bal. col. totals: $79,650

KLOOSTER & ALLEN

WORK SHEET, ADJUSTING, CLOSING, AND REVERSING ENTRIES Ellis Fabric Store shows the trial balance on the following page as of December 31, 20-1.

At the end of the year, the following adjustments need to be made:

(a and b) Merchandise Inventory as of December 31, $28,900.
(c) Unused supplies on hand, $1,350.

(d) Insurance expired, $300.
(e) Depreciation expense for the year, $500.
(f) Wages earned but not paid (Wages Payable), $480.

Ellis Fabric Store
Trial Balance
For Year Ended December 31, 20-1

ACCOUNT TITLE	DEBIT BALANCE					CREDIT BALANCE				
Cash	28	0	0	0	00					
Accounts Receivable	14	2	0	0	00					
Merchandise Inventory	33	0	0	0	00					
Supplies	1	6	0	0	00					
Prepaid Insurance		9	0	0	00					
Equipment	6	6	0	0	00					
Accumulated Depreciation—Equipment						1	0	0	0	00
Accounts Payable						16	6	2	0	00
Wages Payable										
Sales Tax Payable						8	5	0	00	
W. P. Ellis, Capital						71	2	0	0	00
W. P. Ellis, Drawing	21	6	1	0	00					
Income Summary										
Sales						78	5	0	0	00
Sales Returns and Allowances	1	8	5	0	00					
Interest Revenue						1	2	0	0	00
Purchases	41	5	0	0	00					
Purchases Returns and Allowances						1	8	0	0	00
Purchases Discounts						8	3	0	00	
Freight-In		6	6	0	00					
Wages Expense	14	8	8	0	00					
Advertising Expense		8	1	0	00					
Supplies Expense										
Telephone Expense	1	2	1	0	00					
Utilities Expense	3	2	4	0	00					
Insurance Expense										
Depreciation Expense—Equipment										
Miscellaneous Expense		9	2	0	00					
Interest Expense	1	0	2	0	00					
	172	0	0	0	00	172	0	0	0	00

REQUIRED

1. Prepare a work sheet.
2. Prepare adjusting entries.
3. Prepare closing entries.
4. Prepare a post-closing trial balance.
5. Prepare reversing entries.

P 15-9A (LO1/2/3)

✓ Cost of goods sold: $37,740;
Total assets: $39,850

INCOME STATEMENT, STATEMENT OF OWNER'S EQUITY, AND BALANCE SHEET Paulson's Pet Store completed the work sheet on page 609 for the year ended December 31, 20--. Owner's equity as of January 1, 20--, was $21,900. The current portion of Mortgage Payable is $500.

REQUIRED

1. Prepare a multiple-step income statement.

2. Prepare a statement of owner's equity.

3. Prepare a balance sheet.

P 15-10A (LO4)

✓ Working capital: $29,200;
Quick ratio: 2.78 to 1;
Accts. receivable turnover: 22.86

FINANCIAL RATIOS Use the work sheet and financial statements prepared in Problem 15-9A. All sales are credit sales. The Accounts Receivable balance on January 1, 20--, was $3,800.

REQUIRED

Prepare the following financial ratios:

(a) Working capital

(b) Current ratio

(c) Quick ratio

(d) Return on owner's equity

(e) Accounts receivable turnover and average number of days required to collect receivables

(f) Inventory turnover and average number of days required to sell inventory

SERIES B EXERCISES

E 15-1B (LO1)

✓ Net sales: $82,196

REVENUE SECTION, MULTIPLE-STEP INCOME STATEMENT Based on the information that follows, prepare the revenue section of a multiple-step income statement.

Sales	$86,200
Sales Returns and Allowances	2,280
Sales Discounts	1,724

E 15-2B (LO1)

✓ Cost of goods sold: $59,442

COST OF GOODS SOLD SECTION, MULTIPLE-STEP INCOME STATEMENT Based on the information that follows, prepare the cost of goods sold section of a multiple-step income statement.

Merchandise Inventory, January 1, 20--	$13,800
Purchases	71,300
Purchases Returns and Allowances	3,188
Purchases Discounts	1,460
Freight-In	390
Merchandise Inventory, December 31, 20--	21,400

PROBLEM 15-9A

Paulson's Pet Store
Work Sheet
For Year Ended December 31, 20 - -

#	ACCOUNT TITLE	Trial Balance Debit	Trial Balance Credit	Adjustments Debit	Adjustments Credit	Adjusted Trial Balance Debit	Adjusted Trial Balance Credit	Income Statement Debit	Income Statement Credit	Balance Sheet Debit	Balance Sheet Credit
1	Cash	15,860.00				15,860.00				15,860.00	
2	Accounts Receivable	2,340.00				2,340.00				2,340.00	
3	Merchandise Inventory	15,000.00		(b) 16,500.00	(a) 15,000.00	16,500.00				16,500.00	
4	Supplies	800.00			(c) 200.00	600.00				600.00	
5	Prepaid Insurance	600.00			(d) 150.00	450.00				450.00	
6	Equipment	5,000.00				5,000.00				5,000.00	
7	Accum. Depr.—Equipment		4,500.00		(e) 450.00		4,950.00				4,950.00
8	Accounts Payable		4,890.00				4,890.00				4,890.00
9	Wages Payable				(f) 300.00		300.00				300.00
10	Sales Tax Payable		860.00				860.00				860.00
11	Mortgage Payable		4,000.00				4,000.00				4,000.00
12	B. Paulson, Capital		19,850.00				19,850.00				19,850.00
13	B. Paulson, Drawing	1,200.00				1,200.00				1,200.00	
14	Income Summary			(a) 15,000.00	(b) 16,500.00	15,000.00	16,500.00	15,000.00	16,500.00		
15	Sales		71,510.00				71,510.00		71,510.00		
16	Sales Returns and Allowances	1,340.00				1,340.00		1,340.00			
17	Purchases	40,660.00				40,660.00		40,660.00			
18	Purchases Returns and Allowances		1,020.00				1,020.00		1,020.00		
19	Purchases Discounts		800.00				800.00		800.00		
20	Freight-In	400.00				400.00		400.00			
21	Wages Expense	22,300.00		(f) 300.00		22,600.00		22,600.00			
22	Advertising Expense	300.00				300.00		300.00			
23	Supplies Expense			(c) 200.00		200.00		200.00			
24	Telephone Expense	684.00				684.00		684.00			
25	Utilities Expense	716.00				716.00		716.00			
26	Insurance Expense			(d) 150.00		150.00		150.00			
27	Depr. Expense—Equipment			(e) 450.00		450.00		450.00			
28	Miscellaneous Expense	150.00				150.00		150.00			
29	Interest Expense	80.00				80.00		80.00			
30		107,430.00	107,430.00	32,600.00	32,600.00	124,680.00	124,680.00	82,730.00	89,830.00	41,950.00	34,850.00
31	Net Income							7,100.00			7,100.00
32								89,830.00	89,830.00	41,950.00	41,950.00

E 15-3B (LO1)

✓ Cost of goods sold: $109,714;
Net income: $12,040

MULTIPLE-STEP INCOME STATEMENT Use the following information to prepare a multiple-step income statement, including the revenue section and the cost of goods sold section, for Aeito's Plumbing Supplies for the year ended December 31, 20--.

Sales	$166,000
Sales Returns and Allowances	1,620
Sales Discounts	3,320
Interest Revenue	3,184
Merchandise Inventory, January 1, 20--	33,200
Purchases	111,300
Purchases Returns and Allowances	3,600
Purchases Discounts	2,226
Freight-In	640
Merchandise Inventory, December 31, 20--	29,600
Wages Expense	22,000
Supplies Expense	650
Telephone Expense	1,100
Utilities Expense	9,000
Insurance Expense	1,000
Depreciation Expense—Building	4,600
Depreciation Expense—Equipment	2,800
Miscellaneous Expense	214
Interest Expense	1,126

E 15-4B (LO5)

CLOSING ENTRIES From the work sheet on page 611, prepare closing entries for Balloons and Baubbles in a general journal.

E 15-5B (LO6)

REVERSING ENTRIES From the work sheet in Exercise 15-4B, identify the adjusting entry(ies) that should be reversed and prepare the reversing entry(ies).

E 15-6B (LO5/6)

ADJUSTING, CLOSING, AND REVERSING ENTRIES Based on the information that follows, prepare two sets of entries—one that will have a reversing entry and the other without a reversing entry. Enter existing balances and post all entries to two sets of T accounts for Wages Expense and Wages Payable.

(a)   Wages paid during 20-1 are $20,080.
(b)   Wages earned but not paid (accrued) as of December 31, 20-1, are $280.
(c)   On January 3, 20-2, payroll of $840 is paid, which includes the $280 of wages earned but not paid in December.

EXERCISE 15-4B

Balloons and Baubbles
Work Sheet
For Year Ended December 31, 20-1

#	ACCOUNT TITLE	Trial Balance Debit	Trial Balance Credit	Adjustments Debit	Adjustments Credit	Adjusted Trial Balance Debit	Adjusted Trial Balance Credit	Income Statement Debit	Income Statement Credit	Balance Sheet Debit	Balance Sheet Credit
1	Cash	2 8 0 0 00				2 8 0 0 00				2 8 0 0 00	
2	Accounts Receivable	4 2 0 0 00				4 2 0 0 00				4 2 0 0 00	
3	Merchandise Inventory	8 6 0 0 00		(b) 7 5 0 0 00	(a) 8 6 0 0 00	7 5 0 0 00				7 5 0 0 00	
4	Supplies	7 8 0 0 00			(c) 2 8 0 0 00	5 0 0 0 00				5 0 0 0 00	
5	Prepaid Insurance	6 2 0 0 00			(d) 1 2 0 0 00	5 0 0 0 00				5 0 0 0 00	
6	Equipment	3 0 0 0 00				3 0 0 0 00				3 0 0 0 00	
7	Accum. Depr.—Equipment		6 0 0 00		(e) 3 0 0 00		9 0 0 00				9 0 0 00
8	Accounts Payable		1 8 0 0 00				1 8 0 0 00				1 8 0 0 00
9	Wages Payable				(f) 2 0 0 00		2 0 0 00				2 0 0 00
10	Sales Tax Payable		8 0 0 00				8 0 0 00				8 0 0 00
11	L. Marlow, Capital		12 2 0 0 00				12 2 0 0 00				12 2 0 0 00
12	L. Marlow, Drawing	2 0 0 0 00				2 0 0 0 00				2 0 0 0 00	
13	Income Summary			(a) 8 6 0 0 00	(b) 7 5 0 0 00	8 6 0 0 00	7 5 0 0 00	8 6 0 0 00	7 5 0 0 00		
14	Sales		31 0 0 0 00				31 0 0 0 00		31 0 0 0 00		
15	Sales Returns and Allowances	8 0 0 00				8 0 0 00		8 0 0 00			
16	Purchases	22 0 0 0 00				22 0 0 0 00		22 0 0 0 00			
17	Purchases Returns and Allowances		1 8 0 0 00				1 8 0 0 00		1 8 0 0 00		
18	Purchases Discounts		4 0 7 00				4 0 7 00		4 0 7 00		
19	Freight-In	2 0 0 00				2 0 0 00		2 0 0 00			
20	Wages Expense	1 2 0 0 00		(f) 2 0 0 00		1 4 0 0 00		1 4 0 0 00			
21	Advertising Expense	3 0 0 00				3 0 0 00		3 0 0 00			
22	Supplies Expense			(c) 2 8 0 0 00		2 8 0 0 00		2 8 0 0 00			
23	Telephone Expense	7 0 0 00				7 0 0 00		7 0 0 00			
24	Utilities Expense	4 8 0 0 00				4 8 0 0 00		4 8 0 0 00			
25	Insurance Expense			(d) 1 2 0 0 00		1 2 0 0 00		1 2 0 0 00			
26	Depr. Expense—Equipment			(e) 3 0 0 00		3 0 0 00		3 0 0 00			
27	Miscellaneous Expense	1 1 0 00				1 1 0 00		1 1 0 00			
28	Interest Expense	9 7 00				9 7 00		9 7 00			
29		47 8 8 7 00	47 8 8 7 00	17 0 0 0 00	17 0 0 0 00	55 8 8 7 00	55 8 8 7 00	35 3 8 7 00	40 7 0 7 00	20 5 0 0 00	15 1 8 0 00
30	Net Income							5 3 2 0 00			5 3 2 0 00
31								40 7 0 7 00	40 7 0 7 00	20 5 0 0 00	20 5 0 0 00

E 15-7B (LO4)

✓ Current ratio: 3.68 to 1;
Return on owner's equity: 42.6%;
Inventory turnover: 3.42

FINANCIAL RATIOS Based on the financial statements shown below and on the next page for McDonald Carpeting Co. (income statement, statement of owner's equity, and balance sheet), prepare the following financial ratios. All sales are credit sales. The balance of Accounts Receivable on January 1, 20--, was $6,800.

1. Working capital
2. Current ratio
3. Quick ratio
4. Return on owner's equity
5. Accounts receivable turnover and the average number of days required to collect receivables
6. Inventory turnover and the average number of days required to sell inventory

McDonald Carpeting Co. Income Statement For Year Ended December 31, 20 - -						
Revenue from sales:						
Sales			$122 8 0 0 00		
Less sales returns and allowances			1 1 0 0 00		
Net sales				$121 7 0 0 00	
Cost of goods sold:						
Merchandise inventory, January 1, 20- -			$ 19 3 0 0 00		
Purchases		$62 8 0 0 00			
Less: Purchases returns and allowances	$2 8 0 0 00				
Purchases discounts	1 9 4 4 00	4 7 4 4 00			
Net purchases		$58 0 5 6 00			
Add freight-in		9 4 4 00			
Cost of goods purchased			59 0 0 0 00		
Goods available for sale			$ 78 3 0 0 00		
Less merchandise inventory, December 31, 20- -			16 7 0 0 00		
Cost of goods sold				61 6 0 0 00	
Gross profit				$ 60 1 0 0 00	
Operating expenses:					
Wages expense			$ 18 0 0 0 00		
Advertising expense			9 8 0 00		
Supplies expense			3 2 0 00		
Telephone expense			1 2 0 0 00		
Utilities expense			8 0 0 0 00		
Insurance expense			8 0 0 00		
Depreciation expense—building			3 5 0 0 00		
Depreciation expense—equipment			2 5 0 0 00		
Miscellaneous expense			2 0 0 00		
Total operating expenses				35 5 0 0 00	
Income from operations				$ 24 6 0 0 00	
Other revenues:					
Interest revenue			$ 2 8 0 0 00		
Other expenses:					
Interest expense			2 1 0 0 00	7 0 0 00	
Net income				$ 25 3 0 0 00	

McDonald Carpeting Co.									
Statement of Owner's Equity									
For Year Ended December 31, 20 - -									
C. S. McDonald, capital, January 1, 20- -						$52	0	0	0	00
Net income for the year	$25	3	0	0	00				
Less withdrawals for the year	10	4	0	0	00				
Increase in capital						14	9	0	0	00
C. S. McDonald, capital, December 31, 20- -						$66	9	0	0	00

McDonald Carpeting Co.															
Balance Sheet															
December 31, 20 - -															
Assets															
Current assets:															
Cash						$10	4	0	0	00					
Accounts receivable						8	9	0	0	00					
Merchandise inventory						16	7	0	0	00					
Supplies						1	2	0	0	00					
Prepaid insurance							7	0	0	00					
Total current assets											$37	9	0	0	00
Property, plant, and equipment:															
Building	$60	0	0	0	00										
Less accumulated depreciation—building	18	0	0	0	00	$42	0	0	0	00					
Equipment	$22	0	0	0	00										
Less accumulated depreciation—equipment	6	2	0	0	00	15	8	0	0	00					
Total property, plant, and equipment											57	8	0	0	00
Total assets											$95	7	0	0	00
Liabilities															
Current liabilities:															
Accounts payable	$ 8	4	0	0	00										
Wages payable		3	0	0	00										
Sales tax payable	1	0	0	0	00										
Mortgage payable (current portion)		6	0	0	00										
Total current liabilities						$10	3	0	0	00					
Long-term liabilities:															
Mortgage payable	$19	1	0	0	00										
Less current portion		6	0	0	00	18	5	0	0	00					
Total liabilities											$28	8	0	0	00
Owner's Equity															
C. S. McDonald, capital											66	9	0	0	00
Total liabilities and owner's equity											$95	7	0	0	00

SERIES B PROBLEMS

P 15-8B (LO5/6)

✓ Net income: $4,590; Post-closing trial bal. columns: $53,500

WORK SHEET, ADJUSTING, CLOSING, AND REVERSING ENTRIES The trial balance for Darby Kite Store as of December 31, 20-1 is shown on the next page.

At the end of the year, the following adjustments need to be made.

(a and b)   Merchandise inventory as of December 31, $23,600.
(c)   Unused supplies on hand, $1,050.
(d)   Insurance expired, $250.

(*continued*)

Darby Kite Store
Trial Balance
For Year Ended December 31, 20-1

ACCOUNT TITLE	DEBIT BALANCE	CREDIT BALANCE
Cash	11 7 0 0 00	
Accounts Receivable	11 2 0 0 00	
Merchandise Inventory	25 0 0 0 00	
Supplies	1 2 0 0 00	
Prepaid Insurance	8 0 0 00	
Equipment	5 4 0 0 00	
Accumulated Depreciation—Equipment		8 0 0 00
Accounts Payable		7 6 0 0 00
Wages Payable		
Sales Tax Payable		2 5 0 00
M. D. Akins, Capital		50 0 0 0 00
M. D. Akins, Drawing	10 5 0 0 00	
Income Summary		
Sales		57 9 9 0 00
Sales Returns and Allowances	1 4 5 0 00	
Purchases	34 5 0 0 00	
Purchases Returns and Allowances		1 1 0 0 00
Purchases Discounts		6 3 0 00
Freight-In	3 6 0 00	
Wages Expense	10 8 8 0 00	
Advertising Expense	7 4 0 00	
Supplies Expense		
Telephone Expense	1 1 0 0 00	
Utilities Expense	2 3 0 0 00	
Insurance Expense		
Depreciation Expense—Equipment		
Miscellaneous Expense	3 2 0 00	
Interest Expense	9 2 0 00	
	118 3 7 0 00	118 3 7 0 00

(e) Depreciation expense for the year, $400.
(f) Wages earned but not paid (Wages Payable), $360.

REQUIRED

1. Prepare a work sheet.

2. Prepare adjusting entries.

3. Prepare closing entries.

4. Prepare a post-closing trial balance.

5. Prepare reversing entries.

P 15-9B (LO1/2/3)

✓ Cost of goods sold: $75,350;
Total assets: $117,750

INCOME STATEMENT, STATEMENT OF OWNER'S EQUITY, AND BALANCE SHEET Backlund Farm Supply completed the work sheet on page 615 for the year ended December 31, 20--. Owner's equity as of January 1, 20--, was $50,000. The current portion of Mortgage Payable is $1,000.

REQUIRED

1. Prepare a multiple-step income statement.

2. Prepare a statement of owner's equity.

3. Prepare a balance sheet.

PROBLEM 15-9B

Backlund Farm Supply
Work Sheet
For Year Ended December 31, 20 - 1

#	Account Title	Trial Balance Debit	Trial Balance Credit	Adjustments Debit	Adjustments Credit	Adjusted Trial Balance Debit	Adjusted Trial Balance Credit	Income Statement Debit	Income Statement Credit	Balance Sheet Debit	Balance Sheet Credit
1	Cash	10 1 8 0 00				10 1 8 0 00				10 1 8 0 00	
2	Accounts Receivable	26 4 2 0 00				26 4 2 0 00				26 4 2 0 00	
3	Merchandise Inventory	42 1 6 0 00		(b) 44 3 0 0 00	(a) 42 1 6 0 00	44 3 0 0 00				44 3 0 0 00	
4	Supplies	4 3 6 0 00			(c) 8 6 0 00	3 5 0 0 00				3 5 0 0 00	
5	Prepaid Insurance	3 0 0 0 00			(d) 7 5 0 00	2 2 5 0 00				2 2 5 0 00	
6	Equipment	38 0 0 0 00				38 0 0 0 00				38 0 0 0 00	
7	Accum. Depr.—Equipment		6 0 0 0 00		(e) 9 0 0 00		6 9 0 0 00				6 9 0 0 00
8	Accounts Payable		41 2 0 0 00				41 2 0 0 00				41 2 0 0 00
9	Wages Payable				(f) 4 2 0 00		4 2 0 00				4 2 0 00
10	Sales Tax Payable		8 0 0 0 00				8 0 0 0 00				8 0 0 0 00
11	Mortgage Payable		8 0 0 0 00				8 0 0 0 00				8 0 0 0 00
12	J. Backlund, Capital		57 0 0 0 00				57 0 0 0 00				57 0 0 0 00
13	J. Backlund, Drawing	6 8 0 0 00				6 8 0 0 00				6 8 0 0 00	
14	Income Summary			(a) 42 1 6 0 00	(b) 44 3 0 0 00	42 1 6 0 00	44 3 0 0 00	42 1 6 0 00	44 3 0 0 00		
15	Sales		141 8 0 0 00				141 8 0 0 00		141 8 0 0 00		
16	Sales Returns and Allowances	1 3 1 0 00				1 3 1 0 00		1 3 1 0 00			
17	Purchases	81 3 0 0 00				81 3 0 0 00		81 3 0 0 00			
18	Purchases Returns and Allowances		2 9 0 0 00				2 9 0 0 00		2 9 0 0 00		
19	Purchases Discounts		1 5 1 0 00				1 5 1 0 00		1 5 1 0 00		
20	Freight-In	6 0 0 0 00				6 0 0 0 00		6 0 0 0 00			
21	Wages Expense	41 3 0 0 00		(f) 4 2 0 00		41 7 2 0 00		41 7 2 0 00			
22	Advertising Expense	4 0 0 0 00				4 0 0 0 00		4 0 0 0 00			
23	Supplies Expense			(c) 8 6 0 00		8 6 0 00		8 6 0 00			
24	Telephone Expense	8 0 0 0 00				8 0 0 0 00		8 0 0 0 00			
25	Utilities Expense	1 3 0 0 00				1 3 0 0 00		1 3 0 0 00			
26	Insurance Expense			(d) 7 5 0 00		7 5 0 00		7 5 0 00			
27	Depr. Expense—Equipment			(e) 9 0 0 00		9 0 0 00		9 0 0 00			
28	Miscellaneous Expense	2 0 0 0 00				2 0 0 0 00		2 0 0 0 00			
29	Interest Expense	1 0 8 0 00				1 0 8 0 00		1 0 8 0 00			
30		259 2 1 0 00	259 2 1 0 00	89 3 9 0 00	89 3 9 0 00	304 8 3 0 00	304 8 3 0 00	173 3 8 0 00	190 5 1 0 00	131 4 5 0 00	114 3 2 0 00
31	Net Income							17 1 3 0 00			17 1 3 0 00
32								190 5 1 0 00	190 5 1 0 00	131 4 5 0 00	131 4 5 0 00

P 15-10B (LO4)

✓ Working capital: $43,230;
Quick ratio: 0.84 to 1;
Accts. receivable turnover: 4.35

FINANCIAL RATIOS Use the work sheet and financial statements prepared in Problem 15-9B. All sales are credit sales. The Accounts Receivable balance on January 1 was $38,200.

REQUIRED

Prepare the following financial ratios:

(a)   Working capital
(b)   Current ratio
(c)   Quick ratio
(d)   Return on owner's equity
(e)   Accounts receivable turnover and the average number of days required to collect receivables
(f)   Inventory turnover and the average number of days required to sell inventory

MANAGING YOUR WRITING

A friend of yours has the opportunity to invest in a small business. She has come to you for advice on how she might determine whether this would be a good investment. In particular, she is concerned about how long it takes to sell the merchandise and collect receivables. Draft a memo suggesting various ratios that should be computed to evaluate the business's profitability, ability to pay its current obligations, and time required to sell inventory and collect receivables.

ETHICS CASE

Brian Marlow recently was hired to prepare Louise Michener Consulting's year-end financial statements. Brian just earned his CPA certificate, and Louise Michener was one of his first clients. Louise employs a bookkeeper, Martha Halling, who does the daily journal entries and prepares a year-to-date trial balance at the end of each month. Martha gives the December 31 trial balance to a CPA to make the adjustments and generate the financial statements. As Brian was looking through Louise Michener's books, he noticed two things. First, in each of the last three years, a different CPA had prepared the financial statements. Second, the amount shown on the December 31 trial balance for miscellaneous expense was quite high this year compared to prior years. Brian called Martha to find out if she knew why miscellaneous expense had such a high balance. Martha's response was "I just do what Louise tells me to do. If she wants to charge personal expenses to the company, it's none of my business."

1.   What should Brian do?

2.   How might Brian's decision affect Martha? Has Martha done anything unethical?

3.   Write a short letter from Brian to Louise explaining why personal items should not be charged to a business.

4.   In small groups, discuss the ethical responsibilities of an accountant relating to a client's books.

MASTERY PROBLEM

Dominique Fouque owns and operates Dominique's Doll House. She has a small shop in which she sells new and antique dolls. She is particularly well known for her collection of antique Ken and Barbie dolls. A completed work sheet for 20-3 is shown on the next page. Fouque made no additional investments during the year and the long-term note payable is due in 20-9. No portion of the long-term note is due within the next year. Net credit sales for 20-3 were $35,300 and receivables on January 1 were $2,500.

REQUIRED

1. Prepare a multiple-step income statement.

2. Prepare a statement of owner's equity.

3. Prepare a balance sheet.

4. Compute the following measures of performance and financial condition for 20-3:

    (a) Current ratio
    (b) Quick ratio
    (c) Working capital
    (d) Return on owner's equity
    (e) Accounts receivable turnover and average number of days required to collect receivables
    (f) Inventory turnover and the average number of days required to sell inventory

5. Prepare adjusting entries and indicate which should be reversed and why.

6. Prepare closing entries.

7. Prepare reversing entries for the adjustments where appropriate.

CHALLENGE PROBLEM

John Byers owns and operates Byers Building Supplies. The following information was taken from his financial statements:

Balance Sheet	12/31/-2	12/31/-1
Accounts Receivable	$700	$500
Inventory	300	100

Income Statement	
Net Credit Sales	$7,200
Cost of Goods Sold	5,000

All sales are made on account.

REQUIRED

Based on the above information, on average, approximately how many days pass from the time Byers purchases inventory until he receives cash from customers?

MASTERY PROBLEM

Dominique's Doll House
Work Sheet
For Year Ended December 31, 20-3

#	Account Title	Trial Balance Debit	Trial Balance Credit	Adjustments Debit	Adjustments Credit	Adjusted Trial Balance Debit	Adjusted Trial Balance Credit	Income Statement Debit	Income Statement Credit	Balance Sheet Debit	Balance Sheet Credit
1	Cash	5,200.00				5,200.00				5,200.00	
2	Accounts Receivable	3,200.00				3,200.00				3,200.00	
3	Merchandise Inventory	22,300.00		(b) 24,600.00	(a) 22,300.00	24,600.00				24,600.00	
4	Office Supplies	800.00			(c) 600.00	200.00				200.00	
5	Prepaid Insurance	1,200.00			(d) 400.00	800.00				800.00	
6	Store Equipment	85,000.00				85,000.00				85,000.00	
7	Accum. Depr.—Store Equipment		15,000.00		(e) 5,000.00		20,000.00				20,000.00
8	Notes Payable		6,000.00				6,000.00				6,000.00
9	Accounts Payable		5,500.00				5,500.00				5,500.00
10	Wages Payable				(g) 200.00		200.00				200.00
11	Sales Tax Payable		850.00				850.00				850.00
12	Unearned Rent Revenue		1,000.00	(f) 700.00			300.00				300.00
13	Long-Term Note Payable		10,000.00				10,000.00				10,000.00
14	Dominique Fouque, Capital		75,800.00				75,800.00				75,800.00
15	Dominique Fouque, Drawing	21,000.00				21,000.00				21,000.00	
16	Income Summary			(a) 22,300.00	(b) 24,600.00	22,300.00	24,600.00	22,300.00	24,600.00		
17	Sales		130,500.00				130,500.00		130,500.00		
18	Sales Returns and Allowances	900.00				900.00		900.00			
19	Rent Revenue		25,000.00		(f) 700.00		25,700.00		25,700.00		
20	Purchases	72,000.00				72,000.00		72,000.00			
21	Purchases Discounts		750.00				750.00		750.00		
22	Freight-In	1,200.00				1,200.00		1,200.00			
23	Wages Expense	42,000.00		(g) 200.00		42,200.00		42,200.00			
24	Rent Expense	6,000.00				6,000.00		6,000.00			
25	Office Supplies Expense			(c) 600.00		600.00		600.00			
26	Telephone Expense	1,500.00				1,500.00		1,500.00			
27	Utilities Expense	7,600.00				7,600.00		7,600.00			
28	Insurance Expense			(d) 400.00		400.00		400.00			
29	Depr. Expense—Store Equipment			(e) 5,000.00		5,000.00		5,000.00			
30	Interest Expense	5,000.00				5,000.00		5,000.00			
31		270,400.00	270,400.00	53,800.00	53,800.00	300,200.00	300,200.00	160,200.00	181,550.00	140,000.00	118,650.00
32	Net Income							21,350.00			21,350.00
33								181,550.00	181,550.00	140,000.00	140,000.00

COMPREHENSIVE PROBLEM 2: ACCOUNTING CYCLE WITH SUBSIDIARY LEDGERS, PART 1

During the month of December 20-1, TJ's Specialty Shop engaged in the following transactions:

Dec. 1	Sold merchandise on account to Anne Clark, $2,000, plus tax of $100. Sale no. 637.
2	Issued check no. 806 to Owen Enterprises in payment of December 1 balance of $1,600, less 2% discount.
3	Issued check no. 807 to Nathen Co. in payment of December 1 balance of $3,000, less 2% discount.
4	Purchased merchandise on account from Owen Enterprises, $1,550. Invoice no. 763, dated December 4, terms 2/10, n/30.
4	Issued check no. 808 in payment of telephone expense for the month of November, $180.
6	Purchased merchandise on account from Evans Essentials, $2,350. Invoice no. 621, dated December 5, terms net 30.
8	Sold merchandise for cash, $4,840, plus tax of $242.
9	Received payment from Heather Waters in full settlement of account, $490.
9	Sold merchandise on account to Lucy Greene, $800, plus tax of $40. Sale no. 638.
10	Issued check no. 809 to West Wholesalers in payment of December 1 balance of $1,000.
11	Issued check no. 810 in payment of advertising expense for the month of December, $400.
12	Sold merchandise on account to Martha Boyle, $1,260, plus tax of $63. Sale no. 639.
12	Received payment from Anne Clark on account, $1,340.
13	Issued check no. 811 to Owen Enterprises in payment of December 4 purchase. Invoice no. 763, less 2% discount.
13	Martha Boyle returned merchandise for a credit, $740, plus sales tax of $37.
15	Issued check no. 812 in payment of wages (Wages Expense) for the two-week period ending December 14, $1,100.
15	Received payment from Lucy Greene on account, $1,960.
16	Sold merchandise on account to Kim Fields, $160, plus sales tax of $8. Sale no. 640.
17	Returned merchandise to Evans Essentials for credit, $150.
18	Issued check no. 813 to Evans Essentials in payment of December 1 balance of $1,250, less the credit received on December 17.
19	Sold merchandise on account to Lucy Greene, $620, plus tax of $31. Sale no. 641.
22	Received payment from John Dempsey on account, $1,560.
23	Issued check no. 814 for the purchase of supplies, $120. (Debit Supplies)

(*continued*)

Dec. 24   Purchased merchandise on account from West Wholesalers, $1,200.
Invoice no. 465, dated December 24, terms net 30.

26   Purchased merchandise on account from Nathen Co., $800.
Invoice no. 817, dated December 26, terms 2/10, n/30.

27   Issued check no. 815 in payment of utilities expense for the month of
November, $630.

27   Sold merchandise on account to John Dempsey, $2,020, plus tax of $101.
Sale no. 642.

29   Received payment from Martha Boyle on account, $2,473.

29   Issued check no. 816 in payment of wages (Wages Expense) for the two-week
period ending December 28, $1,100.

30   Issued check no. 817 to Meyers Trophy Shop for a cash purchase of
merchandise, $200.

As of December 1, TJ's account balances were as follows:

Account	Account No.	Debit	Credit
Cash	101	$ 11,500	
Accounts Receivable	122	8,600	
Merchandise Inventory	131	21,800	
Supplies	141	1,035	
Prepaid Insurance	145	1,380	
Land	161	8,700	
Building	171	52,000	
Accum. Depr.—Building	171.1		$ 9,200
Store Equipment	181	28,750	
Accum. Depr.—Store Equipment	181.1		9,300
Accounts Payable	202		6,850
Wages Payable	219		
Sales Tax Payable	231		970
Mortgage Payable	251		12,525
Tom Jones, Capital	311		90,000
Tom Jones, Drawing	312	8,500	
Income Summary	313		
Sales	401		116,000
Sales Returns and Allowances	401.1	690	
Purchases	501	60,500	
Purchases Returns and Allowances	501.1		460
Purchases Discounts	501.2		575
Freight-In	502	175	
Wages Expense	511	25,000	
Advertising Expense	512	4,300	
Supplies Expense	524		
Telephone Expense	525	2,000	
Utilities Expense	533	6,900	
Insurance Expense	535		
Depr. Expense—Building	540		
Depr. Expense—Store Equipment	541		
Miscellaneous Expense	549	2,700	
Interest Expense	551	1,350	
		$245,880	$245,880

TJ's also had the following subsidiary ledger balances as of December 1:

Accounts Receivable Ledger			*Accounts Payable Ledger*	
Customer	Balance		Vendor	Balance
Martha Boyle			Evans Essentials	
12 Jude Lane			34 Harry Ave.	
Hartford, CT 06117	$3,250		East Hartford, CT 05234	$1,250
Anne Clark			Nathen Co.	
52 Juniper Road			1009 Drake Rd.	
Hartford, CT 06118	1,340		Farmington, CT 06082	3,000
John Dempsey			Owen Enterprises	
700 Hobbes Dr.			43 Lucky Lane	
Avon, CT 06108	1,560		Bristol, CT 06007	1,600
Kim Fields			West Wholesalers	
5200 Hamilton Ave.			888 Anders Street	
Hartford, CT 06117	—		Newington, CT 06789	1,000
Lucy Greene				
236 Bally Lane				
Simsbury, CT 06123	1,960			
Heather Waters				
447 Drury Lane				
West Hartford, CT 06107	490			

At the end of the year, the following adjustments (a)–(g) need to be made:

(a, b) Merchandise inventory as of December 31, $19,700.

(c) Unused supplies on hand, $525.

(d) Unexpired insurance on December 31, $1,000.

(e) Depreciation expense on the building for the year, $800.

(f) Depreciation expense on the store equipment for the year, $450.

(g) Wages earned but not paid as of December 31, $330.

Requirements and working papers for this problem are provided in two versions: General Journal based and Special Journals based. Complete the version as directed by your instructor.

REQUIRED—GENERAL JOURNAL

1. If you are not using the working papers, open a general ledger, an accounts receivable ledger, and an accounts payable ledger as of December 1. Enter the December 1 balance of each of the accounts, with a check mark in the Posting Reference column.

2. Enter transactions for the month of December in the general journal. Post immediately to the accounts receivable and accounts payable ledgers.

3. Post from the journal to the general ledger.

REQUIRED—SPECIAL JOURNALS

1. If you are not using the working papers, open a general ledger, an accounts receivable ledger, and an accounts payable ledger as of December 1. Enter the December 1 balance of each of the accounts, with a check mark in the Posting Reference column.

2. Enter transactions for the month of December in the proper journals. Post immediately to the accounts receivable and accounts payable ledgers.

3. Post from the journals to the general ledger. Post the journals in the following order: general, sales, purchases, cash receipts, and cash payments.

(*continued*)

REQUIRED—GENERAL JOURNAL *(continued)*

4. Prepare schedules of accounts receivable and accounts payable.

5. Prepare a year-end work sheet, an income statement, a statement of owner's equity, and a balance sheet. The mortgage payable includes $600 that is due within one year.

6. Journalize and post adjusting entries.

7. Journalize and post closing entries. (*Hint:* Close all expense and revenue account balances listed in the Income Statement columns of the work sheet. Then, close Income Summary and Tom Jones, Drawing to Tom Jones, Capital.)

8. Prepare a post-closing trial balance.

9. Journalize and post reversing entries for the adjustments where appropriate, as of January 1, 20-2.

REQUIRED—SPECIAL JOURNALS *(continued)*

4. Prepare schedules of accounts receivable and accounts payable.

5. Prepare a year-end work sheet, an income statement, a statement of owner's equity, and a balance sheet. The mortgage payable includes $600 that is due within one year.

6. Journalize and post adjusting entries.

7. Journalize and post closing entries. (*Hint:* Close all expense and revenue account balances listed in the Income Statement columns of the work sheet. Then, close Income Summary and Tom Jones, Drawing to Tom Jones, Capital.)

8. Prepare a post-closing trial balance.

9. Journalize and post reversing entries for the adjustments where appropriate, as of January 1, 20-2.

COMPREHENSIVE PROBLEM 2: ACCOUNTING CYCLE WITH SUBSIDIARY LEDGERS, PART 2

During the month of January 20-2, TJ's Specialty Shop engaged in the following transactions:

Jan. 1 Sold merchandise on account to Anne Clark, $3,000, plus tax of $150. Sale no. 643.

2 Issued check no. 818 to Nathen Co. in payment of January 1 balance of $800, less 2% discount.

3 Purchased merchandise on account from West Wholesalers, $1,500. Invoice no. 678, dated January 3, terms 2/15, n/30.

4 Purchased merchandise on account from Owen Enterprises, $2,000. Invoice no. 767, dated January 4, terms 2/10, n/30.

4 Issued check no. 819 in payment of telephone expense for the month of December, $180.

8 Sold merchandise for cash, $3,600, plus tax of $180.

9 Received payment from Lucy Greene in full settlement of account, $1,491.

10 Issued check no. 820 to West Wholesalers in payment of January 1 balance in amount of $1,200.

12 Sold merchandise on account to Martha Boyle, $1,000, plus tax of $50. Sale no. 644.

12 Received payment from Anne Clark on account, $2,100.

12 Issued check no. 821 in payment of wages (Wages Expense) for the two-week period ending January 11, $1,100.

Jan. 13   Issued check no. 822 to Owen Enterprises in payment of January 4 purchase. Invoice no. 767, less 2% discount.

13   Martha Boyle returned merchandise for a credit, $800, plus sales tax of $40.

17   Returned merchandise to Evans Essentials for credit, $300.

22   Received payment from John Dempsey on account, $2,121.

26   Issued check no. 823 in payment of wages (Wages Expense) for the two-week period ending January 25, $1,100.

27   Issued check no. 824 in payment of utilities expense for the month of December, $630.

27   Sold merchandise on account to John Dempsey, $2,000, plus tax of $100. Sale no. 645.

Late in January, TJ's agreed to sell the business to a competitor. To agree on a selling price, financial statements are needed as of January 31 and for the month of January 20-2. To prepare these financial statements, TJ's must perform the same procedures it normally does at year-end.

At the end of January, the following adjustments (a)–(g) need to be made:

(a, b)   Merchandise inventory as of January 31, $19,000.
(c)   Unused supplies on hand, $115.
(d)   Unexpired insurance on January 31, $968.
(e)   Depreciation expense on the building for the month, $67.
(f)   Depreciation expense on the store equipment for the month, $38.
(g)   Wages earned but not paid as of January 31, $330.

REQUIRED—GENERAL JOURNAL

1.   If you are not using the working papers, open a general ledger, accounts receivable ledger, and accounts payable ledger as of January 1. Enter the January 1 balance of each of the accounts, with a check mark in the Posting Reference column. The beginning balances for Part 2 are the same as the balances from your solution to Part 1 of Comprehensive Problem 2.

2.   Enter transactions for the month of January in the general journal. Post immediately to the accounts receivable and accounts payable ledgers.

3.   Post from the journal to the general ledger.

4.   Prepare schedules of accounts receivable and accounts payable.

5.   Prepare a month-end work sheet, income statement, statement of owner's equity, and balance sheet. The mortgage payable includes $600 that is due within one year.

REQUIRED—SPECIAL JOURNALS

1.   If you are not using the working papers, open a general ledger, accounts receivable ledger, and accounts payable ledger as of January 1. Enter the January 1 balance of each of the accounts, with a check mark in the Posting Reference column. The beginning balances for Part 2 are the same as the balances from your solution to Part 1 of Comprehensive Problem 2.

2.   Enter transactions for the month of January in the proper journals. Post immediately to the accounts receivable and accounts payable ledgers.

3.   Post from the journals to the general ledger. Post the journals in the following order: general, sales, purchases, cash receipts, and cash payments.

4.   Prepare schedules of accounts receivable and accounts payable.

5.   Prepare a month-end work sheet, income statement, statement of owner's equity, and balance sheet. The mortgage payable includes $600 that is due within one year.

(continued)

REQUIRED—GENERAL JOURNAL *(continued)*

6. Journalize and post adjusting entries.

7. Journalize and post closing entries. (*Hint:* Close all expense and revenue account balances listed in the Income Statement columns of the work sheet. Then close Income Summary and Tom Jones, Drawing to Tom Jones, Capital.)

8. Prepare a post-closing trial balance.

REQUIRED—SPECIAL JOURNALS *(continued)*

6. Journalize and post adjusting entries.

7. Journalize and post closing entries. (*Hint:* Close all expense and revenue account balances listed in the Income Statement columns of the work sheet. Then close Income Summary and Tom Jones, Drawing to Tom Jones, Capital.)

8. Prepare a post-closing trial balance.

Accounting for a Professional Service Business: The Combination Journal

Careful study of this module should enable you to:

LO1 Explain the differences between the modified cash and accrual bases of accounting.

LO2 Describe special records for a professional service business using the modified cash basis.

LO3 Describe and use a combination journal to record transactions of a professional service business.

LO4 Post from the combination journal to the general ledger.

LO5 Prepare a work sheet, financial statements, and adjusting and closing entries for a professional service business.

Professional service businesses include law, dentistry, medicine, optometry, architecture, engineering, and accounting. As discussed in Chapter 5, many small professional service businesses do not need to prepare financial statements in strict compliance with generally accepted accounting principles (GAAP). This is because they don't need to raise large amounts of money from investors or creditors who expect GAAP financial statements. Thus, many of these businesses use the modified cash basis. This simplifies the accounting process and provides results similar to the accrual basis if receivables and payables are minimal. If at some point GAAP financial statements are needed, an accountant can convert the modified cash basis statements to the accrual basis which is required under GAAP.

Small professional service businesses may also use a combination journal as the book of original entry, instead of a general journal, or special journals (illustrated in Chapter 12). The purpose of this module is to illustrate accounting for a professional service business using the modified cash basis of accounting and a combination journal.

THE MODIFIED CASH AND ACCRUAL BASES OF ACCOUNTING

LO1 Explain the differences between the modified cash and accrual bases of accounting.

The modified cash and accrual bases of accounting are the same except for three types of events. The accounting differences for these three events are shown in Figure M1-1. First, expenses for services received are not recorded until paid. Thus, accounts payable is not used under the modified cash basis for services received. Second, under the modified cash basis, accrued expenses are not recognized. Examples of accrued expenses include wages that were earned by the employees, but not yet paid, and interest expense that has been incurred, but not yet paid. Thus, no end-of-period adjusting entries are made for these types of events. This means that other records must be used to maintain information on amounts owed for wages, interest, and other expenses. Typically, these bills are filed chronologically by due date.

FIGURE M1-1   Modified Cash Basis vs. Accrual Basis of Accounting

DIFFERENCES BETWEEN MODIFIED CASH AND ACCRUAL BASES OF ACCOUNTING		
EVENT	**ACCRUAL BASIS**	**MODIFIED CASH BASIS**

Expenses
  Bills for services received,
  but not yet paid.
	Expense
	  Accounts Payable
		No entry.
		(Record when paid.)

Wages earned by employees,
  but not yet paid.
	Wages Expense
	  Wages Payable
		No entry.
		(Record when paid.)

Revenues
  Services provided on account.
	Accounts Receivable
	  Professional Fees
		No entry.
		(Record when cash is received.)

The modified cash basis is the same as the accrual basis, except receivables and payables are not recognized for revenues and operating expenses.

Finally, under the modified cash basis, revenues from services performed on account are not recorded until cash is received. Thus, no accounts receivable are entered in the accounting system. This means that other records must be used to maintain information on amounts owed by clients and patients. These records generally include an appointment record and a client or patient ledger record. These records are illustrated in Figures M1-2 and M1-3.

ACCOUNTING FOR A PROFESSIONAL SERVICE BUSINESS

LO2 Describe special records for a professional service business using the modified cash basis.

The appointment record, shown in Figure M1-2, is used to schedule appointments and to maintain a record of the services rendered, fees charged, and payments received. It also serves as a source document for the patient ledger records, shown in Figure M1-3, which show the amount owed by each client or patient for services performed. A copy of this record may also be used for billing purposes.

FIGURE M1-2   Appointment Record

Date: 6/4/--

Time	Patient	Medical Service	Fees	Payments
8:00	Dennis Rogan	OV	40.00	40.00
15				
30	Rick Cosier	OV;EKG	120.00	
45				
9:00	George Hettenhouse	OV;MISC	50.00	
15				
30	Sam Frumer	OV;LAB	75.00	75.00
45				
10:00	Dan Dalton	OV	40.00	
15				
30	Louis Biagioni	OV;X	65.00	
45				
11:00	Mike Groomer	X	40.00	40.00
15				
30				
45				
12:00				
15				
30				
45				
1:00	Mike Tiller	OV;LAB	80.00	
15				
30	Peggy Hite	OV;PHYS	190.00	
45				
2:00				
15				
30				
45				
3:00	Vivian Winston	OV;MISC	40.00	
15				
30				
45				
4:00	Hank Davis	OV	40.00	40.00
15				
30				
45				
	Bill Sharp			150.00
	Phil Jones			80.00
	Diane Gallagher			200.00
			780.00	625.00

FIGURE M1-3   Client or Patient Ledger Account

Patient Name	Dennis Rogan
Address	1542 Hamilton Avenue Cincinnati OH 45240-5524
Phone Number	555-1683

Date	Service Rendered	Time	Debit	Credit	Balance
20-- June 4	Office Visit	8:00	40.00		40.00
4				40.00	—

THE COMBINATION JOURNAL

The two-column general journal illustrated in Chapter 4 can be used to enter every transaction of a business. However, in most businesses, there are many similar transactions that involve the same account or accounts. Cash receipts and payments are good examples. Suppose that in a typical month there are 30 transactions that result in an increase in cash and 40 transactions that cause a decrease in cash. In a two-column general journal, this would require entering the account Cash 70 times, using a journal line each time.

A considerable amount of time and space is saved if a journal contains **special columns** for cash debits and cash credits. At the end of the month, the special columns for cash debits and credits are totaled. The total of the Cash Debit column is posted as one amount to the debit side of the cash account and the total of the Cash Credit column is posted as one amount to the credit side of the cash account. Thus, instead of receiving 70 postings, Cash receives only two: one debit and one credit. This method requires much less time and reduces the risk of making posting errors.

If other accounts are used frequently, special columns can be added for these accounts. **General Debit** and **General Credit columns** are used for accounts not affected by many transactions. A journal with such special and general columns is called a **combination journal**.

Many small professional enterprises use a combination journal to record business transactions. To demonstrate the use of a combination journal, let's consider the medical practice of Dr. Ray Bonita. Bonita uses the modified cash basis of accounting. The chart of accounts for his medical practice is shown in Figure M1-4. The transactions for the month of June, his first month in practice, are provided in Figure M1-5.

A combination journal for Bonita's medical practice is illustrated in Figure M1-6 on page 631. Note that special columns were set up for Cash (Debit and Credit), Medical Fees (Credit), Wages Expense (Debit), Laboratory

FIGURE M1-4   Chart of Accounts

RAY BONITA, M.D. CHART OF ACCOUNTS				
Assets			**Revenue**	
101	Cash		401	Medical Fees
141	Medical Supplies			
142	Office Supplies		**Expenses**	
145	Prepaid Insurance		511	Wages Expense
182	Office Furniture		521	Rent Expense
182.1	Accum. Depr.—Office Furn.		523	Office Supplies Expense
185	Medical Equipment		524	Medical Supplies Expense
185.1	Accum. Depr.—Med. Equip.		525	Telephone Expense
			526	Laboratory Expense
Liabilities			535	Insurance Expense
202	Accounts Payable		541	Depr. Exp.—Office Furn.
			542	Depr. Exp.—Med. Equip.
Owner's Equity				
311	Ray Bonita, Capital			
312	Ray Bonita, Drawing			
313	Income Summary			

FIGURE M1-5   Summary of Transactions for Ray Bonita's Medical Practice

June 1	Ray Bonita invested cash to start a medical practice, $50,000.
2	Paid for a one-year liability insurance policy, $6,000. Coverage began on June 1.
3	Purchased medical equipment for cash, $22,000.
4	Paid bill for laboratory work, $300.
5	Purchased office furniture on credit from Bittle's Furniture, $9,000.
6	Received cash from patients and insurance companies for medical services rendered, $5,000.
7	Paid June office rent, $2,000.
8	Paid part-time wages, $3,000.
9	Purchased medical supplies for cash, $250.
15	Paid telephone bill, $150.
15	Received cash from patients and insurance companies for medical services rendered, $10,000.
16	Paid bill for laboratory work, $280.
17	Paid part-time wages, $3,000.
19	Purchased office supplies for cash, $150.
20	Received cash from patients and insurance companies for medical services rendered, $3,200.
22	Paid the first installment to Bittle's Furniture, $3,300.
23	Purchased medical supplies for cash, $200.
24	Paid bill for laboratory work, $400.
25	Purchased additional furniture from Bittle's Furniture, $4,000. A down payment of $500 was made, with the remaining payments expected over the next four months.
27	Paid part-time wages, $2,500.
30	Received cash from patients and insurance companies for medical services rendered, $7,000.
30	Bonita withdrew cash for personal use, $10,000.

LEARNING KEY

Set up special columns for the most frequently used accounts.

Expense (Debit), Medical Supplies (Debit), and Office Supplies (Debit). Special columns were set up for these accounts because they will be used frequently in this business. Other businesses might set up special columns for different accounts depending on the frequency of their use. Of course, General Debit and Credit columns for transactions affecting other accounts are also needed.

Journalizing in a Combination Journal

The following procedures were used to enter the transactions for Bonita for June:

General Columns

Enter transactions in the *general columns* in a manner similar to that used for the *general journal*. Look at the entry for June 5 in Figure M1-6.

(a)   Enter the name of the debited account (Office Furniture) first at the extreme left of the Description column.

(b)   Enter the amount in the General Debit column.

(c)   Enter the name of the account credited (Accounts Payable—Bittle's Furniture) on the next line, indented.

(d)   Enter the amount in the General Credit column.

General and Special Accounts

Some transactions affect both a *general account and a special account*. Look at the entry for June 1 in Figure M1-6.

(a)   Enter the name of the general account in the Description column.

(b)   Enter the amount in the General Debit or Credit column.

(c)   Enter the amount of the debit or credit for the special account in the appropriate special column.

Enter all of this information on the same line.

Special Accounts

Many transactions affect only *special accounts*. Look at the entry for June 6 in Figure M1-6.

(a)   Enter the amounts in the appropriate special debit and credit columns.

(b)   Do not enter anything in the Description column.

(c)   Place a dash in the Posting Reference column to indicate that this amount is not posted individually. It will be posted as part of the total of the special column at the end of the month. (The posting process is described later in this chapter.)

Description Column

In general, the **Description column** is used for the following:

(a)   To enter the account titles for the General Debit and General Credit columns.

(b)   To identify specific creditors when assets are purchased on account (see entry for June 5).

  Note: For firms using the accrual basis of accounting, this column also would be used to identify specific customers receiving services on account (accounts receivable) and specific businesses that provided services on account (accounts payable).

(c)   To identify specific creditors when payments are made on account (see entry for June 22).

(d)   To identify adjusting and closing entries.

(e)   To identify amounts forwarded. When more than one page is required during an accounting period, amounts from the previous page are brought forward. In this situation, "Amounts Forwarded" is entered in the Description column on the first line.

Proving the Combination Journal

At the end of the accounting period, all columns of the combination journal should be totaled and ruled. The sum of the debit columns should be compared with the sum of the credit columns to verify that they are equal. The proving of Bonita's combination journal for the month of June is shown at the bottom of Figure M1-6 on page 631.

FIGURE M1-6 Combination Journal: Modified Cash Basis

COMBINATION JOURNAL
PAGE 1

DATE	CASH DEBIT	CASH CREDIT	DESCRIPTION	POST. REF.	GENERAL DEBIT	GENERAL CREDIT	MEDICAL FEES CREDIT	WAGES EXPENSE DEBIT	LABORATORY EXPENSE DEBIT	MEDICAL SUPPLIES DEBIT	OFFICE SUPPLIES DEBIT	
20-- June 1	50 0 0 0 00		Ray Bonita, Capital	311		50 0 0 0 00						1
2		6 0 0 0 00	Prepaid Insurance	145	6 0 0 0 00							2
3		22 0 0 0 00	Medical Equipment	185	22 0 0 0 00							3
		3 0 0 00		—					3 0 0 00			4
			Office Furniture	182	9 0 0 0 00							5
			Accounts Payable—Bittle's Furn.	202		9 0 0 0 00						6
	5 0 0 0 00			—			5 0 0 0 00					7
		2 0 0 0 00	Rent Expense	521	2 0 0 0 00							8
		2 5 0 00		—						2 5 0 00		9
		3 0 0 0 00		—				3 0 0 0 00				10
		1 5 0 00	Telephone Expense	525	1 5 0 00							11
		2 8 0 00		—					2 8 0 00			12
	10 0 0 0 00			—			10 0 0 0 00					13
		3 0 0 0 00		—				3 0 0 0 00				14
		1 5 0 00		—							1 5 0 00	15
	3 2 0 0 00			—			3 2 0 0 00					16
		3 3 0 0 00	Accounts Payable—Bittle's Furniture	202	3 3 0 0 00							17
		2 0 0 00		—						2 0 0 00		18
		4 0 0 00		—					4 0 0 00			19
		5 0 0 00	Office Furniture	182	4 0 0 0 00							20
			Accounts Payable—Bittle's Furn.	202		3 5 0 0 00						21
		2 5 0 0 00		—				2 5 0 0 00				22
	7 0 0 0 00			—			7 0 0 0 00					23
30		10 0 0 0 00	Ray Bonita, Drawing	312	10 0 0 0 00							24
	75 2 0 0 00	54 0 3 0 00			56 4 5 0 00	62 5 0 0 00	25 2 0 0 00	8 5 0 0 00	9 8 0 00	4 5 0 00	1 5 0 0 00	25
	(1 0 1)	(1 0 1)			(✓)	(✓)	(4 0 1)	(5 1 1)	(5 2 6)	(1 4 1)	(1 4 2)	26

Proving the Combination Journal

Debit Columns	
Cash	75,200
General	56,450
Wages Expense	8,500
Laboratory Expense	980
Medical Supplies	450
Office Supplies	150
	141,730

Credit Columns	
Cash	54,030
General	62,500
Medical Fees	25,200
	141,730

Note: The account numbers in the Posting Reference column and at the bottom of the special columns are inserted as posting is completed. The same is true for the (✓) at the bottom of the General Debit and Credit columns.

POSTING FROM THE COMBINATION JOURNAL

LO4 Post from the combination journal to the general ledger.

The procedures for posting a special column are different from the procedures used when posting a general column. Accounts debited or credited in the general columns are posted individually throughout the month in the same manner followed for the general journal. A different procedure is used for special columns. Figure M1-7 describes the procedures to follow in posting from the combination journal.

FIGURE M1-7   Posting from a Combination Journal

GENERAL COLUMNS	Since a combination journal is being used, enter "CJ" and the page number in each general ledger account's **Posting Reference column**. Once the amount has been posted to the general ledger account, the account number is entered in the Posting Reference column of the combination journal. Accounts in the general column should be posted daily. The check marks at the bottom of the General Debit and Credit columns are entered at the end of the month and serve as a reminder that these totals should not be posted.
SPECIAL COLUMNS	1. Post the totals of the special columns to the appropriate general ledger accounts. 2. Once posted, enter the account number (in parentheses) beneath the column and "CJ" and the page number in each general ledger account's Posting Reference column.

LEARNING KEY

Amounts in the General column are posted individually. Only the totals of the special columns are posted.

Portions of the combination journal in Figure M1-6 and general ledger accounts for Cash, Office Furniture, Accounts Payable, and Medical Fees are shown in Figure M1-8 to illustrate the effects of this posting process. Note that the individual debits and credits in the General columns are posted individually throughout the month. Only the totals of the special columns are posted at the end of the month.

To see the advantages of posting a combination journal compared with the general journal, simply compare the accounts in Figure M1-8 with the same accounts in Chapter 4, Figure 4-12. Note the number of postings required for the general journal and combination journal.

	Number of Postings		
	General Journal	Combination Journal	
Cash	13	2	(Special columns for cash)
Delivery Equip./Office Furniture	3	2	(No special column)
Accounts Payable	3	3	(No special column)
Delivery/Medical Fees	3	1	(Special column for Medical Fees)

Clearly, using the combination journal can be quite efficient.

FIGURE M1-8   Posting the Combination Journal

COMBINATION JOURNAL (only selected transactions are shown)   PAGE 1

	DATE		CASH DEBIT	CASH CREDIT	DESCRIPTION	POST. REF.	GENERAL DEBIT	GENERAL CREDIT	MEDICAL FEES CREDIT	
5	20-- June	5			Office Furniture	182	9 0 0 0 00			5
6					Accts. Payable—Bittle's Furn.	202		9 0 0 0 00		6
7		6	5 0 0 0 00			—			5 0 0 0 00	7
12		15	10 0 0 0 00			—			10 0 0 0 00	12
16		20	3 2 0 0 00			—			3 2 0 0 00	16
17		22		3 3 0 0 00	Accts. Payable—Bittle's Furn.	202	3 3 0 0 00			17
20		25		5 0 0 00	Office Furniture	182	4 0 0 0 00			20
21					Accts. Payable—Bittle's Furn.	202		3 5 0 0 00		21
23		30	7 0 0 0 00			—			7 0 0 0 00	23
25			75 2 0 0 00	54 0 3 0 00			56 4 5 0 00	62 5 0 0 00	25 2 0 0 00	25
26			(1 0 1)	(1 0 1)			(✓)	(✓)	(4 0 1)	26

GENERAL LEDGER

ACCOUNT: Cash   ACCOUNT NO. 101

DATE	ITEM	POST. REF.	DEBIT	CREDIT	BALANCE DEBIT	BALANCE CREDIT
20-- June 30		CJ1	75 2 0 0 00		75 2 0 0 00	
30		CJ1		54 0 3 0 00	21 1 7 0 00	

ACCOUNT: Office Furniture   ACCOUNT NO. 182

DATE	ITEM	POST. REF.	DEBIT	CREDIT	BALANCE DEBIT	BALANCE CREDIT
20-- June 5		CJ1	9 0 0 0 00		9 0 0 0 00	
25		CJ1	4 0 0 0 00		13 0 0 0 00	

ACCOUNT: Accounts Payable   ACCOUNT NO. 202

DATE	ITEM	POST. REF.	DEBIT	CREDIT	BALANCE DEBIT	BALANCE CREDIT
20-- June 5		CJ1		9 0 0 0 00		9 0 0 0 00
22		CJ1	3 3 0 0 00			5 7 0 0 00
25		CJ1		3 5 0 0 00		9 2 0 0 00

ACCOUNT: Medical Fees   ACCOUNT NO. 401

DATE	ITEM	POST. REF.	DEBIT	CREDIT	BALANCE DEBIT	BALANCE CREDIT
20-- June 30		CJ1		25 2 0 0 00		25 2 0 0 00

LO5 Prepare a work sheet, financial statements, and adjusting and closing entries for a professional service business.

Determining the Cash Balance

The debits and credits to Cash are not posted until the end of the accounting period. Therefore, the cash balance must be computed when this information is needed. The cash balance may be computed at any time during the month by taking the beginning balance and adding total cash debits and subtracting total cash credits to date. Figure M1-9 shows the calculation of Bonita's cash balance on June 15.

PERFORMING END-OF-PERIOD WORK FOR A PROFESSIONAL SERVICE BUSINESS

Once the combination journal has been posted to the general ledger, the end-of-period work sheet is prepared in the same way as described in Chapter 5. Recall that financial statements are prepared and end-of-period work is normally performed at the end of the fiscal year. For illustration purposes, we will perform these activities at the end of Bonita's first month of operations.

Preparing the Work Sheet

Bonita's work sheet is illustrated in Figure M1-10 on page 636. Adjustments were made for the following items:

(a)   Medical supplies remaining on June 30, $350.

(b)   Office supplies remaining on June 30, $100.

(c)   Prepaid insurance expired during June, $500.

(d)   Depreciation on office furniture for June, $200.

(e)   Depreciation on medical equipment for June, $300.

Preparing Financial Statements

Dr. Bonita made no additional investment during June. Thus, as we saw in Chapter 6, the financial statements can be prepared directly from the work sheet. Recall that if Bonita had made an additional investment, this amount would be identified by reviewing Bonita's capital account and would need to be reported in the statement of owner's equity. Bonita's financial statements are illustrated in Figure M1-11 on page 637.

FIGURE M1-9   Determining the Cash Balance

COMBINATION JOURNAL

PAGE 1

DATE	CASH DEBIT	CASH CREDIT	DESCRIPTION	POST. REF.	GENERAL DEBIT	GENERAL CREDIT	MEDICAL FEES CREDIT	WAGES EXPENSE DEBIT	LABORATORY EXPENSE DEBIT	MEDICAL SUPPLIES DEBIT	OFFICE SUPPLIES DEBIT	
20– June 1	50 0 0 0 00		Ray Bonita, Capital	311		50 0 0 0 00						1
2		6 0 0 0 00	Prepaid Insurance	145	6 0 0 0 00							2
3		22 0 0 0 00	Medical Equipment	185	22 0 0 0 00							3
4		3 0 0 00		—					3 0 0 00			4
5			Office Furniture	182	9 0 0 0 00							5
6			Accounts Payable—Bittle's Furn.	202		9 0 0 0 00						6
7	5 0 0 0 00			—			5 0 0 0 00					7
8		2 0 0 0 00	Rent Expense	521	2 0 0 0 00							8
9		3 0 0 0 00		—				3 0 0 0 00				9
10		2 5 0 00		—						2 5 0 00		10
11		1 5 0 00	Telephone Expense	525	1 5 0 00							11
12	10 0 0 0 00			—			10 0 0 0 00					12
13	65 0 0 0 00	33 7 0 0 00										13

Beginning balance $ 0
Add cash debits   65,000
Total $65,000
Less cash credits   33,700
Cash balance, June 15 $31,300

FIGURE M1-10   Work Sheet for Ray Bonita, M.D.

Ray Bonita, M.D.
Work Sheet
For Month Ended June 30, 20 - -

ACCOUNT TITLE	Trial Balance Debit	Trial Balance Credit	Adjustments Debit	Adjustments Credit	Adjusted Trial Balance Debit	Adjusted Trial Balance Credit	Income Statement Debit	Income Statement Credit	Balance Sheet Debit	Balance Sheet Credit	
1 Cash	21 1 7 0 00				21 1 7 0 00				21 1 7 0 00		1
2 Medical Supplies	4 5 0 00			(a) 1 0 0 00	3 5 0 00				3 5 0 00		2
3 Office Supplies	1 5 0 00			(b) 5 0 00	1 0 0 00				1 0 0 00		3
4 Prepaid Insurance	6 0 0 0 00			(c) 5 0 0 00	5 5 0 0 00				5 5 0 0 00		4
5 Office Furniture	13 0 0 0 00				13 0 0 0 00				13 0 0 0 00		5
6 Accum. Depr.—Office Furniture				(d) 2 0 0 00		2 0 0 00				2 0 0 00	6
7 Medical Equipment	22 0 0 0 00				22 0 0 0 00				22 0 0 0 00		7
8 Accum. Depr.—Medical Equipment				(e) 3 0 0 00		3 0 0 00				3 0 0 00	8
9 Accounts Payable		9 2 0 0 00				9 2 0 0 00				9 2 0 0 00	9
10 Ray Bonita, Capital		50 0 0 0 00				50 0 0 0 00				50 0 0 0 00	10
11 Ray Bonita, Drawing	10 0 0 0 00				10 0 0 0 00				10 0 0 0 00		11
12 Medical Fees		25 2 0 0 00				25 2 0 0 00		25 2 0 0 00			12
13 Wages Expense	8 5 0 0 00				8 5 0 0 00		8 5 0 0 00				13
14 Rent Expense	2 0 0 0 00				2 0 0 0 00		2 0 0 0 00				14
15 Office Supplies Expense			(b) 5 0 00		5 0 00		5 0 00				15
16 Medical Supplies Expense			(a) 1 0 0 00		1 0 0 00		1 0 0 00				16
17 Telephone Expense	1 5 0 00				1 5 0 00		1 5 0 00				17
18 Laboratory Expense	9 8 0 00				9 8 0 00		9 8 0 00				18
19 Insurance Expense			(c) 5 0 0 00		5 0 0 00		5 0 0 00				19
20 Depr. Expense—Office Furniture			(d) 2 0 0 00		2 0 0 00		2 0 0 00				20
21 Depr. Expense—Medical Equipment			(e) 3 0 0 00		3 0 0 00		3 0 0 00				21
22	84 4 0 0 00	84 4 0 0 00	1 1 5 0 00	1 1 5 0 00	84 9 0 0 00	84 9 0 0 00	12 7 8 0 00	25 2 0 0 00	72 1 2 0 00	59 7 0 0 00	22
23 Net Income							12 4 2 0 00			12 4 2 0 00	23
24							25 2 0 0 00	25 2 0 0 00	72 1 2 0 00	72 1 2 0 00	24
25											25
26											26
27											27
28											28
29											29
30											30

FIGURE M1-11   Financial Statements for Ray Bonita, M.D.

Ray Bonita, M.D.
Income Statement
For Month Ended June 30, 20 - -

Revenue:											
Medical fees							$ 25	2	0	0	00
Expenses:											
Wages expense	$8	5	0	0	00						
Rent expense	2	0	0	0	00						
Office supplies expense			5	0	00						
Medical supplies expense		1	0	0	00						
Telephone expense		1	5	0	00						
Laboratory expense		9	8	0	00						
Insurance expense		5	0	0	00						
Depreciation expense—office furniture		2	0	0	00						
Depreciation expense—medical equipment		3	0	0	00						
Total expenses							12	7	8	0	00
Net income							$12	4	2	0	00

Ray Bonita, M.D.
Statement of Owner's Equity
For Month Ended June 30, 20 - -

Ray Bonita, capital, June 1, 20 - -							$50	0	0	0	00
Net income for June	$12	4	2	0	00						
Less withdrawals for June	10	0	0	0	00						
Increase in capital							2	4	2	0	00
Ray Bonita, capital, June 30, 20 - -							$52	4	2	0	00

Ray Bonita, M.D.
Balance Sheet
June 30, 20 - -

Assets											
Current assets:											
Cash	$21	1	7	0	00						
Medical supplies		3	5	0	00						
Office supplies		1	0	0	00						
Prepaid insurance	5	5	0	0	00						
Total current assets							$27	1	2	0	00
Property, plant, and equipment:											
Office furniture	$13	0	0	0	00						
Less accumulated depreciation		2	0	0	00		12	8	0	0	00
Medical equipment	$22	0	0	0	00						
Less accumulated depreciation		3	0	0	00		21	7	0	0	00
Total assets							$61	6	2	0	00
Liabilities											
Current liabilities:											
Accounts payable							$ 9	2	0	0	00
Owner's Equity											
Ray Bonita, capital							52	4	2	0	00
Total liabilities and owner's equity							$61	6	2	0	00

Preparing Adjusting and Closing Entries

Adjusting and closing entries are made in the combination journal in the same manner demonstrated for the general journal in Chapter 6. We simply use the Description and General Debit and Credit columns. These posted entries are illustrated in Figures M1-12 and M1-13.

FIGURE M1-12 Adjusting Entries

COMBINATION JOURNAL

	DATE		CASH DEBIT	CASH CREDIT	DESCRIPTION	POST. REF.	GENERAL DEBIT	GENERAL CREDIT	
1					Adjusting Entries				1
2	20-- June	30			Medical Supplies Expense	524	1 0 0 00		2
3					Medical Supplies	141		1 0 0 00	3
4		30			Office Supplies Expense	523	5 0 00		4
5					Office Supplies	142		5 0 00	5
6		30			Insurance Expense	535	5 0 0 00		6
7					Prepaid Insurance	145		5 0 0 00	7
8		30			Depr. Expense—Office Furniture	541	2 0 0 00		8
9					Accum. Depr.—Office Furn.	182.1		2 0 0 00	9
10		30			Depr. Expense—Medical Equip.	542	3 0 0 00		10
11					Accum. Depr.—Medical Equip.	185.1		3 0 0 00	11

FIGURE M1-13 Closing Entries

COMBINATION JOURNAL

	DATE		CASH DEBIT	CASH CREDIT	DESCRIPTION	POST. REF.	GENERAL DEBIT	GENERAL CREDIT	
12									12
13					Closing Entries				13
14	20-- June	30			Medical Fees	401	25 2 0 0 00		14
15					Income Summary	313		25 2 0 0 00	15
16		30			Income Summary	313	12 7 8 0 00		16
17					Wages Expense	511		8 5 0 0 00	17
18					Rent Expense	521		2 0 0 0 00	18
19					Office Supplies Expense	523		5 0 00	19
20					Medical Supplies Expense	524		1 0 0 00	20
21					Telephone Expense	525		1 5 0 00	21
22					Laboratory Expense	526		9 8 0 00	22
23					Insurance Expense	535		5 0 0 00	23
24					Depr. Expense—Office Furn.	541		2 0 0 00	24
25					Depr. Expense—Med. Equip.	542		3 0 0 00	25
26		30			Income Summary	313	12 4 2 0 00		26
27					Ray Bonita, Capital	311		12 4 2 0 00	27
28		30			Ray Bonita, Capital	311	10 0 0 0 00		28
29					Ray Bonita, Drawing	312		10 0 0 0 00	29

Learning Objectives	Key Points to Remember
LO1 Explain the differences between the modified cash and accrual bases of accounting.	As shown below, there are three basic differences between the modified cash and accrual bases of accounting.

DIFFERENCES BETWEEN MODIFIED CASH AND ACCRUAL BASES OF ACCOUNTING

EVENT	ACCRUAL BASIS	MODIFIED CASH BASIS
Expenses		
Bills for services received, but not yet paid.	Expense Accounts Payable	No entry. (Record when paid.)
Wages earned by employees, but not yet paid.	Wages Expense Wages Payable	No entry. (Record when paid.)
Revenues		
Services provided on account.	Accounts Receivable Professional Fees	No entry. (Record when cash is received.)

Learning Objectives	Key Points to Remember
LO2 Describe special records for a professional service business using the modified cash basis.	Special records are required for a professional service business using the modified cash basis. Since accounts receivable are not entered in the accounting system, other records must be maintained to keep track of amounts owed by clients and patients. These records generally include an appointment record and a client or patient ledger record.
LO3 Describe and use a combination journal to record transactions of a professional service business.	A combination journal is used by some businesses to improve the efficiency of recording and posting transactions. It includes general and special columns. The headings for a typical combination journal for a doctor's office are shown below.

COMBINATION JOURNAL PAGE 1

DATE	CASH		DESCRIPTION	POST. REF.	GENERAL		MEDICAL FEES CREDIT	WAGES EXPENSE DEBIT	LABORATORY EXPENSE DEBIT	MEDICAL SUPPLIES DEBIT	OFFICE SUPPLIES DEBIT
	DEBIT	CREDIT			DEBIT	CREDIT					

Learning Objectives	Key Points to Remember
LO4 Post from the combination journal to the general ledger.	Rules for posting a combination journal are as follows: 1. Amounts entered in the general columns are posted individually to the general ledger on a daily basis. 2. The totals of the special columns are posted to the general ledger at the end of the month.
LO5 Prepare a work sheet, financial statements, and adjusting and closing entries for a professional service business.	The work sheet, financial statements, adjusting entries, and closing entries are prepared in the same manner as discussed in Chapters 5 and 6. Remember, however, that under the modified cash basis, adjustments are made only for prepaid items and depreciation of plant and equipment.

DEMONSTRATION PROBLEM

Maria Vietor is a financial planning consultant. She developed the following chart of accounts for her business:

Vietor Financial Planning
Chart of Accounts

Assets	Revenues
101 Cash	401 Professional Fees
142 Office Supplies	
	Expenses
Liabilities	511 Wages Expense
202 Accounts Payable	521 Rent Expense
	523 Office Supplies Expense
Owner's Equity	525 Telephone Expense
311 Maria Vietor, Capital	526 Automobile Expense
312 Maria Vietor, Drawing	533 Utilities Expense
313 Income Summary	534 Charitable Contributions Expense

Vietor completed the following transactions during the month of December of the current year:

Dec. 1	Vietor invested cash to start a consulting business, $20,000.
3	Paid December office rent, $1,000.
4	Received a check from Aaron Bisno, a client, for services, $2,500.
6	Paid Union Electric for December heating and light, $75.
7	Received a check from Will Carter, a client, for services, $2,000.
12	Paid Smith's Super Service for gasoline and oil purchases, $60.
14	Paid Comphelp for temporary secretarial services obtained through them during the past two weeks, $600.
17	Purchased office supplies on account from Cleat Office Supply, $280.
20	Paid Cress Telephone Co. for local and long-distance business calls during the past month, $100.
21	Vietor withdrew cash for personal use, $1,100.
24	Made donation to the National Multiple Sclerosis Society, $100.
27	Received a check from Ellen Thaler, a client, for services, $2,000.
28	Paid Comphelp for temporary secretarial services obtained through them during the past two weeks, $600.
29	Made payment on account to Cleat Office Supply, $100.

REQUIRED

1. Enter the transactions in a combination journal. Establish special columns for Professional Fees, Wages Expense, and Automobile Expense. Vietor uses the modified cash basis of accounting. (Refer to the Chapter 4 Demonstration Problem to see how similar transactions were recorded in a general journal. Notice that the combination journal is much more efficient.)

2. Prove the combination journal.

3. Post these transactions to a general ledger.

4. Prepare a trial balance.

(continued)

Solution 1. and 2.

COMBINATION JOURNAL   PAGE 1

Line	DATE	DESCRIPTION	POST. REF.	CASH DEBIT	CASH CREDIT	GENERAL DEBIT	GENERAL CREDIT	PROFESSIONAL FEES CREDIT	WAGES EXPENSE DEBIT	AUTOMOBILE EXPENSE DEBIT
1	20-- Dec. 1	Maria Vietor, Capital	311	20 0 0 0 00			20 0 0 0 00			
2	3	Rent Expense	521		1 0 0 0 00	1 0 0 0 00				
3	4		—	2 5 0 0 00				2 5 0 0 00		
4	6	Utilities Expense	533		7 5 00	7 5 00				
5	7		—	2 0 0 0 00				2 0 0 0 00		
6	12		—		6 0 0 00					6 0 0 00
7	14		—		6 0 0 00				6 0 0 00	
8	17	Office Supplies	142			2 8 0 00				
9		Accounts Payable—Cleat Office Supply	202				2 8 0 00			
10	20	Telephone Expense	525		1 0 0 00	1 0 0 00				
11	21	Maria Vietor, Drawing	312		1 1 0 0 00	1 1 0 0 00				
12	24	Charitable Contributions Expense	534		1 0 0 00	1 0 0 00				
13	27		—	2 0 0 0 00				2 0 0 0 00		
14	28		—		6 0 0 00				6 0 0 00	
15	29	Accounts Payable—Cleat Office Supply	202		1 0 0 00	1 0 0 00				
16				26 5 0 0 00	3 7 3 5 00	2 7 5 5 00	20 2 8 0 00	6 5 0 0 00	1 2 0 0 00	6 0 0 00
17				(1 0 1)	(1 0 1)	(✓)	(✓)	(4 0 1)	(5 1 1)	(5 2 6)
18										

Proving the Combination Journal

Debit Columns		Credit Columns	
Cash	26,500	Cash	3,735
General	2,755	General	20,280
Wages Expense	1,200	Professional Fees	6,500
Automobile Expense	60		
	30,515		30,515

3.

GENERAL LEDGER

ACCOUNT: Cash   ACCOUNT NO. 101

DATE		ITEM	POST. REF.	DEBIT	CREDIT	BALANCE	
						DEBIT	CREDIT
20-- Dec.	31		C J 1	26 5 0 0 00		26 5 0 0 00	
	31		C J 1		3 7 3 5 00	22 7 6 5 00	

ACCOUNT: Office Supplies   ACCOUNT NO. 142

DATE		ITEM	POST. REF.	DEBIT	CREDIT	BALANCE	
						DEBIT	CREDIT
20-- Dec.	17		C J 1	2 8 0 00		2 8 0 00	

ACCOUNT: Accounts Payable   ACCOUNT NO. 202

DATE		ITEM	POST. REF.	DEBIT	CREDIT	BALANCE	
						DEBIT	CREDIT
20-- Dec.	17		C J 1		2 8 0 00		2 8 0 00
	29		C J 1	1 0 0 00			1 8 0 00

ACCOUNT: Maria Vietor, Capital   ACCOUNT NO. 311

DATE		ITEM	POST. REF.	DEBIT	CREDIT	BALANCE	
						DEBIT	CREDIT
20-- Dec.	1		C J 1		20 0 0 0 00		20 0 0 0 00

ACCOUNT: Maria Vietor, Drawing   ACCOUNT NO. 312

DATE		ITEM	POST. REF.	DEBIT	CREDIT	BALANCE	
						DEBIT	CREDIT
20-- Dec.	21		C J 1	1 1 0 0 00		1 1 0 0 00	

ACCOUNT: Income Summary   ACCOUNT NO. 313

DATE	ITEM	POST. REF.	DEBIT	CREDIT	BALANCE	
					DEBIT	CREDIT
20--						

ACCOUNT: Professional Fees   ACCOUNT NO. 401

DATE		ITEM	POST. REF.	DEBIT	CREDIT	BALANCE	
						DEBIT	CREDIT
20-- Dec.	31		C J 1		6 5 0 0 00		6 5 0 0 00

ACCOUNT: Wages Expense   ACCOUNT NO. 511

DATE		ITEM	POST. REF.	DEBIT	CREDIT	BALANCE	
						DEBIT	CREDIT
20-- Dec.	31		C J 1	1 2 0 0 00		1 2 0 0 00	

(continued)

ACCOUNT: Rent Expense   ACCOUNT NO. 521

DATE	ITEM	POST. REF.	DEBIT	CREDIT	BALANCE DEBIT	BALANCE CREDIT
20-- Dec. 3		C J 1	1 0 0 0 00		1 0 0 0 00	

ACCOUNT: Office Supplies Expense   ACCOUNT NO. 523

DATE	ITEM	POST. REF.	DEBIT	CREDIT	BALANCE DEBIT	BALANCE CREDIT
20--						

ACCOUNT: Telephone Expense   ACCOUNT NO. 525

DATE	ITEM	POST. REF.	DEBIT	CREDIT	BALANCE DEBIT	BALANCE CREDIT
20-- Dec. 20		C J 1	1 0 0 00		1 0 0 00	

ACCOUNT: Automobile Expense   ACCOUNT NO. 526

DATE	ITEM	POST. REF.	DEBIT	CREDIT	BALANCE DEBIT	BALANCE CREDIT
20-- Dec. 31		C J 1	6 0 00		6 0 00	

ACCOUNT: Utilities Expense   ACCOUNT NO. 533

DATE	ITEM	POST. REF.	DEBIT	CREDIT	BALANCE DEBIT	BALANCE CREDIT
20-- Dec. 6		C J 1	7 5 00		7 5 00	

ACCOUNT: Charitable Contributions Expense   ACCOUNT NO. 534

DATE	ITEM	POST. REF.	DEBIT	CREDIT	BALANCE DEBIT	BALANCE CREDIT
20-- Dec. 24		C J 1	1 0 0 00		1 0 0 00	

4.

Vietor Financial Planning
Trial Balance
December 31, 20 - -

ACCOUNT TITLE	ACCOUNT NO.	DEBIT BALANCE	CREDIT BALANCE
Cash	101	22 7 6 5 00	
Office Supplies	142	2 8 0 00	
Accounts Payable	202		1 8 0 00
Maria Vietor, Capital	311		20 0 0 0 00
Maria Vietor, Drawing	312	1 1 0 0 00	
Professional Fees	401		6 5 0 0 00
Wages Expense	511	1 2 0 0 00	
Rent Expense	521	1 0 0 0 00	
Telephone Expense	525	1 0 0 00	
Automobile Expense	526	6 0 00	
Utilities Expense	533	7 5 00	
Charitable Contributions Expense	534	1 0 0 00	
		26 6 8 0 00	26 6 8 0 00

KEY TERMS

combination journal (628)   A journal with special and general columns.

Description column (630)   The column in the combination journal used to enter the account titles for the General Debit and General Credit columns; to identify specific creditors when assets are purchased, or payments made, on account; to identify amounts forwarded; and to identify adjusting, closing, and reversing entries.

General Credit column (628)   The column in the combination journal used to credit accounts that are used infrequently.

General Debit column (628)   The column in the combination journal used to debit accounts that are used infrequently.

Posting Reference column (632)   The column in the combination journal where the account number is entered after posting to accounts from the general debit and credit columns.

special columns (628)   Columns in combination journals for frequently used accounts.

Self-Study Test Questions

True/False

1. Under the accrual basis of accounting, revenues are recorded when earned.
2. The modified cash basis of accounting is used by most large businesses.
3. The modified cash basis uses the accrual basis when recording revenues and expenses.
4. Under the modified cash basis, interest expense is recorded when paid.
5. Many small professional service businesses use the modified cash basis.

Multiple Choice

1. Which of these would make the best "special column" in a combination journal?

   (a) Office Equipment   (c) Revenue
   (b) Prepaid Insurance   (d) Telephone Expense

2. Verifying that debit column totals equal credit column totals is the process of

   (a) debiting.   (c) closing.
   (b) proving.   (d) adjusting.

3. Posting from the combination journal is accomplished by placing " _____ " and the page number in the Posting Reference column of the general ledger account.

   (a) G   (c) J
   (b) DJ   (d) CJ

4. Using the modified cash basis, when a business provides services on account, _____ is debited.

   (a) no entry   (c) Cash
   (b) Accounts Receivable   (d) Owner's Equity

5. Using the modified cash basis, when wages are earned but not paid, _____ is debited.

   (a) Wages Expense   (c) Wages Payable
   (b) no entry   (d) Accrued Wages

The answers to the Self-Study Test Questions are at the end of the text.

REVIEW QUESTIONS

LO1	1. Explain when revenues are recorded under the modified cash basis and accrual basis of accounting.
LO1	2. Explain when wages expense is recorded under the modified cash basis and accrual basis of accounting.
LO2	3. Explain the purpose of an appointment record.
LO2	4. Explain the purpose of a patient ledger account.
LO3	5. Explain the purpose of a special column in the combination journal.
LO3	6. Explain the purpose of the General columns in the combination journal.
LO3/4	7. How does the use of the combination journal save time and space in entering cash transactions?
LO3	8. Explain the purpose of the Description column in the combination journal.
LO3	9. What is the purpose of proving the totals in the combination journal?
LO4	10. When an entry is posted from the combination journal to a ledger account, what information is entered in the Posting Reference column of the combination journal? In the Posting Reference column of the ledger account?

SERIES A EXERCISES

E M1-1A (LO1/3)
✓ **General Debit total: $2,715;**
Cash debit total: $11,100

JOURNAL ENTRIES Jean Akins opened a consulting business. Journalize the following transactions that occurred during the month of January of the current year using the modified cash basis and a combination journal. Set up special columns for Consulting Fees (credit) and Wages Expense (debit).

Jan.	1	Invested cash in the business, $10,000.
	2	Paid office rent, $500.
	3	Purchased office equipment on account from Business Machines, Inc., $1,500.
	5	Received cash for services rendered, $750.
	8	Paid telephone bill, $65.
	10	Paid for a magazine subscription (miscellaneous expense), $15.
	11	Purchased office supplies on account from Leo's Office Supplies, $300.
	15	Paid for one-year liability insurance policy, $150.
	18	Paid part-time help, $500.
	21	Received cash for services rendered, $350.
	25	Paid electricity bill, $85.
	27	Withdrew cash for personal use, $100.
	29	Paid part-time help, $500.

E M1-2A (LO1/3)

✓ Total debits: $19,191

JOURNAL ENTRIES Bill Rackes opened a bicycle repair shop. Journalize the following transactions that occurred during the month of October of the current year. Use the modified cash basis and a combination journal with special columns for Repair Fees (credit) and Wages Expense (debit). Prove the combination journal.

Oct.	1	Invested cash in the business, $15,000.
	2	Paid shop rental for the month, $300.
	3	Purchased bicycle parts on account from Tracker's Bicycle Parts, $2,000.
	5	Purchased office supplies on account from Downtown Office Supplies, $250.
	8	Paid telephone bill, $38.
	9	Received cash for services, $140.
	11	Paid for a sports magazine subscription (miscellaneous expense), $15.
	12	Made payment on account for parts previously purchased, $100.
	14	Paid part-time help, $300.
	15	Received cash for services, $350.
	16	Paid electricity bill, $48.
	19	Received cash for services, $250.
	23	Withdrew cash for personal use, $50.
	25	Made payment on account for office supplies previously purchased, $50.
	29	Paid part-time help, $300.

SERIES A PROBLEMS

P M1-3A (LO3/4/5)

✓ 2. Cash bal., 1/12: $10,310;

3. Total journal credits: $15,499;

5. Trial bal. total debits: $13,460

KA
KLOOSTER & ALLEN

JOURNALIZING AND POSTING TRANSACTIONS AND PREPARING A TRIAL BALANCE Angela McWharton opened an on-call nursing services business. She rented a small office space and pays a part-time worker to answer the telephone. Her chart of accounts is shown below.

Angela McWharton Nursing Services
Chart of Accounts

Assets		Revenues	
101	Cash	401	Nursing Care Fees
142	Office Supplies		
181	Office Equipment	Expenses	
		511	Wages Expense
Liabilities		512	Advertising Expense
202	Accounts Payable	521	Rent Expense
		525	Telephone Expense
Owner's Equity		526	Transportation Expense
311	Angela McWharton, Capital	533	Electricity Expense
312	Angela McWharton, Drawing	549	Miscellaneous Expense
313	Income Summary		

(continued)

McWharton's transactions for the first month of business are as follows:

Jan. 1   Invested cash in the business, $10,000.

      1   Paid January rent, $500.

      2   Purchased office supplies on account from Crestline Office Supplies, $300.

      4   Purchased office equipment on account from Office Technology, Inc., $1,500.

      6   Received cash for nursing services rendered, $580.

      7   Paid telephone bill, $42.

      8   Paid electricity bill, $38.

     10   Received cash for nursing services rendered, $360.

     12   Made payment on account for office supplies previously purchased, $50.

     13   Reimbursed part-time worker for use of personal automobile (transportation expense), $150.

     15   Paid part-time worker, $360.

     17   Received cash for nursing services rendered, $420.

     18   Withdrew cash for personal use, $100.

     20   Paid for newspaper advertising, $26.

     22   Paid for gas and oil, $35.

     24   Paid subscription for journal on nursing care practices (miscellaneous expense), $28.

     25   Received cash for nursing services rendered, $320.

     27   Made payment on account for office equipment previously purchased, $150.

     29   Paid part-time worker, $360.

     30   Received cash for nursing services rendered, $180.

REQUIRED

1.   Journalize the transactions for January using the modified cash basis and page 1 of a combination journal. Set up special columns for Nursing Care Fees (credit), Wages Expense (debit), and Transportation Expense (debit).

2.   Determine the cash balance as of January 12 (using the combination journal).

3.   Prove the combination journal.

4.   Set up general ledger accounts from the chart of accounts and post the transactions from the combination journal.

5.   Prepare a trial balance.

P M1-4A (LO3/4/5)

✓ 2. Cash bal., 11/12: $5,949;

3. Total journal credits: $6,499;

5. Trial Bal. total debits: $18,155;

Adjusted Trial Bal. total debits: $18,455; Net income: $1,842;

7. Capital, 11/30: $6,772;

Total assets, 11/30: $13,947

KLOOSTER & ALLEN

JOURNALIZING AND POSTING TRANSACTIONS AND PREPARING FINANCIAL STATEMENTS Sue Reyton owns a suit tailoring shop. She opened her business in September. She rents a small work space and has an assistant to receive job orders and process claim tickets. Her trial balance shows her account balances for the first two months of business (September and October). No adjustments were made in September or October.

Sue Reyton Tailors
Trial Balance
October 31, 20 - -

ACCOUNT TITLE	ACCOUNT NO.	DEBIT BALANCE	CREDIT BALANCE
Cash	101	5 7 1 1 00	
Tailoring Supplies	141	1 0 0 0 00	
Office Supplies	142	4 8 5 00	
Prepaid Insurance	145	1 0 0 00	
Tailoring Equipment	188	3 8 0 0 00	
Accumulated Depreciation—Tailoring Equipment	188.1		
Accounts Payable	202		4 1 2 5 00
Sue Reyton, Capital	311		5 4 3 0 00
Sue Reyton, Drawing	312	5 0 0 00	
Tailoring Fees	401		3 6 0 0 00
Wages Expense	511	8 0 0 00	
Advertising Expense	512	3 3 00	
Rent Expense	521	6 0 0 00	
Telephone Expense	525	6 0 00	
Electricity Expense	533	4 4 00	
Miscellaneous Expense	549	2 2 00	
		13 1 5 5 00	13 1 5 5 00

Reyton's transactions for November are as follows:

Nov. 1   Paid November rent, $300.

2   Purchased tailoring supplies on account from Sew Easy Supplies, $150.

3   Purchased a new button hole machine on account from Seam's Sewing Machines, $3,000.

5   Earned first week's revenue: $400 in cash.

8   Paid for newspaper advertising, $13.

9   Paid telephone bill, $28.

10   Paid electricity bill, $21.

12   Earned second week's revenue: $200 in cash, $300 on account.

15   Paid part-time worker, $400.

16   Made payment on account for tailoring supplies, $100.

17   Paid for magazine subscription (miscellaneous expense), $12.

19   Earned third week's revenue: $450 in cash.

21   Paid for prepaid insurance for the year, $500.

23   Received cash from customers (previously owed), $300.

(continued)

Nov. 24   Paid for newspaper advertising, $13.

26   Paid for special delivery fee (miscellaneous expense), $12.

29   Earned fourth week's revenue: $600 in cash.

Additional accounts needed are as follows:

313   Income Summary
523   Office Supplies Expense
524   Tailoring Supplies Expense
535   Insurance Expense
542   Depreciation Expense—Tailoring Equipment

November 30 adjustments are as follows:

(a)   Tailoring supplies on hand, $450.
(b)   Office supplies on hand, $285.
(c)   Prepaid insurance expired over past three months, $150.
(d)   Depreciation on tailoring equipment for the last three months, $300.

REQUIRED

1.   Journalize the transactions for November using the modified cash basis and page 5 of a combination journal. Set up special columns for Tailoring Fees (credit), Wages Expense (debit), and Advertising Expense (debit).

2.   Determine the cash balance as of November 12.

3.   Prove the combination journal.

4.   Set up general ledger accounts, including the additional accounts listed above, entering the balances as of November 1, 20--. Post the entries from the combination journal.

5.   Prepare a work sheet for the three months ended November 30, 20--.

6.   Record the adjusting entries on page 6 of the combination journal and post to the general ledger accounts.

7.   Prepare an income statement and statement of owner's equity for the three months ended November 30, and a balance sheet as of November 30, 20--. (Assume that Reyton made an investment of $5,430 on September 1, 20--.)

8.   Record closing entries on page 6 of the combination journal and post to the general ledger accounts.

SERIES B EXERCISES

E M1-1B (LO1/3)

✓ **General Debit total: $2,129;**
Cash debit total; $9,400

JOURNAL ENTRIES Bill Miller opened a bookkeeping service business. Journalize the following transactions that occurred during the month of March of the current year. Use the modified cash basis and a combination journal with special columns for Bookkeeping Fees (credit) and Wages Expense (debit).

Mar. 1   Invested cash in the business, $7,500.

3   Paid March office rent, $500.

Mar. 5   Purchased office equipment on account from Desk Top Office Equipment, $800.

6   Received cash for services rendered, $400.

8   Paid telephone bill, $48.

10   Paid for a magazine subscription (miscellaneous expense), $25.

11   Purchased office supplies, $200.

14   Received cash for services rendered, $520.

16   Paid for a one-year insurance policy, $200.

18   Paid part-time worker, $400.

21   Received cash for services rendered, $380.

22   Made payment on account for office equipment previously purchased, $100.

24   Paid electricity bill, $56.

27   Withdrew cash for personal use, $200.

29   Paid part-time worker, $400.

30   Received cash for services rendered, $600.

E M1-2B (LO1/3)

✓ **Total debits: $14,349**

JOURNAL ENTRIES Amy Anjelo opened a delivery service. Journalize the following transactions that occurred in January of the current year. Use the modified cash basis and a combination journal with special columns for Delivery Fees (credit) and Wages Expense (debit). Prove the combination journal.

Jan. 1   Invested cash in the business, $10,000.

2   Paid shop rental for the month, $400.

3   Purchased a delivery cart on account from Walt's Wheels, $1,000.

5   Purchased office supplies, $250.

6   Paid telephone bill, $51.

8   Received cash for delivery services, $428.

11   Paid electricity bill, $37.

12   Paid part-time employee, $480.

13   Paid for postage stamps (miscellaneous expense), $29.

15   Received cash for delivery services, $382.

18   Made payment on account for delivery cart previously purchased, $90.

21   Withdrew cash for personal use, $250.

24   Paid for a one-year liability insurance policy, $180.

26   Received cash for delivery services, $292.

29   Paid part-time employee, $480.

SERIES B PROBLEMS

P M1-3B (LO3/4/5)

✓ 2. Cash bal., 7/14: $4,786;
3. Total journal credits: $9,472;
5. Trial bal. total debits: $8,190

JOURNALIZING AND POSTING TRANSACTIONS AND PREPARING A TRIAL BALANCE J. B. Hoyt opened a training center at the marina where he provides private water-skiing lessons. He rented a small building at the marina and has a part-time worker to assist him. His chart of accounts is shown below.

Water Walking by Hoyt
Chart of Accounts

Assets		Revenues	
101	Cash	401	Training Fees
142	Office Supplies		
183	Skiing Equipment	Expenses	
		511	Wages Expense
Liabilities		521	Rent Expense
202	Accounts Payable	525	Telephone Expense
		526	Transportation Expense
Owner's Equity		533	Electricity Expense
311	J. B. Hoyt, Capital	537	Repair Expense
312	J. B. Hoyt, Drawing	549	Miscellaneous Expense
313	Income Summary		

Transactions for the first month of business are as follows:

July	1	Invested cash in the business, $5,000.
	2	Paid rent for the month, $250.
	3	Purchased office supplies, $150.
	4	Purchased skiing equipment on account from Water Fun, Inc., $2,000.
	6	Paid telephone bill, $36.
	7	Received cash for skiing lessons, $200.
	10	Paid electricity bill, $28.
	12	Paid part-time worker, $250.
	14	Received cash for skiing lessons, $300.
	16	Paid for gas and oil (transportation expense), $60.
	17	Received cash for skiing lessons, $250.
	20	Paid for repair to ski rope, $20.
	21	Made payment on account for skiing equipment previously purchased, $100.
	24	Received cash for skiing lessons, $310.
	26	Paid for award certificates (miscellaneous expense), $18.
	28	Paid part-time worker, $250.
	30	Received cash for skiing lessons, $230.
	31	Paid for repair to life jacket, $20.

REQUIRED

1. Journalize the transactions for July using the modified cash basis and page 1 of a combination journal. Set up special columns for Training Fees (credit), Wages Expense (debit), and Repair Expense (debit).

2. Determine the cash balance as of July 14, 20--.

3. Prove the combination journal.

4. Set up general ledger accounts from the chart of accounts and post the transactions from the combination journal.

5. Prepare a trial balance.

P M1-4B (LO3/4/5)

✓ 2. Cash bal., 6/12: $4,832;

3. Total journal credits: $4,587;

5. Trial Bal. total debits: $13,023;

Adjusted Trial Bal. total debits: $13,283; Net income: $2,928;

7. Capital, 6/30: $7,028;

Total assets, 6/30: $9,008

KLOOSTER & ALLEN

JOURNALIZING AND POSTING TRANSACTIONS AND PREPARING FINANCIAL STATEMENTS Molly Claussen owns a lawn care business. She opened her business in April. She rents a small shop area where she stores her equipment and has an assistant to receive orders and process accounts. Her trial balance shows her account balances for the first two months of business (April and May). No adjustments were made at the end of April or May.

Molly Claussen's Green Thumb
Trial Balance
May 31, 20 - -

ACCOUNT TITLE	ACCOUNT NO.	DEBIT BALANCE	CREDIT BALANCE
Cash	101	4 6 0 4 00	
Lawn Care Supplies	141	5 8 8 00	
Office Supplies	142	2 4 3 00	
Prepaid Insurance	145	1 5 0 00	
Lawn Care Equipment	189	2 4 0 8 00	
Accumulated Depreciation—Lawn Care Equipment	189.1		
Accounts Payable	202		1 0 8 0 00
Molly Claussen, Capital	311		5 0 0 0 00
Molly Claussen, Drawing	312	8 0 0 00	
Lawn Care Fees	401		4 0 3 3 00
Wages Expense	511	6 0 0 00	
Rent Expense	521	4 0 0 00	
Telephone Expense	525	8 8 00	
Electricity Expense	533	6 2 00	
Repair Expense	537	5 0 00	
Gas and Oil Expense	538	1 2 0 00	
		10 1 1 3 00	10 1 1 3 00

Transactions for June are as follows:

June 1 Paid shop rent, $200.

2 Purchased office supplies, $230.

3 Purchased new landscaping equipment on account from Earth Care, Inc., $1,000.

5 Paid telephone bill, $31.

6 Received cash for lawn care fees, $640.

(continued)

June 8   Paid electricity bill, $31.

10   Paid part-time worker, $300.

11   Received cash for lawn care fees, $580.

12   Paid for a one-year insurance policy, $200.

14   Made payment on account for landscaping equipment previously purchased, $100.

15   Paid for gas and oil, $40.

19   Paid for mower repairs, $25.

21   Received $310 cash for lawn care fees and earned $480 on account.

24   Withdrew cash for personal use, $100.

26   Paid for edging equipment repairs, $20.

28   Received cash from customers (previously owed), $480.

29   Paid part-time worker, $300.

Additional accounts needed are as follows:

313   Income Summary
523   Office Supplies Expense
524   Lawn Care Supplies Expense
535   Insurance Expense
542   Depreciation Expense—Lawn Care Equipment

June 30 adjustments are as follows:

(a)   Office supplies on hand, $273.
(b)   Lawn care supplies on hand, $300.
(c)   Prepaid insurance expired over past three months, $100.
(d)   Depreciation on lawn care equipment for past three months, $260.

REQUIRED

1.   Journalize the transactions for June using the modified cash basis and page 5 of a combination journal. Set up special columns for Lawn Care Fees (credit), Repair Expense (debit), and Wages Expense (debit).

2.   Determine the cash balance as of June 12.

3.   Prove the combination journal.

4.   Set up general ledger accounts including the additional accounts listed above, entering balances as of June 1, 20--. Post the entries from the combination journal.

5.   Prepare a work sheet for the three months ended June 30, 20--.

6.   Record the adjusting entries on page 6 of the combination journal and post to the general ledger accounts.

7.   Prepare an income statement and statement of owner's equity for the three months ended June 30, and a balance sheet as of June 30, 20--. Assume that Claussen invested $5,000 on April 1, 20--.

8.   Record the closing entries on page 6 of the combination journal and post to the general ledger accounts.

MANAGING YOUR WRITING

Your friend is planning to start her own business and has asked you for advice. In particular, she is concerned about which method of accounting she should use. She has heard about the modified cash and accrual methods of accounting. However, she does not really understand the differences. Write a memo that explains each method and the type of business for which each method is most appropriate.

ETHICS CASE

Nancy Bowles, the owner of Bowles Services, a sole proprietorship, rushed into the office late Monday morning carrying a deposit receipt from the bank. Upon handing the receipt to Sarah, the accountant, she instructed her to debit Cash and credit Professional Fees for the full $10,000. When Sarah examined the source document, she saw that the cash had come from the account of Richard Bowles, Nancy's father. Nancy explained to Sarah that she was applying for a bank loan and needed to "show that her company earned more year-to-date income than it actually had." Nancy used the rationale that the company would earn at least $10,000 in revenue during the next few months but the financial statements the bank required were as of the end of this month.

1.   Does Nancy's explanation make sense? Is it ethical?

2.   How should this transaction be entered in Bowles Services' books? Does it matter whether the modified cash basis or accrual basis of accounting is used?

3.   Make a written list of all the consequences Nancy might face as a result of recording this transaction as a debit to Cash and a credit to Professional Fees.

4.   Break up into groups of two and role play Nancy's and Sarah's point of view in this situation.

MASTERY PROBLEM

✓ 1. Total debits to General Dr. col. of CJ: $112,705; 2. Total debits of CJ: $305,305; 4. Total debits on Trial Bal.: $232,200

John McRoe opened a tennis resort in June 20--. Most guests register for one week, arriving on Sunday afternoon and returning home the following Saturday afternoon. Guests stay at an adjacent hotel. The tennis resort provides lunch and dinner. Dining and exercise facilities are provided in a building rented by McRoe. A dietitian, masseuse, physical therapist, and athletic trainers are on call to assure the proper combination of diet and exercise. The chart of accounts and transactions for the month of June are provided below. McRoe uses the modified cash basis of accounting.

(continued)

McRoe Tennis Resort
Chart of Accounts

Assets

101	Cash
142	Office Supplies
144	Food Supplies
184	Tennis Facilities
184.1	Accum. Depr.—Tennis Facilities
186	Exercise Equipment
186.1	Accum. Depr.—Exercise Equip.

Liabilities

202	Accounts Payable

Owner's Equity

311	John McRoe, Capital
312	John McRoe, Drawing
313	Income Summary

Revenue

401	Registration Fees

Expenses

511	Wages Expense
521	Rent Expense
523	Office Supplies Expense
524	Food Supplies Expense
525	Telephone Expense
533	Utilities Expense
535	Insurance Expense
536	Postage Expense
541	Depr. Exp.—Tennis Facilities
542	Depr. Exp.—Exercise Equip.

June 1   McRoe invested cash in the business, $90,000.

1   Paid for new exercise equipment, $9,000.

2   Deposited registration fees in the bank, $15,000.

2   Paid rent for month of June on building and land, $2,500.

2   Rogers Construction completed work on new tennis courts that cost $70,000. The estimated useful life of the facility is five years, at which time the courts will have to be resurfaced. Arrangements were made to pay the bill in July.

3   Purchased food supplies on account from Au Naturel Foods, $5,000.

5   Purchased office supplies on account from Gordon Office Supplies, $300.

7   Deposited registration fees in the bank, $16,200.

10   Purchased food supplies on account from Au Naturel Foods, $6,200.

10   Paid wages to staff, $500.

14   Deposited registration fees in the bank, $13,500.

16   Purchased food supplies on account from Au Naturel Foods, $4,000.

17   Paid wages to staff, $500.

18   Paid postage, $85.

21   Deposited registration fees in the bank, $15,200.

24   Purchased food supplies on account from Au Naturel Foods, $5,500.

24   Paid wages to staff, $500.

28   Deposited registration fees in the bank, $14,000.

30   Purchased food supplies on account from Au Naturel Foods, $6,000.

30   Paid wages to staff, $500.

30   Paid Au Naturel Foods on account, $28,700.

June 30   Paid utility bill, $500.

30   Paid telephone bill, $120.

30   McRoe withdrew cash for personal use, $1,500.

REQUIRED

1.   Enter the transactions in a combination journal (page 1). Establish special columns for Registration Fees (credit), Wages Expense (debit), and Food Supplies (debit).

2.   Prove the combination journal.

3.   Post these transactions to a general ledger.

4.   Prepare a trial balance as of June 30.

CHALLENGE PROBLEM

This problem challenges you to apply your cumulative accounting knowledge to move a step beyond the material in the module.

✓ **NI modified cash basis: $7,000; NI accrual basis: $7,300**

Gerald Resler recently opened a financial consulting business. Summary transactions for the month of June, his second month of operation, are provided below.

1.   Cash collected from clients for consulting fees, $10,000. $1,500 of the $10,000 was for consulting fees earned in May, but received in June.

2.   Consulting fees earned in June, but to be received in July, $2,000.

3.   Supplies on hand at the beginning of June amounted to $500. All purchases of supplies are made on account. Supplies purchased during June, $1,000. At the end of June, $600 worth of supplies remained unused.

4.   Paid cash on account to suppliers during June, $800. $200 of the $800 was for purchases of supplies made in May.

5.   Wages paid to an assistant, $2,000. Of this $2,000, $300 had been earned in May. In addition, the assistant earned $500 in June, which will be paid next month.

6.   Purchased a laptop. Paid $1,200 cash in June and will pay the balance of $1,200 in July. Gerald expects to use the laptop for two years at which time he expects that it will be obsolete and have a zero salvage value.

REQUIRED

Prepare income statements for the month of June using the modified cash and accrual bases.

ANSWERS TO SELF-STUDY TEST QUESTIONS

CHAPTER 2

True/False
1. T   2. F (A/P is a liability)
3. T   4. T
5. F (other changes could occur: capital could increase, revenue could increase, etc.)
6. F (net income)   7. T

Multiple Choice
1. c   2. a   3. b   4. d   5. c

CHAPTER 3

True/False
1. T
2. F (liability accounts normally have credit balances)
3. T   4. F (credit balances)
5. T   6. F (increase)

Multiple Choice
1. c   2. c   3. b   4. d   5. a

CHAPTER 4

True/False
1. T   2. T   3. T
4. F (A, L, OE, R, E)   5. T

Multiple Choice
1. b   2. c   3. b   4. a   5. d

CHAPTER 5

True/False
1. F (match revenues and expenses)
2. F (to bring accounts up-to-date)
3. T
4. F (depreciable cost = cost − salvage value)
5. F (to match cost of asset against revenues it will help generate)

Multiple Choice
1. a   2. c   3. d   4. c   5. a

CHAPTER 6

True/False
1. T
2. F (additional investments are added to the beginning balance)
3. F   4. T   5. T

Multiple Choice
1. b   2. d   3. a   4. c   5. b

CHAPTER 7

True/False
1. F (primary purpose is to reconcile book balance with bank balance)
2. F (deducted from book balance)   3. T
4. F (deducted from book balance)
5. F (entries are not posted from petty cash record to general ledger)

Multiple Choice
1. b   2. a   3. c   4. b   5. d

CHAPTER 8

True/False
1. F (does *not* work under control and direction)
2. T   3. F (is called wages)
4. T   5. T

Multiple Choice
1. c   2. b   3. d   4. a   5. d

CHAPTER 9

True/False
1. F (these taxes are paid by the employer)
2. T   3. T
4. F (FUTA tax is levied on employers)
5. F (this form is W-2)

Multiple Choice
1. b   2. d   3. b   4. d   5. a

CHAPTER 10

True/False
1. T   2. T   3. T
4. F (the debit *excludes* the sales tax)   5. T

Multiple Choice
1. d   2. c   3. b   4. b   5. a

CHAPTER 11

True/False
1. F (purchase requisition)   2. T
3. T   4. F (credited)   5. F (buyer)

Multiple Choice

1. d   2. a   3. a   4. d   5. b

CHAPTER 12

True/False

1. T   2. F (general journal is still needed)
3. F (only credit sales)   4. T   5. T

Multiple Choice

1. a   2. a   3. c   4. c   5. a

CHAPTER 13

True/False

1. T   2. T
3. F (this is true for the periodic method)
4. T   5. F (the buyer pays)

Multiple Choice

1. b   2. c   3. a   4. c   5. b

CHAPTER 14

True/False

1. T   2. T   3. T
4. F (revenue is recognized)
5. F (contra-revenue account)

Multiple Choice

1. b   2. a   3. b   4. b   5. b

CHAPTER 15

True/False

1. T   2. F (whichever is longer)
3. T   4. T
5. F (number of times accounts receivable turned over)

Multiple Choice

1. c   2. a   3. b   4. d   5. c

MODULE 1

True/False

1. T   2. F (Large businesses use the accrual basis.)
3. F (See Figure M1-1.)
4. T   5. T

Multiple Choice

1. c   2. b   3. d   4. a   5. b

*Page references in bold indicate defined terms.

A

AAA (American Accounting Association), 6
ABA (American Bankers Association) Number, **234**
account, **22**
account form of balance sheet, **185**
account tiles, **22**
accountants, 8–10
accounting, **4**
    career opportunities in, 8–13, *fig.*, 8
    computers and, 35–36, 195–198, 335–336, 458, 460–461
    double-entry, 54
    methods of, 147–150
    purpose of, 4
    systems, 7
accounting clerks, **8**
accounting cycle, **194**, 225–226
    period 2, 227–229
    with subsidiary ledgers, part 1, 619–622
    with subsidiary legers, part 2, 622–624
accounting elements, 20–21
accounting equation, **21–22**, *fig.*, 56
    effect of transactions on, 22–30
    expanding, 24–25
accounting Information systems, **9**
    users of, *fig.*, 4
accounting period concept, **25**
accounting process, 4–5, *fig.*, 5
    overview of, 34
accounts payable, **20**
    schedule of, 412–414, *fig.*, 414
accounts payable ledger, **409**
    after posting, *fig.*, 413
    posting cash payments to, 411–412, *fig.*, 412
    posting from cash payments journal to, *fig.*, 459
    posting from purchases journal to, *fig.*, 454
    posting purchases to, 409–410, *fig.*, 409
accounts receivable, **20**
    schedule of, 371–373, *fig.*, 372
accounts receivable ledger, **365**
    after posting, *fig.*, 372
    posting cash receipts to, 370–371, *fig.*, 371
    posting from cash receipts journal to, *fig.*, 450
    posting from sales journal to, *fig.*, 445
    posting sales to, 365–367, *fig.*, 366

accounts receivable turnover, **584**
accrual basis of accounting, **147**, 625–626, *fig.*, 148, *fig.*, 149, *fig.*, 626
adjusted trail balance, 144, *fig.*, 144D
adjusted trial balance columns, **144**, *fig.*, 542
adjusting entries, **134**, 135, 544, *fig.*, 145, *fig.*, 539, *fig.*, 544, *fig.*, 589, *fig.*, 638
    journalizing, 145
    posting, 146–147, *fig.*, 146–147
    preparing, 638
    under perpetual inventory system, 544–545
    under expense method, 571–572
    which to reverse, *fig.*, 590
    See also correcting entry; reversing entries; work sheet
adjustments, work sheet, 143, *fig.*, 144C, *fig.*, 541
Aetna, 190
AICPA. *See* American Institute of Certified Public Accountants
American Accounting Association (AAA), 6
American Bankers Association (ABA) Number, 234
American Institute of Certified Public Accountants (AICPA), 6, 9
analyzing, **5**
    business transactions, 22
    See also transaction analysis
Anderson, Jeanette, 64
appointment record, *fig.*, 627
asset accounts, debits and credits in, 58–60
asset method, **572**
assets, **20**, 55
    and records, protection of, internal control, 272
    contra-, 140
    current, 185
    long-term, 185
    plant, 139, 185
    quick, 583
ATMs. *See* automated teller machines
auditing, **9**
automated teller machines (ATMs), **236**, *fig.*, 236
Automatic Data Processing, Inc. (ADP), 333
average collection period, **584**
average cost method, **499–500**
average days to sell inventory, **586**

B

balance, **54**
balance sheet, **33**, 185, 580–583, *fig.*, 184
    analysis, 583
balance sheet columns, **144**, *fig.*, 144E, *fig.*, 543
bank reconciliation, **241**, 242–243, *fig.*, 242, *fig.*, 243, *fig.*, 244
bank statement, **239**, *fig.*, 239
    reconciling, 240–245
    See also checking account
blank endorsement, **234**
book of original entry, **93**
book value, **140**, 582
bookkeepers, **8**
bookkeeping, computerized, 446
budgeting, **10**
business activities, types of, 219
business entity, **20**
business entity concept, 20–21
business transactions, **22**
    analyzing, 22
    See also transaction analysis
businesses, types of, 7, *fig.*, 7

C

canceled checks, **239**
capital, **20**
capital account, *fig.*, 580
cash, **234**, 400–401, *fig.*, 150
    determining balance, 634, *fig.*, 635
    management, discounts matter, 405
    short and over, 250
    T account, *fig.*, 55, *fig.*, 221
    See also checking account; petty cash fund; statement of cash flows
cash basis of accounting, **148**
    comparison of methods, *fig.*, 148, *fig.*, 149
cash discounts, **362**
cash payments, 240, 411, *fig.*, 240, *fig.*, 411
    internal controls over, 273–277
    journalizing and posting of transactions, 407–412
    posting to general ledger and accounts payable ledger, 411–412, *fig.*, 412
cash payments journal, **455–459**, *figs.*, 455
    posting from, 456–459, *fig.*, 457, *fig.*, 459

cash receipts, 367–369, *fig.*, 369
  internal controls over, 272–273
  journalizing and posting of transactions, 363–371
  posting to general ledger and accounts receivable ledger, 370–371, *fig.*, 371
cash receipts journal, **444–450**, *fig.*, 446–447
  posting from, 447–450, *fig.*, 449, *fig.*, 450
cash register tape summary, *fig.*, 356
Certified Internal Auditor (CIA), **10**
Certified Management Accountant (CMA), **10**
Certified Public Accountant (CPA), **9**
change fund, 249–250
chart of accounts, 90–91, *fig.*, 91, *fig.*, 536, *fig.*, 628
  expanded, 141, 536–537, *fig.*, 142
check, **237**, *fig.*, 238
check register, **277**
check stub, **237**, *fig.*, 238
checking account, 234–239
  bank statement, 239
  making deposits, 234–237
  opening, 234
  writing checks, 237–239
CIA. *See* Certified Internal Auditor
Circular E—Employers Tax Guide, 288, 324
classified balance sheet, **185**, *fig.*, 581
classifying, accounting process, **5**
Clifton, Jeff, 138
closing entries, 586–588, *fig.*, 189, *fig.*, 191, *fig.*, 587, *fig.*, 589, *fig.*, 638
  journalize, 190
  post, 190–193, *fig.*, 192–193
  preparing, 638
closing process, **187–193**, *fig.*, 188, *fig.*, 586
CMA. *See* Certified Management Accountant
collections, bank reconciliation, 241
combination journal, **628–631**
  journalizing in, 629–630
  modified cash basis, *fig.*, 631
  posting from, 632–634, *fig.*, 632, *fig.*, 633
  proving, 630–631
compound entries, **96**
computerized bookkeeping, 446
computers and accounting, 35–36, 195–198, 335–336, 458, 460–461
conservatism, **503**
consignee, **497**
consignment, **496**
consignor, **497**

consistency, **499**
contra-asset, **140**
contra-cost accounts, **536**
contra-revenue accounts, **536**
control activities, internal control, 271–272
control environment, internal control, 271
controller, **9**
controlling account, **365**
corporation, **7**
correcting entry, **108**, *fig.*, 108
  See also adjusting entries; errors
cost, **503**
cost accounting, **10**
cost flows of inventory, 501
cost of goods sold, 405, *fig.*, 533
  allocation of goods available for sale to, *fig.*, 497
  assigning cost to, 495–504
  estimating, 504–506
cost of merchandise sold, 405
CPA. *See* Certified Public Accountant
credit, **55–57**
credit balances, **57**
credit memo, **242**, 358–359, *fig.*, 359
credit terms, *fig.*, 362
cross-reference, **100**
current assets, **185**, **582**
current liabilities, **185**, **582**
current ratio, **583**

D

data
  flow of, 90, *fig.*, 90
  year-end adjustment, *fig.*, 539
  See also chart of accounts; general journal; general ledger; source documents; trial balance
database software, 35
Davis Homes LLC, 414
Davis, Ken, 12–13
Davis, Lisa, 238
DeBartolo Properties Management, Inc., 138
debit, **55–57**
debit balances, **56**
debit memos, **242**
deductions, other, 299
Deloitte and Touche, 9
deposit rules, summary of, *fig.*, 325
deposit ticket, **234**, *fig.*, 235
deposits, 240, *fig.*, 240
deposits in transit, **241**
depreciable cost, **139**
depreciation, **139**, *fig.*, 140, *figs.*, 141
  double-declining-balance method, *fig.*, 177

expense, 139–141
  modified accelerated cost recovery system, *fig.*, 177
  straight-line method, *fig.*, 176
  sum-of-the-years-digits method, *fig.*, 176
Description column, **630**
direct deposit, **294**
discussion memorandum, **5**
Disney. *See* Walt Disney Company, The
documents and records, internal control, 272
double-declining-balance depreciation method, **176–177**
double-entry accounting, **54**
  See also credit; debit; T account; transaction analysis; trial balance
drawee, **237**
drawer, **237**
drawing, **25**, 56
  debits and credits including, 60–68
duties, segregation of, internal control, 271

E

earnings, 285–287
  in stock market, 190
EFT. *See* electronic funds transfer
EFTPS. *See* Electronic Federal Tax Payment System
EIN. *See* employer identification number
Electronic Federal Tax Payment System (EFTPS), **325**
electronic funds transfer (EFT), **245**, 294
electronic payroll system, *fig.*, 300
electronic source documents, 92
electronic system, **300**
e-mail software, 35
employee, **284**
  and employer taxes, summary of, *fig.*, 332
  FICA tax withholding, 291
  income tax payable, 299
  total payroll cost of, 323–324
  wage and tax statement, 330–331
  wages and taxes, summary of, 331
employee earnings and deductions, 284–292
  accounting for, 296–299
employee earnings record, **296**, *fig.*, 296–297
Employees Withholding Allowance Certificate (Form W-4), 287, *fig.*, 288

employer
and employee taxes, summary of, *fig.*, 332
FICA taxes, **318–319**
FUTA tax, 320
payroll taxes, 318–321, 321–324
SUTA tax, 320
employer identification number (EIN), 234, **325**
Employers Annual Federal Unemployment (FUTA) Tax Return (Form 940-EZ), *fig.*, 329
Employers Quarterly Federal Tax Return, Form 941, 326, *fig.*, 327–328
Employers Tax Guide (Circular E), 288, 324
end-of-period adjustments, 134–142
end-of-period work for a professional service business, 634–638
endorsement, **234**
Enron, 9
Ernst & Young, 9
errors
bank reconciliation, 241
in the trial balance, 106–108, *fig.*, 106
on the work sheet, 145, *fig.*, 145
expense method, **571**
adjusting entries under, 571–572
expenses, **24–25**, 56
debits and credits including, 60–68
effect of on accounting equation, 25–30
exposure draft, **6**

F

Fair Labor Standards Act (FLSA), **285**
FASB. *See* Financial Accounting Standards Board
federal income tax withholding, 324–326
Federal Insurance Contributions Act. *See* FICA
Federal Tax Deposit Coupon, Form 8109, 325–326, *fig.*, 325
Federal Unemployment Tax Act. *See* FUTA (Federal Unemployment Tax Act) tax
federal withholding tax table, *fig.*, 289–290
FEI. *See* Financial Executives Institute
FICA (Federal Insurance Contributions Act), 291
FICA taxes, **291**
employee, 291
employer, 318–319

FIFO (first-in, first-out) method, 499, *fig.*, 499
financial accounting, **9**
Financial Accounting Standards Board (FASB), 5
Financial Executives Institute (FEI), 6
financial ratios, tracking, 585
financial statement analysis, 583–586
financial statements, 31–34, 182–186, *fig.*, 32, *fig.*, 637
and trial balance, linkages between, *fig.*, 71
effect of adjusting entry on, *fig.*, 136, *fig.*, 137, *fig.*, 138, *figs.*, 141
impact of merchandise inventory on, 492–493
preparing, 634
financing activities, **219**
first-in, first-out (FIFO) method, **499**
fiscal year, **25**, **134**, 190
FISH (first-in, still here), 501
FLSA. *See* Fair Labor Standards Act
FOB destination, **404**
FOB shipping point, **404**
footings, **54**
Form 1099, 284
Form 8109, Federal Tax Deposit Coupon, 325–326, *fig.*, 325
Form 940, 329
Form 940-EZ, Employers Annual Federal Unemployment (FUTA) Tax Return, *fig.*, 329
Form 941, Employers Quarterly Federal Tax Return, 326, *fig.*, 327–328
Form W-2, Wage and Tax Statement, *fig.*, 330
Form W-3, Transmittal of Wage and Tax Statements, 331
Form W-4 (Employees Withholding Allowance Certificate), 287, *fig.*, 288
fraud, 244
freight-in account, 404–405
FUTA (Federal Unemployment Tax Act) tax, **320**, 326–330
computation of, *fig.*, 320
payable, 323

G

GAAP. *See* generally accepted accounting principles
general accounts, 630
general columns, 629
General Credit column, **628**
General Debit column, **628**

general expenses, **578**
general journal, 93–97, *fig.*, 96, *figs.*, 101–102, *fig.*, 364, *fig.*, 369, *fig.*, 407, *fig.*, 411, *fig.*, 441
general ledger, 98–105
after posting, *figs.*, 103–104, *fig.*, 372, *fig.*, 413
posting cash payments to, 411–412, *fig.*, 412
posting cash receipts to, 370–371, *fig.*, 371
posting purchases to, 408, *fig.*, 408
posting sales to, 364–365, *fig.*, 365
posting to, *figs.*, 99–100, *fig.*, 443, *fig.*, 449, *fig.*, 452, *fig.*, 457
general ledger account, **98**
and T account, comparison of, *fig.*, 98
General Motors, 21
generally accepted accounting principles (GAAP), **5–6**
governmental accounting, 10
gross margin, **405**, **576**
gross pay, **287**
gross profit, **405**, **576**
computation of, 405–406, *fig.*, 406
gross profit method, **505**, *fig.*, 505
gross-price method, **435**

H

Haas Transfer Warehouse, 295
historical cost principle, **139**

I

IBM, 195
IMA. *See* Institute of Management Accountants
in transit, **496**
income from operations, **576**
income statement, 31–33, 182, 576–579, *fig.*, 183, *fig.*, 362, *fig.*, 363
income statement columns, **144**, *fig.*, 144E, *fig.*, 543
Income Summary, **187**
income tax withholding, 287
independent contractor, **284**
information and communication system, internal control, 272
input, 34, *fig.*, 34
Institute of Management Accountants (IMA), 6
internal auditing, **10**
internal control, **234**, *fig.*, 270
importance of, 269–270
key components of, 270–272

over cash payments, 273–277
over cash receipts, 272–273
interpreting, accounting process, **5**
interstatement analysis, **584**
inventory
   allocation of goods available for sale
      to ending, *fig.*, 497
   assigning cost to, 495–504
   cost flows of, 501
   errors, effect of on net income,
      fig., 493
   estimating ending, 504–506
   importance of, 534
   loss on write-down of, 504
   methods, comparison of, 501,
      fig., 501
   physical flows of, 501
   systems, types of, 494
   See also merchandise inventory
inventory sheet, **495**, *fig.*, 496
Inventory Short and Over, **545**
inventory turnover, **585**
investing activities, **219**
investments by the owner,
   additional, 186
invoice, **400**

J

Jacuzzi Brands, Inc., 269, 270
job opportunities, 10–13
   expected demand, *fig.*, 11
   expected growth, *fig.*, 11
journal, **93**, *fig.*, 440
journal entries, 243–245, *fig.*, 244
journalize closing entries, 190
journalizing, 93–97
   adjusting entries, 145, 544–545
   employer payroll taxes, 321–322
   in combination journal, 629–630
   payroll transactions, 296–298
   purchases and cash payments
      transactions, 407–412
   sales and cash receipts transactions,
      363–371

K

Kendall Square, 585
KPMG, 9
Kramer Iron, Inc., 244

L

last-in, first-out (LIFO) method, **500**
ledger account, *fig.*, 627
liabilities, **20**, 55, 185

liability accounts, debits and credits in,
   58–60
LIFO (last-in, fist-out) method, **500**,
   fig., 500
liquidity, **34**, **582**
LISH (last-in, still here), **502**
long-term assets, **185**
long-term debt, **185**
long-term liabilities, **185**, **582**
loss on write-down of inventory, **504**
lower-of-cost-or-market method,
   503–504

M

MACRS. *See* Modified Accelerated
   Cost Recovery System
magnetic ink character recognition
   (MICR) code, **234**
management advisory services, **9**
managerial accounting, 9
manual system, **300**
manufacturing business, 7
market, **503**
market value, **139**
marketing chain, *fig.*, 357
MasterCard, 355
matching principle, **134**
Mattel, Inc., 135
Medicare taxes, 324–326
   payable, 299, 322
merchandise inventory
   adjustment for, 532–535
   impact of on financial statements,
      492–493
   See also inventory
merchandise purchases accounts,
   401–406
merchandise purchases transactions,
   398–401, *fig.*, 402
merchandise sales accounts,
   359–363
merchandise sales transactions,
   356–359, *fig.*, 360
merchandising business, 7, **356**
   closing entries for, *fig.*, 587
   preparing a work sheet for,
      537–543, *fig.*, 538
merit-rating system, **320**
MICR (magnetic ink character recognition) code, **234**
Microsoft, 195
Modified Accelerated Cost Recovery
   System (MACRS), **177**
modified cash basis, **149**, 625–626
   combination journal, *fig.*, 631
   comparison of methods, *fig.*, 149,
      fig., 626

monitoring processes, internal
   control, 272
mortgage, **582**
Mortgage Payable, **582**
multiple-step income statement, **576**,
   fig., 579

N

natural business year, **495**
net income, **24**, *fig.*, 144H, *fig.*, 189,
   fig., 493, *fig.*, 543
net loss, **24**, *fig.*, 144H, *fig.*, 189
net pay, **287**, computing, 292
net sales, **576**
net worth, **20**
net-price method, 435–436
normal balance, **56–57**, *fig.*, 57
not sufficient funds (NSF) checks, **241**
notes payable, **20**
not-for-profit accounting, 10

O

operating activities, **219**
operating cycle, **185**, **582**
operating income, **576**
operating statement, **31**
Oracle, 195
output, **34**, *fig.*, 34
outstanding checks, **241**
owners capital, 56
owners equity, **20**, 55, **583**
   accounts, debits and credits in,
      58–60
   return on, 584
   statement of, 580, *fig.*, 580
   umbrella, 55, *fig.*, 56
   See also statement of owners equity
ownership structures, three types of,
   6–7, *fig.*, 6

P

paid vouchers file, **277**
para-accountants, **8**
partnership, **6**
paycheck and earnings statement,
   fig., 295
payee, **237**
payment and reporting responsibilities,
   324–333
payment process, voucher system, 276,
   fig., 276
payments, summary of, 331–333
payroll
   accounting for, *fig.*, 298

calendar, *fig.*, 332
check, 294
complexity, dealing with, 333
cost of an employee, total, 323–324
fraud, 295
record-keeping methods, 300
records, 293–296
transactions, journalizing, 296–298
payroll processing center, 300
payroll register, **293–294**, *fig.*, 292–293, *fig.*, 318–319
payroll taxes expense, 322, *fig.*, 322
periodic inventory system, **494**, 498–502, *fig.*, 495, *fig.*, 545
adjustment for merchandise inventory, 532–535
permanent accounts, **187**
perpetual inventory system, **494**, 502–503, *fig.*, 495, *fig.*, 545
preparing and journalizing adjusting entries under, 544–545
record: FIFO method, *fig.*, 503
perpetual LIFO inventory method, 525–526, *fig.*, 526
perpetual moving-average inventory method, 526–527, *fig.*, 527
personal identification number (PIN), 236
petty cash fund, **245–249**
petty cash payments record, **246–248**, *fig.*, 247
petty cash voucher, **246**, *fig.*, 246
physical flows of inventory, 501
physical inventory, **495–497**
PIN. *See* personal identification number
plant assets, **139**, **185**
post closing entries, 190–193
post-closing trial balance, **193–194**, 588, *fig.*, 193, *fig.*, 588
posting, **99**
adjusting entries, 146–147, *fig.*, 146–147
cash payments to general ledger and accounts payable ledger, 411–412, *fig.*, 412
cash receipts to general ledger and accounts receivable ledger, 370–371, *fig.*, 371
from cash payments journal, 456–459, *fig.*, 457, *fig.*, 459
from cash receipts journal, 447–450, *fig.*, 449, *fig.*, 450
from combination journal, 632–634, *fig.*, 632, *fig.*, 633
from purchases journal, 452–454, *fig.*, 452, *fig.*, 454
from sales journal, 442–444, *fig.*, 445

purchases and cash payments transactions, 407–412, *fig.*, 408, *fig.*, 409
sales and cash receipts transactions, 363–371, *fig.*, 365, *fig.*, 366
sales journal to general ledger, *fig.*, 443
to the general ledger, *figs.*, 99–100
Posting Reference column, **632**
prepaid insurance, 137, *figs.*, 137
presentation software, 35
PricewaterhouseCoopers, 9
private accounting, 9
processing, **34**, *fig.*, 34
professional service business
accounting for, 626–627
performing end-of-period work for, 634–638
profit and loss statement, 31
property, plant, and equipment, **185**, **582**
protection of assets and records, internal control, 272
public accounting, 9
public hearings, **5**
publicly held companies, **269**
purchase invoice, **400**, *fig.*, 400, *fig.*, 401
purchase of merchandise, review of entries for, *fig.*, 532
purchase order, **399**, *fig.*, 399
purchase requisition, **398**, *fig.*, 399
purchases, **398**, 407
account, 402–403
discounts account, 403–404
entered in general journal, *fig.*, 407
journalizing and posting of transaction, 407–412
posting to accounts payable ledger, 409–410, *fig.*, 409
posting to general ledger, 408, *fig.*, 408
purchases journal, **451–454**, *fig.*, 451, *fig.*, 452
posting from, 452–454, *fig.*, 452, *fig.*, 454
purchases returns and allowances, 410, *fig.*, 410
account, 403
purchasing process
document, *fig.*, 398
voucher system, 273, *fig.*, 274

Q

quick assets, **583**
quick ratio, **583**

R

Rankin, Christy, 414
ratios, 583
tracking financial, 585
receiving report, **400**
recording, accounting process, 5
records and documents, internal control, 272
report form of balance sheet, **185**
reporting, 5
and payment responsibilities, 324–333
reports, summary of, 331–333
restrictive endorsement, **234**, *fig.*, 236
retail method, **505**, *fig.*, 506
retailer, 356–357
return on owners equity, **584**
revenues, **24**, **56**
debits and credits including, 60–68
effect of on accounting equation, 25–30
unearned, 535–537, *fig.*, 535
reversing entries, 588–591, *fig.*, 589, *fig.*, 591
risk assessment, internal control, 271
ruling method, **107**, *fig.*, 107

S

salary, **284–285**
sales, **356**, 363–364, 370, *fig.*, 364, *fig.*, 441
account, 360
journalizing and posting of transactions, 363–371
of merchandise, review of entries for, *fig.*, 532
posting to accounts receivable ledger, 365–367, *fig.*, 366
posting to the general ledger, 364–365, *fig.*, 365
tax payable account, 361
sales allowance, **358**
See also sales returns and allowances
sales discounts, **362**, *fig.*, 363
account, 362–363
sales invoice, **358**, *fig.*, 358
sales journal, **441–444**, *figs.*, 442
posting from, 442–444, *fig.*, 443, *fig.*, 445
sales return, **358**
sales returns and allowances, 367, *fig.*, 362, *fig.*, 368
account, 361–362
sales ticket, **357**, *fig.*, 357
salvage value, **139**

Sarbanes-Oxley Act (SOX), **9**, 269
schedule of accounts payable, 412–414, **413**, *fig.*, 414
schedule of accounts receivable, 371–373, *fig.*, 372
Sears, 92
Section 404 internal control report, *fig.*, 270
Securities and Exchange Commission (SEC), 5
segregation of duties, internal control, 271
self-employment income, **319**
self-employment tax, **319**
selling expenses, **576**
service business, **7**
    accounting for a professional, 626–627
    performing end-of-period work for a professional, 634–638
service charges, **241**
SFAS. *See* statement of financial accounting standards
signature card, **234**, *fig.*, 235
single-step income statement, **576**, *fig.*, 578
slide error, **106**
Social Security taxes, 324–326
    payable, 299, 322
sole proprietorship, **6**
source document, 91–92, *fig.*, 92
special accounts, 630
special columns, **628**
special journal, **440**
specific identification method, **498**, *fig.*, 498
spreadsheet software, 35
state unemployment tax. *See* SUTA (state unemployment tax) tax
statement of cash flows, 220–222, *fig.*, 221
statement of financial accounting standards (SFAS), **6**
statement of financial condition, **33**
statement of financial position, **33**
statement of owners equity, **33**, 182, 580, *fig.*, 184, *fig.*, 580
    with additional investment, *fig.*, 186
    with net loss, *fig.*, 33
    See also owners equity
stock market, earnings in, 190
straight-line depreciation method, 175–176
straight-line method, **139**
subsidiary ledgers
    part 1 accounting cycle, 619–622
    part 2 accounting cycle, 622–624
summarizing, accounting process, 5

sum-of-the-years-digits, **176**
sum-of-the-years-digits depreciation method, **176**
supplies, 135–136, *figs.*, 136
    asset or expense, 63
SUTA (state unemployment tax) tax, 320, 330, *fig.*, 321
    payable, 323

T

T account, 54, *fig.*, 98, *fig.*, 189
    balancing of, 54–55
tax accounting, **10**
taxation, **9**
taxes
    electronic federal tax payment system, 325
    employee, 299, 331, *fig.*, 332
    employer payroll, 321–324, *fig.*, 332
    FICA, 291, 318–319
    FUTA, 320, 323, 326–330
    income tax withholding, 287, 324–326
    Medicare, 299, 322, 324–326
    self-employment, 319
    Social Security, 299, 322, 324–326
    summary of, 331–333
    SUTA, 320, 323, 330
taxpayer identification number (TIN), 234
temporary accounts, **187**
10-column work sheet, 142
time card, *fig.*, 285, *fig.*, 286
TIN. *See* taxpayer identification number
trade discount, **400**–401, *fig.*, 401
transaction analysis, 57–70, *fig.*, 57, *figs.*, 58–69
transactions, summary of, 69–70, *fig.*, 30, *fig.*, 94, *fig.*, 220, *fig.*, 629
Transmittal of Wage and Tax Statements (Form W-3), 331
transposition error, **106**
trial balance, 70–71, **105**, *fig.*, 70, *fig.*, 71, *fig.*, 105, *fig.*, 134, *fig.*, 135, *fig.*, 144B, *fig.*, 540
    finding and correcting errors in, 106–108
    work sheet, 143
two-column general journal, **93**, *fig.*, 93

U

undepreciated cost, **140**, **582**
unearned revenue, 535–537, *fig.*, 535

unpaid vouchers file, **274**
useful life, **139**

V

Visa, 355
voluntary deductions, 292
voucher, **273**, *fig.*, 275
voucher check, **276**, *fig.*, 277
voucher register, **274**
voucher system, **273**
    payment process, *fig.*, 276
    purchasing process, *fig.*, 274

W

Wage and Tax Statement, Form W-2, *fig.*, 330
wage-bracket method, **288**
wages, **284**–285, *figs.*, 138, *fig.*, 589
    summary of employee, 331
wages expense, 138, 298
Wal-Mart, 496
Walt Disney Company, The, 135
web browser software, 36
weighted-average method, **499**–500
wholesale sales transaction process, *fig.*, 358
wholesaler, 357–358
withdrawals, **25**
    effect of on accounting equation, 25–30
withholding allowance, **287**
word-processing software, 35
work sheet, **142**–144H, *fig.*, 144A, *fig.*, 183, *fig.*, 184, *fig.*, 577, *fig.*, 579, *fig.*, 581, *fig.*, 636
    completing, 144F, 144H, *fig.*, 543
    errors on, 145, *fig.*, 145
    for a merchandising business, 537–543, *fig.*, 538
    preparing, 142–144H, 634
    10-column, 142
workers compensation insurance, 333–335
working capital, **583**
WorldCom, 9
writing, managing of, 12–13

Z

Zegarelli Associates, 238

Note: While for a specific company each account number used would have only one title, titles vary from company to company as needed.

Assets (100–199)

100s—Cash Related Accounts
- 101 Cash
- 105 Petty Cash

120s—Receivables
- 121 Notes Receivable
- 122 Accounts Receivable
- 122.1 Allowance for Bad Debts
- 123 Interest Receivable (Also Accrued Interest Receivable)

130s—Inventories
- 131 Merchandise Inventory
- 132 Raw Materials
- 133 Work in Process
- 134 Finished Goods

140s—Prepaid Items
- 141 Supplies (Specialty items like Medical, Bicycle, Tailoring, etc.)
- 142 Office Supplies
- 144 Food Supplies
- 145 Prepaid Insurance

150s—Long-Term Investments
- 153 Bond Sinking Fund

160s—Land
- 161 Land
- 162 Natural Resources
- 162.1 Accumulated Depletion

170s—Buildings
- 171 Buildings
- 171.1 Accumulated Depreciation—Buildings

180s—Equipment
- 181 Office Equipment (Also Store Equipment)
- 181.1 Accumulated Depreciation—Office Equipment (Also Store Equipment)
- 182 Office Furniture
- 182.1 Accumulated Depreciation—Office Furniture
- 183 Athletic Equipment (Also Tailoring, Lawn, Cleaning)
- 183.1 Accumulated Depreciation—Athletic Equipment (Also Tailoring, Lawn, Cleaning)
- 184 Tennis Facilities (Also Basketball Facilities)
- 184.1 Accumulated Depreciation—Tennis Facilities (Also Basketball Facilities)
- 185 Delivery Equipment (Also Medical, Van)
- 185.1 Accumulated Depreciation—Delivery Equipment (Also Medical, Van)
- 186 Exercise Equipment
- 186.1 Accumulated Depreciation—Exercise Equipment
- 187 Computer Equipment
- 187.1 Accumulated Depreciation—Computer Equipment

190s—Intangibles
- 191 Patents
- 192 Copyrights

Liabilities (200–299)

200s—Short-Term Payables
- 201 Notes Payable
- 201.1 Discount on Notes Payable
- 202 Accounts Payable (Also Vouchers Payable)
- 203 United Way Contribution Payable
- 204 Income Tax Payable
- 205 Common Dividends Payable
- 206 Preferred Dividends Payable
- 207 Interest Payable (Also Bond Interest Payable)

210s—Employee Payroll Related Payables
- 211 Employee Income Tax Payable
- 212 Social Security Tax Payable
- 213 Medicare Tax Payable
- 215 City Earnings Tax Payable
- 216 Health Insurance Premiums Payable
- 217 Credit Union Payable
- 218 Savings Bond Deductions Payable
- 219 Wages Payable

220s—Employer Payroll Related Payables
- 221 FUTA Tax Payable
- 222 SUTA Tax Payable
- 223 Workers' Compensation Insurance Payable

230s—Sales Tax
- 231 Sales Tax Payable

240s—Deferred Revenues and Current Portion of Long-Term Debt
- 241 Unearned Subscription Revenue (Also Unearned Ticket Revenue, Unearned Repair Fees)
- 242 Current Portion of Mortgage Payable

250s—Long-Term Liabilities
- 251 Mortgage Payable
- 252 Bonds Payable
- 252.1 Discount on Bonds Payable
- 253 Premium on Bonds Payable